RELIGION AND POLITICS IN GERMAN HISTORY

Also by Frank Eyck

G. P. GOOCH: A Study in History and Politics

THE FRANKFURT PARLIAMENT: 1848–1849

THE GERMAN PUBLIC MIND IN THE NINETEENTH CENTURY (*editor*)

THE PRINCE CONSORT: A Political Biography

THE REVOLUTIONS OF 1848–49 (*editor*)

Religion and Politics in German History

From the Beginnings to the French Revolution

Frank Eyck

First published in Great Britain 1998 by
MACMILLAN PRESS LTD
Houndmills, Basingstoke, Hampshire RG21 6XS and London
Companies and representatives throughout the world

A catalogue record for this book is available from the British Library.

ISBN 0–333–71094–0

First published in the United States of America 1998 by
ST. MARTIN'S PRESS, INC.,
Scholarly and Reference Division,
175 Fifth Avenue, New York, N.Y. 10010

ISBN 0–312–21130–9

Library of Congress Cataloging-in-Publication Data
Eyck, Frank.
Religion and politics in German history : from the beginnings to
the French Revolution / Frank Eyck.
p. cm.
Includes bibliographical references and index.
ISBN 0–312–21130–9 (cloth)
1. Church and state—Germany.   2. Church and state—Holy Roman
Empire.   3. Germany—Church history—To 843.   4. Germany—Church
history—843–1517.   5. Germany—Politics and government—1517–1648.
6. Germany—Church history—18th century.   7. Germany—Politics and
government—To 1517.   8. Christianity and politics—Germany-
-History.   9. Germany—Politics and government—1648–1789.
I. Title.
BR854.E93 1998
322'.1'0943—dc21   97–37276
                                                        CIP

This book is printed on paper suitable for recycling and made from fully managed and
sustained forest sources.

10   9   8   7   6   5   4   3   2   1
07   06   05   04   03   02   01   00   99   98

Printed and bound in Great Britain by
Antony Rowe Ltd, Chippenham, Wiltshire

To Rosemarie

Contents

List of Maps and Genealogical Tables

Maps

Genealogical Tables

Preface

During the 1980s, I did some research on the relations between church and state in Germany, but initially confined myself to the last three centuries. Gradually, however, I came to the conclusion that my perspective required lengthening and that I needed to go back further into the past for a better understanding of how religion and politics affected each other in German history. In recent years I therefore concentrated on the pre-1789 period. The present book is the result of these endeavours.

In view of the long time-span covered in this volume, I needed all the help I could get from the expertise of friends and colleagues in various periods and aspects. While gratefully acknowledging their assistance, I want to emphasise that any shortcomings are entirely due to myself.

I am deeply thankful for the encouragement and suggestions I received from the late Reverend Professor Frederick Copleston SJ, whose vast learning, high intelligence, humility and charity made a lasting impression on me. It is sad that owing to the early death of Professor Karl Leyser, a fellow student in the senior history class at St Paul's School in London before the Second World War, I could not take advantage of his wisdom.

Professor Christopher Brooke (Cambridge) read the early chapters and I profited greatly from his detailed advice, as I did from that of Professor Donald Bullough (St Andrews). I also derived considerable benefit from suggestions made by Professor Rudolf Lill (Karlsruhe), Professor Heribert Smolinsky (Freiburg), Professor Adolf Birke (Munich), Professors Joseph Becker and Anton Rauscher (Augsburg), Professor Heinz Schilling (Berlin), Dr Benjamin Arnold (Reading), Professor Gordon Hamilton (Huron College), Canon Douglas Skoyles (Calgary), Rev. Burke Hoschka (Cochrane, Alberta), and Timothy Wild (Calgary).

I appreciated particularly the intellectual companionship given to me during the writing of the book by many friends and colleagues at the University of Calgary, including Professors Hugo Meynell, Irving Hexham, Karla Poewe, Haijo Westra, Holger Herwig, Anthony Parel, Martin Staum, Francine Michaud, Mark Konnert, Cyril Challice, and Ted Regehr. I am grateful to them for the time they took to read the whole or part of the manuscript, and for the comments they made.

During the earlier part of my work I received valuable suggestions, on research trips around Germany, from the late Professor Thomas Nipperdey, as well as Professors Eberhard Weis, Trutz Rendtorff and Georg Schwaiger (Munich), from the late Professor Karl-Georg Faber (Münster), from Professors Hans- Ulrich Wehler, Jürgen Kocka, Klaus Schreiner and Reinhart Koselleck (all at that time in Bielefeld), the late Professor Walter Lipgens

(Saarbrücken), Professor Wolfgang Schieder (now Cologne), Professor Konrad Repgen (Bonn), and Professor Christoph Weber (Düsseldorf). A visiting professorship at Würzburg University in 1982 allowed me to live for some months in a historic episcopal city and to reside in Germany for the first time as a civilian adult.

Once more my gratitude goes out to the University of Calgary for all the intellectual and technical support and encouragement I have received on campus, particularly from the Department of History and the Faculty of Social Sciences, and for being allowed to continue to share in the life of the university even after formal retirement. Particular thanks go to the University Library and its staff.

I am very grateful for the support I had for my research from the German Academic Exchange Service for help with expenses incurred on travel in Germany, to the Social Sciences and Humanities Research Council of Canada for a leave fellowship, to the Calgary Institute for the Humanities for an annual fellowship providing considerable relief from teaching, and to the University of Calgary for regular sabbatic leaves, as well as other financial support for my research.

I wish to express my gratitude to Wendy Amero for typing final changes to the text and for helping me with the trials and tribulations of word processing, and to Peter Atkins for some checking of sources for the final version. It is a particular pleasure to thank our son Andrew for helping to prepare the manuscript for the publisher, as I assisted my father, Erich Eyck, in 1949 with seeing his *Bismarck and the German Empire* through the press during his absence overseas.[1] My wife helped me patiently with this book right through the many years it took to complete it, and it is to her that the book is dedicated.

In order to provide more ease of reading, the dignities of ecclesiastical and secular dignitaries have been largely capitalised. In some other matters, such as the omission of the apostrophe in Thirty Years War, I have followed Macmillan house style.

In the end-notes, full details of titles are normally given at first mention in each chapter, and thereafter short titles. Readers may wish to refer back to the first entry on a work in a chapter. Where the source for a quotation is in German, I have translated the extract from the original German.

The publishers and author wish to thank the following for permission to adapt maps published by them: Map 1 (Division of Carolingian Empire) adapted from Map 6 in *Germany: a History* by John E. Rodes, copyright © 1964 by Holt, Rinehart and Winston and renewed 1992 by John E. Rodes, reproduced by permission of the publisher; Map 2 (The Empire and Italy) from map 3, entitled 'The Hohenstaufen Empire', on p. 39 of *Germany: A Short History* by Donald S. Detwiler, 2nd edn, rev., Carbondale, 1989. Copyright © 1989 by the Board of Trustees, Southern Illinois University;

Map 3 (Religions of Central Europe) from *A History of Modern Germany* by Hajo Holborn, Copyright © 1964 by Hajo Holborn, reprinted by permission of Alfred A. Knopf, Inc. My thanks go to Dr Monika Rieger of the Department of Geography, University of Calgary, for compiling and redesigning the maps.

Genealogical tables are given for the main imperial dynasties and the Hohenzollern. Thanks go to Wendy Amero for word-processing the tables.

Department of History   FRANK EYCK
University of Calgary

1 Parameters of the Book

Even today, religion and politics are not as distinct from each other as may appear at first sight. During the past there has rarely been agreement as to where religion ends and politics begins, and vice versa. That this is not merely an academic question is clear from the bitter struggles that took place, even before there was a full realisation of a distinction between them, to determine which matters come under the State (the secular authorities) or under the Church. These conflicts are not over by any means, as the clashes between Church and State about such subjects as abortion, divorce and education in our own day show.

So far nobody has been able to produce a definition of religion that is generally acceptable. Within the context of Judaism and Christianity, 'religion' is here visualised as a belief in a superior power that shapes the fate of both individuals and communities – what Schleiermacher called 'a feeling of absolute dependence'.[1] Tentatively politics is used to denote the secular as opposed to the ecclesiastical or spiritual, the state and its representatives in contrast to the church, the emperor rather than the pope, sword and sceptre rather than mitre.

The importance attached to relative boundaries between the spiritual and the secular sphere is illustrated by the many attempts made over time to delineate them more clearly. Among the most outstanding of these are St Augustine's famous *City of God* (composed between 413 and 426), later in the fifth century the doctrinal statements by Pope Gelasius I (492–6), and in the sixteenth Martin Luther's writings on the Two Kingdoms. Connected with this, there was also concern from ancient times onwards with the question as to whether one of these spheres – the secular, or the spiritual – was superior to the other, and if so which. The doctrines that were put forward to solve these problems were usually the result of deep thought, faith and prayer. They were not always easy to interpret, and could not necessarily be applied at the time in which they were formulated. Some of them were saved up for later, more propitious situations. For example, many of the claims made by the papacy with regard to the Empire had to wait for their implementation, which depended to some extent on the relative strengths of the two parties, and indeed also on the international constellation and the fortunes of war. Popes and bishops were not above leading armies into battle. At the same time, in another context, the churches tried to restrain local feuding and to limit the days on which such fighting could take place. However, it was the papacy itself which organised 'holy wars' culminating in the crusades. During the events covered by this book, there occurred a variety of types of wars, including some fought largely for

1

religious reasons against 'heathens' and 'infidels', others between Christian powers, and after the Reformation between different Christian confessions. The ebb and flow in the religious component of war is some indication of the general importance of matters of faith. Thus international relations and war are of great interest in connection with this work. There were, in fact, few public aspects of life on which the Church did not at some time or other take a stand. Thus this study of necessity has to range widely over a large field.

The Teutonic or German kings as Holy Roman Emperors had close links with the papacy and with Italy, at any rate with Lombardy and Rome. Thus the history of the Church, including its leadership, its problems and its achievements, is followed in some detail, and not simply to the extent that it had an effect on 'Germany'. A country of that name is hard to define in any meaningful way before the nineteenth century and similar problems arise with such concepts as 'the German Church'. However, this book makes no claim to providing a comprehensive history of the relations between popes and emperors, or more universally between the spiritual and the secular power.

The present work arises from a combination of interests in a number of subjects, such as certain aspects of German nationalism, and more generally the relationship between religion and politics. The term 'German nationalism' is here used in the sense of movements arising first in the French Revolutionary and Napoleonic eras. The Germans were as much entitled as, say, the Italians to form something like a national state, or to follow the earlier example of the French. To nineteenth-century historians supporting what one might summarise as the German national movement, the unification of the country was the natural outcome of its previous history. Conversely, the history of Germany was interpreted in the light of this apparently logical (or even inevitable or predestined) development. But was there a straight line that led from the Holy Roman Empire that ended in 1806 and the German Confederation of 1815–66 to the modern German national state? After all, as late as 1848 the national movement was divided on the question as to what territories, such as – above all – Austria, should be included. Obviously a Greater Germany (*Großdeutschland*) including the whole or parts of the Habsburg Monarchy, would have been completely different from the Lesser Germany (*Kleindeutschland*) that emerged under Bismarck; the former was not an impossibility in the middle of the nineteenth century. For a Greater Germany under a Roman Catholic emperor there would have been much more continuity with the Holy Roman Empire than there was for a Germany under Protestant Prussian leadership. Thus later development affected, and was liable to distort, the interpretation of the past. It therefore seemed worth while to take a fresh look at the development of the Germanic peoples and their role in the Holy Roman Empire, if one could do so without judging them from the angle of the modern German national state.

The religious factor certainly complicated the interpretation of German history. As already mentioned, the decision for a Lesser or Greater Germany had religious implications affecting the leadership of the new state. The Catholic majority in Greater Germany became a minority in the Lesser Germany. Its Protestant majority viewed the medieval Christian heritage, and particularly the relationship of Germanic rulers with the papacy and in some ways with Italy, in quite a different light from Catholics. In this connection, a historical treatment aware of these tensions and trying to rise above them also seemed to be worth attempting. In view of the many connections between religious and political factors, an examination of the history of what was to become Germany conducted within the framework of the relationship between religion and politics appeared to hold out some promise of elucidation. It is hoped that this has been realised in the book.

It is this relationship between religion and politics, between the ecclesiastical and secular spheres, which provides the thread from the Christianisation of the Germanic peoples to, at the very least, the Peace of Westphalia of 1648 ending the Thirty Years War. For most of the period from the eighth to the sixteenth century, intermittently from the second half of the thirteenth century to the abdication of Emperor Charles V in 1556, the story is dominated by the relationship of the Germanic kings, as emperors, with the papacy. In the book, Church and 'State' are, so far as possible, given equal weight. The successes and failures of papal and imperial plans are only explicable in terms of the events and personalities connected with their implementation. They therefore require narrative, as well as analysis, as will be seen in the chapters that follow.

2 The Germanic Peoples, the Roman Empire and Christianity (until 814)

The history of the people that was (Austria apart) largely included in the newly formed German Reich in 1870–1 was shaped by a combination of Germanic traditions with those of antiquity, Judaism and Christianity. Germany was not, however, unique in this. The Germanic tribes that settled in such areas as the Rhineland, the present Lower Saxony, Thuringia and Bavaria were part of a larger family of peoples that helped to establish the English and Scandinavian kingdoms. The destinies of these Germanic peoples were deeply affected by both classical antiquity and Christianity, as mediated through their contact with a Roman Empire that eventually adopted Christianity. Thus Italy played a vital role in the history of many of the Germanic peoples, in view of the position of Rome as the capital of the (Western) Empire and as the centre of Latin Christianity, indeed eventually as the seat of the papacy. In this way the Germanic peoples became part of a Christian order that had absorbed much of the heritage of classical antiquity, not only Latin, but also Greek. The East Roman (Byzantine) Empire was based on Greek culture, in both church and state, and through the Eastern Church many Greek influences continued to enter Christianity, and therefore to influence the Germanic peoples.

The Germanic peoples were attracted to the Roman Empire, with its achievements and wealth, as peaceful settlers, as soldiers, as confederate auxiliaries and eventually as invaders and conquerors. They focused on the Empire even after the abdication of the last emperor in the West in 476 and the general decline (except for intermittent periods of resurgence) of the Empire in the East. One reason is that for the 'barbarian' (in the sense of somebody who was neither a Roman nor a Greek), the attainments of Roman and Greek culture became even more awe-inspiring through the mysteries of the Christian religion. Thanks to the establishment and growing importance of the papacy, Rome became the very symbol of church and state in the ancient world, drawing many migrating peoples to Rome and Italy.

Altogether, through their ability to assimilate ancient cultures, the Germanic peoples were able to act as a link between classical and medieval civilisation, to provide European continuity.[1] In this sense the Germanic world has been called the greatest and the most permanent creation of the political-military genius of Rome.[2] The Germanic peoples that conquered many parts of Europe were comparatively few in numbers in relation to the populations of the countries over which they ruled. This necessarily required co-operation and compromise between the new and the old. The price the Germanic peoples paid for their successful assimilation of previous cultures was that most of them – with the notable exception of the Franks – lost their identity by becoming merged with the populations they conquered.[3] Thus such events as the abdication of the last West Roman emperor in 476 were less of a break than has previously been thought. In Italy at that time the transition from a (West) Roman Empire requiring support from the Germanic soldiery to the technically mixed Germanic–Byzantine regime that followed involved only limited change.

The German national movement in the nineteenth century emphasised more what separated Germans from other Europeans than what united their people with them. For anyone who writes in English, there is a special problem in dealing with this period. Germans in their language can distinguish between *Germanen* (Old or Ancient Germans, Germanic peoples) and *Deutsche* (modern Germans), whereas the English term 'Germans' covers both without differentiating between them. Thus a German historian can say succinctly: '*Germanentum und Deutschtum sind nicht identisch*'[4], which can hardly be rendered elegantly in English. The literal translation would be: 'Germanicness [referring to the Old Germans] and [modern] Germanness are not identical.' In the present work an attempt will be made to keep these concepts apart, in spite of the linguistic and stylistic difficulties.

Any treatment of the Germanic peoples before they come into contact with the Roman Empire and Christianity suffers from two major problems: the information is sparse and there is no agreement on the interpretation of the little we know. While the former is easily understandable, the latter requires explanation. On the face of it one might assume that the more recent an event, the more controversial it might be, with the corollary that happenings two thousand years ago were not so likely to arouse the passions. But such a conclusion would be mistaken. In some respects the engagement and sometimes even the bitterness in discussions among German historians of early Germanic origins shares overtones with the more famous and better publicised *Historikerstreit* (historians' dispute) of recent years about the Nazi regime.[5]

Why should an examination of the remote Germanic past stir the emotions? It has something to do with Germany being a 'belated nation',[6] with disagreement over the record of the comparatively brief period of the unified German state established by Bismarck, and with Germany's place in Europe and European civilisation; this is once more a topical subject with the achievement of German reunification. The more 'nationalist' German historians in recent years tend to emphasise a Germanic identity which by a process of continuity led to the modern Germany. They abhor receptiveness to foreign influences, often regarding these as harmful and as destructive of 'good German' traditions, among which they rank representative institutions and a freedom peculiar to Germanic tribes. These historians tend to attribute the delay in German unification until 1870 to preoccupation with matters that had little relevance to Germany itself, as well as to outside interference, particularly by the papacy. Although many generations separate them from the great writers of the German national movement in the nineteenth century, both were looking to the past for answers about the present and future of their country.

Strong opposition to these rather nationalistic views has been voiced in Germany during recent decades by scholars of a more cosmopolitan outlook who regard the quest for pure Germanic peoples as futile. Countering racial doctrines, they have pointed out that very early on, during migrations, the Germanic tribes absorbed other peoples, such as Celts. These scholars also emphasise that for our historical accounts of the Germanic peoples we have to rely on observers like Julius Caesar and Tacitus, who were bound to see things through Roman spectacles, thus unwittingly becoming responsible for some distortion. In any case, by the time Caesar and Tacitus wrote, the Germanic tribes were already in the process of being exposed to Roman culture. The 'internationalists' criticise their opponents for assuming that they can view the Germanic peoples in a kind of static or timeless position, in isolation from their environment and from the cultures with which they came into contact. Instead of objecting to receptiveness to other influences, they view the interaction with the Roman Empire and the Christian Church positively. Unfortunately the sparsity of historical information leaves the field open to all those who have political and religious axes to grind.

Before their conversion to Christianity, the Germanic tribes had various religions which can be described neutrally as pre-Christian. They have also been called heathen. The term 'heathenism', in the sense of a sub-group of paganism, ought not to be used in a disparaging sense, certainly not in that of denoting an absence of religion. The non-Christian Germanic peoples are sometimes classified as heathen, as opposed to the 'pagan' religions of, for instance, Greece and Rome. The German language incidentally, only has the term *heidnisch*. Without wishing to minimise the differences between Christianity and pre-Christian religions, there is now an increasing recognition of their overlaps and the difficulty of making a clear distinction between magic and religion. After all, even Pope Gregory I in 597 recommended 'not the destruction, but the adaptation of pagan shrines and celebrations'.[7]

Germanic religion and cult gave a coherence to each tribe, which was based on the extended family, the *Sippe*. Tribal leadership was in the hands of certain men who were regarded as especially *edel* (noble) because of some outstanding feat they – or their ancestors – had performed in the past, for instance in battle. The nobility were the leaders who chose from among themselves as their chieftain, duke or king someone they credited with particular charisma. This ruler, who occupied a very special position marked by his assumed divine descent, was also a kind of high priest. Sometimes these two functions were in different hands, with the king ranking higher than the high priest, though the latter had a security of tenure which in the case of the ruler was dependent on continued success. Fortune in war and peace were regarded as favourable signs from the gods. But what happened if the chieftain or the dynasty he had founded lost his *Heil*, his divine charisma, and became unlucky? There was always liable to be tension between the divine status of the royal family and earthly realities, if the charisma gradually disappeared, as it did for instance first with the Merovingians, and then with the succeeding Carolingians. Though the chieftain was elected by the nobles, this was not necessarily incompatible with the special position of a ruling family. Election might simply confirm the charisma, or select certain members of the ruling dynasty in preference to others, though the charisma applied to the whole family, or at any rate to its male members. Formal primogeniture was still unknown and the extension of the charisma to all sons was liable to lead to partitions of the inheritance.

The duke or king was not an absolute ruler. The nobility exercised some independent judgment and the king could not count on its unconditional allegiance. Germanic institutions may be called an aristocracy with a monarchical head. Indeed, not only the nobility, but even lesser families were entitled to secure justice for themselves. The religious cult helped to regulate relations between different sections of society and to keep the clan together, as well as to differentiate it from others.

We can assume that organisation and customs were modified by the Germanic tribes (*Stämme*) as they began their migrations, fought for land and eventually settled permanently. These different challenges were bound to affect the position of the duke or king. He began as leader of a certain following (*Gefolgschaft*), then became a military chieftain (*Heereskönig*) and eventually a territorial ruler. As a war leader the chieftain would also recruit outside his tribe, or he might take charge of a larger tribal group. If successful, he would thus become the territorial ruler not only of his own people, but of those he had conquered. In more settled conditions, ruler and nobility would represent the interests of the *Stamm* in the new region. The acquired territory then received the name of the conquering tribe. In general, the organisation sketched proved remarkably adaptable in seeing the Germanic peoples through the various phases in their development. However, they were bound to be affected by contact with the Roman Empire and with the peoples they conquered.

Julius Caesar began the conquest of the territory inhabited by Germanic tribes in 55 BC. But the Roman advance was checked during the reign of the Emperor Augustus. In AD 9, the Roman general, Varus, was decisively beaten by Arminius, a chieftain of the Germanic *Cherusker*, who had earlier served with distinction in the Roman army and had received Roman citizenship. German legend has – probably quite inaccurately – immortalised him as Hermann. Arminius' victory in battle had profound consequences for the future of Germany and indeed of Europe. A large-scale Roman conquest of the whole of what later became Germany, similar to what happened – for instance – in France, never took place. In most of the territory east of the Rhine and north of the Danube there was thus nothing parallel to the fusion of Roman culture with local traditions that produced a mainly Celtic–Roman civilisation (with some Germanic elements) in Gaul. Only a comparatively small part of modern Germany, largely west of the Rhine and south of the Danube, ever came under Roman rule and shared Roman culture and law. The greater part of Germany, including the state which was to take over leadership in the nineteenth century, Brandenburg–Prussia, had no part in the Roman experience.

There were, however, many contacts between the independent Germanic tribes and the Roman Empire. These took place in spite of the establishment of a military border by the Romans, the *Limes*, largely along the Rhine and the Danube. Roman civilisation and good pay attracted many Germans to the Roman legions, some of them even becoming body-guards to the emperors as early as the reign of Augustus. Well before the great migration of peoples (*Völkerwanderung*) and the foundation of the Germanic states in Italy, Germans were accustomed to serving there: and whole tribes were incorporated in the Roman Empire as confederates (*foederati*). From the beginning, relations between the Germanic tribes and Roman Empire were ambivalent, increasingly so as the grip of the Romans on their own Empire loosened. Germanic tribes were liable to alternate between loyalty and hostility to the Empire, depending on changing circumstances, besides often warring among themselves.

In the long term, relations of the Germanic tribes with the Roman Empire, as well as between themselves, were decisively affected by Emperor Constantine's abandonment of the struggle against Christianity, followed by the gradual Christianisation of the Empire. In view of the role played by the religious cult in holding a tribe together, the eventual conversion of the Germanic tribes to a major supranational religion cutting across tribal boundaries was bound to have a profound effect on them, weakening traditional frameworks and removing obstacles to acculturation. After the Roman Empire, Christianity – in many cases taken over from the Romans – was the second great cultural influence to which the Germanic peoples became exposed, opening up to them even further parts of the heritage of antiquity.

The process of Christianisation took many centuries. In the generations after Constantine I (306–37) and Theodosius I (379–95), the Church was initially too preoccupied with its struggle against paganism in Roman society to have much time and energy to convert Germanic tribes. At a later stage, missionary efforts were made among the Germanic peoples within the boundaries of the Roman Empire. A number of German tribes, or parts of them – sometimes as 'confederate' allies of the Romans or serving in their armies, sometimes as conquerors of imperial territory – gave up their indigenous religion and accepted baptism. It so happened that at a crucial time after the year 350 Arianism, rather than Catholicism, was in the ascendant at Constantinople under the Emperor Constantius.

Arius, a presbyter in Alexandria, had earlier, during the reign of Emperor Constantine, put forward an interpretation of the Trinity according to which Christ the Son, although the highest of all creatures, was still a creature and that he had a beginning of existence. Arius' contention was opposed by another Alexandrian cleric, Athanasius, who affirmed that man's eternal salvation was imperilled if the relationship of the Son to the Father was not eternal and unchangeable. Christ could only be the mediator in the relationship between humanity and divinity if, while fully human, he was eternally divine. Athanasius resisted reducing Christ to a subordinate god, which might lead to the kind of polytheism practised by the pagans. The unity of the Trinity was in danger from dualism, from the Arian separation of the creature from the creator, just as the Gnostics had separated body and spirit.[8] The doctrinal cleavage presented a threat to the unity of the Church. Although Christianity had not yet become the official religion of the Roman Empire, the emperor took action to restore stability. Constantine therefore summoned a general council of the episcopate to Nicaea in 325. Under presssure from the emperor, Arianism was rejected by the acceptance of the formulation that the Son is of one substance with the Father, and that the Father and the Son are 'the same'.

The Germanic tribes in the Balkans were, however, converted by Arian missionaries south of the Danube.[9] These tribes eventually settled mainly in the Western parts of the Empire, where Catholicism prevailed and where Arianism had never been so strong as in the East. Perhaps in this connection no move was more crucial than that of the Ostrogoths from the East, where they had been baptised as Arians, to the West, at the very moment when important changes were taking place there.

Generally it can be said that while invaders, mainly Germanic, at times penetrated both halves of the Empire, they were militarily more successful in the West than in the East. Whereas they effectively disrupted the political life in the West, they failed to secure control in the East.[10] The Germanic tribes were able to establish a strong position for themselves in Italy, mainly as the allies of the West Roman emperors. In 476 the Germanic commander Odoaker was proclaimed king by his troops in Rome and the last West Roman emperor was overthrown. Thus Germanic peoples found themselves

residual heirs to power in the West Roman Empire, though at first technically under the authority of the East Roman (Byzantine) emperor. For a time
Odoaker ruled in Italy with Byzantine approval, but eventually he got
involved in a dispute with the Emperor Zeno.

Odoaker was not the only Germanic ruler with whom Zeno was having
difficulties. There was also Zeno's nominal ally, the Ostrogoth king Theodoric, who periodically intervened against Byzantium in order to better his
bargaining position. With his base in the Balkans, Theodoric was too close to
the eastern capital, Constantinople, for the emperor's comfort. Zeno was
able to achieve a dual objective when he persuaded the Ostrogoth king to
take his army to Italy. On the one hand, he removed a threat to Constantinople, on the other he secured an ally against his troublesome subordinate
Odoaker in Italy. Zeno promised Theodoric that he could rule in Italy as the
Emperor's deputy once he had achieved victory over Odoaker, until he
could personally assume power there. It took Theodoric from 488 to 493
to defeat his rival, whom he murdered treacherously,[11] and he was eventually recognised by Byzantium as the emperor's deputy in Italy. Theodoric's
rule in Italy, though to some extent following in Odoaker's footsteps, made a
much stronger impact on posterity, setting a pattern of which later Germanic
rulers, like the Carolingians, were not to be unmindful.

Thanks to his imperial commission and to his great ability, the former
chieftain of a wandering tribe in the Balkans became the founder of a
kingdom in Italy. Here Theodoric drew support not only from his own
people, who merely formed a small fraction of the total population, but
also from native Italians. He had a dual legitimacy. First, as the son and
designated heir of an Ostrogoth king, he had proved his mettle in battle as a
Heereskönig and had been himself proclaimed king by his victorious army in
471. The Gothic army he took to Italy, which contained many elements of
other peoples, was one of the pillars of his rule. Secondly, through his
appointment as consul by the emperor, he had acquired Roman citizenship.
Theodoric was adopted by the emperor and took the name of a Roman
imperial dynasty, calling himself *Flavius Theodoricus rex* as master of Italy[12]
rather than *rex Gothorum*. He had the title of *princeps Romanus* and some
Romans acclaimed him as *dominus*, their master, and as *Augustus*.

With the end of the West Roman emperorship, some of the republican
Roman institutions went through a process of revitalisation, and the senate
became more active. Theodoric determined membership of this body. He
controlled the Roman bureaucracy and made appointments up to its higher
senatorial–patrician ranks.

One of the most remarkable aspects of Theodoric's regime was the
manner in which this 'barbarian' military chieftain, who had learned much
from Byzantium (where he had spent some years as a hostage) was able to
integrate Gothic with Roman institutions. He applied a general territorial

law in the Italian kingdom, which did not differentiate between various ethnic groups and from which even his Gothic followers were not exempt. He tried to get them to acknowledge in public life an undivided state, a common *civilitas*.

Although himself an Arian, Theodoric, as the emperor's deputy, had authority over the Catholic Church. Except during his final years, Theodoric's relations with that church and in particular with the papacy were generally good. The Ostrogoth ruler of Italy did not follow the example of some Arian kings in persecuting Catholicism. The son of a Catholic mother, Theodoric was tolerant towards Catholicism. He even gave a helping hand to attempts aimed at healing the theological disputes between the papacy and the Byzantine emperors, though he must have been aware that any understanding between them might affect his own position adversely.

In fact, Theodoric's position was weakened when emperor and pope moved closer to each other. Thus, after ruling with great success for many years, Theodoric encountered grave political and religious problems during the final stages of his reign. After reaching agreement with Byzantium on his proposed successor, the designated heir died. In the ensuing confusion, Theodoric took severe measures against Roman senate leaders – among them the famous statesman and philosopher Boethius – who wished to safeguard the future. In turn these actions were viewed in Constantinople as persecution of Catholics and led to the issuing of anti-Arian decrees in the East. Theodoric, desperate to obtain a more favourable atmosphere for himself in Constantinople, pressed Pope John I into service and in 525 compelled the spiritual head of Catholics to undertake an embassy to the emperor to plead on the king's behalf and on that of his Arian co-religionists. Thus one mistake was compounded by another. The pope was received with great respect by the emperor. Neither side had any interest in making concessions to Theodoric. When the pope returned, the king put him into prison, where he died, to be followed to the grave within a few weeks by Theodoric himself, in August 526. Theodoric's fame outlived him and he appears as Dietrich von Bern (Verona) in the German heroic songs, the *Heldenlieder*.[13]

Theodoric's reign ended in failure. Neither his dynasty nor the Ostrogoth kingdom in Italy survived his death for very long. But the long-term historical consequences of Theodoric's creation must not be underrated. It is due to some extent to Odoaker, but even more to the Ostrogoth king, that the conquerors saw the wisdom of building on what earlier generations had achieved, and that the culture, political theory and law of antiquity survived the Germanic invasions. Thus Theodoric was able to set an example to his brother-in-law, Clovis, King of the Franks, at times his enemy and at others his friend. This helps to explain the success of the same policy of co-operation in more auspicious circumstances, facilitated by Clovis' conversion to

Catholicism. The Franks 'were not, like the Goths, isolated in the midst of an alien population, but still remained in contact with the other German peoples', over some of which they extended their rule, such as the Thuringians.[14]

Theodoric for most of his reign followed a constructive policy based on establishing harmony between Roman and Germanic culture. Except at the very end of his reign, he managed to manoeuvre, on the whole, skilfully between the various cultural, religious, political, diplomatic and military interests. He had to take into account the emperor, the leading senatorial caste in Rome and the pope, as well as a multitude of factors in foreign policy, from the Visigoths in Spain (over whom he also ruled for a time)[15] to other Germanic peoples, such as the Franks. The strength of his position in Italy was mainly due to his bringing about a prolonged period of comparative quiet and prosperity. Theodoric enjoyed the respect of both Ostrogoths and Romans. Why did his state not prove more lasting? The main reason was probably that the Byzantine emperors were not prepared, in the long run, to accept such a strong deputy in Italy. In the year following Theodoric's death, Justinian became emperor in Constantinople, determined to destroy Ostrogoth rule in Italy. More generally, religious differences between the Arian Ostrogoths and the Catholic Italians, through hampering social intercourse and intermarriage, proved an obstacle to the fusion of the two cultures and peoples.[16]

After Theodoric's death, the Ostrogoth state in Italy gradually disintegrated from internal dissensions within the dynasty. This provided an opportunity for Justinian to conquer parts of the West Roman Empire, which he claimed as the remaining Roman emperor. After initial Byzantine successes, the Ostrogoths under King Totila prevailed for a time, but were in the end defeated in 552 by Byzantium with the help of Germanic auxiliary troops. Totila was killed in battle and the Ostrogoth state in Italy ceased to exist. The historian Felix Dahn, who published numerous scholarly volumes on the early Germanic peoples, popularised the struggle of the Ostrogoths against Byzantium to hundreds of thousands of German readers in successive generations in his novel *Kampf um Rom (A Struggle for Rome)*, first published in the early days of the Bismarckian Empire, in 1876.

For a few years Italy was a Byzantine province. However in 568, invasions by another Germanic tribe, the Arian *Langobarden* (later called Lombards), soon considerably reduced the Byzantine hold over Italy. All these events were of great interest to the bishops of Rome and to the institution of the papacy.

The increasing importance of the Bishop of Rome was among the notable developments in the growth of the Church during its first centuries. During the early decades, the Church at Jerusalem occupied a leading position. The extensive damage done to Jerusalem by the Romans in the year 70 eliminated the city as the natural centre of the Church, although it remained one of the apostolic patriarchates, with Antioch and Alexandria. The Roman congregation was generally accepted as having a special place in Christionity, because Peter and Paul had occupied the chief position in Rome, and had suffered martyrdom and been buried there.

The significance of certain centres in the early Church must not, however, be exaggerated. Initially the Church in each region was largely autonomous. By the third century, bishops had been recognised generally as the leaders of their congregations in what has been called the monarchic episcopate. Bishops had both the internal function of watching over the orthodoxy of their flock – priests and laity – as well as the external task of keeping their diocese in touch with others. As the Church grew, a number of dioceses were grouped together in provinces, which often conformed to the corresponding secular divisions, under a metropolitan bishop, so called because he resided in the metropolis of the area. Above the metropolitans there were those bishops who were accorded the status of patriarchs. This rank was due, in the case of Rome, Alexandria, Antioch, as well as Jerusalem (which was only recognised later in this capacity) to the apostolic origins of their bishoprics. Only in that of Constantinople was it a consequence of its recently acquired status as the 'New Rome'.

Eventually the bishop, rather than the congregation of Rome, began to be accorded a special status in the Christian Church as a whole, in due course to be recognised as pope. It is remarkable that the seat of the papacy was thus placed in a city which witnessed not only the beginning of the persecution of Christians at the time of Nero, but also some of the most brutal acts committed by the Roman authorities at any time during the centuries of oppression against adherents of the new faith. The hegemony of the Bishop of Rome was very much advanced by Pope Stephen I (254–7), who demanded that – in conformity with Roman practice – other Catholic churches should cease to rebaptise on their admission those who had already received baptism elsewhere. Although not the first bishop of Rome convinced of the primacy of his see, it was Stephen who made the first known formal claim in this respect based on St Matthew's gospel (16: 18–19)[17]: 'you are Peter, and on this rock I will build my church, and the gates of Hades will not prevail against it. I will give you the keys of the kingdom of heaven, and whatever you bind on earth will be bound in heaven, and whatever you loose on earth will be loosed in heaven.'

According to gradually developing papal interpretation, based on a continuous pursuit of a remarkable 'unity of themes' as well as a 'consistency of principles',[18] this text provided the basis for the foundation of the Church as the body of all the faithful, and for the establishment at the same time of the government over this institution. Both the authority and the Church over which this authority was to be exercised were held to have been instituted in one and the same act. It was further argued that as St Peter had directed the Church from Rome, and had in a sense been the first Bishop of Rome, so the occupant of the Roman bishopric was thereby the successor of St Peter and thus possessed primacy over all the Church.

These claims, which began to be made during the third century, when the position of the Church was still precarious, were far-reaching in themselves, but they were taken even further by a number of assertions. It was held that so far as his office was concerned, the pope was not part of the Church, but above the Church; also that he was not accountable to anybody in the Church; and finally that he alone was a kind of link between humanity and divinity, as his actions in binding and loosing on earth had consequences in heaven. To buttress this position, it was maintained that the pope – even if he so wished – could not divest himself of powers which had been biblically entrusted to him as the successor of St Peter himself.

Personally, popes tended to regard themselves as unworthy of their position, but they distinguished between person and office, arguing that the validity of their official acts was not affected by any personal short-comings. The implications of this interpretation of the text from St Matthew both for papal authority within the Church and for the pope's relationship with secular Christian rulers were enormous. But the latter could hardly be visualised during the papacy of Stephen I under non-Christian emperors. Indeed, whatever the theological merits of the position of the popes, in the long term recognition of their claims would depend at least partly on political developments. Stephen, interestingly, did not have his way over those who opposed his policy with regard to rebaptism.

The events during Constantine's reign were bound to affect the position of the papacy, though not only positively. In one sense the authority of all bishops declined as a result of the influence the emperor exercised over the Church. In particular the Bishop of Rome was overshadowed more by a Christian than by a pagan emperor, especially by a Christian emperor present in Rome. Constantine's transfer of the capital to Byzantium, though strengthening the pope's position in Rome itself, rendered it more difficult to make papal views felt at the imperial court in its new Greek environment. Bishop Hosius of Cordova and not the Bishop of Rome was Constantine's main ecclesiastical adviser. Even towards the end of the fourth century, after the establishment of Christianity as the state religion, when Theodosius I was present in Italy, it was Ambrose, Bishop of Milan (which was then the capital), rather than the Bishop of Rome who had the ear of the emperor on ecclesiastical matters. Papal leadership in the Church was not yet fully established. Distance from the main capital Constantinople meant less influence at court, but also opened up the possibility of greater independence from the emperor. The Bishop of Rome thus escaped the fate of becoming a high-level imperial chaplain, such as the

Patriarch of Constantinople may have been at times. The popes certainly took full advantage of their comparative independence during the following centuries.

The definite division of the Empire into West Rome and East Rome after the death of Theodosius I in 395 was a final recognition not only of the extreme difficulty of governing a large empire from one centre, but also of the failure of a synthesis between Latin and Greek culture. Interestingly enough the Church had to some extent anticipated the administrative division when in the course of the third century, the Christians of the West had ceased to use the Greek language.[19] Thus both in religion and politics, West and East were going their own way. In religion this meant that achieving doctrinal harmony all over the Empire was bound to prove hard to attain, though it was in fact achieved intermittently. Even more, rites – such as those used in liturgy – were bound to vary between the Latin West and the Greek East.

For the papacy the gulf between the two parts of the Empire had both benefits and drawbacks. In the Latin West, Rome was the only apostolic see and was thus unchallenged by those found in the East, such as Alexandria, Antioch and Jerusalem. However, there was little chance of the Bishop of Rome asserting authority over the Eastern Church. This was not only because of different theological approaches, but also because the Byzantine emperors exercised a degree of control over church matters. This the papacy was not prepared to accept and thus opposed with great determination by most popes, just as they had previously resisted the occasional encroachments on the spiritual sphere by West Roman emperors. Popes – although they generally had no problem with recognising the authority of the emperor in temporal matters – deliberately asserted a position distinct from the imperial authorities. By preserving its independence from the state, the papacy thus emerged all the stronger when the line of West Roman emperors came to an end. Unlike in the West, in the East relations between Church and emperors were based on quite a different concept, namely that of the interdependence of Church and State, of a single society in harmony with the emperor as the earthly counterpart of the divine monarch. The term 'caesaropapism' has often been applied to the position of the Byzantine emperors, but should probably not be used generally and indiscriminately for the whole existence of the Empire, but only for certain periods, such as those of Justinian's reign or the iconoclastic regime.[20]

The popes painstakingly built up their position by consolidating and extending their theological claims and applying them by means of a thorough administrative system that owed a great deal to imperial Roman example. Papal rulings were modelled on the rescripts of the Roman emperors. Excellent archives, for example, took care to preserve records on which future papal claims could be based.

Certain popes did very much to buttress the position of their office on the basis of the Petrine text, always using the ground already gained by their predecessors. Thus after Stephen I, a new landmark was reached with the pontificate of Damasus (366–84), who claimed somewhat dubiously that the unique authority of the decisions of the Council of Nicaea was due to the fact that they had been approved by his predecessor. In the view of Leo I (440–61), the pope as the legal heir of St Peter could claim a fullness of power (*plenitudo potestatis*) which *inter alia* gave him full authority over other bishops. Leo's attempt to introduce into the West a scheme of unified ecclesiastical control through metropolitans of provinces under the central direction of the pope has been called 'premature but not fruitless.'[21] When Leo had trouble with Hilary, bishop of Arles, he received from the West Roman Emperor, Valentinian III, in 445 confirmation that the primacy of the popes did not require imperial approval for its application.

For the West, it was Pope Gelasius I (492–6) who elaborated the relationship between pope and emperor. Gelasius resisted the intervention of the Byzantine Emperor, Anastasius I, in ecclesiastical affairs and reminded him of the statement by Bishop Ambrose to Theodosius that the emperor is a son and not a bishop of the Church. Building on rudiments found in Augustine, Gelasius in 494 formulated the doctrine of the relations between the two powers, the ecclesiastical and the secular, the sacred authority of the bishops and the authority of the emperor, each with responsibility for its own sphere. In matters of faith even the emperor had to submit to those charged with the care of the Church. In secular matters, however, the bishops had to obey the laws of the emperor, whose rule was instituted by God.[22]

The popes, as bishops of Rome were, at least nominally, elected by the clergy and people of that diocese. They provided a strain of continuity for the population under changing circumstances, during 'barbarian' invasions and governments, as well as during the comparatively brief period of Byzantine rule following the defeat of the Ostrogoth regime. In a sense the Byzantine campaign returned Italy to its rightful rulers, the only Roman emperors after 476. The popes had never ceased to recognise the authority of the Byzantine emperors, to whom they reported their election and after whose reigns they dated their documents. They now answered in a number of matters to the East Roman official in charge of the newly created exarchate of Ravenna as the emperor's representative. Thus they had to secure his approval for their election before they could be consecrated, an inconvenient procedure that was liable to lead to considerable delays. In some periods, exarch and emperor seem to have dictated elections. For a number of reasons, however, the Byzantine presence in Italy did not lead to stability in Rome itself. Constantinople was shaken by a whole series of plots, some of which involved the exarchate of Ravenna. Also the Greek Church under various emperors deviated from the teaching of the Catholic

Church, culminating in the iconoclasm of the eighth century. Many popes with great courage opposed the intervention of emperors in matters of faith as a breach of the Gelasian doctrine of the distinctness of the two powers. The reality of the risk they took is illustrated by the fate of Pope Martin I, who in 653 was deposed by imperial decree because of his rejection of Byzantine theological innovations, forcibly removed from Rome and deported to Constantinople for trial. He died in miserable conditions in exile as a martyr to the faith in 655. The emperor who was responsible for the treatment he received, Constantine II, temporarily moved his court from Constantinople to Italy and was in residence in Rome for a time during 663, before returning home.

In some periods, the popes were virtually dukes of the Roman duchy. At first they did not seek this rule, which was forced upon them by circumstances. However, they eventually felt that measures were required to counter threats to their independence, as we have seen in ecclesiastical matters from the Byzantine emperors, then fleetingly from a generally quite helpful Theodoric, and finally later on from the Langobards. This led them to look for a protector. Their choice finally in the eighth century fell on the Franks, a Germanic tribe, who during the previous two and a half centuries had become the leading military power on the European continent.

In 486, the Merovingian Clovis, King of the Salic Franks, united by conquest the various Frankish peoples under his rule, destroyed the remnants of the West Roman Empire in Gaul and in the following years also defeated the Germanic tribes of the Thuringians and the Alemanni. He began founding a kingdom that contained parts of what later became France and Germany, as well as the Low Countries. Initially Clovis was a heathen. Under their traditions, the Germanic tribes had accorded sacral status to their rulers, ascribing their ancestry in some supernatural way to gods or to sea-beasts, part man, part bull, from whom the Merovingians claimed to be descended.[23] To what extent the Franks conformed to any general Germanic pattern (if there was one) is still being argued by historians.[24] At any rate Germanic kings – probably largely including those of the Franks – were believed to possess *Heil*, a special charisma or grace, which was passed on to their male descendants. Their families were supposed to be descended from gods, that is from divinities that were liable to vary from tribe to tribe, who were believed to bring them good harvests and to secure them victories in battle with their enemies. The *stirps regia* (royal line) had a status raised above all others, which had been acquired by establishing its rule, thus showing the possession of divine favour. On conversion to Christianity, the old genealogy had to be abandoned. Clovis and his clerical advisers were well aware of the risks the Merovingians were taking. Was Clovis' good luck going to be affected by his insult to gods sacred to his house, from whom he claimed descent? Would *sanctitas* replace *fortuna*?

Between 496 and 506, Clovis converted to Catholicism with his followers, thus nullifying the assumption that a Germanic ruler on the European continent had to be either a heathen or an Arian Christian. The story of these happenings is somewhat more complicated than the straightforward conversion of Clovis described by the historian Gregory, Bishop of Tours, two generations or so later.[25] Contrary to Gregory's account, Clovis may not have converted directly from heathenism to Catholicism, but may have passed through an intermediate Arian or quasi-Arian phase. Also the realities of this world could well have had a greater effect on his decision to become a Catholic than Gregory allows. In the bishop's account there are – probably correctly – parallels with Constantine's conversion in the desire of both rulers to enlist Christ as a powerful, victory-giving ally on their behalf.

Clovis understood the connection between religion and international power politics. The great Germanic states, such as those of Goths both Western and Eastern, were Arian. In one sense – from an ethnic point of view – they were his natural allies. A sister of Clovis was married to Theodoric, for whose power he always had a healthy respect. But the Goths were also rivals for power. Clovis did not feel any obligations towards remote kith and kin any more than he did towards his own family, among which he killed, without mercy or apparent remorse, anybody who seemed to stand in his way. His conversion did not restrain him in these efforts. He was an expansionist and soon spotted the comparative weakness of the Visigothic kingdom of Toulouse which lay on his path of conquest towards the South. His adherence to Catholicism increased the likelihood of the Gallo-Roman aristocracies in the neighbouring kingdoms switching their support from their Arian rulers to him. In this sense Clovis' adoption of Catholicism presented a Frankish challenge to Gothic dominance. In the end, the Merovingians weathered the religious transition with most of their following by retaining a kingship still at least partly based on pagan ideas[26] and thus preserving enough of their ancestral charisma. The shrines of holy people, and especially of martyrs, became the homes of Frankish piety, the substitute for pagan temples.[27] Indeed, through the deeds of King Clovis, his dynasty, the Merovingians, strengthened their charisma and thus their claim to kingship. The old habit of interpreting success as a divine favour did not disappear under Christianity.

Clovis' religious decision certainly formed a new departure, whose crucial importance cannot be exaggerated. Through Catholicism the Franks became part of the international community centred in the papacy in Rome, which would have been denied to them through adherence to Arianism. Irish and Anglo-Saxon missionaries, who played a vital part in the conversion of Germanic peoples, constituted a great accession of strength for the Frankish Church. This made possible the cultural flowering under the Carolingians and enabled Charlemagne to play a leading part in Western Christendom. The pre-condition for all this was the fusion of Germanic and Roman peoples and cultures, which could take place under Catholicism. This would have been denied by an Arian conversion, as Theodoric's regime in Italy with the two solitudes of the Catholic Roman population and the Arian Gothic army had shown.

To the Byzantine emperors, the Catholic Franks were a useful instrument against the Arian Goths. It was as the ally of Byzantium that Clovis in 507 defeated the Visigoths, whose main base was in Spain, and deprived them of much of their territory in Gaul. The expedition was co-ordinated with Byzantine fleet movements off the Italian coast which prevented Theodoric from coming to the aid of the Visigoths. For the rulers in Constantinople, the greater distance of Gaul and Germany from vital Byzantine interests made the Franks a less dangerous and much more desirable ally than the Ostrogoths in Italy. Emperor Anastasius recognised Clovis as an honorary consul, strengthening his authority over the newly-won Gallo-Romans.[28] The Frankish kingdom was thus able to build on the tradition of Rome, both imperial and Catholic. Whatever the negative aspects of Clovis' reign, the king showed remarkable ability in preserving continuity with Gallo-Roman civilisation. After Clovis' conquests, the Frankish kingdom formed the centre of gravity in the West.

As the conversion of Clovis had considerable repercussions on German history, we may pause to look more closely at the question as to how much of a change in religion did in fact take place.[29] As we have seen, we cannot fully reconstruct from what to what Clovis was converted. It is safe to assume that the break with heathenism and the acceptance of Christianity, in his case and that of his followers, was not so clear cut as was usually presumed by historians in previous ages. Western European indigenous religions in late antiquity were of a syncretistic nature and had in some respects adopted beliefs that were close to those of the monotheistic religions. At the same time, converts to Christianity did not abandon all the pagan attitudes of the past. Thus, in spite of the absolute rejection of all paganism by the Church, there had in fact been some convergence of faith. Also, whenever the Church makes converts, these contribute to changing the institution itself, partly because some at least temporary concessions to former beliefs are inevitable. According to iconographical evidence, even by the seventh century Frankish Christianity was largely an adaptation of paganism, and one could not be sure that 'the symbolic content of...paganism had disappeared from the minds of makers or users'.[30]

This is not to minimise the difference that conversion to Christianity made in this era. In many respects the step was an enormous one. That is not necessarily so in the sense of a fresh acquisition of religiosity (which may well have been previously present to a considerable extent), or in that of an impact on ethical standards. But certainly the Christian convert had to abjure beliefs that went very deep, as they related him to his ancestors and to the past of his tribe, that set it aside from others and helped to give identity to an ethnic group.[31] It was thus no easy feat for the Franks to cease believing in tribal gods and to accept a deity that knew no national boundaries. Indeed, this matter was so crucial to the Franks that the Church to some extent gave way. The converted Franks were, almost of necessity, allowed to go on as a people 'living and thinking in terms of kindreds and families. It gave them a past and a future, uniting them as kindreds with their ancestors.'[32] Actually under Christianity, family loyalties could be preserved in proprietary churches (*Eigenkirchen*) and monasteries owned by families of rank. These ecclesiastical establishments over the generations provided a link with ancestors through prayers for them, through patronage, clerical and monastic service, as well as the possession of the family cemetery, and possibly even of a local or dynastic saint. The social ends of the Franks had not been affected very much by conversion. Indeed, by accepting Christianity, the Franks – a people in which warriors played a leading part – shifted social emphasis in the kingdom towards warfare. In Christianity the elements of miracle and magic, though present before, were given even greater emphasis. The Frankish Church had been made by Gallo-Romans, but it was a church for the Germanic people.[33]

At least in theory, the new faith took precedence over ethnic traditions. Where the latter were absolutely incompatible with the former, they had to be abandoned, such as the continuing worshipping of pagan shrines and idols,[34] or the persisting habit of obtaining a bride by violence,[35] or concubinage, a custom that died hard.[36] The repeated prohibitions by successive church councils and synods of actions of this kind show that old practices disappeared but slowly. The continuing fear of humanity faced with an uncertain future elicits somewhat different responses in the pre-Christian and Christian eras. Whereas formerly human beings had sacrificed to the gods to propitiate them, now they prayed to the God of the Christians, asked Christ to intercede for them, fulfilled the requirement of charity, helped to set up ecclesiastical foundations and put their faith in the local saint. We cannot look into the hearts and souls of men and women to determine in what spirit they prayed or did charitable works, though the latter will, in any case, usually have been helpful in themselves. Who is to draw the precise line of division between superstition on the one hand and genuine religious manifestation and experience on the other?

Actually Christianity could build on the past, as the converted Germans were already religious people. 'Their lives, as individuals and as members of communities, were conditioned by the sense they had of good and evil, life and death, gods and demons.'[37] Now they became exposed to a religion which emphasised the spiritual and preached the message of divine judgment and divine salvation. Christianity, instead of following existing practice of judging the value of a faith by the worldly success it bestowed, taught the transitory nature of earthly existence and the importance of the after-life. In a period of violence, of invasion and of war, of sudden changes of fortune, the eschatological aspects of Christianity came very much to the fore. 'To that age the saints and ascetics were living and visible witnesses to the power of the world to come.'[38] In the world described by Gregory of Tours, 'the fear of the wrath of God and the vengeance of the saints was the only power capable of intimidating the lawless ruffians who were so common among the new ruling class in the semi-barbarous Frankish state'.[39]

Clergy and laity were agreed on the importance of religion for life. Lay people, who worried about the beyond, frequently turned to the priests for reassurance and advice. Both clergy and laity had their part to play and within the framework of a Christian order there was not initially, and did not necessarily have to develop, any conflict between them. As to the modern concept of a separation between church and state, this is based on assumptions of distinction and specialisation that would have been quite alien to the post-conversion Merovingian era. It was common ground that bishops and kings should act in a unified Christian manner, though there was bound to be disagreement at times on what this implied and involved. The church accepted the authority of kings and dukes in many ecclesiastical matters. It was the Frankish rulers who called church councils and synods, and presided over them, as the Emperor Constantine had done. It was they who decided whether missionaries from outside might enter their territories or should be compelled to leave them.

It was an age in which monarchs assumed some ecclesiastical responsibilities, as bishops also had to shoulder some secular ones. Earlier, during the Roman Empire, the bishops – although they were leaders of an official *cultus* closely controlled by imperial legislation – were not secular administrators, as they were to become to some extent during the Merovingian period.[40] But during the gradual decline and eventual break-up of the West Roman Empire, they had to take the place of secular Roman officials. In this period, the bishops had thus become key figures in their local communities. They had stood firm with their congregations during the foreign invasions and had 'passed into the period of barbarian settlements with a name for staying put, identified in trial with their communities, and their communities identified with them.'[41] One of the many advantages accruing to Clovis by his acceptance of the Catholic faith was that he gained direct control over the Gallo-Roman bishops who belonged to the Gallo-Roman elite that really ran Gaul.[42] This elite was able to play an important part in the Merovingian regime, because the Franks, like many of the other Germanic peoples, were prepared to work with existing institutions and to learn from them. Thus in both education and religion, which went closely hand in hand, the new masters in some respects became the apprentices of the leaders of the people they subjugated.

Clovis exercised control over the bishops in a way that was new. After defeating the Visigoths of Aquitaine, he called a council at Orléans in 511, which was attended by 32 bishops, including four metropolitans. The bishops of Northern Gaul were, however, absent.[43] Generally the bishop was an important link between his own diocese and the wider Church. He was the leader of his community, which he represented at assemblies of the Church, where he acted as a member of an episcopal college, which – in spite of disagreements and clashes of personality – fostered a corporate spirit. The king specified certain matters for discussion and stipulated that the canons passed by the council required his approval.[44] Clovis' successors for a time continued the tradition of summoning councils and synods, but later, during the Merovingian minority troubles, these assemblies for a while fell into disuse.[45]

The bishops as leaders of the institution that had preserved the greatest continuity from the Roman imperial period – the Church – drew their strength both from their ecclesiastical position and from their personal standing in society. Initially during Merovingian rule, they came from the Gallo-Roman elite. Their only possible rival for local influence was the count of the city, but during the break-up of the Roman Empire, civil government had all but disappeared and this had left the count's authority weakened. Thus by Merovingian times, the position of bishop was considered to be on a higher rung of the ladder than that of the count.[46] Indeed the latter office was often a stepping-stone to the former, giving the bishop useful previous administrative experience. Eventually the appointment of a count was normally made subject to the bishop's agreement. Under the Merovingians, the bishops were able to preserve a considerable independence, which was only undermined from the time of Charles Martel in the first half of the eighth century onwards.

The Frankish Church under the Merovingians initially did not develop much of an indigenous missionary impulse. The internal pace of Christianisation was slow, impeded by the poor state of learning, and it took time until the Frankish nobility began to play an important part in ecclesiastical affairs. For men of action the often quite complex teaching of the New Testament will have presented greater difficulties of comprehension than the historical books of the Old Testament, with its more familiar story of kings, wars, victories and defeats. While in the long run the Bible was the book that did more for educating peoples than any other, in the short term the effectiveness of biblical interpretation may have been hampered by the limited literacy of many of those at whom it was directed. In view of these factors, the liturgy assumed a great importance and attuned the mind of gentiles and 'barbarians' to 'a new view of life and a new concept of history'.[47]

The impulse for greater religious activity in the kingdom of the Franks, in Francia, came at first from Irish monks. Ireland had not been part of the

Roman Empire, and its Christianity had some features that differentiated it from that found elsewhere. The culture of Ireland was rural rather than urban. Under the Irish model, the abbot controlled a monastery and the territory under its aegis. The Irish monks alone in Western Europe (probably under oriental influence) preserved the ascetic ideal of *peregrinatio*, of regarding life on this earth as a constant pilgrimage from place to place in preparation for a heavenly home. In pursuit of this ideal they left their beloved homes, preaching and founding monastic cells in various places. Their missionary work was incidental to their fundamental pilgrimage.

The Irish mission to the European continent was begun by St Columbanus (c. 540–615), who landed on the coast of Brittany with 12 followers in 590 or 591. Columbanus was distinguished by the penitential severity of his behaviour and by his learning. Through his personal influence and his focus on God and God's relationship with humanity, he provided a gust of fresh air for the Frankish Church.

Unlike his Anglo-Saxon successors, Columbanus had no official mission to the Frankish church, though he was in touch with the papacy. He depended on establishing *ad hoc* relations with rulers and bishops, which were not always satisfactory. Columbanus, whose reliance on kings was considerable,[48] did not get on well with all the princes in the territories where he did his missionary work and was indeed expelled in 610 by King Theuderich II of Burgundy. Columbanus paid little attention to existing ecclesiastical law and institutions, as he was not particularly interested in organisation, concerning which stipulations are lacking in his severe monastic rules. These deviate in some respects from the Rule of St Benedict, which was favoured by the papacy. While acknowledging the place of public penance and reconciliation by a bishop – for instance, in the case of heresy – Columbanus emphasised the importance of private penance, which had the dual purpose of regret for sins committed and the aim of the avoidance of further sin. He founded three monasteries in Burgundy, of which the main was at Luxeuil, but his influence spread far beyond their cells through the intimate priestly relationship, based on confession and penance, that he established with the laity and particularly with the nobility in the neighbourhood. The monasteries thus played an important part in spreading Christianity to the countryside and acted as centres of education, though this was not their primary or original function. This rural dimension received strong support from the nobility, who founded churches and monasteries on their estates. Generally they were subjected to old Germanic land law and thus became the property of the landlord (*Eigenkirchen*). These private foundations certainly helped to give Christianity a wider geographical and social diffusion, extending to the peasantry, too.[49]

While the flourishing of Frankish monastic life – over a brief period – owed most to Columbanus, it would have been impossible without the active patronage of the Merovingian royal family.[50] Politics and religion were never very far apart, even in this period, and Franco-Irish missionaries were apt to be looked at askance when they ventured outside the Frankish kingdom. Other rulers, such as the Duke of Bavaria, were liable to regard them as a kind of Frankish 'fifth column'. Actually, the missionaries initially found themselves more often than not doing their work among lapsed or not very convinced Christians, rather than among genuine heathens.

A series of minorities, beginning after King Dagobert I's death in 637, brought about a prolonged period of political instability which in turn adversely affected the Church, leading to a weakening of clerical discipline and a slowing down of missionary work. A new impulse to the Frankish Church was, however, given by a second wave of foreign missionaries, this time from the Anglo-Saxon kingdoms, beginning in 678 with Wilfrid of Hexham, Bishop of York, continuing with Willibrord, and culminating in Winfrith, better known as St Boniface. These religious developments coincided with the strengthening of the position of the family later called the Carolingians after Charlemagne, who in 687 were able to extend their office of *Hausmeier* or Steward to the whole of the Frankish kingdom.[51]

The Anglo-Saxons had not – like the Franks – come to Christianity mainly through the medium of a well-established local culture, but through the Irish and papal mission from outside. Their activity in the Frankish kingdom thus led to a fresh beginning on a Germanic and Christian basis, in which the culture of antiquity was experienced indirectly through Christianity.[52]

While the Irish pilgrims, consistent with their attitude, had failed to leave a firm institutional framework, though providing great personal and spiritual stimulation, the Anglo-Saxons were first-class organisers. They always remained in touch with their native country, from which they drew much spiritual strength. The Anglo-Saxon missionaries worked unremittingly with both the Frankish rulers and the popes. Their links with Rome, which went back to the very foundation of the Anglo-Saxon Church, were very close, and they sought guidance from the papacy as a matter of course. Adopting the episcopal church pattern from Rome, they were respectful of the Rule of St Benedict without regarding it as normative. The Rule was composed around 540 by St Benedict of Nursia, then Abbot of Monte Cassino. In it he 'outlined...the government, discipline and observance of a self-contained monastic family occupied with common prayer, private meditative reading and active work'.[53] It was based on a concept of monastic life that was 'essentially social and co-operative', and had a 'strongly practical character'.[54] Altogether, the Anglo-Saxon Church made a major contribution to the partial preservation of the culture of antiquity.

After a short Frisian mission undertaken by Wilfrid, Bishop of York, in 678, his pupil Willibrord began the work on a more regular basis in 690, exactly a century after Columbanus had landed in Brittany. He arrived at an opportune moment, for the Carolingian *maior domus* (Steward), Pippin II, had just conquered Frisia. Willibrord here worked closely with Pippin, for – even more than their Irish predecessors – the Anglo-Saxons deliberately allied themselves with rulers. Thus Christianisation and Frankish conquest could go hand in hand. Willibrord also went to Rome to secure the pope's consent for his missionary work. To complete the triangle, it was he who established the first contact between the Carolingians and the papacy, whose co-operation was to play so important a part in the future. The result of this trilateral co-operation was the foundation of a missionary bishopric for Willibrord.

The Anglo-Saxon mission was crowned by St Boniface, born Winfrith in Wessex (perhaps near Exeter) in the late or middle 670s as the son of parents of substantial means.[55] He entered a Benedictine monastery. Inspired by reports of Willibrord's missionary work in Frisia, he decided to join him there in 716, but owing to difficulties in the area at the time returned to England the following year. However, in 718 he was back on the European continent, where he was to spend the rest of his life, this time beginning by going straight to Rome. He was the man of the hour, for his arrival coincided with both the forward push of the Carolingians into Germany and the awakening of the popes to the missionary possibilities of the region. The task he received from the papacy was to report back to Rome on the situation of Christianity in Germanic territory, just when Pippin II's son, Charles Martel, was forcing the invading Saxons to retreat into central Germany. Between 719 and 722 Willibrord and Boniface collaborated in the re-establishment of the Frisian church under Frankish protection. But some of the most important work done by Boniface was carried out in Hesse, Thuringia and Franconia, where he operated by establishing missionary stations as advanced bases, 'Benedictine monasteries as points of acculturation and bishoprics as centers of ecclesiastical control'.[56] Boniface – who had a kind of roving commission from the papacy – evangelised on a considerable scale, holding mass baptisms.

Naturally Boniface encountered some resistance from local bishops who were not happy with his papal commission where it appeared to infringe their diocesan rights. He weathered this resistance thanks to a measure of support given to him at the express wish of the papacy by Charles Martel (who often, however, appeared to be unconcerned with his efforts).[57] The nobility were unhappy about the insistence of Boniface that church property should be restored. Those noblemen who had become bishops were rather unresponsive to his appeal for a less worldly life on their part. Not surprisingly they opposed his plans for a metropolitan system, with suffragan bishops subordinate to archbishops, which would have curbed their powers. As its leader, Charles Martel, was very much dependent on the support of the nobility, he did not want to antagonise it by raising contentious issues. This applied particularly to the highly sensitive question of church property. It had been used to reward followers, both by Charles and his predecessors in the office of mayor of the palace, and was, indeed, part of the explanation for the decline of the Frankish Church. However, it should be remembered that the *maior domus* had many other preoccupations.[58] It would be wrong to see in Charles an enemy of the Church; like his predecessors and successors, he was generous in his donations to episcopal churches and monasteries.[59]

Boniface was consecrated a bishop in Rome in 722, without a see, but charged with a mission to all Germanic peoples east of the Rhine. Around 732, Pope Gregory III bestowed on him the archbishop's *pallium*, the ecclesiastical pall as a sign of his office. On a third and final visit to Rome in 738 he was, as papal legate and vicar for Germany, given the task of organising the Church in some of the territories there. Thus he visited the more or less autonomous Bavaria not as a Frankish, but as a papal representative, and 'as such was welcomed'.[60] It is characteristic of his approach that he founded in Bavaria not an ecclesiastical province, but a ducal church, though naturally under Rome. This suited the Duke of Bavaria, who needed support south of the Alps as a counter-weight against Frankish hegemony.

Normally Boniface worked in close conjunction with temporal rulers, who benefited from his missionary successes, as these consolidated their rule. He introduced more homogeneity through the establishment of a Catholic faith backed by an efficient ecclesiastical organisation, helping to create greater stability. As most of the missionary work done by Boniface took place in territories that were either already Frankish or were targets for their expansion, it was the Franks and effectively the Carolingians who gained most from his achievements. But Boniface was never a mere instrument in the hands of those on whose support he had to rely, whether rulers or popes. However, he realised, for instance in Saxony, that to be lasting, his missionary work required the success of Frankish arms. Where Frankish control of Saxon territory remained spasmodic, conversion was also precarious.

Boniface, who like his Irish predecessors had responded to the commands of pilgrimage, was never quite happy in the role of clerical politician and administrator, though – like the other Anglo-Saxon missionaries – he was in fact an excellent organiser. But no summary of his activities on the European continent would be balanced without giving his reform of the Frankish Church equal place with his closely associated missionary work.

There has been much discussion of the weakness of the Church under the Merovingians. Undoubtedly that church had many shortcomings, such as corruption and the personal failings of some bishops, but in these matters what happened under the Carolingians – for instance under Charles Martel – was not all positive. The Merovingian period constituted a beginning on which the Carolingians could build. Indeed, there is no abrupt break between the one and the other dynasty, but a gradual transition. When the ability of the Merovingians declined – though not so rapidly and fully as was later claimed – the heads of the various kings' households in the different Frankish kingdoms, who held the office of *maior domus*, in effect took over the exercise of royal powers. Eventually one family virtually governed the whole kingdom as mayors of the palace. After their ancestors, Arnulf, Bishop of Metz, and Pippin I, they were named Arnulfings or Pippinids, and later called Carolingians in honour of Charlemagne (Table 2.1). The Carolingians had their power base in the more Germanic Eastern Frankish kingdom of Austrasia, with its strongly entrenched nobility of which the Carolingians were the chief. Their victory meant a greater Germanic preponderance in the united kingdom of the Franks in which the Roman–Celtic culture of Neustria (based on Gaul) had so far mainly prevailed. Unlike Gaul, Austrasia did not possess the Roman institutional foundations that had been preserved in Neustria. Lay education dating from late Roman times was entirely absent in Austrasia and was even gradually dying out in Neustria.

Table 2.1   The Carolingians

Charles Martel, Mayor of the Palace 714–41

Carloman	Pippin III (The Younger)
Mayor of Palace 741–7 † 754	Mayor of Palace 741–51, King 751 † 768

Charlemagne, King 768, Emperor 800 † 814   Carloman, Co-King 768 † 771

Pippin, King of   Louis I (The Pious), Sole Emperor 814 † 840
Italy † 810

	EMPIRE, ITALY	E. FRANKISH KINGDOM	W. FRANKISH KINGDOM
Bernard, King of Italy † 818	Lothar I, Emperor Succeeded 840 † 855	Louis (The German) East Frankish ruler † 876	Charles II (The Bald) West Frankish ruler Emperor 875 † 877
			KINGS OF FRANCE

Louis II	Carloman, King	Charles III (The Fat)
Emperor † 875	876 † 880	King 876, Emperor 881 abd. 887 † 888

Arnulf, King 887, Emperor 896 † 899

Louis IV (The Child), King 900 † 911

As *maior domus* between 714 and 741, the grandfather of Charlemagne, Charles Martel, not only defended the kingdom against invading heathen Germanic tribes, but also protected Christian Europe against the Muslim Arabs by defeating them in the battle of Tours and Poitiers in 732. Charles, governing nominally in the name of Merovingian kings, in effect ruled over the Frankish kingdom as a kind of *princeps*, asserting royal authority over most of the outlying dependencies, with the notable exception of Bavaria in particular. He centralised government by weakening local control. In this process, because he used monastic and episcopal offices to consolidate his power during a bitter civil war, he was also responsible for undermining the independence of bishops. According to tradition, bishops were supposed to be elected by the clergy and people of the diocese, to which, under the Franks, was added the necessity of approval by the king. From the sixth century onwards, bishops were in fact selected by the king, the diocesan clergy and the aristocracy.[61] Under Charles Martel, a bishop mainly required for his election and maintenance in office the support of the *maior domus*.[62]

Charles' dealings with the Church have been generally characterised as 'a mixture of spoliation, eviction and liberality, varying in proportion according to the situation'.[63] He did not initiate the practice of taking church lands, which had existed for some time.[64] Charles had to establish his position and he needed church lands to reward his followers. In order to secure a good supply of mounted soldiers on whom he could call at any any time, he granted benefices to followers, who were to be known as *vassi*, then as *vassalli*. Where the domain was not adequate for this purpose, he resorted to drawing on church property. The grants were made by royal command on a precarial basis as *precaria verbo regis*, in view of the fact that canon law regarded church property as inalienable. The practice, though on a smaller scale, went back to Merovingian times. The land which the vassals took over was thus not granted to them outright, but only leased to them for a time as a benefice (*beneficium*), leaving the property rights of churches and monasteries intact. The Church was paid rent by holders of *precaria verbo regis*. At one time it was wrongly thought that the Church was compensated by the establishment of the tithe.[65] 'Both the Old and the New Testaments contain many references to tithes; and their payment...was based directly upon divine precept.'[66] From this, a universal obligation to tithe income was deduced in the Middle Ages. In practice, however, the clergy were probably not forced to pay tithes,[67] the proceeds of which were mainly used to benefit 'the churches where the sacraments were administered'.[68] Legislation was passed in the Carolingian period for the civil enforcement of tithes.[69] There were, however, many different practices governing their distribution.[70] Historians are not agreed as to whether Charles' measures constituted secularisation.[71] As we have seen, Charles was certainly not an enemy of the Church, as his – at the very least occasional – support for St Boniface and clerical reform exemplifies. But it is no coincidence that he gave some assistance to the reorganisation of the Frankish Church by a non-Frank not particularly sensitive to Frankish tradition and favouring the strengthening of ties with Rome. Boniface was as opposed to episcopal independence on clerical grounds as Charles was against it on political grounds.

St Boniface laboured ceaselessly to establish or restore Roman norms, whether these related to church discipline, church ritual, hierarchy or monastic discipline. His ideal was the Anglo-Saxon Church. But not everybody in the Frankish kingdom was happy with the activities of a foreign-born cleric acting on behalf of Rome, and this certainly applied to the nobility. Boniface did not have it all his own way with the episcopal reorganisation that he was asked to carry out by Charles Martel's sons, Carloman and Pippin III. Among his lasting achievements was the foundation of bishoprics at Würzburg and Eichstätt, and of a monastery at Fulda.

As Archbishop of Mainz, Boniface for a time dominated the Franco-German Church. But he did not succeed in introducing into the Frankish kingdom the Anglo-Saxon model, with territorial archbishops as masters of their provincial suffragans bound to Rome by the gift of the *pallium*. The decisive opposition to this proposal came from the Carolingians, who did not want the Frankish Church to come under the direct control of the pope, but wished to preserve their own rule over the Church (*Kirchenherrschaft*). Once this disagreement was settled in their favour, the Carolingian mayors of the palace had every reason to be satisfied with the reorganisation of the church carried out by Boniface. They welcomed the impetus he had given to reform, and his restructuring allowed them to direct a hierarchically-ordered church.

In 742, Carloman was able to call and to preside over a council of all the bishops in the territory under his rule, which proved to be the model for future church assemblies. Summoned in the spring to coincide with the annual military muster, not only bishops with their clergy, but also secular magnates attended. The decrees of the synods were promulgated in the name of the ruler, and, not, as hitherto, since antiquity, by the bishops themselves.[72] Carloman also – according to Anglo-Saxon precedent – began the Carolingian practice of enforcing the conciliar decrees and incorporating them as capitularies into the law of the kingdom. This was a momentous development:

> Boniface had to suffer the secular ruler to take the initiative in ecclesiastical matters to a degree unprecedented even during the height of Merovingian power. This was the price he had to pay for the advancement of reform and its application to the old Frankish territory.[73]

Pippin followed with a similar council for his territory, and later (after his deeply religious brother, who had given strong support to Boniface, had abdicated in order to enter a monastery) for the united Frankish kingdom. 'Through their support of the missionary bishop, the Carolingians had gained control of a well-disciplined, effective instrument of central control.'[74]

In spite of the tremendous achievements of Boniface, there is also an element of failure – or at least perceived by him – in his work. He had hoped, like other Anglo-Saxons, to bring light to his blood-brothers, the Saxons, but for him these hopes proved premature. In any case, to evangelise them one had to rely on the Franks, the bitter enemies of the Saxons. To some extent, here the objectives of the Franks and of Boniface were irreconcilable from the first. In 754, Boniface returned to Frisia for missionary work, but was murdered. He became a martyr, 'more powerful in death than in life. Even the Franks were impressed.'[75] He was buried in the monastery of Fulda that he had founded and with which he was particularly closely associated. Deeply spiritual and courageous, Boniface was of necessity often worn down by organisational problems and difficulties of co-operation with others. But he, the stranger from another land, prepared the ground so well that the Franks could now take over themselves. One of his most notable achievements was the reorganisation of the Germanic churches, even if it had not gone so far as he wished:

> without the work of Boniface in Germany, drawing north and south towards a common middle ground within a single ecclesiastical pattern, the work of Charlemagne and even the eventual unification of Germany must have followed a very different path.[76]

A long civil war under Charles Martel and his son Pippin III ravaged the kingdom and did considerable harm to learning.[77] In view of the indispensability of conducting some official business in writing, the authorities were more than ever dependent on clerical literacy. This is one of many reasons why the Carolingians, certainly from Charles Martel onwards, leant increasingly on the Church. Whereas previously the importance of the bishop lay in his role as representative and custodian of divine power, it now became connected more – or as much – with his position as a secular magnate.[78] To some extent, the lead in spiritual and cultural life would to pass to monasteries.[79] The patronage of local saints was broken, to be replaced by Roman relics and the papal–Carolingian alliance. It was an alliance that suited both sides, but it was actually the popes who initially needed help from the Franks.

After considering and eventually rejecting the idea of turning either to the Bavarians or the Aquitanians for assistance, the Holy See by the time of Charles Martel seemed at last to be on the brink of finding the outside support against their enemies in Italy – particularly the Langobards – for which they had been looking. The Byzantine emperors were no longer able to help, and in any case for a number of reasons – such as theological differences between the Western and Eastern Churches – reliance on them was not an attractive proposition to the papacy. When the popes were being hard pressed once more by the Langobards in central Italy, Pope Gregory III in 739 appealed to Charles Martel for assistance. Charles, who needed the Langobard alliance to keep the Saracens out of the Provence,[80] managed to settle the current conflict by sending an emissary. However, the long-term problem of the threat to Rome and to the independence of the papacy posed by Langobard kings bent on mastery of Italy remained, and was to be of major concern to later Carolingian generations.

Charles Martel's period of power, which saw the strengthening of central political authority and the beginnings of a reorganisation of the Church under Roman auspices, supported by the mayor of the palace, proved to be a watershed. Charles had ruled but not reigned, while the Merovingians reigned and no longer ruled. Unlike his father, Pippin III as the new mayor of the palace faced continuing challenges to his position as effective ruler from within his own family. While he had been able to assume control of Carloman's territories after his brother's abdication in 747, his half-brother Grifo had rebelled against him with Saxon and Bavarian help. Campaigns were required in 748 and 749 to crush the risings. In these circumstances Pippin felt that his position needed strengthening and that he could thus no longer accept the compromises which had been acceptable for his father. He therefore raised the dynastic question. At stake was more than simply the question as to which family was to occupy the throne of the kingdom of the Franks, but the whole concept of kingship.

Even if the Merovingians of necessity had to shed some of the previous aspects of their Germanic kingship[81] on being baptised, they retained a special position because of the sacred hereditary prestige of the royal blood. The dynasty, though naturally profiting from the exploits of Clovis, which had enhanced its charisma, did not require constant reaffirmation of its vigour, so long as it was able to command respect as 'the embodiment of the life of the nation and . . . of the land'.[82] For this role it was sufficient for a king to be a dignified figurehead, representing, as he did, 'the unity of the kingdom and the tradition of Frankish legitimacy within the context of late antiquity'.[83]

During the later Merovingian period, attitudes to kingship were changing in the Frankish kingdom. A transformation of royal sacredness followed the reconstitution of the Frankish Church under Charles Martel and his sons on the basis of a sacred foundation radically different from that of its Merovingian predecessor. The Romans and Anglo-Saxons who transformed Francia had little sympathy for the old Germanic view of kingship.

Increasingly their alien view of kingship, namely that kings not only reigned but ruled, was coming to be held by the élite of Francia as well.

The Carolingian ecclesiastical system was based on imported Roman sacrality: it was only a matter of time before their [the Carolingians'] own political position would be as well.[84]

Pippin moved very cautiously. He had many connections with the great abbey of St Denis on the outskirts of Paris, where his father had sent him for his schooling, and the strong support given to him by the ecclesiastical establishment there provided a firm base for him. Probably after securing the agreement in principle of the magnates to setting in motion a transfer of the royal dignity to the Carolingians, Pippin as *maior domus* around 749 sent an embassy consisting of an Anglo-Saxon, Burghard (Bishop of Würzburg) and a Frank, Fulrad (soon to be Abbot of St Denis and royal arch-chaplain) to Pope Zacharias in Rome to seek his guidance on this matter. He asked for the pope's opinion as to whether it was good or not to have Frankish kings who did not have any royal power. How could one be king without *potestas*?

It has been pointed out that these were not Frankish, but Roman questions, and that the response was a foregone conclusion.[85] In determining his response, the pope will have borne in mind above all the interests of the Church. There was the obvious necessity of a good relationship with the secular authorities on which the fate of the Frankish Church depended. The pope will not have been unmindful of his need of Pippin's support against the Langobards threatening Rome, and indeed of the role of defenders of the papacy that he contemplated for the Franks. Zacharias therefore instructed (*mandavit*) Pippin that it would be better if that person were called king who had the actual power. This fitted in with the teaching by St Augustine and other Fathers of the Church that there was a correspondence between form and matter in the world order (*ordo*), and that therefore in this case a king's title implied that he ruled. Accordingly, so that the world order would not be disturbed, he commanded by virtue of his papal authority that Pippin should become king. Following the papal judgment, Pippin was in 751 elected king at an assembly 'according to the custom of the Franks'. Afterwards he was anointed by the Frankish bishops, the first King of the Franks to receive this rite. Although the influence of Boniface in the kingdom was by then in decline, these developments owed much to his earlier establishment of contacts with Rome, and thus rounded off his work.[86]

The events connected with the transfer of the royal dignity of the Franks from the Merovingians to Pippin were of considerable importance for the future. It is true that constitutionally, the election by the Frankish assembly was of greater significance than the decision of the pope that preceded it. However, Pippin's approach to the pope shows that he regarded the latter's support, if not necessarily as essential, at least as advisable to secure the election. The religious element was further emphasised by the anointing (going back to the Old Testament), a novelty for Frankish kings, though there were apparently precedents in Visigothic Spain of which the Frankish bishops may have been aware. The anointing 'at the same time confirmed those pagan conceptions of divine kingship which had already been coated with a thin veneer of Christianity'.[87] For the papacy, with its precarious position in Italy, it was certainly useful to have 'a Frankish king conceived somewhat on the lines of the good king of the Old Testament' who might come to its aid against its enemies.[88]

The nature of Frankish kingship was fundamentally altered by the modalities of Pippin's assumption of the throne. An originally heathen hereditary sacrality, which was not to disappear altogether, had Jewish and Christian elements added to it. The king's inauguration and acclamation changed from the profane to the liturgical and now became ecclesiastical, which it had not been in Merovingian times. The position of the ruler in the Church received a sacramental foundation, as the anointing counted as a sacrament, at any rate until the investiture controversy in the eleventh century. These aspects were emphasised liturgically by litanies, the *laudes regiae*, which are likely to have been used at Pippin's coronation and are, in any case, documented for the reign of Charlemagne. The litany, which is peculiar to the Gallo-Frankish Church, begins with the words *Christus vincit, Christus regnat, Christus imperat*:

> The laudes invoke the conquering God – Christ the victor, ruler, and commander – and acclaim in him, with him, or through him his imperial or royal vicars on earth along with all the other powers conquering, ruling, commanding, and safeguarding the order of this present world: the pope and the bishops, the ruler's house, the clergy, the princes, the judges and the army.[89]

There is in the *laudes* a correlation of the present and the transcendental, with one dissolving in the other.

Building on contemporary perceptions of the Old Testament, Carolingian kingship was seen as a revival of the biblical kingship of David. The introduction of the biblical rite of royal unction commended itself to Pippin not merely for political and dynastic reasons. The ritual of the Old Testament and its revival were in full agreement with the trend of the age towards 'liturgifying' the secular sphere and aiming at theocratic solutions of political problems. The Franks, ever since Charles Martel's victory over the Arabs at Tours and Poitiers in 732, had begun to think of themselves as the new people chosen by God. The Holy See referred to them as the 'new sacred people of promise'. Attention has been drawn to the fact that the Franks

> endeavoured...to wheel into Church history as the continuators of Israel's exploits rather than into Roman history as the heirs of pagan

Rome. [The king was] the *novus Moyses*, the *novus David*. He was the priestly king, the *rex et sacerdos*. . . . 'Jerusalem' wandered to Gaul; the only Biblical pattern of a hallowed tribe, Israel, helped to shape the tribe that was to shape Europe.[90]

The anointing of Pippin in 751 was not, however, the end of the story, either in the development of Christian concepts of kingship or in the relations between the Franks and the papacy. For the co-operation between Pippin and the pope constituted the beginning of a close connection between Francia and Rome, that was to affect, positively and negatively, for many centuries, the history of what was to become Germany. There were many implications in the transactions between Pippin and the pope that were not apparent at the time and that bore fruit in combination with other developments: 751 was the first stage in a process which enhanced the Christian and European importance of the Frankish – and later the Teutonic or German – kingdom. But of necessity this brought with it greater Christian and European responsibilities, such as the protection of the pope and (to some extent as a consequence) involvement in the affairs of regions far away from the Frankish heartlands. A crucial second stage in the position of the Frankish kingdom in Western Christendom was reached in 753 with the appeal of Pope Stephen II to King Pippin for help. Through concern for the pope initially in his capacity as spiritual head of the Catholic Church, the Franks now became thoroughly involved in the complex affairs of Italy and the triangular relationship of papacy, Langobards and Byzantine Empire.

The Frankish interest in Italy was not new. Thus the Merovingian ruler, Theudebert I (534–48), pursued a policy of conquest. Taking advantage of the war between the Byzantine Empire and the Ostrogoths, he for a time subjected Upper Italy to Frankish rule. In Constantinople Theudebert was even suspected of a plan to carry out an assault on the city in alliance with the Langobards and of coveting the imperial crown. In general, however, Germanic rulers accepted the position of the (Byzantine) emperor. Theudebert's son, Theudebald I (548–55), after a defeat at the hands of the Byzantine army, had to give up Upper Italy again, though later Merovingian rulers for a time made the Langobards their tributaries.[91] In the middle of the sixth century the Franks succeeded in getting the Bavarians to recognise their overlordship and appointed (eventually hereditary) dukes from the Agilolfing family to rule over them. Right from the beginning, members of this dynasty established close relations with the Langobard kingdom through matrimonial alliances. The Bavarian dukes tended to follow an independent policy, intent on keeping the obligations to their Frankish overlords to a minimum. In times of Frankish strength, they found it prudent to submit to them. But during the many intermittent periods of Frankish weakness, the Bavarians took little notice of the Frankish overlordship, unless they needed their support against Avars and Slavs. It was difficult for the Frankish rulers to ignore what was going on in Italy, if only because Bavaria tended to rely on Langobard support against them.[92]

In Italy, the Langobards themselves were involved in a triangular relationship with Byzantium and the papacy. During the first half of the eighth century, the popes still recognised the Byzantine emperor as their ruler and diplomatically supported the maintenance of the Byzantine exarchate of Ravenna against the encroachments of the Langobards. However, relations between the papacy and the emperors were not made any easier by the increasing divergence of Western and Eastern cultures, complicated by the interaction of religious and political factors. Once more, as during the Arian controversy, a theological issue divided Christianity largely, though not exclusively, between East and West.

The crisis began in 726 with a declaration by the Byzantine Emperor, Leo III, condemning the veneration of sacred images or icons. The emperor probably did not act on his own initiative, but on the urging of a number of bishops of the Byzantine Church, who wished 'to eliminate practices capable of deteriorating into superstitious usage'.[93] The Eastern provinces of the Byzantine Empire, however much they emphasised the religious differences that separated them from their Jewish and Islamic neighbours, largely shared their opposition to any pictorial representation of divinity. In some respects, the Eastern aversion to icons was a continuation of the earlier Arian refusal to affirm the divine as well as the human nature of the incarnate Christ. Unfortunately, while the opponents of images were trying to answer troubling theological questions, the dispute did not remain on the level of religious discussion. The removal of icons by the emperor led to rioting, which was punished with a measure of severity, though no martyrs of image worship were created.

In 730, the emperor issued a decree penalising the use of icons. Iconoclasm, with its breaking of images, now began in earnest. On the whole the monks in the Byzantine Empire continued to support the use of images, and the imperial measures may have been intended at least partly to break the power of monasticism. The iconoclasm of the Byzantine emperors, which continued intermittently until it was abandoned for good in 843, could not but strain still further relations between the Western and the Eastern churches, and between pope and emperor. The Holy See condemned the iconoclasm of Byzantium and in 732 the emperor countered by transferring the Byzantine provinces of Southern Italy and of Illyricum from the ecclesiastical jurisdiction of Rome to that of the Patriarch of Constantinople. This measure was to embitter papal relations with Byzantium for the future, and made it much more difficult for the Holy See to look to its formal sovereign, the emperor, for support. In any case it was by no means certain that Byzantium would be able to give any military assistance. Thus it became clear by the middle of the eighth century that the continued independence of Rome and Ravenna required the goodwill of the Langobards.

Aistulf, who ascended the Langobard throne in 749, was determined to establish dominance over Italy, or – to put it more positively – to unite Italy under his leadership. He occupied Ravenna in 750–1 and during the following years opened a trade war against Rome. When the pope in 752 appealed to Byzantium for assistance, Aistulf countered by demanding that the Romans should recognise his suzerainty and pay him a heavy tribute. The emperor did not provide any help and merely sent an emissary to negotiate a settlement. Pope Stephen, who recognised that he could not expect any decisive assistance from Constantinople, and in any case foresaw that a forthcoming Byzantine church council was bound to exacerbate the religious conflict with Catholicism, decided to turn to King Pippin for aid. In 753 the pope sent him a secret message describing his predicament and asking for an official invitation to the Frankish royal court. A high level delegation bearing the invitation arrived in Rome in the nick of time, when Aistulf was attempting to take the city and thus to face all parties with a *fait accompli*. Although Aistulf adhered to his demands against Rome, he did not dare prevent the pope from proceeding on his visit to Pippin, for which the Byzantine emissary incidentally appears to have given his permission.

On his arrival in the Frankish kingdom, Stephen was received with the reverence and ritual due to a pope. At the beginning of the negotiations, he implored the king for protection against his enemies, which Pippin at once promised in his name and that of his two sons, the future Charlemagne as well as Carloman. In 754, in an attempt at a peaceful settlement, Pippin sent a number of embassies to the Langobard court at Pavia, but Aistulf proved to be a stubborn and dangerous enemy. He realised that there was considerable opposition to intervention in Italy among the Frankish magnates. When an assembly was held to deliberate the matter, Pippin was unable to secure its agreement to sending an army to Italy. Aistulf supported the opposition by causing Pippin's brother Carloman, who had entered a monastery in Italy, to travel to Francia. In this crisis, Stephen and Pippin moved even closer together. Stephen gave Pippin his spiritual support to force Carloman to re-enter and his sons to enter a monastery.[94]

At Easter 754 Pippin received the reluctant assent of the magnates for the Italian campaign.[95] He apparently gave the pope a written undertaking to guarantee to the papacy the territory of Rome and Ravenna, as well as of Venetia and Istria. The declaration has been at the centre of much historical controversy, being regarded by some scholars as a later documentary interpolation, but it is likely to have been authentic. It is not certain that the pope at this stage produced 'a Roman forgery, in which there may well be elements of truth, known as the Donation of Constantine, ... an early step, perhaps the first, towards the birth of the Papal State as the future was to know it'.[96] The first clear evidence of the existence of the 'Donation' occurs 20 years later, in Charlemagne's reign.[97] It is believed that at any rate the substance of the claims contained in the 'Donation' was conveyed to the Franks and is likely to have impressed them.[98] However, there is room for argument as to whether the guarantee of the territories in question also implied their donation to the sovereignty of St Peter and his successors, that is to the Holy See. These stipulations did not necessarily detract from their belonging to the (Roman or Byzantine) Empire. In any case popes since Stephen II claimed the sovereignty of St Peter over all the territories freed from the Langobards by the Franks. Incidentally, Pippin and Charlemagne failed to keep many of the promises they made.

Before the military expedition set out for Italy, the pope solemnly repeated the anointing of Pippin and his sons as kings of the Franks at St Denis. Pippin and his sons were anointed and his wife, Queen Bertrada, blessed by the pope. There is also the assertion by a monk at St Denis that the pope, in addition to anointing the kings, forbade the Franks, under pain of excommunication, to choose as their kings princes of any other blood than that of the Carolingians who had just been anointed by him. The exclusion was a dual one, not only of the Merovingians and other non-Carolingians, but also of Carolingians branches other than the line of Pippin III.

> The pope thus did rather more than repeat the consecration of 751, which from the Frankish point of view was sufficient; he did all that he could to ensure the succession of Pippin's heirs, not merely to the Frankish throne but to the protection of the papacy. They were the men of St Peter in a sense that no Merovingian had ever been.[99]

To underline the new role the Carolingians had assumed, Stephen also bestowed on the three kings the title of *patricius Romanorum*, (protectors of the Romans), probably without the participation of the emperor, who had hitherto made this appointment.

Pippin led two victorious expeditions against the Langobards, in 754 and 756. The elder Carloman died in a monastery in August 754, while Pippin was *en route* to Italy. King Aistulf sued for peace when he found himself besieged in his capital, Pavia. The Langobards succeeded in delaying the carrying out of the peace treaty. Also, the increasing friction between the papacy and an emperor supporting an iconoclast policy, that was bound to be anathema to Catholicism, brought a coalition between the Langobards and Byzantium into the realm of possibility. But Aistulf was too impatient to wait and proceeded to invest Rome, which he had surrounded completely by the beginning of 756. Once more Pippin answered the pope's call for help and besieged Pavia. Here an imperial delegation reached the King of the Franks with the demand that the exarchate of Ravenna be restored to the emperor, which Pippin refused. Aistulf capitulated in June 756.

The conditions of the second peace treaty were considerably harder on the vanquished than the first. The Langobards had to renew the tribute to the Franks dating back initially to the days of the Merovingians. The pope was to receive a number of Frankish conquests from the Langobards: the duchy of Rome, the exarchate of Ravenna and the Pentapolis, that is the area consisting of five maritime towns on the east coast of Italy. Officials and people in these territories swore allegiance to the pope, and a papal administration was built up.[100] These measures were the beginning of the Patrimony of St Peter, later called the papal states. In law, however, the territories still formed part of the (Byzantine) Empire. Indeed, Stephen II and his successors continued to recognise imperial authority. In this very delicate situation, Pippin was determined to prevent a breach with Byzantium, in which he succeeded. He therefore did not use the title of a *patricius Romanorum*.

When King Aistulf died in 756, Desiderius was raised to the Langobard royal dignity in agreement with the pope and with Abbot Fulrad of St Denis, who had the task of watching over the carrying out of the peace treaty. Desiderius initially promised the papacy further cessions of territory, but did not keep his undertakings. Instead he made approaches to Byzantium. King Pippin declined to conduct a further military campaign in Italy, as he was fully occupied with the consolidation of the Frankish kingdom. In order to prevent a coalition between Desiderius and Byzantium, he decided to propitiate the King of the Langobards, and the pope had to fall in with the changed situation. In any case, the papacy was now preoccupied with its relationship with Byzantium, owing to the increasingly vehement iconoclasm emanating from Constantinople. During this period, the papacy was weakened by the contested papal election of 767, when a *coup d'état* by the Roman military nobility led to the installation of a pope in the most dubious circumstances. The opposition took up contacts with the Langobard king, but managed to exclude Desiderius from having any say in the subsequent events which led to the deposition of the pretender and the election of a legitimate pope, Stephen III. Incidentally, ever since the accession in 757 of Paul I, the successor to Stephen II, popes had informed the King of the Franks of their election in the form in which they had previously announced it to the exarch of Ravenna on behalf of the (Byzantine) emperor. By the time Stephen III's embassy arrived at the Carolingian court, Pippin had died (in September 768), and the defence of the Roman Church was now in the hands of his two young sons, Charles (the Great) and Carloman.

With the transfer of the royal dignity from the Merovingians to the Carolingians, an originally Germanic heathen sacrality, which was not to disappear altogether, was overlaid by the Christian concept of a kingship by divine right. Interestingly, though in some ways representing opposite principles, sacral heredity and divine right were soon combined, even during

Pippin's lifetime, with the Pope's apparent recognition of the hereditary claim of a particular branch of the Carolingian dynasty.[101] In this manner, pope and bishops facilitated the transfer of power from one sacral hereditary dynasty to another, but adding a new ecclesiastical element in the case of the Carolingians with the blessing of the Church, making the new dynasty *kirchlich-sakral*. Frankish (including heathen), Jewish and Christian elements came together in the new concept of kingship. As the royal family was sacral, and not just the ruler, the old Germanic custom of dividing the inheritance, which had been practised by the Merovingians, carried on into the new era. This, too, was bound to have weighty consequences.

Pippin emerged from these developments considerably strengthened. It is true that he had allowed the pope to have some say in affairs of the Frankish kingdoms which were not entirely religious. But from Pippin's perspective at the time, this was not a problem, for once he had ascended the throne he was in a stronger position than the pope, particularly when Stephen needed the help of the Franks in Italy. In any case the Carolingians soon began to believe that they received their power direct from God, without the necessity of help from any intermediary, even the pope. 'If none of the charters of Pepin that are preserved in the original carry the formula "king [of the Franks] by the grace of God" (*Dei gratia rex Francorum*) which his successors regularly used, the idea implied in this phrase is already often expressed' in various charters. Phrases such as ' "With the assistance of the Lord, Who has placed us on the throne . . .", may be found at the beginning of a charter of 760'. Formulations of this kind 'are not purely phrases of protocol', but reflect the doctrine that 'the king of the Franks, since Pippin [III] the Short, actually received from God a personal commission to reign over the Frankish people and to bring about with His aid the triumph of the religion of Christ'.[102] From Charlemagne onwards the Frankish rulers used the formula 'by the Grace of God' as part of their title as rulers.

With the accession of Charles in 768, we arrive at the beginning of a reign of crucial importance not only for the kingdom of the Franks, for Francia and Germania, but for Europe and indeed for Christendom. It was during Charlemagne's reign that the foundation was laid both for the Holy Roman Empire and for the kingdoms of the future. Few, if any of the major matters with which Charles was concerned, failed to have some connection with religion, directly or indirectly. Even more than with his father, religion moved right into the centre of royal policy in Charlemagne's reign, though many roots of this trend go back to Pippin III and to Charles Martel. Ever since the latter's victory over the Arabs at Tours and Poitiers, the Franks saw themselves as a people chosen by God to ward off the infidel. Pippin and his brother Carloman took a great interest in the Church and supervised its reform. They supported missionary work in a religio-political context. Unction strengthened the Christian aspect of kingship. Also, Pippin III not only came to the rescue of the Holy See, but promised continuing help in the name of his two sons. Pippin's refusal to adopt the style of *patricius Romanorum* did not affect his obligations to defend the papacy. The main difference between father and son lay in the fact that Pippin had been compelled to devote too much of his energy to the task of establishing himself as ruler to be able to initiate a deliberate policy of making religion the main focus of the ruler's attention. Charles, who succeeded to the throne young and was to have a long and fruitful reign, could quite deliberately set his own agenda, even if he had to face opposition and even rebellion.

The central principle for Charles was that he saw himself as head of the people of God, whose duty it was to make it more Christian, to extend the faith to the heathens, to defend Europe against the 'infidel', and – last, not least – to assist the pope to preserve his independence from those who threatened it. This perception of the functions of a Christian ruler over the leading Christian people accounts, among other events, for his Italian campaigns on behalf of the papacy; for his wars against the heathen Saxons and Frisians as well as the attempts to convert them; for his (successful) campaigns against the 'pagan arch-enemy, "the Huns" (as people were wont to call the Avars)'[103]; for his (largely unsuccessful) expedition to Spain against the Arabs; for his enactment of church legislation as general laws; and finally for his efforts in the field of education.

Unlike his father, Charles was able to begin his rule as king, as the head of a dynasty whose hereditary royal title had been recognised. This comparatively secure start allowed him to build on his father's achievements. There was even some revival of the Germanic idea of dynastic charisma, earlier represented by the Merovingians.[104] Initially Charles shared Pippin's inheritance with his younger brother Carloman. But after Carloman's death in 771, Charles became sole ruler and reigned until his death in 814. Once he had succeeded his brother, he took over the most important kingdom in Europe, with a respected international position. But naturally he also inherited onerous responsibilities and severe problems. The threat from Islam continued in Spain. The coastlines of the kingdom were liable to be harassed by Vikings. The frontier with the Saxons was often in a turbulent state. Various other peoples, such as the Avars, were also pressing on the eastern frontiers, and at times threatening Bavaria. But the main problem concerning Bavaria in the eyes of the Franks was actually the unreliability of its dukes, in spite of the formal Frankish overlordship. The degree of independence the Bavarians achieved troubled the Frankish kings, particularly as the duchy had important connections with Italy, with both the Langobards and the papacy. The rulers of the Langobards and of the Bavarians tended to provide refuge for opponents of the Frankish monarchy, including disaffected members of the Carolingian royal family, such as eventually the widow and the children of Charlemagne's brother Carloman.

Thus the Franks, quite apart from their special responsibilities for the safety of the Holy See, had a stake in the politics and diplomacy of Italy. Again, as during Pippin's reign, the Frankish rulers were drawn into the conflicts between the Holy See and its neighbours. There was also the question of the precise rights of the ruler of Byzantium, who – while he only held part of Italy – as the sole remaining emperor claimed residual authority over the whole of the peninsula, including Rome. Periodic disturbances in Rome affecting papal elections and challenges to papal authority were similarly liable to involve the Franks.

Thus Charles usually found himself simultaneously having to face several tasks, many of which were interconnected and went on for prolonged periods. Rarely was he allowed to devote his attention to a sole problem for any length of time. Although he delegated responsibility and military command, for instance, to his sons when they were sufficiently old, in critical situations matters had to be settled by the ruler himself. In view of the vastness of his territories and interests, Charles had to be prepared to travel great distances. The court in any case moved around from one royal resid-ence to another, until 794 when Aachen (Aix-la-Chapelle) became his permanent place of residence except for periods of enforced absence.[105] Only a person of boundless energy, outstanding ability, strong nerves and a readiness to make decisions, even if unpalatable, could have the capacity to expand the already extensive dominions and to hold them together. Last, not least, Charles was economical of his time by refusing to became excessively involved in detail. Instead he concentrated on the supervision of the organ-isation needed to run his empire, and on suggesting such new policies, for instance in church matters or education, as might be fruitful for the future.

Charles had considerable understanding of the importance of education and culture, and attracted a number of renowned scholars to his court, fostering what has been called the Carolingian Renaissance. The palace school (*schola palatina*) he developed continued a tradition begun under the Merovingians, which in turn was modelled on the court of Constantine the Great. Alcuin, perhaps the most important figure in the palace school, was a Northumbrian of good birth, who received his education at the cathedral school of York, where he later taught. In 782 he was invited to the court of Charlemagne, where he spent most of his time until 801, when he retired to the monastery of St Martin of Tours, of which he was abbot. He died in 804. Among Alcuin's pupils was the Franconian nobleman Einhard, from the Main region, who wrote the life of Charlemagne.

At the Frankish court, the palace school helped to ensure the survival of the culture of classical antiquity, concentrating at the same time on the rudiments of literacy, including clear handwriting itself. Both religious and secular literature was studied. Considerable attention was paid to poetry. While at times the discipline was quite strict, and even the king was liable to chastise pupils for their scholastic shortcomings, a certain spirit of camerad-erie developed between tutors and pupils, which led to lifetime friendships. 'Every member of the circle, pupil or poet, who left the palace to take up a position as bishop or abbot in another part of the kingdom, maintained his connection with his friends by letters.'[106] Thus the palace school was a cultural centre for the senior clergy.

Charles was well aware of the importance of education for the faith and for the integration of his varied dominions on the basis of the Frankish heritage, the Christian religion and Roman tradition. He gave considerable impetus to a cultural development which he had not initiated. Germanic kings before him had shown themselves keen 'to emulate the literary legal culture of the Roman and Judaeo-Christian civilization to which they were heirs', partly to strengthen the ties between king and people.[107] To put Charles' historical achievement into perspective, without in any way dimin-ishing it, one has to remember that Frankish society was not illiterate: 'a Christian society cannot be a wholly illiterate society',[108] particularly one of a wide-spread religiosity. Literacy was not, indeed, confined to the clergy, or rather to its upper echelons. There is plenty of evidence also for a literate lay piety.[109] Royal patronage is splendidly reflected in libraries of the houses it favoured, such as at Reichenau, St Gall and Lorsch.[110]

An interesting aspect of Carolingian policy concerns its endeavours in writing to restore the pure Latin of antiquity. 'Carolingian reformers wanted to reassert uniformity of belief and practice, and to impose uniform standards on lay people.'[111] In a period in which the oral Latin spoken by 'Romance' peoples deviated from the language of the Roman period, that policy increased the gap between the written and the spoken word (now in the vernacular), while making it somewhat easier for the Romance than the Germanic speaker. The measures of the Carolingian reformers thus had a – perhaps unintended, though not necessarily unwelcome – effect in increas-ing exclusiveness. A full command of Latin set the higher clergy and the secular magnates apart from the ranks beneath them.

The support the king gave to religious and cultural education is particu-larly notable during a period when he was for many years involved almost continuously in fighting wars in many different parts of Europe. Many of these wars were (at least from a modern vantage-point) politico-religious, waged – certainly in the case of the Frisians and the Saxons – in the belief that the establishment of peace and settled conditions in the frontier regions required the conversion of subjected peoples to the Christian faith; only then, it was felt, could reliance be placed on them to observe Frankish laws. These wars were fought with a particular bitterness. In 782, following the destruction of a Frankish army by the Saxons, Charles carried out a massacre of about 4500 Saxon prisoners of war after his victory near Verden by the River Weser. 'Military occupation and forced conversion went hand in hand.'[112] Charles initially issued a law code for the Saxons which stipulated the death penalty even for comparatively minor infractions of Christian duties. It was only later, perhaps as the result of criticisms voiced by Alcuin, that the king adopted more humane methods. A new code was issued after deliberations with the Saxons. Within a comparatively short space of time they became willing allies of the Franks, though some adverse long-term effects of conversion by the sword may well have persisted. However unpalatable Charles' methods of conquering the Saxons may appear to the modern reader, the end result has been considered 'one of the fundamental prerequisites of the formation of the German people'.[113]

Charles' practices on the battlefield and in conquered territory throw light on his perception of the relevance of Christian teaching to his role in the world, especially as a warrior. Presumably he was convinced that he was fighting a just war in the Augustinian sense. One of the main functions of the king in those times was as a leader in war. There is very little sign of old heathen Germanic traditions in these matters having been modified by Christianity. One may wonder whether the Church in the Frankish kingdom at the time – with its worldly bishops drawn from the nobility, and a clergy that was often thoroughly mundane – had rethought the practice and morality of warfare in the light of Christian teaching. Perhaps this is a warning not to overlook the dark side of the reign, while giving credit for it considerable achievement. What was in fact the relationship between politics and religion during Charlemagne's reign?

As a believing Catholic Christian, Charles was thoroughly convinced of the importance of his faith for society.[114] Following the example of his father and his grandfather, he regarded the Church in the Frankish kingdom as being under his supervision. Like his father and his uncle, he presided over synods and proclaimed their decisions as general laws. He went further than they did in using his power to attempt the enforcement of Christian ethics and conduct in everyday life, and in personally involving himself in theological questions. The latter may in part have been due to the fact that the reign of Charlemagne lacked the outstanding clerical figures of the previous generation, such as St Boniface. Even more than his father, perhaps in some ways like his grandfather, he treated the appointments of bishops as being in his gift. He went further than his forebears in using bishops in the royal service and for other than strictly episcopal duties.

Here Charles was not simply following a whim, but the definite aim of ensuring the co-operation of the bishops and the secular magnates – drawn from a similar social background – by getting them to serve together in various tasks of governing the kingdom. With the same objective in mind, Charles summoned both secular magnates and senior clergy to the annual general assembly, convened by tradition – initially in the spring – before the ruler departed on the year's campaign. These meetings dealt with a very wide range of topics, both secular and ecclesiastical. In some cases arrangements were made for matters to be discussed separately by the counts on one hand, and the bishops and abbots on the other.[115]

Charles certainly regarded the Frankish Church as his domain, in which he was largely his own master, without reference to the pope, whom he did not consult in the establishment of at least one new bishopric.[116] He made fundamental changes in organisation by the establishment of ecclesiastical provinces in which diocesan bishops were subordinated to archbishops with metropolitan powers over them. The new archbishops were closely attached to Rome, because they were obliged to collect the insignia of their dignity, the *pallium*, from Rome within three months.[117] Later on in the reign, metropolitan (arch-) bishops themselves held synods to reinforce royal decrees; but this in no way represented a reduction in monarchical power. 'Charles was king of all who lived within the area of his territorial authority, whether laymen or ordained clergy, called by God to rule, guide, reward and punish them.'[118] According to Germanic conceptions, every royal decision amounted to a clarification of divine law, as it was not possible to distinguish the secular from the spiritual parts of divine law.[119]

From a positive point of view this blurring of the boundary between the secular and the ecclesiastical provided the opportunity for prelates with deeply spiritual convictions to influence the conduct of affairs of state, though one wonders to what extent that occurred during the reign of Charlemagne. The disadvantage of the practice was that bishops had less time for their dioceses. That they were needed there was beyond doubt. The Church in the Frankish kingdom at that time suffered from many short-comings, and even the bishops themselves were not always of the necessary moral calibre to be able to set an example. Unfortunately exploitation was as rife in the Church as it was in society outside: each level of its hierarchy oppressed the next lower level. At the bottom, there were the clergy of the estate churches (*Eigenkirchen*). Charles is likely to have been aware of the weaknesses of the system, but he was too beholden to the magnates to attempt genuine reform and contented himself with correcting exceptional and glaring abuses. At the same time, the bishops were too dependent on the king to be able to criticise the way he directed the Church. Perhaps one of the main defects of Charlemagne's regime was his reliance on the families of the secular magnates, many of which had been rewarded by his grandfather with church benefices and property for supporting him.

Presumably the main reason for Charlemagne's ability to administer the Church in his kingdom with very little interference from Rome was the comparative weakness of the papacy at the time. His father at times still had to rely on the support of the pope, particularly for becoming king. Charles was too well established, in spite of the revolts against him, to need the help of the pope. But the Holy See frequently required the

assistance of the King of the Franks. Pippin III had defeated the Langobards, but he had not been able to free the Bishops of Rome permanently
from the danger they presented to them. Another instalment of the obligations incurred to the papacy by Pippin, also on behalf of his sons, now
became due. Almost from the beginning of his reign the affairs of the
Holy See and of Italy, with all their international ramifications, were to be
among Charles' most important preoccupations. In view of the lament of
many German historians over the involvement of their rulers in Italy and
papal affairs, and the difficulty of distinguishing between religious and
political factors in these matters, the continuation and even extension of
Pippin's policy in these respects need closer scrutiny.

That Charles was drawn into a conflict with Desiderius, the successor of
Aistulf as King of the Langobards, was due to a number of factors. The
background to the deeper involvement of the Franks in Italy early on in the
reign of Charles includes not only the difficulties of the popes in Rome and
their call for help, but also an abortive attempt to cement Carolingian
relations with Desiderius by means of a dual matrimonial alliance between
the two dynasties. Pippin's widow, Bertrada, who initiated these overtures,
hoped that the Langobard king would then give up his aggressive schemes.
However, Desiderius wished to renew his predecessor's designs on Rome,
which were liable to bring him into conflict with the papacy. In fact it was in
the hope of enlisting his support for these plans that he gave his daughter to
King Charles in marriage. It goes without saying that the pope took strong
exception to this co-operation between the Franks, whom he regarded as his
natural defenders, and the Langobards, his perceived enemies. In spite of
papal threats, the marriage took place in 770.[120] These diplomatic and
politico-religious complications became interwoven with an increasing tension between Charles and his brother Carloman. The pope, in his anger with
Charles, now moved closer to his rival Carloman. But the situation in Rome
added another complication. In the spring of 771 Stephen III unwisely
allowed himself to become enmeshed in a complicated intrigue through
which he hoped to extricate himself from the domination of his senior
court official at the very time that Desiderius was making a bid to seize
control of Rome and of the papacy. This had disastrous consequences for
the pope's personal position.

Charles was dismayed by the developments set off by Desiderius and
saw that the Langobard alliance had led him into a cul-de-sac from
which he could only extricate himself with difficulty. He could tolerate a
Langobard protectorate over Rome no more than an intervention in Italy by
his brother and fellow-king Carloman, who had good connections not only
with the papal court but with Desiderius.[121] Some time in 771 or possibly in
772[122] Charlemagne repudiated his Langobard spouse, though we do not
know whether this was mainly because of events in Italy or because he

wanted to marry the Swabian noblewoman Hildegard, who became his next wife.

While the situation in Italy continued to cause Charles concern, he was relieved of his most troubling dynastic problem by the death of Carloman, nine years his junior, in December 771, aged only 20. Charles set aside the claims of Carloman's two sons – children at the time – and united his brother's dominions with his own. In the light of Charles' later achievements, many scholars have regarded this reuniting of Pippin III's kingdom as fortunate for Francia and for Europe.

> Had he [Charles] subsequently achieved less, however, more stress might have been laid on his ruthlessness and apparent disregard of the possible rights of his nephews, even conceding that at this time there was no law to challenge practical convenience when the heir to a kingdom was a minor.[123]

Carloman's widow fled the Frankish dominions with her two children and eventually found refuge at the Langobard court with King Desiderius, for whom they became useful instruments in his policy of expansion in Italy. For now the Langobard king hoped to make intervention beyond the Alps impossible for Charlemagne by preparing a *coup d'état* in the Frankish kingdom in favour of Carloman's sons. He even tried to have the young princes papally anointed. But Desiderius found his match in the new pope, who had succeeded the unfortunate Stephen III after the latter's death early in 772.

Hadrian I, the scion of an old Roman family, was determined to resist Desiderius' advance and appealed to the King of the Franks for help.[124] Within a few months of receiving the papal request, after securing the agreement of his magnates, Charles, in the spring of 773, set out for Italy with his troops. Thanks to Charles' masterly strategic plan, Desiderius was caught off guard and made the mistake of allowing himself to be encircled in his capital, Pavia, which the Franks were able to besiege. In June 774 Desiderius was forced to surrender unconditionally and to abdicate.

Charles took over the Langobard kingdom and from then on called himself *rex Francorum et Langobardorum*. The authorities disagree on whether this development had been his aim all along.[125] Charles also almost immediately began to use the title of *patricius Romanorum*, which had been conferred by Pope Stephen II on Pippin and his sons in 754, and which none of them had thought prudent to use up to this point. At Easter 774, before Pavia had fallen, Charles was received in Rome by the pope with all the honours due to his patriciate. However, before allowing him to enter the city, the pope asked for a promise that this token of trust would not be abused, while Charles demanded a pledge from Hadrian to provide for his safety.

King and pope judged that the time had come, even before the surrender of Pavia, to arrive at an understanding on the fate of the Langobard kingdom and on their future relations. Unfortunately the terms of the agreement are known only from papal sources, which may well have exaggerated the size of the territory to be given to the Holy See. Obviously considerable effort will have been made to draw a clear line of demarcation between the zones of papal and Frankish expansion in case of a decisive defeat of the Langobard king, in order to avoid possible complications. However, these diplomatic deals failed to avert tension between king and pope once Charles had succeeded to the throne of Pavia, for the annexation of the kingdom of the Langobards by the Franks changed the whole balance of power in Italy and was bound to affect the way Charles looked at the affairs of Italy. Also king and pope saw their agreement and the new situation in Italy in a different light. While the main value of the final elimination of the threat from the Langobards to Charles consisted in his ability to turn to unfinished business elsewhere, such as to the conquest of Saxony, for the pope it was the beginning of an era of fulfilment.

Soon Hadrian was wondering whether it was really preferable to have a nominal ally in Pavia rather than a declared enemy. Whatever the precise terms of the agreement between Charles and Hadrian, subjectively the pope felt that the king had not treated the papacy fairly and that he had not been sufficiently attentive to his task as defender of the see of St Peter.[126] Hadrian appears not to have adequately taken into account Charles' many other royal preoccupations. At the heart of the practical problem at the time lay the question of the right of passage through the papal states (which cut the peninsula into two almost equal parts) for the agents and even the armies of the Frankish king, who controlled territory in both Northern and Southern Italy.

> This created problems which could not be solved unless one of the two powers was in actual practice subordinate to the other in temporal affairs. All the charters in the world – authentic or not – were powerless to resolve the difficulty.[127]

Although Hadrian, a proud pontiff, protested at times, after a few years he was reduced to the role of docile auxiliary to the policy conducted by the Frankish king.[128]

> The papacy had given itself, on the soil of Italy in the person of the Frankish king, an encroaching protector, so that the pope's temporal rule though only just established, was threatened by the very person who had created it.[129]

Charles was beginning to view Rome and the papal states as no more than an extension of the Italy that he was attempting to constitute. Indeed, he was involved in interfering not only with the temporal but also with the ecclesiastical rights of the papacy, such as the choice of an archbishop of Ravenna. The comparative disadvantage of the papacy in its relationship with the Carolingians was bound to be even more severe when Hadrian was replaced by a much weaker pope, who was also facing serious opposition in Rome itself. But before we progress with the story, we may just cast a backward glance.

The developments that led to Charles' first intervention in Italy are described in detail as they show that once the first – not necessarily very far-sighted – steps had been taken by him early in his reign, before he had gathered enough experience as a ruler, the further moves were reasonable reactions to events as they unfolded. They were neither purely religious nor purely political. There was the close relationship with the papacy established by Pippin III: Charlemagne 'clearly appreciated...the dependence of his rule in the eyes of Frankish churchmen on loyal implementation of solemn undertakings made to Rome by his father'.[130] But there was also the harm that Desiderius could do to Charles by using his nephews against him. In any case, Francia and 'Italy' were not clearly separable. In Bavaria, Duke Tassilo, who was not only Charles' cousin, but also Desiderius' son-in-law, was assuming greater liberty of action, though he had had himself recognised as vassal of the Frankish king.[131] He even developed links with Byzantium. In view of the close connections between the Bavarian and Langobard courts, perhaps an indirect reason for doing away with the Langobards was connected with depriving the Bavarians of possible support against the Franks. It took Charles until 788 to eliminate Tassilo and to take possession of the Duchy of Bavaria. This was so although at the time Byzantium was too much interested in good relations with the Frankish ruler to support his enemy, and the pope was too dependent on the king to be able to do anything for a particularly faithful son of the church, such as the Bavarian duke.[132]

As Charles' reign progressed, he was able to consolidate his possessions. By the end of the eighth century, only the far north remained to be pacified. The question arose whether his mastery of the West should be recognised by a general title indicating the overwhelming position he had acquired. During the last years of the century, after the death of Hadrian in December 795, Charles found himself drawn even more deeply into the affairs of the papacy than before. This was due to the fact that Hadrian's successor, Leo III, encountered the opposition of the Roman nobility, particularly of his predecessor's family, possibly prompted by Byzantium,[133] and thus lacked the authority his predecessor had wielded. He had accusations of adultery and perjury levelled against him and in 799 faced an insurrection in Rome, during which he was brutally assaulted and for a time imprisoned. We are not in a position to know whether any of the personal accusations against the pope were justified, or whether there were other charges of a more general nature. However these, whether true or false, must be seen to some extent against the background of a continuing power struggle in Rome between various noble and other factions. They were fought out mainly – in papal elections and rivalry for offices – at the papal court. The tensions were particularly severe as the contest took place in so small an area.[134]

Temporal rule of the Patrimony of St Peter had fundamentally changed the attitude of the Roman aristocracy to the papacy, which had increased its importance in their eyes. To instal a pope or at least to secure an appointment to a papal office (incidentally modelled on Byzantium) became a desirable objective to the leading Roman families vying for influence in the city and striving to deny it to their rivals. From this period may well have dated a strengthening of memories of the Roman senate of which these aristocratic circles regarded themselves as heirs. Quite possibly the enemies of Leo III were motivated partly by aversion to the whole institution of temporal rule for the curious reason that its establishment revived memories of Roman greatness in a remote past and therefore stimulated the wish to exercise power themselves once more. Leo's difficulties may have been due to an incompatibility between the spiritual and temporal functions of the papacy. The struggle of the Romans and the Italians against the temporal rule of the popes has been called the longest in history.[135] The aristocratic *fronde* left Leo no alternative but to appeal to Charles for help to rescue the papacy from its predicament. Thus factional struggles in Rome had repercussions of European dimensions.

Leo travelled to Paderborn to see Charles. The king decided to go to Rome, in order to investigate personally the guilt incurred not only by the conspirators, but also possibly by the pope himself. Leo was escorted back to Rome by the Franks.[136] It was Charles who, on 1 December 800, presided at St Peter's over a council consisting of higher and lower clergy, as well as lay dignitaries, to whom he referred the complaints against the pope. Leo was requested to prove his innocence by an oath. Charlemagne overruled the papal objection that 'the Apostolic See cannot be judged by anyone', and the pope had to yield. On 23 December at St Peter's, in the presence of the king, Leo had to appear before the council. He managed to combine an affirmation of his innocence of the charges made against him with an assertion of popes not 'being judged or constrained by anyone'. The pontiff's declaration was accepted as sufficient for his rehabilitation. Incidentally, on the same day a delegation arrived at Rome from Jerusalem to present Charles, in the name of its patriarch, with a banner and the keys of the Holy Sepulchre of Calvary and of the Holy City itself. Palestine was then under the rule of Caliph Harun ar-Rashid of Baghdad, to whom Charlemagne sent embassies and gifts.[137]

Two days later, on 25 December, Charles' visit to Rome reached its climax when the pope at St Peter's placed on his head a crown while the 'Roman people' acclaimed him as 'Charles Augustus, crowned by God, great and pacific emperor of the Romans'. After this the pope, prostrating himself, 'adored' the new emperor, in a ceremony instituted under Diocletian. The coronation ceremonial was copied from the procedure followed by the Patriarch of Constantinople at coronations of Byzantine emperors since the fifth century,[138] possibly owing to a desire to avoid being faulted by Byzantium for irregularities.

There has been much debate among historians as to whether Charles approved of what had been done, as Einhard in his biography stated that the emperor later voiced his dissatisfaction at the way in which Leo III had proceeded.[139] How did Charles feel about the imperial title, particularly as it was likely to involve him in difficulties with Byzantium? It was claimed by those supporting Charles' new rank that the imperial throne was in fact vacant, as Constantine VI, the legitimate emperor in Constantinople, had been overthrown in 797 by his mother Irene, who now ruled in his place. However, her legitimacy was open to question, not only because of the circumstances in which she had assumed power, but also because of doubts as to whether a woman could succeed to the throne, particularly in view of the special functions of the Byzantine Emperor in relation to the Church.

In any case, difficulties with Byzantium were nothing new for Charles. Earlier, after the defeat of the Lombards, Adalgis, the son of the overthrown king Desiderius, fled to Constantinople, where he was welcomed with open arms and given the very title of *patricius Romanorum* which had been assumed by Charles. There were even plans to support him against Charles in Lower Italy, but these did not come to fruition.[140] Later Byzantium allied itself with Bavaria and Benevento against the Franks, but following the death of the Emperor Leo IV in 780, Empress Irene sought to alleviate tension with Charles by the conclusion of a dynastic alliance.[141] At any rate, though the understanding broke down fairly soon, in the meantime the withdrawal of Byzantine support allowed Charles – as we have seen – to subject Duke Tassilo in Bavaria.

The internal troubles in Constantinople after the assumption of power by Empress Irene came at a convenient time for Charles, who had been trying for a number of years to obtain equality of rank with the Byzantine emperors by raising his own position and discrediting theirs. In pursuit of the first objective he had challenged – quite unnecessarily from a theological point of view – the settlement of the iconoclast controversy reached by the second ecumenical Council of Nicaea in 787. The council, which had met under the presidency of Empress Irene, permitted the use of icons on the clear understanding that only the prototype and not the actual representation was worshipped. In this way the controversy was settled, to the satisfaction of the pope and of the anti-iconoclast party in Constantinople, though unfortunately only for a time. As a counter-stroke, Charles in 794 called a council at Frankfurt under his presidency to annul the decrees of the second ecumenical council at Nicaea. It so happens that from this year onwards, Charles used Aachen as his permanent residence, modelled in many ways on the palaces and churches of Constantinople, apparently with the idea of rivalling that city's ecclesiastical and political importance. Possibly there was also some idea of competition with Rome, though this was not followed up. In order to discredit Byzantium, the emperors there were attacked for idolising themselves and for pretending to be 'divine'.[142] The controversy had substance in one respect, in that Charles genuinely abhorred the cult with which the Byzantine emperor was surrounded. The known rivalry between Aachen and Constantinople is one of several reasons why the enhancement of Charles' status was not a development that should cause surprise.

All in all, we have reason to suppose that the plan for the ceremony is likely to have been known beforehand to the royal court, which may well have agreed with it. In any case, Charles was not the kind of person who voluntarily submitted to anything he opposed; and a weak pope, who had barely overcome a severe personal crisis, would not have risked antagonising the most powerful ruler in Western Christendom. It is just possible, though not very likely, that Charles objected to receiving the imperial crown at the hands of the pope.[143]

What were the pope's aims in crowning Charles emperor? By adapting the Byzantine ceremonial, the pope effectively took the stage as 'emperor-maker'. He incidentally now dated his documents and coins according to Charles' imperial years.[144] To minimise the part played by the pope in the actual coronation, Charles used the phrase 'crowned by God' in his imperial title.[145] Did the pope also want to bind Charles even more strongly to the task of protecting the Holy See? Even if the popes achieved this objective – which is doubtful – they paid a price for it. For their authority in Rome was reduced by the substitution of the title of emperor for that of *patricius Romanorum*. While in 774 Charles visited Rome on the pope's sufferance, in 800 he was in the city as its master. Once more the popes were faced with a West Roman ruler exercising certain well-recognised historical functions, instead of with a remote East Roman emperor. Charles may indeed have already assumed quasi-imperial powers while still only *patricius*. But now he had law on his side. As emperor, he was entitled to notification by a new pope of his election, but this had already been granted to Pippin III as *patricius* in Roman eyes. Now, however, in accordance with the traditions of the Roman Empire, the emperor's consent had to be secured before the pope's consecration. This right was explicitly claimed by Charles' successor when Leo III died in 816. No more than his Carolingian or even

Merovingian predecessors – or for that matter in the previous exercise of his kingship – did Charles as emperor accept the Gelasian doctrine of a limitation of his authority to the temporal or secular sphere. Even less could he agree to a subordination of the temporal to the spiritual sphere as asserted by Pope Gelasius in 494.[146]

In a sense the imperial title simply acknowledged the overwhelming position Charles had acquired in the West. The revival of the old Roman imperial title in his favour helped to legitimise his rule over many territories that had belonged to the West Roman Empire, including Italy itself. There he appeared no longer simply as a foreign conqueror, but as successor to the Roman emperors. However, his connection with Rome was not only secular, but also spiritual, for Charles ruled over a large part of the territories of the Latin rite, in which there was an increasing consciousness during his reign of belonging to a community, to 'the Occident', in contradistinction to the Byzantine *orientale imperium*. While the Byzantine emperor designated himself as *dominus*, Charles deliberately used the title *gubernans*, which may be rendered as directing the Roman Empire. As emperor he exercised supreme power in Rome and the Patrimony of St Peter, while also ruling over the Frankish and Langobard kingdoms. Thus the emperorship, with its deemed divine bestowal, gave him a leading position among the other – also Catholic – rulers of the West.

There is evidence that some of the kings outside the Carolingian territories, like King Offa of Mercia and King Alfonso of Asturia, recognised Charles' special status.[147] Some contemporary writers see the Frankish Empire as *regnum Europae*.[148] Both the political and the religious distinction from the Eastern Empire was becoming more accentuated. For the pope the new situation meant that he was faced mainly with one ruler in his relations with the flock recognising his spiritual authority. This strong block of Frankish dominions, including the Italian possessions, was bound to create problems for the papacy. Perhaps it was assumed in Rome that, in accordance with the normal Germanic practice, unity would be replaced by division of the inheritance on Charles' death. Indeed, the emperor during the following years did make elaborate arrangements for the partition of his dominions among his three surviving sons. However, as two of them predeceased their father, the remaining legitimate son 'Louis' in fact succeeded to the whole of the Carolingian Empire, with the title of emperor. Any expectation on the part of the papacy that an emperorship combined with rule over a united Frankish realm would die with Charlemagne thus proved erroneous. It remained to be seen what effect the continuation of the combination of both dignities would have on the relationship between pope and emperor.

More immediately, the stresses created with Byzantium by the coronation had to be alleviated, particularly as they added to existing tensions. Except for temporary periods of co-operation, Byzantium had observed Charles' progress with jealousy and had only been too ready to aggravate his difficulties, be it in Bavaria or in Italy. The emperors had regarded Frankish penetration into Italy and the Adriatic area as an infringement of their rights. The Franks risked the severe displeasure of Byzantium by annexing Istria and Dalmatia, and by even subjecting Venice in 805. The Byzantine Emperor, Nicephorus I, went to war with Charles over Venice, which the Franks lost temporarily, only to retake it in 810. At last, in 812, a number of issues were settled by mutual compromise. Both the Frankish and Byzantine courts recognised the *de facto* independence of Venice. Charles renounced the Istrian and Dalmatian sea-ports in favour of Byzantium. In return, Constantinople recognised Charles' imperial dignity.[149]

Charles had always been careful to use a form for his title that avoided so far as possible a challenge to the Byzantine rulers as *the* Roman emperors. Therefore the complicated formula of 'emperor directing the Roman empire, who is also king of the Franks and the Langobards' was used.[150] In return, the Byzantine Emperor Michael I agreed no longer to treat Charles as a barbarian king, but to address him as 'brother'.[151] Charles had achieved his object of obtaining something like equality with the Byzantine emperor, on the basis of the independence of each empire on its own territory. However, the problem was not solved once and for all, as his successor, Louis the Pious, still had to contend with Byzantine claims.[152] That the dual emperorship was bound to deepen the division of Christendom was hardly perceived in Aachen, though it was probably felt in Rome.[153]

When Charles died in 814 at the age of about 72, he appeared to be leaving to his son and heir Louis a mighty empire with a solid foundation. The territory covered most of Western and Central, as well as some of Southern Europe. It extended into the fringes of Northern Spain and in the north to the River Elbe, and into parts of what later became Holstein. A wide eastern salient even penetrated Avar territory in Pannonia, which included parts of present-day Hungary. Northern and Central – but not Southern – Italy were included, apart from the Patrimony of St Peter. Yet, well before the end of the century, the unity of the Empire had been irrevocably shattered. Was this due to the incapacity of his successors or to some deep-rooted flaw, perhaps due to its vastness without enough in common to hold the whole structure together, once the ruler who had created it was no longer in charge?

On the positive side, Charlemagne had expanded and consolidated his dominions, managed to assert his authority over unruly vassals and been largely able to defend the frontiers he had established. He kept the nobility in order and used the system based on benefices to integrate imperial officials by means of establishing a feudal hierarchy, with the lord-vassal relationship at a number of levels, so that his own vassal could – in turn – also be the lord of a vassal under him. Noblemen who held offices under Charles were additionally bound to him by the loyalty they owed as his vassals. Some control was kept over the whole system by prohibiting double vassalage. Even if Charles technically did not gain increased legal powers over the Franks and Langobards through obtaining the imperial crown, his authority was considerably strengthened by his additional prestige. And he used his rise in status to impose a new and more stringent oath on all those who owed him allegiance. Charles had already received a public oath of allegiance from the nobility and the middle ranks of society, and eventually from all inhabitants of his empire, following a rising of Thuringian magnates in 786. This oath was probably instituted when, after the crushing of the rebellion, some of the conspirators pleaded that they had not sworn an oath of fealty to Charles and had therefore not broken any obligations.[154] The formula – still extant – dating from 792, is quite short and established a general relationship of fidelity.

Whereas in the period after 786 there was an obvious cause for the institution of an oath of fealty, the only reason for a new procedure was the establishment of the Empire. The duty of fidelity was now much broader and defined much more precisely than previously. The new oath included such religious obligations as making the keeping of the Ten Commandments part of the commitment to the emperor, who felt responsible for the morals of the inhabitants. It has been pointed out that directives issued in his name in this respect could not possibly be enforced, but that he and his successors were liable to be made answerable for their failure to do so, presumably by the Church.[155] Here we have one of several signs of the tensions building up during the last years of Charles' reign, which were only kept in check by his great ability and prestige.

However, this strengthening of the religious element of Charles' regime does not mean that he considered himself or was regarded as a priest-king, even to the extent that this applied to the Byzantine emperors. Charles was compared to King David, but in the Old Testament David, unlike Melchizedek, was not a priest-king. Actually the papacy – for what it was worth – forbade the Byzantine emperors to use any title reserved to Christ alone. Charles never dissented from the view that cultic functions were those of the clergy alone. His famous opening communication to Leo III on his succession to the pontificate in 796 – asking the pope to pray for the welfare of Charles' realm – shows that there was a whole sphere of activity in which the king could never replace him. Propitiating God was the concern of those who had the sacramental power to loose and to bind, above all the popes, in the exercise of which they were never challenged.[156] In any case, for Charles the temporal and the spiritual power were both instituted by God to bring about His rule, and therefore had to work together closely with this aim in mind.[157]

There was, however, a large area of matters in which there was some overlap of jurisdictions. While the pope could lay claim to overlordship of the whole ecclesiastical hierarchy and to the right to be the sole judge in matters of faith, Charles could – and did – base his right to administer the Frankish Church on his duty to protect it. As we have seen, he even intervened in theological questions at the Council of Frankfurt in 794. Although Charles never denied that the pope was supreme judge in matters of faith, he at times ignored this. Comparatively weak popes could hardly challenge a mighty ruler. In practice, here the relative exercise of rights was dependent on relative power. This posed a problem for the future, when rulers in the West were weaker and popes stronger.

Indeed, even during the last decade of the reign, things did not seem to go so well as before, with famine and a serious threat for a time from the Danes. While this disturbed contemporaries, who wondered whether Charles had been abandoned by good fortune, for the historian the underlying problems are more important. Even if Carolingian 'caesaropapism' did not go so far as has at times been thought, it was unlikely that rulers would in the long run be able to live up to what was expected from them in view of the special status they had acquired through papal unction. Fustel de Coulanges put it very well:

> The Carolingians were crushed by the high idea they had of their power. To command in the name of God, to wish to rule through Him and for Him when one is only a human being, that is to become enmeshed in a net of inextricable difficulties.

He concluded that in politics the ideal is always dangerous.[158] But the problems of the Carolingian Empire were not confined to this highest, religio-political level analysed by Fustel de Coulanges. There were many structural difficulties. The size of the territory was so considerable as to tax the ability of one ruler to direct it. It was doubtful whether it would be possible to maintain harmony between the various cultures, such as the Gallo-Germanic of the Frankish kingdom and that of Italy. Unlike the Roman state, the Empire of Charlemagne could not rely on an efficient civil service. Indeed, it was not easy to recruit as officials men with enough public spirit.[159] In many ways, it was only due to a ruler of Charles' outstanding ability that the Carolingian Empire was built up and could function, during his lifetime and for some years after.

3 Later Carolingians and the Saxon Dynasty (814–1024)

The reign of Louis the Pious, who succeeded Charlemagne in 814 and died in 840, is of particular interest, both for what was exceptional (and did not recur) and for what bore fruit and was thus of long-term significance. His emperorship was marked by a series of severe crises, even resulting in Louis' temporary displacement, due to some extent to the ruler changing his policy. In the latter part of the reign, there were serious external threats to the Carolingian dominions. Many historians have regarded Louis as a weak ruler. However, there is an alternative explanation for some of the apparent failures of his reign. As his appellation of 'the Pious' shows, even if it was coined only towards the end of his reign, at least some of Louis' actions were religiously motivated and display spiritual strength rather than weakness. In fact they were part of the problem of finding a satisfactory relationship between religion and politics, which gives the reign importance from the point of view of the themes central to this study.

Louis had been King of Aquitaine since 781 and while still in this capacity had a short spell as joint emperor with his father before succeeding Charlemagne as ruler of the Carolingian dominions. The Goths in this Pyreneean sub-kingdom kept alive their heritage, in which some elements from the past may well have survived. During his kingship Louis had come under the influence of the remarkable Benedict of Aniane (750–821), the scion of a noble Gothic family, who had established a monastery based on his interpretation of the Rule of St Benedict on paternal land in his Gothic-Septimanian (Languedoc) place of birth. Benedict of Aniane's reformed ascetic monasticism, which turned away from the cultural work which had been emphasised under Charlemagne,[1] was widely emulated in the Carolingian Empire. On succeeding to sole rule Louis brought with him not only Benedict, but a whole circle of Aquitanian advisers that helped to give a new direction to the Empire. Devolution through the establishment of sub-kingdoms under the rule of members of the Carolingian dynasty during the reign of Charlemagne had, on balance, assisted in the task of governing a territory of considerable size and variety, but perhaps sometimes – as in this case – made the provision of continuity for Carolingian policy more difficult.

Louis was fortunate in the early years of his reign, during a period of comparative external peace, to be able to concentrate on domestic problems. He regarded his rule over the Empire 'as *munus divinum*, both as a gift from God and as a mandate',[2] to which the highest moral standards had to be applied. While it would go too far to say that he was a monk on the throne, he certainly believed strongly in the monastic ideal of his mentor Benedict of Aniane. The programme he enunciated for his reign was the *renovatio regni Francorum*, which built on what had already been achieved under Charlemagne, but attempted to go much further in the mutual integration of the ecclesiastical and the secular sphere under the supreme direction of the emperor. Louis played an active part in the establishment of a homogeneous church for the whole of the Carolingian Empire, with the purpose of carrying out ecclesiastical reform. A clearer distinction than previously was made between the secular clergy and the regular order of monks. These matters were naturally of great importance to the papacy.

It was in the relations with the papacy that the new reign involved a considerable departure from the previous one. Charlemagne had, on the whole, succeeded in fitting a good relationship with the papacy into the general policy framework. But after his death, the influence of his ecclesiastical advisers declined, as they were superseded by the Aquitanian circle that Louis brought with him to the imperial court. Cordiality with Rome was replaced by a certain coolness, by a deliberate distancing of the Frankish court from the papacy. At the same time, to the pope the time appeared to have come to find out whether Louis insisted on imperial rights in the Patrimony of St Peter to the same extent as his father. Pope Leo III was to discover that Louis' intense religiosity did not make any difference to traditional Carolingian determination to preserve Frankish rights over the Patrimony. Thus the pope had to yield. Unlike his predecessors, Louis did not carry out church reforms in close cooperation with the papacy. It may be that – because of his strong involvement in ecclesiastical affairs and because of his particular perception of the divine nature of his rule – he was less amenable to the influence of the papacy than more secularly inclined rulers.

In order to avoid papal interference, Louis made quite sure that a series of measures of church reform were completed before Stephen IV arrived at Rheims in 816 for discussions with him, as well as for his coronation of Louis and that of his wife. Louis had already been crowned emperor by his father in Aachen in 813, possibly to exclude the papacy from a say in designating an emperor. The pope therefore attached great importance to being able at any rate to confirm the emperor in his position by putting the crown on his head. In 817 Louis crowned his eldest son Lothar emperor, with the consent of the magnates, but without the cooperation of the pope. However, Lothar at Easter 823 gave the pope the opportunity to repeat the coronation ceremony at St Peter's in Rome. From then on medieval rulers seeking the imperial crown had to proceed to Rome and to obtain the cooperation of the pope to achieve their aim.[3] 'Rome did not rule over the globe, but in order to dominate it one had to have power over Rome.'[4]

The visit, however, did not turn out entirely to the pope's satisfaction, as Lothar asserted imperial authority and impartial justice, even where this turned out to the disadvantage of the papacy. The beginnings of a split into a papal and an imperial party in Rome may well date back to this time, with the former being resentful of imperial intervention and the latter opposed to the temporal rule of the papacy. In the following year, the imperial party succeeded in securing the election of Pope Eugenius II, with whom Lothar concluded the *Constitutio Romana* of 824; this declared the inviolability of both papal and imperial protégés. Above all, it was laid down that in future the administration of the papal territory was to be supervised by a commission consisting of a papal and an imperial *missus*, with the duty of reporting annually to the emperor. The canonical mode was sanctioned for papal elections, but before his consecration the new pope was to take an oath to preserve the *status quo*. Lothar strengthened imperial rights even further in 844 when he stipulated that elections were to be held only after the issue of an imperial authorisation; he also prescribed that they were to take place in the presence of imperial *missi*.[5]

In the agreements which were concluded in 816 and during the following years between Empire and papacy, the relationship of the Roman and the Frankish Churches with the emperor was increasingly put on a similar footing in some respects. Thus the Roman bishopric appeared for a time to be in danger of losing its singularity. One of the few advantages of the arrangement was that in principle free elections – though with some supervision by the emperor – were granted for the papacy, just as they were for the other bishoprics in the Empire. In the case of elections to bishoprics, the emperor reserved to himself the right of consent and institution. With the papacy, all that was required was notification of elections after consecration. The autonomy of the Patrimony of St Peter in administration and justice was also confirmed; the emperor was to intervene only in case of refusal of justice.[6] Incidentally, in 816, Stephen IV – going further than his predecessor – immediately after his election had the Roman people swear an oath of allegiance to Louis.[7]

The close connection between religion and politics prevailing at the time can be seen in the regulation of the succession. Leading ecclesiastics, who had been pressing for a unified church in the Empire, helped to prepare the ground for a scheme to preserve the Carolingian Empire as a single unit, at any rate in the sense of one of the brothers – Louis' sons – being master of the whole. They supported imperial unity on the basis that political arrangements should be analogous to the religious ideal of one body, the Church. Louis owed his sole rulership to the fortuitous circumstance that he alone of Charlemagne's legitimate sons survived his father, thus triumphing over the traditional Frankish tendency to divide the inheritance. 'The *ordinatio imperii* of 817 created a balance between the principles of division and unity.'[8] Louis' eldest son Lothar was established as co-emperor and as the future head of an empire in which his brothers would be kings under him.

The settlement was not regarded as a purely practical matter and was made at the imperial assembly in Aachen after prolonged fasting and prayer and justified on theological grounds, namely that the division of the Empire would be a scandal and offensive to God. The pope was reportedly asked to ratify the arrangement.[9] The regulation of the succession was in line with Louis' decision at the beginning of his reign to drop the reference to rulership over the Franks and the Langobards, and to adopt the simple title of *imperator augustus* to demonstrate that his empire had developed beyond ethnic kingship. This new title also reduced friction with Byzantium.

Besides the *ordinatio imperii*, the preamble to the capitularies of 818–19 and the *admonitio ad omnes regni ordines* of 825 are important documents of the new concept of empire. The preamble of 818–19 distinguishes between the mortal person of the emperor and his office. The ruler directs both church and state. Louis granted the right of election to bishoprics and imperial monasteries, subject to his consent and institution. The *admonitio* was passed at the imperial assembly at Aachen in 825, in which the emperorship is described for the first time as a *ministerium*, in analogy to the office of bishop. The two spheres appear under the names of *ecclesia* and *regnum*. There was also the new concept that every magnate participated in the emperor's *ministerium*.

In the meantime, criticism of the emperor's actions had increased. Louis had made many enemies right from the beginning of his reign, when he excluded members of Charlemagne's wider family from his court, though he did so on grounds of public policy rather than because of any personal dislike. The *ordinatio imperii* was resented by Louis' nephew Bernard, King of Italy, because the stipulation that future emperors, too, would have authority over the rulers of kingdoms in the Carolingian Empire appeared to block his ambition to achieve greater independence. Bernard's rebellion was crushed and in 818 he was sentenced to death by an imperial assembly. Louis commuted the punishment to blinding, but unfortunately Bernard died in the process.

After the death of his mentor Benedict of Aniane in 821, Louis recalled to court a number of members of the imperial family, such as his cousins Adalhard and Wala, who were distinguished clerics. The following year Louis did public penance at the imperial assembly in Attigny for his own shortcomings and those of his father as Christian rulers, as well as for his treatment of his relatives, and particularly for the death of his nephew Bernard during his blinding. The bishops also confessed to their failings. Historians have often interpreted Louis' conduct at Attigny as weakness, but it can also be seen as the strength of a ruler with firm religious convictions. Louis took an exalted view of imperial rule, viewing it as a *ministerium* under his leadership, in which those who assisted him in his rule shared. He was impatient of the inevitable compromises, due to human weakness and the necessity of the preservation of power, which were required to translate religious precepts into political realities. Louis regarded these concessions to the world as failures which could only be expiated by doing penance and making reparation.[10] However, the emperor's moral courage, while doing him honour as an individual, may well have weakened his position as a ruler. Eventually, as the bishops did not persist in their repentant attitude, it was the emperor who had to take sole responsibility for what went wrong and was blamed for it. In some ways Attigny proved to be the precursor of a whole series of troubles which were to mar the rest of the reign, particularly from the end of the third decade of the century onwards.

In 828 insecurity increased at the borders, causing a crisis in the Empire, which perhaps Charlemagne might have handled more calmly.[11] It may well be that in some cases foreign intruders were encouraged to undertake their enterprises by news of internal strife. The following decades of instability at home saw many Norman, Saracen and later Magyar invasions affecting wide parts of the Carolingian Empire, mostly without really effective counter-measures being taken. At the imperial assembly in Worms in 829, Louis allotted a share of the Empire to his infant son from a second marriage, to the chagrin of the offspring from the first. Though he did not in principle deviate from the *ordinatio imperii*, which he had proclaimed with so much moral fanfare a decade earlier, the rearrangement was widely seen as a breach of the ordinance. He strained his relationship with his three sons from his first marriage even further by ending the co-regency of the eldest, Lothar, who had become joint emperor. Alienating Lothar may well have been his greatest tactical mistake.

The last two decades of Louis' life were full of almost continuous strife within the imperial family, involving various coalitions of father and sons, culminating in the *coup d'état* of the three elder sons in 833. Lothar certainly wished his father to abdicate in his favour. There was no precedent for dethroning an emperor, and the legal basis for this first had to be created. In view of the conception of the dignity of emperor as a divine mandate and as an ecclesiastical office which had become established during the two previous decades,[12] it was decided to charge the emperor before the bishops for having failed in the duty of his imperial *ministerium*. Though Lothar succeeded in getting Pope Gregory IV to intervene in the dispute, as a reported guarantor of the *ordinatio imperii*, the pontiff actually failed to achieve anything on his visit to the Frankish kingdom, partly because of the strong stand taken against his mission by the bishops supporting the old emperor. In Soissons Louis handed the clergy a list of his own failings, put down his weapons and was clothed as a penitent. The purpose of the process was to make Louis incapable of reigning. However, this could actually only be achieved by tonsuring Louis, or – which was not contemplated – by blinding him. Lothar in effect took over. Louis was virtually his prisoner, but refused to take any decision on abdicating while unfree. Lothar's treatment of his father eventually led to a reaction in favour of Louis, who resumed his rule. But concord was not completely restored, even after the death of Louis' son Pippin, the King of Aquitaine. This allowed the old emperor in 839 – by disinheriting Pippin's sons – to divide the Empire principally between Lothar, the eldest son from his first marriage, and Charles, a son from his second marriage. The other son from the first marriage, Louis, kept Bavaria. Soon after, in 840, Louis the Pious died.

Perhaps more than for any shortcomings of the ruler, the reign is notable for the attempt to achieve an even more far-reaching integration of *regnum* and *ecclesia* than had taken place previously.[13] Both were to be under the overall supervision of the monarch. Louis was sincere in his striving to apply Christian values to affairs of state. At Attigny in 822 and at Soissons in 833 he practised what he preached: he publicly confessed the sins he had committed during his stewardship. Interestingly he allowed himself to be judged by the bishops in moral and religious questions, though he regarded the prelates as coming, at least indirectly, under his authority; the bishops were in any case among his instruments for carrying out his secular duties. A ruler – even an emperor – who confessed could be granted absolution by the bishops. The prelates were thus put into a position of determining whether a ruler who had sinned – even in his public office – could be restored to grace. In the long term it was only a step further for the greatest bishop, the pope, to judge emperors.

There is also the short-term question whether Louis' public repentance – however much credit it did him as a person – did not materially weaken his position by damaging the emperor's prestige and whether it was compatible with the sacrality of imperial monarchy. As with the popes, a distinction was also to some extent made in the case of emperors between the high office they occupied and their personal unworthiness. But this does not solve the problem of the standing of an emperor who had in public confessed to having been seriously derelict in his duties. Louis' repentance at Attigny may thus have been a major cause in the nearly two decades of unrest that followed. Even if some of Louis' ecclesiastical reforms proved lasting, the reign as a whole ended in failure, because the ruler was incapable of preventing disorder and civil war. A positive achievement was Louis' improved treatment of the Jews, which also benefited trade and commerce in his dominions.[14] Overall, succeeding a father of outstanding ability, achievement and reputation was bound to be a difficult undertaking for any heir. At the same time, part of Louis' difficulties in fact lay in problems which his illustrious predecessor had not solved, but merely kept in check by his imperious personality. It was both the strength and the weakness of Charlemagne's Empire that no attempt was made to amalgamate the various ethnic units into one people. Indeed the larger ones formed the core around which the nations of Europe arose. Also the extent and diversity of the dominions rendered sole rule by one monarch an impossibility. But delegation involved loss of control by the centre, particularly because of the poor communications prevailing in the age, and was liable to lead to internal strife, aggravated by Germanic traditions of dividing the inheritance.

Unfortunately even Louis' death did not end the dynastic conflict, which now divided his sons. Lothar I was beaten in battle at Fontenoy in 841 when he attempted to assert his supremacy as emperor over his two younger brothers, Louis, who governed Bavaria, and Charles the Bald, who ruled over territory that was to form part of the later France. The following year Louis and Charles in Strassburg swore oaths that they would continue to support each other against Lothar. The separate paths that Eastern and Western Francia were to take found their first linguistic expression in the reference to the respective use of High German and Old French by their followers.[15] Interestingly it was the magnates, ecclesiastical and secular, who insisted on the termination of the fraternal fighting.

In the Treaty of Verdun of August 843, a redistribution of the Frankish Empire between the three brothers took place (Map I). Lothar as emperor received a middle kingdom stretching from the North Sea to Italy, a share of the Frankish heartlands which included Aachen, and the protectorate over Rome and the Patrimony of St Peter. He abandoned his efforts to assert his supremacy over his brothers, paving the way for an emperorship based primarily on Italy, though the universal idea was not entirely given up.[16] The territory mainly to the east of the Rhine fell to Louis, that to the west of Lothar's empire to Charles the Bald. Chroniclers referred to Louis as *Rex Germaniae* or *Germanorum* (although he was not given this title officially), and Louis has thus gone down in the history books as 'the German'.

The treaty did not dissolve the Carolingian Empire, even if the imperial idea revived in 800 was now in many ways represented by Lothar's portion: the concept of Frankish unity, of one *populus christianus*, was not abandoned, a reciprocal right of inheritance between the three branches of the dynasty continued and did in fact become operative, and attempts at cooperation in home and foreign policy were made periodically. There were also many links between the aristocracy and the episcopate of the various territories.[17] Although Louis' and Charles' *regna* were not yet formally independent, they began to emancipate themselves from the imperial power.[18]

West Francia and East Francia were the territories from which France and Germany were to develop. However, at Verdun frontiers were drawn without consideration of linguistic boundaries,[19] though in effect West Francia was mainly Romance speaking and East Francia primarily used Germanic or Teutonic languages. That does not mean that East Francia had yet developed any sense of German national identity. The idea of a united Frankish Empire under the Carolingians representing Christian culture did not at

Map I

once vanish into history, however much representatives of the dynasty may have undermined it by their dissensions. It needs hardly to be pointed out that at the time – with its complicated network of loyalties to kings, bishops and feudal lords – nothing like modern states existed. In any case the all-pervading influence of a cosmopolitan church and a common allegiance to Christ, not recognising territorial or ethnic boundaries, prevented the development of anything like a latter-day nationalism.

The borders laid down in the Treaty of Verdun did not prove lasting, partly because Lothar I's branch in the Middle Kingdom encountered problems, especially in connection with the matrimonial affairs of his son Lothar II, King of what was called Lotharingia after the founder and from which the name Lorraine is derived. Lothar II had three children from his mistress Waldrada. Later he married Theutberga, from whom, however, he did not have any offspring. In 863, in order to legitimise a son from his liaison with Waldrada to secure the succession, he wished to return to her and to marry her instead of Theutberga. Lothar was supported in his effort to rid himself of Theutberga by the Archbishops of Cologne and Trier.

Pope Nicholas I, one of the strongest pontiffs of the period, however, now intervened, ruling in favour of the marriage to Theutberga and declaring Waldrada to be a concubine. Furthermore, he deposed the two archbishops who had favoured Lothar's matrimonial plans, summoned them to appear before him in the Lateran, and stipulated that their vacancies should only be filled with his consent. Nicholas had his way, because contemporary opinion was pleased with the way the papacy protected a defenceless woman. The pope also on appeal reversed the excommunication of a suffragan bishop by the powerful Archbishop Hincmar of Rheims and reinstated him. Nicholas' intervention is important in extending the pope's jurisdiction and authority over matrimonial law and over archbishops and even kings.

> According to Nicholas I matrimonial matters belong to that wider sphere of matters which directly affect the salvation and faith of the Christian people...and...make ecclesiastical, that is, papal jurisdiction in matrimonial matters imperative.[20]

This extension of ecclesiastical jurisdiction was a momentous measure, of great consequence for the future, and is still of some importance in our day. Not only was the sphere of ecclesiastical power widened considerably, but also the power of the Church over rulers was strengthened, as they became more dependent on obtaining papal dispensations in matrimonial matters. This increasing assertion of the papacy was in line with a forgery called the Pseudo-Isidorian collection of ecclesiastical law. Many of the decrees incorporated in Pseudo-Isidore for example 'contain absolutely nothing new: what the forgers did was to clothe a particular hierocratic and already virtually accepted tenet in the garb of an ancient decree'.[21] The first clearly established use of Pseudo-Isidore was made by Nicholas in his dispute with the Archbishop of Rheims, who had actually supported him over his intervention in Lothar II's matrimonial affairs.[22]

Pseudo-Isidore helped, at a time of Carolingian weakness and division, to give the papacy the opportunity of becoming the centre from which it could institute a uniform pattern of thought and law.[23] Nicholas maintained that papal decrees and judgments had the force of canon law. In many ways he based himself on the Gelasian doctrine of the two powers, standing up for the right of the Church to run itself. He expressed strong opposition to lay patronage, to the validity of the proprietary churches (*Eigenkirchen*) and to any granting of church property as fiefs. Rulers were not to interfere with the election of bishops and they were not to call synods, which he regarded as a prerogative of the papacy. The pope was not to be judged by anybody. The situation was not yet ripe for the enforcement of all the doctrines enunciated by Nicholas, but they certainly foreshadow much of the programme of Gregory VII.[24]

The history of Lothar's line illustrates the changing balance of power between emperor and pope. When the Frankish monarchy was divided and the emperor became a ruler over a part of the Carolingian dominions, like others, the protectorate over the papacy became the only feature that differentiated the emperor from the kings. Thus papal sanctioning of an emperor received greater significance than it had possessed in the case of, for example, Louis I. Unlike his father and grandfather, Lothar I did not simply put the imperial crown on his heir himself.[25] By petitioning Pope Leo IV to anoint and crown his son, Louis II, in 850, he helped to make the imperial coronation by the pope in Rome an essential element in the process. As Louis II later used this argument to defend the legality of his status to Byzantium, this right of imperial coronation could no longer be denied either to Rome or to the papacy.[26] Louis II had in fact earlier, in 844, been crowned King of the Langobards by the pope. This, by making him a king and conferring rule over a large part of Italy on him, was a necessary precondition for the emperorship. Pope Nicholas I already saw in the papal coronation of the emperor the decisive legal element, or at the very least one of equal importance with hereditary legitimacy. Historically these developments were to play an important part after the extinction of Lothar I's line. Interestingly enough, Nicholas – in accordance with Gelasian doctrine – not only recognised the crowned emperor as his ruler in secular matters, but also refrained from claiming temporal power for the Patrimony of St Peter.[27]

When Lothar II died in 869, his illegitimate son Hugh had no chance of succeeding to his father's inheritance. Charles the Bald attempted to annex the whole of Lotharingia. But in the treaty of Meersen (870), he agreed to partition the territory with Louis the German, thus acquiring a common border with his brother. Lothar I's branch was now confined to Italy, as well as to Burgundy and Provence, which were to gain their independence during the following decade. They were ruled by Lothar I's eldest son, Emperor Louis II, the last legitimate offspring of this line, who died in August 875.

The extinction of Lothar I's line created a new situation in the relations between the papacy and the Carolingian dynasty. The papacy had never questioned that its protection and the emperorship were hereditary in his line, though since 850 papal coronation appeared to have become a necessary element.[28] Louis II had designated Carloman, one of the sons of Louis the German, as his heir. Furthermore Louis the German and Charles the Bald had tentatively agreed on sharing the protection of the papacy in this eventuality. However, the papacy now claimed a say in the question of the imperial succession for itself and for the *populus romanus*. This was done not only on the grounds of long-held rights, but also in accordance with a stipulation in the *ordinatio imperii* of 817, which left the choice of a successor in the kind of case that had arisen to the *populus romanus*.

For some years before the death of Louis II, the papacy had held out to Charles the Bald the prospect of the emperorship,[29] although for a time it had been locked in a struggle with the king concerning their respective rights over the Church in the West Frankish kingdom.[30] Pope John VIII, who had succeeded to the papacy in 872, moved quickly after Louis II's death to summon the clergy and senate of Rome to proclaim Charles the Bald as emperor in August 875, thus setting aside the wishes of both the dead ruler and of Louis the German. Charles himself, in September, received the fealty of part of the Italian magnates as King of the Langobards. At Christmas he was crowned emperor by John VIII at St Peter's. In return, Charles cancelled the stipulation that papal elections had to take place in the presence of imperial *missi*. He also charged Pope John with the direction of South Italian policy.[31] In this kind of competitive situation within the dynasty, the papacy was – at least nominally – able to 'elect, nominate and postulate' the emperor. Two years later, on the death of Charles the Bald, John went even further and claimed that prior papal consent was necessary for bestowing what he called the Italian (but what was strictly the Langobard) crown, so important for the Patrimony of St Peter. As this crown was a preliminary to the emperorship, the papacy was thus getting into a position of establishing a papal right to examine and confirm claims to the emperorship, so vital in the later struggles between them.[32]

It seems that Pope John preferred the West Frankish to the East Frankish line in order to secure greater autonomy for the papal states. This might be regarded as an early instance of papal manœuvring between 'France' and 'Germany'. The papacy felt threatened by the power of the East Frankish rulers, just as it had earlier on resented the strong hand of Emperor Louis II of the Lotharingian line. However, what appeared advisable to the papacy from the point of view of Italian politics was not necessarily the best solution for dealing with the external threats the peninsula faced, above all from the Saracens, against which Louis II had been such a useful ally. Charles the Bald showed more interest in following Emperor Lothar I's example of trying to assert his authority over all the Carolingian lines, and with equal lack of success, than in coming to the aid of the papacy against the Saracens, who were playing havoc with Italy.[33] So it was left to the pope himself to take action. In this desperate situation, he mustered and commanded a fleet against the Saracens, securing initial victories, but finally proving unable to stem the tide of the invaders.

Thanks to the opposition of the second son of Louis the German, Louis III (the Younger), Charles' exploits ended in disaster, and he died in 877 while fleeing from his enemies. He was for a short spell succeeded as West Frankish king by his son Louis II, the Stammerer, an insignificant figure.

The pope journeyed to his court after fleeing from Rome following an invasion of the city by an Italian faction dissatisfied with his leanings towards the West Franks, but he was no more successful in his pleas for help than he had been with his father. Some historians have seen, in the failure of the West Frankish monarchy to rally to the aid of the papacy, one of the reasons why the leadership of the West eventually passed to the East Franks and their Saxon successors.[34] Indeed, in 879, Pope John began to turn to the East Frankish line for help. The youngest son of Louis the German, Charles III (the Fat), appeared in Italy in 879 and received the Italian kingship. In 881 he was crowned emperor by Pope John in Rome. But Charles proved unable to give John any help against his external and internal enemies.

The papacy was increasingly caught up in the politics of the Roman nobility, whose pawn it was in danger of becoming. The series of foreign popes had ceased with the death of Zacharias in 752, to be replaced by a succession of Romans, many belonging to leading families. The link between Romans and the papacy was only broken in exceptional cases.[35] There was also a change from an administration in the hands of paid officials to one in which some of the most important offices passed into the hands of the local nobility.[36] John himself apparently fell victim to the increasing disorders in the city, in 882 becoming the first medieval pope to die a violent death, opening a period in which the papacy sank to its nadir.[37]

Interestingly enough the Carolingian Empire increasingly went into decline at about the same time. While the papacy had briefly been able to strengthen its position with the weakening of the emperorship, its power base was too small to allow it to exercise its functions of providing internal stability in the papal states and defence against attack without the help of the emperor. There were times when imperial authority was irksome to the popes, but its absence exposed the papacy to the pressures of local magnates and overmighty neighbouring lords. This in some ways was an even greater threat to the maintenance of high standards in pontiffs and to the independence essential for the exercise of the spiritual functions of the papacy.

Charles III (the Fat) was to reunite the Carolingian dominions briefly in 884, thanks both to genealogical accident and to election by the West Frankish magnates. But this did not stop the movement towards a break-up. Charles may well have failed at least partly because the two kingdoms were beginning to develop something like different ethnic traits.[38] But he was in any case an unimpressive ruler, and the East Frankish nobility, which had come to the conclusion of his incapacity to govern, in 887 decided to overthrow him and found an able leader in Arnulf, Duke of Carinthia. He was an illegitimate grandson of Louis the German and now succeeded to the East Frankish kingdom. To the surprise of the East Franks, the other parts of the Carolingian Empire did not, however, join them in recognising Arnulf as ruler over the whole empire.

Charles' abdication in 887, to be followed the year after by his death, was a signal for other parts of the Empire to break with the Carolingian succession. In the West Frankish kingdom, Duke Odo of Francia, which comprised Paris, took the throne, at least for the time being. He belonged to a family that had immigrated from Saxony and was to become better known as the Capetian dynasty, which – after alternating with the Carolingians until the end of the tenth century – was to displace them permanently. Burgundy and the Langobard kingdom passed to other families. However, as (initially) the only Carolingian, Arnulf received an oath of fealty from all the various rulers, with the exception of Guy of Spoleto, who not only secured most of the Langobard kingdom, but even forced Pope Stephen V to crown him emperor in 891, after an appeal to King Arnulf to come to the pope's aid had failed. Arnulf was then preoccupied with a Norman invasion, which he, however, managed to defeat.

Soon after these events, Formosus succeeded to the papacy. Rome was split between factions supporting the East Franks and the Spoletans, the latter having taken the place formerly held by the West Frankish party. Formosus, who had earlier collaborated with the Spoletan dynasty against John VIII, now saw that family as a threat to the position of the papal states and of the papacy itself. But he found himself unable to resist Guy's pressure to crown his son Lambert as co-emperor. His only hope was to be rescued from dependance on the Spoletans by King Arnulf, who in 894 was able to organise an expedition to Italy which secured him the Langobard crown. The following year he once more took an army to the peninsula and this time reached Rome, where Formosus crowned him emperor in February 896, although Emperor Lambert (of Spoleto) was still alive. Arnulf, however, fell ill, when he was about to campaign against Lambert, and had to return home, where he died in 899. As to the pope, it was only Formosus' death in April 896 that saved him from experiencing the complete reversal of fortunes which now set in, mainly against East Frankish, but perhaps altogether against foreign influence. His successor, Stephen VI, arranged a ghastly and sacrilegious trial of his predecessor's body, finding him guilty on the grounds that he was disqualified from becoming pope through already being a bishop, though the rule had been broken previously. His true offence, presumably, was his opposition to the Spoletans and his cooperation with the East Franks in crowning Arnulf. The gruesome ceremony led to years of civil war between the Formosan and the anti-Formosan factions, in which the papacy was simply a particularly valuable pawn.[39]

Arnulf died in 899 and left a minor as an heir, Louis the Child. The powerlessness of the new king and the need for self-help led to the formation of what modern historians have called stem duchies (*Stammesherzog-*

tümer), whose leaders took over the tasks of internal order and external defence which the king was no longer able to carry out. The chief of each stem duchy was drawn from the leading family, if there was one, such as in Saxony, where the descendants of Liudolf, better known as the Ottonians, took over. The *Stämme*, with a settled leadership, were able to establish stem duchies more quickly than those where it was contested. Thus the Saxons, with the Bavarians, and later the Franks, were able to achieve political influence earlier than, for instance, the Swabians.

When the Carolingians in Eastern Francia died out in 911 with Louis the Child, the dukes of the stem duchies agreed to elect a king from their midst and to submit themselves to him, though up to what point was yet to be clarified in a situation for which there were no legal precedents. The choice of king fell on Conrad, Duke of the Franks, partly because this *Stamm* was associated particularly closely with the *Regnum Francorum*. The events of 912 reveal that there was a considerable coherence among the *Stämme* of East Francia which allowed them to continue the East Frankish kingdom without attempting to recruit a Carolingian from the West Frankish line. The only exception to East Frankish solidarity was Lotharingia, incorporated into in the East Frankish kingdom in 880, which now joined Western Francia.

Though Conrad I had been elected by the dukes and was indeed one of them, he modelled himself on Carolingian centralism, which he regarded as necessary not only for the internal maintenance of the kingdom, but also for its defence against its external enemies; the latter was, however, left to the Bavarians and Swabians. To curb the power of the dukes, he allied himself with the Church. However, the bishops were not everywhere able to oppose the dukes in which their dioceses were situated, least of all in Saxony. In any case, this kind of alliance with the Church required a firm kingship for its effectiveness. Conrad lost his battles in Saxony and Bavaria, as well as in Swabia, where, too, a strong stem duchy was now emerging. By the time Conrad I's reign ended with his death at the end of 918, it had become clear that the stem duchies could no longer be ignored and that some balance had to be established between their interests and those of the kingdom as a whole.[40]

On his death-bed Conrad showed the magnanimity and vision to designate his most serious opponent, the Saxon Duke Henry, as his successor, in the belief that he had the best chance of preserving the unity of the kingdom. Conrad persuaded his younger brother, Eberhard, to consent to his blood claim being passed over. In May 919, Henry I was formally elected king, but without the participation of the Swabian and Bavarian dukes, whose allegiance he had to compel. The new king learned from the failure of his predecessor and did not attempt to govern with the bishops against the dukes. To emphasise the break with the previous reign, he did not make appointments to a royal chapel.[41] He also did not receive a clerical unction, but it is not clear whether he declined to do so or whether he was refused.[42] However, he insisted on the dukes swearing oaths of fealty and vassalage to him. He thus used the system based on benefices (*Lehenswesen*) – which in this way developed into an essential part of the order of government – to tie the dukes to the kingship.

The dukes, with their base of support among the stems they ruled, according to their own laws, became – after the king – participants in the exercise of power in the realm. They were free to run the duchies largely without interference from the king, and in turn secured the allegiance, as vassals, for instance of the counts, who under the Carolingians had been imperial representatives. Similarly they attempted to bring the bishops under their control. However, here Henry drew the line and began, with some success, to reassert royal control over the Church,[43] particularly after he had succeeded in regaining Lotharingia for the Eastern Frankish king-dom in 925. From that time onwards some elements of Henry's previously in some ways federalist policy were increasingly subordinated to strands of Carolingian tradition. In this connection Henry turned to the Church as the natural ally against ducal and ethnic particularism. He re-established a royal chapel and regained disposal of all bishoprics with the exception of Bavaria, which was only brought under control by his son Otto.[44] Increasingly Henry emphasised the dependent character of the dukes, while recognising their value in representing their stems (which applied to all with the exception of Lotharingia, with its ethnic diversity). However, there was no uniformity in the relationship between king and dukes, as this varied from the comparative independence of Bavaria (in ecclesiastical affairs and even in foreign policy) to a considerable degree of subordination to royal author-ity in the case of Franconia.[45]

Henry broke new ground in 929 with his regulation of the succession to the monarchy. Under Germanic and Frankish tradition it was strictly the family or dynasty (*das Geblüt*) and not the individual person that was called to the throne. This accounted for the custom of dividing the inheritance among the sons, which precluded any notion of primogeniture. We have seen that the sole succession of Louis the Pious was only due to his brothers predeceasing their father. The German word for king, *König*, means some-thing like 'descendant of the founder of the lineage'. Kings of new families in turn established fresh dynasties, though an attempt was made to link them to the previous ruling family.[46] Thus the genealogy of Henry I was traced back to Charlemagne,[47] with doubtful historical accuracy.

With the consent of the magnates, Henry abandoned custom and desig-nated the eldest son from his second marriage, Otto, as sole heir (see Table 3.1).[48] As he did not regard himself as committed to the principle of primogeniture, Henry was free to choose the son who in his opinion was

Table 3.1   The Saxon dynasty

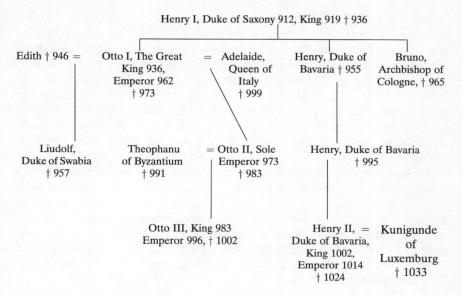

Henry I, Duke of Saxony 912, King 919 † 936

| Edith † 946 = | Otto I, The Great
King 936,
Emperor 962
† 973 | = Adelaide,
Queen of
Italy
† 999 | Henry, Duke of
Bavaria † 955 | Bruno,
Archbishop of
Cologne, † 965 |

| Liudolf,
Duke of Swabia
† 957 | Theophanu
of Byzantium
† 991 | = Otto II, Sole
Emperor 973
† 983 | Henry, Duke of Bavaria
† 995 |

| Otto III, King 983
Emperor 996, † 1002 | Henry II, =
Duke of Bavaria,
King 1002,
Emperor 1014
† 1024 | Kunigunde
of
Luxemburg
† 1033 |

best qualified to succeed him. Thankmar, a son from Henry's first marriage to Hatheburg, which was not recognised by the Church, because she had previously taken vows as a nun, was ignored. However, this was due more to doubts about his personality rather than to objections on the part of the Church.[49] From the offspring of the second marriage, the youngest son, Bruno, was destined for the Church from an early age. The king appears to have passed over his middle son, Henry, because he did not regard him as suitable for the task. When Henry I, in agreement with the magnates, made his final arrangements for the succession in 936, at a time when he felt his end near, Otto also appeared the more appropriate choice because he was already in his mid-twenties, whereas Prince Henry was 10 years younger.[50] The West Franks followed suit in adopting the principle of indivisibility after the demise of the Carolingians. Some historians see Henry's measures as a rejection of the absolute claim of Carolingian concepts of a sacral dynasty which required the partition of the inheritance.[51] However, there is some evidence that not only the king, but to some extent even the Liudolfing (Ottonian) family circle was considered sacral.[52]

Although Henry I only exercised the royal office for something like 17 years, from 919 to 936, his reign opened a new era. He was the first ruler to put on a firm basis the East Frankish kingdom, which had emerged as a separate entity from the break-up of the Carolingian Empire. Internally, the new order was based on the partnership of the stem duchies of the Franks, the Saxons, the Swabians and the Bavarians, to which Henry added the duchy of Lotharingia, which included Aachen, with the Carolingian traditions it contributed to the East Frankish kingdom. With the stipulation of the principle of indivisibility in the royal succession, there was the prospect of an era of stability under one dynasty. Sacral or not, the king was expected to be able to live up to his role. Henry I had not only been able to assert his authority inside the country, but also to defend it. He had defeated the Hungarians in 933 at the Unstrut, had kept the Slavs in check on the eastern frontier and defeated the Danes in the North. He made his influence felt in many parts of Europe, including the West Frankish kingdom.

The initial impulse for the election of Otto I as successor to Henry I in 936 was given by the father's designation of his son as sole heir. Accordingly, after Henry's death, Otto was elected king by 'the Frankish and Saxon people'. However, this was followed by a carefully thought out ceremony in Charlemagne's old imperial palace-church at Aachen. First, in the vestibule of the chapel the dukes and other secular magnates elevated the new ruler on to a specially erected throne and swore fealty to him, 'making him king according to their custom'. Thereupon Otto, in Frankish dress, entered the church, where the Archbishop of Mainz and the people were waiting for him. The archbishop presented the new king to the people, which he asked to consent to the election by the magnates. Thus the acclamation by the people, which formed part of the election, took place in church. The religious act followed at the altar, where the Archbishops of Mainz and Cologne handed the king the insignia of his office during the appropriate prayers, and also anointed and crowned Otto. After this ceremony the prelates accompanied the king to Charlemagne's throne on the gallery, 'where he could see all and be seen by all'. From here, like Charlemagne, he participated in the rest of the service, after which he attended the coronation meal. There he was attended by the Duke of Lotharingia acting as chamberlain, that of Franconia as steward, that of Swabia as cupbearer and that of Bavaria as marshal.[53] These court offices were to play their part in the genesis of the electorates of the Empire.

> If the sacrosanctity of kings...came to them through the anointing and coronation performed by their archbishops – and we may ask whether it only came from that source – it sat more firmly upon them and made them more rather than less commanding with these very men.[54]

This new sacrosanctity may have coexisted with the older type of sacrality connected with 'the charisma of the royal kind and its ancestry'.[55] What was not clear at this stage was how much discretion was vested in the two archbishops who anointed and crowned the king. Could they – as guardians of the sacred – refuse to carry out a ceremony implying the will of God, if in their judgement the elected king was unworthy of his office and therefore unfit to assume a sacral position? These were questions for the future, which had not yet been resolved at Otto I's coronation, in which secular and ecclesiastical elements were found side by side.[56]

The Carolingian tradition, with the choice of Charlemagne's principal residence for the election and coronation, as well as the emphasis on Frankish kingship and dress, is striking. However, there are differences, too. Otto is king not only of the Franks, but also of the Saxons. Indeed all the stems, not only these two, are involved in the ceremonies which have little in common with modern elections. Both federal and centralist aspects are mirrored in the procedures and only the future could tell which of them would predominate. Much would depend on the effectiveness of the new ruler, on the events with which he was confronted and on the manner in which he dealt with them.

Otto was in his mid-twenties when he succeeded to the throne.[57] His ability was soon put to the test, for – in spite of the ground-work laid by his father – only a beginning had been made during the previous reign in dealing with the internal and external tasks facing the kingdom. Not all the dukes were prepared to accept the greater centralisation which Otto, following the example of his father, regarded as necessary. There was resistance to Otto even in his native Saxony.

Otto wished to take advantage of the death of Duke Arnulf in 937 to break the comparative independence of Bavaria. He therefore made his consent to the succession of Arnulf's son Eberhard subject to his renunciation of his authority over the Church in favour of the king. Eberhard declined and refused to do homage to Otto. An invasion of Bavaria by the king was unsuccessful. Otto's set-back was a signal to other malcontents – including the king's half-brother Thankmar and Duke Eberhard of Franconia, the younger brother of the late king, Conrad I – to join in an open rebellion. After some initial successes, the insurgents were defeated. Thankmar was killed while seeking asylum in a church. The opposition of Bavaria was crushed and, under a new duke of the reigning family, agreed to the king instituting bishops and made some concessions of territory. However, an even more serious rising followed, in which Otto's younger brother Henry – who now allied himself to Duke Eberhard of Franconia – was a key figure. As Lotharingia was drawn into the rebellion and threatened to transfer its favours to the West Franks, it became a battlefield between the two Frankish kingdoms. In the end Otto won out, and the Dukes of Franconia and Lotharingia died in the fighting, Henry surrendered to his brother and Lotharingia remained part of Otto's dominions.

In spite of his negative experiences, not least with his relatives, Otto now accentuated existing problems by following a policy of bestowing dukedoms on members of his own family. His brother Henry became Duke of Bavaria and his son Liudolf, Duke of Swabia. Unfortunately there was a great deal of jealousy among the various relatives, especially between Henry and Liudolf. There was also a danger that territorial bases might be misused to threaten the very position of the king himself.

In this situation the bishops acquired a key role in royal centralisation. The Ottonian rulers drew them from the royal chapel, eventually restored by Henry I, which continued Carolingian traditions in creating a circle of clerics that had some internal coherence on the basis of a common attitude to church and ruler. The king was able to appoint bishops but could not remove them so easily. Owing to the requirement of celibacy, which at any rate excluded the possibility of legitimate heirs, bishops could not found dynasties like secular dukes and other nobility. Immunities and jurisdictions granted to bishops by the king weakened the authority of the dukes in their territories, by exempting bishoprics from their authority. Often bishops and abbots were invested with the powers of counts.[58] Bishops became prince-bishops, that peculiar institution of the Empire thus going back to Otto I and continuing to the time of Napoleonic secularisation. Bishops normally exercised secular authority in part of their dioceses.

In Ottonian times, bishops had to divide their time between their primary ecclesiastical tasks and the secular duties the king allocated to them. Perhaps nobody represents this system of government better than Otto I's brother Bruno, who became not only Archbishop of Cologne and Royal Archchaplain, but also Duke of Lotharingia; however, he combined these dignities in a purely personal capacity. From a modern point of view this apparent mixing of functions and what can be seen as the subservience of the prelates to the king might appear strange. But at a time when the Church was not free, and when the papacy was not yet able to assert itself against the authority of the ruler over ecclesiastical matters, royal control was not necessarily the worst solution. For – more than a duke, like that of Bavaria – the king was able to rise above parochial concerns to the level of a general policy in the interest of Christian Europe. The age

> did not yet know the essential distinction between state and Church, but merely the functional distinction between *Sacerdotium* and *Regnum*. Since both powers, as members of one superposed unity under the rule of Christ, regarded themselves as bound to the same religious and political goal, royal service, secular administration, and divine service could all be conceived as one and the same religious and moral accomplishment.[59]

That the king was not regarded merely as a layman made it easier for the bishops to accept his authority. Consecration and anointing could be viewed as a sacrament raising him to the position of vicar of Christ, following the tradition of Charlemagne. The question was to what extent the conditions prevailing at this time would continue in future, such as continued episcopal acceptance of their subservience to the ruler even in many ecclesiastical matters. This would also depend on the degree of control the pope would exercise over the Church in the kingdom, which was often fairly loose, and thus on the general relationship of king and pope.

The organisational changes Otto made took time to bear fruit. They were of importance not only internally, but also externally for the defence of the realm. In both west and south, the East Frankish kingdom faced neighbours sharing the same faith with them. But in the north and the east it found itself next to rulers and populations many of which still adhered to their old religions. Otto believed that a thorough policy of conversion to Christianity on the borders would help to stabilise them, thus going back to Carolingian tradition. He preferred that to the purely military securing of the border practiced during his father's reign. That had proved inadequate immediately after his death, which was the signal for a rising of one of the Slav peoples, the *Redarier*, against Otto.

The Ottonian co-ordination of relations between *regnum* and *sacerdotium* was particularly well adapted to the combination of military operations with missionary activity that was now applied on the eastern and northern borders. In spite of some set-backs, the king was able not only to hold the territory his father had gained, but to extend it and to strengthen the defences by the establishment of marches (*Marken*). In the north, the archbishopric of Hamburg–Bremen carried out missionary activity, to which parts of Denmark had been opened thanks to a victory by Henry I. In the east, *Ostpolitik* and *Ostmission* went hand in hand,[60] as was reflected in the establishment of an (East Frankish) ecclesiastical organisation for the eastern, mainly Slav, territories. Otto was particularly drawn to Magdeburg, which he regarded as an excellent centre from which the missionary work could be undertaken among the Slavs, such as the Wends. There he wished to found an archbishopric, with a number of suffragans, for instance in Brandenburg, where a diocese was established. In 954 he received approval for this scheme from Pope Agapitus II, but it took another decade and a half to be put into operation. This was especially due to the resistance of the Archbishop of Mainz, Otto's son from a liaison with a captured Slav woman from an apparently distinguished family, who did not want to lose control over bishoprics in the east.

Otto's determination to spread Christianity of the Roman rite to the Poles is of particular importance for European history, as Russia was about to be converted to the Orthodox faith. Otto also interested himself in the ecclesiastical organisation of Bohemia, which recognised him as overlord in 950. The friendly relations he established with its duke were richly rewarded when he sent Otto a contingent of troops to combat the most serious threat to his rule, the Hungarian invasion of 955. In a battle at the Lechfeld near Augsburg, Otto defeated the Hungarians so decisively that they gradually abandoned their predatory incursions for good and began to settle down. Otto's victory over the Hungarians, which paved the way for their conversion, was of great significance not only for his own dominions, but also for Europe and Christianity, strengthening even further his already very considerable international position.

His achievement is all the more remarkable, as he had a rebellion on his hands just before the Hungarian invasion. In 953 Liudolf, Otto's eldest legitimate son, then in his early twenties, became the centre of a serious plot against his father. Otto was able to crush the rising by the end of the following year. Liudolf's disaffection was to some extent the consequence of anxieties created for him by his father's second marriage. Otto's first wife, Edith, an Anglo-Saxon princess, had died in 946. The king's second marriage in 951 is part of the story of Otto's increasing involvement in the affairs of Italy, which began even before the final defeat of the Hungarians.

For the first time since Arnulf's death, developments in Italy thus began to impinge directly on the East Frankish kingdom. Arnulf's successor, Conrad I, had no energy to spare during his short reign for matters outside his kingdom. Henry I, towards the end of his reign, had plans to cross the Alps, but first illness and then death frustrated these intentions. What had happened in Italy since the death of Emperor Arnulf at the end of the ninth century?

The decline of the Carolingians, which accelerated in the last quarter of the century, changed the balance of power in Italy. Even in its heyday, the dynasty, while ruling over the Langobard kingdom and exercising some authority over the Patrimony of St Peter, did not have effective power over the whole of Italy. The loss of central control created a power vacuum. This allowed the local nobility, who had originally been imperial officials, to take over the reins in their region. But not even the most important of these were strong enough either to create internal stability over wider areas or to defend the peninsula against invaders, such as the Saracens and the Magyars, who were able to roam about as they pleased almost at will.[61] However, though different parts of the Frankish Empire were allowed to go their own way, a feeling of somehow belonging together did not cease at once. Many links between them continued to exist, particularly among the nobility of the various kingdoms: 'It is no coincidence that Otto the Great's German opponents found allies beyond the borders and that the German king during conflicts with the French king always had followers in the other country.'[62] The Alps, too, did not constitute a barrier to political connections. An Italian potentate like Guy of Spoleto, who happened to be the descendant of an old and respected Frankish family, could be considered for the West Frankish crown,[63] and Hugh of Provence took over the Langobard kingdom. Also Carolingian blood was still regarded as of some value: most of those who wore the Langobard crown were descended from the dynasty in the female line.

Inevitably Rome too, with the papacy, was now dominated by its local nobility and by any Italian ruler strong enough to exercise at least passing authority in the city. The Roman magnates who took over power in the Patrimony of St Peter clothed their authority in titles made famous in Roman history. In the early years of the tenth century a member of a leading noble Roman family, Theophylact, who had been papal financial adviser and commander of the Roman militia, took over power as consul,[64] which his dynasty, later called the Tusculans, exercised for something like half a century. Unfortunately actual control of affairs in the city and the Patrimony of St Peter was gradually taken over by two women of the family, Theophylact's wife Theodora (the Elder) and his daughter Marozia, whose regime was later characterised as pornocracy by the famous sixteenth- century church historian, Cardinal Cesare Baronio.[65] In 932, Marozia's rule was, however, overthrown by her son Alberic II, who as *princeps* and senator of all the Romans gave the city and the patrimony efficient government. During the following decade Alberic asked Abbot Odo of Cluny for help with the reform of the Roman and neighbouring monasteries; Odo visited the city several times during his regime.[66]

For a number of reasons monastic and canonical life had deteriorated during the ninth century. There had been 'secularizing usurpations by rulers, squandering of the property by lay abbots, lack of protection because of the growing weakness of the royal power, and the devastation wrought by Vikings, Muslims, and finally Magyars'.[67] During the tenth century, over a wide area including the Empire and France, both the orders and some lay patrons strove for a monastic renewal, which ushered in a more general church reform movement. One of the regions which made a great impact, particularly on the Empire, was Lotharingia, with for example the monastery at Gorze. Another was France and Burgundy. The famous Cluny Abbey was founded in French Burgundy in 909 by William, Duke of Aquitaine and Count of Auvergne. 'In order that its monks might have autonomy in leading the monastic life, Cluny received a complete freedom in temporal matters from all lordship.'[68] At a time of the decline of royal power and its inability to give sufficient protection, monasteries looked to support from the papacy, and Cluny was not the first one to do so. The monastery was given to St Peter and St Paul, as the apostles and patrons of the Roman see, to whose protection it was commended. Also implicitly Cluny was to have 'full immunity', in the technical sense. In all temporal matters it was to be subject to no outside yoke whatsoever.'[69] While the charter was a starting point, under papal guidance the autonomy of the monastery was strengthened by establishing 'its freedom from all spiritual jurisdiction save that of the Apostolic See'.[70] Cluny developed a special relationship with the papacy and was in sympathy at any rate with many, though not necessarily all, aspects of the church reform movement in the eleventh century.[71] The monastery, which was in the Benedictine tradition, and was concerned with societal renewal, emphasised the liturgy and strict discipline. The Cluniac model was widely accepted elsewhere, even – as mentioned, by *princeps* Alberic in Rome. When Otto began to intervene in Italy, he certainly had to reckon with *princeps* Alberic in Rome.

Why was Otto so concerned with Italy, particularly from the middle of the century onwards, so that he spent most of his time there after becoming emperor, when there was plenty of business for him at home in the East Frankish kingdom?[72] Could he have confined himself to matters north of the Alps? Otto – even more than his father – acquired a leading position in Catholic Europe and he was determined at the very least not to lose it, and if possible to add to it. There were still many fluid frontiers, not only because of invasion from the outside, but also because the collapse of the Carolingian Empire had left a power vacuum in several regions. Otto took very seriously possible rivals for influence in areas of concern to the East Frankish kingdom, such as in Burgundy. He kept a particularly wary eye on the ambitions of Hugh of Provence. Otto regarded the kingdom of Burgundy, bordering on his territories, as a vital interest. He had therefore for many years taken a great interest in the welfare of the Burgundian dynasty and had earlier saved the kingdom from conquest by Hugh. He certainly wished to prevent the establishment of a Burgundian–Italian state in hostile hands.

Hugh now succeeded in arranging a marriage between his son Lothar and Adelaide, the sister of King Conrad III of Burgundy, Otto's particular protégé. When Lothar, who had in the meantime succeeded his father as King of Italy, died in 950, his widow Adelaide, now queen regnant, was taken prisoner by another contender for power in the peninsula, Berengar of Ivrea (a grandson of Emperor Berengar I), who crowned himself king. Otto was particularly displeased with this conduct, as Berengar had sworn him fealty in 941, when fleeing from Hugh.[73] Now he usurped the Italian crown and deprived the rightful queen, Adelaide, of her crown. However, she, with other opponents of Berengar, such as some North Italian magnates,[74] called on Otto for help. In 951 Otto conducted his first Italian campaign, swiftly defeated Berengar, married Adelaide and had himself proclaimed in Pavia as King of the Franks and Langobards, following the precedent of Charlemagne. Similarly, Otto wished to be crowned emperor by the pope in Rome, but Alberic II, who at that time was master of the city, refused him entry. Through controlling Rome and the papacy, Alberic was able to prevent any imperial coronation in his lifetime: Berengar I, who was crowned emperor in 915, did not have a successor after his death in 924. Otto accepted the postponement of imperial coronation because of preoccupations at home.

The conquest of the Langobard kingdom was a logical step for a ruler who regarded himself as the heir of Charlemagne and of the Carolingians. It was not only Hugh and Berengar whom Otto wanted to prevent from acquiring a power base in Northern Italy, but also Duke Liudolf of Swabia, his son, and to some extent Duke Henry of Bavaria, his brother. Their duchies, particularly the latter, had long been active in the Langobard kingdom. At the very least Otto wished to deny Northern Italy to possible rivals. But there was also a positive reason for taking the Langobard crown, for it was an essential preliminary to the emperorship. Again, the achievement of the imperial dignity was natural for Otto in carrying on Carolingian traditions and in wishing to secure for himself a title that would recognise his outstanding position in Europe, confirm his superiority to other kings, and put him on a level with the ruler of Byzantium. In turn, inheriting Carolingian authority over the Patrimony of St Peter would allow him to secure papal support, for example for the foundation of new bishoprics in the East Frankish kingdom. These Otto regarded as essential for missionary work among the Slavs, which in turn was designed to buttress his rule in the East and to secure the borders. On the highest level, there appeared also to be a duty to maintain the Roman Empire. For according to then current interpretation of Daniel's prophecy this was viewed as the fourth and final great empire that had to be preserved for the events leading to the Second Coming and to the beginning of God's rule on earth.[75] To the extent that one can, in that age, distinguish between secular and religious factors, the motives were a mixture of both. On the one hand Rome, because of the papacy, was too important to be left to a local potentate. On the other, a Saxon emperor could also use his control over Rome for raising the standards of the papacy, to the benefit of all the faithful.

It was only when ten years later Berengar – although he served as Otto's vassal in the capacity of King of Italy – without his liege-lord's authorisation attacked the Patrimony of St Peter, that Otto once more took an army to Italy. Alberic II, who died in 954, stipulated that his son, Octavian, should not only succeed him as *princeps*, but that he should also be elected pontiff as soon as a vacancy arose, which happened the following year; as pope, Octavian took the name of John XII. In 960 John, whose unbridled immorality undermined his authority, found himself forced to seek Otto's help against Berengar and invited him to Rome to be crowned emperor. For Otto this was an opportunity to complete the plans in which he had been frustrated in 951 owing to Alberic's grip on Rome and the papacy. In the meantime there had also been a Byzantine advance in Southern Italy, which was a potential threat to the East Frankish position in Italy. Accordingly, in 961 Otto took an army to Italy, and – not finding any resistance – swiftly proceeded to Rome, where the coronation took place in February 962. Queen Adelaide was also crowned and they were both anointed by the pope. The acclamation of Otto as emperor by the Roman people followed his coronation. Then the pope and the Romans swore fealty to the new emperor over St Peter's grave.

Important negotiations took place with the pope during Otto's stay in Rome. At a meeting of a synod, John – with the agreement of those present – gave approval to Otto's plans for the conversion of the Slavs, especially for the creation of a new archbishopric at Magdeburg and for the foundation of new bishoprics on Slav territory.[76] Also a treaty between Otto and John was drawn up which has gone down in history as the *Ottonianum*. Like his predecessors, Otto confirmed the undertakings of previous emperors in relation to the privileges and extent of the Patrimony of St Peter. These imperial *pacta* had probably reached their definitive form in the treaty of Charles the Bald in 876, from which Otto appears to have taken them over. About two-thirds of Italy were allocated to the papal states. However, the new emperor did not have to worry about any obligations arising from this 'Utopian statement', as he was only committed to doing what was in his power.[77] Another part of the treaty between Otto and John concerned the relationship between pope and emperor. The pope was to be elected canonically, that is freely by the clergy and people of Rome. But the newly elected pope had to swear an oath of loyalty to the emperor before his consecration. The emperor was to be a last court of appeal for complaints against papal officials. These stipulations, too, seem to have formed part of agreements between emperors and popes since about 824. Clearly thanks to being crowned emperor, Otto had largely taken over the powers previously held by John as *princeps*.

Because most of Otto's successors as rulers of what had been the East Frankish kingdom and of what was to be called the *regnum teutonicum*,[78] for centuries took armies to Italy and obtained the imperial crown from the pope in Rome, the implications of the events of 962 were very important for the future. They established a unique nexus between the *regnum teutonicum*, the Langobard (or Italian) kingdom and the imperial crown, with the supreme authority over the Patrimony of St Peter that went with it. The 'German' or 'Roman' king as he was to be called appeared to be entitled *eo ipso* to the Langobard and imperial crowns. On this view a special election and coronation in the Langobard kingdom was not necessary. Again according to this interpretation, which was not unchallenged, it was not the pope that transferred the imperial crown to the 'German' king: he merely carried out the formal act of coronation.

Needless to say, the practical enforcement of these theories was bound to depend on the balance of power and on the course of events, just as the application of papal doctrine very much depended on circumstances. In the new constellation, the emperor thus acquired a considerable say over the pope and became the foremost ruler in Italy. Romans and many other

Italians – however divided they were amongst themselves – were not likely to be overjoyed at this foreign entrenchment in their country. This was so especially at a time when they were becoming increasingly conscious of their classical heritage with the spreading of the concept of the *Renovatio Romana*. That made it even more difficult for them to accept subservience to the descendants of those whom their glorious ancestors considered as barbarians.

In the long run, other important Christian rulers were not likely to be satisfied with the spiritual head of their church having this special relationship with one particular monarch. From the point of view of the Saxon rulers and their Salian and Staufen successors, the whole arrangement certainly enhanced their very considerable power even further. Recent historical research has cast doubt on the concept of the 'imperial church system' (*Reichskirchensystem*) of earlier generations,[79] in which the Church was seen 'as the principal instrument of government available' to the Saxon and Salian rulers.[80] Questions have also been raised as to whether their relationship with the papacy allowed the Saxon emperors to increase their influence over their prelates. But a modest claim can still be made, that it was useful for these rulers to have the pope on their side. Thus John's approval of the establishment of a new archbishopric at Magdeburg, in connection with a missionary campaign among the Slavs, was certainly welcome to Otto, even if opposition in Germany was powerful enough to delay implementation. 'Papal approval for the creation of new dioceses was ... necessary, but it was not sufficient.'[81]

Up to a point it can be argued that Italian policy, on the one hand, and colonisation, with Christianisation, in the East, on the other, far from being alternatives or incompatibles, were complementary to each other. But the extent of their dominions and concerns also meant that the emperors had to divide their energy and time between their native kingdom, the Langobard lands and the Papal States, which entailed stays in Italy. The difficulties of holding so many and diverse territories together, while keeping a wary eye on the pope and dealing with the Church–State problems that arose on the national and international level, are readily apparent. They were compounded by the slowness of transportation and communications in the period, requiring extraordinary perception and energy. In any case, often the best plans were ruined by the health hazards of treacherous southern climates and the ravages of epidemics, to which many of those who fought at all levels, including emperors themselves, fell victim.

Although the military campaign was largely successful with Berengar's capture, the situation in Rome had not by any means turned out to Otto's satisfaction. Pope John was dissatisfied with Otto's assertion of his own power in Italy and with what he regarded as inadequate restitution of papal rights, which led him to conspire with Berengar's son Adalbert against

the emperor, violating his oath of loyalty. Otto had to return to Rome and –
ignoring the legal principle that the pope could be judged by no one –
summoned John, who had fled, to a synod to answer the charges against
him. When John refused to appear, Otto had the synod depose him and to
elect another pope, Leo VIII. The obvious breach of the law[82] by Otto not
only led to a rising, but made it easier for John to resume his office when
Otto had left, though he was soon to die a sudden death, apparently in
connection with one of his nightly adventures. When the Romans elected
Benedict V, a person of great integrity, Otto forced Leo on the Romans and
banished Benedict.[83] The emperor now insisted on an imperial confirmation
of each papal election, which brought the Bishop of Rome into a dependance fraught with grave consequences.[84] Otto spent a large part of the last
decade or so of his reign in Italy. At times he used severe methods of
repression. The pattern of events, with emperors constantly being involved
in the affairs of Italy and the papacy, was to repeat itself many times, setting
up resistance to their rule.

The resumption of a Frankish emperorship was bound to put a strain on
relations with Byzantium. After a period of war, during which Otto invaded
Byzantine possessions in the south of Italy, peace was finally achieved in 972.
While Byzantium was left in possession of the territories it held in Southern
Italy, it renounced its claims to Benevento, Capua and Salerno, and implicitly to Rome and Central Italy. Otto's imperial crown was recognised in
Constantinople. To seal the new accord, a Byzantine princess, Theophanu,
was betrothed to Otto the Great's heir, the future Otto II. The following
year, in 973, the emperor died, in his early sixties, after a reign of about three
and a half decades.

With Otto the Great, even more than under his father, what had been the
East Frankish kingdom and was up to a point a forerunner of Germany,
established its hegemony in Europe and in Western Christianity, for the
moment leaving the western part of the former Carolingian Empire well
behind in power and importance. The Lombard and imperial crowns, which
manifested this stature, involved the East Frankish rulers intimately in
the affairs of Italy and of the papacy. This triangular relationship between
the East Frankish kingdom, the Langobard lands and the papacy is thus the
main theme for about three centuries from the imperial coronation of Otto
the Great.

The new ruler, who bore the same name as his distinguished father, had
been crowned co-king in 961 and co-emperor in 967, succeeding to the
throne at the early age of nearly 18 years, because his step-brother, Liudolf,
had died in Italy of malaria in 957, when only 27 years old.[85] This is one of
several instances when, as a consequence of the ravages of diseases against
which individuals from the North of the Alps did not have much immunity,
young princes without experience in government and war were called on to

take over responsibility for the Empire. In a sense, almost a generation of rulers was thus left out in this succession from father to son.

The first five years of Otto II's reign were spent mainly in dealing with the threat to his authority posed by his cousin Henry, Duke of Bavaria, in striking parallel to the rebellion waged by Henry's father of the same name in the previous reign. Fundamentally, the struggle between Otto and his cousin arose from the attempt of the Duke of Bavaria to achieve a commanding position in the south of Germany in alliance with Swabia that any emperor was almost bound to regard as a threat to his rule. In order to curb Henry's ambitions, the emperor therefore took the opportunity to entrust the Swabian duchy when it fell vacant to his friend and cousin Otto, the son of Liudolf, like his father a strong anti-Bavarian. After his rebuff over Swabia, Henry wished to expand elsewhere, but was again resisted by the emperor, who even regarded his existing possessions, which extended into Northern Italy and Istria, as a potential threat to his power. In 974 Henry formed a conspiracy to deprive the emperor of his crown, in which he even tried to enlist the Dukes of Bohemia and Poland, apparently in return for promises to relax their ties with the Empire. Although at this time the Danes carried out an invasion, which was later repulsed, Otto's determination succeeded in crushing Henry's rebellion without the outbreak of a civil war. Henry and his followers were arrested and he himself was suspended as duke. The emperor carried out largely successful wars against the Danes, the Bohemians and the Poles during the following years.

The situation became even more serious in 976 when Henry escaped from arrest and began a fresh rising, securing supporters not only in Bavaria, but also in Saxony, and forcing Otto to undertake a major campaign against him. When things went badly for the insurgents, Henry fled to Bohemia. He was deprived of his Bavarian duchy, which though reduced in size, was given to Otto of Swabia. The Margraviates of Verona and Friuli were detached from Bavaria, as was Carinthia, which now became a duchy of its own. The Bavarian *Ostmark*, which later gave its name to Austria, was awarded to a member of the Babenberg dynasty, which was to play an important part in the future. An expedition Otto led into Bohemia failed. Henry secured allies for a fresh rising and it was only after a further, successful campaign against Bohemia in 977 that the insurgents were forced to surrender and to accept imprisonment. The Dukes of Bohemia and Poland had to recognise Otto's overlordship.

As soon as Henry had been vanquished, the affairs of Lotharingia and relations with the West Frankish kingdom began to preoccupy Otto. He had already intervened in 974 to deal with infringements of the arrangements made for Lotharingia during his father's reign. In 978 matters became even more serious. The West Frankish king, Lothar III, a Carolingian, resented Otto's appointment of Lothar's brother Charles, with whom he was on bad terms, as Duke of Lower Lotharingia. He decided to attempt the conquest of Lotharingia. Without any announcement of hostilities, he tried to secure possession of Otto's person at Aachen by a *coup de main* which nearly succeeded. Otto narrowly escaped capture, not for the last time. The invading West Frankish armies caused considerable devastation, but the emperor was able to gain the initiative after a few months and to penetrate to the outskirts of Paris, though he was unable to take the city. In 980, formal peace was established between the two realms on the basis of the retention of Lotharingia by the East Franks. The head of the rival West Frankish dynasty, Hugh Capet, who had supported Lothar against Otto during the hostilities, did not want to be left out of the understanding and sought Otto's friendship, an interesting reflection of the emperor's leading position in Europe.[86]

Again, however, after overcoming major problems, Otto was faced with new ones, this time in Italy. Actually, Otto's expedition south of the Alps at the end of 980 was originally designed as a peaceful rather than a military venture. The affairs of the papacy required attention. As on previous occasions imperial authority had tended to weaken during the absence of rulers from Italy and therefore needed constant reinforcement. In 974 the anti-imperial party in Rome, which had links with Byzantium, overthrew and murdered Benedict VI, who had been raised to the papacy with Otto I's consent. However, intervention by the imperial *missus* a few weeks afterwards led to the expulsion of an anti-pope, who had been elected earlier and now fled to Byzantium. The new pope was Benedict VII, a church reformer, a grandson of Theophylact, the founder of the Tusculan dynasty,[87] though also related to their rivals, the Crescentians.[88] The Tusculans, who maintained a sturdy independence for Rome earlier in the century under Alberic, were now prepared to try working with the emperor. In 979 Benedict had to leave Rome because of opposition, possibly supported by Byzantium, which gave refuge to the anti-pope, who in 980 made an unsuccessful attempt to return and to take over the papacy once more.

Like many of his predecessors, Otto II undertook his Italian expedition in answer to the pope's appeal for help. Accompanied by the emperor, Benedict was able to return to Rome – from which his opponent Crescentius de Theodora withdrew – in early 981. Unfortunately at about the same time the death of Pandulf of Capua deprived the emperor of his strongest supporter in Central and Southern Italy. Otto now made a radical departure from his father's policy of limited objectives. Otto the Great had undertaken military operations in Southern Italy primarily to achieve a compromise with Byzantium, in which he succeeded. He had also taken the view that the Burgundian and Italian interests of the Empire required the maintenance of peaceful relations with the caliphs in Cordoba and the emirs in Sicily and North Africa.[89] He had carefully avoided getting involved in hostilities with the Saracens in Italy. Otto abandoned his father's policy of attempting to live at peace with Byzantium and with the Saracens. He decided to try expelling them both from Southern Italy, thus challenging the leading regional powers at the same time. He had a strong interest in the area in view of his sovereignty or suzerainty over various territories as King of Italy. For this major operation he required reinforcements from the homeland which came from the Church even more than from the laity.

Otto had considerable success in rolling back Byzantine rule. The authorities in Constantinople had every right to feel aggrieved by the attack of a Christian power on them at the very time when they were trying to defend themselves against the Saracens who were making inroads into their territory, quite apart from the strains arising from internal troubles and Bulgarian expansion.[90] Otto added insult to injury when he assumed at this very time the title of *Romanorum imperator augustus*, which flew in the face of Byzantine claims to their exclusive right to be called Roman emperors. However, in 982, at Cotrone near Cape Colonne the emperor received a serious set-back in a battle with the Saracens, who had responded to the opening of hostilities against them by proclaiming a holy war, a *Jihad*. Otto had to flee ignominiously and once more narrowly avoided capture and never recovered the initiative.

Nevertheless, the princes north of the Alps continued to support him, as they demonstrated at an imperial assembly in Verona in 983. Here at the emperor's request his three-year-old son Otto, the future Otto III, was elected king. When Benedict VII died that same year, the emperor was able to secure the succession of John XIV, who had been in charge of the Italian chancellery. But Italy was not Otto's greatest worry. The most threatening developments took place on the northern and even more on the Slav frontiers. The Danes did considerable harm in an invasion of the Schleswig area. Even more serious were risings of the Slavs which destroyed everything Otto the Great had built up east of the River Elbe. At this critical moment, like so many other rulers and princes from north of the Alps before him, Otto II was attacked by a disease endemic in Italy and particularly dangerous to those from other climates, contracting malaria, from which he died in Rome in December 983 aged 28 – the only emperor in the long line begun by Charlemagne to find his final resting-place there, actually at St Peter's.

Otto II's reign largely ended in failure, but any judgement on his personality must take into account his premature death. His father – or indeed Charlemagne – would not have earned the appellation 'the Great' on the first decade of his rule, which was all that Otto II was allowed. We cannot deduce his potential from the 10 years of his reign. At any rate, as ruler he did not display the sureness of touch which was characteristic for his outstanding predecessors most of the time. Otto II had received a good education and was generally well liked. From the point of view of the future it was ominous that he fought a kind of 'holy war' against Islam while at the same time invading the territory of another Christian ruler, foreshadowing aspects of the Crusades.

The new king was a child of three years and while under Germanic law the fiction prevailed that he could act as ruler, in practice everything depended on the persons who would have the chief influence on him. Until his fifteenth year, the care and education of a king had to be entrusted to a guardian, an office to which the nearest relative was entitled. Henry II, former Duke of Bavaria, who managed to persuade his gaoler to release him, claimed the dignity as the closest male agnate and at first mustered considerable support, even succeeding in having the royal child handed over to him. His fortunes declined, however, when he revealed his ultimate intentions by having himself elected anti-king. However, Henry did not give up easily, even enlisting support outside East Francia proper by allying himself with the Duke of Bohemia.

It was mainly thanks to the determination of Archbishop Willigis of Mainz that the tide turned. Following Henry's election as anti-king, Willigis urged the two empresses, who were still in Italy, to return as quickly as possible. At a diet in Thuringia in June 984, Henry gave up his claim to kingship and surrendered the royal child to his mother Theophanu, who took over the guardianship and with it what amounted to a regency. For about seven years, this gifted and cultured Byzantine princess looked after the interests of the dynasty, mainly north of the Alps, while Empress Adelaide put her considerable influence in Italy at the disposal of her grandson. Apart from doing her best to have the northern and eastern frontiers defended, Theophanu kept a wary eye on developments in the West Frankish kingdom, which still had many links with its eastern neighbour: events there were liable to have an impact on the Ottonian kingdom. There was as yet no complete separation between 'France' and 'Germany': there were many connections between the reigning and noble families, the common Frankish heritage was still a factor (particularly while the Carolingian dynasty survived in the West), and – last not least – diocesan borders and church affairs cut across political frontiers.

The last Carolingian rulers in the West had not been prepared to write off Lotharingia for good. With great skill Theophanu, on the early death of the West Frankish Carolingian Louis V in 987, collaborated with Archbishop Adalbero of Rheims to secure the election of Duke Hugh Capet of Francia to succeed him. Thus she was able to block the election of the nearest male Carolingian agnate, Louis' uncle Charles, Duke of Lower Lotharingia, who had been a vassal of the Saxon rulers, but whose succession to the kingship of the West Franks she regarded as a possible threat to the stability of the Western frontier. Her policy was rewarded by Hugh's renunciation of Lotharingia after ascending the French throne.

The limited effect of territorial boundaries in this age is apparent from the dispute over the succession to the archbishopric of Rheims on the death of the great Adalbero in 989. Though the city was in the West Frankish kingdom, the diocese extended beyond its eastern frontier and the dispute involved East Frankish bishops and in some ways even their ruler. With Hugh's assent Arnulf, an illegitimate son of King Lothar III, was elected to the archbishopric of Rheims, the premier archdiocese in the West Frankish kingdom. When, however, Arnulf treacherously surrendered Rheims to his uncle, the Carolingian claimant to the French throne, the king attempted to secure the consent of the pope to stripping him of his dignity; but when John XV did not respond quickly, Hugh went ahead on his own. He did so although he was warned by a minority at a West Frankish synod that he was acting uncanonically in proceeding against the archbishop without papal consent; he was in fact infringing the Pseudo-Isidorian decretals. The synod acceded to the king's request to remove Archbishop Arnulf from his office. Gerbert of Aurillac, the leading scholar of the century, was chosen to succeed Arnulf as Archbishop of Rheims. However, with the death of Empress Theophanu in 991 Gerbert lost his strongest supporter in the East.

Personalities apart, the East Frankish rulers could not be indifferent to defiance of a papacy with which they were allied and to the resulting diminution of their own authority. The pope, possibly spurred on by Archbishop Willigis of Mainz, was not prepared to allow himself to be ignored in the affairs of so important a diocese and now took a number of measures against the French monarchy; its position was weakened by the contraction of an uncanonical marriage by Hugh's son and co-king Robert. East Frankish bishops were summoned by John XV to participate in synods to settle the issue together with those from the Western kingdom. This was because the pope, to some extent, still thought ecclesiastically in terms of one Frankish kingdom, and also because he believed the eastern bishops might be helpful as a counter-weight to western support for King Hugh's actions. Steady papal pressure on the West Franks to rescind Arnulf's displacement, combined with Gerbert's departure from Rheims because of his unpopularity there, was having some effect. But nothing was definitely settled when Pope John XV died in 996.[91]

In the meantime, Otto III had formally come of age in 995, terminating the guardianship of his grandmother, Empress Adelaide, who had taken over from Empress Theophanu on her death in 991. Adelaide, a remarkable personality of deep religious faith, with a special interest in Cluny, lived on until 999. This Burgundian princess, who had earlier been queen consort of Italy and then queen regnant after the death of her first husband, could look back on a full and eventful life. Even if Otto gradually tired of tutelage and wanted to make his own decisions, his grandmother and his mother must have had a considerable influence on him. The Byzantine heritage on his mother's side, which made a certain impact on the Germanic kingdom, enriched his personality. Having had excellent tutors, the young king was well educated, knew Latin and Greek and could write, an accomplishment that could in that period not be taken for granted even in a ruler. One of the first decisions Otto had to take was to settle the succession to Henry, the erstwhile rebel, in Bavaria after his death. The king confirmed the election of Henry's son of the same name, the future Emperor Henry II, and instituted him in this dignity. But soon the affairs of Italy called, which were to provide the main theme of Otto's reign.

Pope John XV found his position in Rome undermined by (John) Crescentius, a son of the Crescentius de Theodora who had put the papacy under pressure at the beginning of Otto II's reign. Like some of his predecessors, John asked for help from north of the Alps and Otto responded to his call. However, before the king could reach Rome, in the spring of 996 news reached him of the pope's death, actually from natural causes, which could not be taken for granted in this time of violence in the city. Although Otto had only been elected King of Italy and was not yet emperor, the Romans, obviously prompted by their somewhat fearful Crescentius, asked him to propose a successor to the pontiff. Otto III's choice fell on a distant relative, the court chaplain Bruno, a son of Otto of Carinthia and a great-grandson of Otto the Great, the first East Frank to assume the dignity. Bruno, who became Gregory V as pope, was a young ecclesiastic of integrity and determination, thus quite acceptable to those who believed that the Church was in need of reform. On the papal throne he was by no means a subservient follower of his imperial relative. Gregory crowned Otto III emperor in Rome in May 996. As his title Otto chose that used toward the end of his father's reign: *Romanorum imperator augustus*. In every way Otto was determined to have parity of rank with Constantinople. He had already despatched an embassy to the Bosporus to sue for a Byzantine princess. The mission was led by a Greek from Calabria, John Philagathus, Bishop of Piacenza, who had been one of Otto's tutors.

Italy appealed tremendously to the half-Byzantine emperor. Perhaps the vision of Rome and Italy that influenced him most strongly was that of Gerbert, who had left Rheims and was only too glad to accept an honourable invitation from Otto to his court. Gerbert may have been fickle in his allegiance to people and causes: few of his contemporaries were able to change sides with the same adroitness. Undoubtedly, he was very ambitious. But he did have convictions and faith. With his extensive learning, he fascinated the young ruler by his synthesis of classical antiquity with Christianity, in which he did not by any means always give priority to the latter. Otto was also strongly influenced by an Italian cleric, Leo, whom he raised to the bishopric of Vercelli. Leo advocated a renewal of the Roman

Church and the Roman Empire through the mutual cooperation of pope and emperor, with both of them aiding each other, but with the ruler possessing a slight superiority.[92] If Gerbert opened the emperor's eyes to the magnificence of the cultural heritage of antiquity, it was mainly through Leo that Otto was won for the greatness of the old Rome and of the *imperium Romanorum*.[93]

The ideas of Gerbert and Leo provided the basis for the programme Otto gradually formulated from 998 onwards, of the *Renovatio Imperii Romanorum*. The plan met a certain spiritual need in view of a widespread contemporary 'messianic' renewal expectation in its pagan–Roman form. This expectation was combined with the Christian, ultimately oriental–cosmological teaching which saw the Roman Empire as the last of the great empires, which would continue to the end of time.[94] Thus, in this view, a new lease of life for this empire constituted a positive and constructive step. In a sense Otto only responded to a growing movement in Rome and Italy. For a time he seemed to be getting plenty of support south of the Alps. The emphasis given to Rome did not in Otto's eyes diminish for him the importance of Aachen, with its tradition of Charlemagne; there was in fact no contradiction in promoting both.

Unfortunately, Otto's return to his homeland left Gregory exposed to attacks by the Crescentians and he had to depart from the city. Crescentius now persuaded John Philagathus, who had just returned from his expedition to Constantinople to secure a Byzantine bride for Otto, to allow himself to be elected anti-pope as John XVI. Apparently he was supported in his papal ambitions by the Byzantine envoy Leo, who had come back with the East Frankish delegation. In 998 the emperor was back in Rome, where Crescentius put up a fierce, but in the end hopeless, resistance. He was beheaded and his corpse subjected to barbarous treatment. The anti-pope was horribly mutilated and then forced to submit to all the indignities of a ceremony in which he was stripped of his papal office. No doubt this kind of treatment was not unique in a period of violence, and many a ruler would not have had any pangs of conscience about his part in it. But Otto III was different. A person for whom he had a particular reverence, the hermit abbot Nilus from Gaeta, a Greek like Philagathus and one of the most respected men in Italy, had unsuccessfully asked for mercy for his compatriot.[95]

Otto went through a deep spiritual crisis, partly from remorse for failing to save his former tutor from his horrible fate. He was in any case immensely attracted both by the hermits' ideal of a withdrawal from the sinful world and by the search for martyrdom, which another person he venerated, Adalbert, who had been Bishop of Prague, had suffered at the hands of heathen Prussians the previous year. He was also, like his grandmother Adelaide, drawn to the Cluniac movement and he befriended the Abbot Odilo.

No other emperor has been so much in the centre of the religious life of his age as Otto III; his glory is that he absorbed it in all its pulsations and thus became a symbol of the religious as well as the intellectual life of his age.[96]

There were many occasions on which the emperor subjected himself to severe penitential punishment. Otto's attempt to live his religion illustrates the problems a ruler faced in this quest. However much he was drawn to the ideal of withdrawal from the affairs of this world, that was the last thing he could do as emperor. To escape his dilemma, he was believed in some quarters to have taken a vow to abdicate within a certain number of years.

Perhaps Otto got closest in his search of combining his religious aims with his functions as ruler in his expedition to Poland to pay his respects at the grave of St Adalbert in the Polish capital of Gnesen, where Duke Boleslav of the Piast dynasty had the saint's body buried after ransoming it from the Prussians. The duke, whose father had converted to Christianity and made a gift of his recently united country Polonia to St Peter, wished to buttress his demand for the establishment of a separate Polish Church by the possession of the relics of a bishop of Slav descent. This appeared particularly appropriate in view of the veneration Otto had for Adalbert, which he demonstrated by entering the saint's burial grounds barefoot like a pilgrim.

Only the religious character of the journey could justify the disregard for hierarchical order manifested by an overlord visiting his tributary vassal.

It was a pilgrimage, not a state visit, yet seldom have religion and politics been intermixed so closely. That could hardly be otherwise, for in the idea of the young emperor of the rebirth of the Roman Empire, political and religious notions had long been fused into a inseparable unity.[97]

Otto released the duke from his obligation to pay tribute. He appears to have regarded countries like Poland, as well as Hungary, to which he also devoted his attention, as satellites of the renewed Roman Empire around the core territories of the East Frankish and Italian kingdoms. Otto, in spite of the opposition of East Frankish bishops, granted Boleslav his wish of the foundation of a Polish archdiocese, which was established in his capital at Gnesen, with suffragan bishops for Kolberg, Cracow and Breslau.

During the Polish pilgrimage Otto adopted the title of *Servus Jesu Christi*, which St Paul had used in his letters, thus raising him above the pope, who was merely *Servus servorum Dei*. Otto regarded himself as being on an apostolic mission. He was able to extend his functions because the papacy was no longer in the hands of Gregory V, who had watched its prerogatives, but had died in 999, apparently only in the second half of his twenties. His successor was Gerbert, former Archbishop of Rheims, and Archbishop of

Ravenna at the time of his election as Supreme Pontiff. He owed his appointments both to Ravenna and to the papacy to his patron Otto, for they were in this period practically in the gift of the emperor, with subsequent election constituting a mere formality.

Otto and Gerbert were united by strong bonds of friendship and by a common allegiance to the concept of the *Renovatio Imperii Romanorum*, as well as to that of close cooperation between emperor and pope. Gerbert's assumption of the name of Sylvester II as pope provided a motto for his reign, with Otto as a new Constantine. It was not so much that Pope Sylvester was submissive to the emperor, as that he was concerned more with ends than means, more with what was achieved than with ensuring Gelasian purity in making sure that each power kept within its sphere.

However, Otto was not quite prepared to re-enact the part played by the Roman Emperor according to papal interpretation through the 'Donation of Constantine'. Contrary to its version, Otto took up residence in Rome in spite of the fact that it was the seat of the papacy. In 1001 Otto had a document drawn up for the papacy concerning the Pentapolis, the area south of Ravenna important for both emperor and papacy because of its communications with Rome. In it Otto formally declared the 'Donation of Constantine' to have been a papal forgery. Similarly he denied the validity of papal claims to lands granted to the Patrimony of St Peter by Charles the Bald, as the emperor had already been removed from his dignity by that time. The *Ottonianum*, Otto the Great's pact with John XII, was not confirmed. Apparently to undermine the continuing validity of the *Ottonianum*, the new document contained a strong attack on past popes who had squandered the property of the Church and had then tried to make it up by robbing the Empire. Rome was both the imperial and the apostolic city, in contradiction of the 'Donation of Constantine'. But the Roman Church was the mother of all churches. Fundamentally, the Gelasian doctrine of the two spheres was not challenged. Finally, in what was the document's main practical function, the territories in the Pentapolis were given to St Peter for the increase of Sylvester's apostolate and of Otto's empire. This curious phrase has been interpreted as meaning that while the Pentapolis passed from possession by the Empire to the Patrimony of St Peter, the emperor did not surrender all rights over the territory. For he also acted as the secular arm of the papacy, as its defender, a capacity strengthened by his new title of *servus apostolorum*, adopted from early on in 1001.

It is believed that in Otto's vision of the new order, his reservation of rights over the Patrimony of St Peter as its protector had a wider application, for instance in relation to Hungary:

Even the strange contradiction that Hungary was raised 'by favour and on the urging' of Otto to a kingdom and at the same time handed over to

St Peter can be resolved, if the assumption is correct that Otto reserved to himself special rights in the possessions of the apostle.[98]

Pope and emperor shared with the Cluniac movement and with Gallican reformers the view that reform of the Church required above all reform of the papacy. Sylvester regarded Otto as an essential instrument for carrying out the necessary measures to improve the state of the Church. Incidentally, as pope he had to wind up the long dispute over the position of Archbishop of Rheims, in which he had at one time been a contender. He now confirmed Arnulf in his office, though at the same time administering a stinging rebuke to this unworthy ecclesiastic. 'What Gerbert, as Arnulf's rival had declared to be wicked and invalid, he had unhesitatingly done as pope.'[99] It may be noted that, just as the Capetian dynasty increasingly weakened its links with its eastern neighbour, the archdiocese of Rheims ceased to have intimate contacts with East Francia.[100]

After his Polish expedition, Otto appeared to have achieved a dominant position, but it rapidly became apparent that the general concept of his policy caused increasing dissatisfaction on both sides of the Alps. It was a severe crisis in Rome, which occupied so important a place in Otto's plans, that first challenged his whole scheme of things. The Romans felt their freedom of action, including their ability to engage in feuding with each other, impeded by the heavy-handed rule and financial exactions of a resident foreign emperor, who also restricted their influence over the papacy. Otto did not have the local knowledge and skills that Alberic, an early member of what was to be called the Tusculan dynasty, had displayed during the reign of his grandfather in preventing rivalries between various factions from threatening his position in Rome and the Patrimony. The mercy the emperor showed to neighbouring Tivoli, which had risen against him, was resented by the Tusculan family, who had designs on that city and now turned against him. The head of the dynasty, Count Gregory of Tusculum, a senior imperial official, early in 1001 organised a rebellion against Otto. The emperor was shattered by the reverse, and in a speech of which the essence was recorded told the Romans how he felt let down by them. He said that it was through love for them that he had left his Saxons and all the *theotiscos* (Germanic peoples), his own blood; he had adopted them as sons, preferring them to all others.[101]

Although Otto's appeal to the Romans, seconded by the approach of his troops, had some effect, he decided that his position in the city had become untenable. Reinforcements were on the way and a new siege of Rome was in prospect, but before this could come about, the emperor had fallen a victim to the Italian climate, like so many other rulers from north of the Alps, dying in January 1002 not far from Rome, probably of malaria.[102] He asked to be buried in Aachen, for which, with Charlemagne's throne and its relics, he

had shown great veneration. But could this wish perhaps have also manifested a certain doubt as to whether he had acted wisely in absenting himself
for a long period from the effective centre and strength of his empire?
However, to be fair, it also has to be pointed out that, compared with
many rulers before and after, his death at so early an age did not give him
a second chance.

While perhaps it was not surprising that Italians were not necessarily
enamoured of their transalpine conquerors, what was certainly more
remarkable and worrying was the loss of support for Otto III in his home
base. In the East Frankish kingdom there was some breakdown of law and
order. Discontent arising from the neglect due to the emperor's prolonged
absences sometimes took the form of disobedience. These sentiments did
not only affect the secular sphere, but began to undermine the close co-
operation and coordination of *regnum* and *sacerdotium*, on which depended
the smooth government not only of the home kingdom, but also of the
Empire as a whole. An interdiocesan dispute relating to a nunnery threatened the stability of the Ottonian government because of the absence of the
ruler south of the Alps. In the time of Louis the German, the ancestor of the
Saxon dynasty, Count Liudolf, had founded a nunnery at Gandersheim in
the Harz region, which in the course of time became an object of dispute
between the Archbishop of Mainz and the Bishop of Hildesheim, each of
which claimed it for his diocese. However, during the longest period the
Bishop of Hildesheim had in fact exercised jurisdiction at Gandersheim. In
the year 1000, Archbishop Willigis of Mainz took the law into his own hands
and had a synod affirm his title to the nunnery. When the Bishop of
Hildesheim complained against this wilful act to the emperor and the pope
in Rome, an assembly of numerous bishops from both sides of the Alps
under the joint chairmanship of Otto and Sylvester restored the bishop's
jurisdiction over the monastery. Willigis defied this decree and was suspended by the papal legate. What was perceived as an insult to a leading
metropolitan was widely resented in the Ottonian kingdom north of the
Alps.[103]

The success of the negotiations with Byzantium for another dynastic
marriage came too late. When the Byzantine princess destined to be Otto
III's bride landed in Bari, she was greeted by the news of his death the
previous month and returned home.

Like every other Saxon ruler, Otto III left a strong personal mark on his
reign, but owing to his early death ultimate judgements on him are difficult
to make. The key to his policy was his genuine attempt to live and act his
religion, to do what he could as ruler to spread the gospel, but to avoid so far
as possible any actions that would endanger the salvation of his soul. He
believed that he could fulfil his objectives by ruling over an *imperium
christianum* which would be given new strength by a Roman revival through

his programme of the *renovatio*. He saw himself as an apostle who could do his work through combining in his own person the supreme secular and ecclesiastical leadership. He was convinced his ideas would have such a strong appeal to all concerned that he could count on sufficient support to carry out his policies. In his scheme of things the Romans, or at least the ruling circles among them, formed an essential element.

Otto miscalculated badly by believing that he, a ruler from north of the Alps, could lead a Roman revival. The insurrection in Rome shows that its citizens were not prepared to accept voluntarily as their master, in the long term, an emperor residing in their city who primarily ruled over a kingdom north of the Alps. They did not want to relinquish permanently some say in elections to the papacy, as they realised that this more than anything else enhanced their influence. They could identify with a Langobard king or with somebody like Alberic, even if they were partly of Germanic origin, so long as they regarded ruling over Italian territory as their first priority. If the emperor was in the first place a ruler north of the Alps, they wanted him to make his interventions in Italy as brief as possible and to depart for home at the earliest moment. Italian national – or at any rate cultural – feeling, however divided in its practical manifestations, or at least Roman patriotism, received a considerable boost during the reign of Otto III in this trial of strength with the foreigner. Similarly the East Franks or 'Teutons', including the emperor himself, as his speech showed, also saw themselves more distinctly as a people different from others, such as the Italians. It need hardly be added that all this happened without taking on the political over-tones of modern nationalism.

Otto was genuinely concerned with raising the quality of the Church. But the question was whether it was good for the emperor or for the Church that the Gelasian distinction between the ecclesiastical and the secular sphere and, incidentally the Augustinian differentiation between the two cities, should be set aside. For Otto himself the heightened sacrality only com-pounded his personal problems. His strong sense of sin received fresh nourishment from events like the brutal treatment of the anti-pope Phila-gathus (who had, after all, been his teacher), which he had been unable to prevent. The sacerdotal side was too easily neglected in the attempt to be a priest-king. For a ruler there was no easy way out. Otto could not emulate either the hermit St Nilus or the martyr St Adalbert.

Otto III's early death threw his empire into crisis, for he left no male relative closer than the Duke of Bavaria, the grandson of Otto the Great's brother Henry of the same name and duchy. The younger Henry had been a loyal supporter of his second-cousin, the late emperor. While heredity was regarded as important, the right of election had not been superseded. Hermann II, Duke of Swabia, of the younger line of the Conradine dynasty, from which King Conrad I had sprung, provided the most serious challenge to Henry's bid for the crown. Interestingly enough, another contender, the Margrave Ekkehard of Meissen, was bluntly told by a fellow-nobleman that he lacked an essential qualification, that is relationship to the ruling dynasty.

Henry won out through his determination, bordering on ruthlessness, as well as the support of some bishops, particularly of Archbishop Willigis of Mainz, who – as we have seen – had been in trouble with both the emperor and the pope in the previous reign. Willigis at Mainz in June 1002 not only took charge of the election proceedings, in which both the secular and the ecclesiastical princes participated, but also crowned Henry. He thus acted decisively in the new as he had done in the old reign, when he had urged the two widowed empresses to come home as quickly as possible during the critical period following the death of Otto II. As Ekkehard of Meissen had in the meantime been murdered by his personal enemies, only Hermann of Swabia continued his bid for the throne, but after Henry's coronation he was left in the position of a rebel. As mutual fighting and devastation failed to end the stalemate, King Henry in the meantime sought recognition from the other *Stämme*, which he obtained through concessions to them. Thus the Saxons were promised the maintenance of their old laws. Henry's visit to Lotharingia brought about the turning-point, for there he was greeted by the magnates as king and according to custom formally put on the throne in Aachen. Thereafter, following a short campaign, he also obtained the homage of Hermann and invested him with Swabia. Henry thus secured the victory for a hereditary succession based on royal blood, with its charisma, and therefore for some continuity even in a genealogically far from straightforward situation.

King Henry II was born in 973, and was just under 30 years of age when he succeeded to the throne.[104] Initially he may have been destined for a career in the Church. He received a good education, and when his father was restored to the Bavarian duchy, he was groomed for the succession. As duke, he took a strong interest in religious life, to which he brought a genuine piety. Both as duke, and as king and emperor, he was determined to direct the affairs of the Church on his territory, thus insisting on his right to institute bishops and to obtain financial and military support from the Church. Henry was eminently a good practical organiser, who insisted on the best possible use being made of all, including ecclesiastical, resources.

Although Henry was in general appreciative of his predecessor's achievements, he had his feet planted more firmly on the ground than Otto. The new ruler realised better than his cousin that priority had to be given to the territory north of the Alps. He thus abandoned the *Renovatio imperii Romanorum* as the central concept and proclaimed as his programme the *Renovatio regni Francorum*. Here, Henry's most persistent problem concerned his relations with Duke Boleslav of Poland, which occupied him for many years and involved him in a series of wars which were only brought to a

peaceful conclusion in 1018. Fundamentally, the conflict was due to Boleslav's attempt to build up a large Slav empire, including Bohemia, and to his
penetrations of eastern regions of the Frankish kingdom. In addition, Boleslav strove to free himself from the king's overlordship. Henry realised that
he would no longer have the power to assert an overlordship over Boleslav
once his vassal had acquired control over a large territory. Some German
historians have held that Henry was only having to pay the price for the
concessions Otto III had made to the Poles,[105] and, incidentally, also to the
Hungarians, and thus weakening the East Frankish kingdom in relation to
them. However, the Saxon rulers could no more prevent the establishment
of strong states on their eastern than on their northern and eventually on
their western border. Indeed, the greater the coherence in the East Frankish
kingdom, recently confirmed by the strong unity displayed on the extinction
of the main Ottonian line, the more likely were attempts at emulation
among the neighbours. In any case, the matter was not seen at the time
in purely secular terms, because Christianisation was regarded as a good in
itself, whatever the 'political' consequences. Also there was an expectation,
or at least a hope, that religious conversion would result in pacification and
in better relations between peoples and rulers.

There may have been some confusion here in contemporary thinking.
While, up to a point, a common religion bound a particular kingdom more
closely together, shared allegiance to the Latin rite had not stopped wars
between princes and nobles. Conversely, the differences between religions,
such as between Christianity and Islam, or between opposed interpretations
of the same faith, such as between the Catholics and the Orthodox, did not
in themselves necessarily lead to the outbreak of hostilities. At any rate,
however the situation had arisen, by this time the greatest Slav threat to the
Frankish kingdom in the East no longer came from independent, heathen
tribes, but from another important Christian state. The situation was complicated by the uneven pace of Christianisation in the East, which resulted in
enclaves inhabited by Slavs adhering to their old heathen religion wedged
in between Christian Franks and Poles. So far, Frankish advance on the
eastern border and missionary activity, *Ostpolitik* and *Ostmission*, had gone
hand in hand. This strategy was, however, no longer always feasible with
the Liutizen, a heathen Slav people, who occupied territory between Elbe
and Oder, Mecklenburg and Lusatia. The Liutizen called on King Henry for
help against the Poles and once more recognised him as overlord. Henry
agreed to come to their assistance and to fight the Poles in alliance with
them on the only basis acceptable to the Liutizen: they were allowed to
continue adhering to their religion, which they were not prepared to give up
voluntarily.

This method of proceeding was unusual in this period for a Christian king,
who was supposed to be both *defensor ecclesiae* and *propagator fidei*. The

alliance attracted considerable criticism at the time and caused some friction with Christian military formations in the field. The difficulties were very real, just as they were more recently, in our time, during the Gulf War between allies of different religions. However, if Henry had declined to help the Liutizen, or had insisted on their conversion – which could only be a forced one – before coming to their assistance, that would have constituted the subordination of pressing secular – may we say political? – interests to the dictates of theology. Not even a pious Christian like Henry was prepared to do that. Whether the Liutizen alliance actually helped Henry is difficult to know.

In the wars with Boleslav, Henry fell short of achieving all his aims. While he did manage to break the Polish hold over Bohemia, his reconquest of Lusatia was only temporary. In the final peace settlement in 1018, Boleslav retained the territory, though formally as a fief bestowed by the king. Apart from that arrangement, he established his independence from the Frankish kingdom. He only concluded the treaty because he wanted to have his hands free for a campaign against the Russian Empire in Kiev, which he conquered. Besides creating more stability on the eastern frontier, a further advantage of the peace for Henry was that it deprived his internal enemies, who sometimes found refuge with Boleslav, of outside support.

Breaks in the wars with the Poles allowed Henry to devote some attention to Italy. The final phase of Otto III's reign had led to a breakdown of the East Frankish position in the country. Pope Sylvester II ceased to exercise any influence after Otto's death and died in 1003. A local potentate, Margrave Arduin of Ivrea, succeeded in getting himself elected King of Italy, though his rule, which in any case did not cover the whole of the country, was challenged even in traditional parts of the Langobard kingdom, on which the Italian crown was based. The country was deeply split between a predominantly national or ethnic Italian and a pro-Frankish faction. The latter was led by Bishop Leo of Vercelli, who had played so important a part in the previous reign. Leo travelled to Henry's court to enlist his support against Arduin. While the king could not come in person, he entrusted Duke Otto of Carinthia, the father of the late Pope Gregory V, with a small army to undertake an expedition to Italy. Otto was, however, defeated by Arduin in January 1003. It took Henry another year, before he could himself take troops to Italy, routing Arduin.

Henry received strong Italian support, and in May 1004 was elected King of the Langobards and enthroned in Pavia, recognising the Upper Italian–Langobard kingdom as a separate entity, united in personal union with the East Frankish kingdom. However, during the festivities following the coronation, fighting erupted between Henry's entourage and the Italians, which led to the intervention of the king's troops outside Pavia and to a barbarous devastation of the city. But, as Boleslav was still the main enemy, Henry soon returned home, without proceeding to Rome. More than Otto, Henry gave priority to his kingdom north of the Alps and kept his stays in the south to an absolute minimum. Henry's departure largely left the field to Arduin for the time being. Only in 1013, after what proved to be a temporary peace settlement with the Poles, was the king able to cross the Alps once more, to neutralise Arduin, as well as to go to Rome and to deal with the affairs of the papacy.

In Rome, following the set-backs suffered by Otto III at the end of his reign, the Crescentians had resumed their rule, under the leadership of another John Crescentius, son of the head of the anti-imperial party of the same name executed in 998. However, the *patricius* was careful not to antagonise Henry II and above all to keep him away from the city. He had to face the opposition of the rival Tusculans, who had by now reverted to the imperial side and wished Henry to undertake an expedition to Rome. The king himself acted cautiously and confined himself to corresponding with the popes who were in office during John's patriciate and dependent on him. Sergius IV, who had become pope three years previously, and the *patricius* John, died within a week of each other in May 1012. The Crescentian regime did not survive John's death, and this allowed the more pro-Frankish dynasty of the Counts of Tusculum to resume their influence over Rome and the papacy.[106] Thus began an unbroken line of Tusculan popes that continued until 1046, beginning with another Theophylact, who took the title of Benedict VIII. The Crescentians actually had their own papal candidate, Gregory (VI) who was, however, driven out of the Patrimony by Benedict and travelled to Henry's court as a fugitive to enlist his support. The decision on who was the rightful pope was virtually placed in the king's hands. Henry favoured Benedict VIII, who was in possession. The king was obviously not in any way predisposed to a candidate of the Crescentians with their anti-imperial record. At Henry's request, Benedict confirmed the foundation of the Bamberg diocese, one of the projects dearest to Henry and to his wife Kunigunde, who shared her husband's piety. He also offered to crown him emperor, which he did in February 1014 at St Peter's in Rome.

Soon after emperor and pope jointly presided over a synod at Ravenna, which – in the effort to exterminate simony – forbade the levying of dues for consecrations. An attempt was also made to promote the restoration of alienated church property by means of a compilation of inventories. Carrying out this policy soon ran into trouble over a dispute which the famous royal Benedictine monastery of Farfa in the Sabina not far north from Rome had with the Crescentians; this concerned the monastery's territorial rights.[107] When the emperor in accordance with advice given to him by local judges found against the Crescentians and instructed the pope to carry out the judgment, Benedict was disobeyed. The Crescentians, or some of them, rebelled, and were joined by other groups of nobility. Arduin once morej took over the anti-imperial leadership, but he was defeated by Henry's allies, among whom the bishops played a prominent part, as indeed Henry in Italy relied for his rule mainly on the clergy. The rebellion was crushed, after the emperor's departure mainly thanks to the great determination of the pope. Arduin renounced his dignity and retired into a monastery, where he died soon afterwards.

The three Tusculan pontiffs did their best, in difficult circumstances, to guard the interests of the Church and of the papacy, even pursuing the cause of reform, such as of monasteries. If they humoured the wishes of the East Frankish kings and emperors more than those of other rulers, such as of King Cnut of England and Denmark, or of the King of France, they were only respecting the restraints under which they held office. At home, whereas during the Crescentian regime the key part had been played by the head of the house as lay *patricius*, under the Tusculans this office was not filled and the pope himself tried to influence secular life through a strong papacy. Most of the time Benedict, who was personally pious, was successful in preventing the nobility from threatening the papal position through following a skilful policy of *divide et impera*.

Benedict not only restored order in the Patrimony of St Peter, but also organised the defence against Muslim advances, in 1016 defeating the Moors, and freeing Sardinia. He was also active in resisting Greek ecclesiastical encroachment on the sphere of the Roman Church in Southern Italy by cultivating the Latin bishops in the Langobard principalities who were subject to the emperor in Constantinople. Some of these measures were even taken at the initiative of Henry II. There was clearly a certain identity of interests between the East Frankish ruler and the pope in attempting to curb Byzantine influence in Southern Italy. When Norman knights appeared in Rome during the spring of 1017, Benedict enlisted them against Byzantium.[108] However, the Greeks managed to turn the tables on the rebels, entered Langobard territory and even for a time threatened Rome.

In 1020 Benedict journeyed to Henry at Bamberg to enlist his help. On this occasion, Henry renewed Otto the Great's pact with the papacy, the *Ottonianum*, which Otto III had earlier rejected. In 1022 Henry attacked Byzantine positions in Southern Italy, stopped the Greek advance and recovered Capua and Salerno. Altogether, however, Henry failed to effect any permanent change in the situation in Southern Italy, which after his departure returned to the previous unstable state of affairs. Still, although the Byzantine position in the region was not even called into question, the papacy – partly as a result of its cooperation with the emperor – had succeeded in taking the initiative in extending its activities southwards.

Henry developed further the supervision of the church that his Saxon predecessors had begun. 'The third Otto, Henry II and the Salians often became canons in their cathedrals and royal collegiate churches like

Charlemagne's foundation at Aachen.'[109] Thus they constituted the centre of the *Reichskirche*, 'giving it what solidarity it possessed'.[110] Several times Henry called synods. Even to a greater extent than his predecessors had done, he nominated to bishoprics, mainly from the court chapel, leaving very little if any of that free consent of the electors which constituted the essence of the *electio canonica*. Actually Henry's nominees were of good calibre, equally adept at ecclesiastical and secular duties, 'genuine princes of the Church in the sense of Archbishop Bruno of Cologne',[111] the brother of Otto the Great. A strong ruler like Henry was able to create the settled conditions in which church life could flourish. But he did so at the cost of integrating the Church into the framework of the *regnum*, as opposed to the West Frankish kingdom where – with a weaker monarchy – the churches retained more independence from the secular power.[112]

In some cases Henry appointed wealthy noblemen to bishoprics with meagre financial resources, expecting them to subsidise their dioceses and to leave their fortunes to them. Often richly endowing churches, he, however, also utilised their resources, for instance regularly burdening bishoprics with the expenses of the itinerant court where earlier kings had done so only occasionally. So far as the monasteries which came under the king (*Reichsklöster*) were concerned, Henry acted in a proprietary capacity, as *Eigenkirchenherr*. All monasteries had to render him fixed dues, the *servitium regale*, and even had to accept his investiture of secular vassals with monastic property. His interference with their possessions was due not only to his material needs as ruler, but also to a sincere interest in church reform and the best use of resources, for instance by transferring monastic property to bishoprics. Being deeply religious, he felt particularly impelled to intervene in the affairs of the Church, believing that he did so for its own good.

Henry was influenced more by the Lotharingian than by the Cluniac monastic reform movement. In Lotharingia most of the monasteries were royal or imperial. The development of the Benedictine monastic reform movement there incidentally owed much to the activities and donations of a few families belonging to the high nobility. The continuing interest of the patrons of the Lotharingian monasteries promoted autonomy, rather than the Cluniac system of linked congregations coordinated from the centre. The position of the Lotharingian abbeys was legally more secure than that of their French counterparts. Unlike those modelled on Cluny, they did not for the preservation of their rights require exemption from diocesan control and direct subordination to the papacy. For all these reasons, preference was given to the Lotharingian rather than the Cluniac pattern not only in Lotharingia, but in parts of the Frankish kingdom.[113]

Henry's ecclesiastical activities in Italy culminated in the synod at Pavia in 1022, over which he presided together with the pope. Mainly with a view to the preservation of church property and to prevent its alienation to the children of clerics, the pope successfully insisted on passing decrees enforcing, down to the rank of sub-deacon, the duty of celibacy which had fallen into neglect. Apparently the emperor was very pleased with the zeal shown by the pope and at once published the decisions of the synod in an imperial edict.[114] Actions which were were taken in the first instance mainly because of considerations relating to property, assumed all the greater importance when later in the century they became part of a strong reform movement that concentrated on the character of the priesthood and the spiritual significance of the wealth of the church.

An active reign came to an end when Henry II died in July 1024, about three months after Benedict VIII, with whom he had collaborated so closely. Henry had laid down that he should be buried in the cathedral at Bamberg, in the heart of the diocese he had founded for the good of his soul and for which the childless ruler had chosen God as his heir.[115] The placing of a new bishopric there was due not merely to Henry's fancy. With the assumption of the royal dignity by a duke of Bavaria at the beginning of the reign, the Bavarians had joined the Saxons and Franconians as pillars of the kingdom. Saxon Magdeburg, Lotharingian Aachen and Bavarian Regensburg were the main royal residences. Main–Franconia, with Bamberg, owing to its central position thus formed an important link.[116]

As so often with Henry, religious devotion went hand in hand with political considerations. The disaffection of a major magnate in the area and the division of his territory had left a void in the defence of this border region.[117] It is characteristic for Henry that – in spite of considerable ecclesiastical opposition – he created a diocese, rather than a secular principality, for this purpose, underlining once more the essential part played by bishops in the administration of the kingdom, including the raising of troops. 'The field armies of the period would have been much smaller without the episcopal and abbatial contingents.'[118] At the same time the Bishop of Bamberg could also fulfil important primarily ecclesiastical functions by undertaking missionary activities among those who had not yet been won to the faith, such as among the Slavs. Bamberg Cathedral, which in its thirteenth-century form constituted one of the great achievements of ecclesiastical architecture, became a lasting monument to this ruler who combined the realism of the statesman with deep piety. This was recognised in his canonisation by Pope Eugenius III in 1146, which – though resting to some extent on an idealising legend – recognised that the emperor strove hard to be a model Christian ruler.[119] He suffered deep remorse when he sensed that he was straying from this path, such as in his alliance with non-Christians against another Christian power.

The emperor was survived by his wife Kunigunde, from the rising Luxemburg (Lützelburg) dynasty, who lived her faith when soon after the emperor's death she retired to a monastery, where she did duty as a gatekeeper, never leaving its walls. She was buried next to her husband when she died in 1033, being canonised in 1200. It was part of the legend that developed around Henry and Kunigunde that their childlessness was due to deliberately abstaining from matrimonial relations. At any rate, it was a fact that with Henry the Saxon dynasty became extinct in the male line, except for his younger brother Bruno, Bishop of Augsburg, who survived him until 1029, but was not eligible for the succession to the throne as as he was in holy orders. The question of the succession arose in an even more acute form than on the death of Otto III, for a new dynasty had to be found.

4 The Salians: from Cooperation to Struggle with the Papacy (1024–1125)

On the death of Henry II, when the Saxon dynasty could no longer muster an eligible candidate for the throne, there were two contenders for the crown: the cousins Conrad – the elder and the younger – of the senior Conradine line of the Rhenish-Franconian Salian family. They could trace back their descent in the female line to kings of two families: to King Conrad I, as well as to Otto the Great through his daughter Liutgart and her marriage to Conrad the Red, Duke of Lorraine. Though closely related to the Saxon dynasty, the Salians had not always seen eye to eye with the reigning family. Henry II had certainly not been particularly partial to them.

The elder Conrad, who as Conrad II founded the imperial Salian dynasty which reigned until 1125 (Table 4.1), was born around 990. He seems to have received only a comparatively small part of the family inheritance, which went mainly to the Worms branch to which the younger Conrad belonged. He considerably improved his position around 1016 by marrying – as her third husband – Gisela, a member of the junior line of the Salian dynasty and daughter of Duke Hermann II of Swabia. Gisela, who was descended from the Carolingians through her mother Gerberga of Burgundy, was the widow of Hermann's successor as duke, the Babenberg Prince Ernest I, from whom she had two sons. Conrad may have abducted his bride. In any case there was some question about the validity of the marriage in canon law owing to the spouses being related to each other, if only rather distantly. Henry II raised objections to the marriage. Both Conrads were nephews of Bruno of Carinthia, who had been elected pope on the nomination of his distant cousin, Emperor Otto III, and had taken the name of Gregory V.

Archbishop Aribo of Mainz called the election for the kingship, which was held about seven weeks after the death of Emperor Henry II on the right bank of the Rhine opposite Oppenheim. For the first time in the history of what was to become Germany, the electors had a genuine choice between two candidates.[1] Aribo, as presiding officer, was the first to cast his vote, and chose the elder Conrad. His lead was followed by a number of ecclesiastics, and then by the secular lords, led by the younger Conrad. 'The people', who had formed a ring around the ecclesiastical and secular lords, affirmed the election carried out by the dignitaries.

In a solemn ceremony, Kunigunde, the widow of Henry II, handed over the imperial insignia to the new ruler. The election was unanimous, but only

Table 4.1   The Salian and Staufen dynasties

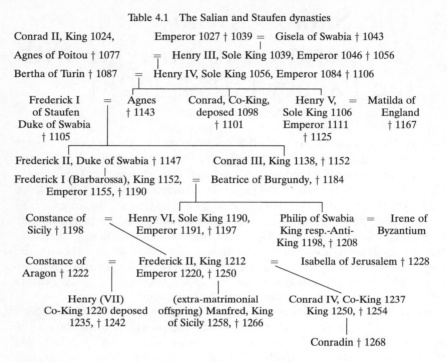

of those present. Many who had a different view-point, such as Archbishop Pilgrim of Cologne, stayed away. Immediately after the election Aribo crowned the elder Conrad king, but refused to act similarly for Queen Gisela in view of scruples about the validity of their marriage on the grounds of consanguinity. Interestingly enough, Archbishop Pilgrim of Cologne, a relative of Henry II, who had opposed the elder Conrad but accepted the verdict of the election, now crowned Gisela.[2] This action paved the way for transfer in 1028 of the right to anoint and crown the king at Aachen from the Archbishop of Mainz to that of Cologne, though challenged by the former for many centuries.[3] Gradually Conrad secured the allegiance of those magnates who had stood out against him. In 1024 the beginnings of a tension between an elective and a hereditary kingship, which was to play an increasing part in the history of the country, can already be seen. However the problem did not appear clearly, because Conrad II was of royal blood with all its sacral connotations, so that election and heredity balanced each other.[4]

So far the term 'German kingdom' has been avoided in this account. To what extent does the term gain currency and meaning in the Salian period? These matters are of considerable importance in the context of the development of a German nation and of the way the German national movement in the nineteenth century looked at German history. There has also been a great deal of interest shown in the questions why and to what degree Germany developed along a different path (*Sonderweg*) from other countries. Research has shown that whereas elsewhere the name of the people (*Stamm*) or the country comes first, only in the case of the Germans was the name of the language the older and provided the basis for the name of the people and the country. Since the end of the ninth century the name of the language and of the people that spoke it, called *theodiscus/teutonicus*, was taken over by the developing German people.[5] The concept of the *regnum teutonicorum/teutonicum*, which gradually superseded the term *Francia* from the first quarter of the eleventh century, first gained currency in Italy rather than Germany. North of the Alps the expression *regnum teutonicum* assumed importance initially during the reign of Henry IV, to some extent in connection with the Investiture Conflict. In any case, the term, when mentioned in official documents or by chroniclers, must not be interpreted in a post-1789 sense of state and nation. Incidentally, in official documents, the king still appeared as *rex francorum*. In the early Salian period the person of the sacral ruler with obligations to the papacy, supported by an aristocracy that occupied the highest rungs of the ladder in both *regnum* and *sacerdotium* in a system founded on benefices on some kind of a feudal basis, cannot be fitted into neat nineteenth-century or twentieth-century political and legal concepts.[6]

The 'stern unlettered realist',[7] Conrad II, made his main contribution primarily in the secular aspects of consolidating the kingdom and empire, of distinguishing more clearly between the office and the person of the king, and in strengthening the position of the rear-vassals and to some extent of the towns.[8] He recognised the military and administrative value to the crown of rear-vassals, who were often on a servile and certainly a precarious tenure. He saw that these counts and knights constituted important military resources and also that they could be used in the royal service. They were to be the backbone of the *ministeriales* who were to become the king's officials. Also the rear-vassals were useful to the king against a rebellious magnate, such as Gisela's son, Duke Ernest II of Swabia, when they refused to follow him into rebellion against his step-father in 1025. Among other matters the duke was dissatisfied with Conrad II as heir to Emperor Henry II cutting him out of prospects for the Burgundian inheritance to which he felt entitled as a great-grandson of Conrad III of Burgundy. The rear-vassals placed their loyalty to the 'supreme protector of their freedom on earth', the king, before that to their duke.[9] Ernest carried out a number of uprisings against the king, sometimes with other princes, until he died in battle in 1030. Conrad the Younger also for a period fought the king. One of the most important measures Conrad II instituted for the East Frankish kingdom was to make the fiefs of the rear-vassals hereditary.

Like his predecessors, Conrad found himself involved in the affairs of Italy. Distinguishing between the permanent rights of the crown and the persons of the rulers, he made it quite clear that the death of Emperor Henry II and the extinction of the old dynasty in no way affected the legal basis of the continuance of the Empire north and south of the Alps over which his predecessor had ruled. In his eyes, the Italian crown, as well as the protectorship over the papacy and the claim to imperial coronation, were implicit in his election and coronation in the Rhineland. Indeed, precedent had established a tradition for the East Frankish kings that made it incumbent on them to undertake an expedition to Italy as soon as possible in order to take possession of the Italian kingdom and to receive the imperial crown from the pope. Whatever the legal rights and precedents, opposition to Saxon and now to Salian rule was still current in Italy, in spite of the existence of a fairly strong imperial party, to some extent among the bishops and particularly among the lay magnates. Remembering the fate of Arduin of Ivrea, none of the leading secular lords in Lombardy and Tuscany was prepared to take the risk of bidding for the crown, but they offered it to the heir of the King of France and, after his refusal, to the powerful Duke William V of Aquitaine for his son, who also eventually declined. For a time, the threat of an international alliance against Conrad loomed on the horizon. Count Odo of Champagne, a nephew of King Conrad III of Burgundy, hoped to inherit that kingdom on the death of King Rudolf III and so to deprive the East Frankish kingdom of the rich prize promised to Henry II. Thus it became essential for Conrad to secure his position in Italy, if only to prevent others, like Odo, or the King of France, from establishing themselves there.

Actually, all attempts to bypass Conrad as King of Italy foundered on the resistance of some prelates, led by Heribert, Archbishop of Milan, and Leo, Bishop of Vercelli, as well as on the disunity among the potential anti-Salian allies. Urged by Heribert not to delay his expedition, and assured of his coronation as king of Italy, Conrad was able to cross the Alps in the spring of 1026. He achieved his objectives, but at great cost, for it became even more patent than before that the East Frankish kings had to conquer the country, much of which was hostile to them and regarded them as foreign invaders. Italian resistance was crushed, ruthlessly, often by systematically destroying the habitations and livelihood of those resisting, in accordance with a form of warfare typical for the age. The East Frankish armies certainly did not make friends among the Italians. Pavia, where the royal palace had been destroyed after Henry II's death, feared punishment and was therefore afraid to admit Conrad, who was crowned instead in Milan, by Archbishop Heribert. Only after the reduction of Pavia could the king undertake the journey to Rome, where he was crowned emperor at Easter 1027 by Pope John XIX of the Tusculan dynasty. John had previously governed Rome, but had been raised to the papacy from the laity on the death of his brother, Benedict VIII, in 1024.

The new pontiff had considerable success in conciliating the opponents of the Tusculan regime and had even succeeded in subjecting his brother Alberic III to papal control by moving him from the position of city prefect to an office at the Lateran. He was a staunch supporter of the East Frankish connection and of Conrad's candidature as king. He showed his sympathy for the reform movement by exempting the Cluny monastery from any episcopal ban or interdict. The ceremony at St Peter's was all the more impressive, as the coronation was attended by two kings, Cnut from England and Rudolf III from Burgundy (to be distinguished from the duchy of the same name). However, as happened so often during the Italian expeditions of the Saxons and the Salians, the celebrations were marred by street-fighting between the troops and the local population, in this instance as on other occasions caused by incidents of no intrinsic importance.

Conrad showed Pope John little gratitude for his support. When he came to Rome for his coronation, he refused to give the pope the usual assurances on entering the city or to confirm the privileges which his predecessors had granted to the Holy See. The emperor regarded himself as the superior of the popes, to whom he showed scant respect and whom he degraded to executive assistants. At a synod held jointly by emperor and pope at the Lateran after the coronation, John was forced by Conrad to reverse his previous decision supporting the patriarch of the Adriatic island of Grado in his dispute with his brother of Aquileja/Friuli, a strong imperial interest. The emperor ended his first Italian expedition by showing the imperial flag in southern Italy. In this region both the imperial and the papal position had deteriorated following the release, soon after Conrad II's accession, of some south Italian princes captured during Henry II's reign.[10] However, the emperor had to return home to suppress risings against his rule there. At Easter 1028, Conrad as emperor took steps to secure the succession in the dynasty by having his ten-year-old son, Henry, elected king.

The early 1030s were a period of Polish and Hungarian invasions, which Conrad was able to contain after some initial set-backs, though in the case of the Hungarians at the price of some cession of territory arranged by his son, King Henry, not entirely to his father's satisfaction. In 1032 Rudolf III of Burgundy died and Conrad claimed the kingdom, which lay between France and Italy, on the basis of treaties initially concluded with Rudolf by his predecessor Henry II. He did so on the grounds of heredity, not just in his personal capacity, but on behalf of the East Frankish kingdom. However, Odo of Champagne, another relative of Rudolf, took advantage of the emperor's preoccupation in the East to subject large parts of Burgundy to his rule and would have been crowned king if Conrad had not taken swift military and diplomatic action. In February 1033, Conrad was himself crowned King of Burgundy, though his rival did not give up. Fortunately, the emperor was able to secure the co-operation of King Henry I of France, who was opposed to any increase of power for his restless and ambitious rival Odo. By the summer of 1034, the war of the Burgundian succession was over.

To mark the beginning of a new era and to demonstrate the union of the three kingdoms, Conrad attended a festival in St Peter's Church in Geneva accompanied by a solemn procession of East Frankish, Italian and Burgundian magnates. With Conrad's reign the designations *Romanorum imperium* and *regnum* became standard. The three kingdoms were regarded constitutionally as an entity, with the East Frankish crown constituting a title to the other two kingdoms. The acquisition of the kingdom of Burgundy, with its centres of learning and its monasteries, was of great importance for the Empire, increasing the influence of the church (or at any rate the monastic) reform movement radiating from the cultural, literary and religious eminence of Cluny in the neighbouring duchy of Burgundy. Strategically the addition of the Burgundian to the East Frankish and Italian kingdoms barred France from expanding into Italy. For the Empire now controlled all the passes over the Alps,[11] which Conrad had to cross once more at the end of 1036.

The situation in Northern Italy again required the emperor's attention, because an ugly conflict had broken out between the greater lords and their lower vassals, the *valvassors*. The latter wished to have security of tenure, but Archbishop Heribert of Milan, who had been Conrad's ally, opposed this. In fighting that ensued over this issue in Lombardy, the lords, supported by higher vassals, were defeated by the rear-vassals. Both parties now appealed to the emperor to settle the dispute, with the emperor tending to support the principle of hereditary fiefs for rear-vassals, as he did north of the Alps. However, the burghers of Milan started a revolt against him in which the archbishop may possibly have been involved. The emperor besieged the city, proclaiming his famous *constitutio de feudis*, which was meant to reconcile the higher vassals, the *capitani* with the sub-vassals, the *valvassors*, and to put the feudal relations between them on a secure legal basis. All vassals, including the *valvassors*, were guaranteed the heredity of their fiefs.

The emperor's option against the mighty Archbishop of Milan and his support for the vassals was due partly to his reliance on the military prowess of the lesser knights. It also accorded with his promotion of the importance of the *ministeriales* in the imperial service north of the Alps. However, unlike in the East Frankish kingdom, Conrad was unable to secure the help of the cities, and by his policy – as was already the case during Milan's resistance under Heribert – brought about an alliance between them and their bishops. The loss of episcopal support at least in parts of Italy was a serious disadvantage not only in mainly secular terms in the short run, but was of considerable consequence in the ecclesiastical struggles to come. Conrad's proceedings against Archbishop Heribert, not only deposing him, but also appointing a successor to him without any judgment of a church court, was bound to make cooperation between *ecclesia* and *regnum* more difficult in future. Conrad hardly seems to have been aware of the dangers of future friction between the two spheres that he was inviting. The emperor had no hesitation in disavowing the pope's actions even in matters that clearly fell within the latter's jurisdiction, such as in the case of the grant of privileges to the Reichenau monastery, which were reversed by Conrad on the intervention of the Bishop of Constance. It is not clear whether the long-suffering pope still received news of this indignity, for he died in October 1032.

Through concessions to the electors and to the nobility, John's brother Alberic succeeded in securing the papal election of his son Theophylact, a layman, thereby hoping to gain the kind of influence in Rome to which he aspired and which had eluded him during the pontificates of his two brothers. But Benedict IX, who was probably in his twenties, contrary to tendentious reports that he was a boy at the time of his consecration, frustrated his father's plans. The new pope skilfully directed the Church for 12 years. While his predecessor had – for whatever reason – allowed the papacy to be used as Conrad's instrument, Benedict was more successful in preserving some independence from the emperor. He demonstrated this attitude when he – to Conrad's surprise – initially refused to accede to a demand from the emperor to excommunicate Heribert.

Conrad's struggle with Heribert foreshadowed other dangers to the imperial position in Italy. The archbishop invited Odo of Champagne to take over not only the Italian kingship, but also the imperial crown. Several Italian bishops were involved in the plot, were arrested, convicted of high treason and transported to the East Frankish kingdom. Heribert was safe behind the walls of Milan. It was only when the evidence of the archbishop's treasonable activities became patent that Pope Benedict IX excommunicated him. The pontiff also needed the cooperation of the emperor, as he was on the point of reverting to his uncle Benedict VIII's active policy in southern Italy.[12] Odo was defeated and killed in battle in November 1037 when he invaded Lotharingia as the ally of the Italian insurgents.

Although Conrad was never able to subdue Milan, he did succeed in 1038 in restoring imperial authority in the Langobard principalities in southern Italy, north of the Byzantine sphere of influence. One action on the part of the emperor in ordering the affairs of the region was of considerable importance for the future. For the last two decades, ever since Pope Benedict VIII had recruited them, Norman warriors had participated in local wars, utilising the rivalries of the various Langobard principalities, and supporting in turn practically all sides – papal, Byzantine, as well as rulers and abbots in the area – though never the Saracens. Conrad II now confirmed the title of the Norman knight Rainulf to the countship of Aversa as vassal of the Prince of Salerno, which made him the emperor's rear-vassal. This formed a further stage in the recognition given to Norman rule in southern Italy and to the eventual formation of a strong Norman dominion there that was to play a major part in history and to have considerable effects on Conrad's eventual successors.[13] However, as so often before, the imperial army during the heat of the summer suffered from the outbreak of an epidemic, which necessitated a retreat to north of the Alps. The wife of Conrad's son and heir, King Henry, who was a daughter of King Cnut, was one of many who fell victim to the disease. Conrad himself died at Utrecht in June 1039, probably aged just under 50, less than a year after his return home, possibly from the consequences of an illness he had contracted in Italy, or weakened by gout. He was buried in the cathedral at Speyer, whose construction he had begun.

Though less pious than his predecessor or his successor, Conrad II in many ways continued Henry II's religious policy, both in supporting the Lotharingian monastic reform movement and in developing further the organisation of the East Frankish church. In substance there was little difference between the practice of the last Saxon and the first Salian ruler relating to the institution of bishops and abbots, or in their use of bishoprics and monasteries in the service of the Empire. 'But while Henry II clothed his rule over the church in the aura of his own priest-kingship and tempered it in a subtle way, the Salian claimed the unlimited rule over the *Reich* Church without any adornment.'[14]

Like Henry II, Conrad demanded a fee in the case of appointments to wealthy sees. It was a sign of the change in the times when this was soon to be regarded as simony – as the sale or purchase of ecclesiastical dignities – by the reform movement. Actually, Conrad may simply have made an attempt, which was then perfectly legal within the framework of the system of benefices, to combine investiture with the obligation to render service to the king, with the *servitium regale*. Within the context of the actual situation during his reign, Conrad was perhaps wanting in not fully recognising the importance of the reform movement and of establishing close contact with it, as his son Henry III did. However, it should not be forgotten that the first great reforming pope in the following reign, Leo IX, who was related to the imperial family, was initially raised to the bishopric of Toul by Conrad. The emperor exacted the same loyalty from his ecclesiastical as he did from his secular dignitaries, which explains his uncanonical treatment of Heribert, Archbishop of Milan. Conrad, who enjoyed wide popularity, with great determination strengthened the secular foundations of the monarchy. He increased the imperial resources, while in general holding back on donations to the Church.[15] A new emphasis was to be given to the role of the monarchy by his son and successor, who had already shown as crowned king during his father's reign that he had his own ideas.

Henry III succeeded to the throne smoothly and without opposition. He was born in October 1017, before the Salian dynasty succeeded to the throne. At the beginning of 1026, when he was eight years old, he was designated king by Conrad with the agreement of the magnates, and thus ear-marked for the succession. As heir to the throne, unlike his father, he received an excellent religious and political education. The last surviving descendant of the Saxon dynasty in the male line, Henry II's younger brother, Bishop Bruno of Augsburg, who died in 1029, was entrusted with his education. At Easter 1027, Henry witnessed the imperial coronation of his father in Rome. Soon after, he was invested by Conrad with the Duchy of Bavaria and, as we have seen, at Easter 1028 was crowned and anointed king. In 1038 he was also invested with the vacant duchy of Swabia and proclaimed King of Burgundy. While heir to the throne, Henry took part in his father's rule and sometimes expressed his dissent from actions proposed by Conrad, for instance over the measures taken against Archbishop Heribert of Milan.

Henry placed greater emphasis on the sacral element in his rule than his father, taking very seriously his position as king-priest. There can be little doubt about his deep religiosity. Unlike his father, he found it difficult to relax, probably because of his unrelenting concern with his sacral position. He inherited his father's quick and imperious temper, without his easy popularity. Henry appears to have been somewhat morose and to have been prone to antagonise those with whom he had to deal.

Coming to the throne allowed Henry to correct a policy of his father with which he had disagreed as heir. The new ruler reached an understanding with Archbishop Heribert of Milan, thus ending a dispute that had weakened Salian power in Italy. But it was some time before he could devote his attentions to matters south of the Alps. His first years were taken up with the affairs of Bohemia, Poland and Hungary, and involved some vigorous campaigning, which was partly successful. Henry for a time asserted the traditional East Frankish overlordship over these countries, but by the end of his reign Hungary had moved out of the Salian sphere of influence and the overlordship over Poland had been loosened.

Internally, Henry attempted to strengthen royal authority over the duchies. Through a combination of circumstances, the king early in his reign controlled Bavaria, Swabia and Carinthia. He did not intend to keep these duchies permanently in his hands, but wanted to make sure that the dukes would exercise their authority in the interests of the kingdom as a whole and that the local nobility, which tended to be unruly, in Bavaria and in the south for instance, would be kept in order; actually a duke appointed from outside the territory sometimes tended to compound the problem of a restless nobility.[16] Accordingly he was not prepared to accept invariably the principle of hereditary succession in the case of the dukes. Thus on the death of Duke Gozilo of Lorraine in 1044, possibly in accordance with his testamentary disposition,[17] the king refused to invest his eldest son Godfrey with the whole of the duchy. He restricted him to Upper Lorraine, while entrusting Lower Lorraine to Godfrey's younger brother. Whatever the legal complexities, here Henry overreached himself, making an enemy of Godfrey not only for himself, but for his dynasty – with important consequences for the future. Situated as his territories were on the western fringes of the Teutonic dominions, Godfrey was able, at various times, during a series of rebellions, to ally for a time with the King of France, as well as with the counts of Flanders and Holland. It took Henry until the end of 1049, and even then only with the help of English and Danish naval forces, to crush his enemies.

Where the king did invest others with duchies, he often selected those who were strangers to the territory they were to rule. He was not always lucky in his choices, as particularly the last years of his reign were to show. Henry also encountered difficulties when he attempted to tighten royal authority over the duchies by relying on the support of the bishops and by strengthening the royal domain, particularly in Saxony. The building of a royal palace (*Pfalz*) at Goslar and the encroachment of the ecclesiastical and territorial powers of Archbishop Adalbert of Hamburg–Bremen on the duchy were resented by the Billung Dukes of Saxony and by many of the Saxon nobility.

Through most of his reign, Henry was greatly concerned with the disturbance arising from irregular warfare. In attempting to curb the incidence of fighting that took place, both on a larger scale and on the level of individual feuding, Henry based himself not only on the well-recognised duty of the king to maintain peace and justice, but also on the priestly functions of his rule. He deliberately went beyond the concept of the Peace of God and the Truce of God, propagated in Western Europe by the Church and particularly by some bishops and the monastic movement; it tried to protect ecclesiastical property and the poor, and forbade knightly feuding on certain days.[18] Henry was not satisfied with half-measures: 'he wanted to put the heavenly ideal into earthly practice'.[19] By forgiving his enemies and by personal and public acts of penance, for instance at a synod held in Constance in 1043 and after the victory over the Hungarians the following year, he hoped to convert his vassals to his high conception of conduct and to end fighting.

The seriousness with which Henry took his role as the 'anointed of the lord', raised high above the general ranks of the laity, is also reflected in his method of investing bishops with ring and staff. It is only since the reign of Henry III that there is evidence of the handing over of the bishop's ring during the ceremony.[20] If the king introduced this aspect into the installation of bishops, he may well have contributed to the eventual outbreak of the investiture conflict by going beyond the Gelasian line of demarcation and intervening in the purely spiritual sphere. However, royal investiture of bishops with ring and staff became problematic only during the following reign because of the increasing tension between king and pope, thus changing the whole nature and impact of the movement for reform of the Church.

During Henry III's lifetime, the reform movement did not threaten the interests of the monarchy, for it was prepared to function within a theocratic framework, particularly as the king and emperor put his dual authority as *rex et sacerdos* at its disposal. Indeed, Henry believed that one of the main purposes of the preservation of his inherited powers was to cleanse the Church of abuses. Where necessary he was ready to change royal practice to achieve this objective. Thus he agreed with the condemnation of simony – the purchase and sale of church offices – by the reformers. It may well be that there was a certain connection between the growing concern about simony and the rise of a money economy that was taking place at the time.[21] Accordingly, he was careful not to accept any fees in connection with the appointment of bishops. However, to raise the revenue he needed, he had to levy fees from secular officials and feudatories.[22] He tolerated the refusal of Abbot Halinard as a monk to swear fealty to him on becoming Archbishop of Lyons, possibly because of the ambiguous position of the city on the frontiers of France and the Empire. Perhaps the system of government was not endangered by making a single exception, but what would be the result if the exception became the rule? There were also at least rumblings of a questioning of the whole theocratic order. Bishop Wazo of Liège in 1046 challenged Henry's right to depose an Italian archbishop in accordance with the judgment of an East Frankish synod, arguing along Gelasian lines of the division into two spheres that such matters were reserved to the pope. Wazo also revived doctrines about the superiority of the priestly over the secular order.

Henry's judgment in ecclesiastical matters was put to a severe test when a confusing situation arose over the papacy. The third of the Tusculan popes, Benedict IX, had for many years been successful in preserving stability in Rome. However, in September 1044 a rising took place in the city, probably organised by the Stephanian section of the Crescentians (the old enemies of the Tusculans), possibly taking advantage of uncertainties caused by the death of the head of the Tusculan family, Alberic III, the pope's father. The Stephanians now got the Romans to elect John, the Bishop of Sabina – the region which provided their power base – as Pope Sylvester III. When

Benedict after a temporary setback secured his re-entry into the city, Sylvester fled and returned to his diocese in the Sabina, from which the lawful pope, who had by now become a mere pawn to the ambitions of power-hungry noble factions, was unable to dislodge him.[23]

Abhorring the prospect of spilling more Roman blood and recognising the hopelessness of his position, Benedict in May 1045 took the unusual step of renouncing the papacy in favour of his godson, the pious arch-priest John Gratian, who took the name of Gregory VI as pope. At first Gregory's elevation was well received, for instance by the Prior Peter Damian, a leader of the church reform movement, and he was recognised by Henry III. However, soon certain financial transactions in connection with the transfer of power became known and led to suspicions of simony, that is to the belief that Benedict had sold his dignity to Gregory. It was on the basis of this interpretation that Henry III, who in the autumn of 1046 began his journey south to receive the imperial crown, turned against Gregory, regarding him guilty of simony, which the king generally condemned as a sin at a synod in Pavia held while on his way to Rome. However, recent research has thrown considerable doubt on the simoniac version of the transactions between the old and the new pope. Although Benedict gave up his pontificate, that still left the problem of the troops that had been recruited and commanded by him, and these had to be bought off. The money that passed between the popes may have been used for this purpose and may have only nominally passed through the hands of Benedict as commander of the troops. If this is so, the stories current at the time, which have since been embroidered in the history books and have made good anti-papal copy, such as Benedict's wish to get married, fall to the ground.

It seems likely that Gregory could have maintained himself as pope if Henry had not taken action against him. However, in December 1046, at synods in Sutri and Rome, Henry decreed the deposition not only of Sylvester (which was clearly justified) and of Benedict (who had already abdicated), but also of Gregory. While the two other popes were allowed to retire with dignity, with Sylvester even retaining his bishopric in the Sabina, Gregory was subjected to great indignities at the synod which stripped him of his high office. He was sent into exile in the Rhineland, accompanied by his chaplain Hildebrand, the later Gregory VII. Towards the end of 1047, this worthy pope, a mere victim of circumstances, died in exile, worn out by the humiliating treatment he had received.

Henry marked a new departure by selecting for the Holy See bishops from his dominions north of the Alps. His choices were on the whole well received by the reform movement, which was quite prepared to accept theocratic rule in the interest of the Church at this time. These popes, presumably at Henry's behest, retained their bishoprics and thus their allegiance to the emperor, though in the case of Leo IX only for a time.[24]

Henry nominated to the vacant papacy Bishop Suidger of Bamberg, a Saxon nobleman, who took the name of Clement II and bestowed the imperial crown on the king and his wife Agnes. Clement at once called a synod, to undertake a major reform of the Church. Whereas Charlemagne had merged the title of *patricius* in the imperial dignity, Henry found it necessary to revive for himself this rank, a dignity last held by John Crescentius, who died in 1012. After a period in which emperor and pope had to some extent led parallel existences, it was no longer certain that the emperorship included the right of nomination for the papacy. It was only by having himself elected *patricius* that the emperor made sure of securing for himself this entitlement to designate the pope, subject to formal ratification by the clergy and people of Rome. Additionally, the emperor as *patricius Romanorum* did something to block the establishment of a new local ruler in Rome, who could endanger the cause of papal and church reform.[25]

Emperor and pope proceeded to Southern Italy to assert the traditional imperial overlordship. Henry accepted the allegiance of the new Norman rulers in Apulia[26] and abandoned the territory of the rebellious princes of Benevento to them.[27] Thus, by extending recognition to them, he helped to pave the way for the establishment of a mighty Norman dominion in southern Italy, which was to make a decisive impact both on the Empire and the papacy, as well as on the relations between them. Presumably both Conrad II and Henry III showed favour to the Normans because they regarded them as potential allies not only against the Saracens, but also against Byzantium. Henry's time in Italy was, however, limited, as he was soon caught up once more in affairs north of the Alps with the great Lotharingian rising in 1047 that was only terminated two years later.

In the meantime, the situation in Rome deteriorated. Pope Clement II died in October 1047 and this allowed Benedict IX to resume the papacy. Apparently the Tusculan pontiff was able to exercise his functions once the initial opposition, which may have come from a small imperial party rather than the *Romanorum plebs*, had crumbled within a few weeks. But Rome was not to remain at peace, for the emperor and *patricius* could not accept the defiance of the papal settlement of 1046, although an expert opinion he had requested from Bishop Wazo of Liège had recognised the title of Benedict IX to the papacy. Instead he nominated to the Holy See Bishop Poppo of Brixen, a Bavarian nobleman. The emperor's personal intervention was required to overcome the unwillingness of Margrave Boniface of Canossa-Tuscany to escort Poppo to Rome, as he regarded Benedict as fully in charge of the situation there. The new pope, who took the title of Damasus II, could only be installed in Rome as Boniface managed to persuade Benedict to withdraw from the city. Whereas Benedict's second pontificate lasted eight months, Damasus died in August 1048 after reigning for only three weeks. Even then the hold of the Tusculans on Rome was not broken.

Henry's choice for the papal throne for the third time fell on a bishop of noble origin, this time on Bishop Bruno of Toul, of the family of the Alsatian counts of Egisheim, to whom the emperor was related through his paternal grandmother. Bruno informed the emperor that he would only assume his new duties if the clergy and people of Rome unanimously elected him pope. He did so in order to emphasise the importance of conforming to canon law, not to challenge the emperor's right of designation, though in principle he did not want interference from the secular power in the affairs of the Church. In February 1049 he entered Rome as a pilgrim and ascended the papal throne after his election.

With Leo IX the first of the great reforming popes succeeded to the Holy See. Having distinguished himself as a bishop in his zeal against simony, he was in touch with many of the leaders of the reform movement, such as Abbot Hugh of Cluny, Archbishop Halinard of Lyons, as well as Peter Damian, the hermit leader and prolific writer on important church questions of the day. Lotharingia, in which Toul was situated, was in the forefront of the reform movement. Leo brought with him a number of advisers who were to play a decisive part in the future: Humbert, later Cardinal-Bishop of Silva Candida, and Hugh Candidus, who was to be a cardinal-priest, had been monks in Leo's diocese; there were also Frederick of Lorraine, Godfrey's brother and Archdeacon of Liège, later Pope Stephen IX; and – last not least – Hildebrand. He was available for new tasks following the death of Gregory VI, whose chaplain he had been; the future Pope Gregory VII now became a subdeacon. Through the appointment of men like Humbert, Hugh and Frederick, the College of Cardinals was considerably strengthened. Thanks to Leo's initiative, the college, which had so far mainly supported the Bishop of Rome at pontifical masses and at other ecclesiastical functions in the city, now began to assist the pope in the administration of the Church as a whole. The apparatus of the papal curia was also reorganised to become more effective.

The new pope, a charismatic personality of great piety, with his boundless energy and zest for travel was able to propagate both to the south and the north of the Alps the basic aim of the reform movement, to Christianise society by penetrating the world with the moral principles of the Church. This was part of a fundamental change of attitude on the part of the papacy and the episcopacy, of a move away 'from an inward and negative view towards the world into an outward and positive one'.[28] The Church was to become more conscious of its place in and its obligations to the external world. Part of this was a changed view of war. There were purposes for which fighting was a suitable instrument, not merely the 'just war' of St Augustine, but also 'holy wars', which could be undertaken either against non-Christians, or against Christians who were deemed to have offended in some way against the Church. The Peace of God and the Truce of God recognised the continuation of some warfare going on, but sought to limit the activity. The cultivation of a Christian knighthood aimed at drawing the nobility away from their traditional petty feuding into the service for a higher cause. This would at the same time allow its members to expiate their sins, or rather to be freed from penance for them by the grant of an indulgence. The long-established unarmed pilgrimage to the Holy Land could be supplemented by a kind of armed pilgrimage to help fellow Christians against the Muslims, or indeed – in the long term – to attempt the recovery of Palestine from the Arabs. The elements which were later combined into the crusades were thus present.

To some extent a more positive attitude to war is not surprising in the reform movement in view of its at times rather combative nature. Perhaps the development was also encouraged at the level of the papacy by the background of the popes Henry III selected, of noblemen presumably coming from a martial Germanic tradition and established in bishoprics. As deacon in the bishopric of Toul, the future Leo IX had led a military levy of his diocese in Italy, and as bishop he had mustered forces against the plunderers of church property. With 'impeccable religious credentials', he at the same time 'appeared to his contemporaries as a warlike shepherd.' Leo was not, like previous bishops and pontiffs, a warrior in spite of his spiritual office, but he 'was the first pope to derive the basis of his wars from religion, harmonizing them with the commands of the Church and infusing religious meaning into the warlike mentality of the army'.[29]

Before Leo could concentrate on his endeavours to reform the Church, he had to secure his position in Rome. A great coalition of the nobility led by the Tusculans, who were now apparently allied to their traditional enemies, the Crescentians, subjected Rome to daily attacks, without however being able to take the city. The pope found himself under pressure from the Romans to take strong action against the attackers, but as he was mainly concerned with destroying Benedict-Theophylact's claims to the papacy, he first attempted to have him tried by a synod for simony. When this way of proceeding failed because of the non-appearance of those cited, he anathemised them and took military action. In the interest of church reform Leo IX not merely fought a traditional campaign, but conducted a kind of holy war against the local enemies of his papacy.[30] From his period in Toul he was familiar with the practice of the Church of calling to arms men from various level of society and forming them into armies accompanied by priests carrying church flags, in order to fight those who broke the peace.[31] These measures were taken by the Church partly by default, for instance in France, because the secular power, whose monopoly the maintenance of law and order had largely been, often proved unable to act effectively. The reform papacy thus began to take advantage of this extension of the activities of the Church to encroach on the traditional secular sphere. With Leo's 'holy war', the age of the crusades is not far distant.

This use of novel methods does not mean, however, that from a practical point of view Leo always succeeded in his undertakings. In the Patrimony of St Peter, in spite of the employment of a formidable array of spiritual and martial weapons, Leo's 'campaign of devastation' of Tusculan territory could not break the resistance of Benedict and his friends. Eventually, when Leo needed a secure base in the Patrimony for his campaign against the Normans, he lifted the siege of the castles of the Tusculans and may have even allied with them for a time. But he seems to have remained convinced to the end that the transactions between Benedict and Gregory were tainted with simony.[32] Before we take leave of the Tusculan popes, the story that has been told makes it clear why they failed to receive credit for their achievements in looking after the Holy See at a difficult time from either the imperial or the papal side in the emerging conflict. The partisans of the Salian dynasty were not prepared to admit that the Tusculans, whom they displaced, had any real merit. The papal reform movement after 1046 was jealous of reforming precursors and would not recognise the concern the Tusculan popes had shown for the upholding of canon law and the activity they had displayed on the international scene.[33]

The new pope was a person of considerable education and culture, even if he was not a scholar of the first order. He was a fascinating personality, full of religious fervour and a preacher of extraordinary power. He gave the papacy an unprecedented exposure, making it into a truly international institution. Instead of regularly residing in Rome, he was almost constantly on the move. He crossed the Alps three times as pope, travelling not only within the territory of the Salian rulers, but to France and to Hungary. From 1050 to his death in 1054, Southern Italy required his presence annually. Leo to a considerable extent exercised direct supervision over the various parts of the Western Church, not always to the liking of the episcopate, both through developing a papal chancery and through personally presiding over synods. His intervention – above all against simony – was particularly strong in France, to the dismay of the king (who boycotted some of the papal endeavours), and to some extent in Italy. In the Salian dominions north of the Alps Leo relied mainly on the emperor's well-known opposition to simony.[34] He regarded this enhanced profile he gave to the papacy as necessary to infuse a new spirit into the Church not only to fight simony, to which his principal effort was directed, but also to curb priestly immorality and to strengthen celibacy. In the process the pope became comparable – certainly in his methods – to secular rulers, particularly as he did not shrink from warfare. Like every other ruler, he had to make hard choices and at times had to sacrifice justice to expediency, even if he conducted his military operations in the name of a 'holy war'. He was also the first pope whose personality could rival that of a Salian – or for that matter a Saxon – emperor. In some ways Leo outshone the able emperor who had himself nominated him to the Holy See. It is not out of the question that Henry began to feel a certain rivalry in his relationship with Leo, which may help to explain at least in part the disaster that eventually befell the pope in southern Italy, at any rate in worldly or material terms.

By the time Leo succeeded to the papacy, the Normans had made considerable progress in annexing Lombard territory, partly as a result of Henry III's action in allowing them to take over whatever they could conquer of the principality of Benevento. Initially, Leo did not adopt a hostile attitude to them and indeed in 1050 accepted their fealty on behalf of the emperor and himself. He certainly hoped to use them to reclaim papal jurisdiction for southern Italy from the Orthodox Church. In the long run, however, the pope could not ignore the complaints of the population about their treatment at the hands of their Norman conquerors, particularly as he – perhaps unwisely – accepted the lordship over Benevento which the inhabitants offered him. In any case this increased papal activity in the region fitted in with the forged *Donation of Constantine*, which provided the basis for claiming southern Italy for the Patrimony of St Peter. The Normans did not take lightly papal intervention in what they regarded as their domain, and relations between the two sides deteriorated so badly, possibly with infringements of papal territory, that Leo determined to attempt their expulsion from their dominions.

In spite of the many theological differences separating them, the pope wished to achieve his military objectives in alliance with Byzantium. He also sought help from the emperor. When Leo crossed the Alps in 1052 to discuss the matter with Henry, the emperor apparently took a favourable view of the pope's plans for an attack on the Normans. Henry, in return for papal counter-concessions, granted the pope the principality of Benevento and some other Italian possessions, either for himself or on behalf of the imperial power. Henry seems, however, to have been prevented by his chancellor, Bishop Gebhard of Eichstätt, ironically Leo's successor as pope, from making effective military help against the Normans available to the pontiff. Surely Henry could have had his own way and given more help, had he so wished. Possibly the emperor resented the independence the pope had displayed in his whole policy and was not too unhappy to see him checked. In the meantime Leo recruited knights from the East Frankish kingdom, whom he led to Southern Italy, together with some Italian troops he procured. Before he could achieve a junction with a Byzantine army, he was beaten in battle by the Normans near Civitate in the countship of Apulia in June 1053. The pope became their prisoner and was kept in honourable captivity at Benevento.

Leo's defeat was also a blow to Byzantine interests in the region. Thus an alliance between the papacy and Constantinople advocated by the local Byzantine commander in southern Italy appeared to have become even more necessary to the maintenance of Greek power. As the Byzantine emperor rightly regarded the restoration of harmony between the Western and Eastern Churches as a prerequisite for a political alliance, Leo from his captivity at Benevento despatched a mission to Constantinople in an effort to remove doctrinal obstacles to religious understanding. Unfortunately he chose as leader of the delegation the impetuous Cardinal Humbert of Silva Candida, who was accompanied by Cardinal Frederick of Lorraine. No more disastrous appointment could have been made. Although the papal legates were received with great friendliness by the Emperor Constantine IX, they soon ran into difficulty with the patriarch Kerullarios, who in no way yielded pride of place to Humbert in the vehemence and acrimony of his statements. The outcome was the famous mutual anathemisation by Humbert and Kerullarios in July 1054. In the end the emperor advised the legates to depart in the interest of their own safety. Humbert, by aggravating the tension with the Orthodox Church, certainly thwarted the pope's urgent need for a better understanding with Constantinople to help him in his Norman predicament. Although to speak of a final schism of the two churches overstates the position, still obviously considerable – while not irreparable – harm was done to their relations. Humbert's dramatic actions may well have lacked legal authority, for Pope Leo IX, who had sent the cardinal to Constantinople, had in the meantime died in Rome on 19 April 1054, shortly after his release from captivity, worn out by what he had gone through in the previous months. It is a moot point whether the legates were aware of this event towards the end of their mission.[35]

In spite of his reverses, Leo IX raised the papacy to new heights.

> He had manifested the authority of Rome north of the Alps, emphasised the binding power of canon law, given a new and dramatic life to the campaign against simony and clerical marriage, provided a startling precedent for papally conducted warfare, and set a stamp on future dealings with the Greek Church.[36]

He took great care to keep on good terms with the emperor, whom he supported for instance by excommunicating Godfrey of Lorraine in 1049. However, cracks in the relationship between the pope and the emperor were already beginning to appear. The lack of understanding over imperial military help for the pope against the Normans was a straw in the wind. The pope was beginning to act on his own as a ruler and as a commander on the European stage in a major way. But he was not an ordinary ruler, for he claimed special religious and moral authority as the successor of St Peter. Leo fought two 'holy wars', against the Tusculans and the Normans, not against 'infidels', but hierarchical wars in the direct service of the papacy. He personally supervised the various territorial churches, intervening in their affairs, at times to the vexation of local rulers and prelates. And – last not least – he drew tremendous strength from having taken over the leadership of the church reform movement, which directly or indirectly affected all the faithful. The theocratic emperor still had considerable powers, such as over the appointment of bishops, whom Henry III was able to recruit from the cathedral schools in which he took a strong interest.[37] But the papacy at the end of Leo IX's reign was becoming a serious challenger.

For the fourth time in his reign, Henry III had to nominate a successor to the papacy. The emperor chose his chancellor, Bishop Gebhard of Eichstätt. He was another of Henry's relatives, whom we encountered earlier as an opponent of an imperial expedition to help Leo IX against the Normans. Gebhard took the title of Victor II. The new pope 'secured from Henry a promise that he would render to St Peter what was rightly his'[38] and, although he had been connected with imperial policy more than his predecessor, vigorously pursued the cause of reform and generally kept on Leo IX's advisers.[39]

In Italy Henry III had lost an important supporter with the death in 1052 of the Margrave Boniface of the house of Canossa, who had been invested with Tuscany by Conrad II. Godfrey of Lorraine, at the end of 1054, without the emperor's permission, secretly married the margrave's widow Beatrice, though the union may not have been valid in canon law owing to too close a consanguinity.[40] He succeeded Boniface as the strongest ruler in central Italy. The match created immense problems for Henry III, who in 1055 undertook a military expedition to Italy. Beatrice and her daughter, the famous Countess Matilda of Tuscany of the following reign, before whose castle of Canossa Henry IV was to do penance to Pope Gregory VII in 1077, were imprisoned. Godfrey fled to Lorraine, where he began another rebellion against the emperor in alliance with Flanders.

Godfrey was not the only one plotting against the emperor in the Salian dominions. Henry's relations with his own appointees to duchies, such as with Conrad, the son of a Lotharingian count palatine, whom he had invested with the Bavarian duchy in 1049, were not always smooth. In 1053 Conrad was removed from his office by a court of princes for feuding with the Bishop of Regensburg, a relative of the Salian house. Conrad may well have resented Henry's close relations with the Bavarian bishops as diminishing his ducal authority.[41] It appears that Conrad had some support among the Bavarian nobility, who were also unhappy with Henry III's regime. After his displacement, Conrad fled to Hungary and raided imperial territory in alliance with the Hungarians. Worse was to come when in 1055 he plotted with Duke Welf III of Carinthia, another appointee of Henry III, and his erstwhile enemy, the Bishop of Regensburg, to overthrow the emperor.

Henry was forced to come back from Italy to deal with the conspiracy, which, however, collapsed with the deaths of the two secular magnates,[42] before it could become even more dangerous through the involvement of Godfrey of Lorraine, who now decided to surrender to the emperor. This submission was all the more important, as relations between the two kingdoms that had arisen from the Frankish monarchy were deteriorating at this time. A meeting between Henry III and the Capetian King of France, Henry I, in May 1056 led to the termination of their alliance and to a breach between them. While the sources are not clear on the reasons for the friction, it appears that the French ruler was making some claims to Lotharingia. Henry I was probably displeased with the emperor's support for reforming popes who were interfering with the French Church and royal rights over it. Characteristically, Henry III offered to settle the dispute through an ordeal by battle, which the King of France refused.[43]

The flare-up of hostility in the Salian kingdom illuminates the continuing antagonism between the central and particularist powers, which was to remain a theme of German history and which had not been removed by the apparent victory of the royal monarchy. If the Ottonian structure enabled the Salian regime to survive the strain of civil war, this was above all due to the bishops, who proved to be reliable pillars of the existing order. Thus the investiture conflict in the following reign, which called into question the right of the king and emperor to nominate to bishoprics that had not been affected by the campaign against simony, struck at the very roots of the whole system of government.

These matters were, however, not yet acute when Henry III died in October 1056, aged only 39, his health possibly having been weakened for many years by the exposure to the epidemic in Italy during 1038 to which his first wife had fallen victim. Already in 1045, Henry had been close to death. Thus he did not have enough resistance to withstand infection when he again found himself in a malaria area in Italy in 1055 during the campaign.[44]

Henry III left a son of just under six years of age to succeed him. The princes had elected the future Henry IV king in 1053, but had apparently made their future obedience dependent on just rule. In view of this reservation, the emperor on his death-bed asked all the princes present to repeat the election of his son as king. Among these happened to be Pope Victor II, who was at the court to prepare a solution of the Norman question, and who participated as Bishop of Eichstätt. The emperor asked the pope to give his special protection to the heir to the throne. The early death of Henry III and the succession of a small boy have been called a major catastrophe.[45] This has to be taken into account in an assessment of the emperor.

Under Henry III, the emperorship reached the apex of its power through achieving supremacy both in the secular sphere of the Salian dominions and the spiritual sphere of the Western Church. But cracks were already appearing in the magnificent edifice. In response to the campaign against simony, Henry agreed to a considerable weakening of royal and imperial authority by forgoing the levying of fees for ecclesiastical investitures. This in turn forced him to augment his financial levies on the laity, further increasing ducal and noble dissatisfaction with his rule, which was reflected in frequent and often dangerous rebellions. There was already some questioning of Henry's theocracy. It has been argued that it was not least through the mistakes of his policy that the four powers arose that were to bring calamity to his successor: the opposition of the Saxon and south German lay aristocracy, the connection of Lorraine with Tuscany, a papacy claiming increased independence and the consolidation of Norman rule in southern Italy.[46] As to the first, the lay aristocracy was bound to adopt a negative attitude to any attempt by the king to strengthen central authority at the expense of particularist powers. In dealing with Godfrey of Lorraine, Henry was on the horns of a dilemma, for on the one hand he could not let him become too powerful, but on the other if he tried to restrain him, he could not avoid incurring his hostility. Could at least part of the difficulty in the case of Henry III – like that of Louis the Pious – have been that the appeal to religious values and the granting of forgiveness sometimes obstructed a sober appraisal of political and military realities?

Henry cannot be made entirely responsible for the increasing hold of the Normans on Southern Italy, for which Leo IX's rashness may have been more to blame. At the same time, with hindsight, it can perhaps be argued that Henry ought to have tried to control papal military plans more closely and possibly to provide Leo with substantial aid against the Normans. However, the increasing emancipation of the popes from imperial tutelage may at least partly explain the reluctance of the imperial authorities to intervene effectively in southern Italy in support of Leo IX. It is, indeed, true that Henry III set in train the process of strengthening the papacy by nominating at least one outstanding pontiff, Leo IX. But, in selecting candidates of quality for the most important spiritual office in Western Christendom, he was only doing what could be expected from a conscientious and profoundly religious ruler concerned with the well-being of the Church, both at the level of the papacy and in his territories. To claim that he was neglecting 'German' interests is to put a completely unhistorical interpretation on his actions.[47] In any case in some ways the personalities of the period were merely responding to the dynamic of the age,[48] such as the impact of literacy.[49] The balance between emperors and popes was in the long run likely to be affected by the new strength gained for the Church and the papacy by Leo IX, even if its effect was for the time being masked by the general atmosphere of cooperation between them.

Even if there had not been a minority, there would have been enough problems in the Salian Empire during the period after 1056 to tax the ability of the strongest ruler, for the middle of the eleventh century was a time of great changes in many spheres. Thanks to the cessation of invasions from outside after the troubles of the tenth century, and to the large measure of stability provided by the Saxon and Salian rulers, there was a growth of population, accommodated by intensive clearance of forests for the purpose of cultivation and aided by technological improvement. On the eastern borders of the Salian Empire north of the Alps, Slav territories were colonised and the inhabitants Christianised. This opened up great opportunities to enterprising noblemen to establish themselves on virgin soil. The increase in agricultural output made possible the emergence and growth of cities, thus supplying a ready market for the produce from the countryside. The cities generally had good facilities for education, and cathedral schools, which 'were emerging as a major intellectual force',[50] took over to some extent the teaching role of the monasteries. The increase in transcontinental trade enhanced the importance of many cities, in particularly in Italy, leading to the establishment of communes with elected officers that frequently superseded the secular authority of the bishop.

These developments, although not uniformly favouring one side, certainly contributed to a change in the balance of strength between empire and papacy. The disintegration of imperial control south of the Alps was hastened, though in the north of Italy the cities, or some factions in them, provided a reservoir of potential allies for the emperor. For the papacy, the increasing independence as well as political volatility of civic ruling circles in the peninsula made it more difficult to function in Rome, forcing it for whole periods at a time to operate from what has been called a travelling household.[51] But the instability of the age also provided the appropriate setting for the parties of movement, such as that propagating church reform, in which the papacy took the lead.

The expanding role of money brought about by the growth in economic activity affected the Church in numerous ways. Without material prosperity, the building of architecturally impressive cathedrals, as well as pilgrimages to the Holy Land, and eventually the crusades, could not have been financed. But at the same time, there was a religious reaction against the commercial and careerist atmosphere in the city on the part of some of the orders, like the Cistercians and the Premonstratensians.

Last, but not least, there was 'an apparent link between the growing concern about simony and the rise of a money economy'.[52] With an increasing emphasis on a money economy, the transactions associated for instance with the investiture of bishops could more easily assume the appearance of simoniacal dealings. The question of simony and the related matter of lay investiture was to loom large in the dispute between the papacy and Henry IV. In this state of flux, the situation became even more volatile owing to the removal of the firm hand of the greatest ruler in Western Christendom and the succession of a small boy. At the same time the papacy became increasingly assertive in leading the church reform movement.

Such fundamental adjustments as the movement of population from the countryside to the cities in turn brought about considerable social change. There were economic and social winners and losers. Some of the population exchanged the comparative security of their ancestral villages for poverty in the city, instead of the improvement in their situation which they hoped to find there. This kind of 'pauperism' was a new problem for the period.

The beginning of the reign of Henry IV showed no signs of the tensions between the Salian rulers and the papacy that were to come. The regent, the widowed Empress Agnes, the young king's mother, was deeply pious and a devout churchwoman.[53] In turn, Pope Victor II did his best to justify the confidence that Henry III had shown him on his death-bed and has been called 'the heir to the imperial policy'.[54] But he followed the emperor into the grave within a few months, terminating the series of imperial nominees from the East Frankish dominions to the papacy and putting an end to the close cooperation between pontiff and emperor.

A royal minority was not anything new in the East Frankish, Teutonic kingdom. During the time of the Saxon dynasty, Otto III was able to take over a well functioning monarchy after a minority, thanks to the remarkable ability shown by his two regents, his mother Theophanu and – after her death – his grandmother Adelaide. The latter had herself been a ruler before her marriage to Otto the Great. Theophanu had clearly learned a great deal about politics before her marriage by closely studying the happenings at the Byzantine court where she grew up. Unfortunately, Agnes does not appear to have been properly initiated into the affairs of the Salian monarchy by her husband. She was invested with the duchy of Bavaria by Henry III, but it is not clear whether she concerned herself much with its administration. However, when compared with events during her son's active reign, the regent does not appear to have done too badly.

The young king reached his majority in 1065 at the age of 15, profoundly influenced by the unfortunate experiences of his minority, and especially by his being kidnapped from his mother's care by Archbishop Anno of Cologne in 1062. In those years, when he was not yet his own master, but during which it was valuable to have control over him, he may well have learned to dissemble when necessary, an art he was to practise later to escape from situations in which he found himself cornered. The lesson he learned from the uncertainties of his childhood was a determination to strengthen the authority of the ruler to the utmost.

By the early 1070s Henry was able to formulate his own policies and to attempt to put them into practice. His foremost objective initially was to regain the rights the crown had lost during his minority. He began by strengthening his hold on Saxony, where he reclaimed lands that had at one time belonged to the Salian dynasty as heir to the Ottonians, and where he built castles to dominate the region. His long-term plan was to make of the Saxon duchy something like a *Reichsland* under the direct control of the king. All these activities, however logical they were, and whatever parallels they had at the time and were to have in other European kingdoms, were bound to stir up the opposition not only of vested interests, but even more widely of a people proud of its tradition. The Saxon nobles found their powers reduced. Resentment was caused by the king continuing his grandfather's policy of using as *ministeriales* in his service, men of low social origin, often previously unfree, who received the right to bear arms. The change in the social order marked by this development, which widely substituted the criterion of professional function for that of traditional right, also brought about with it the reduction to serfdom of free peasants who did not manage to enter the knighthood. Thus not only the Saxon nobility, but also the peasants resented the king's activities in the duchy. Further more Henry, from a position of comparative weakness after a minority, was seeking a radical solution not only to perennial difficulties with Saxony, but to the wider general problem of the king's relations with the stem duchies and their dukes, whom he wished to bring under greater royal control.

In the summer of 1073 a rebellion against Henry broke out in Saxony, led by the duke and supported by the high nobility, most bishops, and the peasantry. The nobles demanded the destruction of all the fortifications Henry had built, the restitution of the lands they had lost, the dismissal of what they perceived as his unworthy advisers and their restoration to his councils. The king rejected the ultimatum and fled to the Harzburg, the almost impenetrable fortification he had erected close to the royal residence at Goslar. There he was surrounded by his enemies, but still managed to elude them, in the first of several extremely hazardous escapes that were to mark his reign. The peasants wished to continue their resistance to the king. But the aristocratic leaders were not interested in strengthening the position of the peasants at their own expense. Peace was therefore concluded between the Saxon nobility and the king in February 1074. Only the Harzburg was exempted from a general razing of the royal fortifications in Saxony and Thuringia laid down in the treaty. But the peasants regarded the Harzburg as a symbol of their oppression by the king. Without the knowledge of the aristocratic leadership they stormed and destroyed the unguarded castle, plundered the royal graves, scattering their remains, and burned down the castle church. These wanton acts led to a reaction in the king's favour. Henry was now able to declare an imperial war against Saxony and to assemble a large army against the rebels, who were defeated in June 1075. Even then the insurgents fought on for a time, but in October they surrendered and the ringleaders were imprisoned. Henry was at the height of his power, but he was about to face an even more dangerous foe, Pope Gregory VII.

The struggle between Henry IV and Gregory VII that was to follow cannot be grasped either in the context of a contest between 'church and state', or simply as an encounter between a national secular and a higher international spiritual authority (as indeed the pope liked to have it represented). As to the former, there were at that time no clear boundary lines between 'church' and 'state', and between the secular and the ecclesiastical or spiritual sphere. Henry IV stood in the Ottonian-Salian tradition of sacral kingship, thus in his understanding of his own position transcending the purely secular. At the same time, Gregory VII did not see the papacy as confined to the purely spiritual domain, on the model of the Carolingian pope whom Charlemagne expected to pray while he himself went to war. Not only did Gregory claim a monopoly of spiritual authority for the Church, but he also asserted the superiority of the ecclesiastical over the secular power, of the papacy over worldly rulers. In the case of the relations of the curia with the East Frankish – Teutonic – kings and emperors, this was a complete breach with tradition. For the Frankish, East Frankish or Teutonic king, particularly once he had been crowned emperor – also partly in his capacity of *patricius* – acquired certain rights in connection with the nomination and election of popes. He was traditionally the protector of the papacy, heir to the Lombard (Langobard) crown, and – again as *patricius* – held some authority in Rome itself. Gregory used theological arguments to override custom. He claimed that he was simply restoring the position that ought to have prevailed all along, for which he quoted Biblical authority, sincerely but selectively, interpreting the Holy Script on the basis of certain assumptions he made. For a long time papal assertions of their rights in these matters had been largely on paper. But now a strong personality had ascended the papal throne who was determined to translate theory into practice. How was something within the realm of possibility in the 1070s which would have been considered completely unrealistic less than two decades previously?

The changed balance of power between the Teutonic rulers and the popes was due to the weakness of the former and the increasing strength of the latter in the years following the death of Henry III in 1056. The authority of the Frankish, East Frankish and Teutonic kings and emperors had to be demonstrated constantly not only to the north, but also to the south of the Alps, for otherwise there was the danger of its falling into abeyance, or at the very least of becoming harder to enforce. The full realisation of their prerogatives required a monarch who combined superb statesmanship and generalship with robust and continuing health. Before a new ruler could set out for Italy to make his influence felt there in the Lombard kingdom in the north, in Rome and in the south of Italy, he had to achieve stability at home. An unduly prolonged absence south of the Alps might be too much of a temptation to resist for unruly elements bent on boosting their position. A minority was liable to lead to a weakening of the Teutonic position in Italy, for a boy ruler could neither give help to the papacy and to potential allies in the peninsula, nor inspire the necessary awe.

In 1057, after the death of Victor II, the last of the popes to work in close cooperation with the emperors, the reformers in the curia were determined to prevent the papacy from again becoming the prize in a power struggle between various Roman factions, including the Tusculans. So far the reformers had been quite prepared to work with the Teutonic emperors to deal with abuses in the church and to improve clerical standards. But at this time the regent, the Empress-widow Agnes, pious though she was, could not spare any resources for the Church, as she had her hands full with problems north of the Alps. The only potentate with the military means of helping the papacy was the late emperor's enemy, Godfrey, Duke of Lorraine, who was married to Beatrice, the Margravine of Tuscany. The reformers therefore elected as pope Godfrey's brother Frederick, Abbot of Monte Cassino, who took the name of Stephen IX, and later also picked his two successors, Nicholas II and Alexander II, who were chosen from the Tuscan episcopate. The empress recognised Stephen as pope, though she had not been consulted about his election. Thanks to the intervention of Hildebrand, the later Pope Gregory VII, Agnes in 1058 also supported Nicholas, elected at Siena against the Tusculan candidate, who had been chosen earlier in Rome, the proper venue for this act. By meeting outside Rome, the reformers thus set aside custom in the interest of a greater cause, that of securing the freedom of the Church from local Roman influences.

The decree issued by Nicholas II in 1059 on procedures for papal elections followed the ideas of the reforming circle. Its purpose was both to regularise Nicholas' election and to establish a mode of election to the papacy which conformed to the general principles of canonical elections. The decree is not to be understood in the sense of a modern election, so there is no specific body of electors. It was rather similar to the traditional ritual for king-making, with the three stages of designation, acceptance and acclamation. The cardinal-bishops (the senior level of cardinals) designated, the rest of the cardinal-priests accepted and were followed by the Roman clergy, and the outcome was acclaimed by the Roman people. In case of any substantial threat to the freedom of election in the city, the cardinal-bishops were entitled to arrange for the election to be held outside Rome; the new pontiff was to have full authority even before his formal enthronement in Rome. It is generally agreed that the decree aimed at making the papacy independent of Roman factions.[55]

Pope Nicholas II, partly to rid himself of the anti-pope who maintained himself close to Rome, also took another step to strengthen the position of the papacy in Central Italy, by coming to terms with the Norman rulers in southern Italy. In 1059 these swore oaths of fealty to the pope and in return received from him as vassals not only the territories they had already sub-jugated, but also prospectively Sicily, should they be able to conquer the island from the Saracens. These arrangements affected the Salian rulers at least in two ways. First of all, they were designed to make the popes independent of the protection they had traditionally received from the Frankish and then the East Frankish – Teutonic kings. Secondly, they inter-fered with imperial titles in southern Italy. The papacy made up for its lack of any basis in feudal law for disposing of southern Italy by deriving its rights directly from the religious sphere. The Norman ruler Robert Guiscard, when later rejecting Henry IV's claims to overlordship, is reported to have replied that, in order to obtain God's help and the intercession of Saints Peter and Paul, he had subjected himself to their vicar the pope, and had thus achieved his victories. 'A daring metamorphosis equated public law and religion, politics and piety. What need of a special legal title when such motives were present?'[56] The Sicilian campaign had aspects of a 'holy war' under papal auspices.

The Normans, whose duties as vassals were to protect the Patrimony of St Peter and the papacy in general, proceeded to break into the strongholds of the anti-pope and delivered him to Nicholas as a prisoner. So long as the curia could rely on Norman support (which was not always the case), it could dispense with the traditional protectorship of the East Frankish Teutonic rulers. The papacy had also in one fell swoop acquired the overlordship over a considerable part of Italy. Although the intention was not necessarily to exclude Henry IV's feudal rights, the papal deal with the Normans may well have led to a deterioration of Agnes' relations with the curia at the end of Nicholas' reign. Whatever the reason, in 1061 the election of Alexander II, the choice of the reformers, was not accepted by the then ruling circles at Henry IV's court, who put up an anti-pope. However the kidnapping of the young king by Archbishop Anno of Cologne, a supporter of church reform, led to a change of policy and to acceptance of Alexander II. During his pontificate, the Byzantine Empire lost its final foothold in Southern Italy and the Normans began their conquest of Sicily from the Muslims.

In the final years of Alexander's reign, papal relations with Henry IV's court again took a turn for the worse. This was due to the crisis in Milan, where a 'half ecclesiastical, half socio-popular movement'[57] called the Pataria, attempted to eliminate married and simoniac clergy, if necessary by the use of force. The papacy under Alexander II, with the encouragement of Hildebrand, not only, as was to be expected, supported the objectives of the party, but even endorsed its revolutionary methods. Alexander bestowed on its military leader a victory banner, the *Vexillum Sancti Petri*. This struggle rather neatly fitted into one of the three categories for which a holy war could be fought, a 'war within the church for religious and moral aims and in behalf of ecclesiastical factions'; the other two were a war against the heathen, and – ever since Leo IX – 'the "hierarchical" war in the direct service of the papacy or the Papal States'.[58] In 1072 the papacy backed the Patarine candidate for the archbishopric of Milan against the prelate invested by Henry IV.[59] As Henry adhered to his choice, Alexander at the Easter synod in 1073, shortly before his death, excommunicated under the accusation of simony five royal counsellors for their part in the investiture of the king's candidate for the Milan archbishopric.[60] Thus, by the time Alexander died in April 1073, an actual conflict was in progress, which brought to the surface different conceptions of the relative roles of the Salian rulers and the popes that were difficult to reconcile.

Alexander II's successor was Hildebrand, his closest adviser, who took the name of Gregory VII, presumably mainly modelling himself on Gregory I, the Great, but also bearing in mind the ill-fated Gregory VI whom he had accompanied, as his chaplain, into exile in Germany after his deposition. Hildebrand was proclaimed pope by the Roman people in the Lateran Church during the funeral of Alexander II, and only afterwards formally elected by the cardinals and the city clergy, not exactly in accordance with Nicholas II's election decree. Whatever view is taken of Gregory VII's exercise of his high office, the strength of his personality and the intensity of his spirituality stand out. Few popes, indeed few rulers, have left their mark in history to the same extent. Gregory VII was the greatest of the remarkable circle of reformers that Leo IX had assembled around him. He was a complex personality. In history he has gone down mainly as the fervent and uncompromising believer in the superiority of the ecclesiastical over the secular power, as well as in the central role of the papacy. What has not been sufficiently emphasised is that for tactical reasons on some occasions he was prepared to forgo or delay the application of his principles. 'The controversial question how far his motives were religious and how far political is virtually insoluble, since both motives merged in him; his politics were religious, and his religion political.'[61] Some of these tensions are reflected in Peter Damian (who had to be compelled to abandon his life as a hermit to become a cardinal bishop) regarding Gregory as a 'holy devil'.[62] The pope was capable both of the highest idealism and of plain resort to expediency. His inconsistencies, his strong temperament and, at times, his temper were very human.

Like Leo IX, Gregory VII was well versed in raising soldiers, an activity in which he had been engaged while papal archdeacon during various troubles in Rome. He endowed the phrase of the *militia Christi* with a mainly military, rather than its previously primarily spiritual meaning, and gave currency to the concept of a knighthood of St Peter, a *militia sancti Petri*, under the direct control of the papacy. He was prepared to carry on a papally controlled holy war against the enemies of the curia, wherever they were to be found, whether it was against the King of France, or against Henry IV, or against the Normans if need be. All this was part of a move away from a primarily other-worldly attitude of the Church, to a strong concern with what was happening here and now. Incidentally, reliance was no longer put so much in kings, and it was useful to the papacy to be able to mobilise other social strata, such as the knights, in its support.

As was to be expected, the new pope stepped up his predecessors' efforts against simony. But, particularly for a man of his fervent personality, he initially showed remarkable forbearance with regard to the way the Salian rulers handled ecclesiastical appointments in their own kingdom, which he was to call *regnum teutonicorum*, as opposed to those in Burgundy and Italy. This fitted in with his policy of treating Henry IV as one of many Christian kings, rather than as heir to the wider role in Western Christendom played by his predecessors. Gregory quite deliberately introduced the terms *rex teutonicus* and *regnum teutonicorum* not previously much in use.[63] In a rather curious way, Gregory is thus of one of the sponsors of the early antecedents of what was later on to become Germany.

For a time after Gregory's accession in 1073, his relations with Henry IV seemed to be good. The pope even informed Henry that he would ask him to look after the interests of the Church while he was away on his planned campaign to the Near East, which he wanted to command in person, to recover territory lost to the Muslims. Actually the expedition was never undertaken, because of Gregory's more urgent preoccupations, later on above all with his struggle against Henry. In the early days of his pontificate, the pope misinterpreted the comparative calm, which was due to the king's usual inclination to fight one enemy at a time and to dissemble to others before he was ready to strike. Gregory's misjudgment that he could rely on Henry's meekness helps to explain the tone of the letter he sent to the king and which, together with a verbal message, was delivered by a papal embassy on New Year's Day, 1076. The pontiff gave the king his apostolic blessing only on condition that Henry obeyed his demands, which were that he should do contrite penance for his dealings with the excommunicated royal counsellors; otherwise he would exclude him from the community of the Church. Gregory registered an energetic protest against Henry's audacity in instituting an archbishop in Milan and some bishops elsewhere in Italy. The whole emphasis in the letter was on the papal demand for the strict obedience which the king owed him as the successor of St Peter. Christ had entrusted his herd to the pope and had given him the power, from which not even kings were exempt, to bind and to loose in heaven as on earth.[64]

Not surprisingly, Henry refused to accept the subordination of his kingship to the supreme authority of the pope, which was quite unprecedented and had never been demanded before. In resisting the papal ultimatum, he was supported by many of the imperial bishops, largely drawn from the high nobility, who resented the increased enforcement of papal primacy resulting in a degree of central control they regarded as unacceptable. At a synod at Worms attended by the majority of the German episcopate soon afterwards, feelings against the pontiff were even further inflamed by slanderous accusations against the pope made by Hugh Candidus,[65] a cardinal-priest who had abandoned Gregory VII early in his pontificate.[66] In any case, Henry decided to give up the conciliatory policy towards Gregory he had followed earlier, partly in the hope of securing the imperial coronation from another pope, after Gregory's deposition. In these moves he was motivated in some ways by a desire to control the kingdom of Italy, which was also an aim of the papacy. 'Henry persuaded or compelled his bishops to renounce their obedience to the pope.'[67] The king himself wrote to 'the monk Hildebrand' demanding his abdication and called on the clergy and people of the Roman Church to depose the pope.

Gregory's response was not long in coming. At the Roman synod in February 1076, he solemnly excommunicated the king and all the bishops who had voluntarily signed the Worms declaration, probably suspended rather than deposed the king[68] and absolved his subjects from their allegiance.[69] While Henry IV's predecessors had removed popes, there was no precedent for a pope on his own initiative displacing an East Frankish or Teutonic ruler. However, even if Henry IV's father had dethroned popes, that does not mean that his son was necessarily wise to follow in his footsteps in an entirely different situation and also without appropriate follow-up. For the power of the papacy and its relative strength in proportion to that of the Salian rulers had increased considerably since the days of Sutri in 1046; moreover Henry III had to deal with a schism and had gone to Italy in person to lend weight to his decisions. Henry IV overrated his own influence and underrated that of Gregory VII if he believed that he could simply decree the latter's dismissal from his position by a stroke of the pen. At any rate, a struggle was begun which was to continue between the two protagonists until Gregory's death in 1085, and which proved to be the beginning of a number of bitter conflicts between popes and emperors. The period of close cooperation between the popes and the Frankish, then the East Frankish and eventually the Teutonic rulers, which had begun in the reign of Pippin III in the second half of the eighth century, was abruptly brought to a close. The harmony between the secular and the ecclesiastical power, which – even if not always practiced – had been the ideal, was over.

Even more than the details of the struggle, the essential ones of which are in any case quite well known, the comparative effectiveness of secular and spiritual weapons, as well as the relative strengths of Henry and Gregory, are of interest to us in our context. The outcome was not predetermined from the beginning, and there were many ups and downs for each side. At first, the excommunication of Henry as well as of the bishops supporting him, coupled with the deposition or suspension of the king, appeared to have had more effect than the measures taken against Gregory. Very skilfully, the pope had left the way open for bishops who had second thoughts about the Worms declaration, and soon most of them had gone over to Gregory. The pope's absolution of the king's vassals from their fealty to him provided an opportunity for the many enemies Henry had at home to come out into the open against him. Saxony rebelled once more, under the leadership of the able Otto of Northeim, soon supported by the south German princely opposition. At Tribur, near Mainz, in October 1076 the election of a new king, which was demanded by his more radical adversaries, was only prevented by the resistance of the papal legates. The papacy was more interested at that stage in the submission of the old than the enthronement of a new king, which points to Gregory's earlier pronouncement having been a suspension rather than deposition. Henry was forced to take an oath that he would dismiss the banned counsellors, render to the pope the obedience due to him and do penance. The princes, however, resolved not to maintain their recognition of Henry as king if he continued to be under excommunication for longer than a year. They invited Gregory to an imperial assembly to be held in Augsburg early in February 1077 to settle their dispute with Henry. This formula allowed the alliance of the papacy with the opposition princes, which had already begun to drift apart, to coalesce once more. Gregory was delighted to be asked to arbitrate, for this would allow him to assume a position above the parties and to demonstrate that the successor to St Peter was the supreme judge in the Catholic world.

For Henry, the position could not have been more serious. The pope refused to receive him in Rome, and indeed at once proceeded north on his way to Augsburg. But Gregory was never to play his allotted part there, for Henry forestalled him. The king quickly realised that the only way out of his predicament was to appear before the pope in person as a penitent before the date fixed for the meeting of the Augsburg assembly, to seek an absolution which in these circumstances Gregory would find it hard to refuse. It was therefore important for him to intercept the pope in Italy before he had crossed the Alps. In spite of great difficulties, the king with his wife and their three-year-old son carried out the dangerous journey across the mountains in the middle of winter. When Gregory heard that Henry was approaching, he sought refuge in the castle of his leading supporter, the Margravine Matilda of Tuscany, at Canossa. The pope reported that Henry 'for three days [25–7 January 1077]...remained before the castle gate, without any royal ornament, pitiful in appearance, barefoot and clad in woollen garments, and he continued tearfully to beg for apostolic help and consolation'.[70]

Gregory was in a dilemma. In order to achieve his aims to the full, his best course was to defer absolution until he had arbitrated at Augsburg. But excommunication, though at times used to enforce policies, was primarily a spiritual measure against a particular person. As the supreme shepherd of the sheep on earth, the pope could hardly refuse absolution to a contrite penitent. Otherwise he would incur the suspicion of vengefulness and political calculation. In the castle, not only the Margravine Matilda, but also Henry's mother-in-law Adelaide of Turin, and his godfather Abbot Hugh of Cluny all appealed to Gregory's mercy on behalf of the king, to which the pope eventually yielded, though with some reluctance. On the third day, Gregory lifted Henry's excommunication and restored him to communion. But did the pope also reinstate the penitent ruler in his kingship? Unfortunately pope and king differed in their interpretation of the practical effects of what had in fact taken place at Canossa. Gregory regarded the events as a preliminary to his arbitrating the affairs of the Teutonic kingdom at an imperial assembly north of the Alps. But Henry was of the opinion that, as he had met the condition of the princes (to have the papal ban lifted within a year), his right to the throne could no longer be questioned. In spite of undertakings to the contrary and thus demonstrating his continued unreliability, Henry put every obstacle in the way of the pope's visit to the Teutonic kingdom. Canossa therefore did not lead to a settlement. It was merely to be a stage in a conflict between the Teutonic rulers and the papacy that was to continue, albeit with some interruption, until the final defeat of the Staufen dynasty in the third quarter of the thirteenth century. Henry gained an advantage in the short run. But by humbling himself in front of the pope he paid a heavy price in terms of the long-term future by disturbing the aura of sacrality that had hitherto surrounded the Carolingian, Saxon and Salian kingship and emperorship, thus undermining its claim to theocracy.

The comparative effectiveness of spiritual and secular weapons in the struggle between emperor and pope is of great interest to us in connection with the theme of this book. In view of the existing, widespread disaffection with the king, Gregory's initial excommunication of Henry in 1076 proved very effective, particularly through absolving his subjects from their loyalty to him. Undeterred by the revocation of the excommunication and by the opposition of the papal legates (who still wanted the pope to arbitrate), the princely opposition proceeded to the election of an anti-king, Rudolf of Rheinfelden, Duke of Swabia, Henry's brother-in-law. Even without direct papal support, resistance to Henry in the Teutonic kingdom proved formidable. However, to anticipate a situation in which Gregory might, after all, have to recognise Henry formally as king, the pope in November 1078 issued a decree that no clerk was allowed to receive investiture of a bishopric, abbey or church from any emperor, king or other lay person. 'The new decree would protect the imperial Church from any future relapse into simony on his [Henry IV's] part.'[71]

In spite of some military defeats, Henry early in 1080 felt strong enough for a fresh show-down with the pope in order to bring to an end a civil war which took a severe toll of the country. He demanded that the pope put the anti-king under the ban of the Church and, in case of Gregory's refusal, threatened the election of an anti-pope. Gregory responded by excommunicating Henry once more and bestowing the Teutonic and Italian kingdoms on Rudolf. Henry summoned a synod of German and Italian bishops at Brixen, which in June 1080 deposed Gregory. By virtue of his authority as *patricius*, Henry appointed as pope Wibert, who had been removed by Gregory as Archbishop of Ravenna and put under the ban; the anti-pope took the title of Clement III. There were now two kings and two popes. In October 1080 the anti-king died from wounds received in a battle he had won against Henry. Although somewhat later a new anti-king, Hermann of Salm, from the house of the Counts of Luxemburg, was elected, the death of the widely respected Rudolf proved a severe loss for the princely opposition.

In the spring of 1081 the time had come for Henry to attack his archenemy on his home territory. But Gregory stood his ground in Rome and it was only at the third attempt in the spring of 1084 that Henry succeeded in taking parts of the city, including St. Peter's, where the anti-pope was installed and crowned Henry emperor. Henry's triumph was short-lived, for the Normans at last responded to Gregory's cry for help. Robert Guiscard had been waging a campaign to conquer Constantinople. This had brought the Byzantine Emperor and Henry closer together, so that Robert feared an alliance between them that might dislodge him from his possessions in southern Italy. Guiscard's impending approach made Henry beat a hasty retreat from Rome, which left the Romans, including his supporters, at the mercy of the Normans. In May 1084 Robert freed the pope, who had been restricted to Castel St, Angelo. Tragically, the Normans and their Saracen auxiliaries plundered, burned and ravaged the city when they encountered resistance, and sold numerous men, women and children into slavery. By this time, Gregory through his autocracy and intransigence had lost the support of many of the cardinals. The conduct of his allies made it unsafe for Gregory to remain in the city. The pope accompanied the Norman troops to Salerno, where he died in May 1085. His last words are reported to have been: 'I have loved righteousness and hated iniquity – therefore I die in exile.'[72]

The fight to the finish between Henry IV and Gregory VII was the first controversy in the medieval Christian world in which the propaganda conducted by both sides played an important part. While the contribution made at this time to political and theological thought should not be underrated, the ferocity and fanaticism of the debate with its oversimplification provided a bitter legacy for the future. During these beginnings of a public debate a pattern of intolerance was set. Each side had a fervent belief in the right-eousness of its cause and the immorality and even satanical nature of its opponents. These attitudes made any settlement of the conflict extremely difficult and led to its prolongation, exacting its toll of destruction and casualties on the way.

Why did the dispute between Henry IV and Gregory VII develop into an all-out struggle to the bitter end, in which no compromise proved possible? That this was so was at least in part due to the unhappy interaction of the personalities of the two key figures who – however different they were in other ways – shared a most unfortunate impetuosity. This made them take snap decisions on questions of great importance on the spur of the moment, without full consideration of the consequences. That is apparent, for instance, in Henry's hasty reaction to the pope's communication delivered on New Year's Day 1076, and in turn in Gregory's suspension of the king which followed. However, the sequence of these fateful events was provoked by the unprecedented and unacceptable manner of the pontiff's commun-ication to the king. While Nicholas II and Alexander II had already done much to strengthen the power of the curia in relation to the Teutonic kings, their successor, Gregory VII, staked out claims for the papacy which cannot be seen simply as a continuation and intensification of their policy, but broke new ground altogether.

As evidenced by the *dictatus papae*, his memorandum on the rights of the papacy,[73] Gregory was convinced not only of the superiority of the spiritual to the secular power in general, but also quite specifically of the, in many ways, unlimited power of the pope not only over bishops, but also over kings. The attempt to establish the primacy of the Bishop of Rome among the bishops of the Catholic and, if possible, the Orthodox Church is a continua-tion of the traditional policy of the curia. But the endeavour to give practical effect to the well-established teaching of the superiority of the spiritual over the secular power by asserting a general papal authority over kings and emperors was quite different from what had gone on before and amounted to an attempt at a radical rearrangement of relationships. Gregory VII had a utopian view of the power of the papacy which he wanted to turn at once into reality. Impatient with the elliptical and allegorical language based on biblical quotation in which papal claims had so far been couched, and which left room for negotiation, Gregory spelled out his demands to Henry with the utmost clarity. Unless it can be assumed that the pope was at that early stage wanting to pick a quarrel, which is unlikely, the tone of his message was based on a misjudgment of the situation at Henry's court. Obviously, in hindsight, it was clear that he had misinterpreted the earlier submissive style of the king's communications. Henry was prepared to say anything to the pope so long as he had his hands full with the Saxons. That he misled the pope is only one example of the trouble that arose from his frequently practiced dissembling.

When it comes to matters of substance, a major point at issue between pope and king was the relative influence each was going to have over the (Lombard) kingdom of Italy. The test case was Milan and the question whether it was the pope, in pursuit of his primacy and his natural interest in northern Italy, or the Teutonic king, who was going to have the decisive say in the election of an archbishop. Investiture came into it, but not initially as the kind of overriding principle it was to become later. In many ways it was a practical matter over which accommodation was not impossible to achieve. Henry may well have exacerbated tensions by twice investing archbishops in Milan, who were both contested.

In the struggle between them, neither king nor pope could count on the loyalty of all who owed them obedience. This was partly due to the fact that both encountered considerable opposition in their own ranks owing to their centralising tendencies, which weakened them in their struggle with their main antagonist. During the earlier, decisive periods this was probably less damaging for the pope than for the king. But towards the end of his reign Gregory was seriously handicapped by the dissatisfaction of many cardinals with his refusal to compromise. Gregory does not seem to have been successful in carrying a united curia with him. Perhaps the inspiration he felt as the vicar on earth of St Peter and St Paul, and indeed of Christ, did not allow him to listen sufficiently to the counsel of his advisers. It must have been difficult to reconcile the requirements of his spiritual mission, as he interpreted it, with those of leadership of the Church in the world, with all the mundane considerations involved.

It was the king far more than the pope who was hindered by internal opposition. The rebellions of the period must not be viewed too critically, for they should be seen in the context of prevailing attitudes. The risings find support in contemporary Germanic concepts of law, which was regarded as something static, expressing traditional rights. In the pre-Gregorian period, the Teutonic king was deemed to be endowed with a sacrality which originated in Germanic notions, but had been translated into Christian terms. One of the most important duties of the king, in addition to exercising justice, was to maintain the law, a law that he had inherited and could not easily change. There were thus severe limitations on his power, and his sacrality did not carry with it the absolutism which the divine hereditary right of kings was to claim for the monarch in the early modern period. What was later to be called sovereignty was not vested solely in the Teutonic king, but was shared with the people. So that a just order pleasing to God could be preserved, the people not only had the right, but even the duty, to resist any breaches of this order by the king. But in turn the ruler, in order to fulfil his obligation of

curbing disorder, might find himself under the necessity of infringing established rights, and therefore the 'law'. Thus the Teutonic king had to walk a
tight-rope in securing for himself all the power he needed to govern, without
giving the people the grounds for rebellion, an almost impossible task.[74]

This put the king at a disadvantage in a conflict with the papacy, an
institution that had been remarkably successful in using the law to
strengthen its power, demonstrating a flexibility which was not feasible in
Henry's case, for example. The papacy was not shackled to existing law and
to traditional rights in the same way as the German king. For the
papacy from the time of Gregory VII onwards claimed the right, where it
regarded this as necessary, to mould existing law[75] by doctrinal announcement to which the law of the church – canon law – had to conform, in a way
no secular ruler could. Thus the Church was able to annex a vast mass of
causes with religious aspects, such as sin, oaths and testaments,[76] which
opened up to the canon law such important subjects as inheritance, marriage, property and contract.[77] The papacy could occupy the high spiritual
ground on behalf of the Church for the attainment of spiritual goals, such as
salvation, or of social improvements, like the increased protection for
the female partner in marriage.[78] The secular ruler might easily be
suspected of wishing to amass additional power and wealth in the interest
of his dynasty. The celibate pontiff of the reform papacy was patently
interested in the prerogatives of his office primarily in the service of a
higher cause. The celibate and elective aspects of the pontificate added
enormously to its strength, giving the curia the resilience, when opportunity
beckoned, to realise claims that had existed for a long time, but previously
only in theory.

The Church could not, in the long run, accept a situation in which the
Teutonic king and Roman emperor exercised a great deal of control
over the ecclesiastical establishment, including the papacy. But under
Gregory VII at times the pendulum swung far to the other extreme, with
even a papal deposition of a king. Obviously a proper balance still had to be
found between the legitimate demands on both sides. It was, however, clear
that a return to the old imperial system as practiced by the Saxon and the
previous Salian emperors had been ruled out by Gregory's actions: historically Henry's humiliation at Canossa far outweighed the short-term tactical
advantages he had gained by his submission.

Curiously enough, it was not only the Church and the papacy that
emerged strengthened from the struggle. Even for the secular power in the
Germanic kingdom it was not all loss. The interdependence of the temporal
and spiritual powers had prevented anything like a State from forming. The
growing independence of the ecclesiastical authority also allowed its secular
counterpart to come into its own: 'The Gregorian concept of the Church
almost demanded the invention of the concept of the State.'[79] As the bishops

became less dependable in the imperial service, the king-emperor was forced to build up a system of support independent of them. Incidentally, canon law and the papal bureaucracy were not only a threat to the imperial position, but also a model that was emulated with advantage.[80] In method, structure and thoroughness, canon law, sometimes due to the influence of Roman law, was far in advance of anything German secular law, with its out-of-date ordeals and trials by water or fire, could offer. Similarly, in efficiency the papal was generally ahead of the royal and imperial bureaucracy. In any case, the law played a key role in what has been called the 'papal revolution'.[81] The increasing importance of the law, often at the behest of the Church (for instance in synodal peace decrees[82]), emphasised the importance of the peaceful settlement of disputes, even if it at times encouraged excessive litigiousness. Gregory's achievement of greater freedom for the Church is undeniable, but it is unfortunate that a terrible price in human suffering had to be paid in the process, largely because of the impatience and impetuousness of the two principals, that of the pope perhaps even more than of the king-emperor.

There might well have been a chance of a settlement of the dispute under the new pope, Abbot Desiderius of Monte Cassino, who had earlier been an ally of Henry IV, and took the name of Victor III in memory of the last pro-imperial successor to St Peter. But the new pontiff, who assumed his dignity very reluctantly and after considerable delay, was by then already ill and died after a short reign. It was only in 1088 with the election of his successor, the Cardinal-bishop of Ostia and former Prior of Cluny, who took the name of Urban II, that the papacy emerged from the crisis through which it had passed during and after the reign of Gregory VII. A personality of outstanding ability, Urban continued to apply many Gregorian principles, but with a suppleness and subtlety which his great predecessor had lacked. However, no less than Gregory VII, Urban was determined to strengthen the power of the papacy and to emphasise the superiority of the spiritual over the secular order. Henry IV was not prepared to sacrifice the anti-pope, because it was he who had crowned him emperor. Thus once again, the inability or unwillingness of the regency at the beginning of the reign to obtain an early coronation proved a disadvantage to the Henrician cause, and indeed an obstacle to a settlement. Unlike Gregory VII, Urban was able to continue the dispute with Henry IV while at the same time resurrecting his predecessor's plans of an expedition against Islam, though in a different form. Building on the more positive attitude the Church had adopted to aspects of soldiering during previous reigns, he was able to devote considerable energy to promoting the First Crusade.

In order to resist the pressures of Islamic forces, the Byzantine emperor had asked for the despatch of volunteers from the West to strengthen his forces. Urban in his response used this request for assistance and fitted it into a wider scheme, that of a 'holy war' against the Islamic 'infidel' in the Near East under papal auspices. In the background there was also the hope of thus contributing to the reunification of the Christian Church. In view of the fact that three kings happened to be under the papal ban and that relations with the Teutonic kingdom were under severe strain owing to the dispute with Henry IV, Urban appealed for support to the knights rather than the kings, and to France rather than Germany. However, the alliance with the knights and the decreased emphasis on the position of the kings fitted in with papal policy. While the reaction to the initial impetus (to supply volunteers to Byzantium) faded into the background, 'taking the cross' – in what was only later called a crusade – ingeniously combined several objectives. Knights who had terrorised their neighbourhoods could now as armed pilgrims (a contradiction in terms) serve a good and even holy cause. Their service was accepted by the ecclesiastical authorities as penance for their sins. Soon the meaning of indulgence, which was to cause so much trouble for the Church in the distant future, was stretched to mean the actual forgiveness of sins, whereas in its strict sense the indulgence was the remission of the temporal punishment due to sin.[83]

In 1095, at the synod of Clermont, Urban's call to the crusade started off a movement which resulted in the liberation of Jerusalem and the formation of the Latin kingdom. Instead of strengthening the ties with Byzantium and the Orthodox Church, the First Crusade increased friction between East and West. In all these world-shaking events only the Western – Lotharingian – fringe of the Teutonic kingdom took part, whereas the French nobility was strongly represented, foreshadowing – though dimly – the future alliance between the papacy and the French dynasty. There was, however, one aspect of the First Crusade that affected Germany deeply. Some irregular forces only loosely connected with the crusading movement, while passing through the Teutonic kingdom, robbed and killed or forcibly baptised many Jewish inhabitants and destroyed some flourishing colonies in the Rhineland. Attempts by some bishops to prevent the slaughter met with little success. The set-back to settlement was strongly felt by the Jewish residents, but did not prove to be the last.

The successful conclusion of the First Crusade with the capture of Jerusalem in 1099, and the eventual establishment of the Latin kingdom there, enormously strengthened the position of the papacy. The curia now played an international role, which in some ways was even greater and more daring than that of the emperors from Charlemagne onwards. The papacy largely took over from the secular rulers the leadership in gaining new converts and territory for the Church. Through adopting a more positive attitude to soldiering and directing military energies against infidels, the Church was able to appeal directly to various sections of society, such as the knights, over the heads of the secular rulers to whom they owed allegiance. The crusading effort may in the short run have diverted some attention from the struggle against Henry IV, but particularly with the capture of Jerusalem the papacy emerged strengthened so that it could face the situation in the Teutonic kingdom with even greater confidence. The crusades certainly embittered relations between Christians and Muslims, though in practice they did not always reflect the theory of mutual hostility. As a somewhat perverse consequence of the military expedition of the crusaders, cultural contacts between the two religions actually increased.

Though Urban II had his set-backs in the dispute with the emperor, he was able to score some successes. He arranged an unusual marriage between the redoubtable Margravine Matilda of Tuscany with the 17 year-old Bavarian, Prince Welf, at least 25 years her junior. The alliance between the Bavarian dynasty, which Henry IV had tried to displace, and the Northern Italian principality closed the Alpine passes to the emperor, who found himself cut off south of the Alps for a longer period, while his position on the Teutonic throne was being undermined. The papacy succeeded in alienating Henry's eldest son Conrad, already crowned king, from his father, and by absolving him from his oath to an excommunicate, encouraged him to rebel against the emperor. On his return to his kingdom, Henry had Conrad deposed as Teutonic king. But the emperor's worst trial was yet to come, with the revolt in 1104 of his younger son, the later Henry V, who had replaced Conrad as Teutonic king. In the meantime Urban II had died in 1099, two weeks after the capture of Jerusalem, to be succeeded by Paschal II, a far less able personality than his predecessor.

Like his elder brother, the younger Henry was encouraged by the curia to rise against his father. It is clear from the reign of Henry V that he was a ruler of considerable ability, while we know little of Conrad. Like his father, the future Henry V was brought up in difficult circumstances, with tension between his father and his mother, and later with the intrigues of his stepmother against the emperor. Again, similarly to Henry IV, the younger Henry may have been taught by the experiences of his youth to dissimulate. It is impossible to say to what extent personal ambition played a part in his revolt against his father. While there must always remain a strong distaste for filial disloyalty, as well as disgust with the methods of deceit and brutality used against his father by the future Henry V, we must also grant him a strong and genuine concern for the future of the Salian dominions. These – with some justification – he regarded as endangered by the inability of the ruling monarch to come to terms with the papacy. He was also worried about his father's conflict with Ruthard, Archbishop of Mainz, which had arisen from the emperor's endeavours to grant restitution to Jewish victims of the crusaders' pogroms and to allow those forcibly baptised to return to the faith of their fathers. However, Henry IV had already, in 1090, demanded from the Jews in Worms and Speyer, desirous of baptism, the renunciation of their property, in order to make up for the loss of the special taxes Jews had to pay to the princes and bishops for their protection.[84] Henry V captured and deposed his father, who died in 1106 in Liège, after a final escape, this time from his son's custody.

In retrospect, Henry IV's reign has been overshadowed by the drama of his fight with the papacy. The emperor appeared in the final show-down to triumph over his great enemy Gregory VII, who died in exile, while he maintained himself on the throne. But he himself later suffered the ignominy of being deprived of his rule by his own son acting as the ally of a papacy with which he continued to be at loggerheads. Were spiritual weapons stronger than all the power and might a secular ruler could muster? That might be going too far, but there is no doubt that a papal ban against a king or emperor, which was continued over a long period or renewed, had a corroding effect, particularly if the monarch could not count on a united people.

Henry IV's tragedy was that the internal reforms he was trying to carry out in order to strengthen the position of the Teutonic king created many enemies for him, particularly in influential circles, thus providing plenty of allies for the papal campaign against the excommunicate ruler. Furthermore, the loyalty of the bishops to the king, which had been so important an element in the Ottonian-Salian era, could no longer be taken for granted. Thus the quarrel with the papacy, in which Henry unwisely had allowed himself to be ensnared, undermined the very foundations of the system of government in the Salian kingdom, quite apart from the increasing difficulties in Italy and the intricacies of the investiture question. That Henry had great abilities cannot be denied. He extended the base of support for the monarchy by his popularity with the towns, the lower nobility and even the peasants. He had a genuine concern for the down-trodden and the suffering, as he demonstrated in one sense in the case of the Jews. In better times he might have broadened and strengthened the whole fabric of society. But by being involved in two major endeavours which were bound to impact on each other, he weakened his position in both. Would his heir be able to save something from the rather desperate situation his father had left him?

Henry V had succeeded in his rebellion against his father thanks to the support of the princely opposition and of the papacy. The death of his father confirmed him in the position of Henry IV's successor. However, to what extent would the new ruler honour the obligations he incurred to his allies in a critical hour? In dissembling when he deemed it necessary, Henry V was like his father. Whereas Henry IV had often shown strong feelings, even in his impetuosity, his son was cold and calculating. The enemy of Gregory VII might be severely disliked and hated by some, but he retained a considerable measure of popularity among a wide section of the people, including the disadvantaged, even unto death. Henry IV on his death-bed asked that he should be buried next to his father in Speyer Cathedral, to which his architectural additions 'gave the church a strong Imperial flavour'.[85] But his wish could only be carried out five years later when the papal ban was removed. He was deeply mourned and a strong reaction took place against his exclusion from hallowed ground after his death. Henry V was never given this kind of affection and was, incidentally, much more ruthless in his methods than his predecessor had been.

The first institution to feel the chill wind coming from Henry V's court was the papacy. The king had been only too willing to use the curia to help him into power, but now that he had ascended the throne and was its undisputed occupant, the interests of the monarchy were paramount to him; any personal obligations had to be subordinated to them. In a way, this was only in line with the real reasons for which he had rebelled against his father. Far from wishing to strengthen the position of the papacy or of the princes, but simply using them, he had on the contrary only rebelled because his father had in his view been inept in defending the Salian dynasty against them. He was determined, so far as he could, to avoid fighting a 'war on two fronts', as his father had been compelled to do. He realised that in order to achieve concessions from the curia, he needed the support of the princes, both temporal and spiritual.

At first fate seemed to smile on the new ruler. At a diet in 1110, Henry V received almost unanimous support for an expedition to Italy to secure the imperial crown. Pope Paschal II was in a quandary. He was unable to secure Norman help to defend himself against the considerable military might Henry V mustered against him in Italy. Horrified at the prospect of further loss of life and devastation, he attempted to find ground for a compromise. The great canonist Ivo of Chartres towards the end of the eleventh century had examined the investiture issue in depth and had come to the conclusion that a line could be drawn between the spiritual and the secular aspects of the episcopate. While the conferment of the office of bishop was a sacramental act that could not be entrusted to laymen, the bestowal of temporalities, or *regalia*, such as property, royal offices, and so forth, could be conceded to the king in accordance to the teaching of St Augustine. The pope accepted this reasoning. Gregory VII had opposed this kind of line of division, for he had aimed at a papal feudal overlordship over the emperorship, complete dependence of the episcopate in the Teutonic kingdom on Rome, and the right of free disposal for church property.[86] Paschal seems to have offered to Henry V the abandonment by the Church of the *regalia*, that is of the royal property and rights conferred on the bishops. In return he asked that Henry should give up the claim to the investiture and the oath of fealty of bishops to him.

The proposed solution appeared to have the chance of settling the long and bitter investiture conflict The greatest difficulty in the way of implementing the papal proposals may well have been in defining precisely what was meant by *regalia*, on which the two sides had divergent interpretations.[87] When the papal decree to hand over the *regalia* to Henry was read to the assembled bishops from the Teutonic kingdom at St Peter's, they indignantly protested. They regarded the proposed settlement as sacrilege and as an attack on their status as imperial princes.[88] In the ensuing disorder the pope could not, as had been intended, proceed to the imperial coronation, which the pontiff now refused as Henry withdrew his agreement to give up the right of investiture. The king then arrested the pope with his cardinals, which led to severe street-fighting. After two months' captivity, Paschal surrendered to Henry's demands and agreed that the king should invest with ring and staff a bishop who had been freely elected, without simony, but with his approval. Consecration would only take place after that. Following the conclusion of the treaty, the pope was released and crowned Henry emperor.

Once more Paschal miscalculated, and so did Henry in this instance, for the treaty could not be enforced. What has sometimes been called the 'papal monarchy' was not absolute. Even Gregory VII had found himself disowned by many of his cardinals when he refused, in 1084, to make any attempt at negotiating with Henry IV and sacrificed the safety of the inhabitants of Rome to his intransigence. In spite of the singular position of the pope within the Church, he could not carry the institution with him if he moved too far outside the established consensus. A veritable revolt against the actions of the pope broke out particularly among the reform party, which in 1112 led to a rejection by the Church of the treaty with Henry.[89]

It was only during the reign of Pope Calixtus II, who succeeded in 1119, that a settlement was achieved. The Treaty of Worms of 1122 proved an important landmark. Agreement was reached in the form of simultaneous declarations by the emperor (the *Heinricianum*) and the pope (the *Calixtinum*) in which they made mutual concessions. Henry gave up the right to invest with ring and staff and conceded to all the churches in his empire free canonical election and consecration. He also promised to restore to the pope all the possessions and *regalia* of St Peter, as well other church property. In return the pope agreed to allow the emperor to be present at the elections of bishops and abbots who came directly under the Empire, thus securing him influence in the deliberations and the right of approval, so long as simony and force were not used. In the case of contested elections, the emperor was to decide, after hearing the view of the metropolitan and of the bishops of the church province, which candidate had the better claim. The emperor was to invest the ecclesiastical dignitaries with the sceptre, the symbol of secular rule, so far as the *regalia* were concerned. The secular investiture was to take place before the consecration in the Teutonic kingdom, but within six months afterwards in Burgundy and imperial Italy, thus very much limiting the influence of the ruler over appointments in the two latter territories. Perhaps Henry felt he could accept the arrangements for Italy more easily, because he had succeeded in 1116 in acquiring the Matildine lands after the death of the redoubtable margravine. He may have felt that this 'provided an alternative foundation for royal power in Italy.'[90]

While attempts were made at times by both sides to bend the agreement to their advantage, by and large the concordat of Worms provided a firm legal foundation for the future. The treaty marked real progress in distinguishing – in accordance with the teaching of Ivo of Chartres – between spiritual functions, which were bestowed by the ecclesiastical authorities by consecration, and the secular aspects of ecclesiastical office, for which investiture with the secular symbol of the sceptre was appropriate. In his treaty with Henry, Calixtus conceded to the Teutonic kingdom more than had been granted in the compromises made with England and France, but less for Burgundy and imperial Italy. If Henry IV had early on been prepared to accept the pragmatic distinction between a Teutonic kingdom in which episcopal elections were left largely untroubled by Gregory VII on the one hand, and an imperial Italy watched jealously by the papacy on the other, decades of conflict over investiture might have been avoided. However, the investiture question was only part of a major trial of strength between the papacy and the rulers of the Teutonic kingdom.

It is not so easy to tell who 'won' the struggle between the Salian dynasty and the papacy. The church reform movement, particularly in its Gregorian manifestation, certainly did not have it all its own way. But undoubtedly the papacy emerged strengthened from the conflict. Quite apart from its victory in imperial Italy, its power over the episcopate in the Teutonic kingdom had been enhanced, and that exercised by the emperors diminished proportionately. In spite of the *homagium* which the bishops in fact swore to the Teutonic king, they were far less dependent on the ruler than they had been before. In view of the important part they had played in the royal and imperial government, the change in their status was of significance. From royal appointees and officials, more often than not supporting the central authority against the local rulers, the bishops in their worldly role now technically became vassals of the king, putting them in a similar situation to the secular magnates, each of whom was determined to strengthen his own position. Thus 'particularism', that is the resistance of the magnates to the unifying and centralising policies of the kings and emperors, got a great boost in the Teutonic kingdom. Also, thanks to the growing power of the 'papal monarchy', the kings increasingly had to share the loyalty of the bishops with the popes. Not only Ottonian-Salian church practice, but the entire constitutional arrangements under these dynasties had broken down.

It has been truly said that the main beneficiaries of the struggle between the Salian dynasty and the papacy were the territorial princes. From 1112 these had once more taken advantage of the ruler's preoccupation with his dispute with the papacy to rise against the king. Again Saxony was disaffected, which was doubly dangerous because its duke, Lothar of Supplinburg, was an enemy of Henry V. It may well be that internal strife forced the emperor into compromising with the papacy to a greater extent than he would have done if the situation had been quiet at home.[91]

After a long illness, Henry V died of cancer in 1125. His marriage to the Princess Matilda, daughter of the Norman King Henry I of England, remained without offspring. The dynastic alliance had incidentally involved the Teutonic kingdom in an unsuccessful war with France at the side of England the previous year. Unlike the rather fruitful Capetians in France, the ruling dynasty after about a century once more died out in the Teutonic kingdom with Henry V.

5 The Staufen Conflict with the Papacy (1125–1268)

Henry V, who died childless, had apparently designated Frederick of Staufen, the eldest son of his sister Agnes, as his successor. However, under the influence of the permanent papal legate in the Teutonic kingdom, Archbishop Adalbert of Mainz,[1] who had become a strong opponent of the emperor and of the Concordat of Worms,[2] and of two papal legates *a latere*,[3] the Staufen candidate was rejected precisely because of his hereditary connection with the previous dynasty. The new king, Lothar III, of the Supplinburg family, about 50-years-old on his accession, who was Duke of Saxony and had been at loggerheads with Henry V, had no connection with the Salians.

Quite apart from relief at the disappearance of a dynasty with which the Holy See had recently been in conflict, there were a number of reasons why the curia preferred the election of the Teutonic king and future emperor to be based on the candidate's personal suitability rather than on any hereditary claim. Not only did it appear appropriate that the secular counterpart of the pope should be elected like the supreme pontiff, but also the influence of the Holy See on the selection for the Teutonic crown would be strengthened by the absence of the hereditary principle. 'Of the German kings of the twelfth century only Lothar III...conformed fully to the papal concept of *idoneitas*,'[4] of suitability. From the point of view of moving away from a hereditary succession, it was also useful that Lothar did not have any male heirs. He was seen by the curia as an advocate of the freedom of the Church, though he was by no means its puppet, as his critics have sometimes claimed. However, he recognised the need for a relaxation of tension between the secular and the papal power for which the Concordat of Worms provided an opportunity, as indeed any ruler succeeding Henry V might have done.

Understandably, members of the Staufen dynasty felt aggrieved by Lothar's election. When the new king, as was his duty, demanded from them the return of crown lands of which they had taken possession as heirs of the Salian emperors, Frederick of Swabia refused to do so. Soon after, the Staufen faction elected an anti-king, Conrad, Frederick's younger brother. It is not clear why Conrad was chosen this time in preference to his elder brother, but this may have had something to do with Frederick's loss of one eye disqualifying him from a partly sacral role for which a physical handicap was perceived as a hindrance.[5] In the meantime, Lothar had married his daughter and heiress Gertrude to a member of the Welf dynasty, Henry the Proud, a matrimonial alliance that had probably been promised to

147

him in order to secure his support at the election.[6] Lothar was forced to fight a war against the Staufen dynasty, which was the beginning of a long-lasting dispute later to be continued by the family of his Welf son-in-law, and was to assume a European dimension. The Church supported Lothar, excommunicating Conrad. Although Conrad had some initial successes, even receiving the Lombard crown, he was unable to dislodge his opponent. But Lothar had other preoccupations, which prevented him from concentrating entirely on the threat posed by the Staufen dynasty.

Once more, in 1130, two rival popes were elected owing to deep divisions within the Sacred College. These were aggravated by the determination of the papal chancellor, Cardinal Haimeric, to secure the election of his own candidate, who took the name of Innocent II. While Peter Pierleoni, who called himself Anacletus II, received a slightly larger number of votes than his opponent, Innocent was supported by five out of the six cardinal-bishops, who had been given special authority in elections under the decree of 1059.[7] Anacletus helped to strengthen his Roman base by an alliance with Roger of Sicily, to whom he granted the royal title.[8] But Innocent gradually built up a considerable following outside Italy, including Lothar himself, who received the imperial crown from him at the Lateran in 1133. Lothar was able to ensure that in future bishops would not be able to take possession of their *regalia* without being first enfeoffed with them by the king. However, in the question of the Matildine lands, he agreed to hold them in usufruct from the Holy See for an annual rent, an arrangement that was liable to be misinterpreted in view of a wall-painting in the Lateran whose inscription denoted Lothar as becoming the pope's vassal.[9]

Following the emperor's departure from Italy, King Roger of Sicily drove Innocent out of Rome. It was only after Conrad, who had been able to maintain his strong position in Swabia, had surrendered to Lothar, that the emperor could undertake an expedition to Italy to restore Innocent in Rome, in which he succeeded for the time being. However, serious differences arose between Innocent and Lothar over Southern Italy, as both claimed suzerainty over the principalities there. In this connection, unable to agree as to which of them had the right to invest the Duke of Apulia, they adopted the temporary expedient of doing so jointly.[10] Lothar died soon after, at the end of 1137, which left Innocent defenceless against the Norman supporters of Anacletus.

The election of 1138 showed curious parallels to that of 1125, if in reverse. The Welfs rather than the Staufen now attracted opposition to their candidature, owing to their connection with the previous ruler. Henry the Proud's position as Lothar's son-in-law, as well as the extensive possessions of his family both in the Teutonic kingdom and in Italy (including the Matildine lands, which they held as papal vassals) now counted against them. Thanks to the determination, as well as the ruthlessness, of Albero, Archbishop of

Trier, 'a friend of Bernard of Clairvaux who had excellent connections with the curia under Innocent II,'[11] Henry the Proud was not chosen. Instead, the former Staufen anti-King Conrad, now in his mid-forties, was elected at Koblenz in March 1138 by a minority of the magnates and soon after crowned by a papal legate. The curia was once again happy to move against the hereditary principle for the Teutonic kingship and the emperorship. Furthermore, it was not in the interest of the Holy See to strengthen the power of a dynasty to which Lothar had entrusted the Matildine lands; there appear also to have been some disputes between the papacy and the Welf dynasty.[12] Henry the Proud resigned himself to the abandonment of his hopes for the kingship and handed over the imperial insignia. But he did not do homage to Conrad III. For the king laid down as a constitutional principle that no magnate should hold more than one duchy. He therefore demanded that Henry should give up either Bavaria or the only recently acquired Saxony, which Henry refused to do. Thereupon he was outlawed and deprived of both duchies, which were bestowed on others.

In October 1139 Henry the Proud died, leaving as his heir his son Henry (later called the Lion), then aged ten. The Welf struggle against Conrad was carried on by the Empress Dowager Richenza and by Welf VI, Henry the Proud's brother. In a limited compromise in 1142, which was far from settling the Staufen–Welf dispute, Henry the Lion was enfeoffed with Saxony. This duchy was given up by Albert the Bear, a member of the Ascanian dynasty, who returned to his previous rule in the Nordmark (the later electorate of Brandenburg). Henry had to formally renounce any claim to Bavaria, but did not adhere to his undertaking. In view of their possessions on both sides of the Alps, the Welfs were a dangerous enemy for the king. When Conrad allied with Sicily's foe Byzantium, King Roger gave financial assistance to the Welfs against their common enemy. In the meantime, Roger had lost an ally in Rome when Anacletus died in 1138. Although there had been widespread support for Innocent II among rulers and leading ecclesiastical personalities, the schism was not finally settled until after the death of his rival.[13]

In 1139, Innocent was able to hold the Second Lateran Council, which was well attended and was later recognised as an ecumenical council. But in view of the encroachments of the Normans, his problems were not over, and he only aggravated these by following the ill-fated example of Leo IX in fighting a campaign against them, in which he was similarly defeated and taken prisoner. Innocent had to come to terms with Roger. His pontificate ended with a Roman rising against papal rule and the setting up of a commune in Rome which, harking back to antiquity, called itself the senate.

For some years there was a serious threat to the papal position in the Holy City. For the time being the papacy could not expect any help from Conrad in view of his preoccupation with the Welf problem. In any case, soon all these questions were overshadowed by the deteriorating situation of the Crusader states in the East, which led to the fall of Edessa in 1144. When the Cistercian Abbot Bernard of Pisa, a pupil of Bernard of Clairvaux, in the following year succeeded to the papal throne as Eugenius III, he summoned King Louis VII of France and his magnates to the Second Crusade. Thus, as with the First Crusade, the call was mainly addressed to France, though this time also to its king. The pope wished to reserve the resources of the Teutonic kingdom for aid to the Holy See against the Roman commune and the Sicilian Normans. Bernard of Clairvaux, perhaps the most prominent representative of Western Christendom at the time, received the commission to preach the crusade, and did so with great fervour.

One of the greatest problems for the church authorities during the First Crusade had been to keep control of what was liable to become a spontaneous movement, with all its excesses. The Church could do little to prevent unauthorised preaching of the Second Crusade in countries not earmarked for the purpose, such as the Teutonic kingdom, where fanatical mass movements once more carried out pogroms against the Jews in the Rhenish cities. It may also be that some of the enthusiasm stimulated by the fervour of Bernard's preaching spilled over from France into the Teutonic kingdom and was misunderstood there. In any case, Bernard came to the conclusion that the only hope of preventing further outrages was for him to undertake the official preaching of the crusade in the Teutonic kingdom in person, which he did without previous authorisation from the pope.[14] He thus thwarted the pontiff's plans to obtain Conrad's help with his own problems in Italy. Bernard felt he needed the king's participation to ensure the success of his efforts in the Teutonic kingdom. While Conrad had little inclination to join, he spontaneously decided to take the cross when Bernard addressed him publicly and warned him that he would not be able to answer at the Last Judgment unless he did so. Among members of his family who also went on the crusade to the Holy Land were Conrad's nephew, Frederick, Duke of Swabia (the future Emperor Frederick I), and his half-brother, the historian Bishop Otto of Freising.

In spite of the presence of two eminent European rulers, Conrad III and Louis VII of France, the Second Crusade (1147–9), unlike the First, ended in complete failure. It was particularly unfortunate that, with some support from the local barons, who ought to have known better, the expedition decided to attack the Emir of Damascus, with disastrous results. He was actually a friend of the crusading states and an enemy of Nur-ed-Din, the captor of Edessa. The military reputation of the Christian armies was shattered. While the prospects of the crusading states had, if anything, worsened, the Islamic position in the Near East emerged considerably strengthened. One of the most serious consequences of the failure of the Second Crusade was the distrust it sowed not only between the crusaders and the Byzantine Empire, but also between the French and the Teutonic kingdoms. Early on during the campaign Conrad vented his anger on the Byzantine authorities for their perceived reluctance to help him and his troops. But his relations with the emperor at Constantinople finally assumed considerable cordiality with the reaffirmation of the alliance that Lothar had initiated. Conrad firmly refused to have anything to do with the plans of Bernard of Clairvaux and of Louis VII, now in league with the inveterate enemy of Byzantium, Roger of Sicily, to take vengeance on the Greek Empire for allegedly not supporting the crusading effort sufficiently. In fact, Emperor Manuel I Comnenus was a far better judge of the situation created in the area by the advance of Islam than most of the leaders of the crusaders coming from Europe, kings included.[15] An incidental long-term effect of the Second Crusade was the deep impression made on the young Frederick by the Byzantine emperor cult and its liturgy, which was to bear fruit when he became emperor.[16] He also emerged from the campaign full of suspicions of Byzantine policy.

At the diet in Frankfurt in March 1147, before the Second Crusade, the Saxon princes declared that they would rather conduct their own crusade closer home, against the heathen Slavs on the eastern borders of the Teutonic kingdom, to which the assembly agreed. Bernard of Clairvaux also accepted the idea and assured the crusaders against the Slavs of the same indulgences as those who went to the Holy Land. Bernard laid down that a relentless campaign was to be waged against the Slavs to obtain their conversion. He specifically forbade the conclusion of any treaties allowing them to retain their old religion in exchange for a tribute. The Wendish crusade, in which such leading princes as Henry the Lion and Albert the Bear participated, reflected a mixture of political and religious motives. Some of the magnates were mainly concerned with extending their rule. However in the end they broke off the campaign as self-defeating, when their own territories were being invaded and pillaged. They were also risking a reduction of the tribute to which they were traditionally entitled from lands that they were now themselves destroying by war.[17]

Conrad III died in February 1152, predeceased by his eldest son, who had already been elected king. Conrad's oldest surviving son was still a minor, unlikely to be acceptable to the magnates as ruler. Therefore Conrad had designated his nephew Frederick, Duke of Swabia, son of his elder brother of the same name, as his successor. Frederick's mother was a Welf princess, sister of Welf VI; an important part of her considerable possessions lay in Italy, and she was an aunt of the redoubtable Henry the Lion. It was hoped that Frederick's election would create an opportunity to overcome the bitter disputes between the two families which had disrupted the two previous reigns. Frederick, now just past his mid-twenties, called Barbarossa by the Italians because of the red colour of his beard, was indeed elected by the magnates, though probably not as smoothly as his famous uncle Bishop Otto of Freising made it appear in his writings.[18]

The measures Frederick Barbarossa undertook to secure the throne already displayed the great determination and indeed ruthlessness as well as the exceptional physical stamina that were to characterise his reign. While the new king exercised a natural authority, he showed a strong interest in views presented to him and was fully aware of the need for ample consultation with all concerned, particularly with the secular and ecclesiastical magnates of the Teutonic kingdom. Whatever changes Frederick eventually made in policy and emphasis, his initial steps were largely predetermined. First of all, if only for reasons of commonsense, he had to consolidate his position in the Teutonic kingdom, for that kingdom was the base of his power, from which he drew the resources he required to maintain his standing in Christendom and elsewhere. Only when he had achieved sufficient progress in creating stability in the Teutonic kingdom would he be able to consider the next move that traditionally followed the accession of a king, namely to strive for his imperial coronation, which would also involve him in the affairs of Italy (Map II).

Frederick's first task was to arrive at a settlement with his Welf relations. In Italy Welf VI was invested with the March of Tuscany and the Duchy of Spoleto. Frederick also conceded the Matildine lands to Welf. The Welfs, however, claimed the Bavarian duchy they had lost in the previous reign owing to their rebellion against Conrad III. The territory had been given to a half-brother of Conrad belonging to the Babenberg dynasty. It took Frederick Barbarossa until 1155 to negotiate a mutually agreeable solution. Henry the Lion, already Duke of Saxony, then also became duke of a reduced Bavaria from which the Austrian margraviate was detached, a decision of momentous – both national and international – importance for the future. Frederick gave increased powers and responsibility to the new Austrian dukes. To some extent this was done to make the offer more attractive to the Babenberg dynasty, but it was probably also part of a general policy of delegation, particularly in territories distant from the main Staufen sphere of influence. In some respects, Frederick's treatment of Henry the Lion also reflected this policy of decentralisation desirable for a ruler concerned, not only with the Teutonic kingdom, but also with Burgundy, Italy and the papacy. For about a quarter of a century, Frederick pursued a conciliatory policy towards his cousin, often helping Henry to solve difficulties with his vassals. The settlement with the Welfs left Frederick free to organise his expedition to Italy.

In the nineteenth century some historians supporting German unification, such as Heinrich von Sybel, raised the question whether the interests of their country were served by what they regarded as the preoccupation of rulers like those of the Staufen dynasty with Italy and the papacy. However, earlier

THE EMPIRE AND ITALY DURING THE
STAUFEN PERIOD
—————— Boundary of the Holy Roman Empire
THE MAJOR DUCHIES:
Saxony
Lorraine
Franconia
Swabia
Bavaria
— · — · — Boundaries of other territories
(see preface for sources)

Map II

in the century, Friedrich von Raumer, the author of a six-volume history of the Staufen dynasty, in the introduction to the second edition of 1840 rejected as unhistorical the possibility of a voluntary abandonment of Italy by the Teutonic rulers.[19] One of the problems amongst others with Sybel's thesis was his assumption that there existed, for example at the time of Staufen rule, not only a German national consciousness, but also a clear separation between Italian and German interests. As to the latter, the strong Italian position of Welf VI, who had earlier rebelled against Conrad III, made it important for the ruler of the Teutonic kingdom to keep a wary eye on developments south of the Alps. Similarly, Henry III had been unable to ignore the dangers of the dynastic alliance between Lorraine and Tuscany. In any case, the king was emperor-elect, awaiting coronation by the pope. No ruler of the Teutonic kingdom could deliberately forgo the imperial crown, which considerably added to his spiritual position so important in an age in which religion and politics were interwoven. His position at home was thereby strengthened, quite apart from any economic advantages a foothold in Italy might give. And finally the king could not simply turn down the pope's appeal for help, for the protectorship of the papacy had formed a significant aspect of the Frankish and then East Frankish–Teutonic crown ever since the days of Pippin and Charlemagne. Also, there were many examples of situations in which the failure of the emperor to give adequate assistance to the pope in fact drove him into the arms of the emperor's enemies, such as the kings of Sicily.

However, when all this has been said, and even if there were economic benefits to be gained there, it remains true that Italy at times constituted a considerable financial and military drain on the resources of the Teutonic kingdom. That was the price which had to be paid for a Teutonic prominence in the medieval period particularly admired by some modern German historians, untroubled by the fact that Teutonic military exploits did not necessarily win friends south of the Alps. It is difficult to reconcile this nostalgia for 'German greatness' in the Middle Ages with criticism of the policy of intervention in Italy. One cannot have it both ways. While the ruler of the Teutonic kingdom may not have had any choice in getting involved in Italy and with the papacy, he faced problems of a complexity which did not confront, for example, the kings of England and France. Indeed, while Frederick Barbarossa was in the middle of consolidating his position in the Teutonic kingdom, the pope was asking him for help in Italy which Conrad III had no longer been able to give. But the new king at once made it clear to the papacy that he approached relations with the Church in a different spirit from his two predecessors, and that he would take full advantage of all his rights.

Frederick was the first ruler born – in 1125 or 1126 – after the conclusion of the Concordat of Worms of 1122. Much younger on his accession than his two predecessors, he took a hard look at the position established for emperor and empire by the settlement in the investiture conflict. Frederick was a profoundly conservative personality, with a stubborn determination to revive old rights,[20] attached to tradition, and looking back to the Carolingian, or at the very least to the Ottonian and Salian, religio-political order. In view of the far-reaching claims of the papacy, he may well have regarded the maintenance of the sacrality of the Empire and of the claim to its divine mission as a political and ideological necessity.[21] In the perspective of the period, there was even a vital theological function that only the (Roman) Empire could fulfil: in an age in which eschatological and apocalyptic feelings were strong, it was the duty of every emperor to maintain the last of the great empires in order to delay the End of Time that had been prophesied on its collapse.[22] The conclusion Frederick appears to have drawn from these considerations was to regard the Worms compromise as unworkable and to strive for a restoration of the imperial power over the Church that had prevailed before the investiture conflict, under strong rulers like Charlemagne, Otto I and Henry III.

Thus Frederick did not – like, for instance, Lothar III – ask the pope for confirmation of his election. 'By signing his letter simply as "King of the Romans" [the title used by the Teutonic kings], he implied that…he now expected the Pope to crown him emperor as a matter of course.'[23] But as both sides needed each other at that stage, neither dwelled too much on theoretical differences. For Frederick wished to secure an annulment of his marriage to Adelaide of Vohburg, from whom he did not have any children. Frederick is said to have found out that his wife had committed adultery.[24] The pope required Frederick's help against the Romans as well as against the Normans of the kingdom of Sicily. Eventually, in March 1153, representatives of Frederick and of the curia signed a treaty at Constance, in which the king undertook not to make peace either with the citizens of Rome or with the King of Sicily without the consent of the Holy See. Frederick also bound himself to come to the aid of the papacy against its enemies; implicitly he recognised not only the pope's authority in matters spiritual, but also his full sovereignty over the Patrimony of St Peter.[25] Both king and pope agreed to repulse any invasion on the part of Byzantium and not to cede any territory to it. The pope promised to give Frederick every help in maintaining and augmenting the honour of the kingdom, if necessary by punishing with excommunication those who violated it. He dissolved Frederick's marriage on the grounds of close kinship.

Unfortunately Frederick could only muster a comparatively small force, as the Teutonic princes were at that time more concerned with domestic than with Italian and papal affairs. Crossing the Brenner in October 1154, he was welcomed by some cities, including Pavia, but Milan became increasingly hostile. Furthermore, Pope Anastasius IV, who was friendly to Frederick, died in December 1154, to be replaced by the English Cardinal, Nicholas Breakspear, a firm opponent of any secular interference in ecclesiastical functions, who took the name of Hadrian IV. Although his position in Rome was precarious, the new pontiff rejected approaches for an understanding from William I, the new King of Sicily, who then proceeded to invade the Patrimony. Thus Hadrian was still dependent on Frederick, who, however, realised that his expeditionary force was too small to fight the Normans. In April 1155 Frederick received the iron crown of Italy at Pavia. He made up his mind to recross the Alps after his imperial coronation In the meantime, he helped the curia against the political and religious radical Arnold of Brescia, who supported the Roman Republic that had overthrown papal rule in the city. As a gesture to the pontiff, Frederick, after capturing Arnold, handed him over to the Holy See, which put him to death as a rebel. 'Thus the life of a passionate idealist, dedicated to poverty and simple Christianity, came to a sad and untimely end.'[26] Frederick's concept of his role as the future emperor, seen perhaps in Carolingian terms, was bound to bring him into opposition to Arnold as a critic of the existing spiritual and secular order. Furthermore, the king was unsympathetic to the aspirations of the Italian cities, tending to rely more on the support of bishops and nobles, as he was accustomed to do in the Teutonic kingdom.[27]

The first meeting with Hadrian in June 1155 did not go too well, because Frederick, in order to avoid any appearance of inferiority, initially did not advance to hold the pope's bridle and stirrup, a reverence to which Hadrian felt entitled according to precedent. The king did so at a second meeting, but the seeds of suspicion had been sown in both the pope and some of the cardinals. Even Frederick's refusal – entirely in accordance with his aversion to democratic principles – to accept the imperial crown from the Roman people in rebellion against Hadrian could not restore a harmonious atmosphere. Frederick was crowned emperor by the pope at St Peter's that same month, but soon after the ceremony a Roman riot forced pope and emperor to withdraw from the city. Frederick, whose small force was weakened by the outbreak of an epidemic during the summer heat, decided to withdraw without even having restored Hadrian's authority in the Patrimony, thus leaving to a later day the task he had promised to fulfil in the Treaty of Constance. Perhaps the emperor had no practical alternative, but the consequences of his retreat were to be felt by him for a long time to come. Before crossing the Alps, he razed Spoleto, which had paid him with false money, and put Milan under the ban of the Empire, intending to settle accounts with that city swiftly on his next visit to Italy. But events now took a turn which he had not fully anticipated.

Naturally feelings ran high in the curia when Frederick did not complete his mission of help to the papacy, leaving the Holy See at the mercy of the Normans when William I besieged Benevento, where the pontiff and a number of cardinals happened to be staying. In June 1156, a concordat was concluded between the papacy and Sicily. The Holy See invested William with the Kingdom of Sicily, the Duchy of Apulia and the Principality of Capua. William took the oath of homage to the pope and agreed to pay tribute. Hadrian's settlement with Sicily was regarded in many quarters of the Church as a betrayal. Some cardinals also felt that it constituted a breach of the Treaty of Constance, which it may have been in spirit. But it will be recalled that the actual stipulations only prohibited one party – Frederick – from coming to terms with Sicily. Whatever view is taken of the legal position, from a practical point of view the concordat was at least indirectly a consequence of Frederick's inability to fulfil the aid he had promised to the papacy.

Following the papal arrangement with Sicily, Frederick's policy became more antagonistic to the Holy See. His appointment of Rainald of Dassel to a prominent place in the imperial counsels reinforced this tendency. The emperor made Rainald chancellor in 1156 and secured the archbishopric of Cologne for him in 1159. Dassel was a man of great energy and courage, with a real passion for military pursuits. He 'had no great taste for the clerical life and treated his vocation in a fashion that was cynical even by the standards of the twelfth century'.[28] He only took orders in 1165. Rainald does not appear to have had much sympathy with the church reform movement. He certainly wished to restrict the influence of the curia and drove Frederick further in an anti-papal direction. The reason for the emperor's reliance on Rainald may well have been that his chancellor had the educational attainments and experience of the world that he felt himself lacking, as he had not originally been destined for rulership and therefore did not have the appropriate learning.[29]

The harder line taken by the imperial court towards the papacy soon became apparent. The aged Archbishop of Lund had been kidnapped on Burgundian soil, and Pope Hadrian quite properly demanded punishment of the guilty for this outrage. In the somewhat strained situation following the concordat with Sicily, the emperor simply ignored the papal communication, failing to fulfil his obligations as a ruler. The curia was divided in its assessment of Frederick's overall aims and therefore decided to test the emperor's resolve by lodging a stronger and more general protest, which it was hoped would rally the bishops of the Teutonic kingdom to the papacy. A papal message conveyed by two legates, one of whom was the papal chancellor Cardinal Roland (the future Alexander III), was read to a large assembly of princes at Frederick's court at Besançon in October 1157. Frederick happened to be on a prolonged visit to his Burgundian kingdom to take possession of the inheritance of his second wife, Beatrix of Burgundy.

Hadrian's message included a reference to the *beneficia* the papacy had conferred on the emperor. *Beneficia* had an ambiguous meaning: it could simply mean benefits, but it could also denote a grant of a fief by a lord to his vassal. Rainald of Dassel without hesitation gave the critical words a feudal meaning when he translated the letter, which at once caused an enormous uproar. Apparently one of the papal legates aggravated the situation by exclaiming: 'From whom then does the emperor hold his empire if not from the pope?' Only the emperor's presence of mind prevented a physical assault on the legates, who were ordered out of the country without having been able to settle their business.[30] As things turned out, the legates failed to sway Frederick's clergy from their loyalty to him. But as a result of the incident even the cardinals who had earlier wavered no longer considered an agreement with Frederick possible. Hadrian decided that things had gone far enough and therefore denied that he had used the term *beneficium* in a feudal sense; he asserted that he had never intended to claim temporal sovereignty over the Empire. Though the controversy had forced the pope to climb down, the hardening attitude of the curia towards Frederick boded ill for his future prospects, including his plans for asserting his authority in Italy.

At first, however, fortune seemed to smile on the emperor when he returned to Italy in 1158. Frederick settled his accounts with Milan left over from his first expedition. The city had to capitulate and to accept some humiliating conditions in a settlement that altogether was not overly harsh. Frederick convoked a diet at Roncaglia, where he received from some Bologna jurists a compilation of a long list of royal rights (*regalia*) to which he was entitled according to Roman law and tradition.[31] These included the authority over the nomination of magistrates and over public roads and rivers, as well as over a whole plethora of financial dues. The emperor claimed these rights for himself, unless documentary proof could be produced to the contrary. Unlike the bishops, the cities generally found it difficult to proffer proof of their privileges, and were thus the main victims of Frederick's policy. Indeed the emperor went even further in disadvantaging the cities, for he restored to the bishops certain rights they had lost to the communes, whether legally or otherwise.[32] The critical issue was whether Frederick's far-reaching claims could be enforced in the kingdom of Lombardy. Would his military strength be sufficient to assert his authority? Also, would the emperor be able to restore peace to a region rent by traditional local rivalries and hostilities? Would he be able to offer impartial justice, instead of following the policy of *divide et impera*, and thus becoming a party to the quarrels?

Actually, the resistance of the cities to the Roncaglian decrees was growing. The emperor's limited military resources only allowed him to take on the small city of Crema in July 1159. The city was besieged for six months 'with unparalleled violence and cruelty',[33] and was razed to the ground after its capitulation. The destruction went far beyond any military requirements.

It reflected both Frederick's belief in his sacred duty as emperor to punish those who violated the divine order represented by him, as well as the 'barbarian' invader's jealousy of the works of the more advanced Italian culture, who 'gets even' by their destruction.[34]

The worsening imperial position in Lombardy was not eased by Frederick's increasing intransigence towards the curia under the influence of Rainald von Dassel, no longer moderated by more irenic advisers like the emperor's uncle Bishop Otto of Freising, who had died in 1158. The curia regarded the Roncaglian Decrees as the first stage of Frederick's assertion of power over the whole of Italy, of which the reported despatch of imperial agents to Tuscany and to the Patrimony of St Peter to stir up trouble against the papacy appeared to be further evidence.[35] The Holy See now took steps to bolster its defensive position by approaches to Sicily and to Byzantium. William I of Sicily helped the pope to strengthen the walls of the Holy City, and in return Hadrian successfully pleaded with the Byzantine Emperor Manuel Comnenus to cease his attacks on Sicily.

Above all, the papacy now took the lead in bringing together the traditionally divided Lombard cities against the emperor. When two of them asked Hadrian to settle their differences, Frederick tried to interfere in this process, which led the pope to threaten him with an interdict. In addition, Hadrian refused to confirm Frederick's nominee to the archbishopric of Ravenna. The pontiff was also upset by the emperor changing his form of address to him in a deliberately discourteous manner. In spite of that, the pope made an effort to negotiate a settlement with the emperor. But this foundered on Frederick's refusal to accede to the demand of the curia that he should give up his claim to sovereignty over the Patrimony of St Peter as well as his ultimate authority over the Italian bishops. In June 1159 the pope moved to Anagni to be closer to his Sicilian protector, and established contact with a number of Lombard cities. However, before all these measures could bear fruit, Hadrian died in September 1159. The papal vacancy precipitated a severe crisis.

The Sacred College was deeply split over the question whether the Sicilian alliance should be continued or whether it would be better to make another effort at coming to terms with the emperor. The result was that rival groups of cardinals elected two different popes. The majority gave their votes to the leader of the pro-Sicilian party, the papal chancellor Roland, as Alexander III, and the minority to the pro-imperialist Cardinal Octavian as Victor IV. Both Alexander and Victor had served the curia with distinction. There was mutual recrimination, with Victor's followers alleging that the pro-Sicilian group among the cardinals had in uncanonical fashion pledged itself not to elect anybody outside their number. Alexander's party countered by claiming that Frederick's representative, Otto of Wittelsbach, had interfered in the elections on Victor's behalf. 'It is no longer possible to discover the truth behind these two sets of allegations, but they agree in finding the cause of the schism in political circumstances.'[36]

The emperor claimed that is was his duty, in order to determine who was the true pope, to summon and preside over a council of the Church, which met at Pavia in February 1160. There, however, he studiously left the decision to the bishops. Both popes were invited to attend the council, to which Victor agreed, while Alexander refused, believing himself to be the rightful pope who could be judged by no one. In any case, he did not trust the impartiality of the emperor, who – in view of the importance he was bound to attach to having a pro-imperial and anti-Sicilian pope – could not be expected to be above the battle. Much had changed in Western Christendom since Henry III had settled a papal schism. Following the Norman conquest of England and the establishment of an energetic Norman–Angevin dynasty, and with the strengthening of the power of the French monarchy under the house of Capet, these two royal houses, at any rate, could not be ignored when it came to a decision on the spiritual head of the Church. It was certainly a flaw in the make-up of the council of Pavia that it was an assembly of imperial bishops called to settle an issue affecting all Western Christendom.

At one stage the bishops asked for more time for their deliberations, but Frederick, who was keen to embark on his campaign against Milan, wanted a speedy decision. In the end a majority voted for Victor, partly because the case for Alexander had not been put in view of his refusal to attend, and partly because the imperial bishops present believed that Victor would suit the emperor better than his rival. This is not, however, to suggest that the council came to its conclusion primarily on political grounds. While each candidate had some points in his favour, neither had a conclusive case. The emperor at once accepted the decision of the council and recognised Victor. Alexander thereupon excommunicated Frederick and released his subjects from obedience, but did not follow the precedent of Gregory VII of deposing him.[37] In exercising his option against Alexander, Frederick had made one of the decisive choices of his reign, which was going to have repercussions for a long time to come.

It could not necessarily be foreseen at that stage that Alexander would win out in the end and that Frederick would eventually, after a long struggle, have to acknowledge him as the true pope. Did the emperor mishandle the situation? Frederick was truly in a dilemma, because just as Alexander did not have any confidence in him, so the emperor did not trust this papal claimant. It is not surprising that Frederick preferred the pro-imperial Victor to the pro-Sicilian Alexander on the papal throne. But the emperor was also misled by a belief in the continued validity of rights based on historical precedent, although these, in this particular case, no longer fitted the actual situation; that he was encouraged in this by Rainald of Dassel does not exonerate him. As it turned out, the emperor would have been better off if he had allowed himself more freedom of manœuvre by not presiding over the decision on who was the rightful pope. The chain of events involving Frederick in this dilemma began with his inability to honour in full the stipulation of the Treaty of Constance to aid the pope. As we have seen, this was due to a limitation of military resources partly imposed by the restrictions under which Frederick ruled in the Teutonic kingdom, which made him dependent on the support of the magnates to fit out expeditions to Italy.

The difficulties over Frederick's support for Victor lay in the future. For the time being, the situation in northern Italy seemed to favour the emperor. Milan had to surrender in March 1162 and probably in part to satisfy the lust for revenge of the city's Lombard enemies, Milan was totally destroyed with the help of these neighbours.[38] This does not reveal a ruler standing above the parties and administering justice fairly and without fear or favour. Northern Italy appeared to be in Frederick's hands, but other events were not going so well for him. Support for Victor was generally crumbling and it was becoming clear that the emperor had found his match in Alexander.

With great skill Alexander broadened his international base of support. Partly in order to avoid capture by the emperor in Italy, and following the example of several predecessors since Urban II at the end of the eleventh century,[39] he went to France and was successful in achieving widespread recognition. He was also able to prevent King Louis VII from honouring a commitment to attend a meeting with Frederick, accompanied by Victor, designed to draw the French ruler into his opponent's camp. Rainald of Dassel did not help the cause of the emperor or of his pope when he declared to Louis that 'the emperor had never promised to share with anyone, and certainly not with petty kings (*reguli*), his jurisdiction over the Roman Church'.[40] The exalted position of the emperor was bound to be weakened by the increasing importance of the leading kings (and their kingdoms); it was unwise as well as quite ineffective to say openly that they should be kept in their place. The canonisation of Charlemagne, which was pronounced by Rainald in Aachen in December 1165, can also be seen as a retort to the kings, in annexing the Carolingians to the Teutonic rather than the French kingdom, and as a means of underlining the special status of the Holy Empire.[41] Evidence of the use of the term *Sacrum Imperium* by Frederick and Dassel goes back to the period just before the Besançon meeting of 1157.

Dassel committed a further blunder when on Victor IV's death in April 1164 he at once, without consulting Frederick, asked the Victorine cardinals to elect a successor, who took the name of Paschal III, thus prolonging the schism. Alexander had, in fact, on various occasions attempted to come to terms with the emperor, while at the same time pursuing all means of strengthening his position, though always taking care to keep the possibility of negotiation open. At the same time, Frederick's cause, for example in Italy, was not helped by his support of a papal candidate without international backing. And in the Teutonic kingdom countless difficulties were caused by the emperor's refusal to give up his pope and to recognise Alexander. Even the oaths which Frederick exacted at the Diet in Würzburg at Whitsun 1165 never to recognise Alexander, in which he also bound himself, failed to stop the erosion of the position of the anti-Alexandrine popes.

At the end of 1165 Alexander took advantage of the election of a senate favourable to him to return to Rome and to make a solemn entry into the Holy City. He lost no time in rallying the anti-imperial forces in Italy against Frederick, who at once realised that he had to return to the peninsula, for the fourth time. Once in Italy, he soon made for Rome itself. Thanks to some adroit propaganda moves ostensibly aimed at settling the schism which put Alexander at a disadvantage, he obtained control of the city in July 1167, though only after the sacrilegious burning down of a church. Alexander had to flee and Paschal was solemnly enthroned in St Peter's. Frederick also proclaimed that it was he and not the pope who had authority over Rome. The emperor appeared to be at the peak of his power in Italy, though he had not yet managed to solve either the Lombard or the Sicilian problem. However, if he felt any satisfaction at that moment, it was dispelled a few days later when once again an epidemic broke out among the troops, this time claiming the lives of Rainald of Dassel and of two of Frederick's cousins, Frederick of Swabia and Welf VII. The emperor had no alternative but to retreat in haste to the north of Italy, prior to his return home, at times having to flee in disguise. There was also bad news about the situation in Lombardy.

By his policy Frederick had managed to largely unite a group of cities that had long been at loggerheads with each other. The Lombard cities were certainly not all opposed either to the Empire or to the emperor, but in general they strongly objected to the way Frederick exercised his authority.[42] In December 1167 16 cities formed the Lombard League. They took a mutual oath to fight for their independence, to resist what they regarded as Frederick's encroachments on their rights, and not to make a separate peace.

Though Frederick still held central Italy, he had lost Lombardy. The fortunes of both Lombard urban independence and of Alexander himself were clearly in the ascendant. The emperor's policy of assuming many rights traditionally held by the Lombard communes and of enforcing these by military means, as well as playing off one city against another, simply did not work. In any case it was probably a mistaken policy not to cooperate more fully with the rising economic forces represented by the cities. This may well have been due to Frederick's inadequate knowledge of conditions in Italy. Altogether Frederick had too few allies and too many enemies. He also lacked a major supporter against Alexander among the rulers; he certainly could not rely on Henry II of England, who was preoccupied with many other problems, including his dispute with Archbishop Thomas Becket. The pope favoured by the majority of the Church was his foe, as were most of the Lombard and some other important Italian cities, and the kingdom of Sicily gave help to his enemies. At times influential circles in Rome were friendly to the emperor, but the situation there was quite volatile.

Thus, particularly also after Rainald of Dassel's death, the whole direction of imperial policy needed re-examining. Frederick showed throughout his reign that he was prepared to face realities, if often only with a certain time-lag. He was not winning the battle in Lombardy or over the papal schism, and he could not fail to see that both were connected. Alexander was giving increasing support to the Lombard League, even going so far as to threaten with excommunication any city which broke ranks. He had some theological grounds for action against an excommunicate emperor, but at the same time he was clearly descending into the political arena with his questionable use of spiritual weapons to support his allies in the Lombard League. To Alexander the end, the absolute necessity of terminating the schism at the earliest possible moment through the recognition of his pontificate by Frederick, may have justified the means he used.

For some years war alternated with negotiation, with Frederick attempting unsuccessfully to drive a wedge between the papacy and the Lombard League. In September 1174 Frederick crossed the Alps for the fifth time. But the emperor was short of troops for the task of reducing the Lombard League to obedience and early in 1176 therefore appealed to Henry the Lion for help, who, however, refused.[43] In May 1176, Frederick was decisively defeated by troops of the Lombard League at Legnano, north of Milan. This event finally convinced the emperor that he had to give up the struggle. Thus in the end, Alexander succeeded in defeating the emperor by patiently pursuing his cause and by helping to maintain a united front against Frederick among the Lombard cities. Owing to the loyalty of the Lombard League to the pope, the emperor was forced to arrive a settlement with the Holy See. Actually, as Frederick's negotiators had discovered that Alexander was not likely to back the demands of the League to the hilt, this course of action suited the emperor, so long as he could pocket his pride and humble himself before the pope. Accordingly, in the preliminary agreement with the Holy See in October 1176, Frederick had to give up his anti-pope and to recognise Alexander without reservations. In return the latter agreed to recognise Frederick as emperor and to repeal his excommunication. The two sides compromised on the question of changes in bishoprics Frederick had made during the schism. The emperor had to yield some territorial rights in Italy; thus the Holy See was to appoint the Prefect of Rome. The concessions Alexander made were mainly at the expense of the Lombards, demonstrating that the pope put the interests of the Church as a whole above the obligations the Holy See had incurred to the north Italian cities during their bitter and costly struggle with the emperor. Naturally the members of the Lombard League resented the pope's attitude, but Alexander told them that they could make counter-claims against the emperor.

Thus gradually Frederick was able to make up, through diplomacy, part of the set-backs he had suffered on the battlefield. He succeeded in detaching some cities from the Lombard League. Although negotiations were several times in great danger of collapsing, finally the Peace Treaty of Venice was concluded in July 1177 between the emperor and the Holy See. Frederick agreed to a six years' truce with the Lombard League, during which he undertook not to demand an oath of loyalty from its members or to take any legal action against them. In the treaty with Sicily, with which there was to be a fifteen years' truce, the emperor implicitly recognised Norman authority over the southern half of the peninsula. Compared with the preliminary treaty, Frederick received a major concession from the pope in that he was allowed to retain the Matildine lands for the time being. In Venice the emperor was absolved by three cardinals and later he 'prostrated himself before the pontiff, who, in tears . . . gave him his benediction'.[44] After mass, Frederick held Alexander's stirrup and made ready to lead his horse, a gesture the pope refused to accept; and he blessed him instead.[45] Alexander was able to crown his reign by presiding over the Third Lateran Council in March 1179, at which it was laid down that in future a two-thirds majority of the cardinals was required for the election of a pope. While one of the canons of the council has been called the charter of the crusade against heretics, [46] the pope did try to mediate the dispute with the Waldensians. However, he left the decision as to whether permission should be granted to them to preach to the local bishop. By his refusal of a licence, the Archbishop of Lyons drove the preachers into opposition to the Church.

Throughout his dispute with the papacy, Frederick – unlike Henry IV – succeeded in avoiding any act demeaning his position as emperor, into which actually Alexander, with great skill and compassion, never attempted to force him. At last the schism was over. Although Frederick had been forced to give up the far-reaching claims with which he had begun his activities in Italy, he emerged from his struggles in a remarkably strong position, even in Italy and in regard to the papacy. His rule over the Teutonic kingdom had never been threatened and his excommunication did not weaken his position there, as had been the case with Henry IV. Had these spiritual weapons been used too often by the popes in their conflicts with rulers and had they thus become blunted? Only the future could tell.

What else had the long dispute between Frederick and Alexander revealed about the relative strengths of spiritual and secular forces at the time? The answer to this question is complicated by the fact that the pope did not confine himself to ecclesiastical weapons, but fought the emperor militarily by proxy, mainly through the agency of the cities of Lombardy, and that he used spiritual penalties in at least partly political struggles. Conversely, some of the emperor's most effective aides during his campaign in Italy were archbishops like Rainald of Cologne and Christian of Mainz, who cannot have had very much time for their purely ecclesiastical functions. However, what mainly stands out in this connection is that even the mightiest prince in Europe could not in the end prevent the recognition of a remarkable and deeply spiritual pontiff who – after overcoming some initial resistance – was widely acclaimed throughout Western Christendom. Compared with that, armies, diplomacy and even oaths never to accept Alexander sworn by reluctant bishops at the command of the emperor did not carry great weight. In another sense, Alexander's success in obtaining Frederick's recognition as pope was a reflection of the pontiff's superior tactical skills and of a sophistication going back to a long Italian tradition of which most of his Teutonic opponents, such as Rainald of Dassel, and much of the time also the emperor himself, were not capable. Alexander did not shrink from the application of force when he regarded its use as necessary, but he showed remarkable restraint in its employment, looking beyond the struggle to reconciliation, an attitude Frederick only adopted at a late stage. Perhaps the emperor never fully got the measure of the situation in the peninsula. He was certainly more effective in the Teutonic kingdom, where he was able to assure a large measure of stability, even during long absences. Much of this was due to Frederick's success in ending the feud between the Staufen and Welf dynasties.

For about 25 years, Frederick had been able to maintain harmony with Henry the Lion, although his cousin began to occupy a quasi-royal position. Again and again, the emperor helped to solve disputes in which Henry was involved. But obviously something had begun to change by the time of Frederick's preliminary settlement with the papacy. In 1176, as we have seen, when the emperor badly needed military reinforcements in Italy, Henry had apparently refused his appeal for help.[47] While in the particular circumstances Henry was not obliged under feudal law to supply soldiers to Frederick, he showed considerable ingratitude to the emperor who had protected him for many years against his opponents. In the preliminary settlement with the papacy, Frederick agreed to some stipulations dealing with rearrangements in bishoprics and with the return of ecclesiastical property after the schism which were clearly going to prove unpalatable to Henry. The treaty included a clause reinstating Bishop Ulrich of Halberstadt in his diocese, from which Henry had expelled him. When the bishop took possession of his diocese and demanded from Henry the return of church property alienated during his absence, the duke responded by military action, which resulted in the bishop banning him. A coalition was formed against Henry in Saxony, which led to the opening of hostilities.

When Frederick held a diet in Speyer in November 1178, both parties lodged accusations against each other. It was a sign of the emperor's changed attitude to his cousin, that – far from trying to achieve a compromise as he had previously done – he summoned Henry and his opponents to a further diet at Worms in January 1179. By then the emperor had apparently come to the conclusion that his cousin's use of the territorial position he had built up for himself was becoming a threat to the coherence of the Teutonic kingdom.[48] But Henry did not appear and thus set off a whole series of legal measures against himself. 'The duke's trial was unquestionably political, but it was conducted in full accordance with contemporary legal standards.'[49] The proceedings consisted initially of a case brought under customary law (*Landrecht*) by those of his peers who felt aggrieved by Henry, and later, after the duke formed a plot against the emperor, by Frederick against his cousin under feudal law. The outcome was that Henry was deprived of his Saxon and Bavarian duchies, but was allowed to keep his allodial lands around Brunswick and Lüneburg.[50] Military action by the emperor proved necessary to obtain Henry's surrender and he was banished for a period to the court of his father-in-law, Henry II, in England. The Saxon duchy was divided, the western part put under the Archbishop of Cologne, the eastern section went to the Ascanian dynasty, to a son of Albert the Bear. The Wittelsbach dynasty received most of what remained of Bavaria, where they were to rule until 1918.

In 1183 the emperor was able to make a definitive settlement with the Lombards at Constance, in which he gave up the far-reaching claims he had made earlier. The rights of the cities were recognised, and even the existence of the Lombard League accepted by the emperor as part of the north Italian order. However, imperial rights in the north Italian cities and further south were preserved, altogether giving Frederick a position in Italy which none of his predecessors since the Investiture Contest had been able to achieve.[51] At a meeting with Frederick at Verona that same year, Lucius III, who had followed Alexander III in the papacy on his death in 1181, successfully urged the emperor to join the planned crusade. They also agreed on joint action against heresy, which appeared to be particularly threatening in the south of France and in Northern Italy. In the papal decretal '*Ad abolendam*' in 1184, the 'classical formula' was found, according to which the Church tried and if appropriate condemned the heretic, but left the execution of the judgment and penalty to the secular arm.[52]

In 1184 Frederick's son and heir, Henry VI, who had already been elected king in 1169, was betrothed at the age of 19 to the Sicilian Princess

Constance, 11 years his senior, as part of a Staufen policy to improve relations with the Norman kingdom.[53] It could not, however, then be foreseen that Constance would soon inherit the Sicilian kingdom, as came about owing to the death of her nephew William II without issue in 1189. Perhaps partly as a consequence of this *rapprochement*, imperial relations with the curia soured, particularly after the elevation of the Archbishop of Milan, 'a fierce opponent of the emperor'[54] as Urban III in 1185. A native of this city, he never overcame the bitterness he felt towards those who had destroyed it. The new pope not only maintained the refusal of the curia to have Frederick's heir, Henry VI, who had been elected King of the Romans as a child, crowned emperor during this father's lifetime. He also attacked the royal exercise of rights over the Teutonic Church and determined a disputed episcopal election there against the wishes of the emperor. In retaliation, King Henry occupied the Patrimony of St Peter. Urban now threatened to excommunicate the emperor, but died before he could do so. Relations between the imperial court and the papal curia improved during the following two pontificates. This was partly due to the necessity of a closing of ranks owing to the fall of Jerusalem to Saladin in 1187 and the proclamation of the Third Crusade that followed. Frederick regarded taking a leading part in the crusade as his duty, as part of his imperial mission. As the premier ruler in Western Christendom he could not stand aside in an enterprise in which the kings of France and England participated. In any case, it is quite likely that as a participant in the unsuccessful Second Crusade in his younger days, he was hoping for a more satisfactory outcome this time.

In the light of previous experience, Frederick took great care organising his force and was able to avert the antisemitic outrages which had marred earlier crusades. Setting out in May 1189 ahead of the kings of France and England, Frederick took the land route through the Balkans. He was thus dependent on the cooperation of the Byzantine Emperor Isaac Angelus. Frederick mistrusted Byzantium ever since the Second Crusade. In turn, Isaac was suspicious of Frederick's intentions. But after some hostilities between the two sides, the Greeks decided on a settlement with Frederick. In March 1190 Frederick's expedition crossed into Asia Minor. It was there, in Armenia, that Frederick was drowned in the river Salef in June 1190.[55] As usual, the death of an emperor created an entirely new situation.

King Henry VI had been acting as his father's regent during his absence on crusade. He was a ruler of considerable ability and indeed of learning, of great determination often manifesting itself in brutality, but he lacked his father's popularity. Even before Barbarossa's death a number of complications had arisen. Henry the Lion, who had to go into exile in England as part of the arrangements for the crusade, decided to return home prematurely in the late summer of 1189, breaking his undertakings to Frederick. He also began a military campaign to recover some of his lost possessions, so that

King Henry, as regent, in October 1189 mustered troops against him. Despite repeated attempts at a settlement, this new phase of the conflict between the Welf and Staufen dynasties continued through most of Henry VI's reign.[56] All this came at a particularly awkward time for the king. As was indicated earlier, the death of William II of Sicily in November 1189 made William's aunt, Henry's wife Constance, heiress to the Norman kingdom. Henry therefore wished to take possession of the Sicilian kingdom as soon as possible. However, the Sicilian nobility elected as king Tancred, a member of the royal family of doubtful legitimacy, so that the claims of Constance and of Henry could only be realised by force of arms.

When news of Frederick Barbarossa's drowning was received, Henry succeeded his father in the Teutonic kingdom without difficulty. In the circumstances there was some urgency for the new ruler to proceed to Rome as quickly as possible for his coronation by the pope, and this took place in April 1191. Henry then moved south attempting to gain possession of the kingdom of Sicily, which included the southern Italian mainland, but was unable to take Naples. With his troops decimated by disease, he had to return home at the end of 1191. The papacy was determined to prevent the Patrimony of St Peter from being surrounded by Staufen territory with its Lombard kingdom in the north and the kingdom of Sicily to the south. The curia now openly supported Tancred and concluded a concordat with him in June 1192.

The situation looked grim for the emperor, particularly as he was also faced with a rising in Saxony which gave new strength to the Welf opposition to him. But everything changed in December 1192 with the capture of the King of England, Richard Lionheart, by Duke Leopold of Austria on his return from the crusade, in violation of the protection extended to crusaders by the Church.[57] Richard, who was very hot-tempered, had made many enemies on the crusade, including Leopold, whom he had personally insulted. While King Philip Augustus of France had been Richard's fellow-crusader, their differences in connection with the extensive English possessions in France continued unabated. As Richard supported not only his Welf relatives but also Tancred in Sicily, the emperor had every reason to ally himself with Philip Augustus, who was keen on Henry's support.

The emperor obtained custody of the eminent prisoner from Leopold in return for the promise of a share of the ransom money. However, Henry now risked running foul of the papacy, and not only for imprisoning a crusader. There was also a widespread suspicion that the emperor had been involved in the murder by Germanic knights of Bishop Albert of Liège, who had been elected by a majority of the voters, but rejected by Henry, while his claims were upheld by the pope.[58] There were possible echoes here of the murder of Archbishop Thomas Becket in Canterbury Cathedral. Pope Celestine III was unable to take effective measures to make good his protection of a crusader, because for various reasons the majority of the cardinals was opposed to such action. Some were imperialists, and others feared that intervention on Richard's behalf would only strengthen the emperor's alliance with Philip Augustus.[59] By adroit negotiations Henry managed to avert any church sanctions against himself. Ruthlessly exploiting his wealthy prisoner, who was only released in February 1194, Henry obtained an enormous ransom which allowed him to finance a further expedition to conquer the kingdom of Sicily after Tancred's death the same month. At Christmas 1194 Henry was crowned King of Sicily in Palermo Cathedral, and the following day Constance bore him a son, the future Frederick II.

In the meantime the opposition in the Teutonic kingdom had collapsed and in March 1194 there had even been a reconciliation between the Welf and Staufen families with a love-match between Henry the Lion's eldest son and a cousin of the emperor. Henry the Lion himself died a year later. The Staufen dynasty now had the Teutonic kingdom, Burgundy and the whole of the Italian peninsula, including Sicily, with exception of the Patrimony of St Peter, at its feet. In view of the enormous power wielded by Henry, the papacy was helpless. All the curia could do was to withhold its consent to far-reaching proposals made by Henry which may have involved a hereditary imperial succession as well as certain changes in the relations between Empire and Church which the papacy feared might make the Holy See too dependent on the emperor; unfortunately not enough is known of the details of Henry's scheme.[60] In the Teutonic kingdom the emperor did, however, succeed in having his son Frederick elected King of the Romans at the age of two.

Soon the situation actually changed again. A rebellion broke out in Sicily which Henry crushed with the utmost brutality. The final blow to the Staufen position was Henry VI's death from malaria in September 1197, at the age of thirty-one, as he was about to depart on crusade from Messina. On his death-bed Henry stipulated that Constance and their son, Frederick, were to render homage to the pope for Sicily, and generally to adopt a conciliatory attitude to the curia. The imperial occupation of the Matildine lands and of the Patrimony of St. Peter was to be ended. Through these concessions, Henry hoped to save the connection between the Empire and the kingdom of Sicily under the control of the Staufen dynasty, in the hands of his only child, King Frederick, then not even three years old.[61]

Although Frederick had been elected King of the Romans, it soon became clear to his paternal uncle, Philip, Duke of Swabia, that owing to his tender age his nephew did not at that time have a chance of being chosen by the princes to succeed his father as ruler north of the Alps. Philip would have liked to have confined himself to being regent for his nephew, but in the end he saw that the only chance of maintaining the crown within the Staufen dynasty was for him to accept election as king, which took place in March 1198. There was by then opposition among the princes to the continuation of the family on the throne, which resulted in the election of a Welf candidate, Otto IV, a son of Henry the Lion, in July 1198. As both sides had a substantial following, the Teutonic kingdom faced a severe crisis with this dual election.

What was to have a profound influence on the fate of the two royal candidates was a change in the papacy in the period before their election. In January 1198, Celestine III, the oldest man ever to have been elected pope (in 1191 at the age of 85) died in his early nineties. He was succeeded by Innocent III, who at about 37 was probably the youngest man ever to have become Supreme Pontiff.[62] In spite of his advanced age, Celestine had watched carefully and with determination over the interests of the Holy See. He was now followed by an outstanding personality at the height of his powers, by one of the greatest popes.

Lothar dei Conti of Segni, who took the name of Innocent III, belonged to a family of small land-owners in the Anagni region near Rome.[63] Through his mother, a Scotti, he possessed close connections with the city's patriciate. He studied theology in Paris under a teacher who emphasised the importance of preaching and penance. His stay of several years in France, whose intellectual climate influenced him deeply, was followed by law study at Bologna, though it is doubtful whether he had any formal training as a canonist, as was at one time believed.[64] However, whatever his training, he clearly had a fine mind capable of probing and dissecting the most complicated legal questions.[65] He was a man of great piety, who wrote two works of devotional theology, and he was well known for his care in saying mass.[66] He also had a proven record of administrative efficiency. His maternal uncle, Pope Clement III, had made him a cardinal.[67]

The absence of a clear verdict from the Teutonic electors provided the first major test of Innocent's ability to make the influence of the papacy felt. The whole issue bristled with theological, political, and indeed also international complications.[68] Otto was supported by his uncle, Richard Lionheart of England, who had earlier created him count of Poitou, and therefore – in view of the Anglo-French conflict at the time – his Staufen opponent was aided by King Philip Augustus of France. Unfortunately the Staufen party antagonised the pope, who was considering adjudicating the dispute, by denying that he had any right to do so. In the Declaration of Speyer of May 1199 Philip of Swabia and his supporters claimed that by his election as king he had already acquired imperial rights. Innocent rejected these views, arguing that 'the imperial position was an "apostolic", that is, a papal favour which could be exercised only on the fulfilment of certain conditions'.[69]

In his famous memorandum *Deliberatio de tribus electis* of the turn of 1200 to 1201, Innocent carefully weighed the claims of each candidate, including those of Frederick, which were not, however, practicable at the time. In Philip's case, the main impediment in canon law consisted in his excommunication.[70] The ban went back to the summer of 1196, when the curia was deeply worried about Henry VI's increasing power and the threat thus presented to the very survival of the Patrimony of St Peter and the independence of the papacy. Philip, Duke of Swabia, who had also become Duke of Tuscany and master of the Matildine lands, had infringed the frontier of the Patrimony, to which Pope Celestine III responded by pronouncing the sentence of excommunication on all those who violated the property of St Peter; Philip was not actually mentioned by name.[71] At the same time, without wishing to condemn Philip by family association, the past record of Staufen dealings with the papacy and the church is taken into account in the memorandum. The decision in favour of Otto is based more on Philip's unworthiness than on the merits of the Welf candidate.[72] In 1201 Innocent somewhat prematurely recognised Otto, who accepted the territorial claims of the Church in central Italy and its overlordship over the Sicilian kingdom. The following year, in the decretal *Venerabilem*, the pope asserted his right to examine the suitability of a Teutonic king for the emperorship, before proceeding to a coronation. In particular, the pontiff claimed for his office the adjudication of disputed elections.[73]

Now, however, it was the pope's turn to misjudge the situation in the Teutonic kingdom, just as Frederick Barbarossa as emperor had underrated Alexander III's papal strength. According to one historian, 'Otto was a worthless, inefficient, bungling, totally unreliable braggart.'[74] In 1204, Otto's position, which was already weak at the time of papal recognition, collapsed altogether. Philip was crowned the following year at Aachen by Archbishop Adolf of Cologne, Otto's main original sponsor, who had changed sides, apparently because he had sufficiently 'fleeced the Guelf [Welf] side'.[75] Even Innocent was abandoning Otto and working out arrangements with Philip involving his recognition. But in June 1208, when all that was needed to complete the settlement was ratification by the two kings, Philip of Swabia was killed in a private quarrel. The princes now accepted Otto, who not only confirmed his previous concessions to the papacy, but also abandoned important royal rights over the churches in the Teutonic kingdom.[76]

Innocent was not, however, to find Otto's policy at all palatable once the Welf king was firmly in the saddle. After his imperial coronation in 1209, Otto answered an appeal from parties in the Sicilian kingdom for his intervention. He crossed into its south Italian territories in 1210, throwing down the gauntlet to the pope, who excommunicated him. Both the papacy and Frederick's rule in Sicily were in considerable danger as Otto was overrunning southern Italy and planning a landing in Sicily itself. Not only Innocent, but also Philip Augustus of France, the enemy of Otto's English ally, encouraged the princes in the Teutonic kingdom to depose Otto and to elect in his place Frederick, King of Sicily, which a handful of them did in September 1211 in Nuremberg. For the pope the choice was not as easy as it was for Philip Augustus. But Innocent decided that in the circumstances the only way to rid himself of the menace of the Welf king was to call on the Staufen heir. Frederick had become his ward on the death of his mother, Constance, just over a year after that of his father Henry VI. The pope relinquished his guardianship at the end of 1208, when Frederick came of age on his fourteenth birthday.[77]

Partly owing to a series of events which could hardly be anticipated, Innocent had found himself in turn backing all three candidates for the Teutonic crown. Thus it was difficult for the curia to maintain that it had been able to apply a set of theological principles in an even-handed way. Actually, in the Teutonic kingdom papal support was not necessarily viewed positively. There was considerable resentment at papal intervention, as displayed for instance by the famous poet, the *Minnesänger* Walther von der Vogelweide. However, the continued struggle over the succession had enabled the Holy See to secure definite advantages. The twists and turns of the dispute had allowed Innocent to stake a papal claim to an increased say in the elections for the crown of the Teutonic kingdom. Furthermore, he had been able to extract important concessions from each of the contenders, including finally from Frederick himself. Not all promises were kept. But what proved to be lasting was the abandonment of imperial rights to a number of territories stretching from the Tyrrhenian to the Adriatic Sea which were now incorporated in the Patrimony of St Peter. This helped to create a widened barrier between the north and the south of the peninsula. It was through his policy of what he regarded as the recuperation of territory rightfully belonging to the Holy See that Innocent III was largely able to complete the foundation of the 'papal states'.

When Otto received reports of the growing opposition to him in the Teutonic kingdom and, indeed, also in parts of Lombardy, he made an important decision not only for his own future, but for that of Frederick: he called off his Sicilian invasion, thereby saving the fortune of the young king, who already had a ship at hand for his flight. In spite of the opposition of his Sicilian counsellors, who – like the late Empress Constance – regarded the Teutonic kingdom as a far away land of little interest to them, Frederick decided to accept the transalpine mission. In response to the prompting of the pope, who insisted on the separation of the Norman and Teutonic crowns, Frederick's recently born son Henry, from his marriage to Constance of Aragon, was crowned King of Sicily. Frederick then set off on his perilous journey, whose successful outcome was not by any means assured. He needed all the support he could get and at this stage was prepared to make almost any concession required of him. He gave an undertaking to the pope that he would respect his wishes to keep the crowns separate, swore him homage as King of Sicily and renewed his mother's promises to respect papal authority in the *regno* of Sicily. In return he was acclaimed (though not yet crowned) emperor in Rome and received urgently needed financial help for his war expenses from Innocent.

Northern Italy was divided in its loyalties, and, as so often before, friendship with one city easily brought with it the enmity of another. It was in these years, apparently, that the party names of Guelf (for the Welf side) and of Ghibelline (an Italian corruption of the name of the Staufen castle of Waiblingen in Swabia) began to be used. These appellations were to be retained later on even when they lost their original meaning with the end of the Staufen dynasty. In order to obtain support, Frederick gave privileges to many cities and particularly to his Genoan allies for their trading activities in Sicily.

Frederick had to criss-cross Italy on his way to the Alps in order to avoid capture by his local enemies, which he only managed narrowly. For similar reasons, his passage of the Alps was quite hazardous, but with a comparatively small following he was able to make his way to the gates of Constance, which he reached barely a few hours before his rival was expected there. Refusal of entry into the city would have been a serious blow to Frederick, and everything therefore depended on the decision of a local bishop unwilling to be drawn into the quarrel of the two kings. In this tense situation the presence of a papal legate with Frederick proved decisive. The legate pointed out to the bishop that Otto had been excommunicated and that if he refused to open the city gates to Frederick he would be defying the pope's wishes, to which the ecclesiastic yielded, if reluctantly. From here on Frederick's progress was more rapid and Otto retreated northwards.

Each side sought support from its allies abroad. In this Frederick succeeded quickly. France promised him assistance against Otto and gave him a considerable financial subsidy, which was useful for rewarding princes in the Teutonic kingdom willing to cast their vote for the Staufen side. Thus, in December 1212, Frederick was formally elected king at Frankfurt and crowned King of the Romans at Mainz. Otto allied himself with his uncle King John of England against France, but they were both beaten in Flanders. Otto suffered defeat at the hands of King Philip Augustus at Bouvines in 1214[78] and had to flee. Frederick's success was thus clinched by the victory of his French ally. In this way, the assistance of the pope and of the King of France to the Staufen side played a considerable part in settling the succession in the Teutonic kingdom. The following year Frederick was crowned again, this time at Aachen, the right place according to tradition.

Though Frederick had clearly won, Otto maintained his claim to be the rightful ruler until his death in 1218. Frederick II was for the time being able in effect – in spite of his infant son also being nominally King of Sicily – to reunite the crowns his father had worn briefly during his reign. But the pope had secured his promise to make arrangements to separate the kingdoms and to place them under the rule of different members of the Staufen dynasty.

Particular attention has been paid to the difficulties Frederick had to overcome in order to overthrow Otto IV, because this victory over apparent odds had important consequences for the future. An aura of invincibility and of the miraculous surrounded Frederick, who himself felt that he owed his unexpected rise to the front ranks of European rulers from the brink of the abyss to divine favour which, he believed, would continue to bless him. Owing to this, the extreme caution he had displayed while fighting to secure the Teutonic crown was now abandoned and replaced by over-confidence, by blindness to the danger-signals he encountered on the way.

What sort of a person was Frederick? He was certainly a man of considerable culture and intellectual attainments. He had some of the winning ways of his paternal grandfather, but also some of Barbarossa's and his father's ruthlessness. Throughout his life he displayed a vivid interest in other civilisations and religions, as he was always curious to find out more and to extend his knowledge, which led to – probably unjustified – suspicions of heterodoxy. Indeed he was a particularly rigorous opponent of all heresies. In the famous law code, the Constitutions of Melfi, which he introduced for the kingdom of Sicily in 1231, heretics were seen as enemies not only of God, but of the ruler and of society. They were deemed to have committed treason against the ruler and therefore deserved to be punished by death.[79] He was fully aware of the potential of Sicily as a base for crusading operations, and was in sympathy with the crusading tradition, hoping to follow in the footsteps of his Staufen forebears. At the same time, while in principle at one with the Church in prosecuting Christians who had strayed from orthodoxy into heterodoxy, he appears to have been reasonably tolerant to members of other faiths. This probably had something to do with his upbringing in the Sicilian kingdom, where there were considerable minorities of Muslims and Jews. Frederick had his Saracen bodyguards, whose loyalty to him personally could not be touched by any papal measures taken against him. He stood up for the Jews in the Teutonic kingdom, when wrongful accusations of ritual murder were brought against them.[80]

Frederick certainly brought a wide experience to his task as ruler of territories stretching from Northern Europe into the Mediterranean, but it was drawn more from the south than the north. This was reflected in the length of time spent in each of his dominions. Whereas Barbarossa, in spite of his preoccupations with Italy, operated from north of the Alps for most of his reign, Frederick II only resided in the Teutonic kingdom for a few years altogether. Though he familiarised himself with the affairs of that kingdom, his main attention was directed elsewhere. He was proud of his Staufen heritage, but he may have seen it mainly in imperial rather than strictly

Teutonic terms. And as he became King of Sicily before he acquired his other crowns, that kingdom – which he owed to his mother's heritage – was bound to occupy a very special place in his priorities. There he was an absolutist ruler, which he could never be in the Teutonic kingdom, where he had to consult the magnates on most major matters. In his administration of the kingdom of Sicily, Frederick achieved a high – and possibly excessive – degree of centralisation. He did not have any scruples in enforcing his rule there with the utmost harshness, particularly if he regarded a stern warning to his subjects as necessary. In the Teutonic kingdom he was quite prepared to be much more conciliatory, making many concessions to the magnates.[81] Admittedly that kingdom was the basis of his emperorship, which Frederick regarded as the vital link holding together his extensive empire. Governing so wide an area obviously presented considerable difficulties to any ruler, but was not necessarily an impossible task. In the meantime the papacy was bound to take very seriously the accumulation of power in Frederick's hands, not least because it extended to northern as well as to southern Italy, and thus hemmed in the Patrimony of St Peter.

For a number of reasons relations with the papacy did not reach a critical point during the pontificate of Innocent III. Frederick was still on the whole careful not to antagonise the pope. There appears to have been a special bond between them ever since the days of Innocent's guardianship over the infant king, even if there were sometimes – inevitably – strains between them. On one side there was a certain paternal care for the young ruler, whom the pope helped to regain his Staufen inheritance; on the other the respect of the ward for his former guardian, even if he was critical of certain aspects of the administration of Sicily during his minority. In any case, Innocent was confronted with many other acute problems and in this situation was supple enough to avoid raising any more. His two main current preoccupations were with heresy and with the infidel. On the one hand he was concerned with the perceived threat that aspects of the poverty movement, but even more the Cathars and the Waldensians, presented to the Catholic order. On the other hand, the need to free the Holy Places from Muslim rule through a further crusade continued to enjoy a high priority for him. He was successful in beginning the process of integrating parts of the poverty movement, such as the Franciscan and Dominican orders, into the Church.[82]

While Innocent was determined to maintain church control over all aspects of religious practice and to stem heresy, he wished to exhaust all peaceful means, such as persuasion, before turning to force and repression. Even with the Cathars, who denied the validity of the priesthood and of the sacraments, and did not accept the divinity of Christ,[83] the pope at times gave pacific methods a chance. However, such events as the Albigensian Crusade in the south of France showed that in the end the voice of reason was silenced by demands for action. This was due to a combination of circumstances, which included the murder of the papal legate in Toulouse in 1208, following his excommunication of Count Raymond VI of Toulouse. Also, this outstanding pontiff was unable to exercise adequate control over a later legate in the field, who incited the troops to indiscriminate slaughter of suspected Albigensians.[84] Thus the reign of even this pope of comparatively moderate views saw both the application of the weapon of holy war against mass dissent, and the extirpation of heretics who refused to submit. The regrettable exclusionary policy towards dissenters which is already apparent in St Augustine's attitude to the Donatists, was now taken a step further by heresy being equated for the first time with the *lèse majesté* of Roman law.[85] The Church at the time was too rigid in many aspects of ecclesiastical policy and practice to adopt a positive attitude to critics of the current order who were alienated by its material worldliness and by what was regarded in many quarters as its excessive politicisation. Presumably the authorities, not only spiritual, but also secular, regarded as a threat to the whole order of society those who did not submit to hierarchy. In a sense it was this fear of subversion from its midst that led to harsher treatment of those who had deviated from the Catholic faith than of those who were not Christians, like the Muslims in the East.

Right from the beginning of his pontificate, Innocent was involved in plans for a further crusade. Like his predecessors since Urban II, he regarded crusades very much as the pope's business. The presence of rulers during the campaign was liable to create difficulties for papal leadership. Indeed, the First Crusade, in which European monarchs did not participate, had been the only truly successful one so far. However, papal control was not easy to enforce, even if the armies were accompanied by a papal legate. This was certainly the case during the Fourth Crusade between 1202 and 1204, which took an entirely different course from the one intended by Innocent III. Thus the Venetians, who transported the troops and wanted their money for their services, in spite of the pope's prohibition[86] succeeded in getting the crusaders to help them to recapture and sack the Adriatic port of Zara, which had been held by their fellow-Christian Hungarians.[87] Also, which was even more serious, the expedition became embroiled in the affairs of the Byzantine Empire on the prompting of Philip of Swabia. He was the husband of the Princess Irene, whose father Isaac Angelus had been deposed and blinded earlier on as Byzantine emperor by his brother Alexius III. Philip managed to get the crusaders to break their journey to the Holy Land at Constantinople, to overthrow Alexius III, and to put on the throne Isaac's son Alexius IV, who had fled to Philip's court. Here Philip was only continuing the dynastic policy of his brother Henry VI, whose crusade had been planned partly in order to assert Philip's claim to the Byzantine throne on behalf of his wife.[88] Again the crusaders acted in contravention of papal instructions, for Innocent had beforehand clearly prohibited any further attacks on fellow Christians.[89]

Actually, the reign of Emperor Alexius IV did not last long. In the ensuing complications, the crusaders in 1204 ransacked Constantinople and replaced the Byzantine emperor by a Catholic ruler entirely alien to the orthodox population. Innocent was taken aback by the turn of events, but decided to endorse what had happened, particularly as – at any rate on paper – the schism between the Catholic and Orthodox Churches had been overcome. The treatment meted out by the crusaders to a Christian population was scandalous. It hardly required gifts of prophecy to predict that the so-called Latin Empire at Constantinople would not last, and it was actually overthrown in 1261, with the restoration of the Byzantine Empire. It is ironical that the crusaders weakened the main indigenous Christian bastion against Islam in the Near East by disrupting Byzantine government. Even if the changes made in Constantinople in 1204 were seen in some quarters in the West as positive, the Fourth Crusade, which had failed to achieve anything against Islam, did not generally redound to the credit of the papacy in the short, and certainly not in the long run.

Soon after, however, the crusading movement was to gain a notable recruit. When Frederick II's coronation was repeated at Aachen in 1215, to make up for any defects of the previous one in Mainz, the king took a crusader's vow. While this act was not the result of a sudden – entirely spontaneous – decision, the young ruler was certainly deeply moved by the solemnity of the coronation ceremony. He wished to follow the example of his paternal grandfather and of his father, as well as to put himself in the Carolingian tradition of a fighter against the infidels, which he marked by having the body of Charlemagne reinterred.[90] At the same time, he had in mind the advantages that might accrue to his Sicilian kingdom from his presence in the Near East. He was also staking a claim for a share in the leadership of the crusading movement and striking a blow at papal monopoly over it.[91] We cannot be sure as to what exactly was in Frederick's mind when he took his crusading vows. According to one authority he may simply have wished, at a time when he was still having to consolidate his position in the Teutonic kingdom, to secure the protection against attack to which every crusader was supposed to be entitled.[92]

Innocent was less than pleased with his former ward's action, but in the long run, during the ensuing conflict, the crusading vow taken in 1215 actually provided the strongest weapon in the papal armoury against Frederick. It has been suggested that at Aachen early in his twenties Frederick publicly proclaimed the programme for his reign: crusade, succession to Charlemagne, and world domination.[93] While it is true that Frederick claimed the heritage of Charlemagne, he recognised that with the rise of powerful kings like those of France and England the relative importance of

the emperorship had decreased, and with that the chance of world dominion. But the invocation of Charlemagne's memory certainly carried with it a
rejection of any papal claims to superiority over the emperor. Through his
crusading vow, taken perhaps too eagerly with the intention of accelerating
the stabilisation of his position in Christendom and *vis-à-vis* the papacy,
Frederick presented hostages to fortune and to the curia. He underrated the
time it would take him to regulate the affairs of his various dominions in
such a way that he could be absent for a longer period.

Innocent III, one of the outstanding pontiffs even in spite of all the set-
backs he suffered, died in 1216, soon after presiding over the Fourth Lateran
Council. Frederick was fortunate that the Sacred College elected as his
successor the aged Cardinal Cencius, who as chamberlain had completed
the important *Liber Censuum,* listing papal revenues,[94] and now took the
name of Honorius III. A man of compromise, Honorius strove to preserve a
consensus among the cardinals and saw in a good relationship with Frederick the best way of safeguarding the interests of the papacy. He therefore
acceded to Frederick's request for his imperial coronation, which took place
at St Peter's in November 1220. Honorius met Frederick's wishes to what
might appear to be a surprising extent. Though at one time threatening
excommunication, he in the end accepted a further delay in the emperor's
setting out on crusade.

Frederick never felt quite at home in the Teutonic kingdom, where he
lacked the power he had in Sicily and Southern Italy; he therefore did not
want to give up direct rule of the monarchy in which he had been born and
which had come to him first. Accordingly, Frederick was permitted by
Honorius to keep all his crowns, so long as he did not attempt to integrate
Sicily into the Empire. However, in the meantime the princes in the Teutonic
kingdom had recognised Frederick's nine-year-old son, Henry (VII), as King
of the Romans and therefore, subject to election, as the likely next emperor.
As Henry had already been crowned King of Sicily as an infant, this did not
exactly look like a plan for an eventual partition of the various dominions. In
any case, Henry's dignities could only be exercised at his father's discretion,
particularly so long as he was not of mature years. Furthermore, Frederick
began to legislate in the *regno*, the kingdom of Sicily, by imperial authority.
While these developments caused concern to the curia, the pope perhaps at
the same time sensed a diminution of the Staufen threat to the Patrimony of
St Peter elsewhere, for Frederick in this period seemed to be quite prepared
to see papal influence over the old Lombard kingdom of Italy strengthened.
With this relaxation of tension in the north, the papacy was no longer under
so much pressure from two directions. Also the emperor adopted a conciliatory stance over the Matildine lands, at any rate in the short run.[95]

In the meantime, the catastrophic defeat of the Fifth Crusade at Damietta
in the summer of 1221[96] made Frederick's presence in the East all the more

urgent. Frederick had actually put a strong squadron from the Sicilian navy at the disposal of the crusade, but in this critical situation more was required of him. The papacy was all the more determined to reverse the setback of the Fifth Crusade, as the papal legate, Pelagius, came under considerable criticism for the part he had played in the campaign. Thus the prestige of the papacy was involved, at least indirectly. Pope and emperor met in March 1223 to plan a further crusade and Frederick bound himself to depart for the East in 1225. With the pope's encouragement arrangements were made for Frederick, whose first wife Constance of Aragon had died in 1222, to marry Isabella, heiress of the kingdom of Jerusalem; her father carried the nominal title. Perhaps Honorius saw the chance of gaining in Frederick a strong King of Jerusalem who would secure the Holy Land for Christianity and found a powerful new Latin dynasty there. He hoped that Frederick would then content himself with a kind of imperial overlordship over his various kingdoms without endeavouring to exercise too much direct control over any of them.[97] If this was the pope's expectation, it was quite unrealistic.

It so happened that mustering the necessary resources for a crusade did not prove feasible even in 1225, and with papal agreement at a conference in San Germano, Frederick's departure was fixed for August 1227. Honorius wanted to make absolutely sure that there would be no further delay. Frederick therefore had to have an oath sworn on his behalf laying down that he would fall under the papal ban if he did not set out at the stipulated date.[98]

The pope believed that the most pressing problem in his relations with the emperor had now been settled. However, Frederick's intervention in the affairs of the Sicilian Church proved to be a continuing source of friction between them. As Frederick in his capacity of King of Sicily was technically a vassal of the Holy See, these matters caused particular annoyance to the curia. But the emperor was now about to raise questions which affected the vital interests of the papacy even more closely than arrangements for the crusade or royal interference with the Sicilian Church. To make preparations for his crusade, Frederick summoned the nobility and cities of Lombardy, as well as the magnates of the Teutonic kingdom, to a diet at Cremona, in Lombardy, over Easter 1226. To the Lombards this appeared to herald an attempt on the emperor's part to revive his rights over the (old Lombard) *regnum Italicum* in the north of the peninsula, over what German historians tend to call imperial Italy (*Reichsitalien*), which had been in abeyance since his father's death. Some Lombards, too, were in sympathy with unorthodox religious movements and resented Frederick's promise to suppress heresy.[99]

Honorius had resigned himself to Frederick's breach of his promises to separate his crowns, so long as he did not attempt to exercise rule over northern Italy. He was very sensitive to any Staufen assertion of power there, as that would put pressure on the Patrimony of St Peter from two directions.

The first reaction to the calling of the diet at Cremona came from the cities of the region, which revived the Lombard League that had caused so much difficulty for Frederick Barbarossa. By blocking passes over the Alps, the League prevented the attendance of representatives from the Teutonic kingdom, thus paralysing the diet as well as delaying the crusade. In the end, in the face of Lombard insurgence, the emperor had to call on the pope to mediate. Honorius to a large extent backed the cause of the Lombard cities and Frederick accepted the terms he proposed. The emperor appears to have realised by then that he had made a severe mistake in attempting to reestablish imperial power in Northern Italy before going on crusade. However, before the League had also agreed to the terms of the conciliation, Honorius died in March 1227.[100]

For Frederick and his future relations with the Holy See everything depended on who was going to be elected as Honorius' successor. When the cardinal who was the first choice of the Sacred College for technical reasons refused to accept the dignity, a cousin of Innocent III was raised to the pontificate, taking the name of Gregory IX.[101] The choice of the name, with echoes of Gregory VII, was not in itself conclusive, but was certainly a warning to the emperor to exercise extreme caution. The new pope, a friend of St Francis, had played an important part in the establishment of the Franciscan and Dominican orders. He combined a mild disposition with a 'stormy passion of his temperament, which could increase to a terrifying harshness'.[102]

Soon after his accession the new pope had to make a decision of outstanding significance in relation to the emperor. Frederick set out from Brindisi in September 1227, as stipulated in the treaty of San Germano, but was infected by an epidemic raging among the crusaders and had to return to shore after a few days. Obviously a sick emperor could not lead a crusade. Gregory at once, without hearing a report on the precise circumstances which had led the emperor to interrupt his expedition, under the terms of the Treaty of San Germano excommunicated Frederick for breaking his crusading vows. While the pope was formally entitled to take this step, he could have dispensed the emperor from the penalties incurred by his failure to sail for the East.[103] His decision flew in the face of justice and commonsense, for a higher power had prevented the emperor from fulfilling his commitment at that time; Frederick hoped that it was simply a matter of postponement. The injustice of Gregory's decision was bound to reflect badly on papal claims of high standards of impartiality on which curial jurisdiction prided itself. Frederick replied to the papal ban in measured terms, but Gregory was not to be deterred, and he put under interdict every place where the emperor was staying. The pope now openly supported the Lombards against Frederick and generally tensions between the papal and imperial sides became greatly exacerbated. Thus at Easter 1128, an uprising of the imperial party in Rome forced Gregory to flee from his capital. Frederick's lieutenant in Spoleto, exceeding the emperor's instructions, invaded the Patrimony of St Peter and occupied the territories incorporated by Innocent III.

Frederick now decided to go on crusade as soon as he had recovered his health, even though he was excommunicate. *En route* he asserted imperial authority in Cyprus, in the course of which he made many enemies. He then, by negotiation with the Sultan of Egypt, obtained possession of Jerusalem for a period of ten years and there in March 1229 wore his crown as emperor in the Church of the Holy Sepulchre,[104] an act the patriarch of Jerusalem had tried to prevent. Altogether 'Frederick's crusade left a legacy of conflict and disorder both in Cyprus and in the Holy Land.'[105] If Frederick believed that the liberation of Jerusalem would unite the Christians in the Holy Land behind him and would win over the pope, he was mistaken. Indeed the curia is likely to have been confirmed in its doubts about the emperor's orthodoxy by the manner in which he ignored his excommunicate status by going on crusade.

The emperor was also taking considerable chances by absenting himself from Europe at a time that was bound to be critical for him. When he returned to Italy in June, he found that papal troops had invaded the *regno*, but he was soon able to turn the tables on them. Thanks to the mediation of Hermann of Salza, Grand Master (*Hochmeister*) of the Teutonic Order, the friend of both emperor and pope, and of several bishops and princes from the Teutonic kingdom, Frederick managed to reach a settlement with the pope in July 1230 in a fresh treaty of San Germano. The emperor made far-reaching promises to the curia to loosen his control over the Church in the kingdom of Sicily, and was freed from the papal ban the following month. Many questions in the relationship between Empire and papacy were left open. To mark the reconciliation, Gregory and Frederick dined together, accompanied only by Hermann of Salza, who had done so much for them.

It is not surprising that Hermann played so prominent a part in bringing the two warring parties together. In his historic achievement, the establishment of the Teutonic Order in Prussia, he demonstrated his ability to work with both the temporal and the ecclesiastical power, with emperor and pope. In the negotiations which followed the call of the Polish Duke Conrad of Masovia to the order in 1225 or 1226 to help him against the heathen Prussians, the Grand Master accepted imperial as well as papal privileges. Emperor and pope in a sense competed for the mission against the heathen. Frederick with his 'Golden bull of Rimini' of 1226, granted the order territorial rule (*Landesherrschaft*) over the parts to be conquered. Gregory IX in 1234 took Prussia under the protection of the Holy See.[106] It was, however, mainly due to the imperial charter, granted under the influence of

Frederick's mentor Hermann, that – for better or for worse – a long period
of conquest, Christianisation and colonisation of Prussians and Slavs and
other inhabitants of the Baltic region by Germanic peoples was initiated.
The conquered territories were not incorporated in the Empire; also the
Grand Master of the Teutonic Order was not a Prince of the Empire
(*Reichsfürst*) in the medieval period. However, the order played an important part in the Empire through its *commanderies* (*Balleien*), which were
substantial landholdings that in varying degrees over time supplied
resources for the work in Prussia.[107]

Let us, after this diversion to eastern colonisation, return to the settlement
between pope and emperor to which Hermann of Salza had contributed so
much. Gregory had been very reluctant to absolve Frederick from excommunication so long as the emperor effectively kept rule over all his dominions in his own hands. Presumably he had in the first place put the emperor
under the ban because of his dissatisfaction with Frederick's breach of his
promise to detach Sicily from his other possessions. Thus the emperor's
inability to depart for the crusade at the stipulated date in 1227 owing to
illness may have simply provided a suitable opportunity for excommunication. Gregory in the end accepted the reality of his own military defeat and
of his inability to mobilise sufficient opposition to Frederick in the Teutonic
kingdom, where the emperor's position remained reasonably stable. Also
the pope had found out to his chagrin that the Lombard cities were not
prepared on this occasion to rise against the emperor to support the Holy
See. Once more it became evident that, while Lombard League and curia
were often drawn together against the emperor, their interests were not
identical. Some cities in Lombardy were havens for heretics and were out of
sympathy with the increasingly hard line taken by the Church towards
dissidents.

For Frederick it was important to be freed from excommunication. Once
more this spiritual weapon proved powerful, and to some extent balanced
the emperor's military advantage. Frederick preserved the integrity of the
territories united under his own rule. In this question of great importance to
both sides, the emperor was a clear winner; the papacy had failed in the
objective which it had pursued since Henry VI's reign of preventing or
breaking the union. In return for gaining his most important objective and
for being released from excommunication, Frederick was quite prepared to
make promises about the administration of the Church in the Sicilian kingdom, though it remained to be seen whether the papacy would be content
with the way he carried them out.

For the time being, relations between the curia and Frederick were mainly
positive, although Frederick, with his tendency to raise awkward
issues, opened potential trouble-spots in Sicily and Lombardy. In the
regno, Frederick in the constitutions of Melfi in 1231 considerably

centralised the administration, into which in the long term his concessions to the papacy concerning the Sicilian Church could only be integrated with great difficulty. What proved even more troublesome in the short run was that Frederick re-opened the question of Northern Italy, by again calling a diet to meet there, this time at Ravenna in November 1231, as he had done earlier at Cremona in 1226. The curia could not be indifferent to an attempt by Frederick to strengthen his power in the north of the peninsula. History repeated itself, as earlier during the reign of Honorius III. Once again the Lombard cities rose against the emperor. Interestingly enough, Frederick now even called on Gregory to mediate in the dispute, which was an impossible undertaking as the demands of the two sides were mutually exclusive.

Worse was to come for the emperor. In 1234 Frederick's eldest son, the 23-year-old King Henry (VII) of the Romans, who was his lieutenant in the Teutonic kingdom, rose against his father. Relations between father and son had been tense for some years, one of the problems – apart from the difference of generation – being that they found it difficult to co-ordinate their policies and that Henry was beginning to resent the limitations his father put on his power. He was also unwise enough to think of asserting his authority as King of the Romans in Lombardy, a region which his father regarded as within his primary sphere of influence. In 1235 he even went so far as to ally himself with the Lombards in rebellion against his father. Gregory, who was very much concerned with the spread of heresy in northern Italy and was dissatisfied with the attitude of some of the insurgent Lombard cities in this question, assisted the emperor by excommunicating his son. When Frederick after a prolonged absence thereupon returned to the Teutonic kingdom, without an army, his son's rebellion collapsed. Henry was deposed by his father and imprisoned for the rest of his life; he predeceased his father in 1242. Frederick was able to return to Italy after getting the magnates in the Teutonic kingdom to elect as King of the Romans and thus presumably as a likely future emperor the seven-year-old Conrad, his son from his marriage to Isabella, the heiress to the kingdom of Jerusalem. This election in 1237 is notable in that it was carried out by a college of 'eleven "fathers and luminaries of the Empire" who had accompanied the emperor to Vienna'. They ' "took the place of the Roman Senate" and chose Conrad IV as King of the Romans and future emperor.' Finally discarding what has been called the 'myth of universality', it was hoped to prevent conflicts over elections, such as dual ones taking place in two different places.[108] These efforts are an interesting parallel to those being carried on simultaneously in relation to the choice of popes.

In November 1237 the emperor defeated a Lombard army at Cortenuova, north of Milan. But Frederick spoiled the chance of putting his rule over Northern Italy on a more stable basis by making unacceptable demands, such as the unconditional surrender of Milan. Once again, a Staufen ruler misjudged the degree of resistance of which a major Lombard city was capable. Milan fought on in alliance with some of the other communes, and Frederick was unable to take Brescia in the autumn of 1238, in spite of a considerable international muster of troops.

To add fuel to the fire, in October 1238 the emperor had his illegitimate son Enzio married to the heiress of a large part of Sardinia, without consulting the pope, who regarded himself as the island's feudal overlord. He also strengthened imperial influence in Rome.[109] So once again Frederick was intervening in areas to which the Holy See was bound to be sensitive, thus upsetting the fine balance of power that had been established between Empire and papacy. Gregory therefore brought together a league of anti-imperial Lombard cities, helped to create an alliance between Venice and Genoa against Frederick, and reasserted his position in Rome. The final step taken by Frederick leading to a renewed breach with the papacy was his call, in February 1239, for an all-out war against the hostile Lombard cities. The following month Gregory accordingly excommunicated the emperor once more. While not naming the Lombards, the pontiff justified his measure by asserting that Frederick had not carried out his undertakings of 1230 regarding the Sicilian Church and that he had attempted to dominate Rome. Gregory promulgated a full-scale crusade against the emperor.[110] He also called a general council of the Church to meet in Rome at Easter 1241, but Frederick in a battle at sea took captive most of the foreign representatives, who were being transported in Genoese ships. By doing violence to innocent third parties engaged in their ecclesiastical duties, as well as by now also occupying the Patrimony of St Peter, the emperor demonstrated that he was fighting a war to the finish with the curia. By this action he antagonised King Louis IX of France (St Louis), who was well-disposed towards him and had tried hard to maintain neutrality in the papal-imperial conflict. The King of France deplored the quarrel which in his eyes diverted energy from the far more important issue of the crusades. To some extent he blamed the strife on the intransigence of the curia, notably later on under Innocent IV. In any case he is likely to have had little sympathy with papal depositions of a fellow monarch, 'whose hereditary title was incontestable, and whose culpability had not been judicially proved'.[111] Perhaps the most pious ruler of his age, Louis was yet adamant in his opposition to what he regarded as the interference of ecclesiastical justice in temporal matters.[112]

Frederick ruthlessly attempted to extract every advantage from his captives. As he delayed the release of some of the imprisoned cardinals, he impeded papal elections in succession to Gregory IX, who died in August 1241. Except for the short reign of a pontiff who died after a few days in office, it took nearly two years until a pope, the Genoese Cardinal Fieschi, who took the name of Innocent IV, could be elected in June 1243.

The new pope inherited plenty of problems besides that of the excommunicate emperor. His concerns included the persistence of heresy, the threat posed to Christendom by the Mongols, the critical state of the Latin Empire at Constantinople and the need for a further crusade. Innocent, an outstanding jurist and skilful diplomat, without Gregory's fiery temperament, attempted to come to terms with Frederick, who had opened negotiations. As the struggle between emperor and pope had taken on very personal overtones, Gregory's death provided the opportunity for a reappraisal of the relations between them. But in the end, though an interim treaty was concluded in March 1244, mistrust between the two sides was too great for a settlement; indeed both at once attempted to improve their positions beyond what had been agreed. In order to free himself from the emperor's pressure, and to assemble the general council which Frederick had prevented during the pontificate of Gregory IX, Innocent in the end decided to leave Italy. After being detained in Genoa for some months by sickness, he moved to Lyons, close to France, but still in the Empire, though hopefully out of the emperor's reach. Louis IX objected to Innocent's 'action in settling at Lyons, which risked provoking open war with the Empire; he felt his hand was being forced'.[113]

It was at Lyons that the council met in June and July 1245. The assembly concerned itself with a whole variety of subjects, including measures to be taken against the spread of heresy and against the advance of the Mongols into Russia. A further crusade against the Saracens as well as aid to the Latin Empire in Constantinople were also on the agenda, quite apart from the major question of the emperor's excommunication. Frederick was summoned to the council as an accused person, who had to answer the charges against him. As was to be expected, the emperor refused to be present; he was able to prevent almost entirely the attendance of bishops from his territories. A final attempt to bridge the differences between emperor and pope by negotiation failed. Accordingly, at the last meeting of the council, the bull of deposition was read and approved by the assembly. The grounds given for this action were that Frederick was guilty of perjury (in not keeping the various promises he had made), of a breach of the peace (in invading the Patrimony of St Peter), of the sacrilege of his earlier imprisonment of prelates travelling to a previous council, and of the suspicion of heresy. Frederick was deposed as emperor and king. He was to be stripped of all honours and dignities, his subjects were released from their oaths of fealty, and the magnates in the Teutonic kingdom were called upon to proceed to a fresh election. The pope, as overlord, was to make a decision about the Sicilian kingdom in accordance with the advice of the cardinals.[114] Frederick was in no doubt about the seriousness of the papal challenge to his entire position and to that of his dynasty, and was determined to fight back with all his might. At any rate in their propaganda both sides were in agreement about the theological significance of the struggle and in viewing Frederick in a key eschatological role, his opponents seeing him as a precursor of the anti-Christ and his supporters as the long expected Messiah–Emperor.

It is not necessary here to recount the ups and downs of the conflict in the following years: suffice it to say that the papacy strove to make good its threats to displace Frederick and his family from their rule, both in the Empire and in their various kingdoms. Innocent IV, like Gregory IX earlier, used the crusading weapon against Frederick.[115] In 1246 a conspiracy against Frederick in Sicily, apparently supported by the papacy,[116] was cruelly crushed by him. In the Teutonic kingdom, the curia sponsored a series of anti-kings, initially (also in 1246) the election of the Landgrave of Thuringia, Henry Raspe, who, however, died the following year, to be replaced by Count William of Holland. Frederick maintained a firm hold over Sicily, and his son King Conrad over much of the Teutonic kingdom. The emperor was prevented by a severe military defeat at the hands of the city of Parma from proceeding to Lyons to plead his cause personally before the pope. In 1249, he had one of his main officials in the *regno*, Petrus de Vinea, arrested as a traitor, though one cannot be sure whether the charges levied against him were in fact true; de Vinea died in prison, probably taking his own life.[117] Frederick's son, King Enzio of Sardinia, fell into the hands of the Bolognese, who kept him incarcerated for the rest of his life; he was to live on until 1272. In Central Italy, imperial fortunes improved during 1248 and 1249. Though Frederick was unable to score a clear victory over the papacy, he had certainly not been beaten when he died after a violent bout of dysentery at Castle Fiorentino in Apulia in December 1250.

Frederick named his eldest surviving son Conrad, the offspring of his union with his second wife, Isabella of Jerusalem, as heir of all his kingdoms. Frederick's illegitimate son, Manfred,[118] was endowed with lordships that would allow him to control the whole of Apulia. He was also appointed Conrad's bailiff, ' "especially in the kingdom of Sicily", which gave him almost unlimited powers which his brother could not revoke. Clearly it was on Manfred that Frederick pinned his hopes for seeing his Italian ambitions achieved.'[119] These testamentary arrangements made by the father were not likely to promote the good relations between the brothers on which the smooth working of the new scheme of things depended. Even though Frederick had high hopes for Manfred's role in Italy, he was not prepared to endow him with the Sicilian crown, presumably as he wished to preserve the unity of the Staufen dominions, though this was going to make any settlement with the papacy even more difficult.

The death at this critical moment of this powerful ruler, who in a very personal sense held together all his various dominions, certainly posed serious problems for the Staufen dynasty. Frederick's son, Conrad IV, already King of the Romans, was up to a point able to consolidate his position in the Teutonic kingdom, though he was unable to crush William of Holland, who had defeated him in 1246 during his father's reign. In the Sicilian kingdom, Manfred was actually confronted with extensive revolts on the mainland after the death of the emperor, and attempted to come to an arrangement with the pope. Innocent IV was only prepared to recognise him as Prince of Taranto, a territory bequeathed to him by his father, which Manfred did not regard as sufficient. As Conrad did not fully trust his Sicilian lieutenant, though he was in his way trying his best to look after the interests of the dynasty, the king made the fateful decision of securing his Italian and Sicilian inheritance in person. Leaving behind an undefeated anti-king in the Teutonic kingdom and proceeding to Italy in 1251[120] may well have been a mistake on Conrad's part, even if he scored considerable military successes south of the Alps.

As Conrad had been deposed together with his father at the Council of Lyons, the curia, as overlord of the Sicilian kingdom, looked around for an alternative King of Sicily among the European dynasties and approached Charles of Anjou, the younger brother of King Louis IX. At this stage, though Charles was tempted by the offer, the negotiations foundered over financial matters, and perhaps also because of King Louis' disapproval. Innocent IV appeared to be more successful with Henry III of England, whose second son, Edmund, though still a minor, was in fact invested with the *regno* in 1255 by Innocent's successor, Alexander IV. As, however, Henry sought to reduce the onerous commitments to the papacy he had undertaken to finance an expedition to Sicily to instal Edmund, Alexander annulled the grant of the kingdom in 1258.[121]

Innocent IV, who returned to Italy in 1251, found that things were not going all his own way by any means. There were, in fact, negotiations with Conrad, who very much wished to reach a settlement with the papacy. Conrad had reached the conclusion, to which his father had not been able to bring himself, that harmonious relations with the curia required a separation of the imperial and Sicilian crowns. He was therefore prepared to assign the Sicilian crown to his half-brother Henry, the child of Frederick II's third wife, Isabella, sister of Henry III of England. Unfortunately Henry died prematurely and the negotiations finally came to an end with Conrad's death from a fever in May 1254 at the age of 26 in Southern Italy.[122] Once more the Italian climate claimed a Teutonic king, inflicting a further serious blow on the dynasty. Full success eluded Conrad, not only because of his early death, but also because his suspicions of his half-brother prevented him from utilising Manfred's energy and ability, and from coordinating Staufen approaches to the curia.

The only clearly legitimate surviving male member of the Staufen family was Conrad IV's son, aged two, whom history has named Conradin. This left the field in the Teutonic kingdom free for William of Holland, an able ruler, who, however, died in 1256. In the meantime, in 1254, several major Rhenish cities, in view of the weakness of central authority in the Teutonic kingdom, founded the *Rheinische Bund* to strengthen public order, in which they were joined by a number of archbishops and bishops. The *Bund* demanded that this time there should be an uncontested election. By 1257, when the election took place, the number of electors had been reduced even below that which had participated in Vienna in 1237 during the reign of Frederick II; also it was becoming clearer which princes belonged to the electoral college. In the meantime, in 1252, the princes – and not just the electors – affirmed what was largely implicit in the 1237 election, namely that the person who was chosen king was already thereby entitled to imperial authority, even without papal confirmation.[123]

The full advantages of the new electoral college could not be realised in 1257 as the rivalry between France and England once more, as in the period after the death of Henry VI, had its counterpart in deep divisions among the electors. While the Archbishop of Trier was allied to France, his opposite number in Cologne was in league with England. King Alfonso X of Castile was chosen by the Archbishop of Trier, the Duke of Saxony and the Margrave of Brandenburg; Richard of Cornwall, brother of King Henry III of England, was elected by the Archbishops of Cologne and of Mainz, as well as the Count Palatine of the Rhine. The King of Bohemia, Ottokar II, apparently cast his vote subsequently for each of the two kings. For a time the Duke of Bavaria challenged the right of the King of Bohemia to a seat on the electoral college, but eventually lost out and had to wait until the Thirty Years War to succeed. Thus at least six of the seven electors confirmed in the Golden Bull of Charles IV in 1356 officiated for the first time in 1257. Interestingly enough, both kings had ties to the Staufen dynasty. Alfonso was a grandson of Philip of Swabia, and Richard the brother of Frederick II's third wife.[124] While Alfonso was never able to visit his new kingdom, Richard spent nearly four years there; for much of the time he was preoccupied with the civil war in England. Richard's influence on the Teutonic kingdom was thus limited. The *Rheinische Bund*, incidentally, now disintegrated, having failed to prevent a dual election.

Following Conrad IV's death in 1254, all that was left of the Staufen position was that part of the kingdom of Sicily which was controlled by Manfred, initially acting as regent for his nephew Conradin. While it is difficult to form a clear impression of Conrad in view of his short reign, his half-brother's impact on his time comes through more strongly. The offspring of Frederick II's liaison with the beautiful, highly intelligent Bianca Lancia, who belonged to the Piedmontese nobility, was perhaps the most capable of Frederick II's sons, cultured, personable, courageous, a good commander and an able administrator. Interestingly enough, it seemed at first to suit both Pope Innocent IV and Manfred to try to come to terms.

Manfred, who took over the regency of the *regno* on behalf of his infant nephew Conradin, opened the kingdom to Innocent, who was able to enter Naples in triumph. By papal decree, Manfred became vicar of the southern Italian peninsula. Innocent IV recognised him as regent for the *regno* and as Prince of Taranto, the territory bequeathed to him by his father. But the parties interpreted their agreement in different fashions. Innocent wished to make papal rule over the *regno* a reality, while Manfred intended right from the beginning to emancipate himself from papal tutelage and to run Sicily in his own way; it was not clear at this stage that his ambitions extended to other parts of Italy, too. Also the pontiff intended to reorganise the kingdom and to dismantle or restructure the centralised Norman system of government, to which Manfred was determined to adhere.[125] Cooperation between Manfred and the curia thus broke down. Manfred therefore attempted to restore Staufen authority in the kingdom, without bothering about the pope.[126] Still, further negotiations between them took place from time to time, until the papacy was finally committed to its own candidate for the kingship.[127]

Manfred was gradually able to consolidate his rule over the *regno*, had himself elected king by the Sicilian barons – by-passing papal claims to have a say in this matter – and was crowned at Palermo in 1258. He built up a very considerable international position for himself, concluding marriage alliances with Aragon and with the Greek state of Epirus, which brought him some territory in the Adriatic. The treaty with Aragon, technically a vassal of the Holy See, is evidence that Manfred was widely accepted as ruler of the kingdom of Sicily, papal claims to the contrary. In spite of sporadic negotiations (interrupting repeated hostilities) we cannot be certain that the curia would have been prepared to accept Manfred as ruler of Sicily in the long run. Thus Manfred had to make the difficult choice of either lying low in the hope of a permanent settlement with the curia, or of consolidating his position, running the risk of driving the papacy to find a replacement to dislodge him. In true Staufen fashion, Manfred went over to the offensive. Once he in the early 1260's developed contacts with the Ghibellines in Central and Northern Italy and even received some votes in Rome at an election for senator,[128] the papacy finally determined that it had to turn elsewhere.

The curia did not rest until the last Staufen stronghold had been taken and, as feudal overlords, offered the Sicilian kingdom to princes belonging to a number of dynasties. Eventually, just before his death in 1264, Urban IV, the able Patriarch of Jerusalem and the first of a number of French popes in this period, succeeded in coming to an arrangement with the younger brother of King Louis IX of France, Charles of Anjou, who was also Count of Provence, to undertake the conquest of the *regno* from Manfred. Negotiations to this end had been prolonged, partly because of the reluctance of

Louis IX to have his dynasty involved in the quarrels between the papacy and the Staufen dynasty. Louis, who had become a prisoner during his crusade in 1250, blamed the misfortunes of his expedition to some extent on the misdirection of church resources to the fight against Frederick II. He was convinced that a united Western Church not weakened by internal dissension could have performed much better on crusade in the Holy Land. Louis raised doubts about the legitimacy of the dispossession of the Staufen dynasty, but eventually withdrew his objections to his brother being enfeoffed with the Sicilian kingdom by the pope. At the last moment, in 1263, before the treaty was finally signed, it was Urban's turn to hesitate. This was due to Charles of Anjou being elected senator by the Romans, though actually on the nomination of a cardinal, to thwart the candidature of Manfred's son-in-law, Peter of Aragon. There was now a danger that the proposed servant of the papacy might become its master. Urban died in October 1264, being succeeded by Clement IV, another Frenchman, who had earlier been in the service of the King of France.

Charles was very ambitious, already controlled the Provence and by his 'purchase of the county of Ventimiglia...extended his rule beyond the mountains'. He possessed territories close to Piedmont.[129] Much more than the Staufen rulers, Charles already had a base in Northern Italy, or at least easier access to the region than the Germanic emperors. When he sailed with his expedition from his own territory at Marseilles in May 1265, he was able to reach the mouth of the Tiber in a week.[130] Thanks to naval communications and to greater centralisation, the kingdom of France, which was at least indirectly involved in the Sicilian venture, was thus in the position – if required at some later time – to get troops to Italy more quickly than the Teutonic kingdom.

All this was an advantage to the papacy, in the short run, to dislodge Manfred, admittedly a powerful enemy and a successful diplomat, with wide international contacts. But it remained to be seen whether the Angevin–French connection might not in future be a greater threat to the independence of the papacy than the Staufen dynasty had ever been. That these considerations are not based simply on hindsight is clear from the worries felt by the curia about the activities in which Charles engaged not only in Rome, but in other parts of Italy. Furthermore, the attempt to dislodge a well-established ruler from his throne required massive financial efforts, which were bound to be resented by the churches subjected to special taxation. And the use of the crusading weapon by the papacy against Christians was liable to raise doubts among the faithful.

Obviously not all the faults were on one side. But the papacy was running severe risks by calling in a French prince with an already existing base in northern Italy. It may well be that the curia did not follow up sufficiently the possibilities of coming to terms with a Staufen king of Sicily who was unlikely to succeed his father and grandfather in combining that crown with the dignities of Teutonic king and Roman emperor. In fact, there was some awareness of this at the curia, particularly during the reign of Urban IV, French though he was by origin, for there was a certain scepticism about an enterprise whose outcome was 'almost as much feared as wished for.'[131] Things changed in Charles' favour under Clement IV.

Charles certainly delivered. Within four weeks of entering the kingdom of Sicily, with which he had in the meantime been invested by the pope, he annihilated Manfred's forces at Benevento in February 1266. Manfred, courageous as ever, was killed on the battle-field. Charles now took over the kingdom of Sicily.

In 1268 the 16-year-old Conradin attempted to regain the Sicilian inheritance. He was well received in many parts of Italy, including Rome, and gathered a certain following, but in August he was decisively beaten at Tagliacozzo, east of Rome, not far into the *regno*. Conradin escaped from the battlefield, but was caught and handed over to Charles, who had him and some of his companions publicly beheaded in Naples in October. It must be pointed out, however, that the Angevin marshal, who had been captured in Tuscany, had been executed before the battle on Conradin's orders.[132] The new King of Sicily treated Conradin as a criminal, even refusing him Christian burial at the time. According to a historian of the papacy, the execution of a captured prince reclaiming his inheritance was unprecedented.[133] Charles may well have behaved brutally even by the standards of an age that was not overscrupulous in the use of its methods, and for this he was castigated not least by his ally, the pope.[134] However, there is no surviving evidence that Pope Clement IV opposed this particular act of cruelty.[135]

The popes won their struggle with the Staufen rulers and thereby destroyed the special position the Teutonic kings occupied as emperors in the order of things. After the end of the Staufen dynasty, it was only the occasional Teutonic king and emperor who for periods of time presided over Christendom in anything like the way Charlemagne, Otto the Great and Henry III had done, and that Frederick I, Henry VI and Frederick II attempted to do. Clearly the relationship between emperors and popes had already run into serious difficulties during the last two reigns of the Salian Emperors, Henry IV and Henry V. But following the end of the Salian dynasty there had ben a period of co-operation between them under Lothar III and Conrad III. Why did matters again come to a head under Frederick I?

The Concordat of Worms of 1122 had been an attempt to prevent future strife by going some way in regulating the relations between the two powers. However, not only was it not practicable to cover the whole range of contentious issues, but in a time of movement it was also impossible to 'freeze' the existing state of affairs. On both sides new personalities came into play, reacting in their own way to the constant changes in the situation, in Rome, in Lombardy, or in the kingdom of Sicily. Thus the theoretical, often theological, positions taken up by both sides, which they required to buttress their various claims, were being developed further. The theological claims answered to the spiritual, politico-religious needs of the time and could therefore not be omitted. The drawback was that the theological debate, with its moral overtones, was liable to exacerbate conflict, which might have been solved more easily with a strong dose of pragmatism. The opponent was thus often seen as evil rather than as simply misguided, leaving to posterity an unfortunate heritage for future inter-human relations and attitudes to conflict between various ethnic and religious communities. In this situation the issues that caused strife could not be settled by compromise, and both sides allowed themselves to be driven to measures that were completely out of proportion to the detailed questions in dispute. The countless localities that were destroyed, and the men who were killed or maimed in combat, had to pay the price for this inability of emperors and popes to come to an understanding. Were the matters in contention so difficult to solve that they could only be settled by wars of annihilation?

On the theoretical level it was not easy to reconcile papal claims of superiority to the temporal power with the need of secular rulers, at any rate within certain limits, to make the decisions they regarded as necessary, and on which their safety and that of their peoples and territories might depend. Many territories at times had to submit to papal interference, but none was affected more fundamentally and for longer periods by claims put forward by the Holy See than the Teutonic kingdom in view of its imperial connection.

Theological doctrines, however fervently put forward, were not the primary cause of conflict in the Staufen period, though they contributed considerably to an atmosphere of tension. It is true that Frederick I wanted to go back to the level of imperial power at the time of Henry III's death in 1156. This attitude, taken up by Frederick I, set off considerable strife in Italy and friction with the papacy, but did not in itself lead to the breach of 1160. What actually caused a conflict was not a general disagreement about spheres of power or about one of the many matters constantly in dispute, such as the filling of bishoprics or the validity of royal marriages. As to the latter, the pope in fact agreed to the annulment of his first marriage requested by Frederick. The breach came through an issue that was no part of the regular relations between the imperial court and the curia, but the very special case of a papal schism.

It was proceedings in the Sacred College that started off a sequence of events leading eventually to Frederick's excommunication and to a prolonged war. The emperor got involved because he claimed that it was his duty to call and preside over a council of the Church to decide the question as to who was the true pope. The council was not representative of the Church in general and backed what turned out to be the wrong candidate, in the sense that he did not win or at any rate keep international support. He stuck too long to a series of what proved to be anti-popes, and had to give in eventually. In the end, after abandoning a hopeless policy, Frederick to a considerable extent recovered his position. Even after his reconciliation, he was not always easy for the curia to live with, but they could at least co-exist. However, Barbarossa left what was in many ways a bitter legacy. The curia remembered his brutality to Italian cities and his occupation of the Patrimony of St Peter towards the end of his reign. That affected the way the papacy viewed both his son and his grandson.

Frederick I bequeathed to his son a powerful emperorship, strengthened even further by the bonus of the Sicilian inheritance. Henry VI saw the chance of finally turning the situation in Italy, which had defied his father over long periods, in favour of the Empire. Henry's reign was too short and his achievement too tentative to reach any definitive assessment about him. Would his empire have lasted had he reigned longer?[136] Even more than his father, Henry also left memories of brutality, particularly with the curia, as well as with Italians and Sicilians, which were not going to make things easier for his son Frederick II in due course.

Frederick II was initially very careful in establishing his position. But unfortunately he appears to have taken at their face-value the excessive sacral claims for imperial power advanced by his side, and gradually developed a kind of megalomaniac emperor-complex. He had a sense of a divine mission due to his seemingly miraculous rise to imperial power.[137] All this, combined with the potential of the Sicilian kingdom, with its Mediterranean and crusading possibilities (which he was the first to be able to exploit), gave him an overweening ambition; at the same time it made him strangely complacent and unreasonably sanguine about the outcome of the life and death struggles in which he was involved.

Frederick had a very good start with his Teutonic kingship, because through a strange twist of circumstances he had become the candidate sponsored by the papacy. An outstanding pontiff, Innocent III, provided key support for Frederick in gaining the crown. In return, the pope secured an undertaking from the king to keep the Sicilian monarchy separate from his other crowns. This was a vital necessity for the Holy See in order to prevent a recurrence of the excessive power over Central Italy wielded by Henry VI. Frederick did not keep this undertaking and, whatever the formal reasons for his first excommunication, thereby provoked the initial breach with the papacy. Some historians have admired the way Frederick, in 1220, in spite of solemn undertakings, engineered the election by the Teutonic magnates of his son Henry (VII), already crowned King of Sicily, as King of the Romans.[138] But where did all these 'victories'

over the curia get Frederick? The emperor at the very least wished to remain
in power and to pass on his various crowns to his heirs in the Staufen
dynasty. By breaking his undertakings to the papacy, he put all this at risk
and gambled on a successful outcome of the struggle. Also tactically he was
not always so clever. He gave a handle to the papacy by not being able to
make good his crusading vows. Was he wise to take the oath so early in the
reign? Why did he have to delay so long? In the end he came under time
pressure and could not continue because of illness. He was always trying to
do too much.

Above all, Frederick lacked any sensitivity for the necessity of achieving a
balance of power with the papacy that would allow the Holy See to feel
secure and the Staufen Empire to function without repeated friction with the
curia. He failed to see that the papacy was bound to view an excessive
accumulation of power in his hands, particularly in Italy, as a threat. Did
he think that he could reduce the papacy to dependence on the emperor? If
so, he did not grasp the spiritual and international character of the papacy
any more than his grandfather did when he called a council of the Church to
settle the papal schism. As Innocent IV's move to Lyons shows, the papacy
was determined to preserve its independence, even if the necessity of moving
out of the imperial orbit meant leaving not only Rome and the papal states,
but Italy altogether. In other words, if the emperor made things too difficult
for the pope, the Holy See would leave his sphere of influence, to the
detriment of the emperor's authority. It is doubtful if Frederick II, whatever
his intelligence and culture, was a real statesman grasping a situation
intuitively.

Even if the unacceptability to the papacy of the union of Frederick II's
crowns is taken for granted, the use of spiritual weapons, including that of
the crusade, in the struggle against the emperor remains unfortunate. Gregory IX's vehemence of temper, which could assume a 'terrifying harshness',
is criticised in a Roman Catholic history of the papacy.[139] The curia may in
the end not have had much of an alternative to its use of spiritual weapons,
but these were employed at great cost to the credibility and spirituality of the
Church. However, it would be wrong to blame the collapse of the Staufen
dynasty, and with it of a pervasive imperial power, entirely on the Church.
There was already too much of a discrepancy between the pretensions of the
emperorship and the reality of its power. Also every new ruler had to
establish himself afresh, if not necessarily in the Teutonic kingdom, then
certainly in Italy, braving epidemics which took their toll on them and their
men. An Empire without Sicily had apparently been incomplete and not
quite viable, but with Sicily the main base of power had shifted rather too
much to the south. This constituted a threat to its independence which the
papacy could not disregard. Perhaps the story of the Staufen dynasty shows
that in these circumstances neither a Germanic kingdom extending also to

Italy, nor a Sicilian kingdom that was combined with the Teutonic kingdom, provided a long-term solution.

While the universal pretensions, which papacy and Empire shared, created friction between them, in another sense the two institutions needed each other. They were united in many of their aims, even if they disagreed about each other's functions in their common tasks. Were the House of Anjou and the kingdom of France going to be more comfortable partners for the papacy than the Staufen? The royal dynasties of the Teutonic kingdom, in view of their imperial connection, at least took seriously the international dimension of their mission. Would the kingdom of France and the House of Anjou, after eliminating – at least for the time being – the Teutonic competition, look beyond the frontiers of their territories or merely consult their own interests? There was a potential danger that the fall of one universal or quasi-universal power would be followed by the decline in the influence of the other, the papacy.

6 The Later Middle Ages (1268–1517)

After Conradin's death, the Staufen were no longer able to present a descendant of their male line for the dignities they had held, such as the emperorship, the Teutonic kingship and the Swabian dukedom, even quite apart from the Sicilian kingship. The term 'interregnum' for the period between the death of Conrad IV in 1254 and the election of Rudolf of Habsburg in 1273, in the sense of a rulerless time north of the Alps, is technically incorrect, because there were in fact German kings at that time. But none of these kings, from William of Holland to Richard of Cornwall and Alfonso of Castile, was able to play a prominent part on the European stage in the way their predecessors from the previous major dynasties, from the Carolingians to the Staufen, had done. Thus the papacy for the time being no longer felt threatened by the Teutonic kings, who had actually not held the imperial title since Frederick II. As the term *Regnum Teutonicum* fades away, the least unsatisfactory solution is to refer to the German kingdom, in the sense of a medieval institution which has only a limited resemblance to modern Germany.[1]

The declining role of the German kingdom opened the way for the French to make a bid for European hegemony, for the claims of their kings that they rather than the German rulers were the true heirs of Charlemagne, and for their expansion into the Empire; this eastward pressure was to be a prominent continuing feature of the policy of the French royal dynasties and even beyond. As we have seen, French influence was – at least indirectly – further enhanced by papal use of a Capetian prince, Charles of Anjou, as an instrument for ridding the Holy See of Staufen rule over the Sicilian kingdom. So long as Louis IX occupied the throne, the papacy could rest comparatively easy about French policy; however, the king died on crusade at the siege of Tunis in 1270. Charles was far from accepting the same moral restraints on the use of power as his elder brother. He lacked any scruples about putting pressure on popes and cardinals in the interest of his dynastic ambitions, thus hopelessly splitting the Sacred College into his supporters and opponents. It was due to these divisions mainly created by Charles that a long pontifical vacancy, lasting nearly three years, followed the death of Clement IV in November 1268, the month after Conradin had been publicly executed in Naples.

The paralysis of the Sacred College was all the more serious, as Charles utilised the absence of a pontiff for his own purposes, to establish his authority in many parts of Italy, beyond his Sicilian rule that had received papal blessing. Indeed, this development violated the obvious and time-hallowed interest of the Holy See in preventing any encirclement, by continuing to insist (as in the days of Frederick II) on having southern and northern Italy in separate hands. Even some of the French popes had become worried about increasing Angevin influence in the Italian peninsula. Actually Charles' designs also extended to the Byzantine Empire, where he was hoping, under the guise of a crusade, to revive the Latin Empire overthrown in 1261. Quite apart from the misuse of an appeal to religion in a scheme of secular aggrandisement, it is fascinating to see how Charles carried on certain aspects of Staufen policy, of both Philip of Swabia and Frederick II.

Finally, in September 1271, the cardinals achieved a compromise with the election of the Archdeacon of Liège, Theobald Visconti, who did not belong to the college and was actually in the Holy Land at the time. Gregory X was a deeply religious personality of great moral integrity and proved to be one of the outstanding popes of the century. The new pontiff saw that the curia had for some years been too preoccupied with the succession in the Sicilian kingdom and the situation in Italy, to the neglect of its primary tasks of recovering the Holy Land and ending the schism with the Byzantine Church. He was also determined to reduce the sway held by Charles of Anjou. He combined his various objectives very skilfully. In working for union with the Greek Church, a matter of supreme importance in itself, he was at the same time attempting not only to improve the prospects for a crusade to the Holy Land, but also to deprive Charles of the excuse for a Latin adventure aimed at Constantinople. He certainly curbed the King of Sicily and the influence of France generally.

Shortly after his coronation, Gregory sent out invitations to a General Council of the Church to take place once more at Lyons. The council, which met during the summer of 1274, witnessed preliminary steps for a settlement between the Greek and the Roman Churches. If only for political reasons, to ward off an invasion by Charles of Anjou, the Byzantine Emperor Michael wished to keep the negotiations on union alive. But for a long time to come widespread opposition in the Byzantine Empire to the granting of any concessions to Rome prevented any meaningful progress in this question.[2] Plans were also made for a crusade to the Holy Land.

Perhaps the most striking accomplishment of the council was the new regulation of papal elections in the constitution *Ubi periculum*, which was drawn up in order to prevent the recurrence of prolonged vacancies. After the death of a pontiff, the cardinals were to wait no longer than ten days for the arrival of absent members of the Sacred College. The election was to be held in the place where the pope had died. The cardinals were to meet *in conclave*, that is they were not to have any communication with the outside world until they had elected a new pope; the longer they took over their deliberations, the more rigorous were their conditions of confinement in conclave to be. Also the cardinals were to be deprived of any income during the vacancy. Not surprisingly there was considerable resistance in the Sacred College to the decree, which, however, in essence, is still valid today. In its proceedings, if not in its enduring effect, the Second Council of Lyons (1274) was a convincing sign of the as yet unshaken ecumenical recognition of the papacy, above all in the occident.[3]

One of the pope's priorities during his reign was the normalisation of the situation in the German kingdom, as a preliminary step to restoring the imperial dignity for its ruler. These measures were aimed at creating a counter-weight to France and Anjou, particularly in Italy, and securing imperial leadership for a crusade to the Holy Land. The death of Richard of Cornwall in the month following the papal coronation in March 1272 helped the new pontiff to gain the initiative. Gregory refused to confirm Alfonso of Castile as King of the Romans, as this grandson of Philip of Swabia, who was dabbling simultaneously in too many projects, was sending help to the Ghibellines in Northern Italy.[4] Louis IX's son, Philip III, who was supported by his uncle Charles of Sicily, was – like a number of his successors on the French throne – also a contender for the imperial crown, but was vetoed by Gregory. Another ruler interested in the German kingship was King Ottokar II of Bohemia, who had built up a large empire. Though also a grandson of Philip of Swabia, he was – unlike his cousin Alfonso – for a time able to maintain good relations with the Holy See. But the curia realised that so mighty a potentate was not likely to find favour with those who had to make the decision. In the end seven electors, who on this occasion for the last time included the Duke of Bavaria (in the absence of King Ottokar II of Bohemia) in October 1273 unanimously voted for Count Rudolf of Habsburg (Table 6.1). Like William of Holland earlier on, he was not a Prince of the Empire (*Reichsfürst*), but his family had a predominant position in the Alsace and in what was to become Switzerland; he was, indeed, the most powerful prince in the south-west of the kingdom.

Rudolf I was born in 1218, he was thus in his mid-fifties when he was elected king. He had been a close ally of the Staufen rulers, whose policy he continued in many respects, for example in promoting the interests of the cities. But unlike Ottokar he was not related to them. In the following period direct descent from the deceased ruler was not generally regarded as a recommendation for the succession, as it had been during most of the time previously. Interestingly enough it was the French kings in this period who in their – as it turned out unsuccessful – efforts to gain the imperial crown emphasised their royal blood and claimed descent from Charlemagne.[5]

The Habsburg ruler attempted to reclaim royal rights that had been alienated, thus initiating a policy of 'revindication' which was to play an important part in the following centuries. In these endeavours he came up

Table 6.1   The Luxemburg and Habsburg dynasties

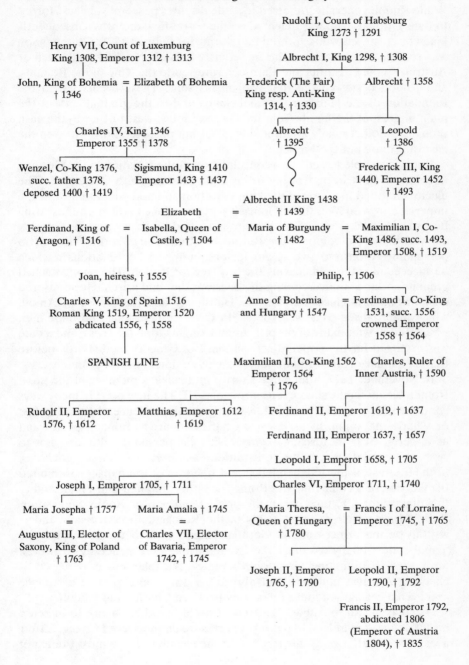

against the resistance of Ottokar, who refused to swear allegiance to him. While Rudolf generally preferred to settle disputes peacefully, he was forced to fight Ottokar, who was defeated on the battle-field and was subsequently killed by Austrians who captured him during his flight in 1278. Ottokar's son was confined to Bohemia. The imperial fiefs his father had held, such as Austria, Styria, Carinthia and Carniola, reverted to the King of the Romans, and Rudolf bestowed the first two on his sons. These events led to the foundation of the Habsburg dynastic lands and to the gradual shift of the main interest of the family from the German south-west further to the east, though Rudolf certainly attempted – somewhat unsuccessfully – to stop the eastward march of the French.

Rudolf was able to achieve a consolidation of the situation in the German kingdom at least in part owing to his good relations with Gregory X. The electors notified the pope of the king's election and asked him to bestow the imperial crown on him. Rudolf himself sent a message to the pontiff assuring him of his loyalty and of his readiness to undertake a crusade. Gregory showed his strong support for Rudolf by strenuously exerting himself in persuading Alfonso to give up any idea of an imperial coronation, in which he succeeded in the end, leaving the way free for Rudolf. The pope attached great importance to overcoming the divisions that had arisen. He sponsored a matrimonial alliance between the Habsburgs and the House of Anjou, which materialised some years later. In October 1275 king and pope met, when Rudolf with many of his princes and knights took the cross, and a date was arranged for the imperial coronation. But Gregory died shortly before that, in January 1276, without being able to complete his programme.

In November 1277, after three short pontificates, a member of the great Roman Orsini family succeeded as Nicholas III. The new pope in many ways continued Gregory X's policy of lessening the dependence of the Holy See on Charles of Anjou. In 1278, when Charles' tenure as Roman senator and as imperial vicar in Tuscany expired, Nicholas persuaded the king not to renew his candidature. In the constitution *Fundamenta militantis*, Nicholas, in the interest of the independence and freedom of the papacy, prohibited the election of secular rulers as Roman senators, and had himself elected to this dignity for life; thus began the papal *signorie* over Rome. Soon after, Rudolf gave up all imperial rights in the Romagna, a concession under-written by the princes of the German kingdom. With the Romagna, the 'papal states' finally assumed the frontiers that were generally to prevail until 1860.[6] Continuing Gregory X's policy, Nicholas not only aimed at checking Angevin ambition, but also at creating some kind of a balance and even a certain amount of harmony between Charles and Rudolf.

Nicholas' death in August 1280 gave Charles another chance to increase his influence, and indeed to put severe pressure on the Sacred College. After a vacancy of half a year, this resulted in the election of 'the most French of all the popes of the thirteenth-century.'[7] Simon de Brion, at one time Louis IX's chancellor, had assisted Charles in the establishment of his rule in Italy. As Martin IV he aligned himself quite openly with the Franco-Angevin and Guelf cause. The Cologne Canon Alexander of Roes condemned his hostility to the German kingdom and to the Ghibellines. Martin supported Charles' ambitions in Italy, even in Rome itself, as well as his plans for attacking the Byzantine Empire, thus destroying any progress that had been made towards union by the Second Council of Lyons. But now Charles suffered a severe set-back.

That earlier papal anxieties about the severity of the Angevin regime in the *regno*, the kingdom of Sicily, as well as its increasingly French colonial character, were fully justified, is shown by the 'Sicilian Vespers' in the spring of 1282. The island of Sicily was lost to Charles when the French garrisons there were murdered by the inhabitants. The rebellion against Angevin rule even spread to the territories of the kingdom of Sicily on mainland Southern Italy, though the Angevins were largely able to maintain themselves here. There are certain parallels between the grievances levelled against Charles and those which were made against the government of Frederick II during the last years of his reign. The French prince to some extent caused his own troubles by insensitivity to the feelings of his new subjects. Actually the insurgents appealed to the pope for protection, wishing 'to place Sicily under his direct authority, as a free community or group of communes'. But Martin IV, as Charles' loyal follower, refused outright. This left the way open to a Staufen connection, King Peter III of Aragon, the husband of Manfred's daughter Constance, to take over the island of Sicily.[8] Thus the Staufen dynasty, at any rate in the female line, preserved at least part of Frederick II's heritage.

The papacy for a long time refused to accept the loss of the island of Sicily as final. In its efforts to recover the island, the Holy See even deposed King Peter III of Aragon as ruler of his native kingdom for refusing to hand over Sicily, and offered his throne to a French prince. The latter conducted a French crusade against Aragon with papal blessing, but unsuccessfully. The island of Sicily remained in the hands of the Aragonese dynasty, and the rule of the house of Anjou was confined to the kingdom of Naples, in mainland Southern Italy. The harm done to the authority of the papacy by its futile struggle for Sicily, which even an anti-Angevin pope like Honorius IV (1285–7) was not prepared to abandon, was considerable. The ecumenical prestige the curia had achieved at the Second Council of Lyons in 1274 was squandered. The severe crisis in which the papacy was soon to find itself owed something to its preoccupation with the Sicilian question and to the split this question caused in the Sacred College.[9] Once more the affairs of the House of Anjou proved divisive for the Church and for Italy. The earlier papal option against the Staufen and for the Angevin dynasty had not turned

out to the advantage of the Holy See. Curiously, the Sicilian rising and its
consequences actually for the time being lessened the threat of Angevin
imperialism to the papacy.[10]

Honorius IV, like Gregory X earlier on, fixed a date for the imperial
coronation of Rudolf I. But once more difficulties arose, this time in the
German kingdom. The electors were worried that, once Rudolf had received
the imperial crown, they might be faced with a hereditary succession in the
House of Habsburg restricting them in their choice of ruler. They realised in
any case that, as emperor, Rudolf would put pressure on them to elect his
unpopular eldest son, Albrecht, King of the Romans. However, Rudolf I
died in 1291 without having been crowned emperor. While it would be going
too far to suggest that the papacy prevented an imperial coronation, the
curia did not always act in this matter with the necessary despatch, perhaps
through being overcareful. The absence of an imperial coronation for
Rudolf certainly proved a set-back for his plan of a Habsburg succession in
the German kingdom, particularly in view of Albrecht's unattractive personality. The electors' choice of a king from a different dynasty was at least in
part due to their determination to bypass Albrecht, but also to their opposition to what amounted in practice, if not necessarily in theory, to a hereditary succession. Actually at the time Albrecht was facing a rebellion of his
own subjects, which he, however, eventually managed to crush.

The election of the next German king took place in a different international setting from that of his predecessor Rudolf, perhaps mainly because
of the succession to the French throne that had taken place in 1285. Philip
IV ('the Fair') was to change the face of Europe during a reign of nearly
three decades, certainly with profound effects for both the German kingdom
and the papacy. Philip's constant reiteration of his claim to be emperor in his
kingdom was bound to have an effect on the position of the German king,[11]
particularly as it was backed by the superior power wielded by a ruler who
was much more master in his own house than his eastern neighbour. The
difference in their respective importance was bound to be all the greater
unless Rudolf's successor could continue endowing the German kingship
with his own dynastic resources. The electors determined otherwise.

The Archbishops of Cologne and Mainz this time quite deliberately
sponsored a minor potentate, Count Adolf of Nassau, who was not a Prince
of the Empire (*Reichsfürst*), in the hope that he would be their instrument,
willing to reward them at the expense of the German kingdom. Most of the
other electors, including Wenzel II of Bohemia, also backed Adolf, who was
elected King of the Romans in May 1292. Albrecht defeated a plan to
despoil him of most of his possessions by making a timely submission; he
recognised Adolf and swore fealty to him for his fiefs.[12]

Honorius IV's successor died a month before Adolf of Nassau was elected
King of the Romans. It took the Sacred College longer than the electors in

the German kingdom to choose a successor. This time the delay was due to a dispute over the rights to certain lands between the two great Roman families, the Ghibelline Colonna and the Guelf Orsini, which paralysed the election process. It was only in July 1294 that a candidate emerged, who had the necessary support in the Sacred College, the hermit Peter of Morrone, who was in his eighties. He accepted after some hesitation and took the name of Celestine V. Many saw in this saintly man the long-expected 'angel pope'. Unfortunately Celestine was quite inexperienced in the ways of this world and very quickly allowed himself to be used by King Charles II of Naples for his own purposes. He soon realised that he was entirely unsuited for his new role, longed for his old solitary life in a hermit cell, and began to think of abdicating the papacy. In this frame of mind he consulted one of the leading cardinals, Benedetto Caetani, who advised him that he could in fact, if he wished to do so, resign his dignities, which he did in December 1194, about five months after his election. The Sacred College at once elected as pope Benedetto Caetani, who took the name of Boniface VIII, the very cardinal whom Celestine had consulted about his abdication. This certainly turned out to be a fateful choice.

Boniface had excellent credentials. He had served the curia with distinction. His family ties to both the Orsini and Colonna families[13] provided grounds for the hope that the new pontificate might inaugurate an era of peace in the Roman region. He had an exalted notion of the powers of his office, in the sincere belief that it was the duty of the Holy See, for the spiritual welfare of Western Christendom, to prevent any violation of the rights of the Church. Actually, during their war against each other, the Kings of France and England had taxed their clergy without the necessary papal consent, contrary to the decrees of the Fourth Lateran Council. In response, during 1296, Boniface – in the bull *Clericis laicos* – declared that any clerical taxation without papal consent would be subject to spiritual penalties, thus making the regulations even more stringent than they had been hitherto. With this bull the pope touched a raw nerve in both kings, as the new rules interfered with their ability to raise money from their clergy quickly in time of war, an essential measure to finance their military operations. King Philip IV of France at once prohibited the export of bullion from his realm, seriously affecting papal revenues. Boniface soon gave in, because he was deeply involved in another matter, which for a time preoccupied his attention.

Unfortunately the pontiff had allowed himself, not entirely without fault from the other side, to be drawn into a fight to the finish with the Colonna family, arising in the first instance from his ambition to acquire more land for his own family, the Caetani. Using his papal power, Boniface carried out a campaign of destruction against the Colonna and stripped the two cardinals belonging to their family of their dignities. He thus made irreconcilable enemies of the rival dynasty. In due course, this was to contribute substantially to his undoing.

When it came to the affairs of the German kingdom, while Boniface was critical of Adolf of Nassau, he was not hostile to him. In 1295, Boniface rebuked Adolf 'for serving as hired soldier in English pay'.[14] Actually not only Adolf, but also the electors at various times took money from foreign kings, ushering in a long period in which rulers of other countries exercised undue influence in the German kingdom, down to the end of the Holy Roman Empire. In spite of Philip IV's increasing antagonism to Boniface, the pope ordered Adolf to come to terms with France. He even went so far as to instruct the Rhenish archbishops to withhold all services if the king were disobedient.[15] However, while the Holy See limited Adolf's room of manoeuvre, the real threat to him came from the electors in the German kingdom.

Adolf faced an insoluble dilemma. Unless he was prepared to remain a cipher, he had to acquire dynastic power, to found a *Hausmacht*. But this was bound to involve him in a struggle with the electors which he could not win. Adolf's chosen area to establish a Nassau stronghold was in a central area of the German kingdom, the margraviate of Meissen. This affected the interests of two of the most powerful electors, the Archbishop of Mainz and the King of Bohemia. In any case Albrecht had simply been biding his time and was waiting for an opportunity to deprive Adolf of the crown.

Open war broke out in the German kingdom in March 1298, and in June the electors deposed Adolf. They claimed that the king had oppressed the Church and committed sacrilege, that he had broken his word and that he had disturbed the peace, apparently charges borrowed from Innocent IV's proclamation against Frederick II.[16] It is characteristic of the rigidity of the medieval constitutional system that at times the levelling of particularly serious accusations, such as those of heresy, seemed to be required to have opponents removed from office, even if they were unfounded. In declaring that an unbanned king had forfeited the throne, the electors usurped the pope's function as a judge and thus set the scene for further conflict between the German kingdom and the Holy See.[17] During the following proceedings, Albrecht of Habsburg was elected king.

In July, Adolf was defeated and killed in the battle of Göllheim in the Palatinate. After a 'second election' of Albrecht I later that month, the electors asked Boniface for recognition of the steps they had taken. But without awaiting a papal reply, Albrecht was crowned King of the Romans at Aachen in August, 'an action which defied all papal theories of the right of confirmation'.[18] Boniface thereupon excommunicated Albrecht, stressing particularly not only the treacherous killing of his lord, King Adolf, but also his actions against the archdiocese of Salzburg; apparently Albrecht had usurped the mining rights of the archbishop.[19] The pope's attitude was one of the reasons that led Albrecht into concluding an alliance with France.[20] Boniface retaliated in 1300 by appointing Diether, the Dominican brother of the late Adolf of Nassau, to the vacant archbishopric of Trier. Diether formed an alliance with the other two Rhenish archbishop-electors against Albrecht. In April 1301, the pope declared all Albrecht's subjects released from their allegiance to him and encouraged the Rhenish prelates in their war against him, thus increasing the king's difficulties in the German kingdom.[21] But the pontiff's attitude to Albrecht changed completely once the Holy See was once more involved in a bitter struggle with France later that same year.

This time the difference that arose between Boniface and Philip concerned Bernard Saisset, first bishop of the diocese of Pamiers, which had been carved out of that of Toulouse. The diocese of Toulouse had always resented this loss of territory, and in the spring of 1301 the current bishop denounced Saisset to King Philip because of doubts about his loyalty to French rule. The area of the Languedoc, to which Pamiers and Toulouse belonged, had not yet beeen fully integrated into the kingdom of France, and continued restive in matters of religion, in spite of the Albigensian crusade, indeed with 'secret heresies growing stronger with suppression'.[22] To Philip, the assertion of his power over Bishop Saisset, the pope's friend, served as a test for three of his policy objectives: the establishment of royal control in a region which still needed taming, rolling back papal influence over the Church in France, and finally making good his independence from Rome. On the basis of 'a hideous perversion of law, by men of great skill as legalists, who know how to twist procedures and claim justice for them',[23] a political and personal case was built up against Saisset. The bishop's immunity was violated and he was kept largely under royal arrest. The case was appealed to Rome and everything now depended on the reaction of the curia.

Boniface at times showed flashes of greatness. He saw at once that unless he took a stand against the King of France on this issue, the papacy would no longer be able to protect the Church in France against royal encroachments and the erosion of its rights. Without hesitation the pope struck back. Exploiting the way in which Philip had put himself in the wrong over the trial of Saisset, Boniface demanded that the bishop be allowed to come freely to Rome and that all his confiscated goods be restored to him. In the bull, *Ausculta fili*, the pope summoned a council of the ecclesiastics of France to meet in Rome in November 1302, to which the king could also come, and to which he could send representatives. Actually many French prelates attended in spite of royal orders to the contrary. Boniface also reinstituted the prohibitions of the bull, *Clericis laicos*, which he had earlier relaxed.[24] The pope struck a blow not only for the rights of the Church in France, but also for the principle of due process in law, which, however, the ecclesiastical authorities themselves frequently violated through the methods employed by the Inquisition. Clearly Boniface had to act. But there is room for discussion as to whether he responded in such a way as would give him a good chance of winning in the end, and as to whether he took sufficient account of the realities of power in Europe and particularly in Italy.

It was now Philip's turn to act. He had the bull burned and circulated a forged version to discredit the actual papal pronouncements. In November 1302, Boniface responded with his most famous announcement, the constitution *Unam sanctam*. In this he decreed what had previously been taught without attaining the status of a dogma, that for salvation it was essential to be subject to the Roman Bishop.

In this changed situation, relations between the curia and Albrecht had improved so much by the beginning of 1303 that negotiations for a settlement could begin in earnest. In April, Boniface promulgated a bull in which he accepted Albrecht as King of the Romans and emperor-elect, who in turn, through his representatives, had sworn an oath to Rome 'of fealty and obedience'. Albrecht 'could console himself that to admit papal claims weakened electoral [ones], and he was prepared to sacrifice theory to practice.' In any case, Boniface gave solid support to the German kingdom and the Empire, contesting French claims to Lyons. Furthermore, in a speech expounding the bull, Boniface stated: 'Let not that Gallic pride exalt itself, saying that it knows no superior. They lie, since by law they are and ought to be subject to the Roman king and emperor.'[25]

In the meantime the French authorities were busy spreading allegations about Boniface designed to destroy him, such as that he was a heretic and that he sinned sexually. There was a systematic propaganda campaign to enlist support for Philip, as champion of the faith, to summon a General Council of the Church in order to depose Boniface and to have a legitimate pope elected. The stage was now set for the dramatic finale. Boniface had a bull excommunicating Philip IV drawn up, which was known to be due for a promulgation on 8 September. In order to prevent Philip's excommunication, the king's chancellor, William of Nogaret, timed an attack on the pope at his residence in Anagni for the previous day. Nogaret was supported by the Colonna, whom Boniface had earlier made his sworn enemies. Accompanied by their troops, Nogaret and his allies entered the town. They demanded that Boniface should renounce the papacy, which the pontiff refused. Fierce fighting ensued, during the course of which the pope was freed from the grip of the conspirators. But he died a broken man in Rome on 12 October 1303.

The reign of Boniface VIII is one of the most dramatic in the hardly uneventful period of the medieval papacy. The pontiff in a remarkable degree combined greatness with pettiness, the highest principles with the lowest pursuit of the interests of his family. He was too inclined to raise matters of principle, such as the superiority of the spiritual over the temporal power, at a time when conditions were far from ideal for stepping up papal demands. The truly great popes, such as Alexander III and Innocent III, and even to some extent Gregory VII, in the pursuit of their aims took into account the actual situation in which they found themselves. Boniface was too inclined to make enemies, through his imperious attitude to others and the vile temper he often displayed. He paid dearly for the enmity of the Colonna, which began with a family dispute that had nothing to do with the interests of the papacy. What led to his downfall was the alliance of his domestic with his foreign enemies, of the Colonna with France. Boniface never got the measure of Philip IV and his circle of officials, like Nogaret. It is true that Gregory VII's reign also ended in defeat, but his death in exile was the price he paid for a great cause, which not only survived his earthly troubles, but was strengthened by them.

Boniface had his supporters, even at the end and beyond. But while he had at times fought on great issues of principle, events had become so confused and the issues so muddied, that he could not emerge as the clear champion of the interests of the Church against an overmighty monarchy. Tragically, one of the most highly intelligent and gifted occupants of the throne of St. Peter was also one of the most disastrous. For in a sense, at least indirectly, the medieval papacy never recovered from the assault of Anagni.

> The French monarchy, by seizing the pope... not only ruined the claims of the head of the church to the domination of Christianity, but also... called into question the whole relationship of spiritual and secular power... in this sphere nothing was to be the same as before.[26]

The blame for this development must rest mainly on the shoulders of the French authorities, and ultimately of King Philip IV, though Boniface contributed to the confrontation with them. That France could become such a threat to the papacy had only been made possible by the weakening of the German kingdom and the Empire in the struggle of the Holy See with the Staufen dynasty, finally conducted with the help of the Angevin dynasty.

The papacy was now paying the price for failing to come to an arrangement with the Staufen dynasty after the death of Frederick II, and for siding with France and Anjou instead. Popes and emperors had been united by an adherence to the concept of a Western Christendom, in which they shared a universal role, even if they at times disagreed about the distribution of these universal powers. It was not in the interest of the German kings and Holy Roman Emperors to contest the international dimension of the papacy, because that also formed a substantial part of the basis of their leading position in Christendom. The kings of France were in an entirely different situation. They were now promoting the national concerns of France and wished to make themselves fully sovereign by removing any constraints on their power, including those of the papacy, if necessary by subjecting the Holy See to subservience. If they sought the emperorship, it was done in the first instance for the aggrandisement of their country, rather than in pursuit of a universal Christian mission.

With the repercussions arising from the assault on Boniface VIII at Anagni and his death soon after, the papacy faced one of the most severe crises in its history. The Patrimony of St Peter was in a state of disorder, incidentally making it very difficult for the next pope to govern from Rome, and much would depend on his personality. The Holy See, after having earlier encouraged an extension of French influence in Italy, now faced a hostile France, thanks to the complications caused during the reign of Boniface VIII. In this predicament, on the one hand, the curia had to make an attempt at mending bridges with the kingdom of France, which had earlier – in the struggle with Germanic emperors – often offered a refuge to the papacy. On the other hand, no self-respecting institution, least of all the papacy, could ignore the part played by the French authorities at Anagni, and allow the crime committed against the head of the Church to go unpunished. Balancing the two almost mutually exclusive objectives required a personality in whom skilfulness and firmness were matched to perfection. Sadly but understandably, one of the many unfortunate con-sequences of the previous pope's troubled reign was the determination of the cardinals not to elect another strong pope. In the difficult circumstances, the somewhat mediocre Nicholas Boccasini, a former Master-General of the Dominicans, who took the title of Benedict XI, was in fact able to achieve some success in improving relations with France. However, apart from excommunicating Nogaret and his accomplices at Anagni,[27] he delayed insisting on the full expiation of the crime against his predecessor until he had left Rome and felt sufficiently safe from attack. By then it was too late, for he died soon after, in July 1304, before he could fully carry out his policy.

After Benedict's short pontificate, there was almost a year's vacancy. The severe divisions between the Bonifatians and their opponents continued. Eventually the pro-French Napoleon Orsini tricked the Bonifatians into agreeing to the election of the Archbishop of Bordeaux, Bertrand de Got, by making it appear that he was one of theirs. Instead of proceeding to Rome, the new pope, who took the title of Clement V, had himself crowned at Lyons and never went to Italy, probably owing to the pressure to which Philip IV subjected him right through his pontificate. The King of France was determined to make Clement amenable to his wishes and, by discredit-ing Boniface's memory, to shield himself, and particularly his chancellor, the excommunicated William of Nogaret, from the full consequences of the involvement in the kidnapping attempt at Anagni. He therefore demanded that the dead pope be tried on such absurd grounds as heresy. Even the weak Clement was bound to try and resist this attempt to destroy the reputation of one of his predecessors, though only with limited success. Eventually this macabre affair came to an end without a verdict on the corpse. But by confronting the pope with a whole series of almost insoluble problems, the manœuvre achieved its objective of softening his resistance to French demands. Thus Clement agreed to have the bulls of Boniface erased from the papal register. And in the end Nogaret was let off very lightly.[28]

The king also forced the pope, against his better judgment, to tolerate French proceedings against the Templars on such charges as sexual perversion and heresy which most historians have since regarded as unjust. It is difficult to be sure of what motivated Philip against the order, but it may have been that he coveted its wealth. After trials that were a travesty of justice, many knights and even the Grand Master of the order were burned by the French. Under intense pressure from Philip, the pope dissolved the whole order at the Council of Vienne in 1312. All these measures brought the Church into discredit. They permanently weakened a papacy which Philip forced to give up the independence for which Gregory VII had fought so hard, and to debase itself by becoming an instrument of the French monarchy.

Following the murder of Albrecht of Habsburg by his nephew in May 1308, Philip even aimed at a further strengthening of his power and of his hold over the papacy by securing the election of his brother Charles of Valois as King of the Romans. It is interesting to note that, still at this juncture, the German kingship was seen as the necessary preliminary to the coveted imperial crown. In view of some electoral vacancies, the decision fell mainly to the Rhenish archbishops, who opted against both Charles of Valois and a Habsburg succession. With Clement's support, in November 1308 the brother of Archbishop Balduin of Trier, Count Henry of Luxemburg, who had close ties with the French monarchy, was chosen. It remained to be seen whether this minor prince would be able to escape the fate of Adolf of Nassau. Actually, with Henry VII, the Luxemburg dynasty rapidly rose to European importance, which gradually allowed it, in the German kingdom and the Empire, to rival the Habsburg and the Wittelsbach families that had so far predominated there. This development owed a great deal to Henry's skill in managing people and affairs, which also distinguished the two other emperors of his dynasty, his grandson Charles IV and his great-grandson Sigismund.

As in similar previous situations, the first problem confronting the new king, initially backed by scant resources, was that of coming to terms with the powerful Habsburgs, who resented their displacement from the royal dignity. Partly in order to satisfy them, the king agreed to take action against Albrecht's murderers; his nephew, John Parricida, died in prison and one of the other conspirators was broken on the wheel. The Habsburgs renounced their claims to the crown of Bohemia, where the male line of the royal family had died out. As King of the Romans, Henry took advantage of this situation to use one of the important privileges that went with the dignity, his prerogative of filling a vacant fief. He bestowed the Bohemian kingship, which carried with it one of the seven electorates, on his son John, to whom a sister of the last king of the old Przemyslid dynasty was given in marriage.

Henry VII was the first German king since the Staufen to be able to undertake an expedition to Italy. The pope actually agreed to a plan for Henry's imperial coronation in Rome. Clement, like some previous popes in this era of French predominance, attempted to create a certain counter-weight to France; Henry's interest in Italy was useful in this context. In view of the far-reaching influence the Angevin kings of Naples had achieved not only in the south, but also in the centre and north of the peninsula, an understanding with King Robert of Naples was essential for the smooth course of Henry's mission. Clement, again in line with certain curial traditions, brokered an agreement between the two kings in order to establish concord in Italy. Robert was keen to strengthen his position in Provence, where his family inheritance was situated, by being enfeoffed with Burgundy, that is the kingdom of Arles, which Henry was quite prepared to do. Philip IV spoiled this plan by putting pressure on the pope to veto the transaction. This French intervention may well have been the main cause of the troubles Henry encountered in Italy. At first, while the pope was still on side, the King of the Romans, who quickly received the iron crown of Lombardy, early in 1311, was widely welcomed in Italy, amongst others by Dante. Indeed he attained a popularity which few German kings had achieved. Henry very much wished to stay above the Italian factions. But when the deal with Naples turned sour and the pope was prevented by Philip from giving Henry support, the latter's progress from Milan to Rome was hindered by the Angevins and the Guelfs. Thus Henry was forced to become a Ghibelline protagonist.

Owing to Neapolitan intervention, the imperial coronation in Rome in June 1312, through cardinals appointed by the pope, only took place with great difficulty. Exasperated by the resistance of Naples to him, Henry used his newly acquired imperial authority to take proceedings against Robert, which brought him into open confrontation with the French monarchy and with a papacy under French tutelage. The pope now openly took the side of the Guelfs, made Robert of Naples senator in Rome and entrusted him with the *signorie* in Florence. Thus Italy, instead of being pacified, was again in flames. Henry's legal proceedings against Robert once more led to the stirring up of old controversies about the powers of an emperor, as both the imperialist and the Neapolitan side submitted expert opinions and memoranda. Dante, who had greeted Henry's arrival in Italy enthusiastically, in his *Monarchy* based the necessity of the Empire on theological grounds, urged the rightfulness of Roman claims to the Empire, and argued the direct dependence of the Empire on God without the mediacy of the pope. The aim of his tract was to demonstrate the emperor's independence in the political sphere. At the other end of the spectrum, the Neapolitans rejected the Germanic Empire as an institution and ascribed many contemporary evils to it.[29]

Henry was making preparations for action against Naples, when he died from malaria near Siena in August 1313, aged just under 40, the last German king to succumb to an infection in Italy. His premature death prevented the establishment of the Luxemburg dynasty on the German throne at that stage. There had not been time to prepare the way for the succession of his son John, the King of Bohemia, who was not even 18 years old. What ensued was an interregnum of more than a year. Then a dual election took place in October 1314, of representatives of the two other major princely families, of the Habsburg Frederick, as well as the Wittelsbach Louis of Bavaria, who was supported by the Luxemburg party. France had tried to promote the candidacy of a younger son of Philip IV, but the electors were united against that. It took until 1322 for the issue of the dual election to be settled, when Louis IV proved victorious in the battle of Mühldorf and Frederick was taken prisoner. Louis had defeated Frederick, but he now faced a greater enemy, the new pope.

In the meantime, Clement V had died in April 1314, bequeathing a difficult heritage. Rome had been left to its own devices, the papacy had largely become dependent on France and thanks to Clement's elevations, French cardinals, most of them from the pope's home territory of the Gascogne, now constituted a majority of the Sacred College; also a thriving provincial nepotism had depleted the resources of the curia. Owing to deep divisions in the Sacred College and to a number of flagrant irregularities, it needed more than two years for another pontiff to emerge, so that the dual election in the German kingdom took place during a papal interregnum. Again it was Napoleon Orsini who broke the deadlock, this time with the election of the 72 year-old Cardinal-bishop of Ostia, Jacques Duèse, who came from the region north of Toulouse and had long been in the service of the kings of Naples. He had earlier been Bishop of Avignon and took the title of John XXII. It was John who established the curia permanently in Avignon, partly in order to improve relations with the French monarchy, which had deteriorated so much during the reign of Boniface VIII. While there were grave objections to removing the curia from Rome and its vicinity, actually the machinery of papal government could function with more normality in Avignon than in the often chaotic conditions prevailing in the Holy City and during the resulting perambulations of the papal court. However, in Avignon, though still outside France and actually in the territory of the Angevin kings of Naples as rulers of Provence, the French could bring pressure to bear from their territory on the other side of the River Rhône. And after Anagni it was impossible to exclude a *coup de main*. Certainly John, though largely voluntarily, supported French and Neapolitan policy. He adopted a neutral attitude in the dispute between the two claimants to the German crown, but adhered to the traditional curial view that the King of the Romans should not exercise any authority in Italy until after his imperial coronation.[30] He thus confirmed his predecessor's appointment of King Robert of Naples as imperial vicar for the whole of Italy.[31]

After his victory over Frederick in 1322, Louis hoped to be recognised by the pope and to make arrangements with him for his imperial coronation. But as soon as he attempted to assert royal rights in Italy, particularly after he had put himself at the head of the Ghibellines and prevented a papal victory over Milan, John reacted sharply against him. Once more, for the last time in the medieval period, a major struggle ensued between the papacy and a German king. Again, claims were made on both sides affecting the relationship between the pope and the King of the Romans as well as their respective powers. Like Innocent III, John asserted the right and even duty of the papacy to closely scrutinise the person of the King of the Romans, as well as the way he had been elected, before agreeing to his imperial coronation. He even went further by claiming that, until a valid successor had been established on the German throne, it was his responsibility to direct the affairs not only of the Italian, but also of the German kingdom. John suspected Louis of heresy by association as the ally of the Milanese, whom he had declared to be guilty of this crime, and accordingly began legal proceedings against him on those grounds. He even denied him the right to call himself king, as he had not been approved and confirmed by the pope, and simply addressed him as 'Louis the Bavarian', the name under which he has gone down in history. Louis in turn accused John of heresy for his condemnation of the teaching of the Spiritual Franciscans who asserted that Jesus and the apostles did not possess anything individually or in common; for obvious reasons, the preaching of poverty presented particular dangers to the papacy. Louis also demanded the summoning of a General Council of the Church.

In 1324, the pontiff excommunicated Louis, and even put the German kingdom under interdict, which led to severe clashes there, as some wished to obey the papal censures, whilst other ignored them. However, Louis' ability to maintain himself in power was not at this stage put at risk by the pope's attitude. Soon, Louis' court began to harbour some of the pope's enemies. John, who did not always have the support of the Sacred College for his policies, such as those directed against Louis, tended to be rather authoritarian, regarding even the secular opponents of the policy of the Holy

See as – at least potential – heretics. Here he was going back to a policy for which Boniface VIII had recently set a bad precedent when he condemned the Colonna cardinals and their followers as heretics. John was responsible for a considerable extension of the Inquisition[32] by taking drastic action against the Spiritual Franciscans, which brought him into conflict with the General of the Franciscans, Michael of Cesena, who was kept under arrest at Avignon. In 1328 Michael as well as the theologian William of Ockham, who had also been detained, escaped from papal imprisonment, and sought refuge with Louis.

In the poverty dispute, as so often in the later Middle Ages, theology and politics, political theory and practical politics mutually affected each other. The theological problems that were raised made a solution of the practical political questions, for instance a settlement of the issue of the legitimacy of Louis' rule, more difficult.[33] In any case, Louis was determined to fight the pope. In 1327 he went to Italy and allied himself with Marsilius of Padua, who had developed the radical concept of a secular state. In accordance with Marsilius' doctrine of popular sovereignty, which was far ahead of its time, Louis accepted the imperial dignity from the Roman people. Under the leadership of Sciarra Colonna, one of the most brutal assailants of Boniface VIII at Anagni, the Romans formed a republic against the absent pope and his helper Robert of Naples.[34] An excommunicated bishop officiated at Louis' consecration and the imperial crown was put on his head by none other than Sciarra Colonna. Whether the emperorship was worth acquiring in circumstances such as these was questionable. Though naturally ignored by the pope, Louis' imperial status was in fact widely accepted, eventually even by the electors. Pope John XXII died at the end of 1334 without having succeeded in overthrowing Louis.

John XXII was a curious mixture. The papacy in this period has been called very political,[35] but John actually also held strong views on theological questions, though these were those of a dilettante. Some of these opinions made him enemies in high places. He was a person of considerable ability, but his reign was marred by an excessive support for French policy in general as well as for strong Franco-Angevin predominance in the whole of Italy. John regarded the firm establishment of the latter as a necessary condition for the return of the papacy to the Patrimony of St Peter, thus delaying the urgently required presence of the pontiff there. So the curia for the time being settled down in residence at Avignon, which was to lead to such grave problems in the future. Another corollary of John's preference for France and Anjou was his attempt to exclude the Empire as well as the Aragonese Frederick of Sicily from any say in Italy. During John's reign, part of the Sacred College, actually under Napoleon Orsini's leadership, had wished to have him condemned, and tried to enlist the support of Louis and the German bishops for this endeavour.

As John XXII died in Avignon, the papal conclave also took place there. In view of the theological dilettantism of the previous pope, the cardinals in December 1334 elected an expert in this field, the Cistercian Jacques Fournier, who had shown fervour and indeed severity in the fight against heresy. He took the title of Benedict XII. Within a few months of his election, the new pope began the building of a big palace in Avignon, thus making a return to Rome even less likely. Benedict at times attempted to make a stand against French policy. But he basically had to continue following the dictates of its kings, actually going further in some respects than his predecessor. Louis made strong efforts to come to terms with Benedict, but even considerable concessions did not manage to move the pontiff, as King Philip VI of France vetoed any reconciliation. In view of this situation in Avignon, the Estates in the German kingdom rallied to Louis. In 1338 a diet at Frankfurt, in the manifesto *Fidem catholicam*, stated that John XXII had been unjust in instituting proceedings against Louis, as the king did not need papal approbation for his dignity, a statement which was reaffirmed by the electors at a meeting in Rhens. A second diet at Frankfurt the same year went even further and proclaimed in the *Reich* law, *Licet iuris*, that whoever had been duly elected King of the Romans was entitled to the imperial crown without confirmation by the pope. In the spring of 1339, the electors even recognised Louis' emperorship. Anti-curial sentiments in the German kingdom increased, as the interdict through its interference with the services provided by the Church took its toll, particularly as Benedict was less inclined than his predecessor to grant exemptions in certain circumstances.

The conflict between France and England, with the beginning of the Hundred Years War in 1339, also affected the German kingdom. At first Louis allied with England, but soon moved closer to France. However, the papacy still under Benedict's successor Clement VI was not interested in coming to terms with Louis, unless papal rights of confirmation were conceded, which was regarded as unacceptable. While Louis had held his own against the papacy, he began to encounter resistance in connection with his plans to expand Wittelsbach dynastic power by acquiring Tirol. This brought him into conflict with the Luxemburg dynasty, one of whose princes had married the heiress of the territory. The Wittelsbach side asserted that the union had not been consummated and was therefore void. Louis at once had the heiress wedded to one of his sons, which led to immediate papal sanctions against him; these carried more conviction in the German kingdom than the previous clerical measures taken against him.

In this situation Charles, the eldest son of John, the blind King of Bohemia, and a grandson of Emperor Henry VII, organised a coalition to overthrow Louis. In April 1346, the pope asked the electors to proceed to the choice of a new King of the Romans. In July, after Louis had been deposed, Charles, with French and papal support, received the votes of the three archbishops, as well as of his father as King of Bohemia, and of the Duke of Saxony. Actually both father and son fought for the French when they were defeated at Crécy in August 1346 by the English. John was killed. Charles was wounded, but was able to escape and succeeded to the Bohemian throne without difficulty. Three months later he was crowned King of the Romans in Bonn, as Aachen, like nearly all the imperial cities, supported Louis, whose position in the kingdom was still strong. Charles was handicapped by appearing to be a *rex clericorum* (*Pfaffenkönig*), an instrument of the priests, which at that time of anticlerical feeling in the German kingdom was a severe disadvantage. However, Louis suddenly died in October 1347 and thus Charles IV, the head of the Luxemburg dynasty, became undisputed ruler, particularly after he had neutralised the anti-king Günther of Schwarzburg elected in 1349, who died the same year.

Charles IV was one of the most important German kings of the later Middle Ages. Born in 1316 as the son of King John of Bohemia and of his wife, the Przemyslid heiress Elizabeth, he spent an unhappy early childhood in Bohemia owing to the tensions between his parents. But from the age of seven onwards he was brought up at the court of his uncle-by-marriage Charles IV of France in Paris. He received an excellent education there; one of his teachers was the later Pope Clement VI. In the early 1330s he spent two years in Italy, before returning to Bohemia to take over the duties of lieutenant for his widely roaming chivalrous father; he also became Margrave of Moravia. From 1340, when his father became totally blind, Charles had to play an even more prominent part in the affairs of his dynasty, which propelled him to the centre of the European stage. He enjoyed good relations with the French court and the papal curia, but was determined to assert his independence from his patrons. In these efforts he was helped by the increasing room for manœuvre given to the German kingdom by the preoccupation of the French monarchy with the Hundred Years War and the loosening of its hold on the papacy whenever the English cause was in the ascendent. He soon established himself as the outstanding ruler in Western Christendom of his time and certainly as one of the shrewdest.

Charles was a very cultured person, though he could also be quite crude. In 1348 he founded the first university in the Empire, the Charles University in Prague. He had a knowledge of languages quite extraordinary for his time. A deeply pious person, he accumulated an enormous collection of relics. He supported the papal Inquisition: 'Whether he moved from conviction, policy, or a mixture of both, there can be no question that he supported the persecution of heresy with more legislation and determination than any German emperor since the time of Frederick II.'[36] His piety, incidentally, did not prevent him from pursuing his own interests and those of his dynasty with ruthlessness and at times without moral restraint, as we shall see. In purely secular terms he was an adversary his opponents underrated at their peril, somebody not to be taken in easily, a master of timing, with endless patience until it was time for him to strike. Like Rudolf of Habsburg, he preferred peaceful settlement to fighting. But conciliation had its own costs and Charles was always trying to raise money. While Charles with the addition of Lower Lusatia in 1369 and particularly of the Brandenburg electorate in 1373 created a very considerable Luxemburg empire, the territories he ruled gained from his capacity for government. The German kingdom and Bohemia were among those of his lands which benefited from his generally wise rule, even if he was at the same time able to serve his own interests.

Perhaps the greatest blemish on Charles' rule was his treatment of the Jews of Nuremberg at the time of the Black Death in 1349. The city, to which Louis IV had granted considerable privileges, was fast becoming the most important trading centre in the south of the German kingdom. Within days of Louis' death, Charles had established his court there and had drawn the city to his side. But the late emperor's son, the Elector Louis of Brandenburg, who had helped to promote the anti-king, did not allow Wittelsbach influence in Nuremberg to be destroyed so easily and helped to organise a coup, which overthrew the city council. In order to regain the support of Nuremberg and to secure the help of Louis of Brandenburg in this endeavour, Charles promised him three Jewish houses of prime quality in Nuremberg, which the Wittelsbach prince could choose, as soon as the Jews there had been 'beaten'. Charles also assured the previously overthrown Nuremberg council, once it had been restored, of impunity if anything happened to the Jews; he furthermore made plans for this eventuality, decreeing that a *Marienkirche* was to take the place of the synagogue. Something did in fact happen to the Jews. One of the beneficiaries from these transactions in Nuremberg recorded that 'on 5 December 1349 the Jews were burned'. A Jewish source reveals that 560 Jews fell victim to the pogroms. 'Apparently, in spite of his not only publicly demonstrated, but actually authenticated attachment to the Church and his piety it touched Charles little that he paved the way for the death of so many Jews.'[37] However, at other times, such as during the plague of 1348–9, Charles IV, with Pope Clement VI, attempted, in vain, to prevent the massacre of the Jewish population.[38]

The comparatively stable situation in the German kingdom allowed Charles to spend many years in Bohemia in order to consolidate his position there. By 1354, he was ready to venture to Italy to claim the imperial crown. Rome had in the meantime gone through a great deal of turmoil. In 1347, the notary Cola di Rienzo, who wished to preserve the remnants of ancient Rome and to bring about a renaissance of its glorious past, had carried out a revolution in the city. He set himself up as a tribune of the people and carried out a draconian regime in which he imitated old Roman constitutional norms. At that stage Rienzo did not include the pope as part of the Roman order and thought in terms of the election of an Italian emperor by representatives of the Roman people. However, a few months later Rienzo was overthrown after eighty members of the Roman city nobility had been murdered. At first he hid with Spiritual Franciscans, whose radical religiosity had provided the background for his political ideology, but this led to his being accused of heresy by the papacy. Rienzo fled to Charles' court in Prague where he was received courteously. But the king was unwilling to become involved with a suspected heretic, and handed him over to the pope in Avignon, where Rienzo came to an arrangement with the curia. He foreswore his Spiritualist ideals, and in 1354 was sent back to Rome, this time as an emissary of the Holy See, to support Cardinal Albornoz' efforts to reorganise the Patrimony of St. Peter preparatory to the return of the papacy to the Holy City. However, in October 1354, Rienzo was murdered by the Roman populace. In 1355 Charles became King of the Lombards and was crowned emperor by a papal legate in Rome. At the request of the Pope, Innocent VI, another southern Frenchman, Charles only spent one day officially in the city. Wisely, unlike his grandfather, he kept out of the internal disputes in Italy, though this caused disappointment among his supporters, such as the poet Petrarca.[39]

Charles gave the German kingdom a period of peace and, in spite of an alliance with France, kept it out of the Hundred Years War. One of his greatest achievements was the issue of the Golden Bull in 1356, which provided the German kingdom and the Empire with a fundamental constitutional law. The Golden Bull consists of a number of laws and decrees, partly based on previous pronouncements, which were deliberated with the nobility and the cities and agreed with them at diets in Nuremberg at the beginning of 1356 and in Metz at the end of that year. The main stipulations concerned the election of the King of the Romans by the electors(*Kurfürsten*), and these were in many respects modelled on the papal conclave. The arrangement followed in recent vacancies received definite sanction, confirming that there were seven electors. These consisted of the three Rhenish Archbishops (of Mainz, Trier and Cologne), of the King of Bohemia, the Elector Palatine of the Rhine, the Duke of Saxony and the Margrave of Brandenburg. The Dukes of Bavaria and Austria were not included among the electors, thus omitting any representation from the south of the kingdom. The main weight of the electoral vote was in the Rhineland, which constituted the majority of the college.

The modalities for the election were regulated in detail. As soon as the Archbishop of Mainz had learned of the death of the king or emperor, he was to invite the other electors to the election and to fix the date for it, which was to take place at Frankfurt within three months. If the archbishop failed to act within thirty days of the ruler's death, the electors were to proceed to

Frankfurt on their own initiative within the three months' period. The personal safety of the electors was to be safeguarded both on their journey and during their stay in Frankfurt, to which each of them was to be allowed to bring not more than two hundred men on horseback, of which only fifty could be armed. During the election the city of Frankfurt had full police powers, even over the electors.

Every effort was to be made to have the election take place within thirty days, otherwise the electors – like the cardinals under the papal election decree of 1274 – were to be put on bread and water; actually this stipulation was not realised. None of the electors, respectively their representatives, were allowed to depart until the election had taken place. Whatever the absolute majority of the electors, that is four out of the seven (even with the candidate voting for himself), determined was to be regarded as the unanimous decision of the college. The Archbishop of Mainz presided over the proceedings, asking each elector in turn, according to a prescribed order, to indicate his choice. The Archbishop himself had the final say, thus exercising a casting vote in case of a tie. As soon as the king had been duly elected, his first act as ruler was to confirm the privileges of the electors, an action he was to repeat as soon as he had been crowned emperor. It was the Archbishop of Cologne who crowned the king at Aachen.

Altogether the position of the electors was considerably strengthened in comparison with that of other princes. In order to avoid any doubt as to who was entitled to cast the electoral vote, a strict order of succession was laid down for each of the secular electorates. Male primogeniture was to apply, with 18 as the age of majority. The electors were granted the right – desired by all princes – of being entitled to be enfeoffed by the king with their territories on succeeding to the inheritance, which was called *Leihezwang*. In fact, perhaps as a result of the privilege granted to the electors, this also became a customary right for all large royal fiefs. The territory of the elector was declared to be indivisible, because the electoral vote was attached to it. Again the reason for the stipulation was to secure absolute clarity as to who was entitled to vote on this very important occasion. Indeed there were some partitions, though most of the electors were saved the debilitating divisions which elsewhere led to the formation of dwarf principalities. Thus they preserved for their territories a size adequate to allow them to play an important part in the affairs of the kingdom. Altogether the electors were given a semi-royal position and any attack on them was to be regarded as a particularly serious crime (*Majestätsverbrechen*). Of the electors, the King of Bohemia received a number of special privileges. During throne vacancies, the Count Palatine on the Rhine and the Duke of Saxony were to act as Vicars of the Empire. It was also laid down that every year after Easter the electors were to meet for four weeks in an imperial city, which, however, failed to happen. Actually, if this stipulation had been implemented, the

College of Electors could have become established as a regular constitutional organ.

The electoral stipulations of the Golden Bull provided the basis for the elections of kings of the Romans to the end of the Empire. They did succeed in preventing dual elections, but only after the death of Charles IV's son Sigismund in 1437. From then onwards they began to be regarded as a fundamental law of the Empire. A notable feature of these sections of the Golden Bull was the absence of any reference to the pope. Thus an emperor who had come to the throne with the aid of the Holy See to displace Louis IV in effect reafffirmed the declaration made by his predecessor and the electors in 1338, rejecting the necessity of papal confirmation for the elected King of the Romans. According to the bull the king assumed his function as soon as he had been elected. Thus a factor of uncertainty in ensuring a smooth succession from one ruler to another was removed. This was all the more important as, unlike other monarchies, the German kingdom – which had arisen from agreement between the various tribes or stems (*Stämme*) – depended for its continued existence on the election of the king and future emperor. In view of these historical origins and the importance of securing the oaths of fealty from the princes all over the kingdom after the election, the appearance of unanimity was of value; in fact, however, the majority principle, taken over from the papal conclave, was now adopted. All these matters were particularly weighty, for, as a precondition for the emperorship, the German royalty had a sacral aspect.

The Golden Bull is not concerned merely with the German kingdom, but also with the Empire. The bull stated clearly that the Holy Roman Empire had 'different laws for nations distinct in customs, modes of life and language' and therefore 'had to carry out the appropriate acts of government'. In view of that the electors were asked to learn several languages, not only German in some form (which they knew from childhood), but also Latin, Italian and (Bohemian)-Czech, 'the languages in which the most important business of the Empire was transacted'. Interestingly, French was omitted from the list of recommended languages. This was not only symbolic for the supranational nature of the Empire, but for the shift in its centre of gravity from the West to the East, which included particularly Bohemia, Austria and Brandenburg.[40] With the increased importance of the electors, a certain dualism between emperor and empire, of *Kaiser und Reich*, of emperor and electors, as well as some oligarchical elements, crept into the constitution of kingdom and empire. Thus matters developed quite differently from, for instance, the increasing centralism adopted by the French monarchy. The Golden Bull resulted from cooperation between emperor and electors, and had the potential of giving more stability to the German kingdom. The bull incidentally also attempted to bring feuding into proper legal form.[41]

Like so many previous German kings and emperors, Charles was deeply concerned about the affairs of the papacy. In 1365, he travelled to Avignon to try and persuade the Pope, Urban V, to come back to Italy. In a second Roman expedition in 1367, Charles managed to lead Urban back to Rome, but the pope soon returned to Avignon. Charles, incidentally, took advantage of his first trip to Avignon to have himself crowned king at Arles, in order to keep for the Empire the overlordship of Burgundian territory annexed by France; he was the last German king or emperor to receive the Burgundian crown. In 1376, Charles, who was always prepared to wait, succeeded in having his eldest son Wenzel elected King of the Romans, thus strengthening the prospects of a continuation of the Luxemburg dynasty at the head of the German kingdom and the Empire. A reign of outstanding achievement came to an end when the Emperor Charles IV died in November 1378, greatly troubled by the Great Schism which had begun earlier in the year.

The crisis had been set off after the death of Gregory XI in Rome in March 1378. Gregory was the last of three popes who came from the Limousin in the south of France and the nephew of the first of these, Clement VI. He was elected in Avignon in 1370. In spite of French opposition, Gregory XI made plans to take up residence in the Patrimony of St Peter, but was unable to do so until 1376, well into his reign; by then there was only rather more than a year left of his pontificate.

Unfortunately, the Roman populace, in its determination not to lose the papacy again, would not allow the cardinals to carry out their important duties in the peace and quiet they required. The crowd assembled outside St. Peter demanded that a Roman, or at least an Italian, be elected pope, making it very difficult to follow proper procedures in conclave. After some discussion of other possible candidates, the majority of the college in April 1378 agreed on an Italian, Bartolomeo Prignani, the Archbishop of Bari; he had been in charge of the papal chancery in the absence of the vice-chancellor in Avignon. But an assault on the conclave interrupted the completion of the necessary formalities for Prignani's election. The cardinals now gave in to mob pressure to select a Roman, and then elected the old Roman Cardinal, Tebaldeschi, who was enthroned in spite of his protests. But later a number of cardinals, who had fled earlier, returned to the conclave and completed the formalities for the election of Prignani, who called himself Urban VI. Had he been duly elected? What could be read into the initial willingness of the cardinals to recognise him and to work with him? Unfortunately Urban was not particularly tactful, and thus spoiled any chance he might have had of stilling the doubts about the legitimacy of his election. Many cardinals therefore approached him to convey to him their opinion that he had not been duly elected, but Urban refused to budge. References were made to the summoning of a general council to settle the problem.

In the end, in a fresh conclave in September, this time in an area under Neapolitan control, the non-Italian Cardinal, Robert of Geneva, was elected pope and took the name of Clement VII. The schism was a reality. There is still no agreement among historians as to who was the legitimate pope. Clement, the more skilful of the two popes, found it impossible to establish himself in Rome and therefore decided to take up residence in Avignon. The prestige of the papacy suffered grievous harm. The two popes vied with each other for the favours of the mighty, being quite prepared to reward their followers with favours, often at the expense of the long-term interests of the Church and the Holy See. Inevitably, the churches in the various countries used the opportunity to emancipate themselves as much as possible from any control by the Holy See. In the German kingdom, it was not so much the kingdom itself that took advantage of the situation, but more the individual princes and to some extent even the cities.[42] The cause of church reform suffered a further set-back. Certainly by the fourteenth century some of the ideas that were to dominate the Reformation came to the fore, such as the demand for general church councils and for a return to the primitive church and its poverty. Reform of the Church was to take place both in its head and its members. The cry for reform of the papacy in particular naturally increased during the schism. There was some doubt whether even an improved papacy would be able to reform the Church as a whole. Increasingly it was realised that each part of the whole had to make its own contribution, including the monastic orders. Unfortunately the Franciscans, for instance, were rent by divisions over the question of poverty.

The Avignon papacy initially had French support, but the greater part of Europe belonged to the Roman 'obedience', including most of the German kingdom, which, however, in the nature of things was divided in this matter. While Wenzel was able to succeed his father Charles IV in the German kingdom, he was preoccupied with Bohemia, where the high nobility rebelled and took him prisoner in 1394. The situation there was becoming increasingly critical, particularly in Prague, where there was deep unrest because of demands for a reform of the Church, and also because of conflicts between those of Czech and those of Germanic stock. In the German kingdom itself, Wenzel came under increasing criticism because of his inability to prevent feuding between the princes and the cities, and also because of his inaction over the schism and his alleged neglect of imperial interests by his appointment of a Visconti as Duke of Milan. Thus the comparatively strong position Charles IV had established for the crown in the German kingdom vanished with his successor. In 1400, as with Adolf of Nassau, the electors – in this case the four Rhenish ones – proceeded to Wenzel's deposition. They elected as king one of their number, Rupert of the Palatinate, a member of the Wittelsbach dynasty, which also ruled in Bavaria. While Wenzel did not accept his displacement, he did not actively set about reclaiming the German throne.

Rupert, an upright ruler without wiles, found the task he faced a very difficult one. In 1401, he undertook an expedition to Italy, but was beaten by Duke Visconti of Milan. The imperial crown eluded him. In the German kingdom itself, the so-called Marbach association (*Marbacher Bund*) of south-western princes and cities was formed against him under the leadership of the Archbishop of Mainz. In the end Rupert also found himself overtaken by developments in the Church which resulted in cardinals from both obediences, without the authority of either pope or of the King of the Romans, summoning a council to Pisa in 1409. The schism had continued because, whenever a vacancy occurred either in Rome or in Avignon, a new pope was elected for that 'obedience'. At Pisa, both popes of the time, Gregory XII in Rome and Benedict XIII in Avignon, were deposed and the philosopher Peter Philargi of Candia was elected in their place as Alexander V. The council and Alexander were supported by France. However, as the two previous popes did not give up, there were now three pontiffs.

The outbreak of civil war in Germany was only averted by the death of Rupert, who was by then completely isolated, in 1410. Actually the king was one of the best territorial rulers of the time, a true Christian who was deeply disturbed by the schism and strove harder than most of his contemporaries to overcome these divisions. Rupert gave asylum to professors of the University of Paris who had been expelled because of their stand against the Avignonese pope. With them he founded, in 1386, the University of Heidelberg, after Prague and Vienna the oldest in the Empire.

In spite of all the good intentions of those who had drawn up the Golden Bull, another dual election took place on Rupert's death. Actually two princes of the Luxemburg dynasty were elected, Wenzel's younger half-brother Sigismund and his cousin Jobst, Margrave of Moravia. As Wenzel had still not accepted his deposition, there were now three kings. However, Jobst died in 1411 and eventually Sigismund came to terms with his half-brother, so that in practice he became the unchallenged German king.

In the meantime, in 1410, the military religious Order of the Teutonic Knights in Prussia had suffered a severe defeat at the hands of the Polish–Lithuanian kingdom in the battle of Grunwald (Tannenberg). Sigismund had in fact tried to prevent the outbreak of hostilities, which proved so disastrous to the order. As was related in the last chapter, the order around 1226 answered the call for help against the heathen Prussians from the Polish Duke Conrad of Masovia, and received imperial and papal privileges for this mission. Like the Templars and the Knights of St John, the Teutonic Knights began in the Holy Land towards the end of the twelfth century. Following the rule of the Templars, they were initially responsible for looking after hospitals in Jerusalem and Acre, which was the seat of the order until 1291. But after the loss of the possessions in the Near East, the Grand Master from 1309 onwards conducted his operations from the Marienburg in West Prussia. Imperial and papal authority formed the basis of the independence of the state of the Teutonic Order in Prussia, whose task it was to spread Christianity among those who had not yet accepted it.[43] However, the *Ordensstaat*, of which one can speak from about 1300, 'was politically based on conquest'.[44] The Christianisation of the heathen *Prussen* of the Baltic encountered lengthy resistance and took about half a century. The order established a sizeable state, which soon dominated the eastern part of the southern Baltic shore up to Livonia. A further advance to the east had been stopped in 1242 by the Prince of Novgorod.

The Teutonic Knights operated outside the territory of the German kingdom and the Empire, from which they drew their recruits and many settlers. It had widespread possessions in other parts of Europe, including the German kingdom. Not only administratively, but also culturally and economically, with its thriving trading cities, above all of Königsberg and Danzig, the *Ordensstaat* was a remarkable achievement. But the way of life of the knights did not exactly encourage them to adhere strictly to their rule, which included poverty, chastity and obedience. Also the justification for their religious mission was somewhat undermined by the baptism of Jagiello, the ruler of Lithuania, in 1382. The order was threatened externally by the Polish–Lithuanian Union and internally by some of the nobility and towns. The price now had to be paid for the failure of the order to take root among the population on its territory owing to its policy of recruiting from the German kingdom. From about 1400 onwards many even of the Germanic nobility and towns preferred Poland–Lithuania to the order. The peace treaty of 1411, to which the order had to submit, marked the beginning of considerable cessions of territory to Poland, which in 1466 led to a recognition of Polish suzerainty for what was left of its territory, and to its secularisation in the Reformation.[45]

From the German unification movement in the nineteenth century onwards, the disaster that befell the Teutonic Knights was very much seen from a national and ethnic point of view, as a struggle between Germans and Slavs. Empire and German kingdom were criticised for not coming to the aid of German culture. These national criteria taken from a later age only helped to distort what actually happened to the Teutonic Order in Prussia. The expansionary policy of the order was sooner or later bound to involve it in difficulties with the Poles, who wished to have access to good Baltic ports. Once Poland and Lithuania had become sufficiently powerful, they were ready to risk a trial of strength with the order, which the latter was unlikely to win. Not even all the resources of the *Ordensstaat* could be thrown into the scale against the enemy, because the authorities had not understood the importance of contented subjects. Like other rulers, the order had its problems with the estates, just as the prince–bishops did with their noble cathedral chapters. Finally, on the deepest level, a question-mark hangs over the viability of the religio-political idea represented by the order. Did it really make sense to establish a permanent military establishment to carry out a limited task, that of Christianisation of local populations, which it was intended to complete within a reasonable number of years, and which would thus deprive the order of its main *raison d'être*? Also, were the rather ruthless methods often used by the order not only with non-Christians, but also with fellow-Christians, such as the Archbishop of Riga, really likely to redound to the credit of Christianity?

Of great importance, but not so relevant to the religio-political theme of the book was another Germanic institution also operating without the aid of the emperor or the great territorial lords, the German Hanseatic League.[46] This was an association of traders from cities like Lübeck, Bremen, Hamburg, Riga and Danzig, who joined together in their dealings with local merchants in the cities with which they did their business. They also formed depots in important centres, such as London, and obtained trading concessions in various places, including, for example, Venice. The League 'exercised a virtual monopoly on all trade in the Baltic and North seas'.[47] It collaborated, but also competed, with the Teutonic Order. The Hanseatic League was involved in hostilities with Denmark in the second half of the fourteenth century over its monopoly on shipping in the Baltic, but in the end won the conflict. The fifteenth century saw both its peak and its gradual decline. Among the reasons for the latter were the collapse of the rule of the Teutonic Knights in Prussia, continuing difficulties with the Scandinavian kings, and the strengthening of north German territories like Brandenburg, which forced their towns to leave the League.[48] It was Sigismund who entrusted the energetic Hohenzollern dynasty with the Brandenburg electorate.

Sigismund was no novice in the art of government. The offspring of Charles IV's fourth and final marriage, with Elizabeth of Pomerania, he took as his wife the elder daughter of the Angevin King, Louis of Hungary, and was able to retain that kingdom even after her death; Poland, the other part of Louis' inheritance, went to his younger daughter. Like his father, Sigismund was a ruler of great ability and determination. He did not evade the most daunting challenge facing him, that of ending the schism. As events had turned out, the Council of Pisa had only aggravated the division, even though the conciliar method pointed the way out of the crisis in the future. In any case, the chances of the Pisa pope being generally accepted were diminished by the death of the respected Alexander V within a year of his election. His successor, John XXIII, did not inspire the same confidence. He had a reputation for cunning and for not always being particularly choosy in the choice of his means.[49] Involving himself deeply in Italian politics, he captured the Holy City from Gregory XII, the pontiff of the Roman line. The Avignon Pope, Benedict XIII, maintained his support in the Iberian peninsula. Negotiations between the different popes failed to end the schism.

The papal problem was complicated by the unstable situation in France, indeed by the concurrence of a civil war with the threat of a fresh attack by the English. The insanity of the French King, Charles VI, led to a power struggle for the regency and for control of the king between his two leading relatives, John the Fearless, Duke of Burgundy, and Louis, Duke of Orléans. In 1407 Louis was assassinated on John's orders, setting off a decade of fighting between the Burgundians and the royal court factions with which the Orléans party was associated. The continuance of this internal disorder was all the more serious, as the English King Henry V, who succeeded to the throne in 1413, made extensive territorial claims on France.

Sigismund regarded a further General Council of the Church as essential for a final resolution of the schism. He was aware that the summoning of a council would be made even more difficult by a state of war between England and France, as well as by the internal unrest in the latter. He thus strained every nerve to secure at least a postponement of the Anglo-French war, so that the council could start meeting. Sigismund therefore undertook a mission of personal diplomacy, travelling to France and to England.[50] The delay in the beginning of the war allowed the council to convene and to begin its work. Sigismund's diplomatic activities are all the more remarkable if account is taken of the slow communications and transportation prevailing at the time. Also, in view of the distance of the Hungarian kingdom from the strategic centres in western Europe, he was unable to bring any actual military power to bear in support of his objectives; however, as ruler of the kingdom most threatened by the Turks, Sigismund occupied a special position in Western Christendom.[51] In reactivating the kind of responsibilities for the papacy that a previous German king like Henry III had exercised in the middle of the eleventh century, Sigismund relied mainly on force of personality.

As so often in the history of the relations between pontiffs and German kings, the troubles in which popes found themselves made them look to these kings for help. When John XXIII had to flee from Rome, he appealed for assistance to Sigismund. The king rightly decided, on the grounds of legitimacy as well as practicability, to work for a solution of the schism with that pope, who incidentally commanded the largest territorial 'obedience',[52] rather than with any of his rivals. Sigismund used John's predicament to drive a hard bargain by insisting that the pontiff should summon a general council of the Church to a city in the Empire, namely to Constance; that he should be personally present there; and that he should undertake in advance to submit to the decisions of the council.[53] The king himself, after negotations with John's emissaries, took no chances and himself issued an announcement about the dates and location of the forthcoming council. This was followed some weeks later by a papal bull confirming the arrangements. The council was opened by John XXIII in November 1414, but it took some weeks to fill up, as there was at first an understandable uncertainty as to whether the synod would actually be able to function. Sigismund arrived in Constance at Christmas.

In a way, the new council had more legitimacy than that of Pisa, which had been summoned by cardinals. The synod at Constance was indeed opened by a pope; but its main business was to sit in judgment on the rival popes, including the one presiding. There were problems with an assembly determining the relative claims of three contenders to an office whose holders regarded themselves as Christ's representatives on earth, and who asserted that they could not be judged by anyone. The matter had to be settled for practical reasons, for the schism could not be allowed to continue.

Two important procedural decisions were made at the outset, one relating to voting rights, the other to the process of arriving at decisions. The first, concerning voting rights, was taken to weaken the position of the bishops. It was believed that the majority of the bishops, particularly the Italians, supported John, and were therefore likely to oppose his removal, which was regarded as necessary by Sigismund and the majority of the 'nations' represented at Constance. In order to weaken the position of the bishops, some of the leading personalities at the council, such as the French Cardinal, d'Ailly,[54] got together and had the right to vote granted to doctors of theology and of canon law, representatives of the cathedral chapters, deputies of absent prelates and ambassadors of princely courts. Another novelty of the Council of Constance was the decision at the behest of the Germanic and the English to vote by 'nations', which followed the practice of the universities, but must not be understood in a modern sense. Each of the 'nations', such as the French, the English (which was joined by the Irish and the Welsh), the Germanic (to which the Netherlands, Switzerland, Hungary, Bohemia, Croatia, Poland and Scandinavia also adhered) and the Italian (with Crete and Cyprus) deliberated separately. In each 'nation' the representatives of princes met with the prelates and doctors, and the council could only come to a resolution if unanimous agreement had been reached between the 'nations'. Even in the absence of the Spaniards, who continued to support a non-cooperative Benedict, the council was establishing its legitimacy as the organ to end the schism, to suppress heresy and to reform the Church.[55]

The solution of the schism proved to be a prolonged affair and indeed took up the attention of the council again and again from the early days nearly to the end. On reform there was little agreement in detail as yet. The *causa fidei*, and especially the enforcement of orthodoxy, which was urgent, appeared to offer the best chance of early action.

> Ideas regarded as heretical, which were maintained in England and Bohemia toward the end of the fourteenth and at the beginning of the fifteenth century, acquired a universal importance because they expressed revolutionary views in the quarrels over the constitution, structure, and life of the Church.[56]

Thus the teaching of John Wyclif and Jan Hus became the focus of investigation and discussion. In May 1415, the council condemned many of Wyclif's writings.

Wyclif, who had died in 1384, spent the greater part of his life at Oxford and probably held a fellowship there, financing his work at the university 'in the usual and necessary fashion of the day' through a number of benefices he held elsewhere as an absentee.[57] His theology was strongly influenced by his philosophy. He started off as a nominalist, taking 'the view that universals have no existence independently of being thought and are mere names'.[58] But he regretted his nominalism as an error of his youth and swung round to the very opposite, becoming an ultrarealist. The key to his metaphysic was now the indestructibility of universals (the qualities of things), which led him to view Scripture as having been 'conceived in the mind of God before creation, and before the material Scriptures were written down'.[59] Thus, as a divine idea the Scriptures had to be taken literally, leading to the adoption of a fundamentalist attitude. As an ultrarealist Wyclif had difficulties with the orthodox doctrine of transubstantiation. While his view on the eucharist made him an outsider, his anticlericalism was popular and secured him friends in high places, who kept the ecclesiastical measures taken against him in check. The high taxation due to the Hundred Years War attracted support to his call for an at least partial disendowment of the Church, whose wealth he castigated as an aberration from its poverty at the beginning. Wyclif held that if the Church could not reform itself, the state should take the measures necessary to bring about the necessary changes.

Particularly during the last six years of his life, from 1378 onwards, Wyclif's view became even more extreme. Arguing that, like Scripture, the Church had existed from eternity, he adopted a predestinarian stance, refusing to allow authority to the visible Church, and regarding it as an anti-Christ. While the elect were immune from the consequences of mortal sin, the ministrations of those who were not predestined had no effect. Thus he clearly contradicted the well-established and, from a practical point of view, eminently sensible teaching of the Church that the validity of sacraments was independent of the moral worth of the officiating priest. Because he advocated a ministry of the elect, which included the laity, he regarded as superfluous a priesthood carrying on ecclesiastical tradition and formulating laws of the Church (both of which he rejected). Only Scripture counted. The important impetus he gave to the vernacular translation of the Bible is thus a logical development of his ideas.

While holding radical ecclesiastical views, 'in secular politics, Wyclif remained profoundly conservative'.[60] It is true that he put forward the view that possession and dominion depended on a state of grace, but he applied the theory mainly to the Church and not to the king and the lay lords, whose sins did not in his eyes invalidate their authority. 'Even tyrants must be accepted.'[61]. He also bore in mind that the secular power might always be needed to reform the Church. In the Peasants' Revolt of 1381, while sympathetic to some of the grievances, Wyclif condemned the peasants for their acts of forcible disappropriation. The Lollards derived much from his ideas, however they developed them, although Wyclif did not actually organise the movement. But an even greater legacy left by him was the ferment of thought he created for the future. Many of those elements represented in the sixteenth-century Reformation which undermined the authority and the hierarchy of the Catholic Church were already present in Wyclif: the predestinarianism, the emphasis on the Scriptures and their availability to the laity, the prescriptive example of the primitive church, altogether coming close to a ministry of all believers.[62] As Wyclif clearly deviated from the official teaching of the Church and refused to see the error of his ways, he was a heretic within the medieval definition. His condemnation proved crucial to the proceedings against the Czech reformer John Hus, who was suspected of being his disciple and had been cited to Constance to answer charges against him.

As we saw earlier, Hus's ruler, King Wenzel, had since his accesssion in 1378 encountered considerable difficulty in dealing with the prevailing social, ethnic and religious unrest in Bohemia. While he lacked the outstanding ability demonstrated both by his father and by his half-brother Sigismund, it would be unfair to blame all the problems on him. Thanks to the initiatives taken by Charles IV, including the foundation of the University of Prague, the city, which was now outranked only by Paris in the number of inhabitants, had become the 'cultural hub of central and eastern Europe'.[63] There was a ferment of ideas in Bohemia, particularly in Prague and at its university, which was testing the outer bounds of orthodoxy. 'In a political, economic, intellectual and clerical centre the distance between that, which Christ had taught, and a clearly different world was bound to be felt more painfully than in other places.'[64] In this connection, the difference between the riches and the power of the princes of the Church on the one hand, and the example set by Christ and the apostles on the other, was particularly glaring.[65] Partly owing to the end of the period of colonisation, there was continuous tension between the Germanic part of the population, which in certain aspects provided the leadership, on the one hand, and the Czech majority on the other; but not all Czechs were by any means poor or uninfluential. This situation provided the background for the emergence of John Hus and the Hussite movement.

John Hus was born into a Czech family about 1369, and after studying at the University of Paris returned to his native Bohemia in 1381, gravely disturbed by the Great Schism, and became active in Prague in the cause of the reform of the Church and especially of the clergy. For a time he collaborated with Zbynek, the Archbishop of Prague, but became embroiled in a dispute with him over Wyclif's writings. These had a strong echo at the University of Prague, especially among the Czechs; indeed many of the Germanic elements attacked their Czech colleagues for their support of Wyclif's teaching, partly in order to strengthen their position in the university. Hus led university opposition to the declaration by the curia listing some of Wyclif's writings as heretical. When Zbynek demanded the handing over of Wyclif's writings and had them summarily burned, Hus protested energetically, for which the archbishop excommunicated him temporarily.[66] Over a longer period Hus actually received the support of King Wenzel. Becoming increasingly something like a spiritual leader of the Czechs, Hus sided with the king in supporting the cause of the Council of Pisa in attempting to heal the schism. Actually Wenzel did not only have the general interest in mind in his enthusiasm for a council, but saw a chance of securing support for regaining the German crown from Rupert of the Palatinate in return for his services in the conciliar cause. However, Archbishop Zbynek continued to adhere to the 'Roman' Pope, Gregory XII.

When the question of the council of Pisa was referred to the University of Prague as the highest authority in ecclesiastical law in the land, the conciliar solution was rejected by the Bavarian, Saxon and Polish 'nations' there, most of them actually Germanic. Apparently they were 'mindful of the benefices they might one day wish to have in German-speaking lands of the Roman obedience'.[67] But for the Czechs, including Hus, the priority was church reform, for which they wished to secure conciliar support. They therefore backed the king. In a decree of 1409, Wenzel granted three votes for the Bohemian nation, against one to be held together by the three foreign nations, reversing the previous balance of forces. Thus religious differences exacerbated the tensions between the Czech and Germanic parts of the population still further. That weakened what remained of that inter-ethnic cooperation, to which Bohemia owed some of its greatness, which was of particular importance to the German kingdom in view of the country's unique relationship with the Empire. Bohemia had been a hereditary kingdom since 1212, when it was freed from all financial obligations to the Empire, also no longer requiring imperial confirmation of royal elections. 'Only the fact that Bohemia's kings kept insisting on their role as the ranking temporal electors of the Empire (with the hope of acquiring for themselves the imperial dignity) prevented the complete separation between Bohemia and the Empire.'[68] This complex relationship between them and the crucial part played by the Bohemian electoral vote were to have substantial repercussions on the German kingdom for centuries to come.

The change in voting procedures for the 'nations' at the University of Prague led to the exodus of large numbers of Germanic masters and students, who, incidentally, enabled the Margrave of Meissen, soon to become Elector of Saxony, to found the University of Leipzig. Prague University changed from an international to a national institution: 'while it harmed the prestige which the school had had all over Europe, it established all the more firmly its position as the spiritual centre of the Czech nation.'[69] Hus now took over the rectorship of the university from a Germanic predecessor. The reform and national movement largely merged. Hus, who stood out in the way he cared for the low and down-trodden, saw help for them rather in the 'moral decency and the humane ethics commanded by Christ and the Scriptures',[70] than in changes in the social order. He inveighed against simony, vehemently protested against the sale of indulgences by John XXIII, and challenged the pope's right to demand general obedience. John wished to use the proceeds of these indulgences to finance a crusade against the allies of the pope of the Roman obedience, Gregory XII. He now confirmed Hus' excommunication, demanded the demolition of the Church of Bethlehem, Hus' centre of activities in Prague, and put the city under interdict. At Wenzel's request, to draw the interdict away from the capital, Hus went into voluntary exile in the Bohemian countryside, where his preaching had a considerable echo among the peasants.[71]

In the autumn of 1414, the Prague magistrate Jacobellus, a radical follower of Hus, during the latter's absence and without consultation with him, introduced communion in both kinds (*sub utraque specie*). The 'cup for the laity' in fact merely restored the state of affairs that prevailed before the middle of the thirteenth century, after which it had been generally withdrawn. With his action Jacobellus wished to deprive the clergy of a symbol of superiority over the laity. The council fathers in Constance regarded Hus' views, as well as the administration of the cup to the laity contrary to the prevailing sacramental regulations, as threats to the whole church order requiring their urgent attention.[72]

Hus accepted the summons to Constance, where he received a safe conduct from King Sigismund as protector of the council. Like the childless reigning King Wenzel, his heir presumptive Sigismund did not want to have any extreme action taken against Hus or indeed against the practice of communion in both kinds. He did his best to have Hus protected by his knights and would have liked to have had the whole question of the 'cup for the laity' looked at more carefully, before any conclusions were reached. But all attempts at a compromise and at deflection of the ultimate punishment in the end proved unavailing. The council fathers regarded the interest shown in Wyclif's teaching at the University of Prague, particularly among the Czechs there, as highly dangerous. Hus was tarred too much with the Wyclifite brush, was not given sufficient opportunity to rebut accusations of an identity of views with the English reformer, and was weighed down by the council's recent reaffirmation of the condemnation of the latter's teaching. He was too sincere and too truthful to take advantage of attempts to save him, for instance by accepting a mild abjuration formula. Altogether he was not prepared to obey the existing church order as it stood. He had an ethical and spiritual concept of the Church strongly shaped by Augustinianism.[73] This approach found little understanding from reformers like Gerson with their emphasis on the 'hierarchical structure of the church',[74] which they believed was put at risk by Hus' questioning outlook. For the medieval church, 'the heretic who wilfully persisted in his error was condemned to the pains of hell for eternity... he was ... challenging the fear of damnation, and backing his own judgement ... against a spiritual authority with the power to decide his eternal future'.[75] So in the end there was no compromise and therefore no chance of avoiding the ultimate penalty. Hus died at the stake on 6 July 1415.

The heresy case against Hus is less clear-cut than that against Wyclif. Although Hus defended Wyclif, he did not follow him blindly and adapted many of his ideas;[76] he was not necessarily a follower of Wyclif's heresies. In his writings he gave expression to the view of the Church as a body of the predestined, challenging the existing hierarchical church and the obedience owed to it. That some of Hus' concepts were unacceptable to the church establishment is not surprising. He certainly had to be taken seriously, and in many ways later developments confirmed that necessity. But the question arises whether the methods adopted by the authorities, instead of removing the threat, did not in fact aggravate the situation. The council decided to strike at communion in both kinds, which was prohibited on 15 June 1415, and at Hus. Instead of crushing opposition, the combination of the two measures taken had the reverse effect of what was intended. For the first time in its history, the Church of Rome was openly defied in its attempt to crush heresy by substantial sections of the population in a major country, so that in the end a deviation from usual practice had to be allowed in Bohemia. But before commonsense prevailed, war took its toll of killing and destruction over many years. The 'crusading' armies despatched against the Bohemian dissidents were not victorious.

Did the Church, in enforcing its *magisterium*, have no other way of dealing with Hus, a priest and academic teacher of the highest integrity, a man of deep sensitivity for the sufferings of fellow human beings, than to inflict the horrible punishment of burning? Did these procedures foster the spiritual aims for which the Church existed? To raise these questions is not to expect the fifteenth century to practice tolerance. Hus himself actually was convinced that those *properly* convicted of heresy should be put to death,[77] but he was at loggerheads with the council on both the definition of heresy and the procedures to be followed to determine it. He came to Constance in the expectation that he would be able to debate his theological views with the council fathers, as an equal and not as a prisoner in the dock. His assessment of the situation may have been naïve, but the council would have been wise to have given him a chance to present his case. If that had happened, his eventual conviction, whatever the penalty, would have inspired more confidence, particularly in Bohemia. There would have been a greater chance of justice being seen to be done. The course of events at Constance showed up in a glaring light the general deficiencies in the judicial proceedings conducted by the Church in cases of suspected heresy. However, even if the council erred in linking Hus too much to Wyclif, the Czech reformer certainly questioned the competence of the church authorities to deal with matters of dogma, and therefore set himself up as a judge of the true faith. The ecclesiastical authorities rightly regarded this attitude as liable to lead to a proliferation of faiths, such as indeed was to happen in the following century.

Hus was a mild man, but convinced as he was as a person of deep faith that he held the key to salvation, he felt it was his duty to strive for the acceptance of his beliefs and for the defeat of all obstacles to the spread of his ideas. Thus he could not be tolerant of the views of those who disagreed with him. Potentially he presented a threat to church order and discipline, and therefore, in view of the central function of the Church in medieval society, to the whole social order. Within the mental framework of the age, the question here is simply the extent of the punishment to be inflicted on those who deviated from the teaching of the Church; essentially, whether somebody like Hus had to suffer the final indignities of being stripped of his priesthood and of being handed over to the secular power to be burned.

There is also another issue that has ever since troubled those who have concerned themselves with the fate of Hus at Constance. Why was the safe conduct issued by King Sigismund as protector of the council set aside? The formal answer is that at the time even a safe conduct could not protect a convicted heretic. For Frederick G. Heymann, the Hussite historian,

> there ... is no excuse for this breach short of the fantastic claim that no Christian need keep faith with a heretic, and Sigismund himself acknowledged the flagrant wrong he felt compelled to do ... by violently blushing when the sentence was pronounced and Hus looked at him ... The accusation that he was guilty for the death of Hus followed Sigismund through most of his life and seems to have burdened his conscience, as he

made considerable efforts, throughout the following years, to prove his innocence.[78]

While there may well have been a large measure of agreement in the synod on the questions relating to Hus and to Bohemia, little headway had been made in the main business of the council, to end the schism. To achieve union, the best way of proceeding against any of the rival popes whose elimination appeared essential was to bring accusations of moral turpitude and unworthiness for the high office. This was, in fact, the method used against John XXIII. It was John's flight from Constance in March 1415 which forced the council to focus not merely on the practical problem of ending the schism, but also on the general relationship between councils and popes. There was an understandable fear among the council fathers that their assembly might be transferred to another place or dissolved altogether. Thanks to the determination of Sigismund and of some of the conciliar leaders, such as Jean Gerson, Chancellor of the University of Paris and his king's representative at the synod,[79] the constitution *Haec sancta* was passed by the council in April 1415. This stated that the synod received its authority immediately from Christ and that all, even popes, were obliged to obey its decrees, whether relating to reform or to the schism.[80] 'This was conciliarism in purest form. Here the church no longer existed in its hierarchy, in the pope, the cardinals and the bishops, but in the *aggregatio fidelium*.'[81] The reference to the general body of the faithful reflects the widened composition of the council to include many who were not prelates and who thus did not have responsibility for carrying out the decrees of the council.

John was brought back to Constance as a prisoner and deposed because of simony, bad administration and scandalous morals. Though at the time 'regarded as an unworthy, but not as an unlawful pope',[82] the official roll of the popes does not contain his name, which was thus available to the convenor of the Second Vatican Council. There were now still two claimants to the papacy. Fortunately the pope of the Roman obedience, Gregory XII, a highly respectable ecclesiastic, was prepared to give way. But as he could not be expected to surrender his dignity to a council called by an unworthy rival, he was allowed to have the synod formally summoned in his name at a sitting at which his abdication was subsequently announced; he was appointed a cardinal-bishop by the council.

Benedict XIII still refused to renounce the papacy. Once more Sigismund exerted every effort to find a solution and headed a conciliar mission south. While he did not succeed in obtaining Benedict's abdication, he won the states of the Iberian peninsula, which had belonged to the Avignon obedience, for the council in December 1415. However, it took nearly two years until the Spanish states were represented at the council as the fifth 'nation'. Finally, in July 1417 Benedict was deposed after legal proceedings against him; safe in his Spanish redoubt, he continued to regard himself as the rightful pope until his death in 1423. Now at last the council had succeeded in creating a vacancy which could be filled by the election of a new pope.[83]

Before this could take place, there were, however, a number of problems that had to be resolved. Constance was the scene of tumults. Many of those attending the council, such as the cardinals, felt personally threatened and formed contingent plans to flee. The resumption of hostilities between England and France with the Battle of Agincourt in October 1415 increased tensions in Constance. At times Sigismund had adopted a hostile attitude to the French. Also he was widely suspected of wishing to exercise a decisive influence on the election of the new pope, possibly to delay the event until he had made sufficient preparations for what he regarded as a suitable choice. The council was at the crossroads, what should have priority, reform or the election of the pope? Sigismund now demanded, supported by the Germanic 'nation', that reform of the Church should precede the election of the new pope, only succeeding up to a point. But how close was the council to achieving agreement on an overall plan for the reform of the Church in general and of the curia in particular? Would it be right to delay the main business of the council, the election of a new pope, in the hope of speedily agreeing on a complete reform programme? In fact commissions of the council had been working on the question of reform and had got to the stage of making a number of important recommendations. As to the synod, 'the old and often repeated assertion that it did little for the reform of the Church is completely unjustified'.[84]

There was something to be said for each priority, but as the two questions were linked, only the future could tell who was right. However, 'in the light of later history more understanding should be granted to the call for reform',[85] for it was correctly realised that in the long run only a thorough-going effective reform could preserve church unity. Probably wisely, a compromise was reached between these stark alternatives. Those articles of reform that had already received the consent of the 'nations' were to be published before the papal election and to be put into force. Thus, in October 1417, in the decree *Frequens*, the future pope was committed to the calling of councils within certain time spans, for the first time after five years, then after a further seven years, and finally every ten years. A procedure was laid down for dealing with a future schism. Every newly elected pope was to make a confession of faith. Finally the translation of bishops and prelates against their will, and certain papal dues, were prohibited.[86] The new pope was obliged to accept the reform decrees of the council and to carry out further reforms.[87]

As to the mode of election, a procedure proposed by the French 'nation' was adopted. The new pope was to be elected by the Sacred College and by six representatives of each of the five 'nations'. The 30 representatives of the 'nations' had a slight numerical edge over the 23 cardinals. Both among the cardinals and in each of the nations a two-thirds majority was required. Thus the new pope would be safe from any challenge to his election and politically unassailable.[88]

In spite of the many hurdles a successful candidate had to surmount, the conclave in Constance was in fact able to reach a decision on the second day, on 11 November 1417. Cardinal Oddo Colonna received the requisite two-thirds majorities both among the cardinals and in each of the 'nations'. He accepted the election, the only Colonna to ascend the papal throne, and called himself Martin V. From now on, the council was under the presidency of the new pope.

The electors chose well, perhaps too well from the point of view of conciliar power. Naturally it was a matter of honour and integrity for the council to select the person best fitted for the position. Was a pope of great ability, with a strong personality, liable to be a threat to the existence of councils and to their legitimate aspirations? After the long period of schism and papal impotence, anybody elected pontiff was bound to make the attempt to recover some of the initiative the papacy had lost to the general council. A particularly capable pontiff like Martin V was likely to be especially successful at this, almost inevitably at the expense of the power of general councils. While Martin respected the restrictions imposed on the papacy, at least in the letter, he strengthened the power and organisation of the curia and refounded the Patrimony of St Peter. If he made use of the advantages his permanent executive role gave him over councils that came and went, he was doing nothing unfair or indeed unexpected. The role councils were to play in the future direction of the Church had not been finally settled at Pisa and at Constance, but would depend on the wisdom shown by the leaders of a future council, some years away.

In the meantime, it was left to the new pope to deal with current and urgent issues, ranging from the relationship of the curia with the various territorial churches to the measures to be adopted towards a Bohemia increasingly out of control after the burning of Hus and the prohibition of the chalice for the laity. In 1418 Martin V in his own name proclaimed seven reform decrees already agreed by the council before his election. He also concluded concordats with the five council 'nations', which were generally to run for five years, until the next council. The concordats were designed to secure the reforms laid down by the Council of Constance, particularly in restricting the papal right of clerical nomination. In 1420 Martin was able to enter Rome and to reactivate by stages the Patrimony of St Peter, whose revenues were all the more essential to the curia because the Council of Constance had reduced the papal income; also there were unusual expenditures due to the fusion of the curiae of the three obediences. Little came out of the Council of Pavia/Siena (1423/24), because of Martin's preoccupation with rebuilding the Patrimony, and because of the priority he gave to the restoration of the papal power.

What did not go so well for Martin was the situation in Bohemia. If the council and the pope, who himself had for some time been strongly opposed to Hus, believed that the measures that had been taken would settle the problem, they were mistaken. In a letter of September 1415, about 450 nobles of Bohemia and Moravia, in an unprecedented action, addressed a letter to the council asserting that Hus had been unjustly burned. Already about a year previously, some leading Bohemian nobles had urged Sigismund 'to ensure that Hus was not "furtively abused, to the dishonour of our nationality and of the Bohemian land"'.[89] The manner in which the council had handled the two matters of greatest concern to Bohemia, the chalice for the laity and the question of Hus' theology, created a strong opposition in the country to the proceedings in Constance. For they managed to stir up at the same time national and religious feelings which were both deeply felt; 'the two decisions tended to be lumped together in the minds of the Bohemians and Moravians, and the emotional reaction against the one buttressed the other.'[90] It was this religio-national combination, brought about largely by the actions of the Church, which eventually was to present a major threat to church unity, not only in Bohemia, but also elsewhere. So long as differences between the Church Universal and the different territorial authorities could be settled directly between them, an excessive strain on the unity of the whole Church could be avoided by special deals being made to cope with varying national conditions. But the warnings given to the council by Sigismund and Wenzel, as well as by the nobility in the kingdom, about the dangers inherent in the Bohemian situation, had not been taken sufficiently seriously by the council fathers. As a consequence, the council, and later the pope, had to grapple with a dynamic popular movement, with which it was difficult to negotiate and which – as became apparent – one could not crush, at any rate in the short run. In fact the church authorities lost control over the situation in Bohemia. This became clear in the developments arising from the demand for the cup for the laity.

With the total prohibition of the practice by the council, the chance had passed to allow controlled change, such as the granting of permission for the administration of communion in two kinds in certain circumstances. There was a hardening of the fronts. To some extent owing to the uncompromising attitude taken in Constance, the more radical Hussites in Bohemia took over and carried their demands much further than was necessarily inherent in the original agitation for the chalice for the laity. Going far beyond a request for permission to deviate from normal liturgical practice, there was a movement to make communion in both kinds universal and compulsory. Right from the beginning, the fervour with which those who believed that it was unbiblical to deny the cup to the laity attempted to make communion in both kinds generally available, led to unrest and to acts of violence. 'Giving the chalice to the laity involved more than a mere liturgical change.'[91] Where the Utraquists (so called because of the demand for communion in two kinds, *sub utraque specie*) triumphed, priests who adhered to the old order had no alternative but to leave. Often the crowd took over and enforced the cup on the laity, disturbing church order and liturgical dignity. Individual consciences were subjected to often almost unbearable strain. Divisiveness set in. What was regarded as liturgically correct in one church, even in the same township, was regarded as wrong and as sinful in another. The priest or layman left behind by change, or who had become discontented with existing practices, had to conform unwillingly or to uproot himself, to become a refugee. What happened in Bohemia from about 1415 tragically proved to be curtain raiser for the following centuries.

While King Wenzel at first refused to enforce the prohibition of communion in two kinds decreed by the Council of Constance, he reversed his position in 1419. But when he ordered the closing of most Hussite churches, a rebellion broke out in Prague. Even at this point there was still a certain chance of compromise, but that passed when Wenzel, who had maintained a certain popularity, died from a stroke, without leaving any children of his own. Sigismund was the nearest heir, but he was at that time in his Hungarian kingdom preparing for war against the Turks. In any case, in view of his conduct towards Hus at the Council of Constance, his candidature 'was bound to meet sharp resistance on the side of the more radical Hussites'.[92]

The Hussite movement was not united. It contained many factions, above all the more moderate Utraquists and the more extreme Taborites. Different Hussite factions had varying criteria for orthodoxy and heresy, and did not shrink from numerous executions to enforce them, with even fewer safeguards than the Inquisition provided. In all this the militarily highly successful Hussite commander, John Zizka, took a leading part. 'In extirpating "heretics" and especially those likely to spread and increase heresy, Zizka acted quite fully in accordance with the basic attitude of the medieval Church, differing from it only in determining who was to be regarded as a heretic.'[93] Indeed, the dissensions among the Hussites were often fought out with the uttermost bitterness and cruelty. Sigismund would have liked to settle with the Hussites, in order to assume his rule over Bohemia as his brother's heir. But so long as the pope and the church authorities were not prepared to make the concessions even moderate Hussites regarded as necessary, these had no option but to collaborate with the more radical sections of the movement. They realised that unless they all hung together, they would hang separately. Thus in a sense it was the uncompromising policy of the curia that kept moderate and radical Hussites together, at least to a certain extent.

Actually the Hussites were not only able to defend themselves, to defeat crusading armies and Sigismund himself, but to go over to the offensive, invading neighbouring countries. From the point of view of spreading the gospel outside Bohemia and assuming importance outside national boundaries, their offensive was largely counter-productive. Hussitism did not gain that many converts by the sword, and demonstrated only too clearly the gap between its practice (such as the barbarism of its soldiers) and its spiritual pretensions, the very inconsistency of which it accused the existing Church. It thus remained a national movement, largely confined to Bohemia, and failed to develop into a serious threat to the writ of the Church Universal elsewhere. It was only in 1436, that the conflict was settled, up to a point, not by the reigning Pope, Eugenius IV, but by the Council of Basle, at a high-point of the conciliar movement. By then the papal throne was no longer occupied by Martin V, who died in February 1431.

It is generally agreed that Martin V was a pope of outstanding ability and authority, and that he reigned at a crucial time for the Church, but there is little consensus on the question as to whether he dealt with its problems as effectively as possible. He may well have come to the conclusion that a general reform of the Church was impracticable. He favoured some of the reform movements in the monastic orders, believing that the initiative for a true reform had to originate 'from the monks, clerics, mystics, even from the ordinary faithful'.[94] Martin did in fact succeed, by recreating an effective curia, in restoring a certain amount of discipline in the Church. He demanded from the bishops that they should reside in their dioceses, and made a number of excellent appointments to the Sacred College. Also he forbade inflammatory sermons against the Jews as well as forced baptisms, and insisted on clergy being able to speak the language of their parishioners. In spite of that, and making allowances for the difficulties a pope of a united church had to face after a period of schism, Martin may well have missed a chance at a crucial juncture of doing more for reform. But if timely action to avoid the crisis of the sixteenth century was not taken, the responsibility must also partly rest on the shoulders of Martin's successors.

Just before his death in February 1431, Martin V, in accordance with the regulations on the frequency of council meetings laid down in Constance, summoned a new general synod to meet in Basle, under the presidency of the learned Cardinal Cesarini, who was given the authority to dissolve the assembly fairly quickly. Martin chose Basle, in the German kingdom and the Empire, in preference to a French location, as he even then regarded French Gallicanism as highly dangerous.[95] Martin's successor Eugenius IV (Gabriele Condulmer) confirmed the arrangements for the council. Though possessing some good personal qualities, the new pope was not sufficiently versed in the affairs of this world and tended to be inflexible. He soon ran into considerable difficulties, for instance with the Colonna nephews of his predecessor, and his reign was not one of the happiest.

As Cesarini was engaged in fighting the Hussites, the Council of Basle was opened for him in his absence in July 1431. Following the example of his predecessor, Eugenius decided to dissolve the council after a short meeting, and did so in November of that year. But Cesarini, who had in the meantime arrived in Basle after suffering a military defeat at the hands of the Hussites, with the support of the majority of the cardinals refused to carry out Eugenius' instructions. From now on, for most of the time, council and pope were at loggerheads. This led to a great deal of manœuvring on the part of rulers. Thus Sigismund, while at that time basically supporting the Council of Basle, had himself crowned emperor by Eugenius in Rome in May 1433. There was, however, also a certain period of cooperation between papacy and council, when Eugenius, owing to a crisis in the Patrimony of St Peter, particularly with the Colonnas, revoked his dissolution bull in December 1433; but the harmony did not last. When the pope early on refused repeated invitations to join the council in Basle, the demands of the council fathers became more strident and many of the decrees of the Council of Constance were reaffirmed.

For a time, the initiative in the affairs of the Church passed to the council in Basle, which was attended by a number of eminent personalities, and it looked as if some form of conciliarism, with councils playing a regular part in the government of the Church, might take root. Certainly Cardinal Cesarini in Basle showed himself much more aware than the curia of the crisis which the church was facing. There was a severe threat to Christianity from the Turks, particularly to Byzantium; the Hussite problem was still unresolved, and the need for internal reform of the Church was becoming daily more urgent. And it was Cesarini and the council that began to tackle some of these questions, for example that of the Hussites.[96]

Early in 1437 the Council of Basle ratified a settlement which had been accepted by the Hussites in July 1436. The chalice was granted to Hussites in Bohemia, Moravia and elsewhere, but communion in one kind was still allowed to those who desired it. Thus the Hussites had not succeeded in imposing the cup for the laity on the whole of Bohemia. Also the ministry of all believers was not conceded to them. The punishment of mortal sin was reserved to those 'whose office it is'. Preaching was to be undertaken by 'the priests of the Lord and by worthy deacons'. The Hussites did best in the question of the ownership of land. Priests were not to be owners of estates. A widespread transfer of church and monastic lands to the laity had taken place during the Hussite revolution. This was now accepted by the Church. Sigismund could at last take up his rule in Bohemia and actually guaranteed the *status quo* in this question of former church lands.[97] The papacy ignored the agreement and did not feel bound by it, which stored up trouble for the future. However, even that did not diminish the importance of what had happened. The combination of nationalism with religious dissent demonstrated in the Hussite movement proved to be a powerful solvent of church unity and orthodoxy:

> Substantial doctrinal unity in the Church was maintained partly by force, and partly by a continuing public commitment to the cause of orthodoxy; when this broke down, and beliefs condemned as heretical maintained themselves successfully against all efforts at repression, the Middle Ages was at an end.[98]

The religio-national complications of the Bohemian question constituted a continuing problem not only for the country's rulers and for the Church in general, but also for the German kingdom and the Empire.

Unfortunately the settlement with the Hussites proved to be about the last achievement of the council, whose shortcomings became increasingly evident. These arose to some extent because incorporation in the council, carrying with it a vote, had been granted rather too freely to many who did not have any special claim to be represented; because obedience to the council was enforced as an article of faith, partly through intimidation by a system of personal supervision and delation, which could even result in charges of heresy; and because pressure groups, some of them manipulated by princes, exerted a considerable influence. Demagogy flourished and 'the mass [in the sense of numbers] counted'.[99] In a crucial matter, that of union with the Greek Church, the synod demonstrated its inability to function properly, and thus allowed the initiative to pass to the papacy. It was unfortunate that at a time when the Greeks were hard-pressed by the Turks, the Western Church was largely paralysed by the continuing dispute between the Council of Basle and Pope Eugenius.

The Greeks wished to secure the support of the West by arranging a union. They were not prepared to come to Basle, but wanted to attend a council in Italy in the presence of the pope, who in September 1437 moved the meeting-place to Ferrara. While a minority of the Basle council fathers under the leadership of Cesarini were quite prepared to agree to an Italian location, the populist majority of the council continued to insist on Basle. Thus, after all the papal schisms there was now something new, a conciliar schism.

The question of where to meet the Greeks led to a split at Basle between the moderate minority and the 'conciliarist' majority determined to dictate to the pope, and if necessary to depose him. The moderates, with Cesarini at the head, left Basle. The influential Cardinal Enea Silvio Piccolomini (later Pius II), 'the most important humanist of his century',[100] who had earlier on been a supporter of the council, became quite disenchanted with 'conciliarism'. Only a rump remained at Basle, compensating for the decline in its authority with an ever increasing radicalism.[101] It does not inspire particular confidence in this group to learn that 'the same men who tried Jeanne d'Arc were among those speakers most listened to' at the council.[102] That councils became involved in confrontations with popes, to some extent of necessity at Constance, but without the same compelling circumstances in the case of the radical rump at Basle, was an unfortunate development for the Church. It was, moreover, a contest in which the council was likely to emerge as a loser against the superior resources, above all financial, which curia and papacy could muster.

Some of the greatest popes, such as Alexander III (1159–81) and Innocent III (1198–1216) had taken the initiative to call councils to round off their work. But if future councils were likely to behave like the Basle rump, popes would understandably be very hesitant to summon general synods. Thus the excesses of the later sessions of the Council of Basle were self-defeating for the conciliar movement represented there, and were only too likely to confirm pontiffs in an autocratic course emphasising the fullness of power (*plenitudo potestatis*) so objectionable to the conciliar movement. The Church needed both pope and council, the latter on an *ad hoc* or perhaps regular basis. Confrontation frustrated any attempt to develop a better constitutional system for the Church, in which not only popes and councils could work together in a fruitful relationship, but in which cardinals could have an appropriate input into the papal decision-making process. While there are obvious differences between a secular constitutional order and a church as a guardian of sacred truths, a chance was missed to fit the council into the role of something vaguely resembling an assembly of estates or parliament. Also, in spite of continued attempts, no satisfactory permanent relationship was established between the pope and the Sacred College. Here there was a genuine problem. On the one hand, the ability of the pope, if necessary, to make swift decisions on his own was a great asset, in many ways accounting for the peculiar strength the Catholic Church was to show in all its trials and tribulations; on the other there were great dangers in an absolute 'papal monarchy'. The Church never succeeded in creating a balanced system, which would have allowed the pope adequate executive power while ensuring that an advisory 'cabinet' of cardinals would keep papal shortcomings in check. Admittedly this was a formidable task, in some ways attempting to square the circle.

In the meantime important changes had taken place in the German kingdom and the Empire. In December 1437 Emperor Sigismund died, after a long and eventful reign, and with him the Luxemburg dynasty, which in many ways had dominated the European scene since the time of Charles IV, came to an end. Although, like his father, he had considerable ability, his reign had not been quite so singularly successful. More than any other personality Sigismund had been responsible for the end of the papal schism in 1417; but he had not been able to ensure that the further council of his reign, at Basle, would end on a positive note. However, this council was at least able to undo some of the unfortunate consequences of the actions of its predecessor in the Hussite question. The problems of Bohemia dogged Sigismund for many years and delayed his succession to the throne there until near the end of his life. He could never shake off completely the burden of guilt that clung to him in connection with Hus' burning at the stake in violation of the safe-conduct he had issued as protector of the Council of Constance. Already there, Sigismund had acquired a certain reputation for double-dealing and untrustworthiness. This impression was reinforced during his long-drawn-out efforts to bring about a settlement of the Hussite question, so that he could assume his rule in Bohemia. In these matters, Sigismund was not his own master and was subject to decisions made at general councils and in the curia. Strong like his father in his powers of persuasion, he was less reliable than Charles IV in honouring his undertakings. For a long time after, the issue of Hussite rights was bedevilled by promises Sigismund had made which were not in his power to give.

Perhaps these were the almost inevitable flaws in a ruler who decisively influenced the affairs of Europe and of Western Christendom in his time. The fact that two church councils were held in the Empire, at Constance and at Basle, had a great deal to do with Sigismund's outstanding international position and importance. As King of Hungary, of the Romans, and eventually of Bohemia, and as emperor, he played a central part, for better or for worse, in many of the questions that vitally affected Europe and Christendom, from countering the Turkish danger (particularly as ruler of Hungary) to intervening in the internal problems of the Church. Sigismund shared fully in the European and Christian mission of the house of Luxemburg. He also made at least two decisions which proved fateful for the future of the German kingdom and indeed of Germany, the raising of the Burgrave of Nuremberg, Frederick of Hohenzollern, to the electorate of Brandenburg in 1415, and that of the Margrave Frederick of Meissen to the electorate of Saxony in 1423. Both dynasties continued to reign right to the end of monarchy in Germany in 1918, with the Hohenzollern dynasty (see Table 6.2) increasingly dominating the pages of its history. During the Reformation, the house of Wettin in Saxony exercised a decisive influence at important turning-points, such as in the protection the Ernestine line gave to Luther after the Diet of Worms in 1521, and in the contribution the Albertine line made to the defeat of Emperor Charles V about a generation later.

For some time Sigismund had worked closely with one of the other major dynasties in the German kingdom, the Habsburgs in Austria. He had given his daughter in marriage to the very able Duke Albrecht V of Austria, who had acted decisively in the defence against Hussite invasion. Albrecht virtually inherited the Hungarian and Bohemian crowns from Sigismund, and

Table 6.2   The Hohenzollern dynasty in Brandenburg–Prussia

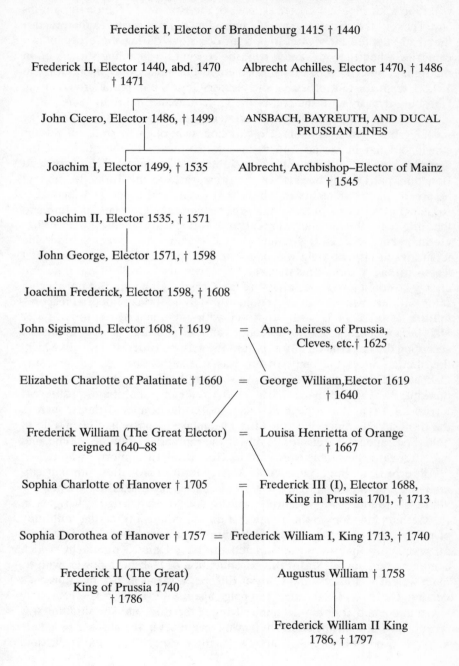

Frederick I, Elector of Brandenburg 1415 † 1440

Frederick II, Elector 1440, abd. 1470   Albrecht Achilles, Elector 1470, † 1486
† 1471

John Cicero, Elector 1486, † 1499   ANSBACH, BAYREUTH, AND DUCAL
PRUSSIAN LINES

Joachim I, Elector 1499, † 1535   Albrecht, Archbishop–Elector of Mainz
† 1545

Joachim II, Elector 1535, † 1571

John George, Elector 1571, † 1598

Joachim Frederick, Elector 1598, † 1608

John Sigismund, Elector 1608, † 1619   =   Anne, heiress of Prussia,
Cleves, etc.† 1625

Elizabeth Charlotte of Palatinate † 1660   =   George William,Elector 1619
† 1640

Frederick William (The Great Elector)   =   Louisa Henrietta of Orange
reigned 1640–88   † 1667

Sophia Charlotte of Hanover † 1705   =   Frederick III (I), Elector 1688,
King in Prussia 1701, † 1713

Sophia Dorothea of Hanover † 1757 = Frederick William I, King 1713, † 1740

Frederick II (The Great)   Augustus William † 1758
King of Prussia 1740
† 1786

Frederick William II King
1786, † 1797

the electors in March 1438 in the end unanimously respected the emperor's wishes in allowing their choice as King of the Romans to fall on his son-in-law. Thus, in the absence of a male heir, they did not revert to the practice they had adopted on several important occasions during the previous two centuries, when they prevented dynastic continuity, including succession in the female line. Indeed, they implemented this policy only once more, in 1742. Except for that occasion, the electors kept the imperial crown in the Habsburg dynasty until the end of the Holy Roman Empire in 1806.

Interestingly enough, Albrecht hesitated for some weeks before accepting the kingship of the Romans. He was honest enough to state openly his conviction that he would find it hard to do justice to the affairs of the German kingdom in view of his commitments in Austria, Hungary, and Bohemia, particularly because of the pressure from the Turks. In the end he accepted. The dilemma of Albrecht II (as he was called as King of the Romans) illustrates a problem that was to haunt the German kingdom and the Empire for the remainder of that constitutional arrangement. Any future German king and Holy Roman Emperor who ruled over considerable territories in his own right was bound to be preoccupied to some extent at least with the affairs of his dynastic lands, which would limit the time and energy he could give to the affairs of the German kingdom. But only such a ruler, with his own *Hausmacht*, could afford to undertake imperial responsibilities, as these were hardly endowed with any financial resources. Later Habsburg emperors lacked Albrecht's candour and became accustomed to accepting the imperial dignity as part of the existing order. If one asks why in the circumstances the emperorship was still sufficiently attractive to the Habsburg dynasty, the high rank, raising the holder to precedence above the kings, was useful, particularly for the ruler of a multitude of different territories. In any case there were certain residual imperial rights, such as the disposal of extinct fiefs; thus the Luxemburg dynasty had been able to hold the Brandenburg electorate during their imperial tenure for a time, and had afterwards been able to reward its Hohenzollern supporter with it.

Albrecht II neither proceeded to Aachen for his coronation, nor participated in the diets of his reign. But he reappointed the administrative personnel of his predecessor, who were accustomed to exercising royal rights in the German kingdom in the absence of the ruler, thus preserving continuity of policy. With Albrecht II, the Habsburgs in the extent of their territorial possessions in many ways anticipated the later Danube monarchy, which came to an end in 1918. But this consolidation of Habsburg power, with its main weight in Eastern and Central Europe, was put at risk by Albrecht's death in October 1439 during a campaign against the Turks in Hungary, only a year and a half after his election as King of the Romans. The situation was complicated not only by Albrecht leaving daughters in the absence of a male heir, but also by his wife, Sigismund's daughter, expecting a child at the time of his death: Ladislas Posthumus, in addition to inheriting his father's share of the Austrian territories of the house of Habsburg, also became King of Bohemia and Hungary, under regency. He died in 1457, bringing to an end the elder Habsburg line. The two kingdoms then passed out of the possession of the Habsburgs for the time being.

In February 1440, the electors chose as successor to Albrecht II as King of the Romans his second-cousin Duke Frederick of Styria, a member of the junior line of the house of Habsburg. Dynastic continuity was preserved, but it remained to be seen how Frederick III would view his functions as German king and future emperor. Although the Luxemburg rulers had certainly not been indifferent to the interests of their house, they had always had enough time and energy to spare for the affairs of Christendom and of Europe. Indeed, in some ways, each of their territories benefited from belonging to a largely hereditary whole. Frederick III for long periods appeared to be preoccupied with dynastic affairs, and for years at a time did not venture outside his Austrian hereditary lands. Admittedly he had to contend with great problems there in view of the earlier abolition of the principle of inheritance by primogeniture in the Habsburg dynasty, which led to the division of territory and to prolonged family disputes.

It is also true that as King of the Romans and later as emperor, Frederick during his reign faced almost unprecedented problems, with the threat to the German kingdom and the Empire in the east from the Turks, and in the west from the rise of Burgundy and the resurgence of France. But he did not show the same determination to deal with these dangers as his predecessors, like Sigismund and Albrecht II. Frederick's policy, unlike that of the Luxemburg rulers, was not such as to convince public opinion that his hereditary lands were being used in a higher interest. Indeed, in his attempt to preserve Habsburg possessions in Switzerland, he weakened the western frontier of the *Reich* in 1442 by summoning into the Alsace against his Swiss enemies French mercenaries, who devastated the territory. In 1443, the French Dauphin Louis, who led these troops, actually claimed the Rhine frontier for France,[103] though he could not enforce this demand. Even if Frederick was often absent from diets, he did devote some attention to the reform of *Reich* institutions, though with limited success. While he may not have been a very inspiring ruler, not all the shortcomings in the situation in the German kingdom were necessarily his fault. They may in part have been due to lack of support from the princes. The poor cooperation between the territorial rulers and the German king certainly weakened the position of the kingdom in relation to the papacy.

Actually in this period, the focus of events shifted increasingly to the council at Ferrara summoned by Eugenius, and it was here that the Greek delegates arrived in March 1438 to negotiate a union. The Greeks were in a desperate situation owing to military pressure from the Turks, and were therefore in a conciliatory mood, which was reciprocated by the Latins. Both sides were determined to prevent old theological disputes from wrecking the negotiations. The union decree of 5 July 1439, passed at Florence, the city to which the council had in the meantime been moved, was the basis of the bull, *Laetentur coeli*, which was signed by the dignitaries present in Latin and Greek the following day. As to *filioque* ('and the Son'), it was agreed that in spite of somewhat different expressions in the creed relating to the Father and the Son, both churches were united in essence on the dogma of the Trinity. It was recognised that the Roman pontiff had the primacy over the whole earth as Christ's deputy, as head of the whole Church and as father and teacher of all Christians, and that he had full power (*plenitudo potestatis*) to govern the entire Church, subject to the preservation of the rights and privileges of the Greek patriarchs.

Unfortunately the Greek embassy to the council was badly received at home and accused of having betrayed the Orthodox faith. The decree of union was only published in Constantinople in December 1452, five months before the fall of the city to the Turks.[104] Clearly the mood of the rank and file in the Byzantine Empire prevented the effectiveness of any union with the Latin Church arranged from above. In spite of the problems with the Greek Church, Eugenius in 1443 organised a military effort to save Byzantium from the Ottomans. But the following year the crusading army was beaten by the Sultan at Varna, where Cardinal Cesarini found his death. 'The last crusading dream expired under the indifference of the West.'[105]

While the Council of Ferrara/Florence under Eugenius' leadership did constructive work in the question of union with the Greeks, the council at Basle deposed the pope in June 1439. The following November in 'a parody of an enclave',[106] the Basle council elected as pontiff Duke Amadeus VIII of Savoy, who took the name of Felix V, bringing about the last papal schism to date. The widower and father of nine children was chosen by the Basle council owing to the awareness that its future was in the hands of the princes, and perhaps also in the hope of receiving support from the resources of his duchy. The secular rulers wished to have control over appointments to the benefices on their territories, above all in view of their financial importance. In principle they therefore preferred Basle over Ferrara/Florence, because they expected less interference from the weaker of the two councils, now also with the weaker pope. Furthermore, the attempt by the Council of Basle to restrict papal power appealed to many princes. Thus King Charles VII of France used Basle decrees, such as those relating to the superiority of councils and the abolition of papal dues, to strengthen his authority over the Church in his territory, at the expense of the papacy, in the Pragmatic Sanction of Bourges in July 1438. But this measure could hardly be regarded as a success for the Council of Basle, as the king claimed the right to interpret or modify its decrees.[107] Indeed

Charles was quite prepared at the same time to come to terms with Eugenius, if his interests so demanded.

In the German kingdom, too, advantage was taken of the dispute between Eugenius and Basle. The Diet of Mainz in March 1439 in some ways modelled itself on the Pragmatic Sanction of Bourges in drawing on many of the reform decrees of Basle. According to Enea Silvio Piccolomini – not an entirely impartial witness in the various stages of his career – this permitted the princes to acquire church estates, and the clergy to be freed from all external authority. It was mainly due to Piccolomini, formerly secretary not only to the Council of Basle, but also to its Pope Felix V, who had since 1442 been in the service of the Habsburg ruler, that Frederick came to an understanding with Eugenius IV in 1445. Frederick recognised Eugenius as pope, and in return was given the right by the curia to make a large number of ecclesiastical appointments in his dominions. While Frederick concluded the agreement with Eugenius on behalf of his own territories, both parties expected the princes in the German kingdom to follow suit in switching their obedience from the Council of Basle and Felix V. In return for this expectation, Eugenius promised Frederick to crown him emperor in Rome, and to make a contribution to his travel expenses. But the princes were not prepared to dance to Frederick's tune. In order to break their opposition, Eugenius unwisely deposed and excommunicated the two main supporters of the Council of Basle among them, the Archbishops of Cologne and Trier. This led to the formation of a league of electors (*Kurfürstenbund*) demanding not only their reinstatement, but also Eugenius' acceptance of the decisions of the Councils of Constance and Basle. Thanks to his diplomatic skills, Piccolomini succeeded in undermining the league at the Frankfurt *Reichstag* in 1446. The following year an undertaking by the curia to allow the two archbishops to resume their sees paved the way for the conclusion of a concordat on the part of the electors with Eugenius, just before the latter's death. This was followed in 1448 by the Concordat of Vienna for the Empire between Frederick III and Eugenius' successor, Pope Nicholas V.[108] That year, in view of Frederick's recognition of Eugenius as pope, the council could no longer sit in Basle and was moved to Lausanne, where it gradually faded out. In 1449, the papal schism was ended with the resignation of the anti-pope. The papacy had won, but in the process had unfortunately acquired a deep aversion to general councils, because it had learned to fear them. The unwillingness of pontiffs to summon general synods made the task of reform even more difficult.[109]

With these events, relations between the Church and the secular powers in the German kingdom settled down to greater calm; there were not many points of friction. On the one hand, Frederick III was mainly concerned with the accumulation of power for his dynasty. On the other, the 'Renaissance' popes from Nicholas V (1447–55) onwards busied themselves with the consolidation of their position in Italy and the Patrimony of St Peter, with crusading efforts to deal with the Turkish threat, as well as with the architectural and artistic development of Rome. Although Nicholas was an excellent choice as pope and was personally quite unexceptionable, it was during his reign that the important decision was made to concentrate on the objectives that have been mentioned, rather than on a genuine church and curial reform.[110] The pontiff affirmed when he was dying in 1455 that the magnificent architectural and artistic developments in Rome he had sponsored were only designed to raise the authority of the Holy See and to impress the people in its weak faith. 'It is not without tragedy that the noblest of the Renaissance popes with good intentions introduced, and laid the basis for, an epoch in the history of the papacy that was soon to darken uncannily.'[111]

Thus, during most of the reigns of the Renaissance papacy, the cause of reform occupied a low place on the agenda. A notable exception was that of Enea Silvio Piccolomini, who became Pope Pius II in 1458, even if he was also the pontiff who began the protracted dispute with Ladislas's successor, King George of Bohemia,[112] and cancelled the compromise with the Hussites concluded by the Council of Basle.[113] He had a considerable amount of work carried out to prepare for reforms, ably assisted by his friend from the German kingdom, Cardinal Nikolaus of Kues, one of the outstanding thinkers, men of faith, and ecclesiastical statesmen of the period. Pius II's all too early death, in 1464, prevented the fruition of reforms. Great hopes similarly attached to the election of his nephew as Pius III in 1503, but these could not be realised owing to his death after a reign of only 26 days.

Regrettably the tone during the years after 1471 was set by a number of pontiffs who attached little importance to their spiritual functions, led disreputable lives, and were often preoccupied with the interests of their families. Some earlier popes had cultivated nepotism, but under certain of the following pontiffs the practice at times assumed proportions that were without recent precedent. The popes of the period after 1471 saw themselves mainly as Italian princes, and several of them were certainly no better and possibly even worse in their political ethics than their secular contemporaries. Francesco della Rovere, who took the title of Sixtus IV (1471–84), is known in history mainly for the Sistine chapel in the Vatican, for whose adornment he secured the greatest talents in this period of the flowering of renaissance art. What may not be equally well known is that Sixtus, through his efforts to reward with a major principality an unworthy nephew, became deeply involved in Italian territorial policy and in several wars to the detriment of the Patrimony of St Peter. He even appears to have supported the unsuccessful attempt to overthrow the Medici regime in Florence in favour of a rival family. The pope cannot be exonerated from responsibility for his criminal complicity in the plot, even if he did not approve of the methods used, which resulted in the assassination of Giuliano Medici and of the wounding of his brother Lorenzo II, the Magnificent, who was the actual ruler of Florence. When Lorenzo inflicted severe punishment on the conspirators and executed the Archbishop of Pisa, who was implicated in the plot, Sixtus imposed the interdict on Florence. The pope could only extricate himself from the fall-out of the *putsch* at the cost of further military complications.[114]

Papal favouritism to their families was particularly objectionable, when the 'nephews' being rewarded were in fact the pontiff's natural sons, as was the case in the reign of Alexander VI (1492–1503), who belonged to the Borja family from Spain. Alexander himself had risen through nepotism as the nephew of a previous Borja pope, Calixtus III, who appointed him a cardinal at a young age. How could a pope claim any spiritual authority, who openly flouted the requirement of celibacy and unashamedly used his pontifical office for the aggrandisement of his children, at least some of whom were completely unworthy of the dignities given to them? Thus Alexander appointed his son Cesare Borja, 'a real *condottiere*, a demonic criminal personality in the grand style',[115] Bishop of Valencia and a cardinal at the age of 17.

The greatest blemish on Alexander's reign was his treatment of Girolamo Savonarola, the Prior of the Dominican Convent of St Marco in Florence. Like the prophets of old, Savonarola called to repentance those who had strayed from their duty, including rulers and priests, even the pope. In his sincere zeal, he allowed himself to be carried beyond the spiritual into the treacherous currents of political and international affairs in Italy. In 1494 he hailed the invading French King, Charles VIII, a frivolous personality, as God's instrument for the reform of the Church, and enforced a theocratic–democratic constitution in Florence after the expulsion of the Medici rulers. His policies brought him into conflict with the pope, who at first bided his time, but struck when Savonarola, with his moral strictness, began to antagonise a considerable section of Florentine public opinion, which had previously given him its backing. In 1497 Savonarola was excommunicated and Florence threatened with the interdict. In April 1498 a mob, which had been incited to violence against Savonarola, stormed the monastery of San Marco. The prior was imprisoned and repeatedly tortured during the mockery of a trial by an ecclesiastical court. The following month he was publicly hanged and his body burned. Thus one of the unworthiest pontiffs ever to have ruled the Church was able to have sentenced to death and executed as 'a heretic, schismatic and scorner of the Holy See' a man of deep spirituality, who emphasised the importance of purity of heart, sincerity of mind and true love.[116]

Like Alexander VI, his successor was the nephew of a pope, this time that of Sixtus IV from the della Rovere family. Julius II (1503–13), a man of great ability and energy, concentrated on the worldly aspects of the papacy and distinguished himself as a ruler and general. He led an unobjectionable life as pope and abstained from nepotism. His predecessor had alienated parts of the Patrimony, mainly in the interests of his family. Julius largely reversed the process and 'established the external foundation of power of the papacy in modern times' with the aim of creating a strong independent Holy See in an Italy free from foreign rule,[117] as will be related in connection with the international developments later in this chapter

Julius was succeeded by Giovanni Medici as Pope Leo X (1513–21), a person of great culture, a patron of the arts, but 'with hardly any spiritual sense of duty',[118] and excessively concerned with the fortunes of his family. It was disastrous that such a person should occupy the papal throne at great turning-points, not only at the advent of Martin Luther in 1517, but also at the death of Emperor Maximilian I in 1519.

One of the reasons why there was so little friction between the papacy and the German king during the long reign of Frederick III was that the King of the Romans for the time being ceased to occupy a special position in Europe and Western Christendom. For the popes the German king was no longer a ruler to be held in awe, as his imperial claim to the kingdoms of Italy and of Arles, – that is, Burgundy – was purely titular, not involving any authority or even in any meaningful sense an overlordship over them. Actually a powerful Duke of Burgundy, like Charles the Bold, himself had imperial ambitions. The popes did not have to fear any interference from Frederick III in the affairs of Italy. Habsburg rule over territories south of the Brenner, such as those belonging to Tirol, was quite acceptable, and the imperial coronation of Frederick III in Rome by the pope in 1452 (the last carried out by the pope in Rome) did not cause any problems. At first almost imperceptibly, chancery language gradually began to reflect the new realities in the relationship between the German kingdom, Italy and the papacy. A *Reich* law of 1442 was the first to distinguish between the Roman Empire and the Germanic nation, and one in 1486 initiated the form that was to be generally used until about 1800, that of the Holy Roman Empire of the Germanic nation (*Germanicae nationis*).[119] Needless to say, these terms are not to be understood in the sense of modern German nationalism. In the changed circumstances, there was no longer any need for the papacy to attempt any kind of control over who was elected King of the Romans and future emperor. In some respects German kingdom and papacy were going their own way, even if they were later to clash occasionally in Italy. But that did not mean all was well.

Frederick was half-hearted in his imperial reforms, so that when their necessity eventually became obvious and a matter of great urgency, the movement to achieve them was naturally directed against the emperor, who was regarded as one of the main obstacles to reform. There is a certain parallel here to the demand in the sphere of the Church for a reform of the head, the papacy and the curia. In the fifteenth century, 'the efforts for a renewal of the Church almost of necessity led to hopes for a reform of the Roman–German Empire'.[120] The movement to *reform* the Church in the medieval sense of the word aimed at restoring it to its original and purer form by freeing the papal Church from its political involvements and thus enabling it to fulfil satisfactorily its role as a universal institution. All this was closely connected with the idea of also reforming the other institution laying a claim to universality, the (Holy) Roman Empire. Thus the tract written by an unknown participant of the Council of Basle published in 1439 under the title *Reformatio Sigismundi* combined discussion of Church reform with that of *Reichsreform*, and rightly so, because 'the decay of one made the restoration of order in the other more difficult'.[121] The author actually attributed the misfortunes of the day to the intermixture of the ecclesiastical and secular estates, and demanded a radical solution, the complete separation of functions,[122] which would have changed the whole character of the Empire.

In an age which did not know many of our modern distinctions, important proposals to reform the Empire were in fact made at the Councils of Constance and Basle by leading figures, among them Nikolaus of Kues, who was mentioned earlier as a friend and collaborator of Pope Pius II. Born in 1401 as the son of a sailor in Kues on the Moselle, Nikolaus became strongly influenced by humanism during his studies in Italy. Following humanist principles of going back to the sources, he demonstrated the spuriousness of the *Donation of Constantine*, on which so many papal claims were based. After receiving a number of benefices in Germany, he joined the Council of Basle, where he finished his important work *De concordantia catholica* on the nature and reform of the Church and the tasks of the council. By including a part dealing with reform of the Empire, he 'produced a significant work on the all-embracing Christian concord in Church and Empire'.[123] At that time he was a moderate conciliarist and regarded the pope as subject to the General Council of the Church. In general he favoured mutual understanding and conciliation, though he was not always very successful in bringing it about in his dealings with others.

He was one of the moderates who abandoned the Council of Basle when it became increasingly radical, and went over to Pope Eugenius and his council. He was appointed a cardinal in 1448 and Bishop of Brixen in 1450, but became involved in a dispute with the Habsburg Prince Sigismund, Count of Tirol; the count's physical measures, such as imprisoning the bishop, at any rate for the moment proved more effective than the ecclesiastical measures taken against him. After release from imprisonment, the bishop withdrew to Rome. As papal legate in the Empire during 1451–2, he was charged with the task of reforming the German Church. Certainly his mission was one of the most important in this matter before the Reformation. The legate's zeal and energy are beyond doubt. In many ways he preached much sense, for example, when, in proclaiming the 1450 jubilee indulgence, he emphasised 'that the important thing was, not the indulgence, but a genuine and sincere conversion, which must begin with a worthy reception of the Sacrament of penance. The Legate strictly forbade the accepting or offering of money for absolution.' But at times he went beyond his brief, displayed 'stubborn views', and was 'out of touch with the reality of the situation', for example when he forbade Jews to lend money to Christians, measures which were annulled by the pope.[124]

Nikolaus had some success in reforming the Benedictine monasteries, but here he found an open ear, following the decision of the Chapter of Benedictine Abbots in 1417 to restore the discipline of the order.[125] But opposition from the mendicants was particularly strong. In spite of his experience of princely intervention in his own diocese, he had no hesitation in calling on the secular arm for the sake of reform. The bishops showed little interest in the legate's mission. They often owed their appointments to political considerations, for example to increase the influence of ruling dynasties beyond their territories. Altogether, the reform mission of the papal legate, while a remarkable effort, only had limited success.[126]

The career of Nikolaus of Kues illustrates many of the strengths and weaknesses of the imperial church towards the end of the Middle Ages. The influence of the Roman curia can be beneficial. Thus it is thanks to papal favour that a cleric of humble family background can enter the ranks of the episcopacy normally reserved mainly to princes and nobles, and that he can even become a cardinal. There is room for talent in the Church, and for plain speaking. Nikolaus of Kues does not become a *persona non grata* to the curia because of his destruction of the credibility of the *Donation of Constantine*. The Church does at times attempt to reform ecclesiastical institutions in a large area with many different interests, but this is only feasible, if at all, when the papacy supports the effort. However, there is not necessarily an adequate appreciation in the German kingdom of the advantages the papacy can at times offer the Church. There was a belief in many quarters at the time that the curia financially exploited Germany, though historical research has largely disproved the accuracy of this notion. A nascent, very rudimentary national feeling had some anti-papal and, indeed, anticlerical overtones.

The schism had laid bare many shortcomings of the Church, and these had attracted particular attention in the German kingdom. A perception persisted of being exploited by the curia and of having to contribute excessively to the papal coffers, which was not necessarily true in comparison with other territories. There was an increasingly strong anti-curial feeling in the Teutonic kingdom, reflected for example in the complaints of the German nation against the Roman court (*Die Gravamina der deutschen Nation gegen den römischen Hof*) in 1451. These sentiments were partly due to the apparent inability of the kingdom to resist papal encroachments owing to the absence of an effective central power – such as in England or France – which could assert itself against Rome. Actually the individual princes and even cities succeeded in obtaining concessions from the papacy which allowed them to increase their hold over the churches in their territory, paving the way to a *Staatskirche*. The advantage of this situation was that church reform could be carried out in many smaller units, such as by cities or by rulers interested in the renewal of church life. 'Germany did not by chance become the country of the Reformation. In no other country had the church reform of the fifteenth century prepared so fruitful a soil for the Reformation of the sixteenth century.'[127]

The successes as well as the failures of Nikolaus of Kues reveal a church that was pluralistic, with all the advantages and disadvantages that entailed. The papal legate's sometimes rather dictatorial methods did not always impress those to whom they are addressed, such as noble abbesses. It is not without irony that an ecclesiastic who was both the possessor of a plurality of benefices and an absentee priest was charged with stamping out abuses in the Church. This is not stated in criticism of Nikolaus of Kues personally, but brings out some of the inconsistencies in the prevailing church system and the difficulty of judging it fairly. In fact, the proceeds from his pluralism (which also provided funds for paying assistants to undertake his duties) helped to finance the important work he did both at the Council of Basle and at the behest of the pope.

Undoubtedly, the debate on reform did some good, certainly so far as the Empire was concerned. In the years from 1485 to 1497, thus extending into the next reign, a constitution was established for the *Reichstag*. This excluded the emperor from its deliberations, and emphasised the position of the estates by turning the acts of the *Reichstag* (*Reichsabschiede*) into treaties between them and the emperor.[128] This dualism in government, shared between emperor and estates, was also in due course to apply to the relations between individual rulers and their estates.

In all these circumstances, it is not surprising that the call for church reform and for *Reich* reform became linked in the German kingdom. There was an increasing realisation of weakness in the kingdom, coupled with a dissatisfaction which arose from comparing an unheroic present with an apparently glorious past.

Two of the elements, without which the Reformation would not have been possible, were already present: on the one hand impatience and resentment of the German population, which were then inflamed by the appeals of the reformers, on the other the territorial states, which knew how to profit from the religious upheavals in order to strengthen their internal cohesion.[129]

Certainly Frederick III worked hard at consolidating the Habsburg dominions and eventually succeeded in virtually reuniting his family's inheritance. He ensured that the Habsburgs, strengthened by their connection with the Luxemburg family, finally overtook the Wittelsbachs, the third of the powerful dynasties of the post-Staufen period in the German kingdom. It was both a strength and a weakness of Habsburg rule that their lands extended from the Austrian east to the German south-west on the Rhine, holding together the German kingdom like a narrow bridge.[130] From the point of view of the interests of the kingdom and its defence this could be an asset, but it could also turn into a disadvantage through overcommitment. In any case, Habsburg power was insufficient to resist a Hungarian invasion into Austria, and in 1485 Frederick was temporarily driven out of his capital, Vienna. Also the Habsburgs gradually lost their hold over Switzerland.

In spite of all setbacks, Frederick doggedly pursued the plan of Habsburg aggrandisement, and in 1477 achieved a remarkable success which was to herald further even more important gains during his son's reign. Under Charles the Bold, the Dukes of Burgundy, a junior line of the French royal family, with their possessions in the Low Countries and elsewhere, had become perhaps the wealthiest rulers in Western Europe. But after his accession in 1467, owing to his excessive ambition Charles had antagonised a number of his neighbours, particularly the French and the Swiss. The duke, whom the emperor refused to raise to royal status, did not have a son. For many years Frederick tried to obtain the hand of his daughter Maria, the heiress, for his son Maximilian, in which he finally succeeded after Charles had been defeated and killed at Nancy in January 1477. The acquisition of most of Charles' territory raised the Habsburgs to major European importance, but at the cost of the hostility of the French Valois dynasty, which now found a major power standing in the way of its expansion to the east and north. This was the beginning of the deep enmity between the Habsburgs and the French monarchy, which continued until the Diplomatic Revolution of 1756, and involved them in a considerable number of wars. These hostilities in turn affected the relationship between the Germanic and the French peoples, with adverse long-term effects on German and French national feelings towards each other.

Maximilian had to defend his wife's inheritance against the French in a war of succession which lasted for fifteen years. He also got into serious difficulty when he attempted to continue his father-in-law's centralist system in the duchy, particularly after his wife's death in 1482. An alliance of the nobility and the big cities, supported by the King of France, for a time succeeded in overthrowing Maximilian's rule, and arranged that his daughter, Margaret, should be betrothed to the French Dauphin, Charles, both children at the time. In the Peace Treaty of Arras of the end of 1482, the actual Duchy of Burgundy, the Franche-Comté and numerous other territories were ceded to France as a dowry. Maximilian added to the friction with France when in 1490 he married by proxy Ann, the heiress of Brittany, who was descended from a junior line of the Capetian dynasty. France was bound to regard this marriage as a threat to its position. The acquisition of this territory did not, in any case, make any geographical sense for the Habsburgs. Charles VIII, who had succeeded his father Louis XI on the French throne in 1483 as a minor, conquered Brittany. He wedded Ann, for which he had her marriage to Maximilian, which had not been consummated, annulled, and cancelled his betrothal to Maximilian's daughter Margaret, who was sent back to her father. 'Maximilian was hit equally hard as husband and as father.'[131] The territories forming the dowry were not returned when the engagement was broken off, embittering even further the relations between the Habsburg and Valois dynasties, which had deteriorated ever since Maximilian's Burgundian marriage. The dispute over Burgundy, at any rate, was at last settled by the peace of Senlis in 1493. France returned the Franche-Comté, and Maximilian thus took over most of his wife's inheritance. But the rivalry between the Habsburgs and the French remained. It was to be severely aggravated later by a further even more important dynastic alliance of the Habsburgs.

In 1490 Frederick was able to return to Vienna after Maximilian had expelled the Hungarians from Austria. The following year a treaty with Hungary secured for the Habsburgs the succession to the throne there in certain circumstances. Frederick died in 1493 and was succeeded in the German kingdom and the Austrian hereditary lands by his son Maximilian, who had been unanimously elected King of the Romans in 1486, interestingly enough on the initiative of the electors. Perhaps the leading princes in the German kingdom were at that stage not unhappy with what gradually became in fact, though not in theory, virtually a hereditary succession, because the Habsburgs at this time, under Frederick III, did not appear to present a threat to their powers. Frederick was not so insignificant as he appeared to his time and to many historians since. But, particularly as he was mainly concerned with the affairs of his dynasty, he did not attach similar importance to the emperorship. If the electors thought that Maximilian would follow in his father's footsteps they were mistaken.

The son of Frederick III and of Eleanor, daughter of the King of Portugal and of an Aragonese princess, was born in 1459. From the time he married the heiress of Burgundy just before reaching the age of 18, he was primarily concerned with establishing Habsburg rule there. His ideas of government were deeply influenced by Burgundian practice, from which he derived an exaggerated ruler cult, a ceremonial reflecting the quasi-divine position of the ruler, and rudimentary antecedents of a military bureaucratic state. Unlike his father, he aimed at the recovery of the kingdom of Italy and at leadership of the Christian world. For these plans he regarded as necessary a reform of the institutions of the German kingdom. This objective brought him into conflict with the estates, which aimed at having the government carried on by themselves, while conceding to the king merely a kind of honorary chairmanship. The attitude of the estates severely limited Maximilian in his foreign policy and in the conduct of his wars. Actually he was blamed by the estates of the German kingdom for set-backs suffered in the *Reich* war against the Swiss, although they were caused chiefly by their withholding aid.

Maximilian was in effect deprived by the Diet of Augsburg in 1500 of his ability to govern. The estates were led by Berthold of Henneberg, the Archbishop-Elector of Mainz,[132] a personality of great integrity and a strong sense of justice, who admirably combined his spiritual and secular tasks. He was a firm supporter of *Reichsreform* and certainly did not wish to hinder the establishment of a strong central authority, but he wanted it to be under the control of the estates. However, these did not do any better than the emperor they had criticised. As the archbishop did not receive sufficient backing, Maximilian through a *coup d'état* was able to dissolve the regiment of the estates that had been set up to supersede him. By taking over crusading indulgences, Maximilian was to some extent able to dispense with aid from the Estates. A number of reforms were attempted, but many of the enacted measures were not carried out for any length of time because of the absence of proper financial support. Perhaps the most lasting achievement was the establishment in 1495 of a supreme judicial body, the *Reichskammergericht*, for which the estates were prepared to pay taxes, as they were interested in a court of law independent of the emperor.[133] Also, 1500 and 1507 saw the institution of Reich circles (*Kreise*), which were to be used for the maintenance of peace and for external defence, but the new arrangements were not put into effect.[134] However, in spite of the fact that the new constitutional order established in these years under Maximilian failed to take firm root, it can still rightly be regarded as an important contribution to imperial reform.[135] Maximilian should not be seen too negatively, even from the point of view of the Empire and the German kingdom. Among the emperors he is outstanding as a friend of the arts and of scholarship. He helped to prepare the way for humanism[136] and in a certain way for a greater awareness of the Germanic cultural heritage.

Maximilian's lack of support from his estates became even more critical when a grave international crisis arose in Italy. Since the peace of Lodi in 1454, the five major Italian powers – Milan, Venice, Florence, the Holy See, and Naples – had been able to maintain sufficient agreement among themselves to secure 40 years of comparative peace and to keep out foreign powers. That era came to an end in 1494, when internal divisions between the Italian powers and dissatisfaction with autocratic excesses in some of the states allowed King Charles VIII of France to invade Italy. A long period of foreign intervention began, which had a negative impact on the fortunes of Western Christendom and the position of the papacy. It overlapped with a time, between 1471 and 1503, when the reputation of the papacy reached one of its lowest points. In his progress through Italy, Charles initially received support from several of the rulers there, including that of Lodovico Sforza, Regent of Milan, whose niece Bianca Maria had become Maximilian's wife. However, particularly once Charles had advanced to Naples in 1495, the Italian states realised their danger and formed the Holy League of Venice, which included Pope Alexander VI, King Ferdinand of Aragon and King Maximilian. For the Holy See the prevention of a union of southern and northern Italy under the same power was essential for the maintenance of its independence, as it had been throughout history. Unlike earlier, the French, and no longer the German kings and emperors, were now the main threat to the papacy.

While Ferdinand was able to expel the French from Naples, Maximilian's intervention was ineffective, for the estates of the German kingdom, in order to assert their power, deliberately starved him of funds, so that he had to turn back without achieving his objectives. These constitutional disputes seriously weakened Maximilian's ability to act when Louis XII became King of France in 1498 and claimed Milan as a descendant of its former ruling dynasty, the Visconti. After taking Milan in 1500, Louis went on to the conquest of Naples with the King of Aragon as an ally, but was cheated by Ferdinand of his share of the booty. Naples (and Sicily) were from then on ruled by Spanish viceroys. During the following years there followed various alignments between the Italian states, including the Holy See, France, Ferdinand of Aragon, his son-in-law Philip of Burgundy, and Maximilian. In 1507 Maximilian wished to assert his rights as King of the Romans in Italy and to proceed there with an army in order to be crowned emperor by the pope in Rome. But the pope, France and Venice would not allow him to come there with an army. As Maximilian found himself blocked by the Venetians and the French from proceeding to Rome, he had himself proclaimed 'elected Roman emperor' in the cathedral at Trent in 1508. The pope confirmed the declaration within a few days.

When Julius II came to the conclusion that France, with its possession of Milan and its control over some other Italian states, was becoming a threat to the independence of the papacy, he took action – with his usual energy – against one of the French satellites in 1510. In retaliation, Louis XII supported a call for a general council at Pisa, to which the pope retaliated by summoning his own council to the Lateran for 1512. Maximilian was at first sympathetic to the Pisan assembly, but after a short time, when it became clear that the papal council mustered the better attendance, switched his support to Julius. Under the new pope, the Medici Leo X, even the French participated in the Fifth Lateran council, which before it was closed in 1517 passed some useful reform decrees, though these were not carried out.[137]

It took Julius until 1512 to have the French expelled from Italy, though not for long. For Italy was soon to become the battle-ground for the great duel between the French and the Habsburgs. From the Habsburg point of view, Maximilian's greatest achievement (though at the same time fraught with future problems) was the marriage of his son Philip in 1496. The bride, Joan, who was to become insane, was the daughter of Isabella of Castile and of Ferdinand of Aragon, and eventual heiress to the united Spain, as well as to its American empire acquired following the expedition of Christopher Columbus in 1492. By the time Philip, who governed the Low Countries, died in 1506, his wife had inherited the claim to the Castilian crown from her mother. In 1516, their son Charles, on the death of his maternal grandfather Ferdinand of Aragon, became King of the united Spain, together with its overseas colonies. In Italy, however, the French were able to recover from the setbacks that had taken place at the end of Louis XII's reign, when the new king, Francis I, during the first year of his reign, reconquered Milan after his victory over the Swiss at Marignano in 1515.

The conflict between France and the Habsburgs was to become bitter after Maximilian's death in 1519, at least indirectly as a consequence of his son Philip's Spanish marriage, which he had arranged. But in the meantime, in 1517 an event had taken place in the German kingdom which was to have repercussions throughout Western Christendom, Martin Luther's formulation of his 95 theses in Wittenberg, the capital of the Saxon electorate.

What was the state of the Church in the German kingdom before Luther made his impact? It would certainly be erroneous to infer that everything was in a bad way. Actually after the Hussite invasions and devastations, heresy was on the decline. There appears to have been, at any rate according to the surviving records, comparatively little radical religious dissent in the German kingdom in the second half of the fifteenth and the early years of the sixteenth century,[138] though the first persecutions of witches also belong to this period. There is testimony, from a foreign witness for 1517, about a degree of church piety particularly high by international standards.[139] The burghers of the flourishing towns set up an unprecedented number of foundations for ecclesiastical purposes.[140] It was the donors who had the – usually hereditary – right of appointment to the new benefices. But the town councils watched the situation carefully and tried to ensure that the patronage was exercised by them as soon as possible.[141] Thus the actual running of the Church, well before the Lutheran Reformation, came increasingly into the hands of lay authorities, not only of the towns, but also of the secular rulers. These certainly – like the towns – were concerned with the spiritual welfare of the people in watching over the administration of the Church. At the same time, the secular rulers were not unmindful of the advantages for the consolidation of their rule over their territories, and indirectly over the nobility, which this extension of their authority over the Church gave them. Increasingly the traditional services provided by the Church, such as the running of schools and hospitals, as well as the relief of the poor, came under lay supervision.[142] It was a characteristic of the age that at any rate the intellectual and commercial leaders of the laity gained a new self-confidence. This was partly due to the humanist movement with its intellectual stimulation, and late in the period also to the invention of the printing press and the wide circulation of the Bible.[143] These laymen were no longer prepared to accept the superiority of the clergy, particularly as the majority of the priests was poorly educated,[144] so that the gap between the cultural standard of the higher laity and of the ordinary priest was increasing to the disadvantage of the latter.

The relationship between faith and learning was causing problems. Among the orders, the universities did not always have the best reputation. Some scholars in their ranks 'were so disgusted by university disputes that they wanted to ban everything from the monastery that reminded them of these'.[145] The last century and a half or so before the Reformation was a prolific period for the foundation of universities in the Germanic part of the Empire. Those at Prague (1348) and Leipzig (1409) have already been mentioned, but other universities that were established included Vienna (1365), Heidelberg (1386), Cologne (1388), Erfurt (by 1392), Freiburg (1457), Tübingen (1477) and, last not least, Wittenberg (1502).

The career prospects of the – in many cases badly remunerated – lower clergy were on the whole dismal, as the upper ranks in the Church, such as those of canons in cathedrals and of bishops, were almost entirely reserved to the nobility and members of ruling dynasties. The prince-bishops of the period tended to concentrate on their secular functions to the detriment of their spiritual ones.[146] These circumstances in the German kingdom, together with the glaring decline in the moral standards of the papacy, and the failure to adhere to the regular calling of councils laid down at Constance, raised doubts about the ability of the Church to provide what was needed. For much more than in the French, English and Spanish monarchies with their comparative centralisation and their increasing ecclesiastical autonomy from Rome, the Church in the German kingdom was dependent on the benefits to be secured from a reformed papacy and curia. For example, any attempt to achieve reform in the German kingdom by breaking vested interests, such as the near-monopoly of the nobility over the bishoprics, had to come from outside, and thus from Rome. In the German kingdom 'what was sought was, strictly speaking, not so much the Church as such, but its possession of the grace of mediating salvation and of truths giving sense' to earthly existence.[147] Thus there were problems, but also possibilities, and the future was open. The answer came in the period after 1517.

7 Reformation and Catholic Reform (1517–64)

In the period from 1517 onwards, the German kingdom that was gradually to develop into the modern Germany once more moved to the centre of the European stage and of Western Christendom. This had not been so since the fall of the Staufen dynasty in the middle of the thirteenth century, a quarter of a millennium earlier. At the same time, for reasons that will emerge, the German kingdom and the Empire soon became more dependent on actions and processes taking place in other countries than had been the case in the recent past and indeed generally throughout the Middle Ages. All this came about as a result of the advent of Martin Luther and of the consequences which flowed directly and indirectly from his activities and the reaction to them.

Luther was born around 1483[1] in Eisleben on the territory of the Counts of Mansfeld, in what is now part of the state of Saxony–Anhalt in the German Federal Republic[2]. His father Hans, who came from fairly modest land-owning peasant stock, was a copper miner who was eventually able to become a smelter master, leasing his smelter from the counts. Hans Luther is an interesting example of the manner in which rapid economic expansion and change at that time provided opportunities for a man of enterprise and energy to rise on the social ladder. His life also illustrates the effects of the increasingly felt vagaries of international trade, because the success of his enterprise, which required a considerable capital investment and thus substantial borrowing, fluctuated with the demand for copper. Although Hans at one stage managed to be clear of debt, very good times at the beginning of the sixteenth century were followed – not untypically – by periods of financial anxiety later in his life. Certainly pictures of Martin Luther's father and of his mother Margarete, who similarly came from a modest propertied peasant background, show signs of hard work and strain.[3] While theories have been advanced to explain Martin Luther's subsequent activities in terms of an autocratic, overly strict father,[4] the severity of Luther's upbringing may not have been at all unusual for the period.[5] The parents had the financial means to give their son a good education, and Martin studied in the arts faculty of Erfurt University from 1501 to 1505. His father wanted him to become a lawyer, in the expectation that this would assure him of a good career, with the social status and income that went with it. However, in July 1505, while on a local journey, Martin was caught up in a violent storm that appeared to threaten his life; during fervent prayers he made a promise that he would become a monk if he survived. While his oath was a spontaneous action when in great peril, he 'had probably thought of becoming a monk before, even though he had not considered it intensively'.[6] In spite of his father's opposition, he made good on this pledge and indeed joined a very strict monastery of the Augustinian Order in Erfurt. Actually, the choice of the particular establishment was probably mainly due to his hope of being able to continue to follow a philosophy and theology similar to the one he with which he had become familiar at Erfurt University.[7] He was ordained priest in 1507.

He experienced a degree of anxiety about his eternal salvation unusual even for his period. He was deeply worried about what he could do for a stern God, who to some later interpreters reflected his strict father. Luther had what in German are called *Anfechtungen*, a difficult term to translate, which might be rendered as challenges to his faith, or doubts, with which he was unable to deal. 'For the theologian, *Anfechtungen* are by no means weaknesses of human nature, but spiritually most significant relationships. As an attack on the whole human being, the *Anfechtung* is always a trial of faith.'[8]

Luther was fortunate in having as a superior in the Augustinian Order and as his confessor the very person he needed in Johann von Staupitz. He was the Vicar General of the Augustinian Observants, that is of the stricter monasteries in which Luther served. A man of wide administrative experience and knowledge in canon law, Staupitz was at the same time a pastor with a human touch and a good sense of humour.[9] He soon spotted that 'part of Luther's problem was neurotic guilt or what the medieval Church called "scruples"', which were encouraged by a 'sense of sin inculcated in the faithful by penitential literature in the late Middle Ages'.[10] Staupitz also 'pointed Luther to the crucified Christ in the midst of his anxieties over election'.[11] He gave him sound traditional pastoral advice, such as that 'while God is merciful to real sinners, imaginary sinners remain trapped in illusions spun out of their own fears'. Partly to divert him from his introspection, he also encouraged him to work for his theological doctorate, which was awarded to him in 1512.[12] Staupitz, who was steeped in Pauline and Augustinian theology, was out of sympathy with the 'quarrelsome distinctions of late scholasticism'.[13] He felt that Luther had been misled by some of his – nominalist – Erfurt teachers.

> He taught Luther that penance begins with the love of God, even though Luther had been given to understand that the love of God is the final step in a process of self-discipline... He warned Luther of the danger of trusting in one's own natural moral energies.[14]

Altogether, Staupitz' importance for Luther can hardly be overrated.[15] The Augustinian superior helped the troubled young monk to overcome a real crisis and thus enabled him to become a useful member of the community. He also stimulated his critical faculties by discussing the shortcomings of the dominant current theology with him. Staupitz thus contributed to Luther's development and increasing importance, though he did not in the long run agree with the path he took.[16] It was thanks to Staupitz that Luther was appointed his successor in the Chair of Sacred Scripture at the recently founded Saxon Electoral University of Wittenberg in 1512. For his lectures on biblical exegesis, which attracted great interest, Luther undertook extensive linguistic studies. He largely mastered Hebrew, Latin, and – up to a point – Greek,[17] pursuing humanist goals in going back to the sources, even if he was not directly influenced by the movement. Luther also rose in the hierarchy of his order, becoming sub-prior of his Wittenberg monastery in 1512. In 1515 he was elected to a three-year term as district vicar over the 10 monasteries of the Augustinian Hermits in Meissen and Thuringia.

Luther's continuing quest for answers to the religious questions that troubled him affected not only his lectures on the Bible, but also his sermons. He became a popular preacher, combining humility with great authority. His pastoral help was very much in demand all through his life. As confessor he was a careful listener who noted the problems of his flock, not only in order to help each individual, but also to keep abreast of general developments.

In matters of faith he stressed the almost exclusive authority of the Bible, to some extent as interpreted by the Church Fathers. On that basis he came to the conclusion that man could only achieve eternal salvation if the grace of God was bestowed on him, through his own deep faith and not through any personal righteousness or good works. To him any theology that placed man's personal merits in the centre diminished the power of God, and in this context he was critical of the strong emphasis the late medieval Church placed on good works (*Werkfrömmigkeit*). Luther's objection was fundamentally to the belief that man could 'work' his way into heaven. A person was 'justified' thanks to God's grace accepted through faith. For Luther 'justification' is the manner in which God brings about salvation, and thus, with the risen Christ, the very centre of Christian faith.[18] However, Luther fully recognised that a 'justified' man was likely to act in a manner beneficial to society through good works and through his righteousness. One of the problems with Luther's teaching on justification was the question of what man could do if he did not receive God's grace.

Increasingly Luther came to the conclusion that the current orthodoxy was inadequate through its failure to provide a proper theology of salvation. He blamed for this state of affairs the prevailing scholastic theology developed during the later Middle Ages from the teaching of St Thomas Aquinas. He also held that the schoolmen had been unduly influenced by philosophy, particularly by Aristotle. He therefore formulated 98 theses for a 'Disputation against Scholastic theology' which were debated at the University of Wittenberg on 4 September 1517. While the wording of the theses, which were formulated pointedly as a basis for debate, is extant, we cannot necessarily infer Luther's precise theological stance from them.[19] He emphasised the consequences of the Fall of Man, which resulted in an alienation from God through sin, leaving man 'so weakened and impotent that he cannot on his own avoid further sin'.[20] These effects could not be overcome, as the scholastics taught, by loving God, which was something that could only follow grace. Basically Luther's view was that a human being could not act meritoriously without grace,[21] which 'is God's instrument in transforming the sick heart of man and making him agreeable and willing in his duties, drawing from him a generous love of God.'[22] The theses also strongly attacked Aristotle as the enemy of grace.[23]

Luther made an important change in his theology in this period, in his lectures on the letter to the Hebrews, which he gave between April and September 1517. Developing ideas taken over from St Bernard, he emphasised the importance of having the conviction that Christ was high priest for oneself personally. He asserted that the essential aspect of receiving Holy Communion was not so much the making of confession or the offering of proper preparatory prayers, but the faith of the individual that he was receiving God's grace (*fides sacramenti*).[24] However, it should not necessarily be inferred from this that Luther thus, as was often claimed later, rejected a 'Church of the sacrament' for a 'Church of the Word'.[25]

Soon, in the following months, the major debate on scholasticism opened in September 1517 was overshadowed by another and historically better known controversy, that on indulgences. This question, though not quite so fundamental theologically, was of considerable immediate practical importance, as well as of great political sensitivity.

'An indulgence is the remission of the temporal punishment due to sin, never of the guilt of sin itself. This remission is worked out either on earth or in purgatory.'[26] But as indulgences became a major source of revenue, especially – but not only – for the Holy See, some of the finer points were soon forgotten. This certainly applied in the case that came to Luther's attention and propelled him into a leading position – or a major problem – in the Empire and indeed in Western Christendom. To fill the third vacancy in the archdiocese of Mainz within a decade, Albrecht of Hohenzollern, the younger brother of Elector Joachim I of Brandenburg, was elected Archbishop-Elector of Mainz in 1514. Each further election triggered the payment of fees to the curia in return for its approval; the diocese was thus heavily in debt.

What made Albrecht such an attractive candidate to his electors was his undertaking to pay off the debts of the diocese. As he wished to remain Archbishop of Magdeburg and Administrator of Halberstadt, he also required a costly papal dispensation for his cumulation of sees. To raise the necessary funds, he obtained a loan from the Augsburg banking house of the Fuggers,[27] while the papacy granted him permission to issue indulgences to finance his transactions. He was allowed to keep half of the proceeds to repay the Fuggers, with the other half going to the Holy See. However, the proceeds from these elaborate arrangements turned out to be disappointing.[28] The indulgences were not sold on the territory of Elector Frederick the Wise of Saxony, whose younger brother had been Albrecht's predecessor at Magdeburg[29], and who was not pleased at an extension of Hohenzollern influence at the expense of the Wettin dynasty.[30] As indulgences were, however, offered in the vicinity of Wittenberg, Luther heard about the way they were handled, largely through his pastoral work. Apparently the Dominican monk and inquisitor Tetzel, who propagated the indulgences, may not have been too scrupulous in the claims he made for them. Luther certainly felt that some of those buying indulgences were given the impression that they were receiving complete remission of their sins and the assurance of going to heaven. It was only 'after long hesitation, and obviously with fear and trembling'[31] that on 31 October 1517 in a reverent, even submissive tone, he addressed a letter on the subject to Archbishop Albrecht of Mainz.[32] He complained to him about the conduct of his indulgence commissioners, but skilfully took the line that the archbishop was presumably unaware of the shortcomings of his servants. He enclosed two documents with his letter, his famous 95 theses on indulgences and his less well known *Treatise on Indulgences*.

It was assumed until recently that on the same day as he sent his letter to Archbishop Albrecht of Mainz, 31 October 1517, Luther also posted his 95 theses about indulgences on the door of the Castle church at Wittenberg, but this has now been questioned.[33] There is in fact no contemporary evidence attesting the affixing of the theses to the door of the Castle church. This question is of some importance in assessing Luther's motives at this time. Probably, as a professor and doctor of theology, he simply wanted to initiate an academic discussion on a theological matter by disputation, as was customary at the time. Actually 'no one came forward for the proposed disputation.'[34] Luther did, however, circulate the 95 theses to a number of people in the vicinity of Wittenberg to obtain their opinions and to gain more certainty for himself on this complex question. He does not seem to have intended at the time to involve the public at large.[35] However, in an age that had not yet developed the concept of copyright, various recipients of the theses had them printed, so that the whole issue soon received wide publicity.[36] To understand Luther's point of view at this time, the theses have to be read together with the *Treatise on Indulgences* which he also sent to Archbishop Albrecht.

In the theses, Luther did not reject indulgences outright. Fundamentally, he focused on the point that indulgences could only release from the punishments laid down by men,[37] especially by the pope, thanks to the power of the keys conferred by Christ.[38] However, 'the remission ... by the pope is by no means to be despised, since it is ... a declaration of divine remission.'[39] Quite apart from the barbed attacks against the instructions issued under Albrecht's authority for the sale of the indulgences,[40] Luther warned against the excessive expectations of plenary remission of punishments aroused by the indulgences; these would only give people a false sense of security about their salvation. Receiving forgiveness required contrition.[41] Apparently, sending the theses and the treatise to Albrecht was only an afterthought, as Luther's postscript to the letter to the archbishop shows, and this accounts for some of the inconsistencies in the package addressed to him. Luther probably felt that he had to go into more details about the theology of indulgences than he had been able to do in his letter.[42]

The *Treatise on Indulgences*, which Luther also enclosed to the archbishop, was drawn up in much more moderate tones than the theses, which were designed to promote debate, and indeed takes a more positive view of indulgences. Presumably Luther put down his considered thoughts on the question at least partly to prepare himself for a disputation. In the treatise, he called the granting and gaining of indulgences 'a most useful practice, in spite of the commerce and avarice which we fear is involved with them'. He could even see a particularly great need for them in his time, as 'more souls go to purgatory today than earlier'. He praised the pope for coming to the aid of the departed.[43] He recognised that the pope 'can ... release a soul from purgatory with regard to the penance he has himself imposed or could impose'.[44] However, in general Luther adopted a dualistic approach, largely distinguishing between the life-long process of 'justification' on the one hand, and sacramental penance imposed or remitted on the other.[45] Throughout, the emphasis is on the deeper spiritual aspects, on the life-long process of healing, on the prayer for grace, as against any excessive concentration on particular sins. The question was now how the church authorities would respond to the matters that Luther had raised.

Let us pause for a moment to consider Luther's position before the beginning of his conflict with the Church. Up to this point, not only did Luther not in any way question his place in the Church, but also could not, any more than the vast majority of the faithful, even visualise a divided Western Church. He was certainly determined to continue his quest for answers to the problems of faith that concerned him, but he did not feel that his position in the Augustinian Order or his professorship at the University of Wittenberg inhibited him in this in any way. Quite the reverse – he was of the opinion that his doctorate in theology in fact obliged him to try and watch over the true faith. He was only too ready to discuss his opinions and to correct them if shown evidence of their erroneousness from the Bible, or possibly also from patristic literature or canon law. For this the particular medium he used, the traditional scholastic format, of well-focused theses formulated to facilitate disputation or at least discussion, seemed to serve his purpose best. In interpreting the theses, we therefore again have to remember that they did not necessarily fully represent his point of view.

Luther's challenging of certain aspects of the teaching of the Church should not, however, blind us to the many areas of agreement. In essentials, his beliefs were orthodox. Nobody could fault his theocentric and christocentric attitude for a lack of faith in God, and in Jesus Christ and his two natures. He continued to adhere to the belief in Christ's Real Presence in the Eucharist. If Luther did not at that time develop much of an ecclesial theology, it is because he respected the hierarchy of the Church in which he had reached a respectable level: just as he expected compliance with his instructions from those under him, he was prepared to show obedience to his superiors and had no problems with the institution of bishops. He did not question either the need for a clergy or the authority of the proper bodies in the Church to lay down dogma and doctrine. Also, at this time, he did not have any problems with the papacy. He visited Rome in 1510 on business for his order: no criticism of the papacy by him is extant from this time. In all sorts of ways Luther was still very much a Christian of the late medieval period, for instance in venerating the saints, though with some reservations. It need hardly be added that he was an exemplary member of a monastic institution, and thus of a movement which was a pillar of the medieval Church.

Like many others, he did not regard all conditions in the Church as ideal and he certainly advocated some changes, some reform, or what was called *reformatio*, as we have seen, above all in the dominant theology and in the question of indulgences. Even in the fall of 1518 Luther still recognised with gratitude that the Roman Church had not so far deviated from the true faith in its decrees and had adhered to the authority of the Bible and of the Church Fathers. He added that he felt bound by its decisions.[46] Up to well into that year he could not imagine that his generally praiseworthy theological activities might get him into trouble, although he was concerned about measures being taken by the Church against others who showed a spirit of independence, such as the humanist Johannes Reuchlin. In Cologne the Dominicans and the university had advocated the burning of Jewish literature to facilitate the conversion of Jews. When Reuchlin in 1510 objected to this measure, the Inquisition proceeded against him, which led to his condemnation by the pope in 1520 for some of his writings in the controversy. Luther could see nothing wrong with the statements Reuchlin had made to justify his objection to the burning of Jewish literature, and he was worried that the Inquisition might arbitrarily accuse people of heresy.[47] But before his clash with the Church, Luther was not by any means in the forefront of the reform movement, certainly not in polemic. Indeed he objected to the 'frivolous, vituperative tone'[48] of such satires as *The Letters of Obscure Men*. These, which were published between 1515 and 1517 in defence of Reuchlin, were directed against the monks in Cologne and partially written by the imperial knight and poet Ulrich von Hutten. Although Luther was at times inclined to extreme statements to make a theological point, his deep faith usually came through. There are not as yet the crude personal attacks on anybody who disagreed with him which were to mar his later writings. Altogether his work before 1518 is of high quality and great spiritual depth and breadth.

Perhaps Luther was naive in thinking that his criticism of the Church in these major aspects would leave him unscathed, but this lack of a 'political' sense at that time does not necessarily reflect badly on him. Luther was driven by what was to be his life's continuing striving, to arrive at true faith, never forgetting that salvation would depend on getting it right.

One of the many questions raised by scholars has concerned the date when Luther made what was called his 'reformatory discovery' about the righteousness of God.[49] According to some authorities this goes back to 1514, to others only to 1518, after Luther's clash with Rome. It is generally agreed that Luther in the years to 1518 developed a theology that increasingly distanced itself from late medieval scholasticism. Ecclesiastically, owing to his emphasis, for example, on the faith of the individual that he was receiving God's grace, his views also implied, or at least could potentially imply, a diminished role for the clergy. However, Luther did not begin to see himself in opposition to the Church until accusations were levied against him in the late spring and early summer of 1518. Indeed, the official theology lacked clarity in many respects,[50] such as the question of indulgences, aspects of which had disturbed even some devout Catholics. Thus Luther could, after all, hope that the points he raised would be utilised by the Church in so far as there was merit in them. He genuinely wished to clarify the issues on which he had focused by promoting discussion on them; he certainly expected to be able to debate and discuss his insights, and to be shown in the light of the authorities, and particularly the Holy Scriptures, where he erred. Thus there is some question whether one can really speak by the early months of 1518 of a reformatory breakthrough in the sense of a theology implying a separation from Rome. Luther's previous views were not *necessarily* incompatible with the doctrine of the Church, only to the extent that they clashed with parts of late medieval scholasticism.[51] The early Luther cannot be seen objectively through the eyes of a divided Christianity. That the gulf between Luther and the teaching of the Church continued to widen in the years from 1518 onwards to the point that it could hardly be bridged is due to the unfolding of events that now began, when he developed his views under the impact of attacks on him and of pressure coming from those who supported him.[52]

Not surprisingly, Tetzel reacted strongly to Luther's criticism. As early as January 1518, he debated a series of theses justifying indulgences, some printed copies of which were burned by students at Wittenberg in March, an action Luther condemned publicly. As the dispute between the two men continued, the tone became increasingly bitter, especially after Tetzel, who was after all also an inquisitor, in late April or early May levelled accusations of heresy against Luther, likening him to Wyclif and Hus.[53] Luther gave as good as he got, in June accusing Tetzel of extraordinary ignorance. According to Luther, Tetzel 'treated the Scriptures as a sow does a feed sack'. He suggested that the inquisitor should content himself 'with wine and fire that smokes from a roasting goose, with which he is better acquainted'.[54] It is noteworthy that he began to adopt the technique of personal vehemence and crude vituperation against anybody who disagreed with him the moment the first accusations of heresy were levelled against him.[55] This tone, which is in German called *Grobianismus*, was not necessarily different from that of protagonists in the different schools and orders in the era of late medieval scholasticism,[56] but for Luther it marked a change of considerable importance. The deeply spiritual theologian and pastor became a fighter in the midst of a dangerous and potentially lethal controversy. The extensive publicity generated by the strong interest in the matters Luther had raised, which revealed for the first time on a considerable scale the effectiveness of the printing press in a matter of major importance, lessened the chances of settling the dispute. The controversy was intensified, indeed aggravated, through the publicity it received, and thus became much more difficult to ignore, or to end quietly by negotiations behind the scenes. Unlike Hus, who taught and suffered before the advent of the printing press, Luther was able to secure wide support through the new medium. This is one of the reasons why it became much more difficult to quietly arrest Luther.

What was even more important than Tetzel's activity was the reaction of the Archbishop of Mainz to Luther's communication about the indulgences to him. He did not reply to Luther, but referred the correspondence to the Holy See. Naturally Albrecht was not predisposed to a favourable view of anybody who was endangering his financial transactions. Also, whatever positive things may be said about him, he was no theologian, 'was incapable of preaching',[57] and does not appear to have fully grasped the importance of the communication addressed to him. He reported Luther to Rome for spreading novel doctrines.[58] Thus the curia, which was another party to the financial arrangements for Mainz, was apprised of the matter in a manner which was unfavourable to Luther and to what he was trying to achieve. Under the influence of Tetzel, who was joined by the redoubtable Ingolstadt Dominican theologian Johannes Eck, up to that time a friend of Luther, even stronger action against the author of the indulgence theses was taken. The Dominican chapter in March decided to accuse Luther in Rome of suspicion of heresy.[59] The pluralism of different kinds of institutions could be a great source of strength for the Church, but in this case the rivalry between the Dominicans and the Augustinians may well have aggravated the situation even further. Similarly, the variety of opinions in universities, which also judged matters of faith, was only liable to proliferate allegations of heresy, many of them unfounded.

Everything now depended on the attitude taken by the papacy. The Medici pope, Leo X, who had succeeded to the pontificate on the death of Julius II in 1513, was a great patron of the arts, especially of Raphael, and always short of money. He was – except for his preoccupation with the threat from the Turks – more interested in Italian politics, including the fortunes of his family, the Medici, than in matters of faith. At a time when the papacy required a pontiff of the calibre, character and deep faith of an Alexander III (1159–81) or of an Innocent III (1198–1216), the Holy See had to make do with a successor of St Peter who in his worldliness failed to grasp the spiritual importance of the issues raised by Luther. After an abortive attempt to 'soothe' Luther through channels of his own order, the papal court theologian, Sylvester Mazzolini from Prierio and thus called Prierias, another Dominican, was asked to prepare a theological opinion on Luther's views. In a hastily written *Latin Dialogue against the Presumptuous Conclusions of Martin Luther*, probably at the beginning of June 1518, Prierias alleged 'suspicion of heresy, disdain for ecclesiastical power, and lack of respect for the papal power of the keys'.[60] The document was completely misnamed, for one thing it prevented, in spite of its title, was in fact what was needed at least as a preliminary step, namely dialogue. Luther was required to appear in Rome within 60 days of receiving the summons, in the absence of which he was threatened with the ban. Even at Rome it was felt later that Prierias' 'perfunctory way of handling the matter' was unfortunate.[61] The issue had now been joined and Luther, whose conduct had not so far been bellicose, turned out not to be the one to shirk a fight, once his religious orthodoxy had been challenged.

Why did the curia act initially in this matter with unusual determination and despatch, and indeed with undue haste? Potentially Luther with his criticism of indulgences was calling into question directly the whole curial system of financing and indirectly papal power itself. In the background there was always the fear of a revival of conciliar authority. The preoccupation of the Holy See with a narrow view of its interests prevented a dispassionate examination of the ideas Luther was putting forward, with a view to ascertaining whether they might in fact contain useful elements. In turn Luther himself could not understand why outside his own order, which was on the whole sympathetic to his views, the authorities were generally not prepared to discuss his writings and to correct him where he was wrong. He simply asked that he should be shown in the light of the Bible, to which he sometimes added the Fathers and canon law, where he had erred. It is very doubtful that he had moved beyond Catholicism by the time he received the summons to Rome, in August 1518.

We are a long way from any definitive view of Luther, perhaps even more so now that more ecumenical interpretations have replaced the straight denominational alternatives, and all that can be done here is to offer a possible hypothesis. Subjectively, Luther certainly did not have any idea of leaving the Church until he was faced with the threat of exclusion. He simply could not understand how an exemplary priest and monk, sub-prior and professor of theology like himself, who was merely trying to save his soul and to point out the way to salvation to his fellow-Christians, could become a heretic. As was already stated in earlier chapters of this book, the hardening of Inquisition procedures during past centuries was increasingly liable to produce grave injustice. That the ecclesiastical authorities should put a leading Catholic scholar in the dock without first exploring whether there was any common ground with him reveals an extraordinary state of affairs. Indeed at the time, in a memorandum in 1520, the humanist Dominican Johann Faber in Augsburg asked for an independent inquiry along those lines.[62] As Faber saw, justice not only had to be done, but to be seen to be done. Instead of isolating Luther, the way the papal proceedings were handled actually strengthened support for him, as we shall see.

The more difficult question to answer is whether a settlement with Luther would have been possible when there was the best chance of achieving it; that is at an early stage, before his position had hardened, or hardened even further. While a person of Luther's brilliance would have tried the patience of any large organisation, he could have enriched the Church if his remark-able energies had been harnessed to a common purpose. That would have required leadership at the curia of persons who combined deep spirituality with the ability to handle others, like Staupitz. Even then, it would not have been easy, perhaps above all because Luther's emphasis on the individual conscience,[63] which resulted in a reduced role for the clergy, had to be integrated with the communal needs of the Church and of its role in society. However, there were other factors which might have allowed a bridging of differences. Luther, who worked very much on his own, had not yet formed a theological system, and in a way never achieved one. There were also contradictions or at least different emphases in some of his writings and utterances. There was certainly room for the ecclesiastical authorities to conduct constructive negotiations with him to try and find a solution; these might, in certain circumstances, have been successful.

The chance was not taken, and under the trauma of accusations of heresy Luther became increasingly radical in his statements. A possible explanation for many of the charges he then hurled against the Church, and particularly against the papacy, is that he never got over the injustice of his treatment and his exclusion from the Old Church, which he began to hate as a result. Luther, through the proceedings taken against him, became one of the great figures of world history, who turned things into new directions. This happened because he found himself unable to participate in what he wanted to do and which he would have been eminently capable of doing, namely strengthening and rejuvenating the Church. Instead he contributed to splitting it, owing to the unresponsiveness of the ecclesiastical authorities. Thus, in spite of all the eminence he achieved, his work can in some ways be seen to have failed and his life was in certain respects a tragedy. The inability to heal the rift in time began a long period in which different Christian churches, which all claimed to represent the true faith and denied it to others, fought each other and inflicted endless suffering on members of opposite confessions. These events were to have a long-term effect on Western Christendom, and not least on the fortunes of the German kingdom and the Empire.

Luther's alleged heresy did not, however, turn out to be a purely theological matter. Luther had spoken out without considering the 'political' implications of the views he was stating, in fact without at the time being fully aware of them. But now, at a stage when he faced a grave situation and when his liberty and indeed his life were in jeopardy, his religious stand benefited from political circumstances. It is true that the papal legate, Thomas de Vio from Gaeta, and therefore called Cajetan, had persuaded Emperor Maximilian to write to the pope in August 1518, drawing his attention to the danger Luther posed for the unity of the faith and promising to support in the Empire the measures to be taken by the Church.[64] But at about this time, Luther secured important backing.

Frederick the Wise, Elector of Saxony, was, if anything, rather conservative in his religious faith and practice. He possessed an enormous collection of relics and secured numerous indulgence privileges; he was too magnanimous to allow Luther's criticism of indulgences to upset him. The elector was concerned with the well-being of the university at Wittenberg, which he had recently founded, as Leipzig with its older university went to the younger – Albertine – line of the House of Wettin in the partition of 1485. Naturally Frederick did not want the electoral university to lose the advantage it had gained in comparison with Leipzig through having Luther as a professor, and thus did not want him to come to any harm. Also the elector will not have been unmindful of the manner in which Luther had – even if unwittingly – somewhat deflated the Hohenzollern rival of the Wettin dynasty, Archbishop Albrecht.

Owing to a conjuncture of circumstances, in this period Frederick's support was at various times needed by both emperor and pope. This proved a great blessing to Luther when, as a result of his replying publicly to charges made against him, a papal *breve* was issued, also in August, in which he was 'charged with a heresy that was notorious and public'.[65] Cajetan was to take Luther into custody, with a view to bringing him before the papal court.

Frederick the Wise was able to get these instructions changed, because he now became a key player in the election of the King of the Romans. Emperor Maximilian wanted to secure this crown for his grandson Charles, King of Spain, to pave the way for his eventual imperial succession, but Frederick and other electors were not prepared to cooperate in this matter, so that the plan had to be dropped. The papacy followed its traditional policy of opposing an increase of power to a ruler well established in Italy. Charles was already King of Naples and Sicily and an interest in Milan could not be excluded in the future. Thus Frederick could be useful to the papacy at the next imperial election; certainly this was not the time to antagonise him over his protégé, 'the Wittenberg monk'. Thus a compromise was reached over Luther. Cardinal Cajetan was to interrogate Luther at Augsburg, where the legate was staying in connection with a session of the diet, and 'to receive his recantation, or otherwise to condemn him',[66] but not to detain him. The citation before the authorities in Rome was thus averted for the time being.

The interrogation took place in October 1518. In accordance with his instructions, the legate did not permit any proper debate, which Luther regarded as necessary. Although Luther in some ways adopted a conciliatory attitude, the gap between his point of view and that of an official spokesman of the Church over such matters as the extent of the authority of the pope, for instance with regard to indulgences, as well as his relationship with councils, was difficult to bridge; it widened even further as a result of the encounter. In spite of all the efforts Cajetan made, also through Staupitz, who was present in Augsburg, Luther would not recant and returned to Wittenberg; but the danger in which he found himself was not over. He realised that he might be excommunicated. In an attempt to forestall that measure, he appealed from the pope to a council of the Church. He thought of leaving Wittenberg, partly to make things easier for the elector. But Frederick was very much concerned for him and certainly did not put any pressure on him to flee. In the meantime, in November, Leo X on the basis of a draft formulated by Cajetan, issued a constitution affirming the validity of indulgences. But this came too late to have any effect.[67]

At the end of 1518 the papal chamberlain, Karl von Miltitz, made an attempt to settle the dispute with Luther during a visit to the Saxon electorate. Luther certainly did his part in trying to arrive at a settlement, so far as his beliefs allowed, but in the end the mission came to nothing. However, soon after, another event occurred which substantially affected Luther's situation for the time being.

Emperor Maximilian died in January 1519. Even more than previously, Frederick the Wise appeared to the papacy as a possible ally against the candidature of Charles for the succession to his grandfather Maximilian. Another contender was King Francis I of France, who, however, was not entirely desirable for the papacy, as he had, right at the beginning of his reign, become ruler of Milan through his victory over the Swiss at Marignano in 1515. In the circumstances, the Holy See tried to persuade Frederick to try for the imperial crown himself, but the elector was too cautious to attempt the uncertain and to him not even entirely desirable prize. Charles in the end won the imperial crown, in June 1519. Even though he had in fact been brought up outside the German kingdom, he appeared to some extent as the 'German' candidate over the French foreigner. He was assisted by Augsburg money, mainly from the Fuggers,[68] though that may not have decided the outcome.[69] After his coronation at Aachen in September 1520 Charles at once assumed the title of 'elected Roman emperor', a custom followed by all his successors. Until the election had taken place, the curia avoided any move that might antagonise Frederick. In the meantime, while Luther certainly still wanted to remain in the Church of Rome, he increasingly developed – at least partly under the impact of the papal proceedings against him – a theology which distanced itself from it, for instance in raising questions concerning the primacy of the pope.

About the time of the imperial election, Luther debated at Leipzig with Johannes Eck, who was Professor of Theology at Ingolstadt, came from a humanistic background and had earlier on been on friendly terms with Luther. Eck was quite critical of aspects of the Church of his day and by no means averse to new ideas, such as in the field of biblical exegesis or in establishing authentic biblical texts closer to the originals than had been achieved previously.[70] He forced Luther into a public expression of his doubts about the primacy of the pope, succeeded in eliciting an indication of sympathy with Hus, and in this connection got him to admit that even councils could err. 'Catholic scholarship credits Eck with being the one who at that time uncovered Luther's remoteness from Rome and his views regarding the structure of the Church that were no longer reformatory [here rather: propagating reform within the Church] but aggressive.'[71] However, it may be argued that little harm could have been done by trying to find common ground, and that something might have been gained – even at this late hour – by a more conciliatory approach, particularly as Luther at this time ranged from extreme views of the papacy to more moderate ones.

Once the imperial election was over, the proceedings against Luther were resumed. In June 1520, the papal bull, *Exsurge Domine*, condemned 41 statements from Luther's writings on several grounds, which varied from heresy to merely being offensive to pious ears, but without designating under which category of censure each of the passages fell. Even Eck, who had a part in the proceedings, was later highly critical of the text and asked for a refutation of the main heresies on the basis of the Holy Scriptures, but without success. The bull remained the only pronouncement of the papal teaching office until the Council of Trent. Luther was to revoke the censured opinions within 60 days of the publication of the bull in the Saxon bishoprics; the writings in which they appeared were to be burned. Unless Luther recanted, which he was not prepared to do as he believed that he would endanger his eternal salvation, he was to be excommunicated; the ecclesiastical ban was promulgated in the bull, *Decet Romanum Pontificem*, of January 1521.

These measures did not deter Luther from questioning the institutions of the Church, quite the reverse. His opposition to the existing ecclesiastical order became more radical. This is shown, for example, in his publication of *A Prelude on the Babylonian Captivity of the Church* in October 1520, which contained unmeasured attacks on the papacy.[72] Obviously any settlement was becoming harder with the passing of every further month, particularly owing to the vehemence of Luther's language against the papacy. It was to become fashionable among Protestants to denigrate as 'papists' those who continued their allegiance to Rome. In a sense it was natural for somebody branded as a heretic in a papal bull to react in this way. But as the battle-lines became drawn between the Old Church and those who disagreed with it, the reunion which both sides desired, or at any rate professed to desire, was bound to become even more difficult to achieve. As antipapalism was a sentiment and indeed a useful slogan to hold together the innovators who increasingly disagreed with each other on many other matters, they could hardly compromise on the papacy, which, in turn, was an institution the Old Church was never prepared to surrender. Another exacerbation of the situation occurred in December 1520, when Luther and some of his followers carried out a book burning, certainly of volumes containing canon law, and probably of the papal bull *Exsurge Domine*.

The stage was now set for the final ban, at the Diet of Worms in April 1521. According to established custom, certainly on his final excommunication by the Church, Luther ought to have been handed over by the secular to the ecclesiastical authorities; Frederick the Wise prevented that. The elector obtained the agreement of the newly elected emperor that Luther should be given a hearing at the Diet of Worms and that a safe conduct should be provided by Charles. By this stage of the proceedings, Luther was no longer alone. He was receiving widespread support and had become a public figure not only of national, but international dimensions. Thus his journey to Worms in April 1521, accompanied by the imperial herald, was like a triumph. But Luther also noted signs of unrest among the people, which worried him, particularly as he feared that social 'tumult' would be blamed on the 'evangelical' movement.[73]

For a fleeting moment at the diet, the two great protagonists, emperor and monk, that were to play such a prominent part in shaping the history of the new age, found themselves face to face. Luther was given a last chance to recant, but refused to do so in a dignified statement:

Unless I am convinced by the testimony of the Scriptures or by clear reason (for I do not trust either in the pope or in councils alone, since it is well known that they have often erred and contradicted themselves) I am bound by the Scriptures I have quoted and my conscience is captive to the Word of God. I cannot and I will not retract anything, since it is neither safe nor right to go against conscience. May God help me. Amen.[74]

Charles wished to proceed at once to the imperial ban, as Luther had not recanted. But the Estates obtained his agreement for making a final attempt at a settlement. Accordingly, negotiations took place between a commission of the Imperial Estates and Luther, but to no avail. Unlike Sigismund with Hus a century previously, Charles honoured the safe-conduct he had granted. The emperor was certainly sincere and honourable in his treatment of Luther. But it is doubtful whether in the circumstances he could have acted differently, for support for Luther in Worms was so strong that any attempt to arrest him might well have provoked a riot.[75]

On his return to Saxony, Luther – in an apparently pre-arranged operation – was ambushed by the elector's horsemen and taken to the Wartburg Castle near Eisenach, where he lived *incognito* as 'Junker Jörg'. In the meantime, the ban of the Empire was inflicted on Luther by the Edict of Worms promulgated by the emperor with the general assent of the Diet in May. Luther and his supporters and abettors were to be arrested and to be delivered to the emperor. The purchase, sale, reading, copying and printing of Luther's writings was prohibited; they were to be destroyed.[76]

It is rare in history for one person by himself to challenge successfully the almost unlimited sway of an institution, particularly a spiritual one backed by overwhelming worldly power, that has existed for more than a millennium; it is unique in the medieval and early modern period of Western Christendom. By the time the ban of the Empire was inflicted on Luther, it was already becoming clear that while he had fought the battle single-handed in the first instance, he was no longer alone. Indeed, during the coming years, not only an increasing number of persons, especially among the monastic orders and the secular clergy as hitherto, but also of rulers and cities began to question the teaching of the Church. Something that was unthinkable in Western Christendom in 1517, apart from the Hussite problem, had become very much a matter of reality within four years. How was that possible? How was it that suddenly the orthodoxy and uniformity imposed by a church that had been taken for granted, again apart from Bohemia, could be challenged?

And this in the case of a church that through the apostolic succession provided continuity with Jesus, above all in celebrating the Eucharist; a church that – whatever its shortcomings – had been administering the sacraments since that time and had been giving spiritual sustenance to the faithful over a long period.

For several centuries, at least from the thirteenth, the Church had been so concerned with breaches of religious orthodoxy as to impede theological discussion. In its quest to maintain the true faith, the Church had spelled out in great detail and with increasing and sometimes confusing complexity its views on many matters, in the process erecting a superstructure that tended to blur central matters of faith. Parallel to this, the apparatus of the Inquisition had been extended, encouraging denunciation, for example from universities and monastic orders, and weakening any safeguards for those accused of heresy. No privileged status was granted to those whose task it was to watch over matters of faith, such as the doctors and professors of theology. Thus St Thomas, who was proclaimed a Doctor of the Church by Pius V in 1567, had been accused of deviation from official doctrine and even of heresy in the years after his death in 1274. By Luther's time theological knowledge on the part of the pope and of many bishops was quite insufficient to appreciate the importance and critical nature of the issues Luther was raising. Also, at least since the pontificates of Gregory IX and Innocent IV, during their struggle with Frederick II, and to some extent even before, the Italian question had unduly influenced papal policy. Secular considerations often gained priority over matters of faith, and this got worse, if anything, during the following periods.

The papal schisms and the transfer of the Holy See to Avignon, with all the competition for support by different 'obediences' that involved, did the institution a great deal of harm. The faithful began to be uncertain as to who was indeed the true pope. To some extent arising out of the papal schisms, the conciliar movement initially aroused great hopes for reform, but eventually proved disappointing. This was partly due to councils attempting to take over executive functions, in some ways in the manner of the French Revolutionary Convention. Indeed, both councils in their attempts to prove their superiority over the papacy, and the Holy See in endeavouring to strengthen what has been called 'the papal monarchy', overreached themselves in the powers they claimed. Neither side strove sufficiently, in the interests of the Church, for a working relationship and some kind of balance between them. Popes were reluctant to summon further councils for fear of a curtailment of pontifical powers. Thus Church reform was delayed and a possible method of dealing with Luther's reinterpretations, by referring them to a General Council of the Church, was regarded as foreclosed by the curia. The worldliness of many popes and senior ecclesiastics was a further obstacle. Actually, even the calling of regional synods to deal with current problems was not always easy to achieve. In this situation Luther appeared to respond to the yearning for reform. These factors, assisted by the printing press, help to explain the enormous echo his writings had.

Why did it fall to somebody in the German kingdom to play the part Luther did, to question the existing ecclesiastical order and to survive to lead a breakaway movement from the Church? Luther's personality was unique and it is probably impossible to prove or to disprove any theory that he had to *come* from Germany to play the part he did. Perhaps the checkered political map of Germany encouraged a strong individualist like Luther. However, for his work to be allowed the time to take root, the German kingdom, or rather the part in which he found himself during the decisive years, was a good place to be. If the local atmosphere in his territory had not been favourable, he could have remedied the situation by moving, as for example Calvin did when he left an unfriendly environment in his native France. It is unlikely that in a centralised kingdom, such as in France or Spain, a person raising fundamental questions about the Church at the time would have been allowed the amount of leeway that was granted to Luther thanks to the protection he was given by his territorial ruler. In the German kingdom and the Empire, the emperor could not so easily, if requested by the pope, enforce his authority against an uncooperative elector or duke, particularly one of the political skills and acumen of a Frederick the Wise. Also the comparative autonomy of walled cities and townships, with their well developed government by council, often supplemented by the participation of guilds and committees of citizens, permitted a measure of independent religious views. Furthermore, public opinion in the German kingdom was strongly anti-Roman and to some extent anticlerical, as the periodic plaints, the *Gravamina* submitted to the *Reichstag*, show. At Worms in 1521 it was actually the staunchly Catholic Duke George of Saxony (of the Albertine line) who with others demanded the reform of abuses in the Church, such as certain payments to the papacy, and the calling of a general council.[77]

Like anti-Romanism, anticlericalism cannot necessarily be equated with a wish to separate from the Old Church. It could simply denote a strong lay religious interest which expressed itself in the demand to have the affairs of the Church conducted in a better or more efficient way, for example in improved preaching from the pulpit. Over long periods, extending into our time, many of the most faithful Catholics have been particularly critical of aspects of Church government and have thus appeared to be anticlerical.[78] There was certainly, in the period at the beginning of the Reformation, a perception that the absence of a strong emperor able to put pressure on the papacy allowed the curia to exploit Germany financially and would continue to do so; but in general the rulers of the largest secular territories, at any rate, objected to a powerful emperor. This is only one of many examples of secular and religious interests pulling in different and often opposite ways. Because of perceived grievances against the Church there had been strong opposition at the Augsburg Diet in 1518 to the granting of aid to the papacy for the campaign against the Turk.[79] The kings of France, by securing the so-called Gallican liberties, had perhaps gone furthest in restricting Roman influence over a territorial church. Even many rulers in the German kingdom, from the Habsburgs downwards, had also obtained concessions from the curia which allowed them a considerably free hand in ecclesiastical appointments.

The situation in the years between 1518 and to at least 1521 should not be seen in terms of a sharp division between those who remained loyal to the Church of Rome and those who joined the reformation movement outside the Old Church, and even less of the establishment of a 'Lutheran' Church. Frederick the Wise, who ensured Luther's survival, is a case in point. As we have seen, he had, with his relics and indulgences, quite conservative religious views, which he continued to practice well past the point when he started to support Luther.[80] He was careful not to expose himself by openly protecting a heretic banned by Church and Empire, and does not appear to have ever personally talked to his famous professor. It was only on his death-bed that he signified some acceptance of the new faith by receiving communion in both kinds.[81] Yet no ruler could have been more assiduous in seeing to Luther's safety and, without coming out into the open, none played a greater part in preventing the enforcement of the Edict of Worms.

Thus a key component of the old order on which so much else depended broke down: hitherto, while it had been up to the ecclesiastical authorities to determine questions of religious orthodoxy and heresy, the secular arm was bound to support the findings and to execute the sentences of church courts. Frederick the Wise, one of the few rulers in this period to earn the epithet given to him, as a consummate politician thus reflected the understandable desire of many of those with responsibilities for governing to postpone taking sides as long as possible. For religion and politics were so closely interwoven that a choice in either sphere was bound to affect the position in the other; also nobody could foresee precisely the balance of forces which would result if Luther secured a measure of support. No Estate of the Empire, whether prince or city, would willingly wish to risk the wrath of the emperor or an adverse reaction of the other Estates, by exposing itself to the charge of heresy or of the support of heresy. Princes and cities had other interests besides religious ones, and though the powers of an emperor were not on a par with those of a king of France, even the withholding of imperial favour might, for example, result in economic disadvantage. Again, we may once more look at the constraints under which Frederick the Wise operated. As head of the elder, Ernestine, line of the House of Wettin, he certainly did not want to give any opportunity to George, the strongly Catholic head of the junior, ducal Albertine, line to fish in troubled waters at his expense and that of his branch of the dynasty.

A more fruitful approach is to think in terms of those who supported Luther's views, or some of these, on the one hand, and those who opposed them on the other. The core of Luther's original support came from the Wittenberg theological school, particularly from Melanchthon and – after a time – from Andreas Bodenstein, who called himself Karlstadt after his birthplace in Lower Franconia; also from his friends at the court of the Saxon elector, like Spalatin, as well as from many members of the Augustinian and Franciscan orders. The young Philipp Melanchthon, whose original name of Schwarzerdt was Graecized by his great-uncle Reuchlin, had been called to the University of Wittenberg as Professor of Greek. The appointment of this rising scholar added fresh lustre to Wittenberg University. Thanks to the publicity Luther's views had received, he secured a wide following of theologians and laymen in numerous cities and townships in the German kingdom. He also impressed many listeners to the debates in which he participated, notably the young Dominican monk Martin Bucer at Heidelberg in 1518. Bucer was to play a leading part in the reformation at Strassburg.

Already at Worms, some of the princes expressed sympathy for Luther and therefore helped to ensure that he would not come to any harm. But it was the cities and towns, both the imperial cities that came directly under emperor and empire (*Reichsstädte*), and the cities that came under the territorial princes (*Landstädte*), from which were drawn the first powerful recruits to adopt some of Luther's ideas. There was no uniform pattern of power relationships in all these varied cities and townships. In many cases, the city had an old-standing quarrel with its bishop. Emancipation from ecclesiastical authority had gone on for some time, with municipalities taking over many of the social functions and appointments to clerical livings that used to be exercised by the Church. Luther's criticisms of the Church could thus be used to take these urban developments even further by increasing lay municipal supervision of matters which had previously been considered the preserve of the ecclesiastical authorities, above all what the priests preached. In many cases the laity demanded that the preacher should adhere closely to the Bible, and especially to the Gospels (*Evangelium*), which gave the new movement its name *evangelisch*, which means according to the Gospel, rather than evangelising, although both could go together.[82] In September 1521, in a letter to Melanchthon, Luther referred to 'Evangelische Freiheit [freedom]'.[83] Melanchthon himself compiled a compendium of the 'evangelische Lehre [teaching or doctrine]' for Landgrave Philip of Hesse.[84] Thus the term is well substantiated contemporarily and was useful as a collective designation for the reformers, at least initially, until the protest at the Diet of Speyer in 1529 allowed the name of Protestantism to be introduced.[85]

Luther had raised a whole number of issues and had thus, without in any sense contriving to do so, been able to attract a whole number of different groups with his ideas. These had developed over the years, earlier on in his cloistered study, more recently in the cut and thrust of controversy. It remained to be seen whether these views, which satisfied Luther's personal religious needs, formed a consistent whole and would be applied in the direction which Luther intended. They were, at least initially, fundamentally theological, but did not constitute or form part of a system. Luther did not regard this as a deficiency, because he was critical of the impact philosophy, particularly Aristotelianism, had made on matters of faith. What we have here was an individual, if a very learned one, single-handedly revising the reigning theology. It only stands to reason that he could not be right on everything, indeed on many matters his initial views were not his final ones. His attitude to the clerical office, for example, went through many changes over the years.[86] It must have been hard for Luther to deny so much of his past, including his monasticism, an institution he attacked with increasing severity.

Luther went further than claiming the right to make up his own mind for himself. He did not consistently advocate the ministry of all believers, certainly not to the extent of wishing to see the clergy abolished altogether. But up to a point the right of every individual to make the decision that suited his own religious view and situation in life could at least be read into his earlier writings and sermons. It was not clear how these individual rights fitted in with Luther's, in many ways, quite conservative outlook. Here the lack of a theological or philosophical system posed considerable hazards, for as we shall see in the ensuing period, it allowed everybody to pick out just what appealed to them. A whole proliferation of different beliefs emerged, as the 'evangelicals' (in the sense of the central position given to the interpretation of the *Evangelium*, that is the gospel) began to disagree with each other. Indeed various reformers, such as Zwingli and Luther, competed with each other for support of those disenchanted with the Church.

Their struggles with each other were initially mainly fought out in the cities that moved away from Catholicism. These constituted the first important group that rallied to the dissidents, leading to the judgment that 'the German Reformation was an urban event at once literary, technological and oratorical'.[87] It is not surprising that the urban centres played an important part in the new religious developments. The absence of strong central institutions had allowed plenty of scope for regional distinctions and thus for the forming of strong specific characteristics not only for the imperial cities, but also for the townships which came under some territorial jurisdiction. The period of the Reformation coincided with economic prosperity due mainly to the expanding trade to the south over the Alps to Venice and the Mediterranean on the one hand, and the booming Baltic commerce from the Netherlands in the west as far as Danzig and beyond on the other. There was also, though more noticeable somewhat later in the century, the boost given through the discovery of the Americas. With all this, and with the increasing influence exercised by banking houses such as the Fuggers and Welsers in Augsburg, came a greater assertiveness of the cities and a determination to shape their own destinies. This was accompanied by a strong interest in religious matters, not only among the leading citizens, but also among the artisans, coupled with an increasingly critical attitude towards the existing Church and its clergy. The impact of the printing press, with its emphasis on matters of faith in general and on original biblical texts in particular, encouraged an enhanced lay interest in the way the Church was run, especially in the effectiveness of preaching from the pulpit. There was a great demand for biblical exegesis. Luther received some support from his prince, and was not so dependent initially on the support of the cities. These were also influenced by others besides him, above all in this period by Luther's almost exact contemporary Zwingli.

Huldrych (Ulrich) Zwingli, like Luther, came from a reasonably well-to-do peasant background. He was born, soon after Luther, in 1484 in the jurisdiction of the famous ancient abbey of St Gall to the south of the Lake of Constance, actually within the Empire, but outside the territory of the Swiss Confederation as constituted at that time.[88] Somehow paying his way, the young Zwingli was able to study in Vienna and afterwards in Basle, where the university was strongly influenced by humanism and indeed by Erasmus, who resided there for many years. He read liberal arts and was thus able to master the kind of *sophisterey* which was to stand him in good stead later on when he participated in public debates during the Swiss Reformation. Like other members of his family he pursued a clerical career. From 1506 to 1516 he was parish priest of the small Swiss cantonal township of Glarus, to the south-west of his birthplace at Wildhaus. Even though he went about his pastoral work with great diligence, he had plenty of time for study. Paying heed to the humanist principle of emphasising the necessity of going back to the sources, he learned to master Hellenistic Greek, studied Erasmus' publication of the original Greek text of the New Testament and began to see Jesus in a new light.[89] But while still a parish priest at Glarus, he also began to witness the Swiss involvement in international affairs at first hand.

In this period, the Swiss, who had earlier largely emancipated themselves from Habsburg overlordship, asserted themselves strongly on the international scene, expanding their confederation (*Eidgenossenschaft*) and acquiring a foothold beyond its borders. Thanks to the reputation for military prowess they had acquired, their mercenaries were very much in demand. In view of unfavourable economic conditions in many parts of the country, the money obtained through the sale of mercenaries (*Reislaufen*) was an attractive proposition. When the new King of France, Francis I, took the offensive in Northern Italy in 1515, the Swiss Confederation sided with his opponents – Duke Maximilian Sforza of Milan, Emperor Maximilian, the pope and Ferdinand of Aragon – and supported them with troops. As chaplain, Zwingli accompanied on the campaign his parishioners serving in the allied army, and preached to them on their duty of giving steadfast support to the pope.[90] He witnessed the severe defeat Francis inflicted on his enemies at Marignano, which allowed him to take Milan. Over ten thousand Swiss were killed. The experience reinforced two convictions Zwingli held, that mercenary service was immoral, and that 'Swiss unity [with which he identified himself] was an indispensable prerequisite for future achievement'.[91] In this period he was a strong supporter of the papacy, from which he incidentally received a pension.[92] He regretted that following the defeat, many of his Swiss countrymen distanced themselves from the papal alliance and tended to favour France. But at the same time he was becoming more pensive on a great many matters to do with the Church.

He was no longer satisfied with some traditional explanations. Under humanist influences he increasingly went back to the sources, from which he concluded that the Church should return to the practices and teaching of the Apostles, thus emphasising one of the main tenets of the Reformation. In the process he became critical of the papacy, now regarding it as the institution that had spoiled the purity of the primitive Church. In 1516, at his own request, he was transferred to the post of stipendiary priest (*Leutpriester*) at Einsiedeln, not far from Glarus. There was, however, as yet no suspicion in Rome of any problem with Zwingli, who received the honorific title of papal chaplain in 1518. By the end of 1518, Zwingli had become so well known as a preacher and as a humanist scholar that the chapter of the Great Minster at Zurich appointed him foundation preacher with parochial responsibilities. It was with the city of Zurich, one of the pillars of the Swiss Confederation, that he was to be associated for the rest of his life and it was there that he was to leave his mark on history.

On taking over his new duties in January 1519, Zwingli at once made changes in the church service. Ignoring the prescribed readings, he began a series of sermons expounding the Gospel, basing himself on the actual text and discarding scholastic explanations. He was a powerful preacher, taking great care to make his sermons well understood by his listeners, whom – as also the hierarchy – he called to repentance. Although he carried out many clerical duties, such as saying mass regularly and taking part in processions, he was 'fast becoming completely scripture-dominated'.[93] For him the authority of the Bible was beyond question, and he – at any rate at that stage – supported the right of the individual to acquire the necessary knowledge to form his own judgment on the text irrespective of the existing official interpretation. Nobody applied himself more diligently to this task of biblical exegesis than Zwingli himself, who accumulated a very considerable library for studying the Bible.

Already at Einsiedeln, Zwingli – like Luther – had been confronted with the problem of indulgences. He still accepted the fact of purgatory and the authority of the pope, and was not directly interested in the whole issue of indulgences. But he disapproved of some of the practices used to propagate them by Bernhardin Sanson on behalf of the diocese of Constance, and perhaps helped to exclude him from Einsiedeln.[94] The matter cropped up again during his first weeks at Zurich, when he was questioned by his parishioners about the manner in which Sanson offered indulgences at the city gates; the city council had earlier prohibited this indulgence-preaching on its territory. Zwingli, again without challenging the doctrine on which indulgences were based, criticised the lack of information given by Sanson to those who purchased them. The reaction of the ecclesiastical authorities was different to that accorded to Luther's criticisms in this matter nearly two years earlier. The Bishop of Constance signalled that he did not support Sanson. The papacy wanted to prevent the dispute which had begun in Wittenberg from spilling over into Switzerland, its ally and source for mercenaries. It was noted in Rome that Zwingli had not so far attacked the pope. Sanson – unlike Tetzel earlier – was recalled.[95]

In August 1519, Zurich was visited by the plague, but Zwingli refused to leave the city. With great courage and without regard for his own safety ministering to the sick and the dying, he himself caught the disease, which nearly proved fatal. Interestingly enough, his life may have been saved by the action of the papal legate in sending his personal physician to him in Zurich. In his prayers, Zwingli committed himself entirely to God's mercy, accepting whatever fate was in store for him. Surviving, he felt that God had set him aside for a special mission on earth, like one of the prophets of old. These beliefs gave him self-assurance, but also made him intolerant of any opposition.[96]

Zwingli only gradually moved away from the Church of Rome. While his early years owed a great deal to Erasmus, he had an ambivalent relationship with Luther. Though sympathetic to many of Luther's views, Zwingli wished to maintain a separate identity and did not want to be lumped together with 'Wittenbergers' or 'Martinians' even after his breach with the Old Church. To some extent the inability of the two leading reformers to evolve a common position was due to a difference in personalities, but this in turn can hardly be separated from the dissimilarity of the environments into which they had been born or the paths their lives had taken. Conditions in the Swiss Confederation permitted an even greater degree of autonomy to large units, such as cities, than in the Empire. This allowed considerable scope to a reformer of religious practices in a great city like Zurich, but only if he could carry the city council with him. Thus of necessity Zwingli had to enter the political arena to a far greater extent than Luther, who required the support of his ruler, but was not expected to play a part in politics. That suited Luther, who had been propelled into prominence through the force of his theology and who was only gradually compelled by the force of circumstances to think out how that could be fitted into the actual circumstances on this earth.

From an early stage of his ministry, Zwingli found himself in the midst of current and quite controversial issues, such as the question of the sale of Swiss mercenaries abroad. Luther, after leaving Erfurt, spent the rest of his life mainly in a comparatively small town, Wittenberg. He was thus denied the experience of life in one of the thriving big cities, which played so important a part in the history of the Reformation, largely because they were the first to join the movement in great numbers, even before many of the princes followed suit. Cities had for some time attempted to regulate the moral life of their citizens. Thus 'the *Magistrat* [city council] of Basle in the middle of the fifteenth century... regarded it as its task to fight severe sins'.[97] As a secular priest who could move about, rather than as a monk and university professor like Luther, Zwingli had been able to acquire an intensive knowledge of both rural and urban population. As a successful preacher and recognised humanist scholar, who had in the meantime gone beyond his teacher Erasmus, he built up a strong position for himself in Zurich, which he, by stages, began to move out of the Roman Church.

Thus Luther no longer had the main anti-Roman field to himself, and Zwinglian influences are important in some of the dramatic events that began to unfold in the Empire, when religious questions became interconnected with burning social, economic, political and constitutional issues. The relative importance of these various factors will be discussed for many years yet without final resolution, but they should not be viewed as mutually exclusive explanations. It required the courage and the religious single-mindedness of a personality like Luther to call into question an ecclesiastical system that had previously not been generally challenged. At the same time men like Luther and Zwingli, who in different ways reflected the atmosphere of a changing environment, would not have had the effect they did in religious matters, if social, economic, political and constitutional conditions had not predisposed society to openness to their ideas. Similarly, while recognising the importance of matters of faith for those who lived through the Reformation, individual responses were bound to take into account prevailing conditions in each locality, as well as perceived personal interests. It was often difficult to avoid taking sides, but those who had to make personal religious decisions in situations of great future uncertainty in many cases took considerable chances, risking imprisonment, expulsion from their homes and even death.

To put reactions to Luther and to the other reformers into focus, it is worth pondering to what extent the religious future of the German kingdom and the Empire could be foreseen around 1521. It was just at the highest level, such as that of the Elector Frederick of Saxony (who had to consider not only his own position, but the interests of his subjects and dynasty) that any attempt was made to peer, however hesitantly, into the future. The elector simply hedged his bets. It was a time, before a further hardening of the battle-lines and the establishment of mutually hostile denominations or confessions, which is best described as a period of the formation of different religious parties (*Religionsparteien*) not yet necessarily divided by clear denominational barriers. Gradually at least two sides were liable to develop, the Catholic and the Evangelical, with the latter possibly in several versions, though repeated attempts were made to arrive at an agreed non-Catholic position.

The Catholic Church still thought fundamentally in terms of the traditional policy of crushing dissent and did not fully realise the threat the 'Evangelicals' posed to the Church at least in some parts of Western Christendom, like the German kingdom. However, the Dutch pope Hadrian VI, who succeeded succeed Leo X in 1522, coupled his demand for the execution of the Edict of Worms with an admission of grave abuses in the Church, particularly at the curia, and a promise of thorough reform. Luther and those who supported him, like Zwingli, were determined to carry on what they regarded as a fight in a righteous cause, in good heart, but without any assurance of survival and with the acceptance of martyrdom if necessary. All the parties to the dispute thought in terms of preserving Christian unity in some form or other, perhaps on the basis of reforms on which all could agree. Who would have foretold around 1521 the founding of non-Catholic Churches that could not be put down, and the creation of an interconfessional checkmate in the German kingdom and the Empire? At that time even the eventual relative strengths of the leading groups could hardly be guessed or predicted. When the Diet of Worms met in 1521, Roman Catholicism in the Germanic region looked stronger and the opposition weaker than proved to be the case in the end. Many of the early 'Evangelicals' showed great courage in holding convictions with quite an uncertain future.

The greatest Roman Catholic asset in kingdom and Empire appeared to be Emperor Charles V, a convinced Catholic, even at times of the greatest tension with the papacy. The head of the house of Habsburg had normally collaborated with church and papacy, to a greater extent than many kings of France, or earlier the Staufen rulers, though not without looking after his own dynastic interests. There was certainly no political incentive for Charles to abandon the Old Church and to join the evangelical movement.

Charles inherited the Habsburg territories in Austria from his paternal grandfather, Emperor Maximilian, the Low Countries and part of Burgundy from his paternal grandmother Maria, Spain and its overseas empire, as well as the kingdom of Naples, from his mother and maternal grandfather. With some exceptions, Charles' territories were staunchly Catholic. He would have undermined his position as head of the Holy Roman Empire if he had wavered in his Catholic faith. But 'the role of the Christian emperor was in itself contradictory. Politics and religion could not simply be reduced to a common denominator,'[98] as Charles was to find out during his struggle with Luther.

Only a ruler with considerable territorial power, with his own *Hausmacht*, could afford to become emperor, but as in earlier history this posed problems of preoccupation with dynastic interests and possible conflicts of interest. Actually the extent of Charles V's possessions was greater than that of any previous emperor, even than those of Frederick II with his kingdom of Sicily, not to mention the crown of Jerusalem. So there is the curious paradox that Charles, the most powerful ruler in Christendom by far, because of the extent of his dominions, in which he resided in turn, could not usually concentrate on a problem, such as the threat from the Turks, long enough to make an impact on it. This certainly also applies to Germany. Furthermore, the multiplicity of his interests influenced his policy in each of his various territories. Sometimes the policy which was required for one region, such as working with the papacy to find a solution for the religious problems in Germany, ran into difficulty in another region, namely Italy, where a perceived clash of interests brought Charles into conflict with the papacy. For an emperor to carry the Estates of the German kingdom with him was difficult enough anyway, without the additional aggravation caused by the religious problem. Even Roman Catholic rulers were reluctant to strengthen the emperor's power when their religious cause might benefit from it.

Luther secretly paid a short visit to Wittenberg in December 1521. An important consequence of this temporary sojourn there was the encouragement he received from his friends to embark on a translation of the New Testament into German.[99] After his return to the Wartburg he was able to complete the task in the incredibly short time of eleven weeks.[100] He extended the translation to the Old Testament in 1523. Luther was not the first to translate the Bible into German,[101] and contrary to later Protestant legend, he did not 'create' the modern written German language of High German (*Hochdeutsch*).[102] While to some extent fitting his translation into his theology,[103] he displayed a deep spirituality in his Biblical interpretation, which was reflected in the stylistic, at times poetic, beauty of his text. This powerful combination, together with the wide circulation given to his work by the printing press, ensured that his Saxon linguistic version established a commanding lead in the Germanic region and the later Germany. Its impact was especially strong in the areas that were to become Protestant; indeed, 'Jacob Grimm was moved to remark that modern standard German was a "Protestant dialect".'[104]

Politically, for the ability of Germans to rise above their local dialects and to communicate with each other in a common language, and indeed for the long-term future of Germany, Luther's Bible translation was of considerable importance. Again, he did not start the movement, as a 'conscious effort to create a unified language' had already begun earlier during the reigns of Emperor Maximilian I and of Elector Frederick the Wise of Saxony.[105] We must not overstate the political implications of the establishment of a common written language in the sense of a modern national consciousness. The frontiers of the territory in which the writ of the German language ran were still vague. Speaking or writing German does not yet denote a feeling of belonging to a 'Germany', whose area still had to be defined in 1848,[106] and during the moves towards national unification.

However important the eventual political repercussions of the Bible translation were, Luther undertook this task first and foremost from a religious point of view. When he arrived at the Wartburg he had two books with him, the Hebrew Bible and the Greek New Testament, which had been rescued during the ambush from among the things in the wagon in which he had been travelling.[107] The Bible had made him what he was: 'By translating the Scriptures he would...be giving his people access to the source from which he was himself drawing....'[108] Thus, he hoped that by allowing everybody to consult the text of the Bible and to judge for himself, he would be taking a substantial step forward to a ministry of all believers; however, problems concerning this approach soon began, which eventually led to a modification of positions. Though Luther was committed to replacing the current official version of the New Testament, the Latin *Vulgata*, as it contained some inaccurate passages, he did not discard it altogether. Luther's deviations from the *Vulgata* were of great significance, as some key parts of Catholic doctrine were based on the earlier text. Thus, as Erasmus showed, the Vulgate translation of the text on marriage in Ephesians 5:31–2 wrongly rendered the Greek term *musterion* as *sacrament*, instead of as *mystery*. The correction was of considerable importance. For the Vulgate translation, by providing a proof text for including marriage in the list of sacraments, had helped to buttress the sacramental system of the Church, 'one of the most important aspects of medieval theology'. The medieval Church had added five more to the original two sacraments, baptism and the Lord's Supper. Similarly, the Vulgate had mistranslated the opening words in Jesus' exhortation in Matthew 4:17 as *Do Penance*, instead of as *Repent*, before correctly going on to: 'for the Kingdom of heaven is at hand'. Here again the Vulgate rendering had supported the sacramental system, in this case the sacrament of penance, another addition to the original two.[109] Luther was very much helped by Erasmus' Latin translation of the Greek New Testament and his annotations. Modern scholarship has progressed beyond Luther's translation, a work which is all the more remarkable in view of the not exactly ideal conditions for his work at the Wartburg.

Luther – even apart from Zwingli – no longer had the reformation field to himself. This is not surprising and was inherent in the ministry of all believers, even if in the long run this principle could not be fully applied. The formation of different religious groups outside the Old Church was also inevitable from the *sola scriptura* principle, once it became clear that this did not provide the basis for a united front against Catholicism, but was in itself divisive, as interpretation of biblical texts lay in the eyes of the beholder.

Luther's absence from Wittenberg allowed another professor, Karlstadt, to take over the lead there. Karlstadt had earlier been more conservative than Luther, and had in fact adhered to a Catholic position longer. For a time from 1517 onwards he collaborated with Luther and debated Eck with him at Leipzig in 1519.[110] However, he 'could not speak with the fluency and originality of Luther, whose theological development during the last five years had been at a dimension of depth beyond that of Karlstadt'.[111] Eck certainly got the better of Karlstadt. In the aftermath of the Leipzig debate, relations between Karlstadt and Luther became strained and differences between them developed. Like Thomas Müntzer, another radical theologian, Karlstadt for a long time suffered in his historical reputation from being in the shadow of Luther. But this should not blind us to the importance of his work, which anticipated much of later Puritanism, such as 'in the "inward religion" to which Karlstadt's mystical theology corresponded'.[112] There is also in Karlstadt the emphasis on the authority of the congregation and the influence of the laity, elements on which Oliver Cromwell's Independents and the congregational movement arising from it drew.[113] Karlstadt showed courage by participating publicly in the debate, for Eck did not forget his opponent in Leipzig and managed to get his teaching condemned.

In spite of all their differences, Luther and Karlstadt shared many religious views, but they disagreed on the pace of reform, on the methods of bringing it about and on the account to be taken of the views of Elector Frederick. Luther was certainly not subservient to any ruler, but he could see very clearly in what a precarious situation the elector found himself and did not want to increase his difficulties. Indeed, he was prepared to leave the comparative refuge of Electoral Saxony if he could ease Frederick's position. Moreover, he was in sympathy with the elector's cautious policy in matters of religion. He saw that the imposition of radical changes by the authorities would only lead to severe problems of conscience for many people. Luther always had a strong compassion for those who were not particularly well informed on religious matters and were wedded to traditional forms.

Karlstadt for a time took a moderate line and even restrained Melanch-thon, who found it hard to deal with a severe crisis during Luther's absence. But in the end he came down in favour of a policy of enforcing reform. Although the elector forbade any changes, Karlstadt went ahead and on Christmas Day 1521 gave the Eucharist to the faithful in two kinds in the Castle church and made a number of other alterations. Soon after, mobs created disturbances in all the churches in Wittenberg.

A few days later emissaries arrived from another – actually economically quite important – city in the electorate, from Zwickau, where an even more radical direction of 'Evangelicals', going well beyond Karlstadt, had taken over. The movement in Zwickau was led by Thomas Müntzer, who was to play such a dramatic part in the events of the mid-1520s. He was born around 1491 in the Harz mountains of Saxony, and like Karlstadt became a secular priest. He was extremely well read and had a good knowledge of Latin and particularly of Hebrew.[114] Müntzer had actually been recom-mended by Luther for the ministry in Zwickau, which he took up in 1520. He did not last long there because he wanted to force the pace of reform beyond the point acceptable to general opinion, so that he was expelled the following year by the Zwickau city council. But, again like Karlstadt, his contribution to religious development is quite considerable. Müntzer stood more in the mystical and spiritualist tradition than Luther.[115] He had a strong sympathy for the suffering of the common man.

Some leading figures of Müntzer's Zwickau circle tried to spread their mystical ideas in Wittenberg, which contributed to the confusion and dis-order there. Melanchthon, who up to a point had worked with Karlstadt, now felt that the only hope for a stabilisation of the situation lay in inviting Luther to return in order to calm the waters. In spite of the opposition of the elector, Luther left the Wartburg in March 1522 and resumed his residence in Wittenberg.[116] With great humanity and charity, and considerable tact for example towards Karlstadt, Luther emphasised in his sermons that the differences between various reformers had to be interpreted with love. He warned against treating dogmatically questions that did not concern the theological core, such as whether communion should be given in one or two kinds, and pleaded that people should have some choice in these matters.[117] He was not impressed by some of the Zwickau 'prophets', whom he dismissed as *Schwärmer*, a difficult term to translate; perhaps 'dreamer' comes closest to it, with a dose of fanaticism added to it. In any case, Luther was able to restore some order.

Stability was not so easily achieved elsewhere in Germany. Quite under-standably, calling into question the existing religious order had widespread repercussions and thus affected society in general; religious faith was central to the way of life of the population. The critics of the Church benefited from challenging the ecclesiastical authorities at a time of considerable change, including an extension of capitalist practices. There was the development of a whole new set of values which examined, for example, the concept of the mendicant orders from an economic point of view. The reformers were influenced by this atmosphere of change, they had access to printed copies of manuscripts which had earlier not been readily available. In turn they took advantage of the printing press to spread their ideas. There was thus a constant interaction between men, with their ideas, and the conditions and facilities of their existence. Unlike a century earlier with Jan Hus, Luther's activity was carried out in a sensitive part of Germany rather than in the more peripheral – though by no means unimportant – Bohemian region. If Luther had been trying to create a popular and indeed populist movement, which was not in the forefront of his intentions, he could not have been more successful than he actually was with his writings, for they seemed to offer something to everybody. Naturally, now that a choice in religion had been established, if somewhat precariously, people were beginning to ask themselves, which teaching – that of certain reformers, like Luther or Zwingli, or that of the Old Church – would suit them best, not only in the purely religious terms of personal faith, but also in the effect their choice would have on their position. The latter does not mean that they were in any sense insincere or that they were using religion for their own interests, for it was not easy to separate out the one from the other. This forms the background of the revolt of the imperial knights (*Reichsritter*).

The imperial knights, who in the old feudal order held their fiefs 'immediately' of the emperor, had gradually seen their relative position in the hierarchy deteriorating. The introduction of artillery and infantry had largely rendered their cavalry obsolete. They saw their power whittled away through the rise of the territorial state, whose endeavours to put them under their authority they tried to resist. Their particular aversion was directed towards the prince-bishops, although, and perhaps rather, because their positions were mainly filled from their own ranks. The influence, prestige and high status of the prince-bishops in society was resented by those who had to continue to grapple with the problems of their position by staying put in their castles. Here they faced increasing financial difficulties which could no longer so easily be remedied, as in the days of old, by sallying forth from them and robbing passing transports of merchants. Their feuding (*Fehden*) had been outlawed by imperial legislation, recently confirmed at the Nuremberg Diet in 1521. The imperial knights were among Luther's early secular supporters; initially his backing had come mainly from within the monastic orders and the secular clergy.[118]

The revolt was led by two *Reichsritter*, Franz von Sickingen and Ulrich von Hutten. Sickingen was the leader and organiser of a troop of mercenaries, a *condottiere*, who had at one time been in the service of Charles V; actually at the beginning of his reign the emperor was regarded with hope by many critics of the existing state of affairs, both secular and ecclesiastical. As early as 1520, Sickingen had offered Luther the protection of the Main–Franco-nian and Middle-Rhenish knighthood. He was supported by Hutten, the gifted humanist poet, who was in the forefront of the anticlerical movement and who had earlier stood up for Reuchlin in his dispute with the Domin-icans of Cologne. In view of papal threats against him, Hutten sought refuge in Sickingen's castle, Ebernburg (not far from Mainz), where he was joined by the Dominican monk Martin Bucer, whom Sickingen put in charge of one of the parishes of which he was patron.[119] Sickingen at once introduced some reformatory concepts on his territories and in 1521, well ahead of Wittenberg, abolished the daily mass. As the knights regarded themselves as a *Genossenschaft*, a kind of fellowship or corporation, what appealed to them particularly in Luther's teaching was his apparent emphasis on con-gregation and community; they regarded these concepts as bulwarks against the increasing encroachment of the territorial state on their liberties. In August 1522, under Sickingen's leadership, 600 knights from the Upper Rhine formed a fraternal association (*brüderliche Vereinigung*), in which they agreed to settle their differences peacefully in the spirit of concord of Christian brotherhood (*christbrüderliche Eintracht*); they vowed to discon-tinue wild drinking toasts and swearing. This religio-political programme foreshadows something of the covenant theology later to figure prominently in Calvinism.[120]

The military operations undertaken by the knights in 1522 and 1523, particularly against prelates, constituted a serious crisis for the German kingdom, and therefore encountered stiff resistance. In the end the operation failed. The association of imperial knights was incomplete without the sup-port of the king; Charles V and his brother Ferdinand, his deputy in Ger-many, saw no reason for joining them against the princes and bishops. The widespread support from the knighthood on which Sickingen counted did not materialise, because in many regions it was a sufficient deterrent for the princes simply to threaten the knights with the loss of their fiefs if they rebelled. The armies of the Swabian *Bund*, an association of cities and princes, made short shrift of the revolt in the south of Germany. Sickingen engaged in a formal feud with the Archbishop of Trier, but after some initial military successes was himself besieged in his hill fortress Landstuhl, which – previously regarded as impregnable – succumbed to the guns of the artillery. He himself died from injuries inflicted by collapsing walls. Hutten fled to Switzerland, in vain sought support from his fellow humanist Erasmus, and was then given refuge by Zwingli near Zurich, but died soon after. Bucer, who was no longer in Sickingen's service and had in the meantime married, was excommunicated and fled to Strassburg,[121] where he found his life's work.

Without in any way wishing to accuse the imperial knights of hypocrisy, there was a fatal discrepancy between the relevance of their religious declarations on the one hand and the reality of their actions on the other. When all is said and done, they fought for what they perceived were the interests of their order, whose constructive importance for the future they overrated. Instead of improving they worsened their position even more, for the princes, bishops and cities were determined to prevent any further threats from the unruly order and razed many of their castles and palaces to the ground. The knights did have some support from figures that were to play an important part in the Reformation, such as Bucer. But if they believed that Luther's teaching provided a brief for their actions, they committed a tragic misunderstanding. In fact Luther 'saw Sickingen's death as divine judgment'.[122]

After the rising of the imperial knights, which created havoc in several regions of Germany, there was even worse to come, in the shape of what has gone down in history as the Peasants' War (*Bauernkrieg*). Even more than the earlier revolt, the Peasants' War assumed such major proportions because of its reaction to, and its interpretation of, reformatory ideas. While considerable research, much on the local level, has been done on the war in recent years, and while there is a measure of agreement on the social and economic causes which contributed to its outbreak, we are still far from a definitive view. It may well be that an agrarian crisis towards the end of the fourteenth century paved the way for a crisis of feudalism in the sixteenth.[123] There can be no doubt about the existence of genuine grievances, many of which had to do with serfdom (*Leibeigenschaft*).

> Although an industrious peasant in 1400 could still count on accumulating a modest estate to pass on to his children, during the fifteenth century such family estates were very likely destroyed by death taxes. When [noble and ecclesiastical] lords demanded a third or half of a serf's estate, they did not exempt whatever land a peasant might own outright, an abuse that serfs found especially grievous...[124]

While the owners of serfs (*Leibherren*) had relaxed their control in many ways around 1450, the prohibition of free movement (*Freizügigkeit*) remained, and indeed became part of the deliberate policy of the territorial state. The serfs remained tied to a soil (*an die Scholle gebunden*) which had to provide an economic existence for an increasing population, while the agriculturally valuable area could not be augmented.[125] Often monasteries had been particularly culpable of bad treatment of their peasants, in many cases demonstrating 'the incompatibility of spiritual claims and secular striving for power'.[126] Not surprisingly, the peasants' movement shared the anticlericalism of the imperial knights' revolt.[127]

Though economic hardship and genuine suffering explain the participation of large numbers of peasants in the revolt, not all those who fought were necessarily the economically downtrodden. Many of the better-to-do and

more influential men in the villages – the 'village patriciate'[128] – became
engaged, because they wished to restore local self-government which had
been whittled down. Furthermore, not only peasants but miners took part, as
did some townsmen, so that the war has also been called the revolt of 'the
common man',[129] though not without finding contradiction.[130] Even when
the material and political grievances are given full weight, it is the addition of
the religious factor which gives the revolt its scope and intensity. This
emerges from the programme of the Upper Swabian peasants, the 12
Articles formulated with the help of an 'evangelical' priest and a lay theologian[131] in February and March 1525. They 'were a list of grievances, a reform
program, and a political manifesto all in one'.[132]

In the preamble, the peasants defended themselves against the accusation
that the rising was caused by 'evangelical' teaching.[133] They argued that the
reverse was true, that because society had not followed the gospel, the
liberation of the peasants from their slavery was God's will. Recurring
to the theme in the twelfth and last article, the peasants demanded the
harmonisation of the secular order with God's work. If it could be demonstrated by the Bible that any of the 12 articles were unjustified, they would be
dropped;[134] this was similar to Luther's statement about his beliefs at the
Worms Diet. So far the peasants had taken their stand on custom and legal
rights, which varied from one locality to another. Now they demanded
radical changes by laying down a new principle to which everything had to
conform. They denied the validity of existing rights of feudal lords, of land-
lords and of owners of serfs unless they conformed to God's law, of which
the peasants – basing themselves on current 'evangelical' teaching of the
ministry of all believers – regarded themselves as interpreters. In this way
they attempted to take the initiative, trying to put the onus on the lords to
demonstrate that their rights were in accordance with the Bible. This
approach by the peasants constituted a revolutionary act and allowed them
to go beyond localised peasant revolts, which had broken out sporadically
right into this period and which could be fairly easily crushed. On the basis
of their new approach, they succeeded in forming a movement covering a
large part of Germany, if never the whole of it. The peasants had a strong
moral case and it is to be regretted that the Church and the secular authorities did not listen more carefully to the fundamental case they put forward;
one of the few who did was the dying Elector Frederick.[135] But from a
practical point of view it was highly unlikely that those in possession would
simply yield rights which they believed they had legally acquired, because the
peasants made demands backed by the threat of force; many lords, and also
monasteries, would have been ruined.[136] So the inevitable happened:
princes, bishops and cities, incidentally Catholics and 'evangelicals' alike,
prepared for civil war, which played into the hands of peasant radicals and
eventually of Thomas Müntzer. The peasants committed acts of murder and

plunder, and the authorities retaliated with great severity, even brutality. Owing to the extent of the risings, 'from Alsace to the Tirol, and from the Black Forest into Franconia, Hesse and Thuringia'[137] Germany was in a deep state of crisis in 1525.

These events would have taken place, even 'had there been no Thomas Müntzer and had he never said or written a word'.[138] However, though he was not the only advocate among the peasants of a fight to the finish, the religious fervour with which he roused the rebels undoubtedly played an important part in stiffening their determination to stake all on the outcome of battle. Following Zwingli, rather than Luther, he insisted on applying the gospel to the here and now. He went even further than Zwingli in his radical application of the Bible – as he perceived it – to the whole social order. To Müntzer the end justified the means. Murder and destruction, in which he participated, were praiseworthy when directed against the Godless, whom he determined. In fact, he sent thousands to their doom and then fled himself, hiding – in vain – from the victors. He, who believed he was some kind of a prophet, had totally lost touch with reality. If he really wished to promote the welfare of the peasantry and of the other groups which participated in the rising, he brought about the reverse. The authorities gave no quarter. The number of those slain and executed is estimated as probably in excess of fifty thousand.[139] Müntzer himself was subjected to extreme torture, during which he betrayed his co-conspirators, and eventually executed. It is difficult for us to divine his mind during the hostilities, as it may have been also at the time for the peasants who fought with him. Müntzer may have thought of the peasants not so much in terms of their social problems, but as instruments of his apocalyptic expectations, as a stage towards the establishment of the Kingdom of the Just.[140] By the time of the Peasants' War, Müntzer had moved well away from Luther, who had inspired him at one time.

The conflict constituted the moment of truth not only for Müntzer, who sacrificed limb and life, but also for Luther. Though Zwingli's ideas – whether interpreted correctly or not – probably played a greater part in bringing about these events than Luther's, the Wittenberg reformer did not emerge entirely unscathed from the crisis. Through publicising complex theological arguments in the vernacular by means of the printing press, Luther risked being misunderstood by at least the less well-educated part of the lay public. At the same time these laymen may have been encouraged by Luther's initial propagation of the ministry of all believers to feel, for example, that the 12 Articles were based on a correct Biblical interpretation, and that they were justified in the use of force to realise them. Luther's at times quite extreme language, and a certain lack of clarity as to whether his arguments related to the current situation or the world to come, may have also led to misunderstanding. Before the beginning of the revolt Luther attempted to mediate by asking the rulers to grant just demands and by warning the peasants against precipitating a civil war. However, when uprisings did take place, Luther in May 1525 published his tract 'Against the Robbing and Murdering Horde of the Peasants', in which 'he urged the princes to fierce retaliation as a Christian act of mercy.'[141] The treatise is certainly an unfortunate episode in his life. But it should be remembered that Luther at great personal risk to himself preached in the area affected by the rising, and that he wrote his piece to rally the rulers at a time when a victory by the peasants appeared quite possible. But it 'read very differently a week later when, after the complete peasant collapse, it was published during the blood-bath of the Junkers'.[142]

In June 1525 Luther married the former nun Katharina von Bora.[143] Soon after the wedding he replied to critics of his attitude during the conflict in his 'Open Letter about the Harsh Booklet against the Peasants', in which he explained the theological background of his intervention with his famous doctrine of the two kingdoms (*zwei Reiche*):

> There are two kingdoms: one is God's kingdom, the other is the kingdom of the world . . . God's kingdom is a kingdom of grace and mercy, and not a kingdom of wrath and punishment, for in it there is sheer forgiving, caring, loving, serving, doing good, possessing peace and joy . . . But the worldly kingdom is a kingdom of wrath and severity, for in it there is sheer punishing, restraining, judging, and condemning, to crush the evil and protect the upright. For this reason it both possesses and wields the sword, and in Scripture a prince or lord is called God's wrath or God's rod . . . [144]

Elsewhere he warned against trying to govern the world according to the Gospel and eliminating the restraining secular power on the grounds that the Gospel prohibited the use of the sword among Christians; chaos would follow once these chains had been removed.[145] Luther's statement is eminently sensible. This applies particularly to a time when even comparatively moderate *Reformatoren*, like the Christian humanist Bucer, used civic authority to force the pace of religious reform, at times at the cost of causing deep divisions. Thus *Reformatoren* like Bucer also needed allies to put their ideas into practice, in their case not the princes, but the cities, which made them dependent on the burghers, who also had their own social and economic interests to consider. These were certainly not going to support the peasants in their use of force to realise their aims, even if many of them were just. *Reformatoren* did not always consider sufficiently the high expectations they aroused by extreme statements. Thus men like Bucer have been accused of 'sowing, what they did not want to harvest'.[146]

Luther remained uneasy about his intervention in the Peasants' War, being aware of his guilt, which was aggravated by his feeling that he sacrificed the salvation of the peasants' souls. He acted as he did for religious reasons: '...I, too, have killed Müntzer....I did it, because he himself wanted to kill my Christ.'[147] What he did was due neither to a surrender to the princes, about whom he made many scathing remarks, nor to a political quietism.[148]

The losses the peasants and their allies suffered and the bitterness caused by them remained. Interestingly enough, not only was something done after the war to examine the peasants' grievances and to see how those which were justified could be remedied, but the starting point was the 12 Articles. If the recommendations of a committee set up by the Diet of Speyer in 1526 had been carried out by the territorial rulers, they would have gone some way to lessen the burdens of the peasants and to strengthen their legal position. Above all, the committee actually succeeded in having more disputes settled by the courts, though at the same time resort by the peasants to force continued and became more frequent in the seventeenth and eighteenth centuries.[149]

The peasants were not only concerned with their economic and social position, but with religious questions, one of their demands being that congregations should elect their own ministers.[150] Some historians have regretted that the communal reformation (*Gemeindereformation*) was one of the casualties of the defeat of the peasants, and that as a consequence the reformation was now taken over by the princes.[151] The question is to what extent a scheme which allowed each congregation to make its own decision among a variety of choices ever had a chance in the situation of the time. Not only was there an increasing gulf between the old religion and the various kinds of reformers, but the latter also quarrelled among themselves. Mutual vituperation not only between reformers and Catholics, but among reformers, increased. Even a comparatively moderate 'evangelical' like Martin Bucer, in the belief that the end of time had come, felt that reforms had to be carried out at once, whatever the feelings of members of congregations, possibly even majorities. Not only radicals like Müntzer and Karlstadt, but even Bucer split congregations and brought about strife and civil disorder through extreme statements.[152] It was especially Luther who was concerned with the feelings of people and how they would react to religious change, particularly if enforced from above, and who therefore often advocated great caution in carrying out reforms.[153] The eventual confessional division of Germany was bad enough, but the struggle for the domination of congregations would have led to even more instability. The secular authorities were the only ones capable of bringing some order into the religious movement, naturally at a price. Regulation by prince or city replaced the ministry of all believers. This was certainly not what Luther intended, and it was ironical that his theological work should have led to matters of faith being determined to some extent by secular princes without theological qualifications, something he had resisted earlier with Frederick the Wise. After the mid-

1520s, Luther too came round to the view that the secular authorities had to act to fill the void left in some territories by the removal of the authority of the Old Church. Also, only princes above all, and to a lesser extent cities, could protect the nascent reformation.

For a long time, the critics of the Church seemed to have it all their own way. But gradually, even before the resurgence of the Catholic Church, cracks began to appear in the ranks of the opposition. This can perhaps be seen most clearly in the relationship of humanism to the Reformation. Both terms were given to these movements by posterity.[154] In the late Middle Ages and into early modern times *reformatio* in the religious context meant reform of the Church, but within its framework. It was only at the end of the seventeenth century that *reformatio* was used to designate a historical period as we now know it.[155] For the historian of the sixteenth century there is some advantage in at any rate attempting to distinguish 'reformers' (who had no desire to leave the Church) from *Reformatoren*, who were determined to put their ideas into practice even if it meant parting with the Church. Though this division as it appears in the historian's hindsight does not always do justice to the complexities of the situation for contemporaries, increasingly, as the 1520s unfolded, men had to make a choice for or against the Old Church, and for or against Luther and the other *Reformatoren*.

This posed a particularly grave difficulty for Erasmus of Rotterdam, who has been fairly generally accepted by historians as the leading figure among the humanists at the time of Luther. Like the term 'Reformation', that of 'humanism' was devised long after the event, indeed even later. 'The German word *Humanismus* was first coined in 1808, to refer to a form of education which placed emphasis on the Greek and Latin classics.'[156] However, the term 'humanist' goes back to the Renaissance period and was certainly current by the sixteenth century, in the use of the expression *Humanista*, signifying a teacher or student of the humanities or *studia humanitatis*. These scholarly disciplines consisted of grammar, rhetoric, history, poetry and moral philosophy, and included the study of Latin and to some extent of Greek writers from antiquity on these subjects. 'Thus Renaissance humanism was not as such a philosophical tendency or system, but rather a cultural and educational program...'[157] Rhetoric played a key part in humanism through its emphasis on writing and speaking well, for which the writers of antiquity served as a model. Most humanists 'were active either as teachers of the humanities in secondary schools or universities, or as secretaries to princes or cities...'.[158] They put 'emphasis on man, on his dignity and privileged place in the universe...'and on 'the concrete uniqueness of one's feelings'.[159] Humanism made a great contribution to modern historiography by applying critical, including philological, criticism to the sources. In the quest *ad fontes* the achievement of Erasmus

in relation to establishing an authentic text for the Bible is of great importance, particularly in our context.

The scholars and poets of the humanist circle in many countries, who –
with all their considerable regional differences – conducted written correspondence with each other, were not unique in their age in adopting a critical
approach to aspects of their age, including conditions in the Church. But
while there was a rivalry with scholasticism, there is not yet a consensus as to
how deep their differences went,[160] and how typical for these the controversy between the Dominicans in Cologne and Reuchlin was. The issues that
were to divide Western Christendom at the time of the Reformation were
not the ones that were at the heart of humanist thinking in the previous
period.[161] Thus it is not surprising that leading humanists were to be found
on opposite sides after 1517, with Ulrich von Hutten supporting the opposition to Rome, and Reuchlin, the victim of clerical persecution, remaining
faithful to the Old Church; he, in fact, disapproved of the reformatory
activity of his great-nephew Melanchthon.

While there is not yet any agreement as to the extent that humanism in
general, and Erasmus in particular, influenced Luther, it is clear that for a
time the two men had a certain sympathy with an admixture of coolness
for each other. Some mutual criticism appeared fairly early.[162] Erasmus,
who was born some time in the later 1460s, was already established internationally when Luther was first becoming well known around 1517.
Though he intervened to try and get Luther a fair hearing in 1519,[163] by
that time it had become clear that their approach to the religious problems
of the time was different and in some ways diametrically opposed.
Erasmus wanted to get problems settled as quietly as possible. He therefore
disapproved of Luther's appeal to the public concerning complex theological matters, which he regarded as more suitable for scholarly discourse.
One of his main aims was to avert schism in Western Christendom, and in
such a case he certainly wanted to avoid being caught in the middle. But it
was not easy for a prominent figure like Erasmus, however much he disapproved of what he regarded as an avoidable escalation of the dispute by
both sides, to remain on the sidelines. The Church and some of the princes
pressed him to come out clearly against Luther. Erasmus opposed the
radical individualism of the priesthood of all believers, as his thought 'always
stressed the corporate identity and responsibility of the community of the
Church'.[164]

When Erasmus finally in 1524 published a tract against Luther,[165] he
chose as his theme the question of free will:

This clearly demontrated that Erasmus had identified the centre of the
controversy more clearly than had Luther's other opponents ... It seemed
to Erasmus that Luther's denial of the freedom of the will in matters

related to eternal salvation made it difficult to think of any kind of human responsibility. If people have no personal responsibility, Erasmus thought that there was also little reason to try to educate them.

Also, while Erasmus had many reservations about various aspects of the Church of his day, on this question he took an orthodox view.[166] The following year Luther issued his reply,[167] vehemently rejecting Erasmus' views, which sealed the breach between the two men.

However, the debt of the Reformation to humanism remained and thanks to men like Melanchthon, the ancient languages and biblical exegesis continued to be cultivated in 'evangelical' circles. If anything, Erasmus has – in spite of his attack on Luther – been viewed more critically in Catholic than in Protestant circles. Catholic opinion of him at the time was divided. Some of his critics regarded him more as an intellectual than as a man of faith. He did indeed receive some support in high places, but in 1526 the Sorbonne condemned several of his statements as heretical and his French translater was burned. In 1537, the year after his death, the Spanish Inquisition recommended that some of his writings should be banned from the schools. However, the curia did not initiate judicial proceedings against him.[168]

Many humanists who had originally supported Luther left the reformatory camp.[169] 'Erasmus's tragedy was that his humane middle ground, opposed alike to scholastic obscurities, vulgar superstitions, protestant dogmatics, and popular disorder, was steadily deserted by both sides.'[170] Actually, there is also the view that Erasmus harmed Christianity by evading clear decisions and definite loyalties,[171] and that he was a representative of an enlightened moralism that anticipated the eighteenth century.[172]

Even if the 'evangelical' movement by the mid-and late twenties had lost some of its initial support, it still had the initiative in Germany. Why was the Old Church so slow to rally? If the Catholics in Western Christendom or even in the Empire had been united, the budding 'evangelical' movement could have been crushed. But in fact there were deep divisions among the Catholic powers which allowed the Evangelicals to gain strength. Here once again an old dilemma that was previously experienced in German history reappeared. Only a ruler with strong resources could take on the emperorship in any meaningful sense, yet such a monarch obviously had his own concerns quite apart from the imperial crown and the German kingdom. Charles V not only inherited the old enmity with France from his grandfather Maximilian, but presented an even more serious threat to the French because of the greater extent of his dominions, which appeared to encircle them. For the Habsburgs, possession of Northern Italy was essential, because of its importance in the communications between the Spanish kingdom of Naples on the one hand and their possessions in Austria and the Low Countries on the other. Contrariwise, if Francis I was going to break out of his encirclement, he needed to preserve his hold on Milan and if possible dislodge the Spanish from Southern Italy. In turn, the importance of Italy for the two leading continental European powers was bound to trigger a papal reaction. Initially in this period France appeared to present the greater threat to the traditional territorial interests of the papal states, but that changed, particularly after Charles' victory over Francis at Pavia in 1525. The papacy now took sides against the emperor. The pope's and the emperor's preoccupation with Italian affairs, as well as their clash of interests there, prevented their cooperation against Luther. Matters got even worse when imperial *Landsknechte* completely out of control plundered Rome in 1527 in the *sacco di Roma*.

The bad relationship between the papacy and the emperor also came at an awkward time in view of the Turkish advances into Europe, which allowed them to defeat the King of Hungary in the battle of Mohacs in 1526 and to annex large parts of the kingdom. 1529 saw them at the gates of Vienna, which they besieged unsuccessfully. The Turkish advance and almost continuous war with France prevented Charles from giving his full attention to the carrying out of the Edict of Worms and kept him away from Germany for many years. His deputy in Germany, his brother Ferdinand, who inherited the Hungarian crown through marriage, also could not give the religious question adequate priority. In the circumstances, the Diet of Speyer in 1526 decreed a 'standstill', which in effect – for the time being – left the carrying out of the Worms decrees against Luther and his teaching to the discretion of the territorial rulers. Thus the history of the German reformation movement mirrored the extent to which the emperor was engaged elsewhere, ranging from passivity in times of great external preoccupation to bursts of activity if he had his hands free.[173]

In electoral Saxony it became clear in the aftermath of the Wittenberg disturbances connected with Karlstadt and even more of that of the Peasants' War, that the 'reform' movement was being discredited by the variety and often the radicalism of its manifestations. Even Luther complained in 1526 that 'there is no more fear of God, or any discipline; since the pope's excommunication has been abolished, everyone does as he pleases.'[174] Once the electorate under Frederick's successor John was clearly moving in an 'evangelical' direction, something had to be done to fill the void left by the abrogation of the existing Catholic ecclesiastical hierarchy; but who had the authority to act? The problem was that there was not – unlike later in England, for example with Thomas Cranmer – any bishop available to apply an 'evangelical' policy in the electorate. Luther, who advocated a gradual approach to change, eventually became convinced that something had to happen. A historical parallel that appeared relevant to him was the action taken by Emperor Constantine when the unity of the Church was in danger. In Luther's view it was the ruler who had to deal with a situation that had got out of hand, as a kind of emergency bishop (*Notbischof*).[175] The Elector John was prepared to act. He and other 'evangelical' rulers based their right to deviate from the religious order in the Empire on their own rather dubious interpretation of the 'standstill' resolutions of the Speyer Diet of 1526.[176] Luther helped John to draft instructions for ecclesiastical visitations, which took place from 1527 onwards. The principal task of the visitors, who acted as electoral officials,[177] was to examine preachers 'as to whether they cling to the old "popishness", persist in errors of faith, are fit for office, and lead an acceptable style of life'.[178]

Although it could not be foreseen at the time, these measures were the beginning of a development that was to lead to Protestant rulers in the role of *summus episcopus* (supreme bishop) taking over the organisation of the Church in their territories[179]. To some extent the process of the secular power assuming some previously ecclesiastical functions had begun before the Reformation and was thus nothing entirely new.[180] Moreover, after the Reformation many Catholic rulers took a leaf out of the 'evangelical' book and also further strengthened their grip on the Church. At the very least, even if secularising tendencies were nothing new to Catholic rulers, their hand in their relations with the Holy See and their ability to obtain concessions from Rome were strengthened by the Protestant onslaught on the papacy. But what was to happen in Protestant states went far beyond anything done in Catholic territories, which after all retained the old hierarchy and continued to some extent under papal jurisdiction; also the monastic orders had links and obediences beyond the territories. When the *Landes-kirchentum* had fully matured, the Protestant ruler controlled his subject both in his secular and his ecclesiastical role, directly in the former, indirectly through the consistory (*Konsistorium*) in the latter. In any case, in both religious camps the development of the modern princely territorial state took a decisive step forward.

The conclusion of a peace treaty with France in 1529 allowed Charles to adopt a more rigorous policy towards the reformers at the Speyer Diet that year. Ferdinand as his brother's deputy in Germany presented an imperial message demanding the revocation of the 'standstill' resolutions of 1526, claiming that they had been abused. There was a reference to the recent understanding reached between the emperor and the pope, and to the hope that a General Council of the Church could be called at an early date. All religious innovation was to be stopped and the jurisdiction of bishops to be restored where it had been removed. Ferdinand also indirectly reprimanded Landgrave Philip of Hesse, one of the leaders of the evangelical movement, for a breach of the peace he had earlier committed on the basis of false evidence of a Catholic plot.[181] As there was a Catholic majority in the Diet, a law was passed ending the standstill. But the 'evangelical' minority in the Diet now protested, which gave the anti-Catholic movement, at any rate on the European continent, the name of Protestantism. The protest was made by five princes, led by Philip of Hesse and the Elector of Saxony, as well as by 14 cities, including the imperial cities of Strassburg, Nuremberg, Ulm and Constance; some of the cities signing the protest had previously been aligned with Zwingli and Zurich.[182] The signatories argued that a unanimously passed law, the 'standstill' of 1526, could not be abrogated by a majority, and refused to submit. The princes and cities claimed the right of conscience only for themselves, not for their subjects and citizens. Thus the evangelical movement became closely linked with the rights of the *Reich* Estates. The next step in the process was to grant the prince or other secular authority the right to lay down the religious faith of the inhabitants of a territory. Thus freedom in one respect was liable to involve deprivation of freedom in another. 'If this protest pointed the way to modern, individual freedom of conscience, this happened on the basis of the medieval liberties of the estates', which assured its members legal protection and minority rights.[183] There are parallels here to the revolt of the Netherlands against Spain later in the century.

Landgrave Philip of Hesse, who had introduced the Reformation in his territories and founded the first evangelical university at Marburg, took the leading part among the Protestants at this time. He was very concerned with the divisions among the anti-Catholics and arranged a meeting between Luther and Zwingli at Marburg the same year. No agreement could be reached, above all on the question of the Lord's Supper. For Zwingli the celebration was purely commemorative, whereas Luther adhered to the Real Presence. The two men had different political attitudes; Luther was more traditional in his attitude to the princes, Zwingli in cantonal Switzerland more radical. There was too little common ground between them to agree on a position.

The next diet, at Augsburg in 1530, was attended in person by Charles, who had earlier that year – at Bologna – been crowned emperor by the pope, the last time this was done. Strongly imbued with his important imperial responsibilities for Western Christendom, Charles once more attempted to reconcile the religious differences in Germany in order to restore Christian unity in the country. As Luther was unable to appear at the diet because of the ban, his place was taken by Melanchthon, his closest collaborator. The two friends complemented each other's abilities. In his *Loci communes rerum theologicarum*, his 'theological commonplaces', Melanchthon in 1521 produced the 'first evangelical dogmatic', which he revised in each of the following three decades.[184] Particularly from the second half of the 1520s onwards, he was right in the forefront of the efforts to establish a church organisation for the Wittenberg confession and to explain the faith not only to its followers, but also to those who were close to it. He served on the visitation commission for the Saxon electorate, ran a private school for young students, especially gifted ones, and was active in the reform of schools and universities. He 'won the world of education for the Reformation and was regarded as a scholarly, and above all as a pedagogical authority'.[185] One of his main preoccupations from now on was to endeavour, in the face of tremendous odds, to help to bridge the difference between the various interpretations of the Christian faith, attending nearly all the religious colloquies.

It was in his quest for reconciliation that he wrote and presented to the diet the so-called Augsburg Confession (*Confessio Augustana*), which – though composed for a particular situation – is still valid in the Lutheran Churches to this day.[186] The document summarised a number of agreements that had been concluded between various evangelical groups. On the one hand, the confession tried to assure Catholics that the Lutherans, without giving up any of their theological positions, held orthodox beliefs; therefore controversial topics such as the papacy, the ministry of all believers, and indulgences were omitted. On the other hand, a clear line was drawn against Zwinglians, sectarians and spiritualists.[187] The document was quite emphatic on the central Lutheran beliefs of justification, of its concept of the Church and of its understanding of the preaching office. Its tone reflected not only theological and ecclesiastical, but also diplomatic realities and the balance of power in the Empire.[188] Luther does not always seem to have been quite happy about the comparatively conciliatory tone, but as he was not the representative at Augsburg, he accepted the result. Luther 'praised the Confession with the ambiguous compliment that he could not have trodden so softly'. Since that time, Melanchthon could not shake off the reputation of being prepared to compromise too easily.[189] He did his best in negotiations with Catholic representatives to go as far as he could in making concessions to restore Christian unity, often minimising the matters which separated them. Once more Johannes Eck was mainly concerned with showing up the Lutheran side as heretical. It may well be that the gulf was now too wide to be bridged, but Eck certainly made it more difficult to reconcile differences.[190]

In any case, with the Catholic response of a *confutatio* and Melanchthon's less diplomatic *apologia* (which the emperor refused to accept) the attempt at agreement had failed. On the Protestant side the theologians were actually in general more conciliatory than the secular representatives. Thus the imperial cities objected to a restoration of episcopal authority, which for them was closely connected with the restitution of Church property.[191] It became clear that the dispute was no longer merely religious, for the evangelicals had in the meantime made material changes. These, although resulting from religious convictions, nevertheless stood in the way of reconciliation. Altogether the endeavour to overcomeile differences proved counter-productive, for instead of starting from the points of agreement reached at Augsburg, both sides returned to the polemic of the years from 1517 to 1525.[192] In the final decree of the diet, the Protestants were allowed a period of grace of a few months, but were threatened with armed and legal measures after that, unless they conformed.[193]

In January 1531, Ferdinand was elected King of the Romans. The Elector of Saxony opposed the election. But not only the Protestant princes were now dissatisfied, but also some of the Roman Catholic rulers, especially the Duke of Bavaria. This was due to a fear that Charles was attempting to establish a hereditary Habsburg succession in the Empire. Shared constitutional interests again and again proved stronger than even bitter religious differences. Catholic and Protestant princes were certainly united in their opposition to any strengthening of the emperor's power, particularly if linked to a hereditary succession.

The Protestant response to the decrees of the Diet of Augsburg was the formation of the League of Schmalkalden in February 1531 by Elector John of Saxony, Landgrave Philip of Hesse and Duke Ernest of Brunswick–Lüneburg, ancestor of the House of Hanover, as well as by a number of cities, including Magdeburg and Bremen. Rudimentary efforts were made to set up a rival constitution to the Empire. The main bond uniting the league consisted of a common Protestantism in its Lutheran form. But there was also opposition to the tendency to assert greater imperial authority, and in this there was some collaboration with Catholic Bavaria. The League engaged in diplomatic activity, for example with France and England, and concluded an alliance with Denmark.

In October of this fateful year 1531, an event took place which had a considerable effect on German Protestantism. Zwingli was killed in the lost battle of Kappel as a soldier with the Zurich contingent fighting the Swiss Catholic cantons, in a war he regarded as necessary for the sake of religion.[194] Protestant south German cities now joined the League of Schmalkalden, as they could not longer look for support to Switzerland.

Once more external factors prevented the enforcement of the old religion in Germany. In 1532 in the Nuremberg 'standstill', Charles conceded some protection for the Protestants in return for their help in the war against the Turks.

In 1534, with French subsidies, Landgrave Philip of Hesse restored Duke Ulrich of Württemberg in his duchy and expelled the Austrians who had taken over. Ulrich, whose father had been insane, also had an unbalanced personality. He had quarrelled with his estates, but lost out against them and was forced to make constitutional concessions, which were in fact preserved up to the time of the French Revolutionary and Napoleonic upheavals. In 1515, he killed Hans von Hutten, whom he suspected of being his wife's lover. The poet Ulrich von Hutten made himself advocate of his murdered cousin, presenting the duke as a tyrant. Duke Ulrich aroused the enmity of the nobility as well as of his wife's Bavarian relatives and of the Emperor Maximilian, her uncle. He was put under the ban of the Empire in 1516 and forbidden to rule for six years, but returned in 1519 and was expelled by the Swabian League. After his restoration, Ulrich introduced the Lutheran Reformation in Württemberg.

1534 also saw the outbreak of fresh troubles, this time in the then Lutheran city of Münster in Westphalia, in which Dutch Anabaptists and spiritualists from Cleves became active. The name of Anabaptist (*Wiedertäufer*), which is applied to this religious group, is not quite accurate. The Anabaptists rejected infant baptism and regarded only adult baptism as valid. They therefore baptised adults, irrespective of whether they had been baptised as infants, an act which in any case they did not recognise. An extreme wing of these religious movements was driven by expectations of the apocalypse, which they interpreted as requiring a violent upheaval of the whole social order. Anyway, during their rule in Münster, the self-proclaimed radical prophets convinced a considerable number of the inhabitants that the end of the world was about to come, and that only Münster would be saved. At the same time they started a reign of terror, which led to the destruction of altars and statues, and to mass expulsions and executions. The Bishop of Münster besieged the city, and with both Catholic and Protestant help ended the revolutionary regime. For the city of Münster it meant the end of the Reformation once and for all and the permanent restoration of Catholicism, as well as the abolition of municipal self-government. More generally, great harm was done to the evangelical cause by these excesses. The Anabaptists for a long time had to suffer for the violence of some of their extreme followers.[195] This partly explains, while it does not excuse, why Lutherans and Calvinists persecuted Anabaptists and subjected them to the death penalty. 'The idea that everyone had the right and the ability to interpret Scripture faithfully became the sole possession of the radicals',[196] though by no means of all of them.

Also in 1534, Pope Clement VII (elected in 1523) died after one of the most disastrous pontifical reigns in the history of the Church, not only in relation to Germany and Switzerland, but also to England. While he was not the only party responsible, he has to take the main blame for the failure to respond constructively to Luther and to call a timely general council. Clement did not realise that papal fears of conciliarism were irrelevant in a time of mortal danger for the Church; moreover the Medici pope thought too much in terms of Italian politics. Charles V had a much clearer appreciation of the urgency required to deal with the evangelical movement. He realised that trying to solve the problem within Germany was only a second-best alternative to a Churchwide solution, but better than doing nothing. In the absence of a general solution, he could only improvise from one situation to another. With every further year the division continued, restoring unity became infinitely harder.

The new pontiff, Alessandro Farnese, took the title of Paul III. One of his most lasting achievements was his authorisation of the Society of Jesus in 1540. In many ways Paul III continued some of the undesirable traditions of the Renaissance papacy. The worst feature of the reign was his nepotism, which could vie with that of the Borja pope Alexander VI, who had appointed him a cardinal. He bestowed important fiefs on a grandson and made his son Duke of Parma.[197] Nevertheless, with the honourable exception of Hadrian VI, whose reign was tragically cut short, he was the first pope in this period to realise the urgency of the need for reforms and the necessity of summoning a council in order to attempt a restoration of harmony and unity in the Church; he made an early announcement of his intention to call one.[198] However, for various reasons, the actual meeting of the council did not take place until many years later. To some extent this delay was caused by objections raised by secular powers, particularly France; but at times there was a suspicion – unjustified in the end – that the pope did not really have his heart in the whole project.[199]

Paul reformed the curia, raised the standards of membership in the Sacred College and appointed a commission to prepare for the meeting of the council. The report of the commission *Consilium de emendanda Ecclesia*, which was published, frankly revealed the shortcomings of the Church. These were above all 'the poor selection of bishops, the ordination of insufficiently trained priests, the accumulation and misuse of benefices by the curia, the decadence of the orders, [and] the deterioration of preaching...' More controversially, the use of a work of Erasmus[200] in the schools was condemned because it might teach 'godlessness'. Also Paul restored the Inquisition for Italy and intensified the persecution of Protestants there, forcing the Italian supporters of evangelism into exile. 'A particular variety of Catholic reform was thus to disappear in the long run.'[201] In Italy and elsewhere, 'many innocent, upright men became victims of the Roman Inquisition'.[202] An outline of Catholic policy is thus beginning to emerge, although its adoption was not a foregone conclusion. The necessity of reform is accepted, but there is little hope for a reunion with the Protestants, or even some of the main-line groups, like the Lutherans, although it is not yet finally given up. Unfortunately a policy of strengthening Catholicism in this manner was bound to emphasise and define more clearly for what it stood, by differentiating it from Protestantism, and thus to widen the gulf even further.

The postponement of the meeting of the council allowed Lutheranism in Germany to grow in strength, particularly in the north, both in the cities, such as Lübeck, and in the principalities, such as Mecklenburg. Particularly important recruits were the Brandenburg Electorate and the Duchy of

Saxony under the Albertine line (which had been staunchly Catholic under Duke George) around 1540, and part of the Palatinate territories from about the mid-1540s. Outside the Empire, already in 1525, Albrecht of Hohenzollern, a cousin of the Elector of Brandenburg, as Grand Master (*Hochmeister*) of the Teutonic Order had secularised its remaining territory as the Duchy of Prussia, of which he became duke, and introduced the Reformation. Just as the order had earlier failed to come to terms with the German immigrants into the territory of its state, so Albrecht's *coup d'état* had, if anything, estranged Prussia from the *Reich*. 'In no way can one construct from that the line of tradition from the *Ordensstaat* to the Hohenzollern Monarchy which had been so popular for a long time.'[203] Actually the order fulfilled a role in the German kingdom, for example participating in the Hussite and Turkish wars.[204] It survived within the framework of the Holy Roman Empire until the events of the Napoleonic period.[205]

Soon Lutheranism in Germany was to be confronted with a serious competitor in Calvinism. Jean Calvin was born in a small episcopal town in Picardy, France, in 1509. His father 'held a position of some responsibility in the cathedral chapter', in a dispute with which he was later to be excommunicated. Jean's mother died a few years after his birth; his father remarried and sent his son to live with another family. Although his father initially intended him for the priesthood, and sent him to the University of Paris to study, he later decided that he should become a lawyer; there are certain limited parallels with Luther's early life here. Perhaps not unnaturally, Calvin did not retain warm feelings for his father. In Paris he was very much impressed by Erasmus and the humanist movement.[206] In 1533 he fled from Paris when the authorities objected to the public sermon of a close friend, Rector Cop of the University, which they regarded as 'evangelical'[207]; Calvin had probably collaborated in the preparation. After visiting his birthplace to renounce benefices his father had arranged for him earlier, he left France, a country he loved, to become a permanent exile. He followed Cop to Basle where in 1536 he published the first edition of what was to develop into a textbook of his theology, the *Christianae Religionis Institutio*. In 1536, on his way to Strassburg, he passed through Geneva, where Guillaume Farel, who had introduced the Reformation there, begged him stay and help him with his work. The town council, which controlled the Genevan Church, became dissatisfied with Farel and Calvin over their demand that the power of excommunication be transferred to the ministers, and the two men were unceremoniously expelled in 1538. Calvin then went to Strassburg, where he worked closely with Bucer. It was with Bucer that Calvin participated during 1540 and the following year in the official colloquies (*Religionsgespräche*) at Hagenau, Worms and Regensburg. Charles V hoped that these would lead to a settlement of religious differences, but while there was a measure of agreement, some fundamental differences could not be bridged.[208] Thus Calvin was beginning to become a figure of note in matters of religion.

Originally Calvin was strongly influenced by Luther's ideas and he retained a considerable respect for him even when their paths began to diverge. 'He always preferred Luther to Zwingli.'[209] Calvin developed a theology distinguished in many respects from that of these two earlier reformers. For example, in the matter of the Lord's Supper, it stands somewhere between their teaching, 'stressing the real but not corporeal presence and reception by faith'.[210] Calvinism is often associated principally with the doctrine of predestination. However, it has been pointed out that Calvin himself was uncomfortable with the doctrine and that he emphasised predestination could only be understood in the context of faith. For him it 'promotes zeal and industry to live purely'. This purity of life is something that Church discipline could help to enforce. When Calvin was recalled to Geneva in 1541 by its citizens, who now regretted the treatment they had meted out to him earlier, he developed a religio-political order which strictly controlled the morals and views of citizens. Not surprisingly, this kind of regime led to frequent tension between the town council and the ministers of religion, for instance over the question as to who had the right of excommunication. Calvin was intolerant not only in matters of morals, but of theology. He was responsible for the arrest and prosecution of the Spanish theologian and physician Servetus, who had challenged traditional trinitarian thought, and had only just escaped from imprisonment at the hands of the Inquisition in France. Calvin supported the death penalty, even if he would have preferred a less brutal method of execution than having Servetus burned alive, on which the city council insisted.[211]

In 1549, Calvin achieved the absorption of Zwingliism in Calvinism by concluding the *Consensus Tigurinus* with Zwingli's successor Bullinger in Zurich. This reinforced Calvinism became a major factor in Germany during the second half of the sixteenth century, as part of a movement of greater European dimensions than Lutheranism was ever able to achieve. There is not yet agreement on the question to what extent Protestantism, particularly Calvinism, helped the rise of capitalism.[212]

After the failure of the religious colloquies, and once he had his hands free elsewhere, Charles seriously considered the implementation of an ambitious policy. His maximum programme was 'to break Reformation and princely power at one and the same time, and to put in the place of territorialism and of a multiplicity of confessions the Catholicity of a uniform imperial state'.[213] This was a tall order. Past history had shown that even the one objective of subordinating the princes to a stronger imperial authority had proved impossible to achieve. To combine that with restoring religious unity was even harder. An additional complication was that the princes, particularly Protestant ones, could call on France for help; the kings there, who enforced Catholicism at home with severity, were quite prepared to put pressure on their Habsburg enemies by allying with heretics and 'infidels' (the Turks). Also, though the papacy was willing to give Charles some help in crushing Protestantism in Germany, there was no guarantee that the interests of the two parties would continue to coincide. The long-awaited General Council was finally opened in 1545 at Trent, a small episcopal city on the Italian side of the Alps, but with a strong German colony, and still within the Empire; the location was a compromise between France, emperor and pope.[214] Actually, the offer of military and financial help to Charles was given by the curia partly in the hope that his early victory might provide the opportunity 'to get rid of the unloved council.'[215] Finally, Charles was never unmindful of the dynastic interests of the house of Habsburg. In 1543 the emperor managed to extend his hold on the lower Rhenish region by acquiring some territory also claimed by the rulers of Jülich and Cleves, and forcing them to give up their Erasmian policy of a religious *via media*. His masterful policy was bound to make him enemies.

Charles was determined to break the League of Schmalkalden, over which he had a certain hold owing to the bigamy of one of its leaders, Landgrave Philip of Hesse. In 1540 Philip, who was already married and the father of several children, with the consent of his wife (!) concluded a second marriage (in the German literature often called *Nebenehe*, which is untranslatable, but means something like 'a marriage alongside') with a lady at court. Luther and Melanchthon after some hesitation as confessors approved this second marriage. But the affair could not be kept secret, and when it became known, Luther advised denying all knowledge. Philip was now in danger of the death penalty because of his bigamy. Charles exploited this situation in order to force the landgrave to give up his oppositional policy in return for a promise of indemnity unless a general war against the Protestants took place.[216]

Charles won over both the Catholic Duke William of Bavaria and the Lutheran Duke Maurice of Saxony to his side by promising them the electoral dignities held by the elder branches of their dynasties. In the circumstances the emperor took care to keep the religious aspect in the background. Formally he took action against Philip and the Saxon Elector John Frederick, the two main leaders of the League of Schmalkalden, in execution of the ban of the Empire for their earlier illegal capture of the Catholic Duke Henry of Brunswick–Wolfenbüttel, whom Luther had ridiculed as 'Hans Worst'.

Before the fighting began, Luther died in February 1546, during a journey to his birthplace Eisleben while trying to help the Counts of Mansfeld to settle a conflict over their inheritance. Two questions preoccupied him as his life was coming to an end. One concerned the Jews. When he wrote to his wife that he had had a bout of dizziness, he remarked that she would probably regard the Jews living in Eisleben as being responsible for that. Luther was disappointed that so few Jews accepted Christianity and, as time went on, turned increasingly against them.[217] The other question that still troubled him was that of the papacy, particularly in connection with its influence on the Council of Trent. When he was dying, he complained about the persecution he had suffered at the hands of the papacy.[218] One wonders whether he had come to terms with his separation from the Catholic Church. Melanchthon now took over the leadership of the Lutherans. With that began what was perhaps the most trying part of his life. In some important respects, for example his maintenance of the humanist heritage, Melanchthon differed from Luther. Also in his search for compromise, he was – unlike Luther – prepared to give a limited acceptance to papal authority over the bishops.[219] Both were deeply spiritual. Melanchthon, who through force of circumstances had to act on the political stage, was somewhat more hopeful than Luther about what human beings could achieve. Thus Melanchthon was more interested than Luther in questions of organisation, including that of the Church. When Melanchthon was mentally and physically exhausted after his efforts at the Augsburg Diet of 1530, Luther sent him a message: 'We are meant to be human beings and not God. That is the sum total.'[220] The two men had so great a respect for each other that disagreements did not affect their relations and in some ways enhanced them. Together they had weathered many storms, which the younger man now had to face by himself. In any case, succeeding Luther was a difficult act to follow, and Melanchthon did not have his authority. From now on, he had to endure many bitter personal attacks from those who disagreed with him and regarded him as too soft (which was something that could not normally be said of Luther). 'As he was often a party in the theological disputes which now began, he could not rise above the parties and mediate.'[221]

In his time, Luther, with all his faults, and indeed probably partly because of them, was a figure that dominated the scene. He had immense courage, coupled with great intelligence, industriousness, compassion, warmth and humility. At the same time he could be quite unpleasant and crude, but he never pretended to anything he did not feel. The changes that came about in this period were set off, or given the chance to develop, as part of a chain of events he started, although he did not realise what the result of his actions might be, and certainly did not intend many of the consequences that followed. That this deeply religious man, who wanted to reform the Catholic Church, should have been partly responsible for the division of Western Christianity, shows how important a figure he was in historical terms; but at the same time it is in some ways a story of failure, and a tragic one.[222]

Owing to the inability of the League to agree to a joint strategy in the Schmalkaldic war, valuable time was lost and Charles was able to defeat and capture John Frederick at Mühlberg on the Elbe in April 1547.[223] The elector could only save his life by a complete political surrender, but did not compromise on his religious faith. John Frederick and Philip were kept in captivity in the Netherlands. Maurice as head of the younger Albertine line of the House of Wettin received the electoral dignity and the bulk of Saxon territory from the elder Ernestine line, which only kept the Thuringian principalities, such as Coburg. In spite of the emperor's promises, Bavaria did not receive the electorate, which remained with the elder Palatine branch of the Wittelsbach dynasty. Bavarian disappointment did not augur well for Charles' future plans.

The emperor was at the height of his power, but now the pope crossed his policy by allowing the council to deal with central dogmatic questions, which prevented Protestant participation and thus undermined Charles' concept for approaching the religious problem; he also moved the council out of the Empire into the Patrimony of St Peter at Bologna. Charles therefore from a position of strength attempted to impose his own solution, 'essentially a moderate Catholic reformation',[224] on the *Reich* in the so-called *Interim* of 1548 at the Diet of Augsburg. The *Interim*, which – because the Catholics objected to some features – applied to the Protestants only, required the reintroduction of the rites of the Old Church in all their territories, only temporarily conceding communion in two kinds and priestly marriage.

The *Interim* marked a severe setback for Lutheranism and was strongly resisted in the north German Hanseatic cities. During the ensuing siege of Magdeburg, a Lutheran doctrine of resistance was formulated, on which that of the Calvinists was modelled. The *Interim* was carried out in the upper German cities and in Württemberg. About 40 imperial cities complied, in order to escape the fate of Constance, which after a siege lost its status as a Free City, was recatholicised and incorporated into Habsburg territory; the Protestant inhabitants had to leave. Bucer preached firmness and if necessary martyrdom to the citizens of Strassburg, but was overruled. He opposed a compromise the city concluded with the bishop, which allowed the Protestants to continue holding their services in the majority of parish churches. Something like this pattern was a model for some other cities, such as Augsburg, and became part of the arrangements of 1555. After this *rapprochement* between the council and the bishop, Bucer found himself dismissed from his ministry[225] and fled to England, where the Reformation seemed to be firmly established in the reign of Edward VI; he was fortunate enough to die in 1551 before the accession of Queen Mary. In March 1548, Melanchthon was asked to examine the implications of the *Interim* for Saxony. In some cities there, the Estates demanded changes before they were prepared to accept the new law. Under the impression of these developments, Melanchthon addressed a letter to the chancellor of the new elector Maurice, which appeared to indicate a willingness to compromise over the *Interim* that did severe harm to him. For a number of reasons he was now fought hard by the orthodox Lutherans. Melanchthon was so tired of the constant disputes that were carried on, particularly those in reformatory circles because they affected him most, that he looked forward to death as a release 'from the fury of the theologians'.[226] He died in Wittenberg in 1560.

Charles also pursued plans for a German *Bund*, with reduced powers for the territories, in which the emperor would assume the leadership. But by now Charles had made too many enemies and was encountering resistance. Not paying attention to subtle changes in sentiment, he pressed on with his programme. Thus he put the city of Magdeburg, which had refused to carry out the *Interim*, under the ban of the Empire; Charles charged the new Saxon Elector Maurice with the task of enforcing the ban. Maurice was not prepared to assist Charles in undermining the powers of the princes through the establishment of a strong imperial power. He therefore accepted the task, but carried it out in a manner clearly opposed to the emperor's intentions. The elector took the city in 1552, forced it to recognise him as *Burggraf* (literally 'count of the castle') and allowed Magdeburg to retain its Lutheranism. In the meantime Maurice was putting together a strong alliance against the emperor. Generally Charles' imperious manner and his harsh treatment of his princely prisoners made it easy for Maurice to gain allies in Germany, meeting some sympathy even among the Catholic Estates. His main domestic associate in this venture was a son of the imprisoned Landgrave Philip of Hesse. The German princes plotting against the emperor agreed in return for considerable subsidies that the episcopal cities of Cambrai, Metz, Toul and Verdun, which belonged to the Empire, should be given up to France. While historians of the German unification movement in the nineteenth century castigated this concession as 'treason against the German cause', a Hessian broadsheet saw France as 'the avenger of German liberty and of the captive princes'.[227] However, there was a difference in legitimacy between the actions in Germany of a king of Spain who had been elected King of the Romans and crowned emperor on the one hand, and a king of France allying with a coalition of German princes who without any authority ceded part of the *Reich* to France, on the other. The issue is not affected by the inhabitants of the cities concerned speaking French.

In March 1552 the new French king, Henry II, invaded Lorraine and took the cities that had been promised to him. At about the same time Maurice moved his troops against the emperor, nearly capturing him; but Charles managed to escape. The emperor's plans were in tatters. The Empire was also involved in a new Turkish war. Charles saw that he had failed in his life's work. He increasingly left German affairs to his brother Ferdinand, who had a more winning manner than his elder brother, with his rather haughty behaviour. The way was now open for a general settlement in Germany, even if Charles, for the time being, retained the imperial dignity and therefore formally the final say. Maurice found Ferdinand more willing to compromise than his elder brother, and the two rulers laid the groundwork for a comprehensive settlement. The Saxon elector did not live to see its conclusion as he was killed in battle with a former ally who had switched to the emperor's side.

The Religious Peace of Augsburg of 1555 formally abandoned the notion of religious uniformity for the *Reich*, as it had become a legal fiction. The Augsburg Confession of 1530 was formally recognised in the sense that it became officially permitted to adhere to it. Thus there were now two religions in the Empire, the Catholic and the Lutheran. However, this recognition was not extended to other Protestant denominations, such as Zwinglians (who were declining in importance in Germany), Calvinists (who were increasing in numbers), as well as Anabaptists and other more radical groups. Not individuals, but the ruling authorities, mainly the princes, were given the right to choose one or other of these religious denominations for themselves and their subjects. Later the principle was to be summed up in something like the formula *cuius regio, eius religio*, that 'he who possesses the territory determines the religion'. The individual subject was given the right to emigrate with his family after selling his property at a reasonable price and fulfilling existing obligations. Where in Protestant cities Catholic churches and monasteries had been reopened, parity between the two denominations was to be maintained. Thus the authorities in the cities were much more restricted in their decisions about religion than the princes.

In general, as well as for the future of the Electoral College in particular, the question of the position of the ecclesiastical principalities (governed by the 'prince-bishops') was decisive. If the ecclesiastical principalities could be kept in Catholic hands, they would in many regions, such as the west and south of Germany, constitute a barrier to Protestant expansion. In the Electoral College, the three ecclesiastical electors only needed one other vote, such as that of a Catholic king of Bohemia (like Ferdinand of Habsburg at this time), to maintain a Catholic majority. Thus the reformatory tendencies of Hermann of Wied, Archbishop-elector of Cologne, were particularly threatening; Charles deposed him in 1547 after his victory in the Schmalkaldic War. In order to prevent the alienation of ecclesiastical principalities by prelates who became Protestants, Ferdinand drew up the ecclesiastical reservation (*reservatio ecclesiastica*), which he succeeded in including in the Augsburg law, although it was not agreed to by the Protestants. It therefore appeared as an announcement based on imperial authority. The ecclesiastical reservation laid down that all bishops, prelates and other holders of benefices who gave up the old religion had to resign their offices at once, but without prejudice to their honour; those entitled to elect a successor then had to make sure that he was a Catholic.

At the same time Ferdinand also gave a secret undertaking to the Protestants, the *Declaratio Ferdinandea*. The Lutheran subjects of ecclesiastical princes were promised by Ferdinand the right to practice their faith. The prelates reluctantly agreed to this arrangement. Both the reservation and the declaration had their effect. Although the two measures were to some extent self-contradictory, on balance they helped to arrest the decline of Catholicism by preserving a base for it in the ecclesiastical territories. Around the middle of the century, a majority of Germans may well have been Protestants. While the declaration benefited the Protestants, in effect the Catholics did not sacrifice that much, because they simply recognised facts. At that time, Catholicism was not strong enough to enforce restitution. For the future, the options were kept open, particularly if the Council of Trent turned out to be the beginning of a Catholic revival. The religious settlement was complicated by the rise in Germany of Calvinism, which was not recognised in the Augsburg settlement. The clearest winners from the religious peace of 1555 were the princes, whose position had been further strengthened.

Charles V recognised the failure of the mission he had set himself when he abdicated in September 1556. The Habsburg dynasty split into an elder Spanish and a younger Austrian line. The strict Catholic Philip II, Charles' son, took over not only Spain, with its colonies, but also the Low Countries and the Italian possessions of the Habsburgs. Ferdinand, the King of the Romans, now became emperor, ruling also over the Austrian hereditary lands, in addition to his Hungarian and Bohemian crowns. Clearly, it had become too difficult to unite all the Habsburg dominions under one ruler. But above all a mortal blow had been dealt to the old concept of an emperor occupying a leading position in Western Christendom. The link between the universal emperorship and the German kingdom was finally broken. Both the rise of important European states, like France, and the religious divisions, had made these ideas outdated.

In the meantime the council, which had returned to Trent in 1551, continued its work with many interruptions, caused by a variety of factors, such as disagreement between the main Catholic powers, and tensions between pope and council. Finally, during the reign of an energetic pope, Pius IV, who wished to bring the work done at Trent to a successful conclusion, the council closed in December 1563. Protestant emissaries endowed with safe conducts were heard in 1552,[228] but their appearance made little difference to the conclusions reached by the council. Indeed, the proceedings were mainly a response to Protestant teaching, at first primarily to that of Luther, but as time went on more to that of Calvin and Melanchthon,[229] and it was largely anathemised. Comparatively little attention was given to points of agreement. Against the *sola scriptura* principle the council occupied itself with the relationship between Bible and tradition, and decided to give apostolic tradition in some respects equal weight with Holy Scripture. However, the Tridentine profession of faith (*Professio fidei Tridentina*), which was issued straight after the conclusion of the council, made obedience to the whole tradition of the Church obligatory, no longer confining it to apostolic tradition.[230]

Key aspects of Luther's justification by faith were rejected and more emphasis placed on free will. 'Against the radical pessimism of some Reformation theologians, the Tridentine anthropology preserved with the free will the essence of humanism.'[231] The complete list of seven sacraments was confirmed, as against the broad Protestant view recognising as such only baptism and the Eucharist. The efficacy of the sacrament did not depend on the faith of the recipient. Against Protestant criticism, 'transubstantiation' was regarded as helpful in explaining the corporeal presence in the Eucharist. Communion was complete in one kind, but the council was prepared to accept administration in two kinds by papal permission, as demanded by the German participants and the emperor.[232] Emphasis was placed on the character of the mass as a sacrifice and on the Eucharist as the main function of the priesthood. As against the Protestant view, preaching was not regarded as essential for the priest.[233] The hierarchy of bishops and priests was confirmed, no agreement was reached on the relationship between bishops and pope. With certain exceptions for service in Church and State, bishops were to be strictly required to reside in their diocese.[234] The validity of marriage was to require the attendance of the priest of one of the spouses in the presence of witnesses to receive the mutual consent of the bridal couple; this put an end to secret marriages.[235] The belief in purgatory, where the dead could be supported by the intercessions from the living, and especially through the celebration of masses, was reaffirmed.[236]

In general, the council redirected the attention of the Church to the care of souls. Effectively, the power of bishops was strengthened by charging them with this task. Apart from the Jesuits, the religious orders were increasingly put under their authority. In a conciliatory gesture to the papacy, the council almost unanimously, with the exception of the Bishop of Granada, voted to ask the pope to confirm its work, which Pius IV did promptly, describing himself as 'Bishop of the Universal Church'.[237] Together with a new emphasis on pastoral work, and above all the foundation of the Jesuit order, the Catholic Church emerged strengthened and was able to regain lost ground.

Somewhat paradoxically, the new Catholicism benefited from the reforming impulses of Protestantism, while taking care to distinguish itself from the breakaway Churches. The unspoken assumption was the abandonment of Church Reunification, even if in theory the ending of the schism remained an ultimate aim, as in a sense it was an obligation on all Christians. In its pragmatic stance in this respect, Catholicism was adopting an attitude similar to that of Protestantism in general. Certainly the most important surviving leader of the first generation of *Reformatoren*, John Calvin, had long before his death in 1564 discounted the prospect of reunion. Calvin left behind a movement of wider European importance than Luther, the spread of whose theology was confined mainly to parts of Germany and to the Scandinavian countries; in Bohemia and Poland both Lutheranism and Calvinism were represented.[238] The areas where Calvinism prevailed included parts of Switzerland and of Germany; but in the latter it was overshadowed by Lutheranism. Calvin's Reformed Church was firmly established in the Dutch provinces that had broken away from Spanish rule and was very influential in France. 1564 also marked the end of an era in the Empire with the death of Ferdinand I and the succession of his son Maximilian II, who had more sympathy for Protestantism than his father.

The half-century or so before 1564 certainly saw great changes, for instance in the position of the Holy Roman Emperor. In his best times Charles V had been able to visualise his position of emperor as the secular head of Christendom in the tradition of his predecessors in the Saxon, Salian and Staufen eras. At least on paper, the Habsburg dominions in Charles V's day constituted an accumulation of power which would have been the envy of even the mightiest of the medieval East Frankish or later 'German' rulers, such as Otto the Great, Henry III, Frederick Barbarossa and Frederick II. Indeed, both the pope and the emperor's main rival as secular ruler in Europe, the King of France, appeared at times during the 1520s to be at Charles' mercy. In Germany, the emperor tasted the hour of triumph in 1547 with his victory in the Schmalkaldic War. He believed that his dual aim of strengthening imperial power and of establishing a moderate Catholic Reformation in the German kingdom was within his grasp. But the actual gains from Charles' victories over his various opponents proved elusive, both in the 1520s and in the 1540s, because even the mightiest empire in the world could not achieve them at the same time. Long since their earlier setbacks, both the King of France and the pope had regained their room for manœuvre and were able to frustrate Charles' plans. In any case, Charles was to find out what many of his predecessors as emperors had experienced, that while it was sometimes possible to inflict a defeat on an individual pope, the institution of the papacy had a resilience which long outlasted the secular rulers who tried to curb it. Also the time had passed when a major kingdom could be knocked out by the capture of its king, particularly that of France, which had certainly overtaken the German kingdom in importance and power; even for a king of Spain and ruler of the Low Countries, France was a formidable enemy. Finally the odds were considerable against the success of a policy which combined the curbing of both territorial rulers and Protestants in Germany by a mighty emperor. The division of the Habsburg dominions into a Spanish and an Austrian portion recognised the failure of

Charles' papal, French and German policy; it made its repetition well-nigh impossible.

After eight centuries, the special relationship with the papacy established first by the Frankish king in Pippin's reign and later by the 'German' king in that of Otto the Great finally came to an end. The association ranged from close cooperation to bitter enmity. After the end of the Staufen period, it was activated only sporadically, for the last time before the reign of Charles V with the role Emperor Sigismund played at the Council of Constance.

The story of the present book and of its theme of religion and politics in German history was so far held together by the bracket between emperor and pope; this tie is now largely removed. As the current chapter shows, the pace of events quickens radically in the half century or so it covers. There is increasingly more to report on the theme of religion and politics, as Germany is divided among the three main Christian confessions of the West. As the German kingdom and the Empire sever their special relationship with the papacy, and as the various territories assume greater power over their Churches, the general affairs of Western Christendom and in particular of the papacy, which provided a thread of the story, are no longer so central to the treatment. Also, as the divisions in the German kingdom and the Empire become more intense, foreign powers, often in league with one of the battling religious parties, are able to take advantage of the disunity by intervention and annexation. Thus the internal story of Germany becomes part of diplomatic history, adding to the subject matter. However, once more the complex relationship between religion and politics dominates a major event, the Thirty Years War, which occupies much of the next chapter.

8 To the Peace of Westphalia (1564–1648)

Religious division certainly wounded the Holy Roman Empire, though not mortally. In the sixteeenth century schism was bound to cause severe problems for any state or country, but particularly to an institution like the Empire. For its origins and history were linked to the Holy See, and its rulers claimed, and at times exercised, a special position in the Church; thus as late as the previous century Emperor Sigismund had presided over a General Council of the Church to settle a disputed papacy. Now not even a Catholic emperorship could any longer be taken for granted. If a Protestant emperor were to be elected, the customary coronation by one of the Catholic archbishop-electors would have been only one of innumerable problems ensuing. The threat to the Empire arising from schism was, however, somewhat diminished as it constituted a loose association of territories and did not normally exercise its rule directly. Thus the religious problem could be passed down to the princes, the ecclesiastical states and the cities, as was largely done in the Religious Peace of Augsburg of 1555, subject to a general framework laid down then.

For the time being, the compromise achieved at Augsburg appeared to be the only way to avoid future bloodshed. Even then, religious controversy and persecution did not cease, and the ferocity of mutual polemic showed no sign of abating. Measures against dissidents took place at the level of the territories and were not by any means confined to the exchange of recriminations between Protestants and Catholics that one would expect. In the second half of the sixteenth and into the following century, German Protestantism was plagued by bitter doctrinal disputes within its ranks to a far greater extent than Roman Catholicism. In some ways, this was a consequence of the initially proclaimed, but soon abandoned, ministry of all believers, which appeared to allow all the faithful, clergy and laity, to work out their own salvation. Catholicism was certainly not immune from infighting and from all too lightly levelled accusations of heresy, sometimes due to internal rivalries, such as those between monastic orders. There was often excessive severity in the enforcement of orthodoxy, for example by the Inquisition. But through the teaching office of the Church and through the hierarchy, greater doctrinal certainty could be attained than in Protestantism. Thus, whatever else was achieved, in a sense the Reformation had simply exchanged one problem for another, replacing a single orthodoxy by a bewildering choice of different and competing theological claims to salvation.

319

In the long run, by destroying what was in many ways a conformity of belief enforced by the Catholic Church with the help of the secular power, Protestantism helped to bring about more religious freedom. But initially, in the sixteenth century, the 'evangelicals' actually added a number of, to some extent, mutually exclusive orthodoxies to Catholicism. Quite apart from the 'Radical Reformation' of groups like the Anabaptists, even main-line Protestantism, both Lutheran and Calvinist, was deeply split. Still more than Calvinism, Lutheranism in Germany was troubled by many internal divisions. After Luther's death in 1546, Melanchthon had tried to keep the followers of the great *Reformator* together, but had largely failed to do so. The skilful conciliator, who, for the sake of religious unity, was prepared to go some distance in concessions to the other main line religions and to the emperor, was out of place in an age, which – at whatever cost in suffering – put conviction and consistency before compromise. After his death in 1560, Philipp Melanchthon's name was associated mainly with the 'Philippists', that is with Lutherans who wanted to build bridges to the Calvinists; actually Melanchthon had also wished to reach out to the Catholics.

Lutheran relations with the Calvinists were on the whole not very satisfactory. For many Lutherans, Catholicism was more acceptable – perhaps one should say less unacceptable – than Calvinism. The tensions between the two Protestant confessions come out strongly during events in two of the electorates, first in Saxony and then in Brandenburg.

Lutheranism had been established officially in both electorates. However, Calvinism – the 'Reformed' religion – had received a considerable boost in Germany when it was introduced in the Rhenish Palatinate in the mid-1560s by Elector Frederick III. In Saxony, the Philippist wing of Lutheranism was suspect as being too conciliatory to the Reformed religion; there was generally a fear of 'crypto-Calvinists'. In 1574 the Saxon Elector Augustus I, the younger brother and successor of the Maurice who played a key part in the Schmalkaldic War, came to the conclusion that a number of his officials had participated in a plot to try and convert the electorate to the Reformed religion. One of them was tortured and then put to death in the most cruel circumstances; a number of others were kept imprisoned for many years.[1] To strengthen the defences against Calvinism, Augustus regarded the reconciliation of theological differences between the various forms of Lutheranism in Germany as essential. He succeeded in obtaining a large measure of agreement in the *Book of Concord* (*Konkordienformel*) in 1580, but only at the cost of deepening the disagreement with Calvinism. Thus the chance of establishing Protestant unity against a resurgent Catholicism had receded even further into the distance.

Augustus' son Christian I, under the influence of his chancellor Nikolaus Crell, 'turned away from strict Lutheranism and favoured the moderate tendencies of Melanchthonians and Cryptocalvinists'.[2] At the same time he largely excluded the Estates from participation in government, making his chancellor almost all-powerful. On Christian I's early death in 1591, the Estates, in which the orthodox Lutherans predominated, took their revenge on his chancellor. Crell was at once arrested by the strict Lutheran regime that followed and, in spite of the objections by the Imperial Cameral Court to the procedures followed, was executed after being imprisoned for ten years. The Lutheran authorities in Saxony actually sent the files relating to Crell to the Bohemian Court of Appellation in Prague, which was under the influence of the Catholic emperor and confirmed the death sentence. As usual in this period, events were due to a mixture of political and religious factors, but the particular viciousness of the methods employed in the power struggle seems to arise mainly from the latter.

An even more important clash between the two main Protestant confessions developed in Brandenburg. In 1613 Elector John Sigismund publicly announced to his Lutheran electorate his conversion to the Reformed religion. He had been very much impressed by Calvinism during his stay at the court of Elector Palatine Frederick IV at Heidelberg, from whose university the Reformed theology radiated all over Germany. What appealed to him, as well as to a number of able men of the younger generation, was that Calvinism seemed to take a much clearer line than Lutheranism towards Catholic theology and ritual. One gets the impression that at this time the Calvinists felt about the Lutherans very much as Luther and his followers earlier did about Catholicism: that their own ideas were so obviously superior and that thus the future belonged to them. Also Heidelberg Calvinism was in close touch with west European Protestantism and was therefore open to Dutch, French and English influences, unlike a mainly German Lutheranism. John Sigismund became a Calvinist during his stay in the Palatinate, probably in 1606.[3]

Historians have focused on the elector's motives for his conversion, particularly on the question whether they were primarily religious or political, or a mixture of both. In 1609 John Sigismund, on the death of his father-in-law, had inherited a claim to the important Jülich-Cleves possessions in the lower Rhineland. This region was of considerable interest to both the Spanish and Austrian Habsburgs, as well as to the Dutch and the French. John Sigismund reached an understanding with the Palatine Prince Wolfgang William, another claimant to the territory, that they would hold the territories in common. The elector naturally wished to obtain a favourable permanent settlement to replace this makeshift arrangement. It was thought at one time that he may have converted to Calvinism in order to obtain Dutch support. However, this might have been necessary to tip the scale in his favour with the Dutch only while Wolfgang William adhered to his Lutheran faith; the latter secretly became a Catholic in 1613, and publicly in 1614. His own conversion to the Reformed religion probably hindered rather than helped

John Sigismund with the population of Jülich-Cleves, among which Lutherans and Catholics may well have predominated.

In any case, a Calvinist elector surely had to realise that he would have problems with the Lutheran population not only of Brandenburg, but also of the Duchy of Prussia he was about to to inherit. Was it wise to divide the population over which he ruled in a period of crisis in Germany, where a Protestant Union, to which Brandenburg belonged for a time, faced a Catholic League, at one stage actually over the Jülich-Cleves question? Furthermore, with interventions in the territory by the emperor and the Spaniards, countered by that of an Anglo-Dutch army and a French force, there was danger of a general war breaking out at any time, as it actually did in 1618. Also, under the Religious Peace of Augsburg of 1555 Calvinism was not, unlike Lutheranism, one of the confessions permitted in the Empire, so that John Sigismund was risking countermeasures from the Catholic emperor. All this casts doubts on the political advisability, at least in the short term, of a conversion to Calvinism which has long been admired by historians.[4]

John Sigismund seems to have been absolutely sincere in converting on religious grounds. For that reason he wanted his subjects to share in what he regarded as the blessings of his new faith. His act therefore also had a 'political' side. As ruler, he wanted his subjects to follow him in his change of religion. He stated bluntly that 'many absurd dogmas' were being preached in the electorate, and that it was his duty as a Christian ruler to ensure that the gospel was proclaimed properly and the sacraments correctly administered 'without papal additions'.[5] In other words, he was telling his subjects that his great-grandfather, Joachim II, had introduced the wrong kind of Reformation into Brandenburg and that the intervening generations of rulers had been remiss in adhering to a Lutheranism which retained too much Catholicism. Now he, John Sigismund, wanted to correct these errors and start afresh. But neither the population in general nor the Estates were prepared to obey the elector's commands. Riots broke out, on one occasion when the order was given to remove all epitaphs, crucifixes, pictures, and both altars from the Berlin cathedral (*Dom*), which thus took on 'the austere appearance of a Reformed house of worship'.[6] Even when due allowance is made for the way in which Lutherans felt provoked and threatened, their loathing for Calvinists is striking.

The religious feeling aroused by the elector's action was so strong and went so deep that John Sigismund had to give in. After several generations of Lutheranism, it was no longer possible for a ruler to enforce a change of religion. From now on Brandenburg had the paradoxical situation of a Calvinist, supported by a court containing many of his co-religionists, ruling over a mainly Lutheran establishment and population. John Sigismund's ill-considered move to some extent paralysed the Brandenburg electorate at any rate in the early years of the Thirty Years War by antagonising the Estates and thus making it even harder to obtain their essential financial support. Actually, offending the religious feelings of the population and of the Estates was the most effective – or possibly the only – way of strengthening the Estates, conscious of popular support, against the crown. Surely this was not what John Sigismund had intended. Also the conversion strained relations with Brandenburg's Lutheran allies, particularly with neighbouring Saxony. Disagreements among Protestants certainly helped the Counter-Reformation at a critical time, at the beginning of the Thirty Years War.[7] In the long term, the Calvinism of the electors, along with some drawbacks, was to have considerable benefits for Brandenburg–Prussia, but most of these could hardly be foreseen when the religious changes were announced.

The story of the Calvinist conversion of the Brandenburg elector John Sigismund and its connection with the Jülich-Cleves dispute is examined in detail because many of the elements of the imminent Thirty Years War and of the course it took are already present. The disunity of the Protestant side comes out very clearly as well as the actual threat of foreign intervention, which was to play such an important part in the war, and was undoubtedly encouraged or necessitated by the weakness of German Protestantism. One notices a certain Calvinist aggressiveness in John Sigismund's plan to convert the population of his Lutheran electorate, as well as some naïvety and irresponsibility. These were also features in the light-hearted way in which the Calvinist Elector Palatine Frederick V a few years later engaged in his Bohemian adventure without proper consultation with other German Protestant states and with his father-in-law, King James I of England. There was certainly enhanced support for a policy of active recatholicisation with the accession of Duke Maximilian I of Bavaria in 1595 and with the increasing power gained by the future Emperor Ferdinand II following his succession to Inner Austria the year after. On the Catholic as much as on the Protestant side, the elements favouring an offensive strategy were calling the tune. Now the framework of peace and religious coexistence so laboriously built up by men like Ferdinand I and Melanchthon in 1555, which had provided a breathing-space from fighting, was about to crumble under the impact of the Bohemian conflict.

Perhaps the charged atmosphere was a response to a change that had gradually developed in the fundamentals of the inter-confessional situation in the Empire since the Reformation, and not only due to the influence of personalities. Luther had largely been able to hold on to the initiative, because the Old Church had been unable to respond in time to the call for reform and to deal with his ideas in a constructive manner. But later Luther had to compete with other *Reformatoren*, who did not share his ideas and for many of whom he remained too close to the Church of Rome. As a result, Western Christendom was split not just in two ways, but in many more. That in turn discredited the 'evangelicals', who at one time seemed to many to have all the answers, and led to a yearning for the restoration of unity. By the turn of the century, some who had left the Catholic Church were indeed ready to return. Thus the situation was ripe for a Catholic initiative.

On the Protestant side, the Lutherans were largely content with the *status quo*, and in any case really had nowhere to go. They objected to much in Calvinism, and many of the more moderate men among them felt closer to the Catholic Church than to their Protestant brethren, but there were too many obstacles to a return to the old faith. They certainly did not want to stir up trouble in the Empire, and wished to remain on good terms with the Habsburg emperors, Catholic though they might be. Only the Calvinists, at least some of them, thought in terms of going over to the offensive. Utterly convinced that they would find salvation as the elect of God, they also drew strength from being part of an international brotherhood of their faith extending to France, Holland, Switzerland and England. As the Reformed religion had not been officially recognised in the Religious Peace of Augsburg, perhaps the more radical and adventurous elements in German Calvinism felt that they had little to lose if they took action that would upset the delicate inter-confessional balance. Also, following the increased vigour of Catholicism after the Council of Trent, they may have had the impression that the situation in Germany was turning against them, and that it was better to strike sooner rather than later. Generally, before the war, Calvinist rulers favoured tougher resistance to the Counter-Reformation than their Lutheran counterparts.

Calvinist assertiveness had its parallel on the Catholic side, where the Jesuit order was in the forefront of a more active policy of taking the initiative in reclaiming lost ground. The Society of Jesus was founded by the Spaniard, Ignatius of Loyola, with some companions in 1534 and was formally established by Paul III in the papal bull *Regimini militantis ecclesiae* in 1540. The following year Ignatius was elected as the first head of the new order, as *Praepositus generalis*, that is 'general' or overall superior, and not in the sense of a military title.[8]

Though the order has gone down in history as an offensive arm of the Counter-Reformation, its fundamental role according to its rule embodied in the *Formula of the Institute* was primarily the internal task of strengthening the faith of Catholics. But in view of the circumstances of the period, as time went on, the order was increasingly caught up in the task of fighting Protestantism, without, however, losing sight of the purposes for which it was originally founded. This was for 'the propagation of faith and the progress of souls in Christian life and doctrine.' Significantly, the first part was strengthened in 1550 by inserting the words 'the defence and' before 'propagation of faith'.

The Jesuits in some ways saw their main task as helping souls through their ministries. In this connection the *Spiritual Exercises* of Ignatius of Loyola, which 'he began to compose...shortly after his conversion in 1521'[9] are central to what the order was trying to do. They were used as a framework, a kind of 'teacher's manual' by persons helping others to find their faith and their place in it in a 'retreat' from the world. The *Exercises* were designed especially for those 'in a position to make a determinative choice about the future, for example, to marry, to choose a certain profession, or to live henceforth in a notably different style'.[10] They were employed not merely in the selection and training of Jesuits, but also used for their their flock. The *Exercises* provided a path for exploring one's spirituality, of clearing away the obstacles to attaining one's peace with God, and for providing guidance as to where one's vocation lay. Every care was taken to let the person going through the *Exercises* find himself and establish his own relationship with God. Therefore emphasis was placed on colloquy, rather than on a teacher-pupil relationship. The system was very flexible in that the director was as often as not somebody from outside the Society. The *Exercises* were passed on to lay people, who could employ them with others. Thus a very considerable multiplier effect and an extensive active involvement of the laity was achieved. Depending on the circumstances of those who went through the *Exercises*, their completion could involve different scenarios ranging from complete seclusion from the world for several weeks, to a 'part-time' involvement, which allowed the person concerned to carry on broadly with his normal life. The way the whole system of *Exercises* worked was kept under constant review. Both in understanding of human psychology and in organising these activities, the order occupied a leading place in the field and was very much in advance of its time.

The Jesuits came directly under the papacy, but not all pontiffs were their supporters. Thus Paul IV, who belonged to the Carafa dynasty, one of the leading Neapolitan families, was not favourably inclined towards them.[11] Members of the order were obliged to go wherever the pope commanded. They were not tied down to a set pattern of service like their predecessors in the mendicant orders of the Middle Ages. For example, they were not obliged to recite liturgical hours in common. Their activities varied considerably. One of their most important functions was the ministry. They also distinguished themselves as teachers both at universities and at schools. By the time of papal suppression of the order in 1773, they ran more than eight hundred educational institutions, including universities and many excellent schools (to which even some Dutch Calvinists sent their children), in various parts of the world, promoting wide international contacts.[12] The Jesuits, while capable of the deepest spirituality, did not hesitate to take an active part in the affairs of this world, and had no qualms about intervening in politics, which proved to be one of the causes of their eventual undoing.

From its very beginnings, the order aroused both tremendous enthusiasm and great bitterness, the latter not only from Protestants, against whom the Jesuits – like other arms of the Catholic Church – took measures as heretics. Ignatius himself regarded dismissal from university professorships, imprisonment or expulsion, and as a last resort the death penalty, as appropriate for them. But in that respect he was not unusual for his age, on most sides of the religious conflict. At the same time, Jesuits were prepared to risk their lives for their faith, such as in England. What, however, is striking is that the Jesuits were dogged to an unusual extent by accusations of heresy from other orders, perhaps mainly because they were innovators. Indeed Ignatius himself, before the founding of the Society, had to go through several periods of imprisonment at the hands of the Catholic authorities on suspicion of heresy.[13] Ignatius is often considered the Catholic counterpart of Luther,[14] and there are parallels between the impact on society of the initial 'evangelical' movement and that of the Jesuits. But the task of the Jesuits was harder than that of Luther. The *Reformator* in many respects found a 'receptive society',[15] whereas the almost unavoidably often rather shrill call of the Counter-Reformation – a shrillness to which there are parallels in Calvinism rather than Lutheranism – was liable to disturb comfortable patterns of Catholic–Protestant co-existence practiced in various places, such as in Southern Germany.[16] Both Jesuits and Calvinists used reason in the cause of their religious zeal.

The involvement of Jesuits in politics also aroused opposition and criticism. 'In an age when politics and religion were inextricably mingled the confessors of the great, who seemed to wield great power without accountability, were the objects at once of envy and hatred; and the majority of these were Jesuits.'[17] Thus inside the Catholic Church, there was jealousy of an order that appeared to be elitist, that was exempt from diocesan control, that ranged more widely over many functions than other parts of the Church, and that showed high intellectual powers.

The Society of Jesus devoted considerable resources to Germany, partly because of its key importance at the time, but also because it possessed in the Dutchman Peter Canisius, 'the apostle of Germany', a leader who devoted his life to the cause of Catholicism there. In 1552 the order founded the *Collegio Germanico* in Rome to provide training for future priests in Germany and some of the neighbouring countries in the East. Jesuit colleges were founded in many parts of the Empire. Among their pupils at the Bavarian University of Ingolstadt were two cousins who were to play an important part in the future, the Habsburg Archduke Ferdinand and Maximilian of Bavaria.

Ferdinand II, who was elected emperor in August 1619 had already been crowned King of Bohemia in 1617. The Bohemian revolt in the summer of 1618 and the displacement of Ferdinand through the election of Elector

Palatine Frederick V as King of Bohemia in August 1619 could not possibly be accepted by the Habsburg dynasty: neither by the Austrian nor the Spanish branch, if only for religious reasons. Frederick's Bohemian venture was only one move on the religious chessboard, which was assuming increasingly major European proportions, initially on the diplomatic front, but eventually in the military field. 'In spite of the aggressive internationalism of Calvinism, it was the Catholic side that proceeded to an offensive that was brought forward quite systematically.'[18]

The conversion to Catholicism of King Sigismund of Poland, a member of the Vasa dynasty who had been overthrown as King of Sweden, offered an opportunity for the Habsburgs to extend their influence to the Baltic area. This boosted even further the Catholic Austro-Spanish Habsburg bloc, which already extended from Spain and the Spanish Netherlands to Italy, as well as from Austria, Bohemia and Hungary to Freiburg in the south-west of Germany, and thus dominated the European continent. In sheer resources and potential military power, the Protestant territories in Europe, which were in any case divided confessionally among Lutherans, Calvinists and Anglicans, were no match. Furthermore England and Scotland (in personal union under the Stuarts since 1603), the United Provinces of the Netherlands, and the Protestant territories in Germany and Switzerland had other, often divergent, interests to consider. Religion remained an important factor, but not the only one, in the alignment of powers in the following decades, until it was to recede more into the background during the second half of the century, when secular factors largely predominated in decisions on foreign policy.[19] Habsburg predominance contained in itself the seeds of its own destruction, because it constituted a threat to the other leading Catholic power, France, and in some ways even for the papacy, because of the traditional objection of the Holy See to being encircled; the Habsburgs reminded the papacy rather unpleasantly of past chapters in its history, such as the struggle with the Staufen dynasty, also strongly entrenched in Italy.

The Spanish Habsburgs, the elder line of the house, were the senior partner of their Austrian relatives. Their position was in fact strengthened by a genealogical accident, the extinction with the death of Emperor Mathias in 1619 of the Austrian branch descended from Emperor Maximilian II. In a secret treaty concluded in 1617 designed to prevent a dispute over the inheritance, the Spanish line was able to secure the reversion of imperial and dynastic rights in Alsace and Upper Italy. This was designed to hand over to Spain the 'Spanish road' from the Mediterranean via Italy, the Alpine passes and the Upper Rhine to the Netherlands.[20]

The Austrian Habsburgs received valuable military help during the Thirty Years War from Spanish bases in the southern Netherlands and in northern Italy. Furthermore, what was at stake for the Habsburgs was not only their rule over Bohemia, but also the electoral vote in the Empire attached to the

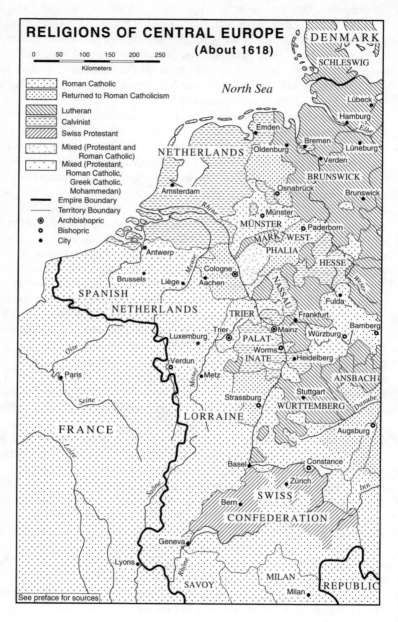

Map III

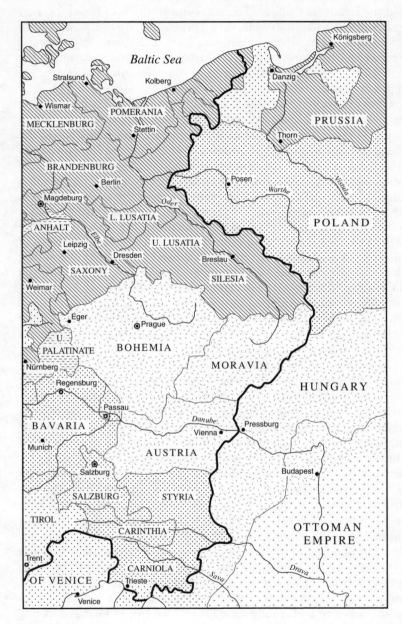

Map III *contd.*

crown, which might tip the scale between a Catholic and a Protestant majority in the Electoral College. The accession of the recatholicising Ferdinand was only too likely to lead to a curtailment of the privileges of Bohemian Protestantism, which in turn was liable to have an impact on its German counterpart. It was in the interest of German Protestantism, to the extent that it had any coherence, to prevent that; however, the Protestant Union kept out of a quarrel not of its own making.

Perhaps it is not only in historical hindsight that Frederick's intervention in Bohemia – in spite of initial successes, with some help from anti-Habsburg elements in Hungary – was a lost cause. Frederick was defeated by the League General Tilly at the White Mountain west of Prague in November 1620 and had to flee. Thus he could not save Bohemian Protestantism, which was at Ferdinand's mercy. Bohemia was largely recatholicised. At the same time Frederick weakened German Protestantism generally and Calvinism in particular by providing an opportunity for the emperor to deprive him of his electoral dignity and to transfer a part of his territory, the Upper Palatinate (north of the Danube), together with the electorship to Duke Maximilian of Bavaria. In spite of military help from the Dutch and English to prevent this, Frederick's Rhenish Palatinate was occupied by Catholic forces, and the Calvinist Church of the Palatinate declared dissolved. By his rash adventure, Frederick inflicted untold suffering on his helpless subjects.

The Thirty Years War illustrates strikingly the complexities of the religio-political relationship. In view of what is well-documented about Lutheran attitudes to Calvinism in John Sigismund's Brandenburg, it is not surprising that the Lutheran elector of Saxony did not rush to the aid of his Calvinist fellow-elector Frederick. John George actually allied with the Catholic emperor against Frederick and the Bohemians. His reward was the Bohemian province of Lusatia. Rulers consulted their interests and those of their territories, as they saw them. John George regarded the moment ripe for some territorial gains. He did not think that he would be hurt, and believed that he might indeed get a better deal from Ferdinand in regard to his secularised Church property and ecclesiastical acqusitions by helping him to an early victory. The prospect of the persecution of Bohemian Protestants, particularly if they were not Lutherans, appears to have had rather a low priority for him. However, Saxony was to have some anxious moments later on in the war. Still, here we have one of the early phases of the alliance between Saxony and Austria which was to persist until Prussia defeated both in 1866. Perhaps the close geographical proximity of Saxony to Habsburg territories also played a part in this Saxon attachment to its neighbour.

A number of 'soldiers of fortune'[21] in the mercenary tradition who were available for hire and mainly raised their own troops emerged during the war. On the Protestant side one of the earliest was Ernst von Mansfeld. The most famous of these mercenary commanders was Wallenstein, who was soon to play a major part in the war on the Catholic side. These *condottieri* lived off the land, making war pay by pillage and showing little distinction between friend and foe. The tragic, wide-spread destruction in war zones was aggravated by this procedure. The Empire and particularly most parts of what was later, broadly, to become Germany, situated in the very heart of Europe, were the scene of military operations, often repeatedly. They were fought over not only by various German armies, but by foreign invaders. There was Spain on the Catholic side. Supporting the Protestant cause were at various times Dutch, English, Danish, Swedish and French troops.

Actually the most important help given to the Protestants for many years was that provided by Catholic France, under Cardinal Richelieu. While the French did not formally enter the war until 1635, they intervened in decisive ways in the meantime. For example, at the end of 1624, they succeeded in arranging to have communications between the Spanish and the Austrian Habsburgs disrupted through the blocking of the Val Telline on the borders between Switzerland and the Republic of Venice. In view of that, combined with the action of the English fleet, Spain could no longer send bullion to Flanders and Austria either by land or by sea.[22] Thus, while the Catholic side was making considerable headway in the Empire, actions by other powers were beginning to affect its future prospects. There was also the threat of a Danish invasion of northern Germany. Elector Maximilian of Bavaria, who controlled the only big army in Germany, persuaded the emperor to find additional forces with which he could resist a European coalition. Wallenstein had submitted proposals to Ferdinand to raise an army at his own expense. In his difficult situation Ferdinand found this offer hard to resist and accepted in the spring of 1625,[23] making one of the most fateful decisions of his reign.

Albrecht von Wallenstein, who was of mixed German and Czech origin and came from a Protestant background, was born in Moravia in the Bohemian kingdom. He converted to Roman Catholicism in his mid-twenties and after the crushing of the Bohemian rising became one of the main beneficiaries from the confiscations of the defeated party. His appointment as the emperor's general was timely, for in the summer of 1625 King Christian IV of Denmark, with some encouragement from foreign governments, intervened in the war. As Duke of Holstein he was a Prince of the Empire and a member of the Lower Saxon Circle, which would dearly liked to have remained neutral, but which he bullied into electing him its president. This was rather dangerous for the Circle, as the League General Tilly was stationed in the neighbourhood. Wallenstein's army also moved to the area.

As was typical for this period, Christian's motives were partly religious and partly political. He genuinely wished to help the Protestant cause, which certainly needed assistance. But at the same time he sought to strengthen Denmark's position in the Baltic and to secure bishoprics for his family,

which brought him right up against the interests of the electors of Brandenburg and Saxony. Tilly defeated Christian on Brunswick territory in 1626,
while elements of Wallenstein's army advanced to Jutland and drove out the
Dukes of Mecklenburg, the general being himself enfeoffed with this dignity
by the emperor. But after reducing the Duke of Pomerania to obedience,
Wallenstein was checked in 1628 at the Baltic seaport of Stralsund, whose
municipality refused to surrender and was defended with Danish and Swedish help. In June 1629 the peace of Lübeck was concluded between the
emperor and Denmark on the basis of the territorial *status quo*. But apart
from undertaking to withdraw from the war in Germany, Christian had to
resign the presidency of the Lower Saxon Circle.

Ferdinand II was at the height of his power. He used the moment, actually
just before the conclusion of the peace with Denmark, to proclaim the Edict
of Restitution in March 1629 on his own authority, without consulting the
diet. He attempted to make a reality of something like the dual policy of
strengthening both Catholicism and imperial power which had helped to
bring down Charles V. All the property of the Church appropriated by
German princes since 1552, as well as all bishoprics and convents that had
become Protestant since 1555, were to be restored to the Old Church. In
other words, while the Ecclesiastical Reservation of 1555 favouring Catholicism was to be enforced, the Declaration of Ferdinand of the same year giving
some protection to Protestantism was dropped. Benefits from the Religious
Peace of 1555 remained restricted to the Lutherans, the 'Augsburg Confession', while the Calvinists continued to be excluded from them. Wallenstein's
armies began at once to enforce the edict, but its application was uneven.
Full enforcement of the edict would have been a severe blow to Protestantism.

It is not surprising that there was great dissatisfaction with the edict
among the Protestant rulers, but actually all princes were largely united in
their dislike of Wallenstein. They resented the way in which the emperor had
built up a 'private army' out of their reach, and had raised up Wallenstein on
his own authority as a Prince of the Empire by depriving the ancient
Mecklenburg dynasty of its rule for supporting Christian of Denmark.
Ferdinand owed Wallenstein such enormous amounts of money that the
only way he could meet these financial obligations was to 'sell' him a
duchy.[24] While the emperor refused to modify the edict, which might have
regained him some Protestant support, he did agree to dismiss Wallenstein,
who was relieved of his command in September 1630. The timing of Wallenstein's dismissal was ill considered, as King Gustavus Adolphus of Sweden
had landed in Pomerania the previous July.

As with Christian IV of Denmark, the Swedish king's motives for entering
the war were partly religious and partly political. The Lutheran king, a man
of sincere faith, certainly took seriously his mission of helping the Lutherans

and to some extent Protestants generally. But he was above all King of Sweden, and as such the enemy of his Catholic cousin Sigismund, who ruled over Poland, but also claimed the Swedish crown. Politically, Gustavus Adolphus was fighting the ally of his Polish cousin in Emperor Ferdinand II, and at the same time endeavouring to extend Swedish power in the Baltic.

In 1631 Richelieu concluded a treaty with Gustavus Adolphus in which he undertook to pay him considerable subsidies for his campaign in Germany. But the fronts were not clear-cut, for Richelieu at one time also came to an agreement with Maximilian of Bavaria, which, however, did not bear fruit. Richelieu hoped that Gustavus Adolphus would serve French interests, but it did not work out that way. Interestingly not only the inveterate enemy of the Habsburgs, France, supported the anti-Habsburg alliance, but also the pope reacted against the growing power of Spain and Austria. While two popes, Paul V (1605–21) and Gregory XV (1621–3) gave considerable subsidies to the emperor and the Catholic League during the early years of the war, their successor did not follow in their footsteps. Maffeo Barberini, who became Pope Urban VIII (1623–44) had been *nuncio* in Paris and was inclined towards a pro-French point of view, though he tried to remain neutral between the Catholic Great Powers during his pontificate. He did indeed, in the first half of the 1620s, attempt to mediate between the Habsburgs and the Bourbons in his striving to restore peace in Europe, to ease the position of the Catholic Church in Germany and to secure stability in Italy.[25] A man of considerable ability, Urban was rather caught up in Italian affairs, which made him especially reluctant to do anything to strengthen the Habsburgs, already firmly entrenched in the peninsula. Regrettably he engaged in nepotism on a considerable scale, enriching his own family. In spite of the entreaties of the emperor and of Maximilian of Bavaria, the pope refused to give substantial financial help to the Catholic side in the Thirty Years War. He pleaded lack of funds, though these were available for his relatives. From the mid-1630s onward, Urban was in the forefront of the movement to restore peace. It was during his reign that the trial of Galileo Galilei took place.[26]

Gustavus Adolphus, who had believed that the Protestants would rally to his side when he appeared on the German scene as their saviour, was disappointed with the reluctance of the major rulers to join him. The important Protestant city of Magdeburg on the Elbe, which was besieged by Tilly, the new imperial commander, fell in May 1631, a victim to the indifference or indecisiveness of the electors of Saxony and Brandenburg. The town and its inhabitants became a prey to the wanton destruction of a soldiery which had run amuck. After some hours, an uncontrollable fire broke out and the city went up in flames. It is not clear who started the blaze, it may not have been the victors; it was hardly in their interest to deprive themselves of their newly conquered base. None of this is conclusive. In any case there was great bitterness among Protestants about the treatment of Magdeburg, whoever was responsible for the conflagration. In September 1631, the Elector of Saxony concluded an alliance with Gustavus Adolphus, but neither party trusted the other. The same month, Gustavus Adolphus inflicted a severe defeat on Tilly at Breitenfeld near Leipzig. The Saxon troops supporting the Swedes performed badly, which undermined Saxon influence over the policy of the victorious coalition.

Ferdinand's position in Germany was now a very poor one, he had to go cap in hand to Wallenstein asking him to resume his command. The general was slow in responding, realising the strength of his position. Actually he was at the same time negotiating secretly with the Protestant side, too. In the meantime, the Saxons, in accordance with allied strategy, invaded Silesia and Bohemia, while the Swedes overran the Main valley and reached Frankfurt, south-western Germany, the Alsace and parts of the Rhineland. If the French thought that Gustavus Adolphus would be their puppet, they were mistaken. In fact the Swedes were becoming too powerful in Germany for the French and moving too close to their sphere of interest. Some historians even believe that the king hankered after the imperial crown.[27] His imperious manner did not go down well with the German princes. Tilly was beaten again by Gustavus Adolphus in April 1632, and died a few weeks later. Wallenstein finally accepted the emperor's commission once more, exacting his own terms. During his second period of service he behaved less like an army commander carrying out the directives of his ruler than like one of principals among the powers, which led to his downfall in the end.

Gustavus Adolphus no longer had things his own way in the theatres of war. In November 1632, he was killed in the battle of Lützen near Leipzig, though the Swedes defeated Wallenstein. Gustavus Adolphus' death was a great loss for the Swedish campaign in Germany, and in a sense for the Protestants in Germany, however critical they may have been of aspects of his policy. His chancellor, Oxenstierna, a gifted man, could not replace his king's rare combination of high statesmanship with skilful generalship. The heir to the Swedish throne, Christina, was still a child, and her mother, the sister of Elector George William of Brandenburg, vain and unreliable. Oxenstierna managed to put together quite a powerful alliance of German Protestant states. In the ensuing fighting, both the Swedes and Wallenstein had some successes. The latter, who continued to maintain secret contacts with his emperor's enemies, eventually stationed himself in Bohemia and refused to move. He was dismissed by the emperor, and murdered by some of his own officers at Eger in Bohemia in February 1634.

The removal of the disobedient general allowed a resumption of the close liaison between the Austrian and the Spanish Habsburgs. In September 1634 the imperial army, as well as the Spaniards – who were hated, certainly by the German Protestants[28] – and the Bavarians inflicted a severe defeat on the Swedes at Nördlingen, north of the River Danube. After about a decade and a half of intermittent fighting, the vast majority of the German territories wanted to restore peace and were prepared to make concessions to end the state of war. In May 1635, the Peace of Prague was concluded between Austria and Saxony, to which nearly all the Empire acceded. Emperor Ferdinand II was now able to make a concession from a position of strength, and withdrew the Edict of Restitution. The effective date for legal title in the case of ecclesiastical dominions was to be 1627, instead of the 1550s. On paper (not very realistically) these matters were to be reviewed after 90 years. While secularisations by Saxony and others east of the Elbe River were not challenged, Catholicism was to prevail in the bishoprics between the Elbe and the Weser. Only Lutherans, and not Calvinists, were to benefit from the relaxation of the Edict of Restitution. But in spite of that restriction, the Calvinist Elector, George William of Brandenburg, decided to accept the treaty, mainly because of resentment of Swedish designs on his prospective Pomeranian inheritance.

Ferdinand II finally, towards the end of his reign, not so long before his death in 1637, achieved a considerable strengthening of imperial power and a consolidation of the existing Catholic position, at least for the time being. But in return, Protestantism in fact, though only Lutheranism in strict law, achieved a greater sense of security of tenure for its position, including its secularisations.

The war might well have ended there and then, but the emperor and the German princes failed to achieve one of the main purposes of the treaty, to free the country from foreign occupation. The Swedes, who did not want to relinquish their foothold in Germany, refused to leave. Richelieu did not consider peace in Germany to be in the interest of France, which was engaged in a persistent struggle with the Habsburgs, though mainly with Spain, against which it formally declared war in 1635. In any case, the French continued their policy of extending their frontiers eastward at the expense of the Empire. Thus by the seventeenth century the German kingdom, which had earlier been able largely to take care of itself, if not to advance its frontiers, was increasingly at the mercy of foreign powers, particularly of France.

The continued fighting and devastation was at last ended by the Peace of Westphalia in October 1648, which brought to an end the Thirty Years War. Negotiations took place at Münster with France and at Osnabrück with Sweden. Peace was made formally by the emperor – since 1637 Ferdinand II's son Ferdinand III – and his allies. The *Reich* Estates signed afterwards. The treaties regulated the relationship of the various religions with the different territories and with the Empire, that of the Estates with Empire and Emperor, as well as that of Germany with foreign countries.

Inside the Empire, or what was to remain of the Empire, the settlement was based on the principles of amnesty and restitution. The ban of the Empire (*Reichsbann*) was lifted on those on whom it had been inflicted, such as the Palatine dynasty. In general, the *status quo* of 1618 was restored, apart from some exceptions, such as that the Palatine electoral vote and the Upper Palatinate remained with Bavaria. However, an eighth electorate was created for the Palatine dynasty.

In effect the Imperial Estates, that is the princes and cities, secured an almost complete sovereignty (*jus territorii et superioritatis*). They were entitled to conclude alliances, so long as they were not directed against Emperor and Empire (*Kaiser und Reich*). In practice, while princes took advantage of this right, they often ignored the qualification. In spite of that and the many inconsistencies in the structure of the Empire, a certain minimum of protection and security was provided for the various estates, particularly the weaker ones that needed it most. This meant that peace and not war was the normal state of affairs between the estates.[29] The final religious settlement after the Thirty Years War will have helped to strengthen the Empire by bringing to an end the severe crisis in which it had found itself. In all governmental acts, such as foreign policy, taxation, and legislation, the emperor was to be dependent on the consent of the estates, which consisted of the College of Electors, the Chamber of Princes and the Curia of Free Imperial Cities.

In matters of religion, there was some modification of previous settlements, such as the Religious Peace of Augsburg of 1555. The principle of *cuius regio, eius religio* was preserved. But it was modified by the stipulation that on the whole each territory should in religion retain the status it had in 1624. Thus a population could not simply be forced to submit to a further change in its religion to conform to that of its ruler. The stipulations did not bind the emperor so far as his hereditary lands were concerned. The arrangement legalised the acquisitions of the Protestants since 1555, that is of territories and their inhabitants, and of Church property of all types, such as bishoprics, monasteries and benefices.

The right of subjects who did not belong to the Church of the territory to private and usually also to public worship was formally laid down. While the subject was entitled to emigrate, if he so wished, the prince was not allowed to compel him to do so. Measures were also taken to prevent the recurrence of the kind of situation in which the 'evangelicals' had been outvoted by the Catholic majority and against which they had protested at Speyer in 1529 (from which the name of 'Protestants' was taken). Accordingly, the diet in all questions concerning religion formed two distinct chambers, the *corpus catholicorum* and the *corpus evangelicorum*, which debated separately. Changes could only be made if both chambers agreed. Parity between Roman Catholics and Protestants was prescribed for appointment to *Reich* bodies, such as the Imperial Cameral Tribunal (*Reichskammergericht*). But the Estates did not succeed in eliminating the *Reichshofrat* (Imperial Aulic Council) in Vienna altogether. Actually the *Reichshofrat* was often used by Germans, because it functioned more expeditiously and because they trusted its impartiality.[30]

In the territorial settlement, Sweden received as fiefs of the Empire (*Reichslehen*) Western Pomerania (*Vorpommern*) with Rügen, as well as the archbishopric of Bremen and another bishopric as secular possessions. Sweden became an Estate of the Empire (*Reichsstand*).

Virtually the whole of Alsace was ceded to France,[31] which also secured bases for an offensive into Germany by receiving the strong fortress of Breisach on the right bank of the Upper Rhine and occupation rights in Philippsburg opposite Speyer. The Lorraine bishoprics of Metz, Toul and Verdun, lost to France in 1552, finally passed out of the Empire.

Saxony retained Lusatia. Brandenburg, which according to valid treaties should have inherited the whole of Pomerania on the extinction of the local dynasty in 1637,[32] obtained merely its comparatively backward eastern part (*Hinterpommern*). Brandenburg received not only the bishopric of Magdeburg, but also those of Halberstadt and Minden. The bishopric of Osnabrück was to alternate between a Roman Catholic and a Protestant. The latter was always to be a member of the Brunswick–Lüneburg dynasty, on which a ninth electorate, the Hanoverian, was to be bestowed in 1692.

Switzerland and the Low Countries, which had for some time gone their own way, were formally separated from the Empire. Sweden received five million *Reichstaler*, a quarter of the sum originally demanded, for the removal of its troops from the Empire. France and Sweden were to be guarantors of peace. Although these two powers were primarily concerned with their own interests, they did help the Protestants to obtain reasonable terms in the peace settlement. The papal *nuncio*, who had participated in the peace negotiations, protested against the stipulations in the treaties which the Holy See regarded as being 'injurious to the Church, but not against the peace as such'. About 20 Catholic imperial estates acceded to the protest. 'In the Peace of Westphalia a new age proclaimed itself; the system of European states freed itself from papal controls. Urban VIII's successor, by whom the protest was made, could do nothing to arrest this development.'[33] It is ironic that after all their struggles, the decline in the general importance of the papacy would follow within a century of that of the Empire with the abdication of Charles V.

The Peace of Westphalia of 1648 largely reaffirmed the Religious Peace of Augsburg of 1555. It is tragic that in the meantime so much blood had to flow and that such extensive suffering was inflicted. The Peace of Westphalia brought to an end a period of strife for the Empire set off by religious differences. Whereas more centralised states, like for example Spain, France and England, could enforce doctrinal uniformity, in the Empire none of the three confessions was strong enough to do so. Thus Catholics and Calvinists in the Empire enlisted foreign help, Austria that of Spain, Frederick of the Palatinate that of Holland and England. That was one of the reasons why the initially primarily religious conflict assumed international proportions. Another was that the internal divisions in the Empire invited foreign intervention, from Denmark, Sweden and France, though there were also elements in the case of the first two of wishing to help their co-religionists. With the French the primary consideration was to prevent the Habsburgs from becoming so strong that they would threaten their security, an early manifestation of rudiments of the balance of power concept. At any rate, the peace settlement entrenched French and Swedish power in Germany.

Internally, the Empire, with its kind of confederate structure, henceforth encouraged a pluralism rare in Europe at the time, not only politically, with a whole range of secular and ecclesiastical principalities as well as cities and imperial knights as hitherto, but also in religion. Coercion in matters of faith did not cease, but it was practiced within, and not between, different territories. The religious dissident in one state was often able, though with sacrifices, to emigrate to one of his faith, not too far away, without having to learn a new language.

It was inherent in the new internal balance that the Habsburgs failed to restore religious uniformity, although Ferdinand II succeeded in largely depriving the Protestants of the initiative and in consolidating Catholicism once more. In the latter objective, he had the support and assistance of Maximilian I of Bavaria. But when a choice had to be made between upholding territorial power against the emperor and spreading Catholicism, the elector opted for the former, even if that meant weakening a catholicising emperor. Thus one can see the receding importance of religion in day-to-day politics even in this pillar of the Counter-Reformation.

Elsewhere, the reaction against the part religion had played in politics was even stronger. Many earnest Christians were deeply disturbed by the manner in which the different religions and the secular authorities enforcing them could proclaim mutually exclusive faiths, all claiming to represent the true faith.[34] Did Christianity have to involve religious wars and the persecution of those who disagreed with the prevailing orthodoxy in the territory concerned? Was it not time to look afresh at the relationship between religion and politics? There were problems for those of deep faith in the manner in which religious matters were laid down minutely in legal form by the authorities in, at any rate, the Protestant territories. Thanks to that feeling, there developed in practice a certain separation between theology and piety.[35] Both in Protestantism and Catholicism a religious revival took place. 'Through turning to inwardness, the withdrawal was accomplished from the alliance between religion and politics, which had been responsible for the suffering of the religious war.'[36]

While internally the Empire was in reasonable shape, it remained to be seen how the defence of Germany and the Empire would fare in the new circumstances. The rallying of the Empire at the time of the relief of the Turkish siege of Vienna in 1683 was a good omen.

The Peace of Westphalia marked a further stage in the increasing complexity of the religio-political relationship, also making it difficult to treat the history of what was to become Germany within this framework. The following chapter will briefly examine the gradually changing role of religion in politics and society in the transition from the age of the religious wars to the French Revolution. Particular attention will be paid to those events and developments which were to have an impact on German nationhood.

9 Epilogue: To the French Revolution (1648–1789)

The Peace of Westphalia of 1648 led to the consolidation of the confessional state.[1] After the breathtaking events of the last one and a quarter centuries, its structure can now be examined more closely in the comparative calm after the Thirty Years War. The formation of confessional states had begun in the 1520s and had made considerable progress in the second half of the sixteenth century after the Religious Peace of Augsburg. For the Catholic territories it was clear by 1555, if not before, that they had to develop their institutions on the basis of a continuing confessional division. For the Protestant states in general, there was more security. Further attempts at recatholicisation could be largely discounted, at least for the time being; for the Calvinists there was at last official recognition as one of the three religions of the Empire.

The religious map of the Empire was a chequered one, ranging from large blocks of territory belonging to a single denomination to confessional frontiers changing every few miles at the other. The mass migrations during and after the Second World War have somewhat blurred the picture so far as the population is concerned. But during walks around some regions of Germany even today, one can still discern when one passes, for example, from a Protestant township to a Catholic countryside, or vice versa. In 1648 Lutheranism almost entirely controlled a large area stretching from Schleswig–Holstein in the north to the Bohemian border in the south, and extending from the Guelph Brunswick (Hanoverian) territories in the west to the Polish border in the east. The main strength of Catholicism lay in two regions: in the south east, that is in Bavaria and the Habsburg territories in Austria and Bohemia, in which the Counter-Reformation repressed a flourishing Protestantism, and in the west, in the Rhenish and Westphalian ecclesiastical territories. Similarly the Franconian bishoprics of Bamberg and Würzburg were of great importance not only for the survival, but also for the recovery of Catholicism. Calvinism was largely confined to the west, to the Rhenish Palatinate, as well as parts of Nassau and Hesse.

Each of these main denominations promoted its own culture. There was the Catholic baroque, after the destruction of the Thirty Years War introduced mainly by Italians, which achieved artistic excellence in the architecture of churches and monasteries, and in the 'residences' of the prince-bishops in the capitals of their ecclesiastical states. The visual beauty and the exquisite proportions of baroque churches, from the largest to the smallest, which must have been so meaningful to the faithful at the time, constitute a precious spiritual heritage for later generations. Catholic culture, again in association with Italian influences, emphasised pictures and colours, as well as music. With its religious processions and carnivals it was strongly rooted in popular piety.

Against that, Protestantism cultivated simplicity in order to concentrate on the Christian message and the Word, uncompromisingly in the case of Calvinism with its iconoclast tradition, in a somewhat more conciliatory approach to the visual element with Lutheranism. The latter appealed even more to the ear than to the eye, excelling in its church music, in its great hymns from Luther's day onwards, and in the cantatas and the arias of composers like Johann Sebastian Bach. His deep spirituality and the manner in which his music reflected the peace he had found with God still gives solace to the believer. Similarly Catholicism rendered important contributions to sacred music through many composers such as Joseph Haydn and Wolfgang Amadeus Mozart. However, Lutheranism made music even more central to divine service than Catholicism by its greater emphasis on congregational participation in singing. The focusing on the Word in the Lutheran service and its emphasis on the sermon, together with the encouragement given to the individual lay person to study the Bible, led to a blossoming of the literary arts. These and the practice of music were cultivated in the Lutheran parsonage which produced future pastors and at least some of the important leaders of intellectual life in the lay sphere, too. Owing to the institution of clerical celibacy there could be no parallel development in Catholicism. One great strength of Catholicism was that, while the quality of the Protestant service was liable to depend on that of the sermon, the Catholic could expect to find his familiar mass wherever he worshipped. While one cannot altogether generalise, the distinct religious practices were bound to contribute to different approaches to life.

Thus what was to become Germany developed mainly two, but to some extent three, cultures based on religious differences. These have largely survived there to this day – up to a point even in a more secular setting – at least in the original *Länder* of the Federal Republic. As it was the princes who could initially after the Reformation settle the religion of their subjects, a considerable theological variety of church doctrine and organisation emerged, even among the Protestant states. Religious change and the strengthening of the power of the territorial rulers went hand in hand. Each territorial state proceeded very much in its own way in both religious and secular affairs. The Reformation and the end of religious unity thus directly and indirectly increased even further the dissimilarities between various parts of Germany. The distinctions due to the many forms of government under which Germans lived, ranging from secular principalities to ecclesiastical ones, from cities to various forms of lordship, which had already existed before the Reformation, were accentuated by religious division. Thus the Empire in some respects was left with even less political unity than before. However, the Empire benefited from the general revulsion against religious wars which bore fruit in the masterly compromise of the Peace of Westphalia removing religious matters from the general arena and relegating them to separate assemblies of Catholics and Protestants. Freed from the bickering over confessional disputes which had gone on over a long time and defied the possibility of compromise, imperial organs including the diet were able to devote their energies to constructive matters in a less contentious atmosphere.

By virtue of his *jus reformandi*, the prince determined what was by common consent at the time the most crucial aspect of life. This was the question of the correct religious faith, for on that eternal salvation, which ultimately ranked higher than all the tribulations of life on earth, appeared to depend. With few exceptions, in the first, Lutheran, Reformation, the princes settled the issue without prior consultation with the Estates.[2] Their decision was facilitated by the situation in the 1520s and for some time afterwards, in which the reformatory movement seemed to carry all before it. A ruler introducing the Lutheran Reformation at a fairly early date, while not expecting to please everybody, could be reasonably sure of substantial support from the leading sections of society as well as some from the broad masses of the people.

With a 'second reformation', however, such as appeared to have been contemplated in Saxony around 1590, and actually attempted in Brandenburg in 1613, only the ruler's personal predilections seem to have counted. Indeed the 'first', Lutheran reformations in these two electorates had taken root so well as to bring about an effective resistance to Calvinisation. In both cases the Estates spearheaded the opposition, in which they were particularly successful as they did not merely represent their own interests, but acted as the voice of a widely held public opinion. The limits to the power of the prince become obvious in this. Generally by the last decade or so of the sixteenth century, and well before the formal prohibition stipulated in the Peace of Westphalia, the ruler of a territory could no longer carry out a second reformation. In no question could the Estates represent public opinion so powerfully as in matters of religious conviction. There are some parallels here to the situation in England, where religio-political questions also became acute in this period.

The prince, however, if he opted to take his territory out of the Catholic Church, had to make further decisions about the religious faith of his subjects. By breaking away from the old faith he freed himself from its hierarchy and had to put something else in its place. He became a kind of bishop, initially perhaps an 'emergency bishop' (*Notbischof*), but as the situation became permanent he virtually developed into a 'supreme bishop' (*summus episcopus*), and was 'pope' in his territory. He governed the Church in his territory through ecclesiastical 'consistories' which he controlled. The governing authorities of the Protestant cities also ruled over their churches. The roughly 65 imperial cities fell into four different constitutional categories, varying from mainly Protestant to principally Catholic cities, as well as some in which Lutherans and Catholics achieved legal equality.[3] Altogether Germans lived in comparatively small and therefore easily controllable states, which fostered authoritarianism, obedience and a passivity due to an indoctrination with the belief that the rulers knew best.

Catholic bishops, who normally exercised secular authority only over the smaller part of their dioceses, did not have to make a decision on religion, though there were cases where they favoured the Reformation and were removed or had to resign. Many prelates were great patrons of the arts, others founded universities in their diocese, like Julius Echter of Mespelbrunn, Bishop of Würzburg from 1573 to 1617. Although in the nature of things the modernisation of government faced difficulties in the prince-bishoprics, they were not by any means all badly run; often the actual administration was in the hands of suffragan bishops (*Weihbischöfe*) who did not belong to the high nobility. But some of the bishoprics, such as Würzburg under Echter, were oppressively counter-reformatory. In a later period, in 1731–2, the expulsion of the Protestants by Leopold Anton of Firmian, Archbishop of Salzburg, was a blow, though largely a temporary one, to hopes of a more relaxed atmosphere between the confessions. However, from about 1750, the Catholic Enlightenment dominated in most episcopal territories. The quality of the bishops varied, but some of them were outstanding personalities and administrators, such as members of the Schönborn dynasty. Their principal sphere of activity was in the Franconian bishoprics on the River Main, though some of them also occupied episcopal seats elsewhere. One of the most capable archbishop-electors was also the last in his principality: Archduke Max Franz, the youngest son of Maria Theresa succeeded to the coveted Cologne archdiocese in 1784; he died in 1801.[4]

A general problem for bishops, who themselves were mostly drawn from princely and aristocratic families, presented itself in their dealings with often uncooperative cathedral chapters; prior to election, members of the chapters had to produce an ever-increasing number of noble ancestors. Because of this resistance from the chapters, the prince-bishops, unlike the secular rulers, could only partially establish absolutism in their dominions. From the beginning of the Seven Years War onwards fears of secularisation grew.[5] Although many of the prelates carried out reforms, the combination of the power of bishop and prince in the ecclesiastical states in some ways assumed an anachronistic appearance.[6]

How far was the power of the secular princes strengthened as a result of the Lutheran Reformation? At first glance the answer appears to be in the affirmative. The religious division of the Empire was an important factor both in preventing a resurrection of the power of the emperor under Charles V and Ferdinand II, and in weakening the coherence of the Empire. In the end the only way the institution could be preserved was by loosening the ties that held together the Empire even further and by abandoning for the time being all attempts at religious reunion. Thus the confessions were allowed to go their own way in matters of faith. This left the princes autonomous, that is to say largely independent, in secular matters. Also, through the *jus reformandi*, they became practically supreme in matters of faith. While between 1555 and 1648 their choice was legally limited to that between Catholicism and Lutheranism, it was also exercised in favour of Calvinism, for instance in the case of the Palatinate. Officially, this third option did not exist at the time. Therefore the repeated exercise of the *jus reformandi*, such as that attempted by Elector John Sigismund of Brandenburg in 1613 to convert the population from Lutheranism to Calvinism, was presumably not envisaged at Augsburg in 1555. The Peace of Westphalia in 1648 wisely clarified the situation in ruling out a further exercise of the *jus reformandi*, while at the same time recognising Calvinism, the 'Reformed' religion, as one of the permitted faiths in the Empire. The *jus reformandi* logically covered not only the initial decision to change to Protestantism, but the establishment of a new church order on the abolition of the old. However, not all historians are in agreement that the possession of the *jus reformandi* and all that went with it in fact furthered the process of consolidation of the princely territorial state.[7]

In the context of the age, the prince thus had power over what his subjects considered a question more important than any other. This was a matter over which many of them were not prepared to compromise their convictions and for which they risked imprisonment, torture or even execution, and for which they were, if necessary, prepared to leave their homes and to emigrate. But as religion affected people so closely and often brought together persons of a variety of social standings and otherwise diverging interests, there were practical limitations on the power of the ruler to use his *jus reformandi*; this applied even if he governed by himself, without the Estates.

The late medieval Empire was dualistic in two respects, both at the *Reich* and the territorial level. It distinguished between the ecclesiastical and the secular sphere, and in government the Estates were generally associated with the prince, for example in financial administration, such as the collection of taxes. So far as the division between the two spheres is concerned, secularisation and the extension of the activities of the secular authorities did not begin with the Reformation, but they were afterwards often accelerated and intensified. The far-reaching princely control over the Church in the Protestant states may well have provided additional encouragement for Roman Catholic princes, for example in Bavaria, to tighten their hold on the

Church. However, in the nature of things, they could not do it quite to the same extent. Certainly in the Protestant states there was some streamlining under the prince's central authority. Secularisation partly did away with a certain pluralism that had arisen for example from the variety of monastic orders. This pluralism had been characteristic of the medieval Church and in some ways even continued in the post-Tridentine era. What also contributed to a strengthening of the power of the state was that princely officials during their visitations were liable to sit in judgment on an individual's personal way of life. This had earlier been the function of the priest and the ecclesiastical authorities. The culture of humanism, with its greater measure of freedom, yielded to a more bureaucratic approach. Control over the individual thus became more 'total', though not in the sense of twentieth century totalitarianism. Still, the safeguards provided by Augustinian and Gelasian doctrines about the two spheres, and more recently by Luther's teaching about the Two Kingdoms, were swept away. These developments removed some of the major obstacles to the eventual establishment of twentieth century totalitarianism.

At the same time that the prince increased his power over the ecclesiastical sphere, he also reduced the power exercised by the Estates, while becoming more independent of the emperor. Thus at the level of his own principality, the prince often acted against the Estates, while in the Empire he insisted on his right as an estate against the authority of the emperor.[8] In theory there is an inconsistency here. In practice the process of strengthening the authority of the ruler in his territory was driven by events, by the lack of unity in the Empire, caused at least partly by the religious division. This had brought in its train the Thirty Years War, including its invasions by both domestic and foreign enemies. In emergency situations, the prince could not always wait for the consent of the different estates of a realm, like Brandenburg–Prussia, which were generally dominated by purely local interests. Obviously large well-armed states had the best chance of surviving at a time like the Thirty Years War; in the West, the danger of invasion continued in view of the threat from France, for example in the Palatinate, as happened later.

Often it was the princes, if only in many cases by being the beneficiaries of hereditary rights or by laying down indivisibility through regulation of the succession, who created large states. The consolidation of their territories appeared to be a necessity in view of the turmoil of the period and the urgency of economic reconstruction after the ravages of the Thirty Years War. The composition of the assembly of estates varied, but typically they represented the estates of the nobility and the towns; in the ecclesiastical principalities their place was taken by the cathedral chapters. The Estates were generally mainly concerned with the interests of the territory or province within the state that they represented.[9] In Brandenburg–Prussia,

there were numerous assemblies of Estates representing different territories. The only chance of overcoming their parochialism might have been
the establishment of Estates-General for the whole of the monarchy, but the
monarchs striving for absolute government in this period objected to this
kind of development; they were prepared to accept provincial assemblies up
to a point, if they did not become too powerful. Particularly a ruler like
Frederick William, the Great Elector of Brandenburg (1640–88), thought
more in terms of limiting the power of the Estates than of their participation.
That left the way clear for autocracy and militarisation which characterised
Brandenburg–Prussia from the reign of the Great Elector onwards; it was
particularly marked under King Frederick William I, the 'soldier king'
(1713–40) and under his son Frederick the Great (1740–86). Generally,
not only in Brandenburg–Prussia, but elsewhere, in most territories in
Germany the rulers succeeded in reducing the influence of the Estates
over the state as a whole and prevented them from exercising or gaining a
representative role. Instead they became privileged corporations. However,
various estates (*Stände*), in particular the nobility, and in the ecclesiastical
states the cathedral chapters, remained of importance in complementing the
power and machinery of the state, such as by patrimonial jurisdiction and in
many administrative matters. In this modified form the *Ständestaat* survived
socially and economically.[10]

The major states established standing armies which were under the sole
control of the ruler and outside that of the Estates. An incidental result of
the organisation and maintenance of troops on a larger scale was an extension of the financial and economic activities of the state, with a strengthening
of the power of the ruler. The armies were used for internal suppression by
the prince, not only in Brandenburg, where the Great Elector ruthlessly
crushed the opposition of the Estates in the only recently acquired duchy of
Prussia. Certainly among major German states, Württemberg, where an
unbroken and in many ways effective Estates representation continued
into the nineteenth century, was the exception.[11] The efficacy of the Estates
was hampered by a clash of interests between the nobility and the burghers
represented in them. Still, the general lack of effective representative institutions weakened the German states when they had to deal with the dynam-
ism of the French Revolution and of Napoleon, and made their transition to
the political and constitutional development of the nineteenth century more
difficult.

Many rulers, particularly those of Brandenburg–Prussia, compensated the
nobility for its loss of influence in the Estates by giving it a leading role in the
administration of the state and by largely reserving commissions in the army
for it. Frederick William, the Great Elector of Brandenburg, came to terms
with the nobility by increasing its power over the peasants, for whom it
became much harder to gain their freedom from serfdom.[12]

An evaluation of the historical position of princes, such as those of Brandenburg–Prussia in this period, is not easy to achieve. It will be recalled from the previous chapter that the rulers of the Protestant electorate of Brandenburg adopted Calvinism just before the Thirty Years War. This step has often been seen as one of the reasons for the rise of Brandenburg–Prussia in the long term. That this state overtook Electoral Saxony in importance may well have owed something to a 'dynamic, aggressive, Calvinism', which thought in world-wide terms, and had its connections with France, Holland, Switzerland and England. Lutheranism, for example in Saxony, tended to be 'fixed on the *status quo*'.[13] Also there was bound to be a certain weakening of confessional exclusiveness if ruler and ruled followed different versions of the Christian faith, without necessarily implying general tolerance or a weakening of autocracy. One action Frederick William, the Great Elector, took certainly came more readily to a Calvinist than a Lutheran ruler. That was the offer of asylum to the Huguenot refugees, his brethren in faith, fleeing from France after the revocation of the Edict of Nantes by Louis XIV in 1685. This gesture had rich rewards, for the skills and cultural accomplishments of the immigrants were of immense benefit to the capital, Berlin, in particular, and to Brandenburg–Prussia in general.[14] Altogether, Frederick William was the first ruler to have a vision of his state which looked to its future importance not only in the Empire, but also on the European stage, to which the recent acquisitions both in the west and in the east appeared to beckon. To achieve that he needed a large standing army, which he wished to finance without having to seek the traditionally required agreement of the Estates to taxes, and which could in turn also be used to curb the Estates. There were implications here for foreign policy, which will be treated in its general context at the end of the chapter.

The next elector, Frederick, took a great interest in the intellectual and artistic development of the state. In 1701 he was able, by arrangement with the Habsburgs (which was not without its cost, as will be shown later) to acquire the royal crown in Prussia. As this was a territory outside the Empire, his new rank did not trespass on Habsburg interests by rivalling the stepping-stone to the emperorship, the kingship of the Romans. Thus Frederick caught up in rank with Augustus the Strong of Saxony, who – also outside the Empire – had become King of Poland a few years earlier. The succession of Elector George of Hanover to the British crown in 1714 followed somewhat of a similar pattern, except that it was just as important for Augustus to be a Catholic in Poland as it was for George not to be one in Britain. After 1714 only two of secular electors – those of the Palatinate and Bavaria, merged in 1777 – were not titular kings.

Frederick's son was Frederick William I, the 'soldier king', who combined irascibility and at times actual cruelty, for instance in his treatment of the

crown prince, with high ethical principles in some respects, as well as outstanding organisational ability. The militarism of the Prussian state may have
gone further than that of the other German monarchies, and already
attracted negative comment at the time, but in the period large standing
armies in the major territories were the norm rather than the exception in
the Empire. The King introduced the 'cantonal' system for military recruit-
ment, under which 'officers and men... were... stationed in their home
districts', incidentally strengthening the hold of the nobility over the peasants.[15] He left his son a full treasury.

Frederick William I was a strict Calvinist and as he agreed with the
spiritual beliefs of the pietists, he encouraged them in his dominions,[16] just
as his father had done when he staffed the theological faculty of the newly
founded University of Halle with them. This movement, that arose within
Lutheranism but outside its official organisation, 'emphasised the practice of
piety, the precedence of life over doctrine, the practical relationship to the
bible, the social impulses'.[17] Pietism in one form was contemplative, but in
another, which predominated for a long time, concerned with practical
reforms of society. Within the context of the Prussian state, pietism helped
to promote an officialdom that based itself on a strict ethical and religious
code; it was almost created for a 'religion of civil servants' (*Beamtenreli-
gion*); it also helped to 'defeudalise' the nobility by bringing together various
social ranks.[18] Pietism has been called the 'great entrance gate of the German Enlightenment'.[19] Both directions of pietism rejected orthodoxy, scholasticism, and any kind of dogmatism.[20]

Frederick William I has often been condemned as a tyrant and excessive
militarist. However for others the King has represented a father who stood
for Christian values diametrically opposed to totalitarian ideology.[21] In his
testament of 1722, the King warned the Crown Prince against an unjust war,
both on religious and practical grounds.[22] The future Frederick the Great
was, unlike his father, strongly influenced by the Enlightenment. How was
he going to deal with the ethical problem his father posed?

The question 'What is the Enlightenment (*Aufklärung*)?' occupied many
of its thinkers in the eighteenth century, including the great philosopher
Immanuel Kant (1724–1804), who emphasised as its essential element
the courage to make use of one's own intelligence (*Verstand*). All spheres
of life were subject to critical examination and open discussion in the light
of reason (*Vernunft*), including religion and church, state and society, as
well as philosophy and science. The Enlightenment stressed the need for
the individual to form his own independent judgment (*Selbstdenken*). For
this Kant regarded freedom as an indispensable prerequisite, in the sense
of 'making use in public of his reason in all matters'.[23] In itself the
Enlightenment was not so much an ideology as a way of thinking. To its
thinkers the process of critical examination was in some ways more

important than its result, which would then in turn be subjected to rigorous critique.

While the German Enlightenment was in one sense part of an international movement, it was bound to be influenced by three factors setting it apart from, say, its English or French counterpart. Germany had an officially sanctioned religious division, it had a multiplicity of territories of different types and, at the time when the movement began, did not yet have a national language in general use. Many legal documents were still drawn up in Latin. French was in fashion for educated people. Thus Frederick the Great was much more at ease in French than in German, for the advances in whose literature he only showed contempt.

Within the context of this book, Enlightenment attitudes to religion are of particular interest. One of the greatest achievements of the Enlightenment in this respect was to imply, as did the philosopher Christian Wolff (1679–1754), that a clear distinction had to be made between knowledge and faith, without, however, in any way questioning the key importance of the latter.[24] The persecution and slaughter of the preceding period certainly led to a questioning of the relationship between church and state, as well as of the methods followed to enforce religious orthodoxy. There was among the educated an increase in the number of deists (who, according to Kant, believed in God) and of theists (who, also according to Kant, believed in an active [*lebendig*] God). Furthermore, unorthodox religious beliefs could readily be found especially among the great writers of the Enlightenment. However, among the rulers in the Empire a freethinker like Frederick the Great was an exception. In Germany (and elsewhere in Europe) the vast majority of the population at all levels in the period of the Enlightenment still followed some version of the Christian faith.

Many theologians took their cue from the Enlightenment without losing faith. While pietists stressed the central position of religious faith, they did not reject Enlightenment attitudes altogether. Indeed, not only Protestants but also Catholics at times found the perspectives of the Enlightenment helpful in increasing their religious understanding. This does not imply that the laity and some of the clergy were necessarily strongly affected in their own fundamental beliefs. But many of them had increasing doubts about the confessional state, for example about the way religious matters were handled by the authorities, both ecclesiastical and secular.

It was initially Catholics who gave important impulses to the Enlightenment in certain respects. Resuming the humanist tradition, which had been under a cloud in the Old Church owing to the controversies of the Reformation period, it was now Catholic theologians and church historians who first applied a critical historical approach to the sources.[25] The French Oratorian Richard Simon (1638–1712) was one of the pioneers of historical Biblical criticism with a work on the Old Testament in 1678; he continued his pursuit undeterred by the suppression of his writing and his expulsion from his order.[26] In spite of the treatment meted out to Simon, the methods he used were in fact employed on a wide scale in many French monasteries in the seventeenth century when Bollandists, Benedictines and Maurists applied critical standards to the sources in their studies of church history, such as the legends of saints. Thus the efforts of enlightened non-Catholic scholars in the eighteenth century had already in some ways been preceded by Catholic church historians.[27] The Catholic Enlightenment, which had a strong impact on Germany, contributed to better teaching in schools and universities, helped to overcome superstition, and led to a greater involvement of the laity in the Church, which became better able to respond to the needs of the time.[28]

Thus at least parts of the Catholic Church, which for much of the Enlightenment represented the forces of darkness, were active in purifying its religious observances. Unfortunately, the unmeasured and often uncomprehending attacks non-Catholics made on the Catholic Church only served to increase the tensions arising from religious disunity, which was bound to hit Germany particularly hard. At the same time there was a much more positive side to the ideas coming from the Protestant Enlightenment in Germany. The decisive influence of philosophers like, above all, Immanuel Kant, but also of Christian Wolff, cannot be overemphasised.

Culture needs its language, and for the German Enlightenment to come fully into its own as an equal in the international community, a language had to be developed that met people's needs at various social levels. It had to be capable of expressing the complex thoughts of specialists, and yet also of being understood by a lay readership. The German language of Gotthold Ephraim Lessing (1729–81), Johann Gottfried Herder (1744–1803), Johann Wolfgang Goethe (1749–1832) and Friedrich Schiller (1759–1805) combined this practical purpose with rare beauty and simplicity of language. These qualities owed something to Shakespearian influences, which were strong in Germany at the time. It is no coincidence that one of the early founders of modern German literature, Lessing, was a profound political as well as religious thinker. His famous drama *Nathan der Weise* in 1779 advocated tolerance towards others religions like Judaism and Islam. The great figures of this flowering of German literature in the second half of the eighteenth century and the early decades of the nineteenth came mainly from writers with a Protestant background.

The Protestant Enlightenment in Germany made a considerable contribution to political development by its insistence on public discussion and on securing the maximum possible freedom for it. Interestingly enough Enlightenment thinkers in Germany looked to the princes to implement their ideas for reform, rather than, for example, to the governments of cities, which were usually oligarchic, often ultra-conservative and not particularly tolerant of dissent.[29] As it was up to a point opposed to a society structured by Estates, the Enlightenment was not particularly sympathetic to assemblies of Estates, from whom it expected little in the way of reform. Alongside a questioning and rather critical attitude, there were also authoritarian elements in the Enlightenment, an 'elitist' intellectual movement which believed that it knew what was best for the populace.

The Enlightenment had an ambivalent attitude to the authoritarianism of princes. On the one hand it looked to 'philosopher-kings' to put its approach into practice. On the other hand it condemned excessive curbs on freedom of expression, for instance through the censorship generally practiced by the princes. The solution to the dilemma appeared to hinge on the success enlightened senior officials had in their attempts to mould the absolutist state in the image of the Enlightenment. This can be seen in Prussia in the activities of Carl Gottlieb Svarez (1746–98), who prepared the new law code, the *Allgemeine Landrecht*, which was commissioned and largely drafted in the reign of Frederick II and proclaimed in 1794 by his successor Frederick William II.[30] The code systematised the law, stated principles which governed rights and duties, and in the process subjected the powers of the monarch to constitutional procedures; the rigid division into 'estates' denoting social status was somewhat watered down.[31]

The general principles (*Allgemeine Grundsätze*) of the code contained remarkable statements on the exercise of religious beliefs, constituting a break with many of the assumptions of the confessional state. Subjecting faith and divine service[32] to compulsory laws was prohibited. Every inhabitant of the state was to enjoy complete freedom of faith and conscience. Nobody was to be harassed, called to account, ridiculed or persecuted because of his religious opinions. The state was only to demand information about the religion of an individual subject if the validity of civic acts depended on that. However, if individuals admitted dissident opinions, the disadvantages arising from them were to be limited strictly to any disqualifications laid down by law.

Remarkably, independent thinkers of great ability like Svarez and the co-author of the law code, Ernst Ferdinand Klein (1744–1810), played a dual role in the process of reform. Although they were officials making submissions to the king, they were able at the same time to discuss the principles of the law reform in which they were engaged freely in societies surrounded by a certain aura of secrecy, out of reach of governmental control. The German rulers were often very well served by highly trained, cultured officials at the most senior levels. These civil servants accepted the limitations on their influence imposed by their status as servants of a near-absolute ruler, like Frederick II of Prussia. Here and elsewhere, the princes strove to create an efficient new bureaucracy based on the nobility, as well as the upper echelons of the bourgeoisie. Often the officials had studied cameral science

(*Kameralwissenschaft*), the science of government, at the universities. This development owed much to rationalism and to the Enlightenment, and gradually contributed to a modification of the nature of the confessional state. For example in the Prussian law code, both the official and minority religions were in an even-handed way in certain respects treated as *Religionsparteien*.

As Frederick II was, unlike his father, a freethinker, he loosened the reins on religious debate and had Voltaire stay at his court, though they eventually quarrelled. In general Frederick ruled autocratically, but he did have some genuine sympathy for the ideals of the Enlightenment. He had an awareness of the importance of publicity which was exceptional for a German ruler of his time. While many Enlightenment thinkers were sharply critical of aspects of his regime, such as its militarism and the heavy hand of the censorship on political debate, they also acknowledged the king's contribution to a relaxation of absolutism in other respects. Certainly Frederick acquired great merits not only through initiating the codification of the law, but also in contributing in many ways to the humanisation of the legal process, for example by the abolition of torture.

In dealing with the question of enlightened monarchs, some confusion was caused by the introduction of the term 'enlightened despotism'. In fact Frederick's advisers like Svarez regarded despotism or tyranny as an abrogation of the duty of the monarch and as a breach of what they saw as the contract between ruler and ruled. However, they did not go so far as to define the circumstances which would justify resistance.

Like Frederick II, Maria Theresa (1740–80) realised the need for reform in her dominions, particularly after her defeat at his hands in the early years of her reign. Indeed, she was quite prepared to learn from her enemy. However, in spite of some common problems, the situation she faced in the Habsburg Monarchy was different from that of Prussia in major respects. While the King of Prussia exercised unchallenged authority over the various parts of his kingdom, which he could largely govern as one unit or make into one, what is called the Habsburg Monarchy by historians did not consist of one state, but was more in the nature of a personal union. Some parts, like Hungary and the Southern Netherlands, possessed certain special rights.

In view of the setbacks it received at the hands of Frederick II, the Habsburg Monarchy seemed to be in more urgent need of reform than even Prussia, which often found itself in desperate situations, particularly during the Seven Years War (1756–63). The financial requirements of the Habsburg Monarchy were certainly very pressing and necessitated a thorough reform of government.[33] Unlike the Habsburg Monarchy, Protestant Prussia did not have a church problem. The estates of the Church including the monasteries had generally been secularised. In various ways the major

Protestant churches in the kingdom came under the authority of the ruler or at least under his influence.

In the Habsburg Monarchy the situation was entirely different. Maria Theresa and her son Joseph II, as the Catholic rulers under various titles of a whole array of territories, only had limited control over the institutions of the Church in their dominions. How much of the wealth in Austria and other parts of the monarchy was in hands of the Church is not easy to establish.[34] Government actions against the Church seemed to historians for a long time to emanate more obviously from Joseph II than from his pious mother, leading to the formulation of the concept of *Josephinismus*.[35] However, the rationale that a pious ruler like Maria Theresa was unlikely to be in the forefront of a movement to interfere with the Church and to reduce its powers and wealth is not conclusive. Maria Theresa was, indeed, a deeply religious person and a firm believer in the Catholic tradition of her family. She still embodied some of the mentality of the Counter-Reformation in her horror of Protestantism and of non-Christian faiths, like Judaism. But she was a person of independent critical judgment and formed her own view on matters of faith. Her reign coincided with quite acrimonious debates within the Church on various issues, such as those which led to the dissolution of the Jesuit order. Others centred on the degree of authority exercised by the pope over bishops, which came to a head in Febronianism in Germany.

The Febronianist controversy began in 1763 with the publication of *De Statu Ecclesiae* in Frankfurt by a writer using the pseudonym Justinus Febronius. The author was the Trier Suffragan Bishop (*Weihbischof*) Nikolaus von Hontheim (1701–90). For quite some time after suspicion fell on him, Hontheim denied authorship, but eventually in 1778 agreed to a formal recantation. Febronius–Hontheim wrote his tract with the intention of clearing away what he regarded as obstacles to efforts to overcome a religious division which he considered to be the *Calamitas Imperii*. For him one of the main stumbling-blocks consisted of many of the monarchical powers claimed by the popes, whom he wanted to reduce to the position of *primus inter pares* among the bishops. He asserted that all bishops were equal and that they were not subject to the jurisdiction of the pope, to whom General Councils of the Church were superior. Febronius' writings could be construed as advocacy of a German National Church, perhaps on Gallican lines, and as paving the way for a measure of state control over the Church in a *Staatskirchentum* or *Josephinismus*. Hontheim's views found considerable support, even among the Catholic authorities in Germany. They had an echo in the protest of the three Ecclesiastical Electors and the Archbishop of Salzburg at the congress of Ems in 1786 against the appointment of a permanent papal *nuncio* in Munich. The famous *Punktation* drawn up by the archbishops asserted the right of bishops to administer their dioceses without

Roman interference.[36] But in the end Febronianism faded from the picture. This was due to contradictions between episcopalianism and the concept of state churches,[37] and to the unwillingness of bishops to support the strengthening of the power of their 'metropolitans' (the heads of church provinces who were normally archbishops) demanded in the *Punktation*.[38] In any case the cataclysmic effects of the French Revolutionary and Napoleonic period overtook these ecclesiastical controversies.[39]

Looked at from the outside, the Catholic Church often created a monolithic impression, such as in its closing of ranks against non-Catholics. But internally there was considerable variety and indeed pluralism, though from time to time in the form of rather unseemly quarrels, some of which were precipitated by the Jesuits. Every fair-minded observer recognised their outstanding achievements as intellectuals and as academic teachers at the universities which had been entrusted to them. Though Catholics were aware of the great services the order had rendered to their Church, many of them, including those supporting ecclesiastical reform, were also critical of many aspects of its activities. The Society of Jesus, which traditionally had strong links with the papacy, often occupied key positions through providing the confessors of rulers. However, the political influence the order was thus believed to have acquired and what one historian calls 'its often questionable manner of exploiting this power' brought it into conflict with reform Catholicism and with the Bourbon courts in Spain, France and Italy.[40] Here one moves in the sphere of hearsay and it is difficult to know which of the allegations made against the order were true. In any case, pressure from courts critical of the Jesuits resulted in a general dissolution of the order by the pope in 1773.

The Jesuits had also incurred intense enmity on account of their attacks on those they perceived to be deviants from the true faith in the Church, such as the Jansenists. These were called after the Dutch theologian and Belgian Bishop Cornelius Jansen (1585–1638), who criticised Catholic doctrines relating to grace and freedom of the will. Jansen's *Augustinus*, which was published posthumously, was condemned by the papacy. After a period in which Jansenist or similar beliefs flourished in France, particularly through the famous convent of Port Royal in Paris, persecution there led to the emigration of some of their leaders and followers to the Low Countries. Actually Jansenists from the Southern Netherlands, which the Austrian Habsburgs had acquired in the peace settlement after the War of the Spanish Succession, were among Maria Theresa's advisers. Though inclining increasingly towards Jansenist piety, which she found particularly consoling in her bereavement after the death of her husband the Emperor Francis, in earlier days she had 'cheerfully employed three Jesuits among Joseph's tutors'.[41] Furthermore, deep attachment to their faith had never prevented Catholic rulers from demanding from the papacy what they regarded as their rights. Finally, though Joseph II did not become sole ruler until his mother's death in 1780, he had considerable influence on his mother's decisions since becoming emperor and co-ruler on his father's death in 1765.

Thus many of the reforms which are often associated with *Josephinismus* took place during the reign of Maria Theresa, and even began in a major way before Joseph's co-rulership. These measures taken by Maria Theresa had strong cameralist aspects, in accordance with the science of the State that had been developed at the universities. Often, but not invariably, the interests of the State took precedence over those of the Church. She took a number of measures to further the economic interests of the State, such as the tightening up of the collection of taxes from the clergy (and the nobility),[42] and reducing the number of holy days.[43] Much of this legislation was motivated by the desire to mobilise in the interest of the State economic resources which the Church was believed to be withholding from the general community, and which were therefore not available for the public good.[44] In accordance with these principles, steps were taken by Maria Theresa in the 1770s to restrict 'the flow of money and property to the church' and to tap 'its wealth to the advantage of the state', as well as to assert 'the authority of the secular power over and against the clergy'.[45] Cameralism and reform Catholicism came together in many of these measures. Certainly this period saw efforts made by the authorities to ensure that the Church provided a better care for the souls and a liturgy related more closely to the people.

Sometimes reforms were taken earlier in Vienna than in Berlin, and went further. The Austrian capital was a melting-pot for ideas which came from various Habsburg dominions. It may have been a disadvantage from a military and administrative point of view that these possessions were scattered over various part of Europe. But culturally it was an asset that the court could draw on many different influences. These included those from the Southern Netherlands, from the German south-west with Freiburg, from Bohemia and from Hungary, and last, not least, from the Habsburg possessions in Italy. The latter were reinforced by the acquisition of Tuscany, where the future Emperor Leopold II was to establish a model enlightened regime.[46] What is particularly impressive in the Habsburg Monarchy is the detailed exchange of views that preceded the actual measures, certainly during the period of co-rule between 1765 and 1780. Many of the memoranda produced by the officials, such as the foreign minister and chancellor Prince Wenzel Anton Kaunitz (1711–94), were of a very high standard.[47] On the whole the disagreements between the reigning monarch and her son served a useful purpose in highlighting the main issues and possible solutions. Eventually Maria Theresa made her decision, which had to be accepted, both by her son and by Kaunitz. But this exceptionally able ruler, to whom the art of governing came naturally, saw to it that all the relevant problems had their airing.[48] How different this was from the way things were handled in Berlin. There Frederick II kept matters very much in his own hands by generally making a ruling one way or the other, usually on written submissions he received; this was, indeed, cabinet government, in the sense of decisions being made solitarily by the king in his cabinet.

If Joseph at times clashed with his mother, this was due only partly to the difference in outlook of the two generations or to the son's difficult temperament. Alongside her 'apparently advanced intentions in ecclesiastical matters'[49] Maria Theresa still remained in some ways a child of the Counter-Reformation, which Joseph assuredly was not. After a number of lingering disagreements, matters came to a head between them in 1780 over the rights and treatment of Moravian Protestants. Joseph and Kaunitz repeatedly pointed out that only the Holy Spirit and not force could bring about a conversion of these Protestants to Catholicism, and that punitive measures were self-defeating, as well as harmful to the State. Indeed their assumption was that where the interests of Catholicism clashed with those of the State, the latter were to prevail. But Maria Theresa remained adamant and in September sentenced 43 Moravians to deportation to Hungary. She died two months later, in November 1780. 'It was...a bitter irony...that only days before her death Maria Theresia seemed prepared to return to the draconian Counter-Reformation policy whose failure in the earlier part of the century had been largely responsible for the ecclesiastical reform impulse of her reign in the first place.'[50] As compared with her son and successor, Maria Theresa was more reluctant to clash with the pope than Joseph. For example the Empress abandoned plans drawn up between 1753 and 1756 'to combat Protestantism by creating new parishes in the Bohemian and Austrian lands, financed by a levy on the secular and regular clergy, and administered by a central Religious Fund' when the pope resisted these measures.[51]

As sole ruler between 1780 and 1790 Joseph had the opportunity to put into practice some of the ideas that his mother had opposed. His main achievement during this period was the granting of a degree of toleration to Lutherans, Calvinists and Jews. He also secularised monasteries on a considerable scale and directed the financial resources realised to improve school education and pastoral care. Joseph acted in relation to the monasteries both as a monarch in the interest of the State, and as a believing Catholic who was dissatisfied with the way the Church responded to its tasks. When Pope Pius VI in 1782 specially travelled to Vienna in an attempt to stop Joseph's measures regarding the Church, no concession of substance was made to him.[52] Little was done to leave to the Church its own sphere, and we are here at an early stage of the *Staatskirchentum*, of the State systematically intervening in the affairs of the Church. This *Staatskirchentum* was to prevail in both Catholic and Protestant Germany in the nineteenth century, probably to the disadvantage of both Church and State. In the long run there were certainly dangers inherent in the state taking over the internal affairs of churches. In some ways the changes made by Joseph II amounted to a relaxation of controls, for example when he transferred censorship of religious literature from the Church to the State.[53]

In the end Joseph's efforts ran into difficulties. This was due to his impatience and to his increasingly autocratic tendencies. He lacked the understanding his mother had for the variety in character of the Habsburg dominions, and managed to antagonise both the Belgians and the Hungarians, so that risings broke out in the two countries towards the end of his reign. In Hungary, for example, many of his measures had to be withdrawn, but the Edict of Toleration was retained. Joseph died in 1790, having witnessed the outbreak of the French Revolution the previous year and being fully aware of the dangerous situation in which his sister, Queen Marie Antoinette, found herself in France.

So far the various component parts of the Empire have been considered in their internal and especially religious aspects. In this section, relations between the various states in the Empire on the one hand, and between them and basically non-German powers on the other, are briefly considered. Although the Habsburg emperors after the Thirty Years War concentrated largely on the affairs of the Danube Monarchy, they continued to attach importance to the imperial crown and to the cultivation of ties with friendly territories. The weaker ones, such as the ecclesiastical principalities, cities and lordships were more dependent on protection from the emperor than the large secular states, but not all of them were in the Habsburg camp. Often the policy of a territory was influenced by the view its ruler took of the European powers – France and Sweden – that had obtained a foothold in the Empire during the Thirty Years War. The right to alliances, which the territories acquired in the Peace of Westphalia, and the complementary prerogative of arming themselves, allowed them to move freely on the European stage,[54] even if technically they were barred from actions against emperor and Empire.

In the *Rheinbund*, which lasted from 1658 to 1667, the three ecclesiastical electorates allied with France. Frederick William, the Great Elector of Brandenburg, was a regular recipient of French subsidies over long periods, which allowed him to finance his standing army without the normally required consent of the Estates to taxation. Rulers like Frederick William were on the whole not deterred from their alliance with France by the relentless pressure Louis XIV exercised to extend French rule into the western territory of the Empire, including the annexation of the famous city and bishopric of Strassburg in 1681. It was only when Louis invaded the United Provinces of the Netherlands in 1672 and when he took action against the Huguenots in 1685 that Frederick William momentarily interrupted his cooperation with France.

The major states of the Empire did, however, rally to its defence when Louis made quite unfounded claims in the Palatinate on the extinction of the main line of the dynasty with the death of the elector in 1685. He based these on rights which he alleged he was exercising on behalf of his brother's wife, the late elector's sister Elizabeth Charlotte ('Liselotte'). Many important princes of the Empire joined the emperor, Spain and Sweden in the League of Augsburg of 1686, to which England and the United Provinces of the Netherlands acceded after the 'Glorious Revolution' of 1688. French troops ravaged the Palatinate and burned down many cities, including the capital Heidelberg. Eventually peace was concluded in 1697 at Ryswick. The Palatinate was restored to its dynasty, to whose electorate a Catholic prince from a junior line of the dynasty now succeeded.[55] Emperor and Empire thus collaborated in to some extent checking Louis XIV's aggressive policy, at least for the time being, as part of a major international coalition.

Considerable efforts were made to settle the Spanish succession before the actual extinction of the male line of the house of Habsburg there, but in the end these proved unavailing. King Charles II of Spain shortly before his death in 1700 appointed Philip of Anjou, a grandson of Louis XIV, who was not in the foreseeable direct line of the French succession, as his sole heir. Philip was to inherit, in addition to the metropolitan country and its American colonies, the Southern Netherlands and the Spanish possessions in Italy. Louis' acceptance of Charles' will on behalf of his grandson in 1701 brought into the grand coalition against him the Austrian Habsburgs under Emperor Leopold I, who also had claims to the Spanish succession, supported by the maritime powers of England and the United Provinces of the Netherlands. In the Empire only the Elector of Bavaria and his younger brother, the Archbishop of Cologne, supported France. The Bavarian Wittelsbach dynasty actually held the Cologne electorate continuously from 1583 until 1761, when it was no longer able to present a male prince for the dignity. All the other Imperial Estates sided with the emperor. Elector Frederick III of Brandenburg was able to get Leopold's agreement to assume a royal crown in Prussia in return for his participation in the War of the Spanish Succession. Bavaria was occupied following Marlborough's victory in the battle of Blenheim in 1704. During the early years of the war Louis XIV suffered a series of defeats. But the death of Emperor Joseph I in 1711 and the succession of his younger brother Charles, the claimant to the Spanish crown, to the Austrian throne changed the situation by threatening to resurrect the empire of Charles V. Thus, because of concerns among the European states with the balance of power, the war ended in a compromise peace in 1713 and 1714 which largely preserved it. The Spanish dominions were divided, the metropolitan country with its colonies went to Philip of Anjou, who renounced all claims to the French throne, but other possessions, for instance in Italy, as well as the Southern Netherlands, passed to the Austrian Habsburgs. Bavaria was, incidentally, restored to its Wittelsbach rulers.

Another major conflict which took place at the same time, the Great Northern War of 1700 to 1721, was also of considerable concern to Germany. In these hostilities the rising power of Russia under Peter the Great challenged the Swedish hold over the Baltic, whereas Sweden under Charles XII, while defending its position, at the same time wanted to settle old scores with Poland. Apart from the importance of the Baltic as a shipping and trading route particularly for northern Germany, the Empire was affected because Sweden still possessed western Pomerania (claimed by Brandenburg–Prussia) and because Elector Augustus the Strong of Saxony had been elected King of Poland in 1697. Augustus was perhaps the most important of many distinguished converts to Catholicism, a step taken in his case to facilitate his election to the Polish crown, at the same time also strengthening the Saxon alliance with Austria. In Germany, with the conversion of a number of rulers (such as in Württemberg) or the hereditary succession of Catholics, such as in the Palatinate in 1685, the Old Church had in many ways regained ground. There were nine electors in the period between 1697 and 1777, when the Elector Palatine inherited Bavaria and the two electoral votes were merged. Of these only two were Protestants, the Elector of Brandenburg (who in 1701 assumed the Prussian crown) and the Elector of Hanover (since 1714 King of Great Britain).

Early in the war Charles defeated Augustus and declared him deposed as King of Poland. But the tide turned when Peter destroyed the Swedish army at Poltava in 1709. In 1713 the new Prussian King Frederick William I joined the anti-Swedish coalition and in the peace settlement, which was concluded in the years between 1718 and 1721, obtained most of western Pomerania for his state. Earlier on, Augustus had been able to reoccupy his Polish kingdom. In territorial terms the great beneficiary was Russia which acquired much of the eastern part of the southern Baltic coast.

In 1740 Frederick II of Prussia disregarded his father's warning against an unjust war, and with Bavarian help and some support from Saxony, challenged Habsburg hegemony in the Empire by invading and then annexing Silesia. In 1742 the election of the Elector Charles of Bavaria interrupted a long line of Habsburg emperors which had begun in the middle of the fifteenth century, though not for long. Emperor Charles VII lost his native electorate and died as an exile in Frankfurt in 1745, to be succeeded by Maria Theresa's husband, Francis I. In the peace settlement, Bavaria, which withdrew from the alliance with Prussia, was once more restored to the Wittelsbach dynasty.

During the three wars which Frederick fought, he was at times very close to defeat in the third of these, the Seven Years War (1756–63), which had considerable international dimensions. The historian Leopold von Ranke believed that the Seven Year War, in which Prussia was allied with Protestant Britain and faced the two major Catholic powers in Europe, France and Austria, was a war of religions; he wrote that this struggle was not an avowed one, but was so by its nature and perceived as such.[56] While there was no permanent international alignment along confessional lines (into which Orthodox Russia could not, in any case, be fitted so easily), the continual rivalry between Austria and Prussia certainly had religious overtones in the long run. In the nineteenth century, a decision for a *Großdeutsch* solution (of German unification including Austria) or a *Kleindeutsch* settlement (without Austria) at the same time determined whether Catholics or Protestants would predominate.[57]

In the Seven Years War, Prussia, which in 1757 demonstrated that it was prepared to defy a declaration of a *Reich* war against it, survived in the face of considerable odds, particularly internationally, and retained its Silesian conquest. The Austro-Prussian dualism in the Empire, in which the Habsburgs had a somewhat superior position, ensued. Frederick did not wish to destroy the Empire or to become emperor himself, which would in any case have been difficult for a non-Catholic.

The Polish Partition of 1772 brought Frederick into alliance with his old Austrian enemy, as well as with Catherine II of Russia, born in Germany as a princess of the minor principality of Anhalt–Zerbst. Prussia gained what became West Prussia, without (at that time) Danzig. However, Frederick II managed to checkmate Austrian plans both in 1778–9 (during the period of joint rule) and in 1785 (under Joseph II) to acquire Bavaria. Clearly Joseph was far less careful than his predecessors to maintain good will in the Empire and his Bavarian designs weakened the Habsburg position in the Empire.

Internally, the Empire still managed to hold together, in spite of all the rivalries between its territories. There had been a certain strengthening of its institutions since the Peace of Westphalia. The diet (*Reichstag*) could function again now that religious questions no longer disrupted its proceedings. In some of the 'circles' (*Reichskreise*) co-operation between the various member territories, often cutting across religious boundaries, had been improved. There was considerable criticism of the *Reichskammergericht*, the law court of the Estates of the Empire, at the time and since for the slowness of its process, some of which was, no doubt, quite justified. But in recent decades historians have pointed out that if things had been quite as bad as they were painted, large numbers of litigants would have hardly taken the trouble of seeking redress in the *Kammergericht* at Speyer, and after the flight from the French in 1693, at Wetzlar. The emperor gained in prestige by providing better service in the Imperial Aulic Council (*Reichshofrat*) in Vienna, which began its existence during the reign of Emperor Maximilian I and became firmly established during the sixteenth century;

following the stipulations of the Treaty of Westphalia, some Protestant members were appointed. Generally, the emperor still had a considerable position in Germany. By the time of the death of Frederick II in 1786 and the outbreak of the French Revolution in 1789 there were no signs that the Empire was about to disintegrate.[58]

Compared with many other countries, including even England, and certainly France, the Empire provided a great deal of tolerance, both in religion and in politics. The different confessions, could, with some notable exceptions, co-exist to a greater extent in the Empire after 1648 than in France, with its campaign to force Huguenots to convert to Catholicism around 1685, or in England with its anti-Catholic hysteria a few years earlier. Politically, the Empire appeared as an absurdity to liberals in the post-Napoleonic period who applied the yardstick of the national state to it. That was a completely unhistorical standard for the period before the early nineteenth century, and therefore not relevant to the Empire which ceased to exist in 1806. With the *reductio ad absurdum* of much of European nationalism culminating in the Second World War, more understanding for the positive points of the Empire has been shown in our age with its supranational institutions. The unification of Germany and the exclusion of Austria showed how difficult it was to fit all or most of German culture into the political boundaries of the new national state. Complications of this kind did not arise in a loose structure like the Empire, which was even diagnosed at the time as not conforming to any of the recognised types of government and which in some ways appeared to be similar to a *monstrum*.[59] Perhaps it was these apparent contradictions which gave it its flexibility so that it could accommodate so much variety in political organisation. Bismarck's extrusion of Austria from 'Germany' in 1866 certainly created other problems.

The defence of the Empire cannot be seen quite so positively as its internal order. It is true that there was a measure of successful co-operation, for example against Turkish invasions. Also Austria, particularly due to the achievements of Prince Eugene of Savoy (1663–1736), succeeded in freeing many of the central and eastern parts of Europe from the Turks. But in the sixteenth and seventeenth centuries the Empire had been unable to resist the French drive towards the east, which had made considerable inroads into its western border areas, such as Alsace and Lorraine. Unfortunately Austria and Prussia, on which the defence of the Empire would mainly depend in the future, often had divergent interests on the European stage. Were they going set their differences aside and wage a united fight for the maintenance of the integrity of the Empire? And how was the Empire going to stand up to the dual threat of foreign invasion and of such concepts as nationalism, republicanism, the equality of all citizens, and the sovereignty of the people, that were bound to be disruptive of its existing order?

In 1789, on the eve of the French Revolution, the religious balance in the German kingdom and the Empire still somewhat favoured Catholicism over Protestantism. The Empire, even if it now permitted Lutheranism and Calvinism, preserved its Catholic character, for instance in the coronation ceremonies, which impressed even non-Catholics. The emperor was a Catholic, so were the majority of the electors, emphasised by the three archbishops among them, who occupied a very special position largely independent of Rome and claimed parity of rank with the Roman cardinals. Catholicism had vibrant cultural centres, with universities, in various parts of the Germanic world, including the Rhineland, Westphalia, Franconia, Bavaria, and – last not least – Austria. Similarly, Protestantism was strongly established, as is clear from this chapter, but could not yet challenge Catholicism for hegemony.

The events during the French Revolutionary and Napoleonic eras between 1789 and 1815 were to put all this to a test.[60]

10 Conclusions

Quite naturally, 'national' histories are written by the various peoples to help their citizens understand their past and to trace their antecedents. This offers comparatively few problems of principle if the country concerned can look back on a history of several centuries, and was able to make the transition from a territorial or dynastic to a national state, largely keeping traditional frontiers; that would apply, for example, to France, and in some ways to England. In the case of Germany, writing its history is a more complicated task, because there was no clearly definable German territorial state from which a national state could emerge with comparative ease. In 1789, there were instead a number of territories in which German language and culture prevailed, from Prussia (except for example in the parts inhabited by Polish populations), Bavaria, Saxony, and so forth, to most of the Austrian hereditary lands. At that time, however, there was not yet a feeling on the part of the inhabitants that they all belonged to what might be called a German nation. The rulers were certainly not prepared to subordinate themselves to a superior authority, like the (usually Austrian) emperor. Indeed the history of the previous centuries documented their striving to emancipate themselves largely from imperial authority.

There existed a 'Teutonic', or later in the Middle Ages and early Modern Times something like a Germanic or German kingdom, which formed a large part of the Holy Roman Empire. Originally this kingdom was one of three that earlier on had all belonged to the Empire; the other two were Burgundy (or Arles) and Italy (which was the old Langobard or Lombard state mainly in the north of Italy). By the end of our period, these two kingdoms had long ceased to be in the Empire, which had also shed many other outlying territories, such as Switzerland and the Low Countries. Historically, the German kingdom had been so closely interwoven with the Holy Roman Empire that it had not acquired so clearly defined an identity as France or England. In the Empire German and non-German peoples lived side by side, such as in Bohemia, whose king was one of the electors. Furthermore not all cultural Germans lived within the Empire, which did not include, for example, the Duchy of Prussia (later East Prussia).

Looking back over the centuries covered in the book, one is struck – at any rate in Ancient Times and the Middle Ages – by the ability of the Germanic peoples to absorb the cultures of peoples with whom they came into contact, for example in Italy. Through a degree of Romanisation and Christianisation, they were able to act as a link between classical and medieval civilisation, thus providing European continuity. When the popes found Rome threatened by the Langobards (another Germanic people) in the middle of the eighth century, they called on the Franks for help. These, unlike other Germanic peoples, had not lost their identity by merging with the populations they conquered, and they had become Catholics rather than Arians on their conversion to Christianity.

The papacy as the spiritual centre of Western Christendom was understandably concerned with its independence, which was threatened at various times by Byzantine emperors, Roman factions and outside forces, like the Langobards, the Saracens and the Normans. The Frankish kings became the protectors of the papacy. The connection was strengthened even further with the imperial coronation of Charlemagne by the pope in Rome in 800. The Frankish rulers thus became the successors of the (West) Roman emperors, now associated with the spiritual and cultural centre of Western Christendom, all the more significant because of the apocalyptic significance attached to the Roman Empire. For the popes as successors of St Peter who was martyred there, their presence in Rome was of great theological importance. But Rome was not a place where they could reside and maintain the necessary administrative apparatus with ease. The city was regarded as a prize not only by local groups, including the nobility, but also by outside forces, with its importance enhanced through the presence of the popes there. For the secular master of Rome was also liable to aim at controlling the papacy itself and elections to it. All this constituted a real problem for the papacy to which there was no easy solution. For the acceptance of protection to preserve its independence might result in dependance on the protector.

Furthermore, Rome could not be seen in isolation, but was part of the general situation in Italy. This is why the politics of Italy inevitably played an important part in papal policy, and thus also in the strategy of the protectors of the Holy See. Only a ruler who had a sufficient foothold in Italy had a chance of coming to the aid of the papacy with adequate dispatch. But this also made him a potential threat to the independence of the Holy See. Here was a dilemma the papacy never quite managed to solve, perhaps because it was almost insoluble. The establishment of the Patrimony of St Peter ('the papal states') was not necessarily the answer. In an age in which religion and politics were closely interwoven and even popes and bishops led soldiers into battle, the endowment of the pope with territory and secular authority is not a surprising development; this was particularly so as the pontiff in some ways bore himself as a kind of monarch.[1] But the power the pope had at his disposal was hardly adequate to deal with his local enemies, and certainly did not provide a sufficient defence against a determined foreign invader.

Interestingly enough, after the splitting up of the Carolingian Empire, it was the East Franks, the Teutons or future Germans, who succeeded to the imperial role, and not the French. In 962 Otto the Great was crowned emperor by the pope, who had sought his aid against his enemies. His grandson Otto III tried to lead a Roman revival, but his reign ended in failure.

The Frankish and then the East Frankish (German) rulers rendered great services to Western Christendom as protectors of the papacy. Again and again during the following centuries, they undertook the arduous and potentially hazardous expedition to Italy to come to the aid of the papacy against its local enemies or to deal with disputed pontifical elections. Their role in connection with the papacy increased their power, because during the course of these activities they became entitled to the Langobard or Lombard crown of mainly Northern Italy. Some control over these territories helped them to keep in check dukes, like those of Bavaria, with possessions in Italy. Imperial coronation by the pope in Rome added to their standing in Western Christendom, raising them over other kings. But there was a price to be paid. The Teutonic or Germanic kings had to go through a complicated process to establish themselves. As soon as they felt that they were sufficiently in control of the Germanic kingdom, they had to prepare for an expedition to Italy, usually accompanied by an army, normally raised with the consent of their magnates. They did not always find Italy welcoming. Their expeditions were liable to involve them in fighting. Relations with popes were sometimes strained. Rome was at times a battle-ground for them. The climate was inhospitable in some places, and many a German ruler or magnate with their troops succumbed to local epidemics to which they were not immune. Italian politics was full of surprises and not all German rulers understood them sufficiently or knew how to deal with them.

The great period of Teutonic influence and power over the papacy climaxed in the reign of Henry III, who found himself faced with a papal schism he had to resolve. Even if the wisdom of some of Henry's decisions can be questioned, there can be no doubt about the high ideals as a Christian ruler with which the emperor approached his task. He sincerely tried to nominate the best possible candidates for the Holy See and through his excellent choice in some cases, above all of Leo IX, initiated the era of the reform papacy. Through raising the standards of the pontificate, he also strengthened the institution. Because he left a minor as heir at his death, this turned out to the disadvantage of the relative power of the Germanic kings and emperors, in circumstances that could not be foreseen. To assume that Henry might have seen a conflict between his role as a protector of the Church and of the papacy on the one hand, and that of emperor on the other, is to apply unhistorical standards to the period. He did not think in national German terms, but simply did his duty as the greatest Christian ruler in the way he perceived it.

Popes and emperors as the spiritual and (primarily, but not only) secular heads of Western Christendom had interlocking responsibilities which were liable to generate friction. There was no agreed demarcation between the two spheres. A price had to be paid for the way papal coronation raised the German king over other monarchs. Could the pope also refuse to crown the king? The papal curia was not averse at times from making claims of the superiority of the spiritual over the secular power, including the right and even the duty to decide who was the rightful German king. Whether these claims could be enforced, depended on the balance of power at the time. Gregory VII felt it was time for the papacy to assert itself.

The reign of Gregory VII marked the beginning of a series of clashes between popes and emperors of a dramatic nature. These had something to do with personality. Both the pope and his opponent Emperor Henry IV bear some responsibility for the disputes which engulfed them. In a deeper sense, Gregory felt that the Church could not in the long run allow itself to be patronised even by the most benevolent of emperors. The pope was determined to establish the independence of the Church in spiritual matters, but at the same time claimed a certain superiority over the secular power. Gregory's fight for the independence of the Church had enormous long-term significance. Henry did penance at Canossa in 1077, but later was able to force Gregory out of Rome so that he had to die in exile. Eventually a settlement between papacy and Empire was reached at Worms in 1122. The cause in which Gregory, one of the great figures of world history, had apparently been defeated was not forgotten by the Church. A much greater assertiveness of the popes in their relationship with the emperors, as well as in the scale of their activities, ensued. It was the popes who initiated and organised the Crusades.

During the period of the Staufen dynasty, especially Frederick I Barbarossa and his grandson Frederick II were involved in bitter conflicts with the papacy. At the same time this was a period of some outstanding pontiffs, of Alexander III who won the struggle with Barbarossa, but never forgot that in the end reconciliation was the only constructive approach to the future. There was Innocent III, who succeeded after the death of Barbarossa's son Henry VI, and found himself guardian to Henry's son, the future Frederick II. Through a strange twist of fate, after successively supporting the two other contenders for the dignity, Innocent in the end saw no alternative to sponsoring a Staufen for the German kingship, in spite of the threat the power of the dynasty in Italy appeared to pose to the Holy See. It can be argued that during the later struggle with Frederick II, there was a certain decline in the standards of the papacy from the spiritual heights it had reached under Alexander III and Innocent III.

Looking back over the history of the relations between emperors and popes, not all the actions towards the papacy by rulers from Henry IV to Frederick II could be justified, or *vice versa* for that matter. Not all of them were necessary to fulfil the emperor's responsibilities to Western

Christendom. Some of them were clearly prompted by Salian or Staufen interests. In any case, it could not be expected that Germanic rulers would repeatedly intervene in Italy and be absent from their main dominions for longer periods, without acquiring some advantage. Still, however much emperors and popes disagreed about their precise functions and relationship, they were largely united by the concept of a bipolar leadership of Western Christendom. Basically, the emperors adhered to this idea, but some of the popes, above all Gregory VII, wished to downgrade Germanic rulers to the position of kings, like others. In a way that was not always apparent, there was a strong linkage between the mutual importance of popes and emperors for each other and of their universalist claims.

In the end, in order to crush the Staufen dynasty for good, mainly because of a clash of interests in Italy, the Holy See offered the Angevins, the younger branch of the French dynasty, the Sicilian crown if they succeeded in expelling the Staufen. This turned out to be a tragic mistake for the curia. Rome and Italy were a great lure to outside powers, enhanced by parts of the latter – like Sicily – in the age of the Crusades also providing good embarkation points for the Holy Land. During the ensuing events, not only Angevin, but actually French influence, over Italy increased to the point that the independence of the papacy was in greater danger than it had ever been under the Staufen. The power vacuum left by the destruction of the Staufen empire was simply filled by others. The French, pursuing a policy based on the perceived interests of their country, had a less universalist commitment to the integrity of the papacy as an institution than the Germanic emperors. It is no coincidence that the decline of the papacy from a position of considerable power followed soon after the end of imperial influence with the fall of the Staufen dynasty.

In 1303, with the participation of a high French official, Pope Boniface VIII, who had attempted to defend papal power against secular interference, was attacked at his residence at Anagni. Though the pope was freed from the grip of the conspirators, he died soon after. This was the kind of blow to the whole position of the papacy which went beyond anything the German kings and emperors had ever done. The latter certainly took action against popes, though not against the papacy. But Philip IV of France – unlike Louis IX earlier – followed an increasingly ruthless policy in pursuit of French interests as he saw them. Earlier on, French kings had given refuge in their dominions to popes who wished to escape from imperial control. Now they encouraged the popes to take up residence at Avignon, close to their kingdom, and even made it more difficult for them to return to Rome. The papacy became subservient to the French kings to an extent it had not previously been to the Germanic emperors. The 'Babylonian captivity' at Avignon did permanent harm to the papacy, from which it could only recover with difficulty.

After the death of Frederick II, Germanic kings and emperors only rarely exercised the kind of authority over Church and papacy that had characterised the periods of the Carolingian, Saxon, Salian and Staufen dynasties. The Germanic kingdom went through some difficult years, until the election of Rudolf I of Habsburg, who was able to consolidate his position with papal help. For a time, the papacy, through claiming the right to approve the ruler, exercised some influence in the Germanic kingdom, but found it just as difficult as Innocent III had done to follow a consistent line.

Henry VII, of the Luxemburg dynasty, was the first German king since the Staufen dynasty to undertake an expedition to Italy, and was widely welcomed there, amongst others by Dante. His attempt to create a certain counterweight to Franco-Angevin influence in cooperation with the papacy was frustrated by Philip IV. Henry's successor Louis ('the Bavarian') was the last German king to become involved in a bitter dispute with the Holy See in the Middle Ages. Later, a papal schism gave Emperor Sigismund the opportunity to reassert the imperial role in connection with the Church once more. The emperor played a vital part in bringing about the Council of Constance, which was able to end the schism, to have a new pope elected and to initiate reforms. It was once more in the reign of Charles V that an emperor who ruled – among many other territories – over the German kingdom, was intimately involved in the problems of the relationship with the papacy that had proved so troublesome in the Salian and Staufen periods. Again – as in the Staufen period – matters were complicated by the emperor's Italian possessions and by the curia's traditional policy of opposing any power liable to threaten its independence. These considerations tended to preoccupy both sides at a time when Martin Luther challenged aspects of the teaching of the Church.

The Reformation fundamentally affected Germany, because the country emerged and remained deeply divided confessionally. The effects of this development for Germany can hardly be overstated and are often underemphasised. The Old Church proved not to be strong enough to defeat Protestantism there. As was to some extent inherent in the Protestant approach to faith, the anti-Catholic side split into a number of factions, mainly into Lutherans and Calvinists, but also into more radical groups. Thus, in turn, Protestantism was not united enough to defeat Catholicism. In the end, after prolonged disputes and two armed conflicts, the Schmalkaldic War and the Thirty Years War, the confessional division was finally accepted in the peace settlement of 1648. The recognition given to the Lutherans in the Religious Peace of Augsburg of 1555 was extended to the Calvinists in the Peace of Westphalia. As distinct from England or France, a limited toleration was practiced in Germany, one of the many positive aspects of the Holy Roman Empire in the period between 1648 and its demise in 1806 that is often ignored. The religious settlement went hand in hand with an increased political decentralisation allowing a large measure of autonomy to the individual states. Apart from certain conflicts, such as the Silesian Wars and the Seven Years War, the different territories, both secular and ecclesiastical, ranging from large states to smaller lordships, could live peacefully side by side. Even the task of defending the frontiers of the Empire was mastered at least in some respects before 1789. But the events of the French Revolutionary and Napoleonic period changed the entire situation.

As a direct or indirect consequence of French intervention in the affairs of Germany, the Catholic position there was dramatically weakened. In each of the successive settlements the Catholics lost out. Secularisation abolished the prince-bishoprics, and with them, for example, the episcopal universities. When the Empire was in its death-throes, the Rhenish archbishops lost their electoral dignity. That weakened not only Catholic influence in Germany, but also the German Catholic Church in relation to Rome. The influences emanating from the curia should not be seen in a mainly negative light, as is so often done. Spiritual and cultural links with Rome and Italy, and indeed with the Mediterranean, gave strength to Catholicism. But the new situation certainly diminished the independence of the German prelates and made them more susceptible to the pressures of what is often disparagingly and somewhat unfairly called ultramontanism. This changed balance of power in the relationship between them was to have consequences into the twentieth century and even to affect the handling of questions relating to the National Socialist regime by the Catholic Church. Rome did not always know better than the local churches.

In the peace settlement at the end of the Napoleonic Wars, the newly established German Confederation preserved only two – admittedly very large – Catholic states, Austria and Bavaria, among just under 40. Catholic majorities were subjected to Protestant states in Baden and Württemberg. Protestant Prussia received the Catholic Rhineland.

Conditions for a German national movement only became ripe after the upheavals of the French Revolutionary and Napoleonic period and the destruction of many Catholic bastions in Germany. Initially the movement was primarily Protestant, as is apparent from the choice of the Wartburg as the meeting-place for the 1817 festival of the national student movement, the *Burschenschaft*. The venue does not show much interest in enlisting Catholics in the national movement.[2] As one would expect, even later on, the idea of German unification appealed more to Protestants than to Catholics,[3] who belonged to an international institution cutting across national boundaries and had links with Rome. The latter valued the medieval heritage of Western Christendom, to which they regarded themselves as standing in direct succession, and were less open to secular ideas than their Protestant brethren. Also they were not likely to be enthused by the prospect of a Protestant majority and head of state, in case of the adoption of the Lesser German (*kleindeutsch*) solution without Austria.

Protestants, and particularly Lutherans, did not have to overcome so many obstacles in joining the national movement. The latter belonged to a confession that was less cosmopolitan than Catholicism, and for that matter Calvinism, and was mainly centred in Germany (apart from Scandinavia). Luther was hailed as the creator of the modern German language, who was thus believed to have contributed to the idea of the German nation. It did not take much to reinterpret him, though with scarce historical accuracy, as a German nationalist who defied the Roman pope, (equally inaccurately) in the tradition of Emperor Henry IV and Emperor Frederick II. Above all, in view of their objections to the papacy, Protestants were critical of much of the medieval Christian heritage, putting in its place their own German nationalist version of the past. In the circumstances, many Protestants, though in no way less religious than their Catholic brethren, were more open to secular influences and to political ideologies like nationalism. Protestant historians like Sybel and Treitschke tried to find historical foundations for the national movement in the past of their forebears. Instead of being proud of the role Germanic emperors had played with regard to the Church and the papacy, they castigated their preoccupation with Italy. They refused to see the complications that would be caused by trying to apply a new principle, that of nationality, to Central Europe, with its mixture of ethnic groups. In the end, the Bismarckian Lesser German solution excluded the rich German culture of Austria from the new state, creating new problems and tensions. The retention of the designation of *Kaiser und Reich* only blurred the issue and made it all the easier to create the impression that Bismarck's *Reich* was similar to the Holy Roman Empire, which was now often simply called the German Empire. Slightly pointedly, one might perhaps say that the Germans were more justified in trying to establish their own state (on condition that they made a success of it) than they were in applying an unhistorical national principle to their past.

Not only did the *Reich* of 1870 exclude much of German culture from the new state, but an unholy alliance between Bismarck and some liberals opened the period of unification in Prussia by divisive and punitive legislation against the Roman Catholic Church hardly compatible with the rule of law. Liberals like the famous pathologist Rudolf Virchow believed themselves to be fighting for culture (*Kulturkampf*) against the dark forces of the Catholic Church. Insufficiently recognising that most other national states, like the French, consisted mainly of one confession, the new Germany did not face up to the very real differences between the main two denominations with a process of healing. Instead, at the very beginning of the new state, the Catholic population of Germany, which tended to constitute a third or so of the population of the Lesser Germany, was alienated and driven into a kind of ghetto. This was liable to increase the 'educational deficit' of the Catholic population, which had begun with the earlier abolition of their educational institutions. The unmeasured anti-Catholicism of Emperor William II only aggravated the situation. It can be argued that some of the excesses of German nationalism were due to doubts about how united the Germans really were, and that one of the main factors for this anxiety was interconfessional tension, which hardly showed any signs of lessening. These divisions played into the hands of the National Socialists with their facile slogans of national unity.

One example connected with our theme may, perhaps, illustrate the situation. Few Roman Catholic historians did as much to promote a more objective interpretation of the Lutheran Reformation in his Church as Joseph Lortz. The debt of the present writer to him is acknowledged in the notes.[4] Actually, Lortz during the early phase of the National Socialist regime believed that Hitler would be able to close what he regarded as 'the deepest wound from which Germany suffered: the religious division'.[5] While he was quite correct in his diagnosis, he soon recognised that he was completely mistaken in the proposed remedy. Thus even a highly cultured Catholic could be taken in by the simplistic solutions Hitler proposed for overcoming deep-seated confessional differences.

The outcome of the Second World War improved the fortunes of Catholicism in Germany by restoring the importance of the Catholic Rhineland and making it a focal point of the original Federal Republic established under Western auspices in 1949. In the west of the country, Germany was thus able to reconnect with much of European Catholicism, including that of Italy, with which it had loosened its contacts under Protestant Prussian leadership. The European Economic Community and Union strengthened these bonds. The continued integration of Germany into the West was not affected by reunification and the move of the capital from Bonn to Berlin. A recognition of the shortcomings of national states in our age will hopefully lead to a better historical understanding for confederate structures like the Holy Roman Empire and the *Deutsche Bund* of 1815–66.

In the space remaining, a footnote might be added to the theme of the more general relationship between religion and politics. Quite conceivably, in the long-term religious example helped to shape political conduct. All too often churches without proper examination rushed into condemning opposite opinions as heretical. This kind of religious intolerance may well have carried over into political life. One can only be saddened by the cruel punishments meted out in the Middle Ages and early Modern Times to those disagreeing with the teaching of the Church. Presumably a challenge to accepted doctrine at the time appeared to threaten the very fabric of society. One wonders whether there was also still a kind of almost pagan fear that the gods would wreak vengeance on communities that displeased them by harbouring dissidents. The heresy hunts of the past, as well as the intolerance members of one church have often shown to those of others, have discredited organised religion, and have led to its decline and loss of influence in state and society. Finally, bringing together the general with the German theme, in a tragic manner the mutual antipathies between the Christian confessions in Germany contributed to the establishment of the Nazi regime, which then proceeded to persecute them all.

Even though conditions have changed, indeed in some ways out of recognition, since the period described in the book, it is hoped that the problems of the interrelationship between religion and politics at that time may have something to say to the present age.

Notes

PREFACE

1. Erich Eyck, *Bismarck and the German Empire* (London: Allen & Unwin, 1950) p. i.

1. THE PARAMETERS OF THE BOOK

1. 'Religion', in I. Hexham *Concise Dictionary of Religion* (Downers Grove, Illinois, 1993) p. 187.

2 THE GERMANIC PEOPLES, THE ROMAN EMPIRE AND CHRISTIANITY (UNTIL 814)

1. For the early Germanic peoples and their contacts with the Roman Empire, see H. Wolfram, *Das Reich und die Germanen – Zwischen Antike und Mittelalter* (Berlin, 1990) p. 34 and *passim*.
2. By P.J. Geary, *Before France and Germany. The Creation and Transformation of the Merovingian World* (New York: Oxford University Press, 1988) p. vi.
3. H.K. Schulze, *Vom Reich der Franken zum Land der Deutschen – Merowinger und Karolinger* (Berlin: Siedler, 1987) pp. 29 f.
4. H. Löwe, 'Deutschland im Fränkischen Reich', in B. Gebhardt *Handbuch der Deutschen Geschichte*, 8th edn, vol. I (Stuttgart, Union 1959) p. 79.
5. Other works consulted (which do not necessarily get directly involved in the controversy) include: J. Fleckenstein, *Grundlagen und Beginn der deutschen Geschichte* (Göttingen, 1988); J.M. Wallace-Hadrill, *Early Germanic Kingship in England and on the Continent* (Oxford, 1971) ch. 1; K. Bosl, 'Die germanische Kontinuität im deutschen Mittelalter (Adel–König–Kirche)', in P. Wilpert (ed.) *Miscellanea Mediaevalia*, vol. I: *Antike und Orient im Mittelalter* (Berlin, 1971) pp. 1–25; W. Kienast, 'Germanische Treue und "Königsheil"', *Historische Zeitschrift*, vol. 227 (1978) pp. 265–324; K. v. See, *Deutsche Germanen-Ideologie* (Frankfurt, 1970) and *Kontinuitätstheorie und Sakraltheorie in der Germanenforschung. Antwort an Otto Höfler* (Frankfurt, 1972); W.H. Maehl, *Germany in Western civilization* (Alabama, 1979); H. Rössler and G. Franz (eds) *Sachwörterbuch zur deutschen Geschichte* (Munich, 1958) *passim*.
6. H. Plessner, *Die verspätete Nation. Über die politische Verführbarkeit bürgerlichen Geistes* (Stuttgart, Kohlhammer, 1959).
7. Quoted in V.I.J. Flint, *The Rise of Magic in Early Medieval Europe* (Oxford: Clarendon press, 1991) p. 77. See A. Murray, 'Missionaries and Magic in Dark-Age Europe', *Past and Present*, 136 (August 1992) p. 191.
8. For a more sympathetic view of Arianism, see M. Wiles, 'Eunomius: hair-splitting dialectician or defender of the accessibility of salvation?', in R. Williams (ed.) *The Making of Orthodoxy: essays in honour of Henry Chadwick* (Cambridge, 1989) pp. 157–72.

9. W. Telfer, 'Arius and Arianism', *Chambers Encyclopaedia*, vol. I, (London, 1959) pp. 593–4.
10. J. Hussey, 'Byzantium', *Chambers Encyclopaedia*, vol. II, (London, 1959) pp. 731 f.
11. H. Wolfram, *History of the Goths*, trans T.J. Dunlap (Berkeley, 1988) p.283.
12. Ibid., p. 286.
13. Ibid., p. 243.
14. C. Dawson, *Religion and the Rise of Western Culture* (London: Sheed & Ward, 1950) p. 84.
15. Wolfram, *History of the Goths*, pp. 309f.
16. Ibid., especially pp. 278–332.
17. H.Chadwick, *The Early Church* (Harmondsworth: Penguin, 1978) p.120.
18. W. Ullmann, *The Growth of Papal Government in the Middle Ages. A study in the ideological relation of clerical to lay power* (London, methuen, 1970) p. 1.
19. C.R. Cheney, 'Papacy', *Chambers Encyclopaedia*, vol. X (London, 1959) p. 393.
20. See Hussey, 'Byzantine Empire', p. 741.
21. C.R. Cheney, 'Leo I', *Chambers Encyclopaedia*, vol. VIII (London: George Newnes, 1959) p. 478.
22. H. Rahner, *Kirche und Staat im frühen Christentum: Dokumente aus acht Jahrhunderten und ihre Deutung* (Munich, 1961) p. 257 and *passim*; K. Baus, 'The Papacy between Byzantium and the German Kingdoms from Hilary (461–8) to Serguis I (687–701)', in H. Jedin and J. Dolan (eds) *History of the Church*, vol. II, trans. by A. Biggs (New York, 1980) pp. 616 ff. This is a continuation of the *Handbook of Church History* under a new title: one or the other is used in the various volumes of this work; Chadwick, *Early Church*, esp. p. 166; Hussey, 'Byzantine Empire', p. 741.
23. J. M. Wallace-Hadrill, *The Frankish Church* (Oxford: Clarendon Press, 1985) p. 19.
24. Wallace-Hadrill in ibid. p. 18, suggests, for instance, that the Scandinavian cult of the gods developed after the Franks had lost continuous contact with the Baltic and that they were influenced to a greater extent by Roman than Germanic gods. In 'The *Via Regia* of the Carolingian Age', in B. Smalley (ed.) *Trends in Medieval Political Thought* (Oxford, 1965) p. 22, he argues that little of kingship of any kind came over the Rhine with the Franks, and that Merovingian kingship was constructed in Gaul out of war leadership and Roman administrative techniques.
25. E. Brehaut (ed.) Gregory, Bishop of Tours, *History of the Franks* (New York, 1965) pp. 39–41.
26. W. Ullmann, *The Carolingian Renaissance and the Idea of Kingship* (London, 1969) p. 43, n. 1, quoting W. Mohr, *Die karolingische Reichsidee* (Münster, 1962) p. 17.
27. Wallace-Hadrill, *The Frankish Church*, pp.25–6.
28. P. J. Geary, *Before France and Germany. The Creation and Transformation of the Merovingian World* (New York, 1988) p. 87.
29. See J. Fleckenstein, *Grundlagen und Beginn der deutschen Geschichte* (Götttingen, 1988) p. 42 f.
30. Wallace-Hadrill, *Frankish Church*, p.29.
31. 'The identity of a gens or people had always been rather artificial; it certainly had no ascertainable racial component, though it could be represented in terms of a fictive shared ancestry.' See Janet L. Nelson on 'The Lord's anointed and the people's choice: Carolingian royal ritual', in D. Cannadine and S. Price (eds) *Rituals of Royalty. Power and Ceremonial in Traditional Societies* (Cambridge University Press, 1987) p. 147.

32. Wallace-Hadrill, *The Frankish Church*, pp. 33–4.
33. Ibid., pp. 53–4.
34. Ibid., p. 96.
35. Ibid., p.102.
36. Geary, *Before France*, p. 106.
37. Wallace-Hadrill, *The Frankish Church*, p. 17.
38. Dawson, *Religion*, p. 36.
39. Ibid., p. 31.
40. Wallace-Hadrill, *The Frankish Church*, p. 3.
41. Ibid., p. 2.
42. Ibid., p. 25.
43. Ibid., p. 95.
44. Ibid.
45. E. Ewig, 'The Conversion of the Franks and Burgundians. Origin and Organization of the Merovingian National Church', in *History of the Church*, vol. II, p. 531.
46. By Geary, *Before France*, pp.130 ff.
47. Dawson, *Religion*, p. 40.
48. Wallace-Hadrill, *The Frankish Church*, p. 63.
49. Fleckenstein, *Grundlagen*, p. 44.
50. Wallace-Hadrill, *The Frankish Church*, pp. 63–70; Geary, *Before France*, pp. 170–78; Fleckenstein, *Grundlagen*, pp. 64–6.
51. Fleckenstein, *Grundlagen*, p. 74.
52. H. Löwe, 'Deutschland im fränkischen Reich', in B. Gebhardt, *Handbuch der Deutschen Geschichte*, vol. I (Stuttgart, 1959) p. 119.
53. M.D. Knowles, 'Benedictines', *Chambers Encyclopaedia*, vol. II (London, 1959) p. 246.
54. Dawson, *Religion*, p. 51.
55. For Boniface see: T. Schieffer, *Winfrid-Bonifatius und die christliche Grundlegung Europas* (Freiburg: Herder, 1954); Wallace-Hadrill, *The Frankish Church*, esp. pp. 150–61; E. Ewig, 'The Papacy's Alienation from Byzantium and Rapprochement with the Franks', in H. Jedin and J. Dolan (eds) *Handbook of Church History*, vol. III, trans. A. Biggs (New York: Herder & Herder, 1969) esp. pp. 9–16; Fleckenstein, *Grundlagen, passim*; Geary, *Before France*, pp. 214–18; Dawson, *Religion*, esp. pp. 66–9, 85–8; W. Levison, 'Saint Boniface', *Chambers Encyclopaedia*, vol. II, pp. 421f.
56. Geary, *Before France* p. 216.
57. H. Fichtenau, *The Carolingian Empire*, trans. P. Munz (Oxford: Blackwell, 1963) p. 16.
58. Schieffer, *Winfrid-Bonifatius*, pp. 129 ff.
59. Ibid., p. 133.
60. Wallace-Hadrill, *The Frankish Church*, p. 154.
61. Geary, *Before France*, p. 133.
62. Ibid., pp. 212 f., 217.
63. Wallace-Hadrill, *The Frankish Church*, p. 136.
64. Ibid., p. 134.
65. G. Constable, *Monastic tithes from their origins to the twelfth century* (Cambridge University Press, 1964) p.29.
66. Constable, *Monastic tithes*, p. 9.
67. Ibid., p.33.
68. Ibid., p.35.

69. Ibid., pp. 31 ff.
70. Ibid., p.54.
71. Fleckenstein, *Grundlagen*, p. 112 uses the term, whereas Löwe, Gebhardt, *Handbuch der Deutschen Geschichte*, vol. I, p. 122, rejects it.
72. Wallace-Hadrill, *The Frankish Church*, p. 156.
73. Fichtenau, *Carolingian Empire*, p. 17.
74. Geary, *Before France*, p. 217.
75. Wallace-Hadrill, *The Frankish Church*, p. 158.
76. Ibid.
77. Geary, *Before France*, p. 213.
78. Ibid., p. 211.
79. Ibid., p. 213.
80. L. Halphen, *Charlemagne and the Carolingian Empire*, trans. G. de Nie (New York: North Holland, 1977) p. 12 (vol. III in the series *Europe in the Middle Ages*).
81. But see earlier discussion of the subject in this chapter, pp. 17–18.
82. Dawson, *Religion*, pp. 79–80.
83. Geary, *Before France*, p. 218.
84. Ibid., pp. 218–19.
85. Ibid., pp. 219–20.
86. T. Schieffer, *Winfrid-Bonifatius*, pp. 257 f.
87. H.A. Myers with H. Wolfram, *Medieval Kingship* (Chicago: Nelson-Hall, 1982) p.107.
88. Wallace-Hadrill, *The Frankish Church*, p.166.
89. E.H. Kantorowicz, *Laudes regiae. A Study in Liturgical Acclamations and Medieval Ruler Worship* (Berkeley: University of California Press, 1958) p. 14.
91. Löwe, 'Deutschland im fränkischen Reich', p. 110.
92. S.v. Riezler, *Geschichte Baierns*, vol. I, p. 1 (Aalen, 1964 reprint of 2nd edn, Stuttgart, 1927) *passim* ; Löwe, 'Deutschland im fränkischen Reich', pp.95 f, 110 f; H.Schiller, *Weltgeschichte. Von den ältesten Zeiten bis zum Anfang des 20. Jahrhunderts*, vol. II (Berlin, 1900) p. 14.
93. J. Hussey, 'Iconoclasm', *Chambers Encyclopaedia*, vol. VII, p. 370; H.-G. Berk, 'The Greek Church in the Epoch of Iconoclasm', pp. 26 ff.
94. Ewig, 'The Papacy's Alienation', p. 22.
95. Wallace-Hadrill, *The Frankish Church*, p.168.
96. Ibid.
97. Ibid.
98. Ibid.
99. Ibid., p. 169.
100. Ewig, 'The Papacy's Alienation', p. 23.
101. Fleckenstein, *Grundlagen*, pp. 77–8.
102. L. Halphen, *Charlemagne*, p. 25.
103. Fichtenau, *Carolingian Empire*, p. 63.
104. G. Tellenbach, 'Europa im Zeitalter der Karolinger', in F. Valjavec (ed.) *Historia Mundi. Ein Handbuch der Weltgeschichte in zehn Bänden*, vol. V (Bern,1956) p. 415.
105. Fichtenau, *The Carolingian Empire*, p. 67; E. Ewig, 'The Age of Charles the Great (768–814)', in H. Jedin and J. Dolan (eds) *Handbook of Church History*, vol. III, trans. A. Biggs (New York: Herder & Herder, 1969) p. 84.
106. Fichtenau, *Carolingian Empire*, p.94.

107. P.Wormald, '*Lex Scripta and Verbum Regis*: Legislation and Germanic King-ship from Euric to Cnut', in P. H. Sawyer and I. N. Wood (eds) *Early Medieval Kingship* (Leeds: University of Leeds, 1977) p. 136.
108. R. McKitterick, *The Carolingians and the Written Word* (Cambridge University Press, 1989) p. 272.
109. Ibid., p. 270.
110. Ibid., p. 185.
111. J.L. Nelson, 'Literacy in Carolingian government', in R. McKitterick (ed.) *The Uses of Literacy in Early Mediaeval Europe* (Cambridge University Press, 1992) p. 264.
112. Wallace-Hadrill, *The Frankish Church*, p. 183.
113. H.K. Schulze, *Vom Reich der Franken zum Land der Deutschen – Merowinger und Karolinger* (Berlin: Siedler, 1987) p. 157.
114. On these aspects see R. McKitterick, *The Frankish Church and the Carolingian Reforms, 789–895* (London, 1977).
115. Halphen, *Charlemagne*, pp. 113–17.
116. D. Bullough, *The Age of Charlemagne* (Toronto: Ryerson Press, 1965) p. 93.
117. E. Ewig, 'The Age of Charles the Great (768–814)', pp. 71 f.
118. D. Bullough, *The Age of Charlemagne*, p. 94.
119. Fichtenau, *The Carolingian Empire*, pp. 58 f.
120. Bullough, *The Age of Charlemagne*, pp. 44 f.
121. Ewig, 'The Age of Charles the Great', vol. III, pp. 55 ff.
122. The authorities disagree on the precise date.
123. Bullough, *The Age of Charlemagne*, p. 45.
124. Halphen, *Charlemagne*, pp. 72 ff.
125. Halphen, *Charlemagne*, pp. 74–5 assumes this, but Bullough, *Age of Charle-magne*, p. 49, believes that Charles took one step at a time, without a pre-conceived plan.
126. Halphen, *Charlemagne*, pp. 78 ff.
127. Ibid., p. 83.
128. Ibid.
129. Ibid.
130. Wallace-Hadrill, *The Frankish Church*, p.185.
131. Halphen, *Charlemagne*, pp. 48 ff.
132. Ibid., pp. 45–6.
133. Tellenbach, 'Europa im Zeitalter der Karolinger', p. 428. But E. Ewig, 'The Age of Charles the Great', p. 90, believes Byzantine support for the insurrection most unlikely.
134. P.E. Schramm, *Kaiser, Rom und Renovatio* (Bad Homburg, 1962) pp. 18 f.
135. By F. Gregorovius, *History of the City of Rome in the Middle Ages*, vol. II, trans. A. Hamilton (London, 1894) pp. 478. See also Schramm, *Kaiser*, pp. 18 ff.
136. Halphen, *Charlemagne*, pp. 87ff.; Ewig, 'The Age of Charles the Great', p. 92.
137. Bullough, *Age of Charlemagne*, p. 167.
138. Halphen, *Charlemagne*, pp.91 ff.
139. Fichtenau, *The Carolingian Empire*, p. 74; Bullough, *The Age of Charlemagne*, p. 183.
140. Fichtenau, *The Carolingian Empire*, p. 66.
141. Ibid., pp. 75–6.
142. Ibid., pp. 67–73.
143. Tellenbach, 'Europa im Zeitalter der Karolinger', p. 432 excludes this hypo-thesis.

144. H.K. Schulze, *Vom Reich der Franken zum Land der Deutschen*, p. 195.
145. Ibid., p. 201.
146. R. Holtzmann, *Geschichte der sächsischen Kaiserzeit (900–1024)* (Munich, 1961) pp.8 ff.
147. Ibid., pp. 6 ff.
148. Tellenbach, 'Europa im Zeitalter der Karolinger', pp. 436–7.
149. H. Schiller, *Weltgeschichte*, vol. II, p. 66.
150. The full title in Latin was: *Karolus serenissimus augustus a Deo coronatus magnus et pacificus imperator Romanum gubernans imperium qui et per misericordiam Dei rex Francorum et Langobardorum.* See Fleckenstein, *Grundlagen*, p.99.
151. Halphen, *Charlemagne*, p. 96.
152. Fichtenau, *The Carolingian Empire*, p. 77.
153. Ewig, 'The Age of Charles the Great', p. 99.
154. Ibid., p. 96.
155. Wallace-Hadrill, *The Frankish Church*, p. 262; see also Fleckenstein, *Grundlagen*, p. 102; Fichtenau, *The Carolingian Empire*, p. 114; Halphen, *Charlemagne*, pp. 117–18.
156. Fichtenau, *The Carolingian Empire*, pp.57–61.
157. Holtzmann, *Sächsische Kaiserzeit*, p. 10.
158. Fustel de Coulanges, *Histoire des Institutions politiques de l'ancienne France*, vol. 6 (Paris, 1892) p. 233.
159. Fichtenau, *The Carolingian Empire*, p. 115.

3.   LATER CAROLINGIANS AND THE SAXON DYNASTY (814–1024)

1. See 'Benedictus von Aniane' in H. Rössler and G. Franz (eds) *Biographisches Wörterbuch zur deutschen Geschichte* (Munich, 1953) p. 56.
2. J. Semmler, '*Renovatio Regni Francorum.* Die Herrschaft Ludwigs des Frommen im Frankenreich, 814–829/830', in P. Godman and R. Collins (eds) *Charlemagne's Heir. New Perspectives on the Reign of Louis the Pious* (814–840) (Oxford: Clarendon Press, 1990) pp. 125f. The section on Louis the Pious owes much to this magnificent volume.
3. H.K. Schulze, *Vom Reich der Franken zum Land der Deutschen. Merowinger und Karolinger* (Berlin: Siedler, 1987) p. 207f.
4. P.E. Schramm, *Kaiser Rom und Renovatio* (Bad Homburg: Hermann Gentner, 1962) p. 21.
5. E. Ewig, 'Climax and Turning Point of the Carolingian Age, 814–840', in H. Jedin and J. Dolan (eds) *Handbook of Church History*, vol. III, trans. A. Biggs (New York, 1969) pp. 112f.
6. Ibid., pp. 107ff; J. Fried, 'Ludwig der Fromme, das Papsttum und die fränkische Kirche', in P. Godman and R. Collins (eds) *Charlemagne's Heir*, pp. 246–9.
7. Fried, 'Ludwig, Papsttum und Kirche', p. 247; F. X. Seppelt and G. Schwaiger, *Geschichte der Päpste* (Munich, 1964) p. 97.
8. H. Löwe, 'Deutschland im fränkischen Reich', in B. Gebhardt, *Handbuch der Deutschen Geschichte*, vol. I (Stuttgart, Union 1959) p. 145. K.F. Werner, in 'Gouverner l'empire chrétien', in Godman and Collins (eds) *Charlemagne's Heir*, p. 19, rightly points out that the *ordinatio* did not prohibit division, but

merely laid down that one of the brothers should be master and the others sub-kings.

9. Fried, 'Ludwig, Papsttum und Kirche' p. 232.
10. Semmler, '*Renovatio Regni Francorum*', p. 137.
11. Ewig, 'Climax and Turning Point', pp. 118–19.
12. Ibid., p. 123.
13. According to J. Semmler in 'Ludwig I, der Fromme', in J. Höfer and K. Rahner (eds) *Lexikon für Theologie und Kirche*, 2nd edn, vol. VI (Freiburg: Herder, 1957ff.) p. 1184, 'the spiritual-political programme of the "Renovatio imperii Francorum" had moved too far away from political reality, the crisis was inevitable.'
14. Werner, 'Gouverner l'empire chrétien', pp. 77 ff.
15. J. Fleckenstein, *Grundlagen und Beginn der deutschen Geschichte* (Göttingen: Vandenhoeck & Ruprecht, 1988) p. 125; Löwe, 'Deutschland im fränkischen Reich', p. 147.
16. Schulze, *Vom Reich der Franken*, p. 330.
17. E. Ewig, 'The Western Church from the Death of Louis the Pious to the end of the Carolingian Period', in H. Jedin and J. Dolan (eds) *Handbook of Church History*, vol. III, trans. A. Biggs (New York: Herder & Herder, 1969) pp. 127f.
18. Fleckenstein, *Grundlagen*, p. 126.
19. W. Kienast, *Deutschland und Frankreich in der Kaiserzeit (900–1270). Weltkaiser und Einzelkönige*, vol. I (Stuttgart, 1974) p. 8.
20. W. Ullmann, *The Growth of Papal Government in the Middle Ages. A study in the ideological relation of clerical to lay power* (London: Methuen, 1970) p. 205.
21. Ibid., p. 178.
22. Though used against Rheims, the forgery probably stemmed from the diocese of Le Mans. See H. Fuhrmann, *Einfluss und Verbreitung der pseudo-isidorischen Fälschungen*, Schriften der Monumenta Germaniae Historica, vol. 24, 1–3 (Stuttgart, 1972–4). Like so much else, I am indebted to Professor Christopher Brooke for pointing this out.
23. W. Ullmann, *A Short History of the Papacy in the Middle Ages* (London, 1972) pp. 99ff.
24. Seppelt and Schwaiger, *Geschichte der Päpste*, pp. 103ff.
25. Ewig, 'The Western Church from the Death of Louis the Pious', pp. 141–2.
26. Schramm, *Kaiser*, p. 46.
27. Ullmann, *A Short History*, p. 95; Ewig, 'The Western Church from the Death of Louis the Pious', pp. 141f.
28. Ewig, 'The Western Church from the Death of Louis the Pious', pp. 151f.
29. Ibid., pp. 143, 152.
30. Ibid., p. 147.
31. Ibid., p. 152.
32. Ullmann, *A Short History*, p. 95.
33. Ewig, 'The Western Church from the Death of Louis the Pious', pp. 152f; F. Gregorovius, *History of the City of Rome in the Middle Ages*, vol. III, trans. A. Hamilton, pp. 180ff.
34. Schulze, *Vom Reich der Franken*, p. 341, quoting J. Haller, 'Die Karolinger und das Papsttum', *Historische Zeitschrift*, vol. 108 (1912) p. 74.
35. Schramm, *Kaiser*, p. 18.
36. Ibid., pp. 19f.
37. Ewig, 'The Western Church from the Death of Louis the Pious', p. 154; Ullmann, *A Short History*, pp. 110ff.; Seppelt and Schwaiger, *Geschichte der Päpste*, p. 115.

38. Schulze, *Vom Reich der Franken*, p. 341.
39. H. Löwe, 'Deutschland im fränkischen Reich', pp. 155ff.; Fleckenstein, *Grundlagen*, pp. 128f.; R. Holtzmann, *Geschichte der sächsischen Kaiserzeit (900–1024)*, (Munich, 1961) pp. 13ff.; Ewig, 'The Western Church from the Death of Louis the Pious', pp. 155f.; Seppelt and Schwaiger, *Geschichte der Päpste*, pp. 113ff.; Ullmann, *A Short History*, p. 112.
40. Fleckenstein, *Grundlagen*, pp. 133ff.
41. Holtzmann, *Geschichte der sächsischen Kaiserzeit*, pp. 69f.
42. F. Kern, *Gottesgnadentum und Widerstandsrecht im Früheren Mittelalter. Zur Entwicklungsgeschichte der Monarchie* (Darmstadt, 1970) p. 85, n. 178.
43. Fleckenstein, *Grundlagen*, pp. 135–7.
44. F. Kempf, 'The Church and the Western Kingdoms from 900 to 1046', in H. Jedin and J. Dolan (eds) *Handbook of Church History*, vol. III, trans. A. Biggs (New York: Herder & Herder, 1959). p. 200f.
45. Holtzmann, *Geschichte der sächsischen Kaiserzeit*, pp. 82f.
46. F. Kern, *Kingship and Law in the Middle Ages* (Westport, Connecticut, 1985) pp. 12ff.
47. Ibid., p. 17.
48. Fleckenstein, *Grundlagen*, pp. 137f.
49. Holtzmann, *Geschichte der sächsischen Kaiserzeit*, pp. 70f.
50. Ibid., pp. 105ff.
51. Fleckenstein, *Grundlagen*, p. 138.
52. 'Striking...is the personal inviolability and immunity of the Liudolfing family circle, despite all the crises and rebellions within it': K.J. Leyser, *Rule and Conflict in an Early Medieval Society: Ottonian Saxony* (London: Arnold, 1979) p. 85.
53. Fleckenstein, *Grundlagen*, pp. 141–2; F. Ernst, 'Das Reich der Ottonen im 10. Jahrhundert', Gebhardt, *Handbuch*, vol. I, p. 175.
54. Leyser, *Rule and Conflict*, p. 80.
55. Ibid.
56. Kern, *Gottesgnadentum*, p. 85, n. 178.
57. See also J.W. Bernhardt, *Itinerant Kingship and Royal Monasteries in Early Medieval Germany c. 936–1075* (Cambridge, 1993) pp. 3ff. and *passim*.
58. G. Barraclough, *The Origins of Modern Germany* (Oxford, 1979) p. 35; Kempf, 'The Church and the Western Kingdoms', pp. 201f.
59. Kempf, 'The Church and the Western Kingdoms', p. 202.
60. Fleckenstein, *Grundlagen*, p. 162.
61. C.M. Ady, 'Italian History', *Chambers Encyclopaedia*, vol. VII, 1959, pp. 778f.
62. G. Tellenbach, 'Kaisertum, Papsttum und Europa im hohen Mittelalter', in F. Valjavec (ed.) *Historia Mundi. Ein Handbuch der Weltgeschichte in zehn Bänden*, vol. VI (Bern, 1958) p. 12.
63. H. Schiller, *Weltgeschichte* (Berlin, 1900) vol. II, pp. 93f.
64. Ullmann, *A Short History*, pp. 112ff.
65. See Holtzmann, *Geschichte der sächischen Kaiserzeit*, pp. 100f.
66. H.E.J. Cowdrey, *The Cluniacs and the Gregorian Reform* (Oxford: Clarendon press, 1970) p. 248.
67. Kempf, 'Renewal and Reform from 900 to 1050', p. 320.
68. Cowdrey, *Cluniacs*, pp. 4ff.; Kempf, 'Renewal and Reform from 900 to 1050', p. 324.
69. Cowdrey, *Cluniacs*, pp. 4ff.
70. Ibid., pp. 6f.

71. For a discussion of the relationship between Cluny and the Gregorian, Reform movement, see the introduction to Cowdrey, *Cluniacs*.
72. Tellenbach, 'Kaisertum', pp. 14ff.
73. Holtzmann, *Geschichte der sächsischen Kaiserzeit*, pp. 143f.
74. F. Ernst, 'Das Reich der Ottonen im 10. Jahrhundert', in B. Gebhardt, *Handbuch der Deutschen Geschichte*, vol. I, p. 183.
75. Holtzmann, *Geschichte der sächsischen Kaiserzeit*, p. 193.
76. Ibid., pp. 198f.; see also H. Mayr-Harting, 'The church of Magdeburg: its trade and its town in the tenth and early eleventh centuries', in D. Abulafia, M. Franklin and M. Rubin (eds) *Church and city 1000–1500: essays in honour of Christopher Brooke* (Cambridge, 1992) pp. 129–50.
77. Kempf, 'The Church and the Western Kingdoms, pp. 208f.
78. See E. Müller-Mertens, *Regnum Teutonicum. Aufkommen und Verbreitung der deutschen Reichs-und Königsauffassung im früheren Mittelalter* (Vienna, 1970).
79. See T. Reuter, 'The "Imperial Church System" of the Ottonian and Salian Rulers: A Reconsideration', *Journal of Ecclesiastical History*, vol. 33 (1982) pp. 347–74.
80. Reuter, 'Imperial Church System', p. 347.
81. Ibid., p. 370 n. 135.
82. F. Kempf, 'The Church and the Western Kingdoms', p. 209.
83. Ibid.
84. Ibid.
85. W. Smidt, *Deutsches Königtum und Deutscher Staat des Hochmittelalters während der Italienischen Heerfahrten. Ein zweihundertjähriger Gelehrtenstreit im Lichte der historischen Methode zur Erneuerung der abendländischen Kaiserwürde durch Otto I* (Wiesbaden, 1964) pp. 76ff.
86. Kienast, *Deutschland und Frankreich*, vol. I, pp. 87ff.
87. Seppelt and Schwaiger, *Geschichte der Päpste*, p. 124.
88. H.K. Schulze, *Hegemoniales Kaisertum. Ottonen und Salier* (Berlin, 1991) p. 253.
89. Tellenbach, 'Kaisertum', p. 16.
90. H. Hunger, 'Byzanz in der Weltpolitik vom Bildersturm bis 1453', in F. Valjavec (ed.) *Historia Mundi. Ein Handbuch der Weltgeschichte in zehn Bänden*, vol. VI (Bern: Francke, 1958) p. 402.
91. Kienast, *Deutschland und Frankreich*, pp. 117ff.; Holtzmann, *Geschichte der sächsischen Kaiserzeit*, pp. 304ff.; Kempf, 'The Church and the Western Kingdoms', p. 194ff., and 'Metropolitans, Primates and Papacy', in H. Jedin and J. Dolan (eds) *Handbook of Church History*, vol. III, trans. A. Biggs (New York: Herder & Herder, 1969) p. 297ff.
92. Schramm, *Kaiser*, pp. 124ff.
93. Ibid., p. 127.
94. Ibid., p. 6.
95. Schulze, *Hegemoniales Kaisertum*, p. 272; for St Nilus see also C. Dawson, *Religion and the Rise of Western Culture* (London, 1950) p. 149.
96. Schramm, *Kaiser*, p. 137.
97. Schulze, *Hegemoniales Kaisertum*, p. 282.
98. Schramm, *Kaiser*, p. 174. See also pp. 161ff.
99. F. Kempf, 'Metropolitans, Primaters and Papacy', p. 299.
100. Kienast, *Deutschland und Frankreich*, pp. 134f.
101. 'Vita Bernwardi episcopi Hildesheimensis auctore Thangmaro', ed. G.H. Pertz, in *Monumenta Germaniae Historica*, Scriptores, vol. IV (1963 reprint of original 1841 edition) p. 770; Schramm, *Kaiser*, pp. 177ff.

102. Smidt, *Deutsches Königtum*, p. 77.
103. Holtzmann, *Geschichte der sächsischen Kaiserzeit*, pp. 369ff.
104. H. Appelt, 'Heinrich II', *Neue Deutsche Biographie*, vol. VIII (Berlin, 1969) pp. 310–13.
105. Holtzmann, *Sachsische Kaiserzeit* p. 359, doubts whether Otto III's concession of a separate church for the Poles through the establishment of the archdiocese of Gnesen was in the interest of the Empire.
106. Ibid., p. 441; K.-J. Herrmann, *Das Tuskulanerpapsttum (1012–1046). Benedikt VIII, Johannes XIX., Benedict IX* (Stuttgart, 1973) pp. 4ff. (vol. 4 in the series *Päpste und Papsttum*)
107. C. B. McClendon, *The Imperial Abbey of Farfa. Architectural currents of the Early Middle Ages* (New Haven, Connecticut, 1987) p. 11.
108. On the importance of the Normans to Montecassino, see H.E.J. Cowdrey, *The Age of Abbot Desiderius. Montecassino, the Papacy and the Normans in the Eleventh and Early Twelfth Centuries* (Oxford, 1983) p. xxviii.
109. Leyser, *Rule and Conflict*, p. 80.
110. Ibid.
111. Fleckenstein, *Grundlagen*, p. 210.
112. Kempf, 'The Church and the Western Kingdoms', p. 196.
113. Kempf, 'Renewal and Reform from 900 to 1050', in H. Jedin and J. Dolan (eds) *Handbook of Church History*, vol. III, trans. A. Biggs (New York: Herder & Herder, 1969) pp. 320ff.; 'Gorzer Reform', in C. Andresen and G. Denzler, *dtv Wörterbuch der Kirchengeschichte* (Munich, 1984) p. 246. But see the view of Holtzmann, *Geschichte der sächsischen Kaiserzeit*, pp. 484f., downplaying the importance of Lotharingian reform for the East Frankish kingdom.
114. Kempf, 'The Church and the Western Kingdoms', pp. 251f.; Herrmann, *Tuskulanerpapsttum* p. 37.
115. Fleckenstein, *Grundlagen*, p. 212.
116. Ibid., p. 204.
117. Holtzmann, *Geschichte der sächsischen Kaiserzeit*, pp. 430ff.
118. Reuter, 'Imperial Church System', p. 364.
119. Kempf, 'The Church and the Western Kingdoms', p. 252.

4. THE SALIANS: FROM CO-OPERATION TO STRUGGLE WITH THE PAPACY (1024–1125)

1. H.K. Schulze, *Hegemoniales Kaisertum. Ottonen und Salier* (Berlin: Siedler, 1991) p. 333.
2. Steindorff, 'Aribo, Archbishop of Mainz', *Allgemeine Deutsche Biographie*, vol. I, (Leipzig, 1875) pp. 524–6; and, 'Konrad II', *Allgemeine Deutsche Biographie*, vol. XVI (Leipzig, 1882) pp. 543–54; H. Appelt, 'Konrad II, Kaiser' *Neue Deutsche Biographie*, vol. XII (Berlin, 1980) pp.492–95; R. Holtzmann, *Geschichte der sächsischen Kaiserzeit (900–1024) (Munich, 1961)* pp. 468ff. F. Kempf, 'Metropolitans, Primates and Papacy', in H. Jedin and J. Dolan (eds) *Handbook of Church History*, vol. III, trans. by A. Biggs (New York: Herder & Herder, 1969) pp. 296 f.
3. 'Köln', in H. Rössler and G. Franz, *Sachwörterbuch zur Deutschen Geschichte* (Munich, 1958) p. 534.

4. J. Fleckenstein, *Grundlagen und Beginn der deutschen Geschichte (Göttingen, 1988) p. 202.*

5. E. Müller-Mertens, *Regnum Teutonicum. Aufkommen und Verbreitung der deutschen Reichs- und Königsauffassung im früheren Mittelalter* (Vienna, 1970) pp. 24 f.

6. Ibid., *passim.*

7. G. Barraclough, *The Origins of Modern Germany* (Oxford: Blackwell, 1979) p. 78.

8. Appelt, 'Konrad II, Kaiser', p. 495.

9. Schulze, *Hegemoniales Kaisertum* p. 352.

10. K. Herrmann, *Tuskulanerpapsttum (1012–1046)* (Stuttgart, 1973) pp. 66 f.

11. K. Hampe, *Germany under the Salian and Hohenstaufen emperors*, trans. R. Bennett (Totowa, New Jersey: Rowman & Littlefield, 1973) p. 40.

12. Herrmann, *Tuskulanerpapsttum*, pp. 42, 106 ff.

13. Hampe, *Germany*, p. 45; 'Normannen', in Rössler and Franz, *Sachwörterbuch*, p. 823.

14. Schulze, *Hegemoniales Kaisertum*, p. 348.

15. Ibid., pp. 348 ff.; F. Kempf, 'The Church and the Western Kingdoms from 900 to 1046', in H. Jedin and J. Dolan (eds) *Handbook of Church History*, vol. III, trans. A. Biggs (New York: Herder & Herder, 1969) pp. 252 f.

16. Hampe, *Germany*, p. 55.

17. Steindorff, 'Gottfried, Herzog v. Lothringen', *Allgemeine Deutsche Biographie*, vol. IX (Leipzig, 1879) p. 464; 'Gottfried der Bärtige von Lothringen', *Neue Deutsche Biographie*, vol. VI (Berlin, 1971) p. 662.

18. F. Kempf, 'Renewal and Reform from 900 to 1050', in H. Jedin and J. Dolan (eds) *Handbook of Church History*, vol. III, trans. A. Biggs (New York: Herder & Herder, 1969) pp. 345 ff.

19. Hampe, *Germany*, p. 48.

20. Theodor Schieffer, 'Kaiser Heinrich III', in H. Heimpel, T. Heuss and B. Reifenberg (eds) *Die Grossen Deutschen*, vol. I (Berlin, 1956) p. 61.

21. C. Morris, *The Papal Monarchy. The Western Church from 1050 to 1250* (Oxford: Clarendon Press 1991) p. 44.

22. Hampe, *Germany*, p. 55.

23. The account closely follows Herrmann, *Tuskulanerpapsttum*, p. 154 and *passim*. For another version see for example, Kempf, 'The Church and the Western Kingdoms', pp. 254 ff.

24. Schulze, *Hegemoniales Kaisertum*, pp. 387–8; T. Lindner, 'Leo IX., Papst', *Allgemeine Deutsche Biographie,* vol. XVIII (Leipzig, 1883) p. 284; R. Schieffer, on the same, *Neue Deutsche Biographie*, vol. XIV (Berlin, 1985) pp. 238–9; 'Victor II', in H. Rössler and G. Franz, *Biographisches Wörterbuch zur Deutschen Geschichte* (Munich, 1953) p. 859.

25. P. Schramm, *Kaiser, Rom und Renovatio* (Bad Homburg, 1962) pp. 229 ff.

26. Th. Schieffer, 'Heinrich III', pp. 63 f.

27. F. Kempf, 'The Gregorian Reform', in H. Jedin and J. Dolan (eds) *Handbook of Church History*, vol. III, trans. A. Biggs (New York: Herder & Herder, 1969) p. 356.

28. M. W. Baldwin in his foreword to C. Erdmann, *The Origin of the Idea of Crusade*, trans. M. W. Baldwin and W. Goffart (Princeton, NJ: Princeton University Press, 1977) p. xxiii.

29. Erdmann, *Origin of the Idea of Crusade*, pp. 118 f.

30. F. Kempf, 'Changes within the Christian West during the Gregorian Reform', in H. Jedin and J. Dolan (eds) *Handbook of Church History*, vol. III, trans. A. Biggs (New York: Herder & Herder, 1969) p. 446.
31. Kempf, 'Renewal and Reform', pp. 347 f.
32. Herrmann, *Tuskulanerpapsttum*, pp. 162 ff.
33. Morris, *Papal Monarchy*, pp. 31 ff.
34. Kempf, 'The Gregorian Reform', pp. 353–4.
35. Ibid., p. 357; H. G. Beck, 'The Byzantine Church from 886 to 1054', in H. Jedin and J. Dolan (eds) *Handbook of Church History*, vol. III, trans. A. Biggs (New, York: Herder &, Herder, 1969) pp. 412–17; H.E.J. Cowdrey, *The Age of Abbot Desiderius. Montecassino, the Papacy, and the Normans in the Eleventh and Early Twelfth Centuries* (Oxford, 1983) pp. 109 f.
36. Morris, *Papal Monarchy*, p. 88.
37. Ibid., pp. 45 f.
38. Ibid., p. 88.
39. Kempf, 'The Gregorian Reform', pp. 357 f.
40. 'Gottfried der Bärtige von Lothringen', p. 662.
41. Hampe, *Germany*, p. 58.
42. Riezler, 'Konrad II, Herzog von Baiern', *Allgemeine Deutsche Biographie*, vol. XVI (Leipzig, 1882) pp. 571 f; A. Gawlik, on the same, *Neue Deutsche Biographie*, vol. XII (Berlin, 1980) pp. 501–2.
43. W. Kienast, *Deutschland und Frankreich in der Kaiserzeit (900–1270)*, vol. I (Stuttgart, 1974) pp. 175 ff.
44. W. Smidt, *Deutsches Königtum und Deutscher Staat* (Wiesbaden, 1964) pp. 78 ff.
45. T. . Schieffer, 'Kaiser Heinrich III', *Die Grossen Deutschen*, vol. I, p. 66.
46. Hampe, *Germany*, pp. 59 f.
47. For a summary of views on this question, see H. Hostenkamp, *Die mittelalterliche Kaiserpolitik in der deutschen Historiographie seit v. Sybel und Ficker* (Vaduz reprint, 1965) in series, *Historische Studien*, vol. 255 (Berlin, 1934), p. 106.
48. *Das Reich der Salier 1024–1125: Katalog zur Ausstellung des Landes Rheinland-Pfalz* (Sigmaringen, 1992) p. 223.
49. See B. Stock, *The Implications of Literacy. Written Language and Models of Interpretation in the Eleventh and Twelfth Centuries* (Princeton, N J, 1983).
50. Morris, *Papal Monarchy*, p. 43.
51. Ibid., p. 42 and *passim,* esp. ch. 2.
52. Ibid., p. 44.
53. For Agnes, see R. W. Southern, *The Making of the Middle Ages* (London, 1965) pp. 76–8.
54. Morris, *Papal Monarchy*, p. 89.
55. W. Ullmann, *The Growth of Papal Government in the Middle Ages. A study in the ideological relation of clerical to lay power* (London, 1970) pp. 323 ff.; K. A. Fink, *Papsttum und Kirche im abendländischen Mittelalter* (Munich, 1981) pp. 25 f. I am greatly indebted to Professor Christopher Brooke for suggestions on this topic.
56. Erdmann, *Origin of the Idea of Crusade*, pp. 132 f.
57. Ibid., p. 140
58. Ibid., p. 144.
59. Morris, *Papal Monarchy*, p. 97.
60. F. Kempf, 'The Gregorian Reform', pp. 365–6.
61. Erdmann, *Origin of the Idea of Crusade*, pp. 149 f.
62. Schulze, *Hegemoniales Kaisertum*, p. 425.

63. Müller-Mertens, *Regnum Teutonicum*, pp. 169 ff and *passim*.
64. Schulze, *Hegemoniales Kaisertum*, p. 420.
65. Ibid., p. 421.
66. I. S. Robinson, *The Papacy 1073–1198: Continuity and Innovation* (New York: Cambridge University Press 1990) p. 37.
67. Ibid., p. 402.
68. Cf. Ibid., p. 403. The translation of the pope's pronouncement by Christopher Brooke, *Europe in the Central Middle Ages 962–1154* (London, 1964) pp. 278 f. suggests suspension rather than deposition.
69. Schulze, *Hegemoniales Kaisertum*, pp. 421 f.; Robinson, *Papacy*, pp. 403 f.
70. Robinson, *Papacy*, p. 406.
71. Ibid., p. 409.
72. Ibid., p. 413.
73. Ibid., p. 18.
74. F. Kern, *Kingship and law in the Middle Ages*, trans. S.B. Chrimes (Oxford, 1939) *passim*.
75. H. J. Berman, *Law and Revolution. The Formation of the Western Legal Tradition* (Cambridge, Mass., 1983) p. 202.
76. Ibid., pp. 222 f.
77. Ibid., ch. 6.
78. Ibid., p. 229.
79. J. R. Strayer, *On the Medieval Origins of the Modern State* (Princeton, NJ: Princeton University Press, 1970) p. 22.
80. Berman, *Law and Revolution*, p. 405.
81. Ibid., and *passim*.
82. Ibid., p. 90.
83. For more details on the question of indulgences, see the account of Luther's involvement in the controversy over them in ch. 7.
84. E. Iserloh, 'The Jews in Mediaeval Christendom', H. Jedin and J. Dolan (eds) *Handbook of Church History*, vol. IV, trans. A. Biggs (New York: Herder & Herder, 1970) p. 613.
85. P. Kidson, *The Medieval World*, in 'Landmarks of the World's Art' series (New York: Mcgraw-Hill, 1967) p. 71.
86. Hampe, *Germany*, pp. 118 f.
87. Robinson, *Papacy*, p. 427.
88. Schulze, *Hegemoniales Kaisertum*, p. 463.
89. To some extent, this follows the account of Schulze, *Hegemoniales Kaisertum*, pp. 463 ff. But see also Robinson, *Papacy*, pp. 426–8.
90. G. Barraclough, *The Origins of Modern Germany* (Oxford, 1979) p. 133.
91. E. Maschke, *Der Kampf zwischen Kaisertum und Papsttum* (Constance, 1955) pp. 20 f.

5. THE STAUFEN CONFLICT WITH THE PAPACY (1125–1268)

1. I. S. Robinson, *The Papacy 1073–1198: Continuity and Innovation* (New York: Cambridge University Press 1990) p. 315.
2. P. Acht, 'Adalbert I, Erzbischof von Mainz', *Neue Deutsche Biographie*, vol. I (Berlin, 1971) p. 44; H. Fuhrmann, *Germany in the High Middle Ages c. 1050–1200*, trans. T. Reuter (Cambridge University Press, 1987) pp. 90, 92, 117 f.

3. Robinson, *Papacy*, p. 441. This refers to 'the *legatus a latere*, "legate from [the pope's] side", sent from the curia on an important mission as papal plenipotentiary' (see Robinson, ibid., p. 147).

4. Ibid., p. 315.

5. H. Boockmann, *Stauferzeit und spätes Mittelalter: Deutschland 1125–1517* (Berlin 1987) pp. 69 f.

6. Fuhrmann, *Germany*, p. 118.

7. C. Morris, *The Papal Monarchy. The Western Church from 1050 to 1250* (Oxford University Press, 1991) p. 168.

8. While Morris, *Papal Monarchy*, p. 184, sees the factions mainly as interest groups, rather than as coherent parties, Robinson, *Papacy*, pp. 382 f. distinguishes between supporters of the Sicilian alliance led by Anacletus, and its opponents, such as Haimerich and Innocent.

9. Fuhrmann, *Germany*, pp. 120 f.

10. Robinson, *Papacy*, p. 385.

11. Fuhrmann, *Germany*, p. 126.

12. Robinson, *Papacy*, p. 455.

13. Morris, *Papal Monarchy*, pp. 183 f.

14. K. Jordan, 'Investiturstreit und frühe Stauferzeit (1056–1197)', in B. Gebhardt *Handbuch der Deutschen Geschichte*, 8th edn, vol. I (Stuttgart, 1959) pp. 295 f.; Boockmann, *Stauferzeit*, pp. 75 f.

15. S. Runciman, *A History of the Crusades*, vol. II (Cambridge, 1957) book III.

16. F. Heer, *Die Tragödie des Heiligen Reiches* (Stuttgart: Kohlhammer, 1952) pp. 207 f.

17. K. Jordan, *Heinrich der Löwe: eine Biographie* (Munich, 1979) pp. 36 ff.

18. Boockmann, *Stauferzeit*, pp. 80 f.; P. Munz, *Frederick Barbarossa: A Study in Medieval Politics* (London: Cornell University Press, 1969) pp. 44 ff.

19. F. von Raumer, *Geschichte der Hohenstaufen und ihrer Zeit*, vol. I (Leipzig, 1857) pp. ix–x.

20. Heer, *Tragödie*, p. 126, refers to 'die Hartnäckigkeit seines Restauratio-Willens.'

21. Ibid., p. 146.

22. Ibid., p. 177.

23. M. Pacaut, *Frederick Barbarossa*, trans. A.J. Pomerans (London: Collins, 1970) pp. 57 f.

24. Munz, *Frederick Barbarossa*, pp. 66 f.

25. Pacaut, *Frederick Barbarossa*, p. 63.

26. Ibid., p. 68.

27. 'Frederick hated the cities (the "Staufer city foundations" are no proof to the contrary).' Heer, *Tragödie*, p. 135.

28. Munz, *Frederick Barbarossa*, p. 95.

29. Heer, *Tragödie*, pp. 86 f.

30. Pacaut, *Frederick Barbarossa*, pp. 80 f. A number of different interpretations have been advanced by other historians, such as Munz, *Frederick Barbarossa*, pp. 142 ff, who believes that Hadrian had set a trap into which Rainald fell. See also H. Wolter, 'The Threats to the Freedom of the Church, 1153 to 1198' in H. Jedin and J. Dolan (eds) *Handbook of Church History*, vol. IV. trans. A. Biggs (New York: Herder & Herder 1970) pp. 54 ff.

31. Roman law did not have any inner meaning for Frederick. 'Like the whole sacral apparatus of antiquity, it was for Frederick only formulation and means, not the expression of an ideology ("*Weltanschauung*")', Heer, *Tragödie*, p. 209.

32. Pacaut, *Frederick Barbarossa*, pp. 84 ff.

33. Ibid., p. 88.
34. Heer, *Tragödie*, pp. 127 ff.
35. Pacaut, *Frederick Barbarossa*, p. 89.
36. Morris, *Papal Monarchy*, p. 193.
37. Munz, *Frederick Barbarossa*, pp. 214 ff; Morris, *Papal Monarchy*, p. 194.
38. Munz, *Frederick Barbarossa*, pp. 182 f; K. Hampe, *Germany under the Salian and Hohenstaufen emperors* (Totowa, New Jersey, 1973) trans. R. Bennett, pp. 179 f.
39. Fuhrmann, *Germany*, p. 103.
40. Pacaut, *Frederick Barbarossa*, p. 107; Munz, *Frederick Barbarossa*, pp. 230 ff.
41. Heer, *Tragödie*, pp. 251 ff.
42. Pacaut, *Frederick Barbarossa*, pp. 126 ff.
43. K. Jordan, *Henry the Lion: a biography*, trans. P. S. Falla (Oxford: Clarendon press, 1986) pp. 161 ff.
44. Pacaut, *Frederick Barbarossa*, p. 164.
45. Munz, *Frederick Barbarossa*, p. 332.
46. Wolter, 'The Threats to the Freedom of the Church', pp. 65 f.
47. Jordan, *Henry*, pp. 161 ff.
48. Ibid., p. 178 f.
49. Jordan, *Henry*, p. 168 f.
50. Fuhrmann, *Germany*, p. 169.
51. Boockmann, *Stauferzeit*, pp. 109 f.
52. Wolter, 'The Threats to the Freedom of the Church', p. 76.
53. Boockmann, *Stauferzeit*, p. 123.
54. Morris, *Papal Monarchy*, p. 200.
55. Runciman, *Crusades*, vol. III, pp. 11 ff.
56. Jordan, *Henry*, pp. 189 ff.
57. As a crusader he was under the special protection of the pope; Robinson, *Papacy*, p. 119.
58. Morris, *Papal Monarchy*, pp. 202 f.
59. Robinson, *Papacy*, p. 119.
60. Boockmann, *Stauferzeit*, p. 131.
61. Fuhrmann, *Germany*, p. 186; Boockmann, *Stauferzeit*, pp. 132 f.
62. Wolter, 'The Threats to the Freedom of the Church', pp. 79 ff; Morris, *Papal Monarchy*, p. 419.
63. J. Sayers, *Innocent III: leader of Europe, 1198–1216* (London, 1994) p. 16 f.
64. Morris, *Papal Monarchy*, p. 418.
65. F. Kempf, *Papsttum und Kaisertum bei Innocenz III. Die geistigen und rechtlichen Grundlagen seiner Thronstreitpolitik* (Rome, 1954) *passim*.
66. There are parallels here with Pope John Paul II, whose pontifical mass the present writer attended in Germany, at Fulda, in the early 1980's. The pope paid great attention to every word he spoke in the service and appeared to be personally addressing each one of us in the huge congregation.
67. H. Wolter, 'The Papacy at the Height of its Power, 1198 to 1216', in H. Jedin and J. Dolan (eds) *Handbook of Church History*, vol. IV, trans A. Biggs (New York: Herder & Herder, 1970) p.138; Sayers, *Innocent III*, p. 16.
68. See for instance the pope's statement on the relative merits of the candidates, *Deliberatio de tribus electis*, at the turn of 1200 to 1201, in Kempf, *Papsttum*, pp. 154 ff.
69. W. Ullmann, *A Short History of the Papacy in the Middle Ages* (London: Methuen, 1972) p. 210.

70. Kempf, *Papsttum*, p. 162.
71. J. Haller, *Das Papsttum. Idee und Wirklichkeit*, vol. III (Esslingen, 1962) p. 286; E. Maschke, *Der Kampf zwischen Kaisertum und Papsttum* (Constance, 1955), p. 55.
72. Kempf, *Papsttum*, pp. 162 f.
73. Morris, *Papal Monarchy*, p. 424.
74. Ullmann, *Short History of the Papacy*, p. 212; Sayers, *Innocent III*, p. 52, also has a negative judgement on Otto.
75. Ullmann, *Short History of the Papacy*, p. 212.
76. Morris, *Papal Monarchy*, pp 424 f.
77. D. Abulafia, *Frederick II: a medieval emperor* (London: Allen Lane, 1988) p. 106. See also F. Baethgen, 'Kaiser Friedrich II. 1194–1250', in H. Heimpel, T. Heuss and B. Reifenberg (eds) *Die Grossen Deutschen*, vol. I (Berlin, 1956) pp. 154–86; H. M. Schaller, 'Friedrich II, Kaiser', *Neue Deutsche Biographie*, vol. V (Berlin, 1971) pp. 478–84.
78. See G. Duby, *The Legend of Bouvines. War, Religion and Culture in the Middle Ages* trans. C. Tihanyi (Cambridge, 1990) *passim*.
79. Abulafia, *Frederick II*, pp. 211 ff.
80. Ibid., pp. 244 f.
81. For instance to the bishops in 1213 and 1220 in relation to the *spolia*, royal rights to a proportion of the property of deceased bishops. See B. Arnold, *Princes and territories in medieval Germany* (Cambridge University Press, 1991) p. 205
82. Wolter, 'The Papacy at the Height of its Power, 1198 to 1216', pp. 173 ff.
83. Sayers, *Innocent III*, p. 157.
84. Ibid., pp. 153 ff, esp. p. 160.
85. Wolter, 'The Papacy at the Height of its Power, 1198 to 1216', p. 163.
86. Ibid., pp. 155f; Sayers, *Innocent III*, p 173.
87. Runciman, *Crusades*, vol. III, pp. 114 f.; Wolter, 'The Papacy at the Height of its Power, 1198 to 1216', pp. 155 f.
88. Boockmann, *Stauferzeit*, p.131; Runciman, *Crusades*, vol. III, pp. 112 ff.
89. Sayers, *Innocent III*, pp. 173 f.; Wolter, 'The Papacy at the Height of its Power, 1198 to 1216', p. 157.
90. Abulafia, *Frederick II*, pp. 120 f.
91. E. Kantorowicz, *Frederick the Second 1194–1250* (New York: Frederick Ungar 1957) trans. E. O. Lorimer, pp. 73 f.
92. Haller, *Papsttum*, vol. IV, p. 20.
93. J. Leuschner, *Deutschland im späten Mittelalter* (Göttingen, 1983) p. 66.
94. Morris, *Papal Monarchy*, p. 214.
95. Abulafia, *Frederick II*, p. 134; Haller, *Papsttum*, vol. IV. p. 12.
96. Runciman, *Crusades*, vol. III, pp. 167 ff.
97. Abulafia, *Frederick II*, p. 150.
98. Haller, *Papsttum*, vol. IV, p. 34.
99. Abulafia, *Frederick II*, p. 155.
100. Haller, *Papsttum*, vol. IV, pp. 37 ff. Abulafia in his *Frederick II*, pp. 154 ff. believes the emperor's intentions in Northern Italy were more limited than they appeared. If that is so, Frederick did not guard sufficiently against misinterpretation of his actions. He was not always particularly felicitous in his gestures or their timing.
101. Haller, *Papsttum*, vol. IV, p. 47.

102. F.X. Seppelt and G. Schwaiger, *Geschichte der Päpste. Von den Anfängen bis zur Gegenwart* (Munich, Kösel, 1964) p. 191.
103. Haller, *Papsttum*, vol. IV, p. 58.
104. Abulafia, *Frederick II*, pp. 186 ff.
105. Ibid., p. 193.
106. H. Heimpel, 'Hermann von Salza', in H. Heimpel, T. Heuss and B. Reifenberg (eds) *Die Grossen Deutschen*, vol. I (Berlin: Propyläen, 1956) pp. 171–86.
107. 'Der Deutsche Orden in Ostmitteleuropa. Jahrestagung des J. G. Herder-- Forschungsrates vom 4. bis 6. April 1990 in Marburg', *AHF Information* (Arbeitsgemeinschaft ausseruniversitärer historischer Forschungseinrichtungen in der Bundesrepublik Deutschland), 54 (6 December 1990) 1–4; see also R. ten Haaf, *Deutschordensstaat und Deutschordensballeien* (Göttingen, 1951) *passim*.
108. Arnold, *Princes and territories*, p. 28.
109. Wolter, 'The Contest for the Leadership of the West, 1216 to 1274', in H. Jedin and J. Dolan (eds) *Handbook of Church History*, vol. IV, trans. A. Biggs (New York: Herder & Herder, 1970) p. 192.
110. Morris, *Papal Monarchy*, p. 485
111. J. Richard, *Saint Louis. Crusader King of France* (Cambridge University Press, 1992) edited S. Lloyd and trans. J. Birrell, pp 101 ff. and *passim*.
112. Richard, *St. Louis*, p. 263.
113. Ibid., p. 218.
114. Haller, *Papsttum*, vol. IV, pp. 173 ff.; Wolter, 'The Contest for the Leadership of the West, 1216 to 1274', pp. 193 ff.
115. Morris, *Papal Monarchy*, p. 485.
116. 'The failure of the 1246 plot revealed how narrow Innocent's support base in southern Italy in fact was.' Abulafia, *Frederick II*, p. 391.
117. Abulafia, *Frederick II*, pp. 401 ff.
118. But with his other brothers he may eventually have been legitimised by his father. See Boockmann, *Stauferzeit*, p. 174.
119. Richard, *Saint Louis*, p. 261.
120. Winkelmann, 'Konrad IV', *Allgemeine Deutsche Biographie*, vol. XVI (Leipzig, 1882) p. 566; H.M. Schaller, on the same, *Neue Deutsche Biographie*, vol. XII (Berlin, 1980) pp. 500–1; Richard, *St. Louis*, p. 261.
121. Richard, *Saint Louis*, p. 262.
122. Ibid.
123. J. Leuschner, *Deutschland im späten Mittelalter* (Göttingen, 1983) pp. 110 f.; Arnold, *Princes and territories*, pp. 27 ff.
124. Leuschner, *Deutschland*, p. 116.
125. Abulafia, *Frederick II*, p. 410; Richard, *St. Louis*, p. 262.
126. Abulafia, *Frederick II*, pp. 410 ff
127. Richard, *Saint Louis*, p. 262.
128. Abulafia, *Frederick II*, p. 412 f.; Richard, *St. Louis*, p. 263.
129. Richard, *Saint Louis*, p. 264. See generally ch. 13.
130. Leuschner, *Deutschland*, p. 101.
131. Richard, *Saint Louis*, p. 265.
132. Ibid., p. 269.
133. Haller, *Papsttum*, vol. IV, p. 353.
134. Ibid., p. 334 and *passim*.
135. Ibid., p. 354.
136. Boockmann, *Stauferzeit*, pp. 132 f doubts it.

137. 'He early conceived his personal fate to be under the immediate law of a higher power'. Kantorowicz, *Frederick the Second*, p. 106.
138. Thus for instance Kantorowicz in *Frederick the Second*, p. 101: 'It was one of the most characteristic gifts of Frederick to win a whole series of positions with one skilful move. He raised it to a high art.' On Kantorowicz see *inter alia* E.Grünewald, *Ernst Kantorowicz und Stefan George. Beiträge zur Biographie des Historikers bis zum Jahre 1938 und zu seinem Jugendwerk "Kaiser Friedrich der Zweite"* (Wiesbaden, Franz Steiner Verlag 1982); R.E. Lerner, 'Ernst Kantorowicz and Theodor E. Mommsen', in H. Lehmann and J.J. Sheehan (eds) *An interrupted past. German-speaking refugee historians in the United States after 1933* (Washington, DC and Cambridge, 1991) pp. 188–205.
139. Seppelt and Schwaiger, *Geschichte der Päpste*, p. 191.

6. THE LATER MIDDLE AGES (1268–1517)

1. Chapter 1 of the recent book by Benjamin Arnold, *Medieval Germany 500–1300* (London: Macmillan, 1997) deals with the question of the kingdom's name.
2. J. Haller, *Das Papsttum. Idee und Wirklichkeit* vol. V, (Stuttgart: Port Verlag, 1953) pp. 44ff.
3. H. Wolter, 'The Crisis of the Papacy and of the Church, 1274 to 1303', in H. Jedin and J. Dolan (eds) *Handbook of Church History*, vol. IV, trans. A. Biggs (New York: Herder & Herder, 1970) p. 267.
4. Haller, *Papsttum*, vol. V, pp. 28, 32; E.E.S. Procter, 'Alfonso X', *Chambers Encyclopaedia*, vol. I (London, 1959) p. 250 .
5. Boockmann, *Stauferzeit und spätes Mittelalter: Deutschland 1125–1517* (Berlin: Siedler, 1987) p. 185.
6. Wolter, 'The Crisis of the Papacy', pp. 235f.
7. Ibid., p. 236.
8. D. Abulafia, *Frederick II: a medieval emperor* (London, 1988) pp. 424ff.
9. Wolter, 'The Crisis of the Papacy', p. 267.
10. Ibid., p. 237.
11. J. Leuschner, *Deutschland im späten Mittelalter* (Göttingen: Vandenhoeck & Ruprecht, 1983) pp. 124f.
12. H. Grundmann, 'Wahlkönigtum, Territorialpolitik und Ostbewegung im 13. und 14. Jahrhundert', in B. Gebhardt (ed.) *Handbuch der Deutschen Geschichte*, 8th edn, vol. I (Stuttgart, 1959) pp. 404f.
13. Wolter, 'The Crisis of the Papacy', p. 269.
14. T.S.R. Boase, *Boniface VIII* (London, Constable, 1933) p. 62.
15. Ibid., p. 66.
16. Ibid., p. 217.
17. Leuschner, *Deutschland*, p. 125f.
18. Boase, *Boniface VIII*, p. 217.
19. Ibid., pp. 217f.
20. Ibid., p. 218.
21. Ibid., p. 265f.
22. Ibid., p. 299.
23. Ibid., p. 300.
24. Ibid., p. 301.
25. All quotations in this paragraph are from ibid. pp. 329 f.

26. A. Vauchez, 'Der Kirchenbegriff im lateinischen Abendland', in M. Mollat du Jourdin, A. Vauchez and B. Schimmelpfennig (eds) *Die Geschichte des Christentums: Religion, Politik, Kultur*, vol. VI (Freiburg: Herder, 1991) p. 269.

27. K.A. Fink, 'The Situation After the Death of Boniface VIII: Benedict XI and Clement V', in H. Jedin and J. Dolan (eds) *Handbook of Church History*, vol. IV, trans. A. Biggs (New York: Herder & Herder, 1970) pp. 291f.

28. Boase, *Boniface VIII*, p. 364.

29. Fink, 'The Situation After the Death of Boniface VIII', p. 306.

30. Boockmann, *Stauferzeit*, p. 218.

31. B. Guillemain, 'Kirche und weltliche Macht in der römischen Christenheit', in M. Mollat du Jourdin, A. Vauchez and B. Schimmelpfennig (eds) *Geschichte des Christentums*, vol. VI (Freiburg: Herder, 1991) p. 578.

32. For some of John XXII's methods, see R.E. Lerner, *The Heresy of the Free Spirit in the Later Middle Ages* (Berkeley, 1972) pp. 26f. and *passim*.

33. Leuschner, *Deutschland*, p. 136; K. A. Fink, 'From John XXII to Clement VI', in H. Jedin and J. Dolan (eds) *Handbook of Church History*, vol. IV, trans. A. Biggs (New York: Herder & Herder, 1970) pp. 311ff.

34. Leuschner, *Deutschland*, p. 137.

35. Fink, 'From John XXII to Clement VI', p. 309.

36. R.E. Lerner, *The Heresy of the Free Spirit in the Later Middle Ages* (Berkeley: University of California Press, 1972) p. 133.

37. Boockmann, *Stauferzeit*, pp. 251–5. The quotation is on p. 255.

38. E. Iserloh, 'The Jews in Mediaeval Christendom', in H. Jedin and J. Dolan (eds) *Handbook of Church History*, vol. IV, trans. A. Biggs (New York: Herder & Herder, 1970) pp. 607f.

39. Boockmann, *Stauferzeit*, pp. 263ff.

40. Leuschner, *Deutschland*, p. 184.

41. Ibid., pp. 178–84; Boockmann, *Stauferzeit*, pp. 267–72.

42. B. Schimmelpfennig, *Das Papsttum: von der Antike bis zur Renaissance* (Darmstadt, 1988) p. 257.

43. On this the historian Treitschke wrote his famous essay *Das deutsche Ordensland Preußen*. The present writer analysed Treitschke's national criteria in this essay, which was originally published in 1862, for a lecture given to the Canadian Historical Association in 1987 and not yet in print.

44. Leuschner, *Deutschland*, pp.154f.

45. See the following chapter.

46. J.E. Rodes, *Germany: a history* (New York: Holt, Rinehart & Winston, 1964) p.7 f.

47. Ibid., p. 7 f.

48. Leuschner, *Deutschland*, pp. 168ff.; Rodes, *Germany*, pp. 77f.

49. Fink, 'The Council of Constance: Martin V', in H. Jedin and J. Dolan (eds) *Handbook of Church History*, vol. IV, trans. A. Biggs (New York: Herder & Herder, 1970) p. 449.

50. P. Ourliac, 'Das Schisma und die Konzilien (1378–1449)', in M. Mollat du Jourdin, A. Vauchez and B. Schimmelpfennig (eds), *Geschichte des Christentums: Religion, Politik, Kultur*, vol. VI, (Freiburg: Herder, 1991) p. 100.

51. Boockmann, *Stauferzeit*, p. 282.

52. Fink, 'The Council of Constance', pp. 449f.

53. Boockmann, *Stauferzeit*, p. 283.

54. See F. Oakley, *The Political Thought of Pierre d'Ailly. The voluntarist tradition* (New Haven, Connecticut 5, 1964) *passim*.

55. Ourliac, 'Das Schisma und die Konzilien', pp. 97.

56. K.A. Fink, 'The Nationalist Heresies: Wyclif and Hus', in H. Jedin and J. Dolan (eds) *Handbook of Church History*, vol. IV, trans. A. Biggs (New York: Herder & Herder, 1970) p. 443.
57. M.D. Lambert, *Medieval Heresy. Popular Movements from Bogomil to Hus* (London, Arnold, 1977) p. 220.
58. A. Flew, *A Dictionary of Philosophy* (London: Macmillan, 1985) p. 250.
59. Lambert, *Medieval Heresy*, p. 222.
60. Ibid., p. 229.
61. Ibid., p. 228.
62. Ibid., p. 233.
63. F.G. Heymann, *John Zizka and the Hussite Revolution* (New York: Russell & Russell, 1969) p.46.
64. Boockmann, *Stauferzeit*, p. 283.
65. Ibid., pp. 283f.
66. Heymann, *John Zizka*, pp. 55f.
67. Lambert, *Medieval Heresy*, p. 288.
68. Heymann, *John Zizka*, p. 36, n. 1.
69. Ibid., p. 55.
70. Ibid., p. 53.
71. A. Vauchez, 'Protest-und Häresiebewegungen in der römischen Kirche', in M. Mollat du Jourdin, A. Vauchez and B. Schimmelpfennig (eds) *Geschichte des Christentums: Religion, Politik, Kultur*, vol. VI (Freiburg: Herder, 1991) p. 340; Heymann, *John Zizka*, pp. 52–6.
72. Vauchez, 'Protest-und Häresiebewegungen' pp. 340f.; Fink, 'The Council of Constance', pp. 456ff.
73. Fink, 'The Council of Constance', p. 459.
74. L.B. Pascoe, *Jean Gerson: Principles of Church Reform* (Leiden: Brill, 1973) p. 40.
75. Lambert, *Medieval Heresy*, pp. 5f.
76. Fink, 'Wyclif and Hus', p. 447.
77. Boockmann, *Stauferzeit*, p. 286.
78. Heymann, *John Zizka*, p. 57.
79. Pascoe, *Gerson* p. 10 and *passim*.
80. For the historical background see B. Tierney, *Foundations of the Conciliar Theory. The Contributions of the Medieval Canonists from Gratian to the Great Schism* (Cambridge, 1955) *passim*. For the development of the movement, see H. Smolinsky, 'Konziliarismus', *Theologische Realenzyklopädie*, vol. XIX, pp. 579–86.
81. P. Ourliac, 'Das Schisma und die Konzilien', p. 99.
82. Fink, 'The Council of Constance', pp. 453f.
83. Ibid., pp. 454f.
84. Ibid., p. 464.
85. Ibid., p. 454.
86. Ourliac, 'Das Schisma und die Konzilien', pp. 100f.
87. Fink, 'The Council of Constance', pp. 464ff.
88. Ourliac, 'Das Schisma und die Konzilien', p. 101; Fink, 'The Council of Constance', pp. 464ff.
89. Lambert, *Medieval Heresy*, pp. 298ff.
90. Ibid., p. 304.
91. Ibid., p. 305.
92. Heymann, *John Zizka*, p.67.
93. Ibid., p. 449.

94. P. Ourliac, 'Das Schisma und die Konzilien', p. 109.
95. F.X. Seppelt and G. Schwaiger, *Geschichte der Päpste. Von den Anfängen bis zur Gegenwart* (Munich: Kösel, 1964) p. 247.
96. Ourliac, 'Das Schisma und die Konzilien', pp. 112ff.
97. Heymann, *John Zizka*, pp. 471ff.; Lambert, *Medieval Heresy*, pp. 330ff.
98. Lambert, *Medieval Heresy*, p; xii.
99. P. Ourliac, 'Das Schisma und die Konzilien', p. 115.
100. Boockmann, *Stauferzeit*, p. 333.
101. Ibid., p. 288.
102. P. Ourliac, 'Das Schisma und die Konzilien', p. 126.
103. Leuschner, *Deutschland*, p. 212.
104. Ourliac, 'Das Schisma und die Konzilien', pp. 119ff.
105. Ibid., p. 120.
106. Ibid., p. 121.
107. K. A. Fink, 'Eugen IV and the Council of Basle–Ferrara–Florence', in H. Jedin and J. Dolan (eds) *Handbook of Church History*, vol. IV, trans. A. Biggs (New York: Herder & Herder, 1970) p. 482; Ourliac, 'Das Schisma und die Konzilien', p. 122.
108. Fink, 'Eugen IV', p. 485f.; Ourliac, 'Das Schisma und die Konzilien', p. 122; Seppelt and Schwaiger, *Geschichte der Päpste*, p. 254.
109. Seppelt and Schwaiger, *Geschichte der Päpste*, p, 253.
110. K.A. Fink, 'Renaissance and Humanism', in H. Jedin and J. Dolan (eds) *Handbook of Church History*, vol. IV, trans. A. Biggs (New York: Herder & Herder, 1970) p. 521.
111. Seppelt and Schwaiger, *Geschichte der Päpste*, p. 256.
112. See F.G. Heymann, *George of Bohemia, King of Heretics* (Princeton, NJ, 1965) *passim*.
113. K.A. Fink, 'The Popes of the Early Renaissance', in H. Jedin and J. Dolan (eds) *Handbook of Church History*, vol. IV, trans. A. Biggs (New York: Herder & Herder, 1970) pp. 537f.
114. Seppelt and Schwaiger, *Geschichte der Päpste*, pp. 260ff.
115. Ibid., p. 264.
116. Ibid., pp. 266f.
117. Ibid., p. 268.
118. Ibid., p. 272.
119. F. Hartung, *Deutsche Verfassungsgeschichte vom 15. Jahrhundert bis zur Gegenwart* (Stuttgart, 1950) pp. 5f.
120. Boockmann, *Stauferzeit*, pp. 347f. The Quotation is on p. 349.
121. Leuschner, *Deutschland*, p. 217.
122. G. Franz, 'Reformation Kaiser Sigmunds', in H. Rössler and G. Franz (eds) *Sachwörterbuch zur Deutschen Geschichte* (Munich, 1958) p. 962.
123. E. Iserloh, 'Theology in the Age of Transition', in H. Jedin and J. Dolan (eds) *Handbook of Church History*, vol. IV, trans. A. Biggs (New York: Herder & Herder, 1970) p. 586.
124. Ibid., p. 589.
125. F. Rapp, 'Die Kirchenprovinzen des Deutschen Reiches', in M. Mollat du Jourdin, A. Vauchez and B. Schimmelpfennig (eds) *Die Geschichte des Christentums: Religion, Politik, Kultur*, vol. VI, (Freiburg: Herder, 1991) pp. 709.
126. Ibid., pp. 706ff.
127. Boockmann, *Stauferzeit*, p.378.
128. Hartung, *Deutsche Verfassungsgeschichte*, pp. 17ff.

129. F. Rapp, 'Die Kirchenprovinzen des Deutschen Reiches', in M. Millat du Jourdin, A. Vauchez and B. Schimmelpfennig (eds) *Geschichte des Christentums*, vol. VI, pp. 705f.; see also pp. 691ff, 703ff.
130. H. Hantsch, *Die Geschichte Österreichs*, vol. I, (Graz, 1951) p. 202.
131. H. Wiesflecker, 'Maximilian I., König (seit 1486), Kaiser (seit 1508)', *Neue Deutsche Biographie*, vol. XVI (Berlin: Duncker & Humblot, 1990) p. 460.
132. E. Bock, 'Berthold von Henneberg', *Neue Deutsche Biographie*, vol. II (Berlin, 1971) pp. 156f.
133. Hartung, *Deutsche Verfassungsgeschichte*, pp. 19ff.
134. Ibid., pp. 21f.
135. Ibid., p.22.
136. H. Wiesflecker, 'Maximilian I', p. 469.
137. Seppelt and Schwaiger, *Geschichte der Päpste*, pp. 269f.
138. Boockmann, *Stauferzeit*, pp. 389f.
139. B. Moeller, *Deutschland im Zeitalter der Reformation* (Göttingen, 1988) p. 38; Boockmann, *Stauferzeit*, p. 399.
140. Boockmann, *Stauferzeit*, pp. 384f.
141. Ibid., pp. 387f.
142. E. Iserloh, 'The Inner Life of the Church', in H. Jedin and J. Dolan (eds) *Handbook of Church History*, vol. IV, trans. A. Biggs (New York: Herder & Herder, 1970) p. 569.
143. Ibid., pp. 579f.
144. Ibid., pp. 575f.
145. F. Rapp, 'Die Kirchenprovinzen des Deutschen Reiches', p. 712.
146. Iserloh, 'The Inner Life of the Church', pp. 575f.
147. B. Moeller, *Deutschland im Zeitalter der Reformation* (Göttingen: Vandenhoeck & Ruprecht, 1988) pp. 38f.

7.   REFORMATION AND CATHOLIC REFORM (1517–64)

1. M. Brecht, *Martin Luther: his road to Reformation, 1483–1521*, trans. J.L. Schaaf (Philadelphia: Fortress Press, 1985) p. 1.
2. *Tatsachen über Deutschland* (Frankfurt: Societäts-Verlag, 1992) p. 62.
3. Brecht, *Luther*, pp. 2ff.
4. For instance by E.H. Erikson, *Young Man Luther: a study in psychoanalysis and history* (New York, 1958).
5. B. Lohse, *Martin Luther: An Introduction to His Life and Work* , trans. R.C. Schultz (Philadelphia: Fortress Press, 1986) p. 21.
6. Ibid., p. 23.
7. Ibid., p. 22.
8. H. Beintker, 'Anfechtung', *Die Religion in Geschichte und Gegenwart. Handwörterbuch für Theologie und Religionswissenschaft*, vol. I (Tübingen, J.C.B. Mohr [Paul Siebeck], 1957) p. 370.
9. D.C. Steinmetz, *Luther and Staupitz. An Essay in the Intellectual Origins of the Protestant Reformation* (Durham, NC: Duke University Press, 1980) p. 8.
10. Ibid., p. 31, including n. 115 drawing on T.N. Tentler, *Sin and Confession on the Eve of the Reformation* (Princeton, NJ, 1977), p. 156.
11. Ibid., p. 32.
12. Ibid., pp. 33ff.
13. Ibid., p. 8.

14. Ibid., p. 33.
15. Brecht, *Luther*, p. 156. For a more critical view of Staupitz's effectiveness as Luther's confessor, see R. Decot (ed.) P. Manns, *Vater im Glauben: Studien zur Theologie Martin Luthers; Festgabe zum 65. Geburtstag am 10. März 1988* (Stuttgart: Franz Steiner, 1988) p. 432.
16. Steinmetz, *Luther*, p. 125.
17. With Greek, 'he never attained the full mastery...as did his humanistic friends.' See H. Bornkamm, *Luther in mid-career, 1521–1530* (Philadelphia: Fortress Press, 1983) p. 45.
18. See on this E. Kinder, 'Rechtfertigung', *Die Religion in Geschichte und Gegenwart. Handwörterbuch für Theologie und Religionswissenschaft*, vol. V (Tübingen, 1961) p. 834.
19. J. Wicks, *Man Yearning for Grace. Luther's early spiritual teaching* (Wiesbaden: Franz Steiner, 1969) pp. 190f.
20. Ibid., p. 192. However, Wicks also points out that in May 1518 Luther clarified his position on this matter by admitting a limited freedom of will, so long as it is not concerned with merit or demerit. See ibid., pp. 192f.
21. On this question, see ibid., p. 193.
22. Ibid., p. 197.
23. Ibid., p. 197; Brecht, *Luther*, pp. 172f.
24. Wicks, *Man Yearning for Grace*, pp. 212ff.
25. R. Decot (ed.), P. Manns, *Vater im Glauben*, p. 438.
26. J. Lortz, *The Reformation in Germany*, trans. R. Walls, vol. I (London: Darton, Longman & Todd, 1968) p. 221.
27. G. v. Pölnitz, *Die Fugger* (Frankfurt, 1960) pp. 112f.
28. Lortz, *The Reformation in Germany*, vol. I, pp. 86ff, 225ff.
29. Flathe, 'Albrecht von Sachsen, Erzbischof von Mainz (1467–1484)', *Allgemeine Deutsche Biographie*, vol. I (Leipzig, 1877) p. 268; Schirrmacher, 'Albrecht von Brandenburg, Erzbischof von Mainz, etc. (1490–1545)', *Allgemeine Deutsche Biographie*, vol. I (Leipzig, 1875), pp. 268–71 and H. Grimm, on the same, *Neue Deutsche Biographie*, vol. I (Berlin, 1971) pp. 166–7; Janicke, Ernst von Sachsen, Erzbischof von Magdeburg (1464–1513), *Allgemeine Deutsche Biographie*, vol. VI (Leipzig, 1877) pp. 291–93. Earlier, a Saxon prince had also sat on the archbishop's throne in Mainz.
30. Brecht, *Luther*, pp. 178ff.
31. Ibid., p. 190.
32. Text in I.D. Kingston Siggins (ed.), *Luther* (Edinburgh, 1972) pp. 56ff.
33. For instance by E. Iserloh, *The Theses Were Not Posted: Luther Between Reform and Reformation*, trans. J. Wicks (Boston, 1968).
34. Brecht, *Luther*, p. 204.
35. Wicks, *Man Yearning for Grace*, pp. 232ff.
36. Brecht, *Luther*, pp. 204f.
37. Thesis 34. See Wicks, *Man Yearning for Grace*, p. 233.
38. Thesis 60. See ibid., p. 234; Brecht, *Luther*, p. 196.
39. Thesis 38, quoted in C.J. Barry, *Readings in Church History*, vol. II (Westminster, Maryland: Newman, 1965) p. 17.
40. Theses 32–9. See Wicks, *Man Yearning for Grace*, p. 233.
41. Theses 30–1. See Wicks, *Man Yearning for Grace*, p. 233.
42. Wicks, *Man Yearning for Grace*, pp. 231, 235.
43. Section 7, see ibid., p. 259.
44. Section 2, see ibid., pp. 243ff.

45. Wicks, *Man Yearning for Grace*, p. 243.
46. E. Iserloh, 'Martin Luther and the Coming of the Reformation (1517–25)', in H. Jedin and J. Dolan (eds) *History of the Church*, vol. v, trans. by A. Biggs and P.W. Becker (New York: Seabury, 1980) p. 54.
47. Brecht, *Luther*, pp. 162f.
48. Ibid., p. 163.
49. Ibid., ch. VI, sec. 5: 'The Inner Turning Point – the Reformatory Discovery'; Lohse, *Luther*, pp. 41 and 157f.
50. Lortz, *The Reformation in Germany*, vol. I, pp. 233f.
51. These questions are discussed, by such distinguished Roman Catholic theologians and church historians as K. Rahner, in *Foundations of Christian Faith*, trans. W.V. Dych (New York, 1978) pp. 357ff., and P. Manns in (R. Decot, ed.) *Vater im Glauben, passim*, and in his introductory lecture 'Was macht Martin Luther zum "Vater im Glauben" für die eine Christenheit', in *Martin Luther 'Reformator und Vater im Glauben'*. Referate aus der Vortragsreihe des Instituts für Europäische Geschichte Mainz (Stuttgart 1985) edited by him, pp. 1–24. See also Cardinal Willebrands' official statement on behalf of the Roman Catholic Church to the meeting of the Lutheran World Federation at Evian in 1970, published in *Herder Korrespondenz*, 24 (1970) pp. 427–31.
52. For a discussion of Luther's development, see B. Moeller, *Deutschland im Zeitalter der Reformation* (Göttingen, 1988) p. 60.
53. Brecht, *Luther*, pp. 206ff.
54. Ibid., p. 210.
55. Ibid.,
56. Lortz, *The Reformation in Germany*, vol. I, p. 72.
57. Brecht, *Luther*, p. 179.
58. Iserloh, 'Martin Luther', p. 52.
59. Ibid., p. 53.
60. Brecht, *Luther*, p. 242
61. Ibid., p. 243.
62. Lortz, *The Reformation in Germany*, vol. I, p. 27.
63. Moeller, *Deutschland*, pp. 51f.
64. Brecht, *Luther*, p. 247; Iserloh, 'Martin Luther', p. 54.
65. Brecht, *Luther*, p. 247.
66. Ibid., p. 250.
67. Iserloh, 'Martin Luther', p. 59; Lortz, *The Reformation in Germany*, vol. I, p. 245.
68. Pölnitz, *Fugger*, pp. 127ff.
69. H. Schilling, *Aufbruch und Krise: Deutschland 1517–1648* (Berlin: Siedler, 1988) pp. 194ff.
70. Lortz, *The Reformation in Germany*, vol. I, esp., pp. 135, 250. See also H. Smolinsky, 'Reform der Theologie? Beobachtungen zu Johannes Ecks exegetischen Vorlesungen an der Universität Ingolstadt', in M. Weitlauff and K. Hausberger (eds) *Papsttum und Kirchenreform. Historische Beiträge. Festschrift für Georg Schwaiger zum 65. Geburtstag* (St Ottilien, 1990) pp. 333–49.
71. Brecht, *Luther*, p. 322. See also Iserloh, 'Martin Luther', p. 63. Lortz, *The Reformation in Germany*, vol. I, pp. 248ff. is more critical of Eck.
72. Brecht, *Luther*, pp. 381ff.
73. Schilling, *Aufbruch und Krise*, p. 157.
74. Brecht, *Luther*, p. 460.
75. Ibid., p. 456.
76. Iserloh, 'Martin Luther', p. 80; Brecht, *Luther*, p. 474.

77. Flathe, 'Georg, Herzog von Sachsen', *Allgemeine Deutsche Biographie* , vol. VIII (Leipzig, 1878) p. 685; E. Werl, 'Georg der Bärtige, Herzog von Sachsen', *Neue Deutsche Biographie*, vol. VI (Berlin, 1971) pp. 224–7.

78. Few statesmen in history can have been more rooted in the Roman Catholic Church than the first German federal chancellor, Konrad Adenauer. Yet Theodor Heuss, the federal president at the time, was struck – as he told the present writer – by what came over as Adenauer's strong anti-clericalism.

79. For details of the critical attitude in the German kingdom to church and papacy, see A.G. Dickens, *The German Nation and Martin Luther* (London: Arnold, 1974) *passim*.

80. Frederick continued to ask the curia for permission to issue indulgences, and in 1519 and 1520 held indulgence celebrations in Wittenberg with considerable financial success. Lortz, *The Reformation in Germany*, vol. I, p. 120.

81. Moeller, *Deutschland*, p. 77.

82. On developments in the cities, see A.G. Dickens, *The German Nation* esp. chs 7–9, who draws on B. Moeller, *Reichsstadt und Reformation* (Gütersloh, 1962) edited and translated by H.C.E. Midelfort and M.U. Edwards, Jr as *Imperial Cities and the Reformation* (Durham, North Carolina, 1982). For comments on Moeller's work, see H. Schilling, *Religion, Political Culture and the Emergence of Early Modern Society. Essays in German and Dutch History* (Leiden, 1992) esp. pp. 63, 67–8, 194.

83. Iserloh, 'Martin Luther und der Aufbruch der Reformation (1517–1525)', in H. Jedin (ed.) *Handbuch der Kirchengeschichte*, vol. V (Freiburg, Herder 1985)', p. 86.

84. R. Stupperich, 'Melanchthon', *Neue Deutsche Biographie*, vol. XVI (Berlin, 1990) p. 742.

85. 'Evangelisch' causes some problems for German ears, as the term was used in connection with the forced Prussian Union of Lutherans and Reformed in 1817, just as 'evangelical' is somewhat confusing in English because of its closeness to evangelising.

86. Lohse, *Luther*, pp. 183ff.

87. A.G. Dickens, *The German Nation*, p. 183 and *passim*; Schilling, *Religion, Political Culture, and the Emergence of Early Modern Society*, esp. chs 2–4.

88. G.R. Potter, *Zwingli* (Cambridge University Press, 1976) pp. 1ff; for Zwingli, see also W.P. Stephens, *Zwingli: an Introduction to his Thought* (Oxford, 1992).

89. Potter, *Zwingli*, pp. 39f.

90. Ibid., p. 38.

91. Ibid., p. 39.

92. Ibid.,

93. Ibid., p. 62.

94. Ibid., p. 44.

95. Ibid., p. 67.

96. Ibid., pp. 69f.

97. F. Rapp, 'Die Kirchenprovinzen des Deutschen Reiches', in M. Mollat du Jourdin, A. Vauchez and B. Schimmelpfennig (eds) *Geschichte des Christentums*, vol. VI (Freiburg: Herder, 1991) p. 705.

98. Brecht, *Luther*, p. 462.

99. Bornkamm, *Luther*, pp. 38f.

100. Ibid., p. 45.

101. Ibid., p. 46.

102. W.A. Coupe (ed.) *A Sixteenth-Century German Reader* (Oxford: Clarendon, 1972) pp. xviii ff.
103. For a more critical view of Luther's exegesis, see R. Rex, 'The unpopular Reformation', *The Times Literary Supplement*, 30 December 1994, p. 25, in which he states *inter alia*: 'Luther's... brutal exegetical method – laying the Scriptures on a procrustean bed of justification and the Law/Gospel dichotomy – will hardly allow him to qualify as a sensitive textual critic.'
104. Coupe (ed.), *A German Reader*, p. xix.
105. Bornkamm, *Luther*, p. 49; Coupe, *A. German Reader*, p. xx.
106. See F. Eyck, *The Frankfurt Parliament, 1848–49* (London: Macmillan, 1968).
107. Bornkamm, *Luther*, p. 1.
108. Ibid., p. 44.
109. A.E. McGrath, *Reformation Thought: an Introduction* (Oxford: Blackwell, 1994) pp. 55ff.
110. Brecht, *Luther, passim*.
111. G. Rupp, *Patterns of Reformation* (London: Fortress, 1969) p. 72.
112. Ibid., p. 152.
113. Ibid., p. 152.
114. Ibid., pp. 158f.
115. Ibid., pp. 254f.
116. Bornkamm, *Luther*, pp. 63ff.
117. Ibid., pp. 69ff.
118. Schilling, *Aufbruch*, pp. 131ff.
119. M. Greschat, *Martin Bucer: ein Reformator und seine Zeit* (Munich, 1990) p. 52.
120. Schilling, *Aufbruch*, p. 133.
121. Greschat, *Bucer*, pp. 53ff.
122. Bornkamm, *Luther*, p. 306.
123. P. Blickle, *The Revolution of 1525: The German Peasants' War from a new perspective*, trans. T.A. Brady, Jr and H.C.E. Midelfort (Baltimore: Johns Hopkins University Press, 1981) p. 49.
124. Blickle, *The Revolution of 1525*, p. 35.
125. Ibid., p. 50.
126. Ibid., p. 34.
127. See S. Hoyer, 'Antiklerikalismus in den Forderungen und Aktionen der Aufständischen von 1524–1525' and H.J. Cohn, 'Changing places: Peasants and Clergy 1525', in P.A. Dykema and H.A. Oberman (eds) *Anticlericalism in late Medieval and Early Modern Europe* (Leiden, 1993) pp. 535–57.
128. Schilling, *Aufbruch*, p. 145.
129. P. Blickle, *The Revolution of 1525*, pp. 105ff.
130. Schilling, *Aufbruch*, pp. 152f.
131. Ibid., p. 146.
132. Blickle, *The Revolution of 1525*, p. 18.
133. On the link between the Reformation, especially Zwingli, and social aspirations, see E. Cameron, *The European Reformation* (Oxford University Press, 1991) pp. 208f.
134. Blickle, *The Revolution of 1525*, p. 20.
135. Bornkamm, *Luther*, pp. 375f.; Rupp, *Patterns*, p. 233.
136. P.Blickle, *The Revolution of 1525*, p. 21.
137. Rupp, *Patterns*, p. 231.
138. Ibid., p. 233.
139. Schilling, *Aufbruch*, p. 159.

140. Something along these lines in Schilling, *Aufbruch*, p. 157.
141. Siggins, *Luther*, p. 99.
142. Rupp, *Patterns*, p. 243; Bornkamm, *Luther*, pp. 386f.
143. Bornkamm, *Luther*, p. 389.
144. I.D. Kingston Siggins (ed.) *Luther* (Edinburgh: Oliver & Boyd, 1972) p. 100.
145. Manns, *Vater im Glauben*, p. 381.
146. Blickle, *The Revolution of 1525*, p. 136.
147. Schilling, *Aufbruch und Krise*, p. 158.
148. On this see *inter alia* S. Ozment, *Protestants: the birth of a revolution* (New York, 1992) ch. 6, 'Luther's Political Legacy'.
149. Blickle, *The Revolution of 1525*, pp. 165ff.
150. Ibid., pp. 19ff.
151. Ibid., pp. 183ff.; on this and related questions see Schilling, *Religion, Political Culture*, pp. 190ff.
152. Greschat, *Bucer*, pp. 56f and *passim*.
153. Bornkamm, *Luther*, pp. 77f.
154. Lohse, *Luther*, p. 63.
155. 'Reformation' in H. Rössler and G. Franz, *Sachwörterbuch zur Deutschen Geschichte* (Munich, 1958) p. 960.
156. A.E. McGrath, *Reformation Thought* (Oxford: Blackwell, 1994) p. 42.
157. P.O. Kristeller, *Renaissance Thought. The Classic, Scholastic and Humanist Strains* (New York, 1961) pp. 9f. On Kristeller's view of humanism, see A.E. McGrath, *Reformation Thought: An Introduction* (Oxford, 1994) p. 45. For humanism see also R.W. Southern, *Scholastic Humanism and the Unification of Europe*, vol. I: 'Foundation' (Oxford, 1995).
158. Kristeller, *Renaissance Thought*, p. 11.
159. Ibid., pp. 20.
160. Ibid., p. 116, says: 'Their controversy... is merely a phase in the battle of the arts, not a struggle for existence.'
161. Cf. ibid., p. 117.
162. Lohse, *Luther*, pp. 63ff.; J. McConica, *Erasmus* (Oxford University Press, 1991) pp. 66ff.
163. McConica, *Erasmus*, pp. 68f.
164. Ibid., p. 77.
165. *De libero arbitrio diatribe*.
166. Lohse, *Luther*, pp. 64f.
167. *De servo arbitrio*.
168. Lortz, *The Reformation in Germany*, vol. I, p. 154.
169. Lohse, *Luther*, pp. 68f.
170. Cameron, *European Reformation*, p. 189.
171. Lortz, *The Reformation in Germany*, vol. I, pp. 149f. It is fascinating to observe that this Catholic church historian shows more respect for Luther than for Erasmus. Lortz calls the latter somebody who remained in the Church 'as a half-Catholic'.
172. Ibid., pp. 151f.
173. Lortz, *The Reformation in Germany*, vol. II:, pp. 5f.
174. B Bornkamm, *Luther*, p. 490.
175. Schilling, *Aufbruch*, p. 210.
176. Lohse, *Luther*, p. 82.
177. Ibid., pp. 82f.
178. Bornkamm, *Luther*, p. 492.

179. *landesherrliches Kirchenregiment*, see Lohse, *Luther*, p. 79 ff
180. Schilling, *Aufbruch*, pp. 210ff.
181. E. Iserloh, 'The Reform in the German Principalities', in H. Jedin and J. Dolan (eds) *History of the Church*, vol. V, trans. A. Biggs and P.W. Becker (New York, 1980) p. 242; Cameron, *European Reformation*, pp. 270.
182. Cameron, *European Reformation*, p. 342.
183. Schilling, *Aufbruch*, p. 211.
184. R. Stupperich, 'Melanchthon', *Neue Deutsche Biographie*. vol XVI (Berlin: Duncker & Humblot, 1990) p. 742.
185. Ibid., p. 745.
186. Schilling, *Aufbruch*, pp. 211f.
187. E. Iserloh, 'The Struggle over the concept of Christian Freedom', in H. Jedin and J. Dolan (eds) *History of the Church*, vol. V, trans. A Biggs and P.W. Becker (New York: Seabury, 1980) pp. 188ff.
188. Schilling, *Aufbruch*, pp. 212f.
189. E. Jüngel, ' "Freiheit – das ist das Christentum" ', *Die Zeit*, overseas edition, no. 8 (21 February 1997) p. 16.
190. E. Iserloh in the Catholic *History of the Church*, vol. V, pp. 256f., is critical of his attitude.
191. Iserloh, 'The Reform in the German Principalities', p. 262.
192. Ibid.
193. Cameron, *European Reformation*, p. 343.
194. Potter, *Zwingli*, ch. 16.
195. Schilling, *Aufbruch*, pp. 174ff.
196. A.E. McGrath, *Reformation Thought: An Introduction*, p. 155.
197. F.X. Seppelt and G. Schwaiger, *Geschichte der Päpste. Von den Anfängen bis zur Gegenwart* (Munich: Kösel, 1964) pp. 285ff.
198. M. Venard, 'Die katholische Kirche', in M. Venard and H. Smolinsky (eds) *Die Geschichte des Christentums: Religion, Politik, Kultur*, vol. VIII (Freiburg: Herder, 1992) p. 251.
199. Ibid., p. 255.
200. *Colloquia familiaria*.
201. M. Venard, 'Die katholische Kirche', pp. 251ff. The quotations are on p. 254.
202. Seppelt and Schwaiger, *Geschichte der Päpste*, p. 287.
203. Quotation from the summary of the opening address by H. Boockmann at the 1990 conference on Teutonic Order. See n. 107 in ch. 5.
204. R. ten Haaf, *Deutschordensstaat und Deutschordensballeien* (Göttingen, 1951) p. 70ff and *passim*.
205. 'Deutscher Ritterorden', in H. Rössler and G. Franz (eds) *Sachwörterbuch zur Deutschen Geschichte* (Munich, 1958) pp. 204f. and *passim*.
206. W.J. Bouwsma, *John Calvin: a sixteenth-century portrait* (New York: Oxford University Press, 1988) pp. 9ff. See also J.T. McNeill, *The History and Character of Calvinism* (New York, 1957).
207. O. Millet, 'Die reformierten Kirchen', in M. Venard and H. Smolinsky (eds) *Geschichte des Christentums*, vol. VIII, Freiburg: Herder, 1992) p. 64.
208. Greschat, *Bucer*, pp. 182ff.
209. Bouwsma, *John Calvin*, p. 18.
210. G.D. Henderson, 'Calvin', *Chambers Encyclopaedia*, vol. II (London 1959) p. 801.
211. Bouwsma, *Calvin*, p. 27.
212. See Max Weber's famous essay *Die protestantische Ethik und der Geist des Kapitalismus* originally published in 1904 and 1905 (English version, for

example, by T. Parsons as *The Protestant Ethic and the Spirit of Capitalism*, 1930) and various commentaries, including G. Poggi, *Calvinism and the Capitalist Spirit: Max Weber's Protestant Ethic* (London, 1983). See also R.H. Tawney, *Religion and the Rise of Capitalism* (Harmondsworth: Penguin, 1938).

213. Schilling, *Aufbruch*, p. 227.
214. Iserloh, 'The Reform in the German Principalities', p. 285.
215. Schilling, *Aufbruch*, p. 229.
216. For an analysis of this affair, see Lohse, *Luther*, pp. 77ff.
217. There is the comparatively favourable *That Jesus was born a Jew* (1523) and the vehement attack in *The Jews and Their Lies* (1543). See J. Brosseder, *Luthers Stellung zu den Juden im Spiegel seiner Interpreten* (Munich, 1972) p. 379 and *passim*.
218. E. Jüngel, 'Ein Spott aus dem Tod ist worden', *Die Zeit* (overseas edn), no. 8, (23 February 1996), p. 16.
219. E. Jüngel, 'Freiheit – das ist das Christentum', *Die Zeit* (overseas edition), No. 8, 21 February 1997, p. 16.
220. Ibid.
221. Stupperich, 'Melanchthon', p. 744.
222. 'An interpretation that one-sidedly concentrates on social history poses the danger of wishing to explain the Reformation without the driving force of the *Reformatoren*. In spite of all the pleasure with the structural, one should see the acting theologians and their adversaries.' H. Smolinsky, 'Stadt und Reformation. Neue Aspekte der reformationsgeschichtlichen Forschung', *Trierer Theologische Zeitschrift*, 92 (1983) p. 44.
223. When Spanish troops conquered Wittenberg in 1547, the Emperor gave orders not to touch Luther's grave. See Jüngel, 'Ein Spott' (see n. 218)
224. Cameron, *European Reformation*, p. 347
225. Greschat, *Bucer*, pp. 228ff.
226. Stupperich, 'Melanchthon', p. 745.
227. Schilling, *Aufbruch*, pp. 237f.
228. H. Jedin, 'Origin and Breakthrough of the Catholic Reform to 1563', in H. Jedin and J. Dolan (eds) *History of the Church*, vol. V, trans. A. Biggs and P. W. Becker (New York, 1980) p. 478.
229. Venard, 'Die katholische Kirche', p. 263.
230. Ibid., p. 264.
231. Ibid., pp. 267f.
232. Ibid., p. 268.
233. Ibid., p. 269.
234. Ibid., pp. 269ff.
235. Ibid., p. 271.
236. Ibid., pp. 271f.
237. Ibid., pp. 272f.
238. B. Nischan, *Prince, People and Confession: the Second Reformation in Brandenburg* (Philadelphia: University of Pennsylvania Press, 1994) p. 239.

8. TO THE PEACE OF WESTPHALIA (1564–1648)

1. Kluckhohn, 'August, Kurfürst von Sachsen', *Allgemeine Deutsche Biographie*, vol. I (Leipzig, 1875) pp. 677f.; H. Rössler, on the same, *Neue Deutsche Biographie*, vol. I (Berlin, 1971) pp. 448–50.

2. C. Schille, 'Nikolaus Crell (Krell)', *Neue Deutsche Biographie*, vol. III (Berlin, Duncker & Humblot 1971) p. 407 f.; M. Ritter, 'Nicolaus R. Krell', *Allgemeine Deutsche Biographie*, vol. XVII (Leipzig, 1883) pp. 121 f.; B. Vogler, 'Die deutschen, schweizerischen und skandinavischen Gebiete', in M. Venard and Heribert Smolinsky (eds) *Geschichte des Christentums*, vol. VIII (Freiburg, 1992) p. 412; H. Schilling, *Aufbruch und Krise: Deutschland 1517–1648* (Berlin, 1988) p. 289.
3. My account is based on the narrative in B. Nischan, *Prince, People and Confession: the Second Reformation in Brandenburg* (Philadelphia: University of Pennsylvania Press, 1994) even if I do not follow him in all his conclusions.
4. Nischan, *Prince*, pp. 94 ff.
5. Ibid., p. 92.
6. Ibid., p. 186.
7. O. Chadwick, *The Reformation* (Harmondsworth: Penguin, 1978) p. 152.
8. J.W. O'Malley, *The First Jesuits* (Cambridge, Mass.: Harvard University Press, 1994) p. 45.
9. Ibid., p. 4.
10. Ibid., p. 38.
11. Ibid., pp. 306 ff.
12. Ibid., p. 16.
13. The Jesuits did not evade challenges, as their polemics against the Jansenists show, but here they were, at least initially, defending themselves.
14. O'Malley, *The First Jesuits*, p. 9; see also H. Schilling, 'Luther, Loyola, Calvin und die europäische Neuzeit', *Archiv für Reformationsgeschichte*, 85 (1994) 5–31.
15. R.J.W. Evans, *The Making of the Habsburg Monarchy, 1550–1700* (Oxford: Clarendon Press, 1984) p. 42.
16. Ibid., also p. 291.
17. M.D. Knowles, 'Jesuits', *Chambers Encyclopaedia*, vol. VIII (London: George Newnes, 1959) p. 81.
18. Schilling, *Aufbruch*, p. 406.
19. Ibid., pp. 406 ff.
20. Ibid., p. 407.
21. H. Holborn, *A History of Modern Germany. The Reformation* (London: Knopf, 1965) p. 308.
22. C. V. Wedgwood, *The Thirty Years War* (New York, 1961) p. 191.
23. Ibid., p. 192; Holborn, *A History of Modern Germany*, pp. 329 f.
24. Schilling, *Aufbruch*, p. 425.
25. Seppelt and Schwaiger, *Geschichte der Päpste. Von den Anfängen bis zur Gegenwart* (Munich, 1964) p. 330.
26. Ibid., p. 332.
27. Holborn, *Modern Germany*, p. 344.
28. Schilling, *Aufbruch*, p. 425.
29. H. Schilling, *Höfe und Allianzen: Deutschland 1648–1763* (Berlin: Siedler, 1989) p. 97.
30. Evans, *Habsburg Monarchy*, p. 151.
31. M. Heckel, *Deutschland im konfessionellen Zeitalter* (Göttingen, 1983) p. 190
32. E. Zeeden, 'Das Zeitalter der Glaubenskämpfe', in B. Gebhardt, *Handbuch der deutschen Geschichte*, 8th edn., vol. II (Stuttgart, 1955) p. 146.

33. H. Jedin, 'European-Counter Reformation and Confessional Absolutism (1605–55)', in H. Jedin and J. Dolan (eds) *History of the Church*, vol. V, trans. by A. Biggs and P.W. Becker (New York: Seabury Press, 1980) p. 628.
34. Heckel, *Deutschland*, part 7, esp. p. 227.
35. Schilling, *Aufbruch*, p. 394.
36. Ibid., p. 396.

9.   EPILOGUE: TO THE FRENCH REVOLUTION (1648–1789)

1. See H. Schilling (ed.) *Die reformierte Konfessionalisierung in Deutschland. Das Problem der 'Zweiten Reformation'*. Wissenschaftliches Symposion des Vereins für Reformationsgeschichte 1985 (Gütersloh, 1986; Schriften des Vereins für Reformationsgeschichte, vol. 195); H.-Ch. Rublack (ed.) *Lutherische Konfessionalisierung* (Gütersloh, 1992); W. Reinhard and H. Schilling (eds) *Katholische Konfessionalisierung*. Wissenschaftliches Symposion der Gesellschaft zur Herausgabe des Corpus Catholicorum und des Vereins für Reformationsgeschichte (Gütersloh/Münster, 1995).
2. F. L. Carsten, *Princes and Parliaments in Germany. From the Fifteenth to the Eighteenth Century* (Oxford: Clarendon, 1959) p. 431
3. R. P.-C. Hsia, *Social Discipline in the Reformation: Central Europe 1550–1750* (London, 1989) p. 73.
4. See M. Braubach, *Maria Theresias jüngster Sohn Max Franz, Letzter Kurfürst von Köln und Fürstbischof von Münster* (Vienna, 1961) and *Kurköln. Gestalten und Ereignisse aus zwei Jahrhunderten rheinischer Geschichte* (Münster, 1949).
5. H. Raab, 'The Decline of the Church of the Empire in the Great Secularization' in H. Jedin and J. Dolan (eds) *History of the Church*, vol. VI, trans. G. J. Holst (New York, 1981) p. 494.
6. H. Raab, 'Geistige Entwicklungen und historische Ereignisse im Vorfeld der Säkularisation', in A. Rauscher (ed.) *Säkularisierung und Säkularisation vor 1800* (Munich, 1976), p. 13.
7. Carsten in *Princes and Parliaments*, p. 437, rejects the thesis that 'the growth of princely power was due to the Reformation, the new position of the Protestant prince as *summus episcopus* of his lands, and the strength he gained through the dissolution of monasteries.' See also p. 440.
8. H.H. Herwig, *Hammer or Anvil? Modern Germany 1648–Present* (Lexington, Mass.: Heath, 1994) p.27: 'a prince could be both absolute in his own state and yet representative in the Reichstag'.
9. But it has also been pointed out that the increase in the power of the princes ran parallel to the development of Estates organisation. See H. Möller, *Fürstenstaat oder Bürgernation: Deutschland 1763–1815* (Berlin: Siedler, 1989), p. 275.
10. Möller, *Fürstenstaat*, pp. 279 f.
11. Carsten, *Princes and Parliaments*, pt I.
12. F.L. Carsten, *The Origins of Prussia* (Oxford, 1954), p. 187.
13. H. Schilling, *Höfe und Allianzen: Deutschland 1648–1763* (Berlin: Siedler, 1989), p. 166.
14. C. Velder, *300 Jahre Französisches Gymnasium Berlin* (Berlin, 1989) on the school that was founded for the Huguenot refugees in Berlin, and which provided a haven of freedom during the National Socialist regime. The present

writer expressed his gratitude to his early school by reading the manuscript
before publication and making suggestions (see p. 562, no. 597).

15. Herwig, *Hammer or Anvil?*, pp. 42 f.
16. H. Möller, *Vernunft und Kritik. Deutsche Aufklärung im 17. und 18. Jahrhundert*
    (Frankfurt/Main: Suhrkamp, 1986) p. 77.
17. Möller, *Vernunft*, p. 76, quoting K. Scholder, 'Grundzüge der theologischen
    Aufklärung in Deutschland', in F. Kopitzsch (ed.) *Aufklärung, Absolutismus und
    Bürgertum in Deutschland* (Munich: Nymphenburg, 1976), p. 313.
18. H.-J. Schoeps, *Preussen. Geschichte eines Staates* (Berlin: Propyläen, 1967), p.
    48. The term *Beamtenreligion* is taken from K. Deppermann, *Der Hallesche
    Pietismus und der preußische Staat unter Friedrich III* (Göttingen, 1961), p. 176.
19. Möller, *Vernunft*, pp. 76 f, quoting C. Hinrichs, 'Der Hallische Pietismus als
    politisch–soziale Reformbewegung des 18. Jahrhunderts', in his *Preußen als
    historisches Problem* ed. G. Oestreich (Berlin: de Grayter 1964), p. 172.
20. Möller, *Vernunft*, p. 77.
21. See J. Klepper, *Der Vater* (1937). Klepper took his life with his wife, who was of
    Jewish origin, and their daughter in Berlin in December 1942.
22. Schoeps, *Preussen*, pp. 57 f.
23. Möller, *Vernunft*, p. 12.
24. Ibid., p. 111.
25. Ibid., pp. 86 f.
26. G.R. Cragg, *The Church and the Age of Reason 1648–1789* (Harmondsworth:
    Penguin, 1970) p. 48.
27. Möller, *Vernunft*, pp. 153 ff.
28. F. Schnabel, *Deutsche Geschichte im neunzehnten Jahrhundert*, vol. IV: 'Die
    Religiösen Kräfte' (Freiburg, 1955) p. 11. The present writer has been deeply
    indebted to Franz Schnabel for his history since reading it for the first time in the
    1950s.
29. Quite generally, both in secular and religious matters 'groups which no longer
    found the approval of the community (*Gemeinde*) had to leave the city'. See H.
    Schilling, 'Alternative Konzepte der Reformation und Zwang zur lutherischen
    Identität. Möglichkeiten und Grenzen religiöser und gesellschaftlicher Differ-
    enzierung zu Beginn der Neuzeit', in G. Vogler (ed.) *Wegscheiden der Reforma-
    tion. Alternatives Denken vom 16. bis zum 18. Jahrhundert* (Weimar: Böhlaus
    Nachfolger, 1994) p. 303.
30. See R. Koselleck, *Preußen zwischen Reform und Revolution* (Stuttgart: Klett,
    1975), esp. ch. 1.
31. 'The *Allgemeine Landrecht* bears a Janus face', combining Enlightened
    state planning with tradition based on estates. See Koselleck, *Preußen*, p. 24.
32. Actually the phrase used in the first paragraph of this section of the *Allgemeine
    Landrecht* is 'der innere Gottesdienst', something like interior divine service.
    For the actual text see E.R. and W. Huber, *Staat und Kirche im 19. und 20.
    Jahrhundert. Dokumente zur Geschichte des deutschen Staatskirchenrechts*, vol. I
    (Berlin, 1973) p. 3.
33. See P.G.M. Dickson, *Finance and Government under Maria Theresia, 1740–
    1780*, 2 vols (Oxford: Clarendon, 1987), esp. vol. II, chrs 1 and 2. See also A.
    Wandruszka, 'Maria Theresia', *Neue Deutsche Biographie*, vol. XVI (Berlin,
    1990) pp. 176–80.
34. Dickson, *Finance*, vol. I, ch. 4.
35. E. Winter, *Der Josefinismus: die Geschichte des österreichischen Reformkatholi-
    zismus 1740–1848* (Berlin, 1962) *passim*.

36. E. Heinen, *Staatliche Macht und Katholizismus in Deutschland*, vol. I (Paderborn, 1969), pp.24 ff.

37. H. Raab, 'Episcopalism in the Church of the Empire from the Middle of the Seventeenth Century to the End of the Eighteenth Century', in H. Jedin and J. Dolan (eds) *History of the Church*, vol. VI, trans. G.J. Holst (New York, 1981) p. 464.

38. H. Smolinsky, *Kirchengeschichte der Neuzeit I* (Düsseldorf, 1993), p. 195.

39. H. Raab, 'N. v. Hontheim', *Neue Deutsche Biographie*, vol. X, pp. 604–5 and 'Episcopalism', esp. pp. 457 ff.; M. O'Callaghan, 'Febronianism', *New Catholic Encyclopedia*, vol. V, pp. 688–9.

40. F.A.J. Szabo, *Kaunitz and Enlightened Absolutism, 1753–1780* (Cambridge University Press, 1994), p. 241.

41. D. Beales, *Joseph II*, vol. I: *In the Shadow of Maria Theresa, 1741–1780* (Cambridge University Press, 1987), p. 56. See also H. Wagner, 'Joseph II', *Neue Deutsche Biographie*, vol. X (Berlin, 1974), pp. 617–22.

42. Dickson, *Finance*, vol. II, p. 267.

43. Beales, *Joseph II*, vol. I, p. 53.

44. Möller, *Fürstenstaat*, p. 299.

45. Beales, *Joseph II*, vol. I, p. 450.

46. A. Wandruszka, 'Leopold II', *Neue Deutsche Biographie*, vol. XIV (Berlin, 1985) pp. 260–6.

47. Szabo, *Kaunitz, passim*.

48. For a more critical view of the system of government, see Dickson, *Finance*, vol. I, p. 207 ff.

49. Beales, *Joseph II*, p. 56.

50. Szabo, *Kaunitz*, p. 257.

51. Dickson, *Finance*, vol. II, p. 33.

52. P. B. Bernard, *Joseph II* (New York, 1968), pp. 112 ff.

53. Bernard, *Joseph II*, pp. 100 ff.

54. Schilling, *Höfe*, p. 133.

55. Schilling, *Höfe*, p. 100.

56. L.v. Ranke, *Zur Geschichte von Österreich und Preußen zwischen den Friedensschlüssen von Aachen und Hubertusburg* (Leipzig, 1875), p. 316, quoted in H. Raab, 'The Decline of the Church of the Empire in the Great Secularization', in H. Jedin and J. Dolan (eds) *History of the Church*, vol. VI, trans. G.J. Holst (New York: Crossroad, 1981) p. 494.

57. See F. Eyck, *The Frankfurt Parliament, passim*.

58. For the situation in the Empire see the somewhat different interpretations in Schilling, *Höfe*, part II, s. 3 and Möller, *Fürstenstaat*, part IV, s. 1.

59. By the German constitutional historian Samuel Pufendorf (1632–94). See Schilling, *Höfe*, pp. 94 ff.

60. For the last two decades or so before 1789 also see *inter alia* J.J. Sheehan, *German History, 1770–1866* (Oxford, 1989); F. Valjavec, *Die Entstehung der politischen Strömungen in Deutschland 1770–1815* (Munich, 1951), and K. O. Freiherr von Aretin, *Heiliges Römisches Reich 1776–1806*, 2 vols (Wiesbaden, 1967).

10. CONCLUSIONS

1. C. Morris, *The Papal Monarchy: the Western Church from 1050 to 1250* (Oxford, 1991) pp. 1f.

2. F. Eyck, 'Liberalismus und Katholizismus in der Zeit des deutschen Vormärz', in W. Schieder (ed.) *Liberalismus in der Gesellschaft des deutschen Vormärz* (Göttingen, 1983), pp. 139f.
3. See F. Eyck, *The Frankfurt Parliament 1848–49* (London: Macmillan, 1968) esp. ch. 8.
4. See Chapter 7 of the current book.
5. E. Iserloh, 'Joseph Lortz – Leben und ökumenische Bedeutung', in R. Decot and R. Vinke (eds) *Zum Gedenken an Joseph Lortz (1887–1975). Beiträge zur Reformationsgeschichte und Ökumene* (Stuttgart: Steiner, 1989) pp. 4–5.

Index